PORTUGUESE VOCABLES IN ASIATIC LANGUAGES

PORTUGUESE VOCABLES IN ASIATIC LANGUAGES

FROM THE PORTUGUESE ORIGINAL
of
MONSIGNOR SEBASTIAO RODOLFO DALGADO

Translated into English with notes, additions and comments

By

ANTHONY XAVIER SOARES, M.A., LL.B., F.RS.L
PROFESSOR OF ENGLISH, BARODA COLLEGE

GYAN

Published by

GYAN

Gyan Publishing House
5, Ansari Road
Daryaganj, New Delhi-110002
Phone: 011-47034999, 9811692060
E-mail: books@gyanbooks.com

Distribution Network
gyanbooks.com
India, USA, Canada, UK, Australia, France

ISBN: 978-81-212-6378-8 (PB)
First Published, 1936

2nd Impression 2022

Printed at: Gyan Press, Delhi.

PORTUGUESE VOCABLES IN ASIATIC LANGUAGES
Author: MONSIGNOR SEBASTIAO RODOLFO DALGADO

PREFACE.

Monsignor S. Rodolfo Dalgado's *Influencia do Vocabulario Portugûes em Linguas Asiaticas (abragendo cerca de cinquenta idiomas)* published by the Academy of Sciences, Lisbon, was issued in 1913, and at once received a very warm welcome from Orientalists all over Europe interested in philological studies.

Sir George Grierson, then in England, thanked the author heartily for his most valuable and interesting work for which, he said, he had been wishing for many years and which would be of the greatest help to him in the linguistic survey of India, just as his excellent Konkani dictionary had been till then. Professors Sylvain Levi and A. Cabaton from Paris, J. Cornu from Austria, and Hugo Schuchardt from Graz, among others, acclaimed the work as an enduring monument to Portugal and a most valuable contribution to Oriental studies, the materials of which, collected with infinite labour, had been put together with great learning and precision.

But except Portuguese India, as was to be expected, no other part of India had heard of the author's name, let alone of this or any other book of his. The irony of the situation is obvious; for though the result of the laborious examination of about fifty different Asiatic languages in search of Portuguese words might make the Portuguese justly and pardonably proud of the part they once played in the cultural history of the East and particularly of India, such a study can have a present-day value and importance only to those in India, Ceylon, Malaya, and other parts of Asia interested in the history and development of their respective vernaculars. The situation was brought about purely because Dr. Dalgado's *Vocabulario*, to give the work the name by which it is generally known, is in Portuguese, and scarcely any Indian Orientalist to-day possesses a working knowledge of that language.

With the object of introducing Dalgado's work to those interested in such studies, I read before the Bombay Branch of the Royal Asiatic Society a paper entitled: *The Portuguese Legacy to the East or the Influence of Portuguese on the Languages of the East with special reference to the Languages of the Bombay Presidency*. This was in 1922. A paragraph from its concluding part will bear quotation here, in as much as it explains my motive in reading it and, at the same time, makes an avowal of my indebtedness for my materials to the *Vocabulario*.

'It remains for me to acknowledge my great and grateful debt to Dr. S. Rodolfo Dalgado's *Influencia do Vocabulario Portugues em Linguas Asiaticas (abrangendo cerca de cinquenta idiomas)*. The student who wishes to study from a scientific and philosophical standpoint the process by which the gradual transplantation of the exotic words on Asiatic soil was affected will find the introduction to this great work of absorbing interest. The book which is published by the University Press, Coimbra, and brought out under the auspices of the Academy of Sciences, Lisbon, is in Portuguese, a language unknown to the majority of scholars in India. I am sure that, on this very account, a few brief remarks on the character of this work as well as on the career and achievements of the indefatigable orientalist and philologist, its author, will not be out of place.' And the very same reasons have determined the inclusion of a sketch of the author's life and work in this volume.

The paper was published in the Society's Journal No. LXXIV, Vol. XXVI, and it was not long before I had the satisfaction of finding that my object had in some measure been realised. The few inquiries which had reached me before, consequent on the brief summary of the paper having appeared in the *Times of India*, Bombay, now increased both in number and in purposefulness. Almost without a single exception my correspondents regretted their inability to read the Monsignor's works in the original and also the absence of an English translation of the most important of them. The *Vocabulario*, in my view, was the one of all his works that would interest scholars in India in as much as it would help them to apprehend the nature and extent of the indebtedness of their own vernaculars to the earliest European language they came into contact with in modern times, just as his *Glossario Luso-Asiatico* would interest Portuguese—one might well say European—students anxious to understand the East and to realise the extent to which Portuguese expansion there, whether commercial, political, or missionary, has enriched their vocabularies.

Accordingly, I applied to the Lisbon Academy of Sciences, —Dr. Dalgado had, meanwhile, after gathering in his rich and abundant harvest, gone to his eternal reward on the 4th of April, 1922,—for permission to bring out an English translation of the *Vocabulario*, and I wish to express here my grateful recognition of its courtesy and kindness in promptly granting my request.

Almost a whole decade had elapsed between the publication of the *Vocabulario* and my decision to present it in English, and during this interval its author had brought out other works on cognate subjects. In these latter he had occasionally arrived at opinions and results different from those he had put forward before, or supported the earlier views with additional evidence, or sometimes provided a fuller and more detailed exposition of a philological or phonetic law which had been concisely set out in the *Vocabulario*. Moreover the bibliography annexed to the present work, very extensive though it is, gives evidence that some sources of information had remained unknown or were inaccessible to the author, whilst others had become available only after the publication of his book, and this was the case particularly with those wherein are to be found a large number of terms derived from Portuguese, once current in Anglo-India. It is true, he has derived his materials under this head from the well-known *Glossary* of Wilson, the *Dictionary* of Whitworth, and Crooke's edition of Yule and Burnell's monumental and fascinating volume; but, since the last-named made its appearance, much published material—new volumes, in the Hakluyt Society's publications, in Foster's *Letters*, and *English Factories in India*, and of the *Indian Antiquary*, etc., ... had become available. The New Oxford English Dictionary which the author does not appear to have known or consulted was also approaching completion.

In view of all this I decided that it would enhance the utility of my translation if I incorporated in it the alterations or additions that the new material had made necessary or possible. The additions have been in the main with reference to Anglo-Indian terms which owe their existence to Portuguese, and they have not been confined to etymological investigations alone but been extended to various other fields—historical, sociological, botanical, zoological, etc. which I thought might provoke the reader's interest, and at the same time relieve to some extent the baldness, as a rule, inseparable from a Vocabulary.

The author, as is but natural, considering the nature of his work, quotes usually from the early Portuguese chronicles in support of the currency of a Portuguese vocable in the East. I thought that it would promote both enquiry and interest among English-speaking readers if I were to give the reference to the relative passage in the English version of the text when such existed, and there are not a few of them in the Hakluyt Society's series. This, with very few instances excepted, I have done.

There are many Anglo-Indian words in the *Vocabulario* for which the author provides quotations; in the case of quite a number of others, he does not do so—the nature of his study did not demand them. I have endeavoured to supply the lacunæ, and, when this had to be done in regard to vocables which had been already dealt with in *Hobson-Jobson*, I aimed at providing, whenever possible, citations other or earlier in point of time than those given by Yule and Burnell. In furnishing references for the various forms sometimes assumed by a term, I have chiefly been moved by considerations of tracing the evolution of its orthography before it became finally stabilised.

Several locutions at one time employed in Anglo-India, as is evidenced by their use in correspondence or accounts of travels, have found neither a place in *Hobson-Jobson* nor the *New Oxford English Dictionary*, or only in one of them, and when such have been listed by me, I thought it useful to mention this fact, or that other one that some of the quotations I have been fortunate to light upon belong to an earlier date than those in either or both these works.

The *Vocabulario* was primarily addressed to the Portuguese, and it was presumably to acquaint even such of them as have no interest in philology with the great linguistic legacy their forefathers have bequeathed to the East, that, at the conclusion of his study, the author provided a general alphabetical list of all the Portuguese words that had found an entry into the languages of Asia, and also separate lists of these words, language by language. I decided to eliminate the general list and in place of it have provided a general index of all words and names in the book. Instead of the separate lists I have prepared for each of the fifty languages an alphabetical index of these very words but in the forms they have assumed in the foreign idioms and, to facilitate reference, have set against each the original Portuguese vocable. In the list of Konkani words derived from Portuguese—their number is legion—the author gives in quite a large number of cases the vernacular idiom which the foreign term has displaced; in those others in which he did not do so I have attempted to supply the omission. The additions made by me, except in the case of the lists, are marked by square brackets, and the material which came to hand after the pages wherein it could have been incorporated had been struck off is put together in a supplement at the close.

The new matter increased the text to almost two and a half times the bulk of the original and the problem of finding the ways and means to bring out the volume would have remained insoluble had it not been for the gracious and personal interest which the Maharaja Gaekwad of Baroda took in the work and the decision of His Highness' Government to finance its publication.

The spontaneous generosity of this great Prince in assisting enterprises that conduce to the cultural or social advancement of his countrymen has become proverbial both in the East and the West. Himself a keen student of languages, Indian and European, he has given proof of his interest in linguistic researches by having had the *Shree Sayaji Shastama Shabda Kalpatri*—a comparative dictionary of administrative terms in seven Indian languages—compiled and published; and everyone in India who has at heart the unification and cultural progress of India is aware how much the movement for making Hindi the lingua franca of India owes to this Ruler. I venture to take this opportunity of recording my indebtedness and grateful thanks to His Highness and his Government.

It remains for me now to thank, besides the many friends who have shown interest in my work, rendered help, and put up with and answered not a few importunate questions, Miss Olive da Cunha, B.A., for offering to let me use her copy of the *Vocabulario* presented to her by the author, which contained corrections and additions made by him—the latter have been shown within parallel lines in the present edition; Dr. Mariano José Saldanha, Professor of Sanskrit, Lisbon University, for his advice regarding the transliteration of certain Konkani phonetics; Mr. Vitus P. de Sá, Solicitor, Bombay, for placing at my disposal letters from Orientalists in Europe received by his uncle, the Monsignor, from which I have quoted; and my daughter Florence who has rendered me very useful assistance in the dreary task of preparing the language lists and the general index and in revising their proofs.

A. X. Soares.

A SKETCH OF THE AUTHOR'S LIFE.

The primary object with which the translation of the *Vocabulario* has been undertaken is to introduce the work to English-knowing students, specially in India, because of the new light it is expected to throw on many a problem which has been baffling lexicographers of modern Indian languages, and also on the question, much discussed at the present day, as to what have been the cultural results that have followed the impact of the West on the East; a secondary, but of no less moment, is to introduce the author to his countrymen—to all who, whether differing in race, creed or political allegiance, claim India as their motherland—and to them he is practically unknown. He is one of India's distinguished sons, born, bred, and nurtured on her soil, notwithstanding which, he has not been accorded by his compatriots the recognition that is his due. One is led to say this because hardly one student of Indology in a hundred has even heard of his name; and because in a publication entitled *Eminent Orientalists* which the well-known publishing house of G. A. Natesan & Co. brought out some few years ago no mention even is made of one who, as will be seen, has claim to an honoured place in the roll of Indian Oriental scholars. And this claim is based not only on his having devoted the greater part of his life to the study of Sanskrit and the many Indo-Aryan tongues derived from it, and to those branches of Oriental research to which one with his knowledge as well of the languages and the scientific method of the West alone could do justice, but also because he never allowed his studies to overshadow his interest in India and his affection for her; far from it, if anything, they helped him to understand better her great past, realise more vividly her present needs, and bestow greater thought on her future.

His eminence in the field of Oriental studies is unquestionable. He was one of the very few Indians enrolled among the 'thirty' whom the Royal Asiatic Society of London at any one time honours with its honorary membership, and we shall at this stage forbear mentioning honours that came to him from other learned societies not as well known to readers in India. There is one fact, however, connected with his life and work which calls for mention even now and it is sure to secure from scholars in India and the East the sympathy and admiration which those of Europe felt for him. During the years he was engaged in compiling his monumental works, in order to avoid worse consequences to his health, he had to undergo surgical operations requiring the amputation of both his legs, one after the other, at the short interval of about three years. And the picture of this ardent and untiring Oriental scholar, alone and away from his home, his only constant companions and faithful friends, the dictionaries of Eastern tongues and Portuguese and other European chronicles, his truncated body resting in an invalid's chair—a veritable Procrustean bed,—from which he lectured to his students, and on which, with heroic resignation, he worked away at his books, is as moving as it is sustaining.

His works are in Portuguese—a language which till the middle of the eighteenth century was the lingua franca of India, but to-day is practically unknown here except to a microscopic section of the population and that limited to a small proportion of the Portuguese possessions in India. Again, he bore a name which could easily lead the indiscriminating to regard him as a non-Indian. What wonder then that his countrymen, had they even heard of him and his works, should have failed to pierce the disguises of name and language and discover in him one of their kindred?

For Sebastião Rodolfo Dalgado was born in Assagão, Bardez, Goa, of a distinguished Brahmin family which for generations had occupied a place of prominence and privilege in the economy of the village. In the sixteenth century, Christianity on the west coast of India was not content with washing off the original sin and subsequent lapses of its recruits, but insisted on wiping away every trace of the ancestral lineage and traditions. It was then that the cognomen of his family 'Desai', so significant, and racy of the soil, was made to yield place to the unmeaning and alien 'Dalgado'. He was one of a family of six brothers and an only sister; one of the brothers died young, two pursued the profession of medicine and two of law.

Young Rodolfo went to school in his village and afterwards at Mapuça, the chief town of his district. Early in life he felt the call towards a priestly vocation and joined the well-known College for ecclesiastical studies at Rachol, in the district of Salsete, Goa, where, after going through his preliminary studies, which included knowledge of English and French and the prescribed course of Philosophy and Theology, in Latin, he was ordained priest in 1881. Very soon afterwards he proceeded to Rome, acquired knowledge of Italian, and joined the University of St. Apollinarius to study Canon and Roman Law. The Doctorate in both these faculties was conferred upon him two years later. As a special case, perhaps because of his noteworthy success in the law schools, he was allowed to sit for the examination of the Doctor's degree in Divinity, which involved his learning Greek and Hebrew, without having to keep terms. He came out of the test with distinction. These results, together with the awards of prizes and medals which accompanied them, brought the Indian cleric to the notice of the then reigning Pope, Leo XIII, who appointed him his Honorary chaplain with the title of 'Monsignor'. This was on the 11th October, 1884, when he was only twenty-nine. Leo XIII, as is well known, was keenly interested in raising the status of the Indian Clergy, and it is believed that it was at his suggestion that Monsignor Dalgado decided to return to India and devote his future labours to his own country. Looking to the contributions he has made to Oriental studies, one feels disposed, at this date, to regard the Pontiff's advice as providential, in as much as the different offices Dr. Dalgado came to hold in various parts of India and in Ceylon brought him into contact with the idioms and cultures of different people, and enabled him to gather materials for the two enduring monuments he was to raise in after years.

From Rome he went to Lisbon where, by a Government order of the 19th November, 1884, he was nominated a missionary of the Crown, with India as his field of activities. He arrived in Goa in April 1885 and in quick succession was appointed to several ecclesiastical offices. We shall refer here only to such as have a direct bearing on his researches in the field of Oriental studies.

On the 19th March, 1886, he was appointed Vicar General of Ceylon, and took charge of his office on the 14th May. As the result of a Concordat between the Holy See and the Portuguese sovereign, the Portuguese Mission in Ceylon became extinct on the 2nd January, 1887, and Dr. Dalgado returned to Goa, but not before he had acquired a working knowledge of Sinhalese and Malay. From May 1887 to April 1890, he was the Vicar General of Bengal, with his headquarters in Calcutta, long enough for him to acquire proficiency in Hindustani and Bengali. In 1893 he was appointed Vicar Forane of Honawar, and he continued in this office till 1895, employing his leisure in learning Kanarese and Tamil. A large part of the three years preceding his taking up his office at Honawar he spent at Savantwadi, a State on the frontiers of Goa, with his eldest brother, Dr. Gelasio D. Dalgado, who was the Civil Surgeon there, studying Marathi and Sanskrit. It was evidently during these years and studies that he realised how closely his own mother tongue, Konkani, was related to Sanskrit, and the recognition of this fact led him to undertake a scientific investigation of the structure and vocabulary of this vernacular. Research was fruitful in helping him to bring out his Konkani-Portuguese Dictionary in 1893, and to write a Grammar of Konkani, on which he was busy at the time of his death and which in its manuscript form he bequeathed to the Public Library of Nova-Goa.

The dictionary has been compiled on a very systematic and scientific basis, the Konkani words being printed in Devanagri characters, and contains an introduction which is as informative as it is lucid. This work which had been executed on a scale and with a method never till then adopted, attracted the attention of the Portuguese authorities in Lisbon, who by an order of the 11th November, 1895, entrusted him with the task of bringing out a Portuguese-Konkani Dictionary, the cost of which was to be defrayed by the State. He had now to proceed to Lisbon to supervise the printing of this work, which ran into over nine hundred pages and dealt with vocables in an orthography with which the compositors at the Government Press were utterly unfamiliar. In the same year 1895, he was elected a fellow of the Geographical Society, Lisbon. The Dictionary came out in 1905 and about this time Dr. Dalgado was made a Domestic Prelate to the Pope. The Lisbon Government exempted him from further missionary service in the East. Such leisure as the exacting task of bringing out the Dictionary left him, he had devoted to the study of Sanskrit and Philology, under Oriental scholars in Portugal, in acquiring a working knowledge of German, and just that much of Arabic as would enable him to consult dictionaries of that language and of Persian. In 1907 he was appointed Professor of Sanskrit at the Lisbon University; and four years later he was elected a corresponding member of the Academy of Sciences, Lisbon. In 1917 the honorary degree of Doctor of Literature was conferred upon him by the Lisbon University.

From the time he brought out his Dictionaries his literary output was prodigious, and his title to be numbered among the eminent philologists of the day grew with every new publication of his that issued from the press. Exclusive of articles he wrote on religious, historical and political subjects for journals in Portugal, Brazil and India, we give below a list of his published writings:

Diccionario Konkani-Portuguez, Philologico-Etymologico. Bombay, 1893, xxx + 562 pp.

Hitopadexa ou Instrucção Útil (translation of Hitopadeśa from the Sanskrit original into Portuguese). Lisbon, 1897, xxii + 292 pp.

Dialecto Indo-Português de Ceylão. Lisbon, 1900, xii + 262 pp.

Dialecto Indo-Português de Goa. Oporto, 1900, 22 pp.

Dialecto Indo-Português de Damão. Lisbon, 1903, 31 pp.

Diccionario Português-Concani. Lisbon, 1905, xxxii + 906 pp.

Dialecto Indo-Português do Norte (the Indo-Portuguese dialect of Bombay and its suburbs). Lisbon, 1906, 62 pp.

Influencia do Vocabulario Português em Linguas Asiaticas. Coimbra, 1913, xcii + 253 pp.

Contribuição para a Lexicologia Luso-Oriental (Contributions towards a study of Luso-Oriental words). Coimbra, 1916, 196 pp.

Historia de Nala e Damyanti (Translation of Nala and Damyanti from the Sanskrit original into Portuguese). Coimbra, 155 pp.

Dialecto Indo-Português de Negapatam. Oporto, 1917, 16 pp.

Gonsalves Viana e a Lexicologia Portuguesa de origem Asiatico-Africana.

Glossario Luso-Asiatico, Vol. I. Coimbra, 1919, lxvii + 535 pp.

Glossario Luso-Asiatico, Vol. II. Lisbon, 1921, vii + 580 pp.

Rudimentos da lingua Sanscrita (Rudiments of Sanskrit, for use of students at the University). 1920.

Florilégio de Provérbios Concanis. Coimbra, 1922, xx + 330 pp.

As will be noticed from the above, his special subject of study was the influence of Portuguese on the languages of the East, and inversely of the idioms of the East upon Portuguese, one might say European, vocabulary. No one before him had attempted this investigation on such a scale, and it can be safely asserted that not one who had touched upon this vast and absorbingly interesting field of study had brought to it the first-hand knowledge and intimacy with so many languages of the East and the West which he did. It was the *Vocabulario* which laid the foundation of his great reputation in the European world of Oriental studies. It represented twenty years' strenuous labours to track down the numerous Portuguese vocables which like nondescripts, without papers or passport, had strayed into the boundaries of Eastern idioms, and so many of whom had lost every semblance which might bespeak their country of origin.

But his *chef d'œuvre* is the *Glossario Luso-Asiatico* in two volumes. It is the complement to the *Vocabulario* and in it the author traces the history of the innumerable Eastern terms met with in Portuguese chronicles, very many of which have become naturalised in Portuguese, and not a few after crossing the frontiers of this language have secured domicile in other European tongues. In the introduction to it he mentions that his original intention was to include in it words derived from African sources, but partly because of the difficulty of obtaining accurate information regarding many of them, and chiefly because of the state of his health, he thought it prudent to circumscribe his investigations to Asia, for fear that the enterprise, as he phrases it, might get shipwrecked before reaching port. Even as it is, to use the words of Sir George Grierson, 'it is a monument of erudition'.

The *Glossario* is not only a Portuguese *Hobson-Jobson* but, as has been fitly pointed out by the late Mr. Longworth Dames, something more besides, because of the peculiar position which the Portuguese language occupies in its relation to the East, a relation very different from that of other European languages. The Portuguese were the first to give new terms and likewise the first to borrow new terms from the East: quite a large number of these latter were adopted by the French and the English.

It is possiblė to realise the magnitude and the monumental character of the work, embodying as it does the result of a quarter century's reading and research, by turning to the Bibliography. Its five hundred and more names of works—several of them running into many volumes—cover practically every book in Portuguese dealing with the East, a very large number of such in Latin, French, Italian, Dutch, Spanish and English, and some even from Arabic, Persian and Chinese sources.

Upon the appearance of the *Glossario* the author was overwhelmed with appreciations from Oriental scholars in different parts of the world. In England, Mr. Longworth Dames, the then Vice-President of the Royal Asiatic Society, reviewed it in the Society's Journal (April 1921) and went so far as to say that he hoped students in England and India who were not acquainted with Portuguese, would endeavour to obtain a sufficient knowledge of that language to enable them to avail themselves of the mass of invaluable information contained in the two volumes. Not long after he was elected an Honorary member of the Royal Asiatic Society.

But his great aspiration was to be a full member or, to use the Portuguese term, 'Sòcio effectivo' of the Lisbon Academy of Sciences, under whose auspices and at whose cost most of his important books had been published. The number of the 'Socios Effectivos', as of the 'Immortels' of the French Academy, is limited, but the death of one of them, Dr. Anselm Jose' Braacamp, had created a vacancy and Dr. Dalgado's name was selected to be placed before the general body at a session on the 27th April, but Providence had willed otherwise, for on the 4th of the same month Dr. Dalgado was summoned by his Maker to receive the due reward of his exemplary sanctity of life, untiring industry, wise use of his rare gifts and his heroic resignation in suffering.

The Portuguese people mourned the passing away of this Indian scholar as a national loss, for they had come to look upon his *Vocabulario* and the *Glossario* as imperishable monuments to their great and glorious past.

At the time of his death he had in the press the *Florilégio de Provérbios Concanis*. It is a fascinating and penetrating study of the everyday philosophy of the Konkani-speaking people. Two thousand one hundred and twenty-seven proverbs which he was able to collect have been translated into Portuguese and grouped under two hundred and twenty-three heads, commented upon and compared with similar sayings in different Asiatic (principally Sanskrit, Marathi, Kanarese) and European (Latin, English, French, Spanish, German) languages.

Early in 1922 he was engaged in preparing at the request of the Lisbon University, a new edition of Duarte Barbosa's famous '*Livro*', but this and a grammar of the Konkani language at which he had been working from 1920 remained unfinished.

Apart from his sacred ministry, love for India and love for Portugal were the two consuming passions of his life. It is in connection with these that his literary activities had their being and around them they moved. The titles of his writings show how he distributed his interest almost equally between these two. But India, as is natural, occupied the first place in his affections. And it is a coincidence, at once significant and arresting, that he should have made his entry on the stage of Oriental scholarship with a dictionary of the Konkani language and that, when the curtain was rung down on his activities, he should have been engaged on an Anthology of Konkani proverbs and a Grammar of Konkani.

From his exiguous resources he endowed a prize for Sanskrit at the Lyceum in Goa, and offered to the Archbishop of Goa a sum of money for the foundation of a chair of Konkani in the seminary of Rachol. The Archbishop did not see his way to accept the offer and he felt disappointed. The Portuguese ecclesiastical authorities, in the past, have been no friends of Konkani, the people's tongue in Goa. Time and again they made relentless efforts to suppress the language of the soil, not unlike those once made by the Normans against Anglo-Saxon speech, and as unsuccessfully. Monsignor Dalgado was surely acquainted with these, but he must have presumed that a newer order had yielded place to the older one.

His intense devotion to India is understandable, but how is it that this Indian with not a trace of Portuguese blood in his veins came to feel the affection he did for Portugal ? A sentence in his preface to this work bears witness to its intensity. 'I have pursued this task with an ardent zeal and unflagging enthusiasm inspired above all by my devotion to Portugal and thought for her glory.' We shall allow Dr. Dalgado himself to answer what on the surface appears to be a very intriguing query :—

"The influence of Portugal in the East which many foreign and some Portuguese writers have characterised as cruel, intolerant and of few beneficial results, presents nevertheless on careful investigation, an aspect and a type which are wholly peculiar, in as much as it has been highly sympathetic and warm-hearted. It is an influence which other nations who regard themselves as being more civilised and more liberal have not up to this day succeeded in exerting in spite of present-day advance in social doctrines. The most striking evidence of this influence, which in itself constitutes a glorious record of the relations that have existed between the conquerors and the conquered, is their effective and legal recognition of political and social equality, without any difference whatsoever, between the Portuguese and their colonials, be they Indians, Chinese, Oceanians or Africans—a policy which as yet remains a desideratum among non-Portuguese colonies, however rich, extensive and cultured.

According to the general theory of the Portuguese, their colonies are not dependencies or centres for exploitation. On the contrary, they are patches of Portugal sown, for her glory, in different climes with races, colours, castes, usages and customs, it is true, very unlike those of the mother country, but not on that account less Portuguese at heart and soul. It is on this account that a Portuguese born in India or Africa of European parents is not ashamed to call himself an Indian or an African.

This fact ought not to cause surprise or be looked upon as an isolated incident or one of recent happening. The primary and most absorbing motive force which impelled the early explorers and conquerors was the idea of extending the temporal and spiritual limits of Portugal and to bind the East and the West with the tender ties of love. Here is an instance of very great value in proof of this. The King of Portugal did not disdain to be treated by the friendly Rajas of Malabar as their brother and the Rajas very naturally were proud to be allowed to claim this relationship. It is useful to remember that no other sovereign of any other power has similarly treated any potentate, Asian or African, even up to the present day, when we are living in an age in which so much is talked about the liberty, equality and fraternity of the human race. Moreover, there is no record of any governor or viceroy of any other power having spoken of an Indian woman as 'my daughter' as the great Affonso Albuquerque used to do without distinction, in respect of the women of Goa, when they were coming over to Christianity and marrying his soldiers and sailors.

These and other facts of a similar nature furnish abundant proof that the Portuguese, who knew how to make themselves dreaded by their enemies and to treat them with severity, possessed, at the same time, the gift of associating themselves without any reserve with the indigenous population and of even identifying themselves with them, and if the latter happened also to belong to their faith, they were looked upon on that very account as their brothers."

It is much to be regretted that since the above was written, and during the last few years, there has been a backward movement in the old Portuguese colonial policy.

The equalitarian and fusionist doctrine of the Portuguese has by many been looked upon as the cause of their failure in the East; there are others, however, who believe, and Dr. Dalgado is one of them, that the true criterion of estimating the success of colonial administration is the affectionate memory and grateful esteem of the rulers by the subject population and, tested by this, the success of the old Portuguese colonial policy has been very great indeed.

It is the earnest desire of present-day statesmanship to see the East and the West understand each other and to have them extend to each other the hand of fraternal sympathy. Dr. Dalgado's *Vocabulario* and *Glossario* will remain abiding monuments of such an alliance between the two civilisations, and he himself, whether regarded as man, priest, or scholar is a splendid exemplar of the happy result to be derived from an intimate association of the East and the West.

THE AUTHOR'S PREFACE

Authorities of indisputable competence have more than once recognised and not less often held forth the great advantage and importance of assembling in one place the large number of Portuguese words, many of them in everyday use, which have been taken over by most of the cultured and some also by the less advanced languages of Southern Asia.

It is now about twenty years that a daily paper in Bombay which has a vast circulation, *The Times of India*, suggested the importance of such a work with reference to India and pointed out to the late Dr. Gerson da Cunha as one suited for carrying it out.

Subsequently Dr. Hugo Schuchardt, an authority on the Romance languages of universal fame who has published so many works on the Portuguese dialects of Asia and Africa and on the diffusion of Portuguese in the East was insistent on the advantage and necessity of preparing a glossary of the Portuguese words introduced into Asiatic tongues.

Dr. Adolfo Coelho, in appreciating an interesting monograph of Mr. Gonçalves Viana on the influence of Portuguese on Malay, declared that this publication imposed upon him the obligation of completing the work he had begun by examining other languages of the Archipelago, a task which, most certainly, he had the competence to perform. But the eminent linguist, in a subsequent edition of his work referred to above, wrote to say that he did not deem himself qualified for undertaking the work and that one already had taken upon himself to execute it, thereby referring to the author of the present book.

Five and twenty years ago when I began the study of the sematology and the etymology of Konkani, the language of Goa, with the aid of dictionaries in Sanskrit, the parent tongue, and of the other languages in use on the frontiers of Goa, I noticed at once that it was not only in Portuguese India but also in British India that many Portuguese words were current; this fact I had on a previous occasion, though of course on a scale much smaller, observed when I was the vicar general and administrator of the Portuguese missions in Ceylon and Bengal. In my Konkani-Portuguese dictionary published in 1903, I indicated by initials placed before the respective word, the six or seven languages, Aryan or Dravidian which used them and which I then knew.

Accepting the suggestion of a friend, I sent him from India in 1892 a very short manuscript study to be put before the International Congress of Orientalists which was to have been held in Lisbon but eventually was not held there. It was a brief study consisting of two distinct parts of the Indo-Portuguese dialect of Ceylon, and of the Portuguese terms, grouped under certain heads, which had been introduced into half a dozen languages of India.

The Geographical Society of Lisbon published, as my contribution to the celebrations in honour of the fourth centenary of the discovery of the sea-route to India, an enlarged study of the Portuguese dialect of Ceylon. But I could not then accede to the pressing request of the late Luciano Cordeiro to put through the press the second part of my essay because I wished to extend the scope of this part of the work and, at greater leisure, to co-ordinate it in the best possible manner.

Since then I have carried on, with interruptions more or less protracted and occasionally with flagging zeal, the arduous task of going through, more than once, a large collection of dictionaries and vocabularies of some fifty languages, some of them voluminous, rare and costly; of acquiring incomplete but published lists of words; of obtaining fresh ones through the help of obliging friends scattered over India, and finally of casting anew the materials thus brought together. And all this has been done in the midst of constant physical sufferings, oftentimes of an excruciating nature, and of not a few moral smarts.

It is but natural that works of the nature of this, especially those taking in an area so extensive and so little surveyed before, are as a rule incomplete and imperfect and full of errors of various sorts, and I should not have even now been rash enough to issue to the public the fruits of my investigations, had it not been for an ever-growing presentiment that Death might come to meet me in the midst of my labours.

What stimulated me in the carrying out of this weary task was not so much my love for literary pursuits as my ardent affection for Portugal. Should the present work, perhaps the last literary product of my leisure hours, with all its shortcomings, contribute in some measure towards her glory, I shall hold myself abundantly repaid for my labour and expense.

I wish to leave recorded here my ever grateful thanks to the Academy of Sciences which gave a most generous welcome to my book and sanctioned its publication; to Mr. Gonçalves Viana who pronounced an opinion on it which I feel was a great deal too complimentary, and who went through the greater part of it and made many judicious and useful suggestions; to Mr. J. A. Dias Coelho of the Government Printing Press, who with very great interest revised the proofs twice over; to Mr. Candido Augusto Nazareth, the manager of the press, who helped so greatly in seeing it being put through quickly and also to its effective get-up; to the missionaries of the Portuguese Government working in the East who furnished me with Portuguese words in the local dialects, and finally to all those who in whatever way have helped me in the execution of this work.

S. Rodolfo Dalgado.

Lisbon, August 1913.

THE AUTHOR'S INTRODUCTION

I. *The Influence of Portugal on the East*

The influence of Portugal on the Orient both as regards its extension and intension has not hitherto, as a whole, been adequately appreciated.

Much has been written about the glorious achievements of her navigators and conquerors, and of the heroic deeds of her captains and governors. There are graphic descriptions of her extensive commercial relations, of her vast emporiums and of the fearful trials and the dazzling luxury of her sons in the colonies. Likewise, in the light of the present-day trend of thought, her policy of cruelty and intolerance and the excesses that flowed from her religious zeal have been the subject matter of severe criticism. And it has been generally held that this influence of Portugal on the East was circumscribed, superficial and ephemeral.

The truth, however, is that the civilizing influence of Portugal in her former dominions and the peoples she came into contact with was, in more senses than one, very extensive, very deep and very abiding. There exist even at the present day numerous and unmistakable vestiges of this influence, and there are irrefutable arguments [1] to support this view.

Dr. Heyligers recognises 'that the influence which the Portuguese exercised in the Indian Archipelago'—and the same can be said of diverse other parts—'was of an absolutely singular character,' and he includes it under three heads: population and

---

[1] 'In the matter of principles, therefore, Portugal was the first country which knew to formulate them in a manner calculated to bring about, by a policy of assimilation between the conquerors and the conquered and without useless severity and futile tyranny, the progress and the civilisation of the most backward regions. And in the matter of practical application we (the Portuguese) gave proofs no less remarkable nor less decisive.' Opinion of the Sub-Committee (Colonial Politics) of the Geographical Society of Lisbon.

race, customs, and language.[1] But there are other aspects by no means of less consequence and which, at the same time, are important factors of civilisation : the introduction of new objects, the flora, the fauna, agriculture and industries.

There is no colonial nation which has less racial egotism and is more inclined to identify itself with the indigenous population than the Portuguese.[2] The discerning mind of Albuquerque found no better means of knitting together the East and the West and of consolidating the Empire which he was founding than by the fusion of the conquerors and the conquered, and towards this end he concentrated all his efforts.[3] If his judicious policy was not resolutely maintained or if it encountered grave difficulties, it did not fail any the less to achieve considerable results. Even at the present time there are to be met with in various parts of Asia groups of families, some small others large, which pride themselves on being the descendants of the European people who were the earliest in modern times to bring their civilisation to the East. These families also glory in designating themselves Portuguese and are proud of their Lusitanian patro-

---

[1] *Traces de Portugais dans les principales langues des Indes Orientales Neerlandaises.*

[2] 'The Portuguese have always been in this matter very tolerant—and this is one of the great qualities of colonisers—and they would never think it a disgrace to contract marriage alliances with the high castes of India, the people with the purest Aryan blood in their veins.' Conde de Ficalho, *Garcia da Orta e o seu tempo*, p. 169.

[3] See João de Barros, Dec. II, V, 11.

'And already at this time there were in Goa four hundred and fifty married men, all servants of His Majesty, the King, and of the Queen, and of the Lords of Portugal; and those who wished to marry were so numerous that Afonso de Albuquerque could hardly grant their requests, for he did not give permission except for the men of proved character to marry.' *Commentaries* of Afonso Albuquerque, III, Ch. 9. [Hak. Soc., Vol. III, p. 41.—Ed.]

'The Portuguese make a marvellous profit all over India. Where they are well received they associate with the natives of the country, who in their turn accompany them in their voyages, so much so, that even all the crews of their ships and pilots are Indians, either Mohammedans or Hindus.' Pyrard de Laval, *Viagem*, Vol. 1, p. 373. [Hak. Soc., Vol. 1, p. 438.—Ed.]

nymics. On this very account they sometimes enjoy rights and privileges which are superior to those granted to the indigenous classes or are the same as those enjoyed by the Europeans as is the case in the Moluccas.[1]

Uptil now we know of no means more effective for civilizing backward peoples than Christianity and its missionary activities; and all colonial nations in greater or less degree employ and support these agencies. The Portuguese colonisers in preference to all other methods made use of religious propaganda as the most effective and enduring way of introducing their culture.[2] And if there were some resultant abuses now exaggerated by hyper-critics, the converts to Christianity are not prepared to admit that they owe more to Europe than to the religion which they

---

1 The Dutch and their proceedings have almost ceased to be remembered by the lowland Sinhalese; but the chiefs of the south and the west perpetuate with pride the honorific title Don, accorded to them by their first European conquerors, and still prefix to their ancient patronymics the sonorous Christian names of the Portuguese.' Sir James Emerson Tennent, *Ceylon, an Account of the Island.*

'In our camps there were four native Modeliares (Mudliars) who were in our service; they were all Christians, and the sons of Columbus, one of the headmen of the Island . . . and they were called Don Aleixo, Don Cosmo, Don Balthazar, and Don Theodozio.' João Ribeiro, *Fatalulade Historica da Ilha de Ceilão*, Bk. II, Ch. I.

2 'The Kings of Portugal always aimed, in their conquest of the East, at combining the two powers, spiritual and temporal, in such a way, that one of them should at no time be exercised without the other.' Diogo do Couto, Dec. VI, IV, 7.

'In Cochin I came across a primary school where children are taught, and I thought that Your Highness would not allow the children to rot now that they are in the school, and I, therefore, gave orders that one of the men who had contracted marriage here should teach the children to read and write; there will be an attendance at the school of nearly one hundred youths and they are the children of the panikars (teachers) and other honest men; the youths are very sharp and take in what is taught them, and that very quickly, and they are all Christians.' Afonso de Albuquerque, *Cartas* (Letters), I, p. 45.

'Antonio Galvão saw to it that the children were taught religious doctrine and to read and write'. Fernão Lopes de Castanheda, *Historia do Descobrimento e Conquista da India* (History of the Discovery and Conquest of India), Bk. VIII, Ch. 203.

profess. And as these converts recall to mind with gratitude the names of those who were the earliest to bring over to them their faith, with ample good will they forgive the Portuguese nation for the lapses they may well have been guilty of.[1] And among the cultured Hindus, who are championing the cause of national self-rule, there are not wanting some who regret, as I myself have had occasion to hear, that Portugal had not converted to her religion the greater part of India.

The Portuguese also promoted the civilisation of the East by her immense trade, bringing over from Europe objects unknown in these parts, introducing these into the domestic life of the people, and by carrying very many objects from parts of Asia to others more remote in the continent; this last fact is testified to by the names of the articles with which are associated their place of origin.[2]

The flora of Asia and, in a especial degree, that of India owes to Portugal the introduction of very many plants, most of

1 'With regard to the influence of Portuguese colonisation on the customs of the indigenous peoples, it is enough to say that since the very beginning Portuguese missionaries preached Christianity and founded Christian schools . . . It is unnecessary to add that the work of the missionaries introduced at the same time, the first elements of European civilisation and that the views of the conquerors, in respect of indigenous customs, began to be mellowed under the influence of Christianity.' Dr. Heyligers, *op. cit.*

'These Catholic populations, which even now are to be found there, in lands over which for long years we have lost our sway, and which combine with reverence for their faith their regard for the name of our land (Portugal), go to prove how deep the teaching and the influence of the Portuguese missionary had penetrated.' Conde do Ficalho, *op. cit.*, p. 160.

2 'Our ancient intercourse has, however, left indelible traces in the language. *Bengarajima*, *Chaujima* and *Santomejima* are fabrics which were imported from the Indian cities of Bengal (Port. *Bengala*), Chaul and St. Thomas (Port. *San Tomé*). *Amakawa-sango* are corals from Macau (formerly called Amacao); *Indengawa*, leather from India; and *Perusyagawa*, that from Persia.' Dr. N. Murakámi, *The Influence of Early Intercourse with Europe*, etc.

'They have also a great quantity of cloths from Cambaya, Chaul, and Dabul; and from Bengal they bring many *synabasos* which are a sort of cloth.' Duarte Barbosa, *Livro*, p. 261. [Hak. Soc. Longworth Dames's Translation, Vol. I, p. 93.]

them of American origin, many of which now grow wild, cover extensive areas and are of conspicuous utility.[1]

In like manner the fauna of the East was enriched, thanks to the Portuguese, by the addition of many specimens till then unknown or not at all common. Proof in support of this will be found in the course of this work.

The cultivation of fields and cocoanut plantations owed no little improvement to the Portuguese and especially to their religious orders who owned extensive but at the same time model estates.[2] And the same may be said with regard to other branches of industry.

II. *The Influence of the Portuguese Language*

The influence which the Portuguese language exercised in the past and even to this day exercises over a large part of Asia, more than any other factor, establishes the great value of the civilizing rôle of Portugal, so wholly singular and without a parallel. That the language of the conquering people will become the official language of a country is to be expected and, as a matter of course, the indigenous inhabitants find themselves under the necessity of learning to speak and write it. But this condition of affairs lasts only so long as the country is under the yoke of the foreigner. Thus we see that Holland, which exercised dominion over various parts of India has left scarcely any trace of its speech unless it be a word or two in one language or another.

It is likewise to be expected that the descendants of the once dominant nation will continue to employ, especially should they represent a large body, their mother tongue long time after their

[1] See Dr. D. G. Dalgado, *Flora de Goa e Savantvadi.* Also see Conde de Ficalho, *Memorias sobre a influencia dos descobrimentos portuguezes no conhecimento das plantas* (A Monograph on the Influence of the Portuguese Discoveries upon the Knowledge of Plants).

[2] 'The excellence of the Goa mangoes is stated to be due to the care and skill of the Jesuits.' *Hobson-Jobson* under *Mango.*

national sovereignty has passed away. This is the case with the Portuguese in Bengal, on both the coasts of the Indian peninsula, and in Malacca and Singapore.

But the phenomenon which one notices in Ceylon is nothing short of a marvel. There, not only the descendants of the Portuguese, but even the children of the Hollanders who exercised a sway over the island during as long a period as the Portuguese, and generally speaking all the Euro-Asiatics and even some of the indigenous inhabitants, have adopted Portuguese as their mother tongue. Besides these, there are the Europeans and the natives who learn the language for the convenience of trade, domestic requirements, or religious services.[1]

And it is yet again a matter for surprise and not a little amazing, that a section of the indigenous population, which cannot lay claim to a drop of Portuguese blood in its veins, should have repudiated its own vernacular and adopted, together with the Christian religion, Portuguese as its mother tongue. This is a phenomenon which one notices in the Presidency of Bombay and also in some parts of the Malabar Coast.[2]

The expansion of the Portuguese language over Asia during the past centuries is astounding. 'The history of the discovery of the Portuguese conquests is likewise the history, generally speaking, of the spread of the Portuguese language,'[3] says Dr. Schuchardt very aptly, and he establishes his thesis with much erudition. To this may be added that the history of the spread of Portuguese missionary activities is, in an equal measure, up to a certain point, the history of the diffusion of the Portuguese language. In those early days Portuguese was

---

1 'Already the language of the Dutch, which they sought to extend by penal enactments, has ceased to be spoken even by their direct descendants, whilst a corrupted Portuguese is to the present day the vernacular of the lower classes in every town of importance.' Emerson Tennent.

See the introduction to *Dialecto Indo-Português de Ceilão* by the author.

2 See *Dialecto Indo-Português do Norte* by the author.

3 *Beiträge zur Kenntniss des kreolischen Romanisch*, V.

regarded as the language of Christianity *par excellence* and a knowledge of it was looked upon as an index of European culture.[1]

Portuguese was spoken in its pure or corrupt form throughout the whole of India, in Malaysia, Pegu, Burma, Siam, Tonquin, Cochin-China, China, in Kamaran in Persia, in Basra of the Turkish Vilayet, and in Mecca in Arabia.[2] And it was spoken not only by the Portuguese and their descendants but by Hindus, Mahommedans, Jews, Malays, and by Europeans of other nationalities in their intercourse with one another or with the indigenous people. It was employed by the Dutch missionaries in their own dominions and, even to this day, English Protestant ministers make use of it in Ceylon. It was therefore for a long time the *lingua franca* of the East.[3]

---

[1] The Chinese converted by Thomas Pires, who were more than three hundred in number and were wont to meet in his daughter's house, used to recite their prayers in Portuguese; and likewise was the case with the Chinese family of Vasco Calvo. See Fernão Mendes Pinto, *Peregrinação* (Travels), Chh. CXI and CXVI. In the Portuguese dialect of Singapore, *papiá cristão* means 'to speak Portuguese.'

'Taken, for certain, to India from the Dominican mission of Larentuka, in the neighbouring island of Flores—from this Larentuka where even to-day Catholic prayers are recited in Portuguese.' Dr. Alberto de Castro, *Flores de Coral*, pp. 147-148.

[2] 'The Portuguese language is spoken and is current from Gujarat to Cape Comorin. It is not unknown on the Coromandel Coast as far as Bengal. It is in common use, in a form more or less pure, in Ceylon, in the Malay Archipelago, and in China. It is understood in Siam and in various groups of the Oceanic Archipelagos, etc.' Cunha Rivara, *Grammatica da Lingua Concani* (Grammar of the Konkani Language).

[3] 'Indo-Portuguese is more or less understood by all classes in the island of Ceylon and all along the whole coast of India; the extreme simplicity of its construction and the facility with which it can be acquired has brought about its extensive use as a medium of intercourse.' *The Bible of Every Land.* See Introduction to *Hobson-Jobson*, and the learned articles of Dr. Adolfo Coelho, published in the Journal of the Geographical Society of Lisbon (2nd, 3rd, and 6th series) under the title *Dialectos Romanicos*; also the same Journal (2nd series, p. 133) with regard to the expansion of Portuguese in Southern Africa. [See also A. X. Soares, *The Portuguese Heritage to the East* (Journal Bombay Branch R.A.S., No. LXXIV, Vol. XXVI).—Ed.]

It is true that to-day the radius of the circulation of Portuguese in Asia is no longer what it used to be; it is much reduced. It has ceased to be the *lingua franca*, and, of its several dialects, some are extinct, others are *in articulo mortis*, and it may well be that yet others shall, after the lapse of ages, have entirely disappeared. But when perchance Portuguese shall have ceased to be spoken in the East, the words from the beautiful tongue of Camoens, adopted and naturalised in a hundred and one of the vernaculars of the East, will continue to exist as long as the vernaculars themselves endure and stand as living and abiding monuments of the Portuguese dominion and civilisation in those parts.

As was to be expected, the languages which most felt the influence of Portuguese were those of India and the Eastern Archipelago. And these are precisely the languages which are the subject of this study, and to these for one reason or another are superadded others. It is on this account that the philological notes that follow in the succeeding chapters have most reference to India.

III. *The Languages of India. General Observations*

India, on a par with her other riches, is rich also in languages and dialects of various species and gradations, which are spoken by an indigenous population of over 300 millions in an area which is equal to that of half Europe.[1]

Especially in the mountainous tracts inhabited by numerous tribes, nomadic and savage or semi-savage there exist so many diverse forms of speech that it is difficult to say whether they are distinct languages, well-defined dialects, or mere variants. In the plains the more important languages spread themselves out as the result of a process of absorption, and many dialects ordinarily limited to provinces or districts are easily reduced to one common

---

[1] [According to the Census of 1921, the population of British India, excluding Ceylon, was reported to be 318,942,480.—Ed.]

type. But there are cities like Bombay and Calcutta which are veritable Babels, where not infrequently one comes across people who can speak, without much difficulty, two or three languages, and educated persons who can express themselves correctly in half a dozen tongues.

But the scientific exploration and the comparative study of this vast language-field may well be said to be yet in its embryonic stage, notwithstanding the valuable investigations on general or special lines which during the last years have seen the light of day thanks to Erskine Perry, John Wilson, Max Müller, George Campbell, Crawfurd, Marsden, Hoernle, Caldwell, Latham, Burnell, Beames, Cust, Grierson, and other eminent orientalists.[1]

Scholars who were absorbed during a long period in the study of the Sanskrit language and its literature, either did not find the time for an analysis of the vernaculars, or perhaps did not deem them worthy of their attention. The early missionaries, as a rule, used to learn the common speech of their zone only so far as was necessary for their work of preaching the Gospel. If they managed to write anything for the use of the public it was no more than what was necessary for teaching religious doctrine to catechumens and neophytes.[2] Even thus, the earliest

---

1 'For nearly thirty years philology has been wandering through the maze of Indian languages with uncertain steps..... Speculations regarding Indian languages must wait till the survey is concluded and all the facts are represented in a convenient form. Till then, even the classification adopted in the following pages must be taken as provisional.' G. Grierson, *The Languages of India*, p. 1.

2 It is but natural that the more proficient should leave behind hand-written notes, grammatical and lexicographical, for the private use of their colleagues and successors in office. 'Father Francisco Anriquez learnt to speak the language and even read and write the script of the country (Malabar) in six months, and within a short time brought out a grammar and a glossary of the language, to the astonishment of the native population and to the great advantage of our Fathers and Lay Brothers who, since then till now, thanks to these and other books which were being produced, study the Malabar language with the same ease with which they do Latin.' Rev. João Lucena, *Historia da Vida do Padre Francisco de Xavier*, Bk. V, Ch. 25.

writings in connection with the languages of the East have come exclusively from the preachers of the Gospel, and in modern times the cultivation of these languages is principally their work.[1]

Since the last fifty years and especially during very recent years the study and the cultivation of the more important living languages has grown apace thanks to the persistent efforts of missionaries and indologists and to the sustained stimulus and generous patronage of the British Government. Everywhere there are to be found mixed vernacular schools, and every year there is published a large number of books in the characters of the various vernaculars, most of them of a didactic nature, not to speak of the large number of periodicals and journals which are read with great avidity by the present generation.[2]

It is, therefore, not to be wondered at that up to now there has been no investigation on scientific lines of the total number of languages and dialects in India nor has there been a unanimous consensus of opinion regarding the limits of the Indian language-field which, of course, varies a great deal from the geographical and political boundaries of India. Robert Cust enumerates no less than two hundred and forty-three languages and two hundred and ninety-six of the dialects grouped under eight families; but he unduly extends the range of the language-field including in it Timor, Madagascar, and the island of Formosa, owing, as he says, to linguistic and ethnic affinities.[3]

In a zone much more circumscribed, but which however included Burma and Siam, Beames in 1868 counted hundreds of

---

1 'To one class of labourers Science is more indebted than to any other. I allude to the Missionaries, both Protestant and Roman Catholic, who have vied with each other in letting light into dark places.' Robert Cust, *A Sketch of the Modern Languages of the East Indies*, p. 21.

2 About eight hundred indigenous periodicals are published in India; they are printed in nineteen different languages. And about seven thousand books are printed each year in the vernacular languages.

3 *Op. cit.*, p. 148.

languages with many of their principal dialects, omitting some and designating others under generic heads.[1]

Sir George Grierson in a more recent publication based upon the British Indian census of 1901, to which he contributed a chapter on the languages of India, computes the total number to be one hundred and forty-seven, including therein the two spoken in Aden (Semitic and Hamitic) and excluding therefrom those of Ceylon (Sinhalese and the language of the Veddas, the aborigines of the island) and of the temporary sojourners in the country. From among the Malayan group of languages he includes only two (Selung and Nicobarese) and he makes Konkani a dialect of Marathi.[2]

IV. *Classification and Division of Languages*

The vernaculars of India and of the Indian Archipelago, actually spoken, can be grouped under five principal families: Aryan (Indic and Iranian branches), Dravidian, Munda or Kolarian, Indo-Chinese (with three sub-families: Mon-Khmer, Tibeto-Burman, Siamo-Chinese), and Malayo-Polynesian.[3]

The Iranian branch has its representatives in Pushtu or Pakhtu and in Baluchi, in the north of India.

The Indic branch includes the Indo-Aryan or Gaurian languages, which stand in the same relation to classical Sanskrit as the Romance languages do to classical Latin.[4] Such are:

---

[1] 'In the Punjab every district has its own dialect and some districts have more than one.'..... 'Munipuri dialects, Koreng dialects, Karen dialects.' John Beames, *Outlines of Indian Philology*.

[2] George Grierson, *The Languages of India, and the Census of 1901*, in *The Asiatic Society Quarterly Review*, April, 1904. See also *Linguistic Survey of India*, by the same author.

[3] Arabic is the sacred, and Persian, the literary tongue of the Mahommedans. The languages of the Andaman Islands and of the gipsies are not classified. European languages and their dialects are excluded.

[4] There are some Sanskritists who believe that Sanskrit was not a living language, in the sense in which Latin and Greek were, spoken by any people, but merely a language elaborated by the Brahmins for their orthodox compositions, on the lines of the old Vedic tongue. 'Sanskrit was only a literary language but never spoken in the sense of a vernacular.' Hoernle and Grierson, *A Com-*

Hindi, Punjabi, Sindhi, Bihari, Bengali, Marathi, Konkani, Gujarati, Assamese, Oriya, Kashmiri, Nepali, Sinhalese.[1] Sir Grierson adds to these eleven others which he designates as Aryan but non-Sanskritic and these are spoken in Gilgit, Chitral, and Kafiristan. The total population of those who speak the Aryan tongues is more than 220 millions.[2]

To the Dravidian family belong Tamil, Malayalam, Telugu, Kanarese, Tulu, Kodagu; Toda, Kota, Kurukh (or Uraon), Malhar (or Rajmahali); Gond, Khond; Kandh, Kolami. The first five and perhaps the Kodagu are cultivated; the rest are not cultivated. The population that employs the Dravidian languages is more than 57 millions.[3]

---

parative Dictionary of the Bihari Language, Introduction. But it is necessary to make a distinction: Sanskrit properly so called or classic Sanskrit could not have been a mother tongue, learnt at the breast of the mother, but yet it is undeniable, according to the data provided by Yaska, Panini, and Patanjali that it was spoken by the cultured classes throughout the length and breadth of Ariavarta (from the Himalayas to the Vindyas), in the same way as Portuguese is in Goa. See Arthur Macdonell, *A History of Sanskrit Literature*. And it is to be noted that in the census of 1901, seven hundred and sixteen individuals declared Sanskrit to be their language.

Sanskrit was evolved from the dialect spoken on the banks of the Sarasvati river almost in the same way as Latin was from the Italian dialect of Latium. Bālabhāshā (literally 'the language of children') corresponds to Low Latin which was spoken by the masses. In many of the Indian languages, inclusive of the Dravidian, the literary idiom differs much from the spoken, as must also have happened, though perhaps not to the same extent, with Latin and Greek. Vid. Robert Caldwell, *A Comparative Grammar of the Dravidian Languages*.

1 With respect to the classification of this language, there is a difference of opinion among indologists and to this we will refer hereafter.

2 The words in the early Indo-Aryan language, mentioned in the Vedas, found their way into the new Indo-Aryan idioms through two channels: directly, through the original Prakrit—a spontaneous and common evolution, and indirectly, through classic Sanskrit, by the labours of the learned. The former are called *tadbhāvas*, and the latter *tatsamas*, which again are divided into ancient and modern. To comprehend the difference: the Portuguese terms *chão* (ground), *cheio* (full), *auto* (action), and *feito* (deed) are *tadbhāvas*, with reference to Latin: *plano* (plain), *pleno* (full), *acto* (action), and *facto* (deed) are *tatsamas*.

3 Brahui, spoken in Baluchistan by about 160,000 people according to the 1921 census report is a remote branch of the Dravidian group. The ancient

The third family—Kolarian—has its original home in the mountainous regions of Western Bengal, and contains ten distinct members, among which are the Santali and the Kol, spoken by 3 millions. The sub-family Mon-Khmer of the Indo-Chinese branch is, at the present day, represented in India by Khassi in Assam, and by Palaung and Wa in the mountains of Upper Burma, and outside India by the languages of Pegu and Cambodia.

Tibetan and Burmese are the two cultivated languages which belong to the other sub-family of the Indo-Chinese branch; they have in the mountainous regions of Northern India innumerable members, most of them little known, and some of them classified in groups, like: Garo, Bodo, Naga, Kuki-chin, Kachin, Himalayan. The Nevari and other dialects of Nepal with the exception of Nepalese are related to Tibetan.

The third sub-family which, outside China, has its principal home in Siam is represented in India by the language of the Shan States and of the Karens of Southern Burma.

Finally the fifth family—Malayan or Malayo-Polynesian—takes in Malacca and Malaysia. Cust makes out ten groups: the Sumatra-Malacca, Java, Celebes, Borneo, Philippines, Molucca, Timor, China, Madagascar and the Alfurese-Negrito group—and enumerates eighty-eight languages and twenty-nine dialects.

With this genealogical classification agrees more or less the morphological. The Indo-Aryan languages are polysyllabic and inflectional, some of them with a tendency towards the analytic stage. The Dravidian are polysyllabic, agglutinative, prone to the use of suffixes, and with a tendency towards a certain degree of inflection. The Kolarian are polysyllabic, agglutinative, suffixive and infixative like the Turkish. The Indo-Chinese languages are monosyllabic and agglutinative. The Malayo-Polynesian are agglutinative but dissyllabic.[1]

Sanskrit writers used to designate the languages of Southern India *andhradrāvidabhāshā*, 'the language of the Andhras and the Dravidas.'

[1] For more details, see Cust, Beames, Caldwell and especially Grierson, *op. cit.*

V. *Geographical Distribution*

It is evident that in the present state of our knowledge, which is far from complete, it is not possible to trace with mathematical accuracy the lines which divide each of the living languages of India, nor would this be possible in respect of certain localities.

Apart from the difficulty referred to above, of determining the territorial boundaries of the languages of India, there arises another of ascertaining whether the hill peoples who are ethnically distinct are also separated by language differences, and if their languages belong to one and the same family.[1]

There are countries where two or more mother tongues or vernaculars exist side by side spoken by different tribes or races; this phenomenon is due to immigration in the remote past.

Besides this, two or more languages become so blended along the frontier of a continuous stretch of territory that, they either go to form one separate dialect with elements taken equally from each language and without any genealogical subordination or one of the two rises superior to the other and preserves its ties of family likeness.

It is not to be expected, therefore, that the linguistic maps which have till now been published are accurate in respect of all the languages; some of them err through excess—by double designation or enlargement of the language-field—others through defect—by omission or contraction of the language area.

The zone of each of the more important languages is sufficiently well known in its general lines and will be marked out in the description that follows of each of these.

---

1 'In the Himalayas the two families, as far as we have data for them, are so intermixed, that it is difficult, if not impossible, to lay down definite boundaries...... Especially is this the case in the large kingdom of Nepal which is still a *terra incognita* in many respects.' Beames, *Outlines of Indian Philology*, p. 9.

The linguistic map that is annexed to this work is an adaptation of the one worked out by Cust, with certain modifications, which I have found very necessary.

VI. *The Scope of this Study*

This work treats of:

1. The Aryan Family, (*a*) Indic branch: Konkani, Marathi, Gujarati, Hindi, Hindustani, Laskari-Hindustani, Nepali, Oriya, Bengali, Assamese, Sindhi, Punjabi, Kashmiri and Sinhalese.—(*b*) Iranian branch: Modern Persian.
2. The Dravidian Family: Tamil, Malayalam, Telugu, Kanarese and Tulu.
3. The Indo-Chinese Family, (*a*) Tibeto-Burman branch: Garo, Burmese, and Tibetan.—(*b*) Mon-Khmer branch: Khassi and Kambojan.—(*c*) Siamo-Chinese branch: Siamese, Annamite and Tonkinese.
4. The Malayo-Polynesian Family: Malay, Achinese, Batta, Sundanese, Javanese, Madurese, Balinese, Dayak, Macassar, Bugui, Nicobarese, Teto, Galoli and Malagasy.
5. The Semitic Family: Eastern Arabic.
6. Japanese, without any classification.
7. Anglo-Indian and Indo-French.
8. Anglo-Chinese or Pidgin-English.
9. Mediately: Some languages of the Malayo-Polynesian family and other origins.

I did not extend the scope of my treatise further than this because I had no materials on hand for doing so and because I did not wish to protract its publication indefinitely. The languages which have not been included in this survey are of very little importance and very little influenced by Portuguese.

VII. *Exotic Elements*

No Asiatic language, generally speaking, and no Indian language in particular, can pride itself on possessing a vocabulary which is purely vernacular, free from a very considerable and, at the same time very necessary admixture indeed, of heterogeneous elements.[1] The exotic elements were first introduced by Sanskrit, whose influence direct or indirect on the Dravidian languages (and on a smaller scale on the Malayan languages) is comparable to that which Latin continues to exercise on the non-Romance languages of Europe. It is divided into old Sanskrit which is in common use and the modern which is confined to literary purposes.

The Mahommedan invasion, in its turn, brought into the country many Arabic and Persian terms but these enriched the vocabularies more of the Aryan than of the Dravidian languages: its influence on these was similar to what it exercised on the languages in the peninsula of Spain.

After them the Portuguese, as was to be expected, gave a large number of words of their own language to almost all the languages, cultivated or uncultivated, what time they themselves were absorbing a large number of words from them into their own tongue. This they effected by direct or indirect means, and they also helped to spread over the country some vernacular expressions derived from one or the other language after they had undergone sometimes a phonetic modification at their hands.

The Dutch, as has been said before, have left very few vestiges of their language and these almost exclusively in Sinhalese; nor, in spite of their long domination, is the influence of their language very great in the languages of Malay, as is admitted by Dr. Fokker.

---

[1] Sanskrit herself borrowed from the Latin *dināru*, denarius, and from the Greek *kalama*, a reed used for writing, *horā*, hour, and other astronomical terms.

Finally, English is at present exercising an influence analogous to that of the Portuguese language, especially in the administrative and commercial terminology, in all the lands subject to its sway. And in course of time this influence will grow more extensive even as the knowledge of the English tongue spreads more among the people.

VIII. *The Agencies at Work and Grounds for the Influence of Portuguese on Asiatic Languages*

The introduction of Portuguese words into Asiatic languages has been effected through agencies which have been working either separately or simultaneously :—

(*a*) direct dominion
(*b*) commercial connection
(*c*) political influence
(*d*) vicinage of Portuguese colonies
(*e*) religious propaganda
(*f*) consociation of many vernaculars in certain cities
(*g*) borrowings from a contiguous language or from a more important language which had already been influenced
(*h*) co-existence of Indo-Portuguese
(*i*) Anglo-Indian vocabulary

The influence of Portuguese and its range is determined by the nature of the cause or combination of causes, and the degree of its action and extent. There are terms in common use which are to be met with in all or almost all the indigenous cultivated languages, and the number of such is small; there are others which are exclusively used by Christians; again there are some which are known to the educated classes and used only in the principal cities.

The directions in which this influence was most felt, and the chief reasons that led to its operation, may be brought under the following heads :—

1. The Christian religion which was propagated and carried on by Portuguese missionaries or by missionaries who though not Portuguese had assimilated Portuguese ways of life and thought; this was so because there were no vernacular terms corresponding exactly with what they wished to teach, or such as were known to the people at large. Again, even when suitable terms or expressions existed in the indigenous languages, they made use of the Portuguese words for fear lest the people might confound Christianity with Hinduism or Mahommedanism and thereby trace resemblances between these three religions. Cf. *cruz* (cross), *igreja* (church), *altar* (altar), *padre* (priest), *casar* (to marry). Likewise the names of ecclesiastical dignitaries, of church vestments and vessels, of ceremonies and liturgical festivities are with few exceptions Portuguese, as: *papa* (Pope), *bispo* (bishop), *arcebíspo* (archbishop), *meirinho* (beadle); *cálix* (chalice), *hóstia*, *particula* (the sacred wafer); *alva* (alb), *estola* (stole), *capa* (cope); *Natal* (Christmas), *Advento* (Advent), *Pascoa* (Easter).[1]

2. The new civilisation which introduced new vocables to signify objects till then unknown or little known, such as: *armário* (ward-robe), *balde* (bucket),

---

[1] For example, in Tamil, not to speak of Konkani, the following ecclesiastical terms are in use: *amito* (amice), *alva* (alb), *cordão* (cord), *casula* (chasuble), *dalmática* (dalmatic), *manípulo* (maniple), *estola* (stole), *capa* (cope), *cálix* (chalice), *patena* (paten), *pala* (?), *bôlsa* (?), *corporal* (corporal), *sanguinho* (a little cloth with which the priest wipes the chalice after receiving the sacrament), *cota* (surplice), *hóstia* (host), *partícula* (wafer), *missal* (missal), *ritual* (ritual), *estante* (a reading desk), *altar* (altar), *cruz* (cross), *castiçal* (candle-stick), *tabernáculo* (tabernacle), *sacramento* (sacrament), *turíbulo* (censer), *naveta* (incense-pan), *caldeirinha* (?), *galheta* (cruet), *pálio* (a canopy carried over the sacrament in processions), *sotaina* (soutane), *loba* (cassock). For the most part such vocables are not referred to in this book.

bomba (pump), *botão* (button), *camisa* (shirt), *fita* (ribbon), *pena* (quill), *pipa* (barrel), *pistola* (pistol), *meia* (sock), *cadeira* (chair).

3. The introduction of new plants; with them were naturally carried the names by which they were known in their places of origin, like: *ananás* (pine-apple), *anona* (bull's heart or the *Anona reticulata*), *caju* (*Anacardium occidentale*), *couve* (cabbage), *papaia* (*Carica papaya*), *pera* (guava or *Psidium guyava*), *tabaco* (tobacco).

4. Foreign words which are often regarded as better adapted to convey an air of distinction or superiority to persons or objects.[1] Cf. *mestre* (master), *pedreiro* (mason), *louvado* (expert, arbitrator), *copo* (cup), *cozinha* (kitchen), *doce* (sweet), *pão* (bread), *jôgo* (game, play), *tronco* (lock-up).

5. Certain words which are adopted by preference because they are simple to pronounce, and are withal expressive and characteristic. Cf. *ama* (nurse), *aia* (ayah), *bacia* (plate), *banco* (bench), *grade* (railing), *leilão* (auction-sale), *sorte* (lottery).

6. Again, there are certain terms the adoption of which to the detriment of or in addition to the vernacular word can solely be explained by the fascination that certain vocables are capable of exercising. Cf. *buraco* (hole), *chave* (key), *paga* (salary), *ponta* (point or end), *renda* (tax).

7. We also come across some words of Asiatic origin which were introduced directly into the other languages from Indo-Portuguese, such as: *achar*

---

[1] As is the case in Portuguese with reference to French and English terms: *soirée, matinée, corbeille, délivrance ; club, lunch, sport.*

(pickle), *chita* (chintz), *gudão* (store-room), *pires* (saucer), *rota* (walking-stick).

IX. *The Morphology of the Exotics*

The greater number of the imported words is made up, as is natural, of substantives which are either the names of persons or objects, and of some abstract nouns, and these are employed sometimes in an extended and, at others, in a limited sense.

Abstract terms and derivatives are formed and the nouns declined in conformity with the general rules of each language. To take an instance, *bebdó* (drunkard), in Konkani, gives *bebdepaṇ* or *bebdikáy* (drunkenness); *bébaduva*, in Sinhalese, gives *bĕbadu-kama*. From *kāzár*, also used as a substantive in Konkani in the sense of 'marriage', is derived: *kāzāri* (married), *kāzārātsó* (marriageable), *kāzró* ('marriage' in a depreciative sense).

Some substantives are employed in an acceptation peculiar to the local Portuguese dialect as in the Sinhalese, *rámuva* (from the Port. dialect, ramo) for 'mould'; *réndaya* (from the Port. dialect, renda) for 'rent, 'toll, tax payable to the State'.

Verbs have very little adaptability and are never much in demand for borrowing purposes. And yet we meet many of them in Konkani and in the Malayan group. In Konkani they remain as a rule unchanged and are conjugated with the vernacular verb corresponding to 'to make' or 'to be' according as it is transitive or intransitive and reflexive. The Malay verbs have no inflexions.

Some words with a verbal form have, in addition or exclusively, the meaning of the substantive, as *casar* (to marry and marriage), *pintar* (to paint and a painting), *jogar* (game of dice), *confessar* (confession).

Some adjectives occur in a few languages, which are also used adverbially as the result of indigenous influence, as, in Goa, *júst* (just and justly), *sert* (certain and certainly). Adverbs proper, conjunctions and prepositions occur only in the Malay group. But we meet with *contra* (against) in Konkani.

X. *Remarks on the Phonetics*

Portuguese words in their transition to Oriental languages suffer as a rule phonetic changes which are more or less important; the same is the case with Asiatic vocables which were introduced into Portuguese. Some of the changes are common to almost all languages and these are consequent on their passage from one language to another or on their obeying the same laws; there are others which are peculiar to each language or to a group or family of languages.

This work being primarily intended for lexicographical purposes, it is not possible to analyse and explain in every case all the phonetic changes that so many words have gone through. On this I think, it would be useful to set down here, in general only the most important changes:

1. The initial vowel when it constitutes a syllable by itself is dropped in the case of polysyllabic words in the same way as in corrupt Portuguese dialects: Thus we have: *kăphlár* from 'acafelar' (to plaster), *nánas* from 'ananás' (pine-apple), *nona* from 'anona' (bull's heart or *Anona reticulata*); *már, murá* (L.-Hindust.) from 'amarra' (cable); *girjá* from 'igreja' (church); *vānjel* (Konk.) from 'evangelho' (evangel); *būrnal* (L.-Hindust.) from 'embornal' (scupper hole in a ship); *duljens* (Konk.) from 'indulgência' (indulgence); *legojo* (Jav.) from 'algoz' (executioner).
2. Sometimes the initial syllable when it begins with a consonant is likewise dropped, as in *míngo* or *míngu* (Mal., Jav.) from 'domingo' (Sunday); *báko* (in many of the Malayo-Polynesian languages) from 'tabaco' (tobacco); *dílu* (Mac.) from 'codilho' (a term employed in a game of cards); *pinéti* (Mal.) from 'alfinete' (pin).

3. The final vowel when preceded by a stressed vowel may also sometimes be dropped as in *almāri* from 'armário' (ward-robe); *basí* from 'bacia' (plate); in Konkani all the post-tonic vowels are eliminated; thus we have, *ālmár* from 'armário' (ward-robe); *vigár* from 'vigário' (vicar); *muzg* from música (music) and músico (musician); *kámbr* from 'câmara' (chamber).
4. The final *a* after a consonant is treated in diverse ways. In the Aryan languages of the South (except Sinhalese) it is silent as in *phít* from 'fita' (ribbon), *kamís* or *kamíj* from 'camisa' (shirt), *bomb* from 'bomba' (pump). In those of the North, ordinarily, it is lengthened out or stressed as in *phītá*, *pīpá*, *gīrjá*, *kamij*, *mêj* from 'fita' (ribbon); 'pipa' (barrel); 'igreja' (church); 'camisa' (shirt); 'mesa' (table). In the Dravidian it is changed into *u̥*, a favourite termination with them: *kamísu* (Tam. *kamisei*), *pistúlu̥*, *rípu̥*, *váru̥* from 'camisa' (shirt), 'pistola' (pistol), 'ripa' (lath), 'vara' (yard). In the Malayan, the final *a* is retained in some words, whilst in others it is changed into the closed *ô*: *renda*, *rendô*, from 'renda' (tax or hire), *roda*, *rodô* from 'roda' (wheel), *ronda*, *rondô* from 'ronda' (patrol).
5. The final *e* mute oscillates between the tonic *í* (Aryan languages) and the atonic *i* (Dravidian and Malayan languages): *bāldí*, *báldi* from 'balde' (bucket); *chāví*, *chávi* from 'chave' (key); *pādrí*, *pádri* from 'padre' (priest). In Konkani and Marathi it is dropped many times, being preceded by the simple consonant: *kôb* from 'couve' (cabbage); *garád* from 'grade' (railing); *búl* (Konk.) from 'bule' (tea-pot); *kôch* (Konk.) from 'coche' (coach).

6. Similarly, the final *o* is dropped in the Aryan languages; it is changed into the short *u* in the Dravidian and into *u* short or the closed *ô* in the Malayan languages. Thus we have *bánk*, *bánku*, *bánkô* from 'banco' (bench); *kald*, *káldu*, *káldô* from 'caldo' (broth); *burákh* (Aryan) from 'buraco' (hole). But *tambākú* or *tamākú* from 'tabaco' (tobacco), in almost all languages.

7. The diphthongs *ei* and *ou* change into *é* or *ê* and *ó*, as in the Portuguese dialects. Thus we have *bandér*, *bandéra*, *banderô* from 'bandeira' (flag); *kadér*, *kadera*, *kadêl* from 'cadeira' (chair); *kôb*, *kôbis* from 'couve,' pl. couves (cabbage); *orívis* (Mal.) from 'ourives' (goldsmith).

8. Some vowels in contact with the labial consonants become nasal: *tambakú* from 'tabaco' (tobacco), *pimp* from 'pipa' (barrel), *bhompḷá* (Mar.) from 'abóbora' (pumpkin). Also *phínt* from 'fita' (ribbon).[1]

9. *Ch* preserves its old sound which is current in the north of Portugal and identical with the oriental *tch*: *tchepém* from 'chapéu' (hat), *tchinél* from 'chinella' (slipper). In some languages as Konkani and Marathi it sounds like *ts* when followed by *a* and *o*. Thus, *tsāví* from 'chave' (key).

10. *V* is almost equivalent to the English *w* especially when it is a medial. Such languages as have no *v* (and sometimes also those that have it) convert it into *b* in the same manner as they change *f* into *p*.

11. The initial *r* is pronounced as though it were a medial. Double *r's* are changed into a single as a

[1] The same phenomenon is also noticeable in Portuguese before mute consonants: *fiandeiro* (spinner) from *fiar* (to spin); *lavandeiro* (washerman) from *lavar* (to wash).

rule, because they are not to be met with in the majority of Asiatic languages; e.g. we have *kareta* from 'carreta' (light cart), *amáru* from 'amarra' (cable), *bora* from 'bôrra' (wine lees), *phôr* from 'fôrro' (lining).

12. *Lh* and *nh* which have no sounds corresponding to them are rendered respectively by *ly* or *l* and *ny* or *n*. Thus we have *tuváliya, tuvála, tuvál, tuvāḷó* from 'toalha' (towel); *veillu, el,* from 'velho' (old); *kunyá* from 'cunha' (wedge); *barkíṇ* from 'barquinha' (a skiff). Konkani, Malayalam and some other languages preserve the original sound in some words representing it by *ñ* or *ññ*. Thus we get *modiñ* or *modinh* (Konk.) from 'modinha' (song), *viññu* (Malayal.) from 'vinho' (wine).

13. *S* intervocalic (=*z*) is generally changed into *j* (sometimes into *s* sibilant) either because many of the languages have no such sound or because it is only associated with the syllables of certain vowels (*a, o, u,* as in Konkani, Marathi, Sindhi). Thus we have *mêj* from 'mesa' (table), *kamíj* or *kamís* from 'camisa' (shirt).[1]

14. *R* and *l* change places in those languages which have these sounds but in those which have only one of them the one is replaced by the other. Thus we have *kadêl, bhobḷó* from 'cadeira' (chair), and 'abóbora' (pumpkin); *boru, charamera* (Jap.) from 'bôlo' (cake), and 'charamela' (bagpipe); *complador, patili* (Pid.-Engl.) from 'comprador' (steward) and 'padre' (priest).

15. Surd consonants frequently become sonant, but rarely does the reverse of this happen. Thus we

---

[1] In Konkani *j* is usually changed into *z* after *a, o, u*: *imáz* from Port. *imagem* (image), *relóz* from Port. *relójio* (watch), *āzúd* from Port. *ajuda* (assistance).

have *alavángu* from 'alavanca' (a hand-spike); *turung* from 'tronco' (lock-up); *práda* from 'prata' (silver); *prek* from 'prego' (nail).

16. Some consonants, especially when they are in contact with *r*, become cerebral as happens in Sanskrit. Thus we have *soḍtí, sorṭí* from 'sorte' (lottery); *korṇel* from 'coronel' (colonel); *bhobḷó*, or *bhompḷá* from 'abóbora' (pumpkin); *barkin* from 'barquinha' (a skiff).

17. There are instances of aspirate consonants, as in *khamís* from 'camisa' (shirt); *khurís* from 'cruz' (cross); *burákh* from 'buraco' (hole); *bhobḷó* or *bhompḷá* from 'abóbora' (pumpkin).

18. There occurs a transposition of *r*, as in *girjá* from 'igreja' (church), *krasa* from 'garça' (heron).

19. The hiatus in the middle of a word is destroyed by the intercalation of a *v*, as in *tuvál* or *tuvāló* from 'toalha' (towel), *baluvárdi* from 'baluarte' (bastion).

20. When there are two consonants together and the second of them is an *r*, a separation is effected between them by the insertion of a vowel (*suarabacti*): *garád* from 'grade' (railing); *paránch* from 'prancha' (scaffolding); *karáb* from 'cravo' (a pink); *turung* from 'tronco' (trunk); *vídur, vídurava* from 'vidro' (glass). Some of the languages do not admit of compound consonants at all; others admit of only double or twin consonants.

XI. *Sources and Difficulties of such a Study*

The most satisfactory way of compiling a complete list of the Portuguese words grafted on to the vocabularies of Asiatic languages, would naturally be to collect the terms by a living and intimate contact with all the different strata of each people, due regard being paid to every phase of their languages. Now, this is well nigh impossible in view of the enormous area and the immense variety of languages to be explored and investigated, not to speak of other obvious difficulties.

Even a seasoned polyglot would find it very difficult to be able to acquire, at the end of many years, complete personal knowledge of about half a dozen languages, and these of one or two language groups only. It is just on this account that there are as yet no comparative dictionaries just as there are comparative grammars of great value.[1] Such as exist are small vocabularies or dictionaries of some dialects or of two or three of cognate languages.[2]

Another way, supplementary but deficient withal, would be to obtain with the help of competent persons a list of Portuguese vocables that have found their way into their respective languages. This again is not easy, because there are few who would show any inclination for a task so thankless, involving the assembling of words which do not spontaneously present themselves to the mind when dissociated from any specific ideas. Even with the help of obliging friends it was not possible for me to secure more than three lists of Tamil, one of Bengali, one of Kanarese, and one of Telugu, and these too were incomplete and summary. I am not aware that such lists of Portuguese words have been made, incomplete though they be, excepting one relating to Hindustani (Schuchardt, *op. cit.*) and some others bearing upon the languages of the Malayo-Polynesian group.

Under these circumstances the only course to take was to run through, word by word, the dictionaries of such languages as

---

1 John Beames, *Comparative Grammar of Aryan Languages.* Robert Caldwell, *A Comparative Grammar of the Dravidian or South Indian Family of Languages.*

2 In 1868 Sir W. W. Hunter published a list of 186 vocables in 120 non-Aryan languages or dialects under the title of *Comparative Dictionary of the Languages of India and High Asia.* F. A. Sevettonham likewise brought out his *Comparative Vocabulary of the Dialects of the Wild Tribes inhabiting the Malayan Peninsula.*

possess them, and hunt them out. But very few are the living languages of Asia which like Marathi, Hindustani or Malay possess a dictionary which may be called a *thesaurus linguæ*. The majority of them have been compiled for school or missionary purposes and some of them do not pretend to satisfy any but the elementary needs. It is, therefore, too much to expect that in such compilations will appear all the words in general or special use.[1]

Dictionary-makers as a rule try to avoid foreign words (I am speaking from experience), perhaps because of a desire to show off the richness of the language, or, when they do mention them, interpret them by descriptions with which the spoken language will have nothing to do. When they point out the etymology of a word, and, there are very few who attempt this, as the greater number of them are not acquainted with Portuguese, they follow the usual tradition and attribute it to a source to which it does not really belong or on the other hand, evade the difficulty by referring it to one of the indigenous languages.[2]

In some cases there are great difficulties in ascertaining whether certain words really owe their existence to Portuguese or whether Portuguese itself received them from other sources; of this kind are terms like *pires* (saucer), *gago* (stammerer), *canga* (yoke), *bafo* (breath); again, whether Portuguese or English is the real source of such words as *biscoito* (biscuit), *botelha* (bottle), *batata* (potato), *estala* (stable); whether certain terms were already known and in use before the Portuguese discoveries and conquests,

---

1 Add to this the fact that some of the most valuable dictionaries are not to be had at all in the book market or are to be had only at very great cost. The public libraries of Portugal possess very few dealing with Asiatic languages; at my pressing request the authorities of the 'Biblioteca Nacional' (National Library), Lisbon, purchased half a dozen of them.

2 There are also some among those presuming to be well informed in these matters who maintain that with the exception of *tôpo* (top), *câmara* (room), *fita* (ribbon), 'and few other words, the Portuguese domination in India left few traces of their language'. *Blackwood's Edinburgh Magazine* quoted by Schuchardt.

such as *tabaco* (tobacco), *arratel* (pound weight), *chá* (tea), *café* (coffee); whether certain terms are in fact not instances of parallelisms, sometimes with very slight change of meaning, such as *chapa* (stamp or mark), *tanque* (tank), *varanda* (veranda).[1]

XII. *The Method observed in this Work*

Among the Portuguese words in this work, there are some whose etymology is evident or almost certain; there are others whose source in the indigenous languages is doubtful or improbable and, finally, there are a few of which it can be said with certainty or with great probability, that they are not the originals of the Asiatic vocables.

Those which come under the second head I have marked with a note of interrogation placed at the very beginning when the doubt embraces all the languages mentioned, or placed before one or more of them when the uncertainty is limited to these. Those of the third class I have distinguished with an asterisk, and I have indicated the reasons for the inclusion of such in my list and also for rejecting them as the etymons of the Asiatic words; I have done this lest it might appear that I had omitted to mention them because I was not acquainted with them.

There are some words which are not genuine Portuguese words and which, therefore, the Portuguese could not have carried with them from Europe; they belong to an Asiatic language or group of languages. But as such words form part of the Asio-Lusitanian vocabulary and were adopted and disseminated by the Portuguese I thought they should have a place in this work after due reservation had been made.

---

[1] 'Derivations of names are much better ascertained in the countries where they originate, and where we know the languages well, than in strange countries where we scarcely know a word much less know the derivations.' Garcia da Orta, *Colloquios dos Simples e Drogas da India*, LVIII. (Markham's Translation, p. 462.)

I have mentioned diverse derivates and compounds of the more important Portuguese words met with in the indigenous languages, and I have done this to prove how the foreign word had acquired a general vogue. In some cases I have also pointed out the zone in which the word is current or the class of people who employ it. Not infrequently I have mentioned the vernacular terms which more or less correspond to the Portuguese words, in order to show that it was not the absolute lack of these in the indigenous languages that led to the adoption of the foreign vocable. I have not carried this process very far because besides making the work too prolix it would involve too great labour.

The vernacular terms, which I have cited as the equivalents of the Portuguese and as common to languages of one family, are reproduced in their original form: in Konkani, in the Indo-Aryan; in Tamil, in the Dravidian; and in Malay, as belonging to the Malayan group.

In the tabulation of Asiatic languages there were two methods open to me, viz. to adopt the geographical or the genealogical, and these do not always coincide. I preferred to make use of the genealogical and the one which traces affinities, at the same time maintaining, whenever possible, the geographical continuity. In this way it is possible to appreciate better the changes that the Portuguese words undergo in cognate idioms. I began with the Indo-Aryan group of languages, taking for my starting point Konkani, and after this I ran through the field of Dravidian languages and then passed on to other families, groups and unrelated languages.

I have collected in a general index all the Portuguese words introduced into the various languages which are the subject matter of this study, and have indicated such as do not figure in the body of the work by italics. From this it will be possible to see very easily the number and the nature of the words that have been adopted into the Asiatic languages.

In order that it may be possible to see at a glance the Portuguese vocables that have been taken over into each of the different languages, I have prepared separate lists of each of them; in these especial lists I have included words employed exclusively in Konkani or in Teto or Galoli, but which I had omitted from the body of the work.

The Portuguese words or such as are presumed to be of Portuguese origin which I have listed in the different Asiatic languages are almost all which are known after reliable scientific inquiry to have been really employed in these several languages. As the result of mere conjectures or inferences, it would have been possible to augment greatly their number in cognate languages.

XIII. *Brief Notes on each of the Languages*[1]

In this chapter I shall present a brief survey of each of the languages which enter into this study in the order in which they figure in it. Besides the filiation and the nature of the language I shall set out the area, the population, the dialects, characters, the antiquity of its literature, etc. I shall indicate also the vehicles by which the Portuguese words found their way into each. In respect of each of these languages I shall quote the various authorities whose studies have reference to the subject of this work.

---

[1] See *Mappa Dialectologico do continente português* (The Dialectical Map of the Portuguese Continent), by J. Leite de Vasconcellos, preceded by a summary classification of languages by A. R. Gonçalves Vianna. Latham, *Elements of Comparative Philology*. Gustav Oppert, *On the Classification of Languages*. Sir Erskine Perry, *On the Geographical Distribution of the Principal Languages of India*, etc. in Journal Bombay Branch R.A.S., Vol. XVI, 1853. H. H. Wilson, *A Glossary of Judicial and Revenue Terms*, the Preface. Robert Cust, *A Sketch of the Modern Languages of the East Indies*. John Beames, *op. cit.*, and *Outlines of Indian Philology*. Caldwell, *op. cit.* George Grierson, *Linguistic Survey of India; The Languages of India, and the Census*.

1. Konkani[1]

Konkani or Concani, formerly called by the Portuguese under a mistaken notion, *Lingua Canarina* or *Canarim*[2] (the Kanarese language) and *Brâmana* (the Brahmin language) is the southernmost representative of the Aryan family in India. It is spoken, according to the opinion of Dr. Gerson da Cunha, by about 2 millions in an area of about 7,000 square miles. Its original home is Goa and on this account and with a view to avoid a confusion between it and a Marathi dialect, it has been called by modern philologists *Gomantaki*, from Gomanta which is the ancient name for Goa.

Konkani extends, due probably in part to the diversity of its political boundaries and in part to emigration, on the north up to Malvan, and on the south to Kanara as far as Mangalore. There are in consequence three principal dialects of it: that of the north, *Kudali*, influenced by Marathi; that of Goa, *Gomantaki*, properly so called, and that of the south influenced by Kanarese and without any special name.

The dialect of Goa is divided into two classes: the language of the Novas Conquistas (New Conquests) which is more influenced by Marathi, and that of the Velhas Conquistas (Old Conquests) which is more under the influence of Portuguese. Again, the vernacular of the Velhas Conquistas is subdivided into the dialect of Bardez and that of Salsete; the former is regarded as purer and is more inflexional, the latter more analytic and

---

1 See Sebastião Rodolfo Dalgado, *Dicionario Konkani-Português* (Introduction). Cunha Rivara, *Ensaio Historico da Lingua Concani*, in the *Grammatica* of Father Thomas Stephen. Gerson da Cunha, *The Konkani Language and Literature*. Angelus Maffei, *An English-Konkani Dictionary*. *Dicionario Portuguez-Concani*, by an Italian missionary. Ramchandra Gunjikar, *Sarasvatī-mandala*.

2 'A long and narrow strip of land, they call Concan, and the people properly **Conquenijs** (Concanese) though our men speak of them as **Canarijs** (Canarese).' João de Barros, Dec. I, IX, 1. 'Orders were thus given to make the proclamation in Portuguese as well as in the **Canarij lingoa** (language) of the country (Goa).' *Id.*, Dec. II, V, 3.

enriched by Portuguese and Kanarese words. The language spoken in Ilhas (the insular portions of Goa) partakes of the characteristics of the dialects of the two afore-mentioned districts.

With regard to the nature and the origin of the Konkani language I shall transcribe what I wrote in my *Konkani-Portuguese* Dictionary: 'From what precedes I will briefly sum up my conclusions : (1) Konkani is an Aryan language and inflexional, not Dravidian and agglutinative ; (2) it resembles *Bālabhāshā* ; (3) it is less removed from Sanskrit in its grammatical structure and in its vocabulary than is Marathi ; (4) it is not a dialect or corruption of Marathi ; (5) it approximates more to ancient Marathi (which in its turn comes very near to *Bālabhāshā*) than to the modern ; (6) it is allied very much in its phonetic structure to the Gaurian languages of the North, specially Bengali ; (7) it represents with much probability Sarasvati which orientalists regard as being extinct, for those who introduced it into the Konkan were emigrants from Tirhotra or Tirhut '.[1]

In Goa, for the purposes of writing, Roman characters with Portuguese sound values are employed; in the north, Marathi *bālbodh* or *moḍí* characters are used ; in Kanara, Kanarese or Roman characters. Old writings in Kanarese as well as in Devanagri are extant and the scripts of these two languages must be regarded as the proper alphabets of Konkani.

The territory in which Konkani is most spoken being under Portuguese rule for four centuries, it is but natural that it should have admitted Portuguese words more largely than any other language. A tenth or perhaps more of the colloquial speech of the Velhas Conquistas is made up of Portuguese words or of words that are derived from Portuguese. In the Dictionary referred to above I included the following : (1) All words of Portuguese origin which had been adopted by one or more of the Oriental

[1] See *Sahyādri-khanda*, edited by Dr. Cunha. Hoernle and Grierson find, 'Konkani has intimate relationship with Hindi, the direct representative of ancient Maharastri.'

languages besides Konkani; because this fact in itself is a sure indication of the need or convenience afforded by such words. (2) All Portuguese vocables that have become so naturalised that they are to be met with in the speech of the people without attracting attention as to their origin; such terms were adopted either with the object of marking a dividing line between the Hindu and the Christian population or because the vernacular terms were not found adequate, or, again, because the indigenous term was not commonly known, or in order to avoid the trouble of coining new terms. (3) Many Portuguese words which are more in use than their corresponding vernacular equivalents. (4) Some Portuguese words that were entirely unnecessary, and this I did in order to show that the language (Konkani) possesses a large number of corresponding equivalents and that only culpable neglect or pedantry could have led to the use of the foreign words.

In the present work I have restricted the choice of the Portuguese vocables in Konkani much further. I have omitted from it all Portuguese words which are used exclusively in Konkani, and are not to be found in any other indigenous language. Such terms which have been left out from the body of the book have been listed however in the special index of this language, appended to this work.[1]

2. Marathi[2]

Marathi is the language spoken in Maharashtra (the great region or country of the Mahars) by 18,237,899 people according

[1] In my *Dicionário Português-Concani*, published by the Portuguese Government in 1905, I have mentioned almost all the words in common use more or less in Gomantaki.

[2] See John Wilson, *Notes on the constituent elements, the diffusion and application of the Marāthī Language*, in Molesworth's Dictionary. Dr. Stevenson, *An Essay on the points of similarity and dissimilarity between the English and Marāthī Languages*, in Candy's Dictionary. Filipe Néri Pires, *Grammatica Maratha.*

to the census of 1901; in this I have included the Konkani that is spoken in British territory. Its zone which takes in a vast area extends from Goa to the river Damaun (*Daman Ganga*), and on its eastern boundaries impinges on Kanarese and Telugu. It has three principal dialects: *Khandesi*, *Dakhini* and *Konkani*; to these some philologists add Gomantaki, more correctly called Konkani.

Marathi owing to its importance occupies the second place in the Gaurian languages. It is much cultivated; there are primary schools in all parts where it is taught and it possesses a rich literature, especially suited for school purposes [1]; its oldest literary specimens which are poetical and religious belong to the 13th century.

Marathi has two alphabets: *Bālbodh* (or *Bāḷbod*) which is, with slight variations, the same as *Devanagri* or Sanskrit, and is employed in the schools and in the press; *Modi* or *Mod*, which is peculiar to it, has fewer characters and makes no distinction between short and long vowels (i, ī, u, ū); it is written in a cursive manner without any separation of letters and is employed for correspondence and in manuscripts.

Its copious vocabulary, consisting of 20,000 words, is made up of the aboriginal Turanic stock, of Prakrit through Magadhi (the ancient language of Behar), of the Sanskrit, through its literature, of Arabic and Persian owing to the Mussulman domination and the influence of Hindustani, and of Portuguese and English.

The infiltration of Portuguese words into the language is due to the former Portuguese dominion over Bombay, Thana, Bassein and Chaul; to commerce (Surat, Bijapur); to the vicinage of Goa and Damaun; to the Portuguese missions in the greater part of the Marathi language-field, and to the Portuguese dialect of the Indian Christians who now go by the name of

---

[1] Molesworth's and Candy's dictionaries deserve especial mention as models in their class.

'East Indians' and who were formerly called '*Norteiros*'[1] (Northeners) because their home was to the north of Goa, the Portuguese metropolis in India.

It is above all in the district of Konkan that the influence of Portuguese is most marked.

3. Gujarati[2]

Gujarati, the language of Gujarat, is bounded on the north by Hindi, and, on the south and east, by Marathi. It is spoken by a population of 10 millions and is very much cultivated at the present day; it is employed a great deal in the periodical press of Bombay. It is the language, the rich and cultured Parsi community (which originally emigrated from Persia) employs as its vernacular, and it is the *lingua franca* of commerce, especially in the city of Bombay.

It has several dialects such as the Surati, Ahmedabadi, Kattiawari and the Mercantile.

The elements that go to constitute its vocabulary are the same as those of Marathi. It likewise has two alphabets: one its own, with few consonants and without distinction of short and long vowels (*i*, *u*), and the other, *Bālbodh* or Devanagri, a little defective and clumsy in form. Gujarati is the vernacular of the Portuguese possessions, Daman and Diu, where there are Government schools in which it is taught; thus the influence of Portuguese in these parts is direct and real with a tendency towards expansion. The dictionaries of the language, which are at present deficient, do not however list all the Portuguese words used in these localities, but only such as form part of the general vocabulary and which found their way into the language as the result of political relations in former times, or of vicinage and commerce.

---

[1] See my *Dialecto Indo-Português do Norte.*

[2] See Shapurjī Edaljī, *A Dictionary Gujarati and English.*

4. Hindi

Hindi is the most important language in India, occupying almost the centre of its language-field whether we look at it from the standpoint of area covering 248,000 square miles ; or of the numbers that speak the language—almost 73 millions ; or from its vitality in ever spreading itself and absorbing other languages, or from the number of its dialects—fifty-eight according to Cust, some of which can pass for real languages. There are philologists who consider that Gujarati, Panjabi and Nepalese should be considered as dialects of Hindi. Beames mentions the following as the principal dialects of the language: Maithili, Magadhi, Bhojpuri, Kosali, Brijbasha, Kanauji, Rajputani (group of dialects), Bundelkhandi. Sir Grierson divides Hindi into two parts : Eastern and Western.

Though Hindi is derived from Indo-Aryan, nevertheless, it contains a large number of words of Turanic descent and a considerable admixture of Arab-Persian loan words. It is generally written in the Devanagri script. Literary Hindi has passed through three stages, archaic, that is at least 700 years old, Hindi of the middle period and the current language.

The influence of Portuguese on it is principally mediate through the intervention of other neighbouring languages. It appears scarcely likely that the influence could have proceeded from politico-commercial relations which were not very frequent.[1]

5. Hindustani

Without entering into the question whether Hindustani is a language by itself or rather a dialect of Hindi, as it is generally supposed to be, I am treating it under a separate head owing to the especial nature of my work. Formed from 16th century Persian which was the language spoken by the Mahommedan

---

1 Shakespear assigns to Hindi a large number of the Portuguese words introduced into Hindustani.

conquerors, and from Hindi, the vernacular of the indigenous population, upon a grammatical structure which is Indo-Aryan, but written usually in a script which is a modification of Arabic and Persian, Hindustani became the mother tongue of the Mahommedans of every part of India and developed into the *lingua franca* of commerce in the principal centres of trade. 'Hindustani is', says Beames, 'by far the most widely spread and commonly understood of all Indian languages, and is spoken as a *lingua franca* by people whose mother tongue it is not, all over India.'

'Hindustani or Urdu is not a territorial dialect,' says Cust, 'it can scarcely correctly be said that it is the common language of any one district though spoken by many classes'. But Sir Grierson maintains that it is the vernacular of the Upper Gangetic plain and of the surrounding country.

It is true that both terms *Urdu* and *Hindustani* are used promiscuously, but Urdu denotes properly speaking, the form of the literary language, purer and more polished, and Hindustani, the common speech diluted by the admixture of exotic words.

The Hindustani of the north is purer and is distinguished from that of the south or Dekkani which is more corrupt. 'A still further degradation or dilution of the language', says Cust, 'takes place by the introduction of Romance-Aryan words in the dialect of the Portuguese settlements on the west coast of India'. In the existing dominions of the Portuguese in India Hindustani is not current.

The influence of Portuguese on Hindustani which is more noticeable in the Dekkani variant is due chiefly to the intercourse and commercial and political relations of former days[1] and to the facility which Hindustani has of assimilating foreign vocables.

---

[1] See J. A. Ismael Gracias, *Uma Dona Portuguesa na Côrte do Grão-Mogol* (A Portuguese Lady at the Moghul Court).

6. Laskari-Hindustani

Lascarí or *lascarim* from the Persian *lashkarī*, first employed by the Portuguese and subsequently adopted by the Dutch and the English in its original meaning, 'soldier',[1] came afterwards to denote the indigenous sailor and is in this sense synonymous with the Arab-Hindustani 'khalasi'.[2] And as it is generally the Mussulmans who are the crews of vessels bound on long voyages, their speech was given the name of Lashkari-Hindustani.

Now, it is but natural that in the formation of this dialect of sea-faring men there should figure very many words from the language of those Europeans who were the first to cross the seas to India and who exclusively dominated them for a long period. The English language is to-day playing a similar, and in an equal measure, a supplementary part. The vocabulary of Lashkari-Hindustani is therefore an admixture of Hindustani, properly so called, of the Portuguese of the 16th and 17th centuries, and of the present-day English.[3]

The study of this 'confusion of tongues' has a special interest because of the variety of forms and the phonetic changes which are represented in the Portuguese words which have issued from the speech of an unlettered people during the long space of

---

1 'What was given as *soldo* (soldier's pay) and rations to the **lascarins** who were in the City.' Castanheda, *Historia do Descobrimento e Conquista da India*.

'They divide among the soldiers of their flag-ships who are called **lascarins.**' Damião de Góis, *Chronica del Rei D. Manuel*, II, Ch. 6.

2 'There were Portuguese sailors fewer than were needed and in their place Mohammedan **lascaris** who as they were interested only in their personal gain and had no experience in the handling of ships were a sort of hindrance.' António Bocarro, Dec. XIII, p. 25.

'With the exception of some (Portuguese) who go as masters or pilots on their own ships or on those of His Majesty, the crew and company are all Mohammedans who are called **Laschares** (whence it is that the soldiers were commonly designated **Lascharis**).' João de Lucena, Bk. IV, Ch. 1.

3 'Dass ursprünglich die ganze Seemannssprache des Laskaren portogiesisch war, das zu vermuten dürfte mit Hinblich auf die vorstehender Abhandlung dargelegten Thatsachen nicht allzuküher sein.' Schuchardt, *Beiträge*, etc.

time they have been current among them. Probably some technical expressions owing to the very mutilated form in which they exist at present have escaped me whilst going through the dictionary of this dialect.[1]

7. Nepali[2]

Nepali, Gorkhali, Khas, and Parbatya are the names of the language of the court and *lingua franca* of Nepal. It is spoken by 3 millions of people who are for the most part Hindus, and the script employed is Devanagri. Its literature is very scanty and of little importance ; it has several dialects.[3]

Strictly speaking Nepali is a dialect of Hindi, deriving its origin from Rajasthani, which is the vernacular of Rajputana. Besides this the numerous non-Aryan languages spoken by the Tibeto-Burman races have influenced its vocabulary. Hunter mentions thirty-six of them in his comparative dictionary.

The influence of Portuguese on this language is entirely mediate by way of Hindi. Unfortunately the English-Nepalese list of words which I have with me is a very concise one. Nevertheless it is safe to assume that a large part of the Portuguese words which are to be found in Hindi have found an entrance into Nepali.

8. Oriya

Oriya, Uriya or Utkala is the language spoken in Orissa by a population of over 9½ millions over an area of 60,000 square miles within the provinces of Bengal and Madras and the Central Provinces. It belongs together with Bihari, Bengali, and Assamese, to the eastern Sanskritic group, which was derived

---

[1] Portuguese words employed both in Hindustani and Lashkari-Hindustani are mentioned in this work only with reference to the former of these two languages in order to avoid repetition.

[2] See Turnbull, *Nepali Grammar and Dictionary*.

[3] Grierson says that Nepali or Eastern Pahari is not the principal language of Nepal but Nevari is. Turnbull, however, maintains that this is not so at present.

immediately from the ancient speech of Magadha, the home of Buddhism.[1]

Oriya has several dialects: the Northern, the Southern, that of Sumbhulpur, of Kalakundi; but that of Cuttack is regarded as the standard. Its alphabet is based on Devanagri with modifications in different parts of the language-field. It is the only one of the North Indian characters to adopt the curvilinear form of the upper strokes which in the other are horizontal.[2] Its earliest literary monuments date back to 400 years.

The Portuguese influence on Oriya is chiefly mediate, through the intervention of Telugu in the south and Bengali in the north, though in former times there was commercial intercourse between the Portuguese and Orissa.[3]

9. Bengali

Bengali, as the name indicates, is the vernacular of Bengal spoken by more than 44 millions, Hindus as well as Mahommedans. It is at the present day much cultivated by the Babus, which is the most cultured and progressive class among the peoples of India. The literary tongue differs a great deal from the spoken, not only in respect of the vocabulary but even in its morphology

---

1 In this work I could not take in Bihari because of the absence of the lexicographical material. Rudolf Hoernle and George Grierson began in 1885 the publication of *A Comparative Dictionary of the Bihari Language*; of this work only two parts have appeared which do not come up to the end of the first letter of the alphabet. Bihari has four principal dialects: Baisvari, Bhojpuri, Magadhi, and Maithili. The last named passed for the standard because it is the most developed and cultivated and because it has literary monuments which go as far back as the 14th century. The natural presumption is that there would be found in it the same Portuguese words as are met with in Hindi.

2 Cust tries to explain this peculiarity by saying that it was necessitated by the writing materials being an iron stylus and a leaf of the fan-palm; straight incised lines would have split the palm. But such materials are or were common to other languages.

3 'The principal sovereigns with whom we had intercourse because of their domains being on the sea coast were: The King of Bisnaga, of **Orixá**, of Bengal, of Pegu, of Siam, and of China.' João de Barros, Dec. I, IX, 2.

and is to a good extent sanskritised. It uses an alphabet which is a picturesque variant of Devanagri.

Bengali has several dialects which are not properly distinguished. Beames groups them under the generic heads of Eastern, Northern, and Southern, that of Central Bengal being the one which is normal. But there are other dialects mixed in character, which have issued from the contact of Bengali with Hindi and Oriya on both frontiers, and also those which have been the result of the contact with non-Aryan languages (Kolarian and Tibeto-Burman) on the east and the west flank, especially by millions of non-Aryans passing into semi-Hinduism, and among these Cust distinguishes those of Purneah, Rungpur, Kuch, Sylhet, Rabha, Meeyang, and Chittagong.

Portugal had a factory at Bandel on the Ugli or Ogolim (Hooghly); it had a large colony in Calcutta, and held constant commercial relations with various parts and, even to-day, owns important missionary stations endowed with extensive estates.[1] From these circumstances sprang a Portuguese dialect, the range of which at present is much circumscribed and which threatens to disappear wholly. These facts explain the introduction of numerous Portuguese words into Bengali. The descendants of European families use many a term relating to sweets and foods (and this happens in other parts of Asia as well) without, so much as, a thought of their origin.

10. Assamese[2]

Assamese is the language spoken in the plain of Assam by the entire population of the Brahmaputra valley which is about a million and a half.[3]

---

1 'Arriving at the port of Chatigão, in the kingdom of Bengala, where at that time there were many Portuguese.' Fernão Pinto, Ch. CLXXII.

'Just like the King of Orixá, and the King of Bengala, who have many ports which we visit and with which we trade.' João de Barros, Dec. III, II, 5.

2 See Bronson, *A Dictionary in Assamese and English*.

3 In the mountainous parts there are non-Aryan tribes, who have a language of their own, one of which, Khassi, is included in this study.

Neither the Ahoms, invaders of the Tai family, in spite of their long domination, nor the Burmese and the Kacharis, members of the Tibeto-Burman family, nor the Mahommedans have left any trace on the language which is closely akin to Bengali.

Assamese is laden with Sanskrit loan words which have been introduced in modern times and, at times, with a modified meaning and pronunciation. It has a script of its own in which the Bible has been translated; but the characters of Bengali are also employed. Since the last two or three centuries it has a literature in prose and verse. The language of the larger number of the poetic compositions differs from that of the Buronjies or Histories which are in prose. At present, as it is the official language of the Provincial Government, it is hoped that it will be extensively cultivated.

The Portuguese words which found an entry into it did so by way of Bengali and Hindustani.

11. Sindhi[1]

Sindhi is the language of the valley of the lower Indus from Multan to the sea; on the east it merges into the Rajputana dialects of Hindi, and on the west into the Beluch dialects. It is spoken by about three million people made up of Hindus and Mussulmans. It is generally written in Arabic characters, with many modifications to represent the cerebrals and aspirates of an Aryan language.[2] Its principal dialects are : Siraí, Vicholi, Lari, Uch, and Kachi.

The vocabulary of Sindhi like that of Hindustani, with the exception of its own original stock, is made up of Sanskrit, Arabic and Persian words. The influence of Pushtu, its Iranic neighbour is especially notable. All the words terminate in vowels as they do in Italian; all those ending in an *u* and *o* being masculine.

---

[1] See George Stack, *A Dictionary English and Sindhi.*

[2] As Sindhi has more sounds than those which are provided for by Devanagri characters, whenever it employs this alphabet, it uses diacritical marks with the ordinary letters in order to distinguish these sounds.

It has no neuter gender. The Portuguese influence on it is, it appears, almost wholly mediate and very limited if we are to judge from the dictionaries of the language hitherto published.

12. Punjabi[1]

Punjabi is the language spoken from the Indus to the Sutlej and from Multan to the mountain ranges; it is the language of about 17 millions and is written in a variety of characters of the Aryan alphabet, the principal of which is Gurmukhi. For official correspondence and for the purposes of general literature the Arabic character is preferred.

Owing to its very close relationship with Hindi, many philologists prefer to regard it as a dialect of the latter. It has a large number of dialects. Beames says that every district of the Punjab has its own dialect, and there are even districts having more than one dialectical variation; Cust who has greater competence to speak on this subject disputes this statement. The more important of these dialects are according to Maya Singh: Punjabi properly so called, Multani, Pathohari, and Pahadi.[2]

In the vocabulary, besides its original stock of Hindi, Arabic and Persian words, many Portuguese terms have found their way through the intervention of Hindustani.

13. Kashmiri

Kashmiri is the vernacular of the Valley of Kashmere, spoken by about three millions or according to Sir Grierson by about a million; it is the most northerly member of the Indo-Aryan language-family. It is not a cultivated language and never has been reduced to writing in its actual form, nor has it a

---

[1] See Bhai Maya Singh, *The Punjabi Dictionary*, Introduction.

[2] Grierson speaks of Multani as Lahnda and regards it as a distinct language very different from Punjabi, and gives it a population of more than three millions. [In the Census report of 1921 Lahnda or Western Punjabi is given a population of over 5½ millions.—ED.]

grammar or a dictionary worthy of the name. It is therefore a spoken language, Persian being the language of the court and of correspondence. Even as such, there are three varieties of Kashmiri spoken: that of the Brahmins, loaded with Sanskrit words; the form used by Mahommedans and sown thickly with Arabic and Persian words; and lastly the one used by the common people, which preserves the old local form and dialectical variations.

This language might well have been left out by me in this work in view of the fact that there exists till now only a vocabulary of the language, in which not even half a dozen of Portuguese words can be traced, some of them being of an uncertain origin. But it appears to me natural that there should be more of them, connected with objects carried into the country by the Mussulman conquerors.

14. Sinhalese[1]

Besides the Vedas, the aboriginal inhabitants of Ceylon whose number is at the present day very much reduced,[2] the two indigenous races that people the island are, the Dravidian, in the north, which emigrated from India in some time immemorial, and the Aryan, brought there by Vijaya in the 6th century B.C. The vernacular of the former is Tamil, and of the latter, Sinhalese or Chinglá, as it is called in the creole language.[3]

It is a much debated question among philologists of the Indian languages as to whether Sinhalese should be classified as an Aryan or a Dravidian tongue. Clough, Max Müller, Cust,

---

[1] See B. Clough, *A Dictionary of the Sinhalese and English Languages*. R. C. Childers, *Notes on the Sinhalese Language*. James D'Alwis, *On the Origin of Sinhalese Language*.

[2] 'There is a class of people whom they call **Bédas**: in colour they are almost like us, and some are dark brown; their language is not understood by any Chingalá or other people of India, and their converse is only with one another.' João Ribeiro, *Fatalidade Historica da Ilha de Ceilão*, Bk. 1, Ch. 24.

[3] Ceylon is a colony—Crown Colony—separated from India. It was on this account not included in the census of India taken in 1901 and 1911.

Alwis lean to the former view. This appears to be more likely in view of the linguistic investigations of Childers.[1]

Sinhalese is at least two thousand years old ; it had a very copious literature dating back from the 4th century and reckons almost two millions who speak it. It has two dialects: the Elu which is the archaic form of the language and which is characterised by the phonetic decadence of Aryan words (*tadbhāvas*) ; and the modern language, the Sinhalese, used by the people, which has admitted in its fold a large number of words without any notable changes from Sanskrit, and from Pali which is the sacred language of the Buddhists to which religion belong the large majority of the Sinhalese.[2] It has its own alphabet which has a few more vowels than Devanagri.[3]

The Portuguese domination asserted itself in Ceylon more intensely and at the same time more extensively than in the different other possessions and exercised an influence so intense and many-sided, that Holland with all her efforts was not able to extinguish it, nor appreciably reduce the traces of its existence. To attest to the truth of this statement there exist two memorials of very high value ; first of all, the Portuguese dialect, which is the most important of all the creole Portuguese languages and which up to this day is full of vitality[4]; secondly, the introduction in the Sinhalese diction, which is otherwise very well stocked, of a host of Portuguese terms. In this latter respect Sinhalese occupies a place second only to Konkani among Indian languages.

---

1 Gustav Oppert classifies Sinhalese among the Aryanised languages.

2 'There exists among them a language which is not used by the common people; it is much like what Latin is among us.' João Ribeiro, Bk. 1, Ch. 16.

3 There are various opinions with regard to the origin of Pali. Westergaard (*Ueber der ältersten Zeitraum der Indischen Geschichte*) derives it from the Ujjaini dialect in the 3rd century B.C. Kern (*Over de Jaartelling der Zuidelijke Buddhisten*) regards it as an artificial language, like the Sauraseni of the dramas, elaborated in the beginning of the Christian era. Oldenberg (*The Vinaya Pitakam*) believes that it is a dialect of Eastern Deccan. See Barth, *The Religions of India*, p. 108.

4 See *Dialecto Indo-Português de Ceilão*, by the author.

It is necessary to realise that this result was in a large measure due to the existence of the creole Portuguese language.

15. Tamil[1]

Tamil is the principal member of the Dravidian family whether we consider it with reference to its splendid culture, or the copiousness of its vocabulary, or the antiquity and the wealth of its literature. No other language, says Rice, 'combines greater force and concision, or is more exact and philosophic in its modes of expressions'.[2]

Its language-field extends from the Ghats to the gulf of Bengal and from Calicut to Cape Comorin. It is also spoken in the southern part of Travancore and in the northern portion of Ceylon and in some other regions. The people speaking the language number about 16½ millions. It has an alphabet of its own which employs 30 letters for its own script and besides four more for writing Sanskrit words which in the latter case is known as *Grantha*. It includes two forms or dialects, the classical or the ancient and the colloquial or the modern called respectively

---

[1] See, especially, for the Dravidian languages the monumental work of Robert Caldwell, from which I have quoted before. and Rev. Henry Rice, *Native Life in South India.*

'The proper spelling of the name Tamil is Tamir, but through the change of *r* into *l* it is often pronounced Tamil and it is often (though erroneously) written Tamul by Europeans.' Caldwell. 'The kingdom of Charamandel, where the language is Tamul.' Duarte Barbosa, *Livro*, p. 291. [Hak. Soc. ed. Longworth Dames, Vol. I, p. 184.]

[2] The Portuguese, according to their practice of giving to a language the name of the country wherein it was spoken called Malayalam, the language current on the West Coast, Malabar, and also by this name designated the language that was in vogue as far as the Coromandel coast, there being a similarity between the two. The other European nations adopted this designation which is at present falling into disuse. 'First of these races whom I call foreigners who dwell in Malabar is a caste called *Chatis*, natives of the province of *Charamandel* .... They speak a tongue which differs from that of Malabar in the same way as Castilians speak a language different from that of the Portuguese.' Duarte Barbosa, p. 340. [Hak. Soc. ed. Longworth Dames, Vol. II, pp. 71 and 73.]

the *Sen* and the *Kodun*,[1] which differ from each other so widely that they might almost be regarded as different languages.

Tamil, jealous of its vernacularity, admits foreign words into it with difficulty; even the importation of Sanskrit words is very limited and these are very little used in classical works, the earliest of which date back more than a thousand years.

The Portuguese influence on it which is not a little considerable arose from various sources: domination of certain tracts of the country, trade, religion and missionary contact, Portuguese creole dialects now almost extinct, and the intercourse between the Tamils and the Portuguese in the various parts under the occupation of the latter.

16. Malayalam[2]

Malayalam is the language spoken along the Malabar coast from Chandraguiri near Mangalore to Trivandrum by about six millions of people. Regarded in its origin as a dialect of Tamil, it developed into a sister language owing to Brahmin influence about the 9th century, by discarding the use of the personal terminations of the verbs and by availing itself of a large number of Sanskrit derivatives. Its alphabet is based upon the Aryan. The Mahommedan inhabitants, called Mappilas, have a dialect of their own and have adopted Arabic characters, though modified, for their script.

Malabar was the country which the Portuguese first discovered and in part conquered and christianised and which for a long time remained under their dominion. Even at the present day there is a Portuguese bishopric in Cochin, and a corrupt form of Portuguese which is in a moribund state[3] is also in use there.

---

1 'A person can make out one without knowing the other.' Rice. According to this author 'Tamil' signifies 'melodiousness'.

2 See Gundert, *A Malayalam and English Dictionary*.

3 Dr. Hugo Schuchardt published a small monograph on this corrupt Portuguese dialect.

Again from or through Malabar were introduced many Indian terms into Portugal, such as: *manga* (mango), *cairo* (coir), *bétel* (betel), *ola* (palm-leaf), *teca* (teak-wood), *chatim* (merchant); there were some that were introduced into Indo-Portuguese, like: *jagra* (jaggery or unrefined sugar), *chuname* (lime), *pinaca* (cocoanut or sesame cake), *mainato* (washerman).

17. Telugu[1]

Telugu or Telinga, in respect of its culture and its glossarial copiousness ranks next to Tamil in the list of the Dravidian languages, but surpasses it in point of euphonic sweetness and the number of those that speak it, viz. over 20 millions.[2]

It ranges from Pulicat to Chicacole and on the west impinges on the boundaries of Marathi. It has a character which is a variation of the Aryan, and its literature dates back as far as the 12th century of our era. Its present-day vocabulary is greatly strewn with exotics, the greater part of which are Sanskrit and Hindustani.

The influence of Portuguese on Telugu is evident from the close and constant relations, political and commercial, that existed between the rulers of Bisnagar or Bisnaga (Vijayanagar) and also from its contiguity to Tamil and Marathi and its contact with Hindustani.

The number of Portuguese words that have been adopted in the popular form of the language is very large and some of them are exclusively borrowed by it and by no other language.

---

1 See C. P. Brown, *A Dictionary of the mixed Dialects and foreign words used in Telugu.*

It is interesting to note how the name *Gentoo* (from the Port. *gentio*, gentile) came to be used by the English for a long time in a restricted sense to the Telugu-speaking Hindus. The Portuguese spoke of this people more correctly as *Badagas*, Tamil *Vadugar*, Kanarese *Badaga*. 'The next province which marches with the kingdom of Narsyngus, they call **Telingu.**' Duarte Barbosa, p. 291. [Hak. Soc. ed. Longworth Dames, Vol. I, p. 183.]

2 'He was appointed Governor of the District of the Talingas, who are the Hindus whose language is more developed than that of any other people in the Deccan'. Diogo do Couto, Dec. IV, X, 4.

18. Kanarese

Kanarese is spoken throughout the plateau of Mysore and in some of the western districts of the Nizam's territory; it is spoken also (together with Konkani, Tulu, and Malayalam but more extensively than any of them) in Kanara, on the Malabar coast, a district which was subjected for centuries to the rule of Kanarese princes.[1] It is the language of over 10 millions of inhabitants.

Kanarese like the other Dravidian tongues has two dialects: the classical or the ancient Kanarese and the colloquial or modern. The former differs from the latter not only in respect of its vocabulary but also because of the use of different inflexional terminations. The Kanarese alphabet is, with very slight changes, identically the same as that of Telugu.

The influence of Portuguese on it is due, in a measure, to domination, to political and commercial relations, to colonists from Goa, to missionary labours and the proximity of other language-fields.

19. Tulu[2]

Tulu or Tulava is the name of a language of not much importance both in respect of population and its language-field; for it is spoken in a limited area bounded by the rivers Chandraguiri and Kalyanpuri, in the district of Kanara, by about 500,000 individuals. Notwithstanding its want of litera-

---

[1] As is evident there was a geographical displacement of the ancient name *Karnata* or *Karnataka,* corrupted into *Kannada, Kanara.* By Carnatic the English mean the eastern footboard of the Ghauts on the Coromandel coast. The old Portuguese, in their turn also, twisted geography and ethnology by speaking of the natives of Goa as 'Canarins' and of their language as 'Canarim' or 'Canarina'. This error has survived even to this day, though it is obvious that the indigenous population of the Konkan ought to be called Konkanis Duarte Barbosa calls modern Canara *Tolinate* 'i.e. *Tulu nādu,* or the modern district of S. Canara'. *Hobson-Jobson.* [Hak. Soc. Longworth Dame's Transl., Vol. 1, p. 183.]

[2] See A. Männer, *Tulu-English Dictionary.*

ture, except for some legends inscribed on palm leaves, it is one of the most highly developed languages of the Dravidian family and is more closely allied to Kanarese than to Malayalam, and has some dialects. Sanskrit, Kanarese, Malayalam, and Hindustani words are grafted on to its original stock. The Malayalam alphabet was formerly employed, but now the Kanarese script has become inseparably associated with the language.

The number of Portuguese words adopted in the language is considerable and more even than in the adjacent languages. I am unable to furnish a reason for this, unless it be the emigration of Hindus from Goa. Religious terms in Portuguese were introduced by Protestant missionaries.

20. Anglo-Indian Vocabulary[1]

The English language has not begotten any bastard variety of itself in India, nor is it likely that any will issue from it in course of time. But the vocabulary of English spoken in India is sown thick, as is but natural, with indigenous terms.

When the English arrived in India, a corrupt form of Portuguese was the *lingua franca* of the country, as much between Europeans and Indians as between the Europeans themselves who belonged to different nationalities.

It is no matter for surprise, therefore, if Portuguese should have furnished a large contingent of words to Anglo-Indian vocabulary, directly or through the medium of the vernaculars. Even so, many indigenous terms found entry into it by way of Portuguese, such as: *areca, betel, benzoin, coir, copra, corge, congee, godown, mandarin, mango, palanquin, monsoon, typhoon*, etc.[2]

Many of the words derived from Portuguese are now obsolete, whilst some are in vogue only in certain parts. On the other

---

[1] See Yule and Burnell, *Hobson-Jobson*. Whitworth, *An Anglo-Indian Dictionary*. Wilson, *A Glossary of Judicial and Revenue Terms*.

[2] 'Even amongst the English, the number of Portuguese terms in daily use is remarkable.' Emerson Tennent, Ceylon.

hand the diffusion of many Portuguese words among the vernaculars is due to it. Hence Anglo-Indian vocabulary has been included in my work.[1]

21. Indo-French Vocabulary[2]

The French arrived late in India, and found there the Portuguese, the Dutch, and the English engaged in a struggle. They exercised scarcely any influence of a general and abiding character on the country. No corrupt form of French is in use in any of its very tiny colonies just as none is current in the English colonies. Indo-Portuguese used to be spoken in them just as it is even now spoken there though on a smaller scale side by side with the Indian vernaculars.[3]

Like the Anglo-Indian vocabulary, the French spoken in India borrowed a number of words which are of genuine Portuguese extraction and very many Asiatic terms that had first been taken over into Portuguese; these, not to speak of such terms as were received directly from the vernacular languages were, generally speaking, carried into it through the agency of Indo-Portuguese. Several of these terms which were used to denote an object peculiar to India travelled over to France and became naturalised there; the same happened when many Anglo-Indian expressions were received into its bosom by European English.

The reasons that led me to include Anglo-Indian vocabulary within the range of my survey have also led me to examine Indo-French, though the importance of the latter is not so great.

---

[1] I have availed myself a great deal of Yule and Burnell's learned glossary.

[2] See Aristide Marre, *Notice sur la langue portugaise dans l' Inde Française et en Malaisie*.

[3] Dr. Schuchardt includes Pondicherry and Chandernagore among the regions in which Indo-Portuguese is spoken, and gives specimens of the Portuguese dialect of Mahe. And E. A. Marre says: 'Il résulte évidemment des propres termes de l'Annuaire que le portugais est parlé par une partie de la population de l'Inde française.'

I do not know of any other work on the subject besides the one cited by me and I turned my attention to Indo-French only at the eleventh hour when I felt convinced that the Portuguese influence on it was not insignificant. It is, therefore, very natural that the list of Portuguese vocables in Indo-French furnished by me should be incomplete.

22. Garo

In the lower part of the Assam valley there is a group of languages of small importance, called Bodo, belonging to the Tibeto-Burman family, and spoken by about 600,000 individuals. One of these languages is Garo, spoken by about 186,000 ; it has various dialects and the language itself has been sufficiently studied. There are schools in which it is taught and school and religious books written in it ; this is due to American missionaries who, however, in teaching it make use of English books in place of the Bengali, and employ largely English terminology in addition to the Aryan.

The Portuguese words which have penetrated into Garo have done so by way of Assamese, and of Bengali, and some of them, perhaps, through the medium of the missionaries.

23. Burmese

Burmese spoken by 7½ millions is an agglutinative and cultivated language. It has many Aryan words which were introduced by Buddhism, the prevailing religion, side by side with Pali literature. It has an alphabet of its own, derived from the Indian. Its principal dialects are: Arakanese, Tavoyee or Taneagsari, and Yo.

Besides Tibetan, Burmese is the only other important member of the Tibeto-Burman linguistic family. Its literature dates back several centuries ; but the language of the literature does not differ much from Siamese.

The influence of Portuguese on it, to judge from the single vocabulary which has come to my hands, is very limited. Some more words that derive their origin from the Portuguese ought naturally to exist, carried into the country either by traders or Portuguese adventurers, or introduced by way of Bengali or Siamese.

24. Tibetan[1]

Tibetan is in a stage of transition from the monosyllabic to the agglutinative type. It possesses a vast literature, ancient and modern, and four different forms of syllabic alphabets, derived from the Aryan and introduced in the 7th century.[2] The literary language is very different from the colloquial. Tibet, according to Bell, is essentially a land of dialects; a proverb much in vogue says, 'each district has its dialect and every Lama his own doctrine'. The most important is the dialect of Lhassa, which is regarded as the standard and is the *lingua franca* for the whole of the country.

The influence of Portuguese on Tibet is almost nil; in a vocabulary of the language I discovered only two words of Portuguese provenance. All the same, there was a Portuguese mission founded in Tibet in 1642 by the Jesuit António de Andrade and carried on subsequently by Fathers Gonçalo de Sousa and João Cabral.[3] At the present time with greater facilities of communication between Tibet and India, it is but natural to expect more Portuguese words to find their way into the language.

25. Khassi[4]

In the southern frontier of the valley of Assam, to the east of India proper, betwixt the Garo and the Naga tribes, is the country of the Khassi-Jyntia tribes whose population is about 200,000 and which speak a language known as Khassi,

---

1 See C. A. Bell, *Manual of Colloquial Tibetan*.

2 'It is to intimate relations thus established, so it seems to me, that Tibet probably owes not only her Buddhism in great measure, but also her written alphabet.' L. A. Waddell, in *Asiatic Quarterly Review*.

3 See Cardinal Saraiva, *Obras Completas* (Complete Works), V, p. 149.

4 See H. Roberts, *An Anglo-Khassi Dictionary*.

or Kossia. In this part is situated Shillong the seat of the Government of the Province of Assam. Morphologically, Khassi belongs to the monosyllabic order; genealogically Beames includes it in the Lohotic or Burmese class. Cust regards it as a family by itself and Grierson basing himself on the authority of Kuhn, affiliates it to the sub-family Mon-Khmer of the Indo-Chinese family.

It has neither character nor literature of its own; the Roman character on account of its convenience has now been adopted in the composition of a grammar and dictionary of the language by English missionaries and in writing school texts.[1]

It has several dialects, the common being the Cheara; it has also a rich vocabulary, composed in a great measure of onomatopoetic terms, and containing an infiltration of Bengali and Hindustani words. It is through the medium of these two languages that Portuguese words have passed into it, without these semi-savages ever having heard the name of Portugal. And this is exactly what will happen in analogous cases.[2]

26. Kambojan

The Kambojan language is at the present day the principal representative of the sub-family Mon-Khmer, Khmer being the indigenous name of the country, now in a state of great decay, and likewise of the people who profess Buddhism. It is spoken by about a million in Cambodia and by about 500,000 in Siam and Annam. It has three dialects, Xong, Samre, and Khamen-Boran.

Kambojan is monosyllabic like the other branches of the family but it has no tones; it is so full of Siamese words that for a long time it was mistaken for Siamese. It likewise has loan words from Pali, Malay, Annamite, and Peguan contracted in the

---

[1] The attempt to introduce the Bengali alphabet was not successful.

[2] Nissor Singh refers to Hindi almost all the Portuguese words introduced into Khassi.

manner required by the tendency of the language. There are two modern characters, the sacred and the vulgar, both of them derived from Devanagri ; it is rich in archaic literary monuments which date back to the 13th century.

The influence of Portuguese on Kambojan which is relatively speaking considerable, is due to the ancient commercial, political and religious relations, and to the influence on it of contiguous languages, especially Malayan.[1] The kingdom being at the present time a French protectorate, many French terms are being introduced in the language, and this of necessity causes doubt as regards the origin of certain Romance words found in it.

27. Siamese[2]

Siamese is the most important representative of the Tai branch of the sub-family Siamo-Chinese, and belongs like Chinese, to the class of monosyllabic, synthetic languages.[3] The name Siam is a corruption of *Sham*, which is another name of the Tai or Thai race, which in the 7th century invaded Upper Burma and afterwards went and settled down in this country and in Assam.[4]

The Siamese language-field is vast ; it extends from Burma to the lake of Cambodia, and from the Gulf of Siam to the confines of Lao. It is spoken by about two million people who profess the Buddhism of the South, and it is written in a script which is of Indian origin and expresses tones by accents. It has an

---

1 See Fr. João dos Santos, *Ethiopia Oriental*, II, Ch. 7.

2 See Michell, *A Siamese-English Dictionary*. Lunet de Lajonquière, *Ditionnaire Français-Siamois*.

3 But the Indo-Chinese languages were formerly inflective as recent investigations have proved. See Grierson, *The Languages of India*, p. 6.

4 The old Portuguese writers call Siam *Sornau*. See Fernão Mendes Pinto. Duarte Barbosa calls it *Danseam*. 'The second kingdom which is a continuation of this along the northern part is *Chaumúa*, the people of which have a language by themselves ; it is properly speaking the kingdom which we call SIÃO (Siam), a name unknown among its people and given to it by foreigners and not by them.' João de Barros, Dec. III, II, 5.

enormous religious and secular literature and three dialects: that of the sacred Buddhistic books, that of the higher orders, and that of the people. Its glossary according to Michell consists of 14,000 words and contains very many foreign words, most of them mutilated and derived from Pali, Sanskrit, Kambojan, Malay, Chinese, and the European languages.

In view of the various kinds of relations that Portugal had with Siam, one should have expected that Siamese would contain many Portuguese vocables; but there is a very small number of such that figure in their dictionaries, and this is a phenomenon that one notes also with regard to the other monosyllabic languages.[1] The educated people coin terms from the Sanskrit to denote new inventions such as telegraph, telephone, stenography; and the journals, and the people in contact with the Europeans prefer words borrowed from the English.[2]

28-29. Annamite and Tonkinese

By Annamite or better still Annamese, is understood the language either of the ancient kingdom of Annam or in a more restricted sense, the Cochin-China dialect, to distinguish it from Tonkinese.[3]

Philologists are not in accord with regard to the classification of Annamese in general. Logan allies it to Mon-Khmer, con-

---

[1] There are in Siam 43 Portuguese, Catholics, who are permanent residents of the place. There are also 250 Portuguese of Chinese origin who have their names inscribed in the register at the consulate. Finally there are 68 more protected Portuguese of Chinese descent residing in Siam. In all 361 Portuguese are to be found in the register. (*Journal* of the Geo. Soc. of Lisbon.) See Fr. João dos Santos, II, Ch. 6; and Frederico Pereira, *Relação de Portugal com Sião*, in *Journal* Geo. Soc. of Lisbon, 8th ser., pp. 385–404.

[2] Such as: bank, bill, boat, boot, foot, madam, mister, minute, agent, hotel, office, pen, police, salute, stamp, station, tape.

[3] 'Which land the Chijs (Chinese) call the kingdom of Cacho, and the Siamese and Malay Cauchinchina; it is different from the Cochij of Malabar.' João de Barros, Dec. III, VIII, 6.

stituting a separate group the Mon-Annan. Cust and Grierson throw doubts on this alleged connection, although there are Khmers in the country. Sylvain Levi traces, as the result of oral information that he has secured, a connection between it and Siamese or Tai, but admits the great influence of Chinese. All the same they don't seem to note in it any vestiges of Indian civilisation which disappears after Cambodia and gives place to the Chinese. The people are Buddhists but of the Chinese type, and possess an abundant literature, and employ a large number of Chinese ideographs used phonetically as a syllabary. The literati, however, prefer the entire Chinese alphabet. In view of the difficulty that the reading of these characters present, the Roman Catholic missionaries have invented an admirable system of adapting the Roman characters to these sounds, which is called Quoc ngu to represent faithfully all the tones and stresses of the language.

This is the system which is generally followed by philologists and according to Lajonquière, by the very natives of Cochin-China.[1]

Tonkinese differs dialectically from Annamite; it has a literature and there are especial books to help its study; but to judge from its vocabulary the difference between the two is not very noticeable.[2] Both use the same European words, but they are very few and as a rule of French origin, except some religious terms which disclose a Portuguese source. Besides commercial intercourse, there were in Tonquin Portuguese missions which were very flourishing and which could count towards the middle

---

1 'Besides Chinese characters, they have characters belonging to the language of the land, which they commonly use and which even the women can learn.' António Francisco Cardim, *Batalhas da Companhia de Jesus*, p. 69.

2 'The inhabitants of Cochin-China are of the same nation as the people of Tonquin and call the entire kingdom Annam; it was the Portuguese who divided it into Cochin-China and Tonquin, both of them being in reality the same people, and in no way differing in language, dress and customs . . . . .' Cardim, p. 69.

of the 17th century 295 churches with a membership of about 200,000 souls.[1]

30. Malay[2]

Of the Asiatic languages, Malay is after Konkani, one of the most important for my work and it was this which induced me to extend the orbit of my investigations outside the limits of India proper.[3]

The Malay language is spoken in Malacca and in the islands of Sumatra (mixed up with other languages), Banca, Billiton, in the Moluccas (or Maluco)[4] and in some other parts. It is said to be spoken by more than 10 million people. There is the Malay language properly so called and what is spoken of as Low Malay. The former, which is the language spoken in Singapore and Malacca, possesses a literature both in prose and verse, written in a modified form of Arabic characters. The other or Low Malay, devoid of difficult sounds (gutturals) and complicated forms, is the *lingua franca* of the whole of the Archipelago, as Hindustani is of India, and as such is spoken by the indigenous population of the maritime ports, even though they be not Malay by race ; it is commonly written in Roman characters.[5]

---

1 See Cardim, *op. cit.*

2 See Favre, *Grammaire de la Langue Malaise*. Swettenham, *Vocabulary of the English and Malay Languages*. Heyligers, *Traces de Portugais*, etc. Gonçalves Viana, *Vocabulário malaio derivado do português*. Fokker, *O Elemento português na lingua malaia*.

3 'It has a language of its own which is called Malay ; it is very sweet and easy to learn.' Castanheda, II, Ch. 112. 'On account of its refinement and its sweetness, Malay has deserved the just claim of being called the Italian of the East.' Favre.

4 'But the most common language and which all use is Malay ; every one took a liking to it because of its sweetness and its agreeable pronunciation.' Diogo do Couto, Dec. IV, VII, 7.

5 'The people of the country are called Malay, and the language of the country is likewise called by the same name ; for purposes of the trade of Malacca with the neighbouring islands, this language is used by almost all the islands and is understood among them.' Lucena, *Historia da vida do Padre Francisco de Xavier*, Bk. III, Ch. 10.

The language of Batavia belongs to Low Malay. Some Portuguese words assume in it especial forms, which are indicated in the present work, just like those which are peculiar to the Moluccas.[1]

Malay has great powers of adaptability and contains many exotics, its vocabulary being laden with Sanskrit, Arabic, Persian, Javanese, Chinese, Telugu and European loan words.[2]

The influence of Portuguese on Malay, especially Low Malay, which has its origin in conquest, prolonged domination, trade, conversions, missions and in the corrupt Portuguese dialects spoken there, is enormous and deep-seated, for it is discernible in a very large number of words and extends even to verbs and particles.

Fortunately, there are many works of a general and special character dealing with this subject. The earliest is the dictionary of Fr. Haex which enters many terms which are not to be found in the present-day works either because they are really obsolete or because they were not in common use but confined and peculiar to missionaries and Christians.[3] Among modern books

---

'The language which is called Malay is among the people of the East what Latin is in our Europe.' Tavernier, *Voyages*, IV, p. 251.

1 The *Samsanas* of Quedda in Malacca who are Siamese by race and Mahommedans by religion use a language which is a mixture of Malay and Siamese.

2 'Both Malay and Hindustani manifest that capacity for the absorption and assimilation of foreign elements, which we recognise as making English the greatest Vernacular that the World has ever seen.' Cust, *The Modern Languages of the East Indies*, p. 150.

'Following the Portuguese came the Dutch, then the English and the Spaniards; in a word the whole of Europe came to plant itself in Malaysia, the language of which had naturally to be enriched by a new series of vocables belonging to different European languages.' Favre.

3 Says the author: 'At the foot of the Malay-Latin Dictionary are appended Portuguese and Tarnatic vocables, which are really in common use and which are mixed up with Malay words in the islands of Amboyana, Banda, Java, and the Moluccas'. As this appendix (pp. 51–54) was wanting in the copy of the National Library which formerly belonged to the old library of Alcobaça, a

the dictionary of Senhor Gonçalves Viana deserves especial mention because in a great measure it takes in its fore-runners.

31. Achinese[1]

Achinese is one of the languages spoken in Sumatra and which has, as its name indicates, its home in Achen (correctly Acheh) which lies in the northern extremity of the island and belongs to Holland.[2] It presents a very close affinity to the Malay language, but is less cultivated and less rich in its vocabulary. Its literature consists of poetical and theological compositions, and of many chronicles. The population is almost entirely Mahommedan and uses the Arabic character.

The influence of Portuguese on this language is not very large, and must have been due directly or indirectly to Malay. The Portuguese had constant relations, as a rule hostile, with the Achinese who in the 16th and 17th centuries represented the most powerful indigenous power in Sumatra.[3]

---

friend sent me a copy on loan from the library of Cardinal Mezzofanti, now brought together in the College of the Propaganda Fide.

[1] See *The Encyclopædia Britannica.*

[2] 'The Portuguese generally called it *Achem* (or frequently, by the adhesion of the genitive preposition, *Dachem*).' *Hobson-Jobson.* António Nunes makes a distinction between 'Dachem grande' (Great Achem) and 'Dachem pequeno' (Little Achem). *Livro dos Pesos da Ymdia.*

[3] [Luis Camoens, the poet, composed an ode to Dom Francisco Coutinho, Count of Redendo, who was Viceroy of Portuguese India from 1561–1564, for the Viceroy had sanctioned the publication of Garcia d'Orta's *Colloquies on the Simples and Drugs of India* and Camoens was d'Orta's intimate friend. This ode is published in d'Orta's book and contains an eloquent address to the Viceroy. Among other things he says of him that perhaps his thoughts are busy with pernicious war (*guerra infesta*) or with bloody Taprobanic Achen, the scourge of the sea (sanguinolento Taprobanico Achem, que o mar molesta). This reference to Achen bears witness to the hostile relations between it and the Portuguese in the 6th century. It is also interesting as proof of the fact that Camoens like many other educated men in his age identified Taprobana of the Greeks in this passage with Sumatra and not with Ceylon.—Ed.]

32. Batta

Batta or Batak is another language of Sumatra which is spoken by a people, pagan and given to cannibalism, and, yet not entirely uncivilised, who are now becoming Mahommedans and Christians.[1] They have a literature both in prose and verse and a character of their own; they write from bottom to top and from left to right.

Cust mentions three dialects of it: Dairi, Toba, and Mandailung. Joustra adds to it Karo, without furnishing much information regarding it.

The influence of Portuguese on this language, which some think has a resemblance to ancient Javanese and others to Malay, is not very great and appears to have been wholly exercised by way of Malay, though the Portuguese had commercial and political intercourse with the country.[2] The words which I have set down as adopted into Batta, belong properly speaking to Karo according to the dictionary of Joustra.

33. Sundanese[3]

Sundanese is the language of the west of Java and probably the ancient language of the island and belongs to the Javanese group. It has no ancient literature. It employs Javanese characters, but in a smaller number, and at the same time the Roman. From its geographical position and the structure of its words it approximates more to Malay than to Javanese, and that is why I mention it before the latter.

---

[1] 'Noted especially for their cannibal institutions.' *Hobson-Jobson.* 'In a part of this island, which they call Bathek, live the anthropophagi..... who hold human heads as objects of value; after severing the heads of their captive enemies, and eating their flesh, they lay up these heads and employ them as a medium of exchange.' Nicolo Conti (1430), *De Varietate Fortunae.* 'They call them **Batas**; they eat human flesh and are a people the most wild and warlike in the whole country.' João de Barros, Dec. III, V, 1.

[2] See Fernão Pinto, Ch. XIII *et seq.*

[3] See especially Rigg, *A Dictionary of the Sunda Language.*

The influence of Portuguese on its vocabulary, which is purer than that of other languages which are allied to it, is both direct and indirect as in the case of Javanese. There existed in Sunda a large Portuguese colony of which Fernão Pinto and other writers make frequent mention.

34. Javanese

'From the linguistic standpoint, Javanese is without doubt the most important of all the Malayo-Polynesian group. It is spoken by many millions of men, belonging to a tribe which occupies unquestionably the first place among the peoples of the Archipelago in development and civilisation. This language, which extends towards the centre of the island of Java as well as towards the east, is distinguished by the copiousness of its vocabulary and its forms, as well as by the richness of its literature.' Heyligers.

It has three principal dialects : High Javanese—a ceremonial dialect ; Low Javanese—the popular dialect ; Middle Javanese—the colloquial dialect. There also exists a poetic form of language, called Kavi, which is charged with Sanskrit terms. The foreign ingredients in the language are the same as in the Malay. Its characters are derived from the Indian, but are much modified and complicated.

It is true the Portuguese never conquered the island but, all the same, they visited its harbours very often and maintained political and commercial relations with it. It is by this means and by the contact of other languages, principally Low Malay, that many Portuguese terms found their way into Javanese.

Some of these as the result of special evolution passed into Krama or High Javanese, in harmony with the nature of the dialect.

35. Madurese

Maduresе is the indigenous language of the island of Madura and of the immigrants who have been established for centuries in the eastern part of Java. It is spoken by about a million and a half and it uses the Javanese alphabet for writing. Its structure is simpler than that of Javanese but its enunciation is more difficult and ruder. It has one dialect, the Sumanap, besides some peculiar forms of the colloquial language.

It appears that the Portuguese did not have much intercourse with the island and that the introduction of the Portuguese vocables into it is due principally to Javanese and to Low Malay. Even so, the number of Portuguese words that are to be found in it is considerable and generally these retain the Javanese form.

36. Balinese[1]

Balinese is the sole language of the island of Bali. It is spoken by about 500,000 people whose religion is still Brahmanical and Buddhist imported from Java and much perverted. According to Cust, the language is more polished than the Sundanese and Madurese. It is generally written on palm leaves in Javanese characters. Its vocabulary betrays traces of Sanskrit through Kavi (the poetic diction of Java), of Javanese, and of Malay. The lower classes speak a dialect which is purer and free from loan words.

In the dictionaries published by the Dutch we find very few Portuguese words, and these too owe their existence in it to mediate influences. But it is likely that there are more of such.

37. Dayak

Dayak or Dyak is the chief of the twelve languages of the extensive island of Borneo. It is also the generic name of the purely indigenous population which is pagan. On the coasts are settled Malays, Javanese, Bugis, and Chinese. The language is an uncultivated one and has neither a literature nor an alphabet.

---

[1] See R. Van Eck, *Eerste Proeve van een Balineesch-Hollandsch Woordenboek.*

The Portuguese had a factory at Borneo (1590–1643). But the Portuguese vocables in this language appear to have found their way chiefly through Malay and other allied tongues. When we consider the way these have been transmitted and the scale of the civilisation of the people and of the language wherein they have been admitted, we must confess that the number of the words thus introduced is remarkable.

38. Macassar[1]

Macassar is the language of the southern part of the Celebes Island which is called by the same name, and belongs to a special group.[2] It is a language that is cultivated, has a literature, and its own characters, preserving the classification of the Devanagri.

In its glossary of words there figure many Malay, Javanese, Sundanese, Chinese, and Arabic terms. It is thus through the agency of Malay and Javanese as well as through direct influence, principally religious,[3] which was very intense that Portuguese words[4] found their way into it.

Bugui[5]

Bugui or Vugui (Bugi or Wugi) is another important language of the Celebes, very much resembling Macassar, and which, according to Cust, has exerted an influence upon the languages of the other islands. It has a copious vocabulary in which many Arabic words have found their way through the influence of Mahommedanism; it has also a rich literature, ancient and

---

[1] See Matthes, *Makassarsch-Hollandsch Woordenboek.*

[2] 'According to Crawfurd this name (Celebes) is unknown to the natives, not only of the great island itself but of the Archipelago generally, and must have arisen from some Portuguese misunderstanding or corruption.' *Hobson-Jobson.* Fernão Pinto calls it 'The Island of Selebres.'

[3] See Diogo do Couto, Dec. V, VII, 2.

[4] It is not known when and by whom the Portuguese terms belonging to the card game of quadrille were introduced; they are not to be met with in any other of the languages except this and in Bugui.

[5] See Matthes, *Boegineesch-Hollandsch Woordenboek.*

modern, and also an archaic language. Its alphabet is the same as that of the Macassar.

The influence of Portuguese on Bugui must have been both direct and indirect, as in the case of Macassar. The large number of words of Portuguese origin, some of which cannot be traced in the other Malayo-Polynesian languages is a proof of the extensive and deep-seated influence of Portuguese civilisation in these parts.

Note.—There are many other languages belonging to different groups of the Archipelago, but I have no materials to enable me to investigate them. It is possible to conjecture from the allied languages that are treated in this work, that even in such, provided they are not entirely the speech of savages cut off from all contact with civilisation, Portuguese words must have found a way, especially such as are in common use, and which have no equivalents in the vernaculars.

40. Nicobarese

Nicobarese, the language of the Nicobar group of islands, is connected in respect of its present-day structure with the Malayo-Polynesian family of languages, but its substratum is provided by another language now extinct. With regard to this older language Sir Grierson says, 'It must be admitted that at the bottom of the languages spoken by the Kols, of the language of the Mon-Khmers and of the Nicobarese and Orang Utans, there is a common substratum which in the case, at least of the Mon-Khmers and the Nicobarese, inasmuch as it shows clear vestiges of its existence, was superimposed by a language belonging to a family of languages entirely different.'

Nicobarese is not a cultivated language, and has no characters of its own ; but it has a variety of dialects, which vary according to the islands and their people.

The Portuguese must have often touched at these islands on their voyages from India and Ceylon to Malacca and must have handed over to them many of their terms, such as *rei* (king), *chumbo* (lead), *sal* (salt), *lebre* (hare), *cabra* (goat), which are not to be found in the other languages.[1] The others which are met with in Nicobarese must have found their way in a great measure through Malay. Again there were Catholic missions on these islands during the 17th century.

41. Teto[2]

The Portuguese colony of Timor has an indigenous population of a million, which is composed of Malay new-comers, and the aboriginal negritos. They speak in the country five languages or principal dialects which are very closely related and having local variations: they are, Teto, Galoli, Uaima, Macaque, and Midic.[3]

Teto is the one generally used over the island[4]; it is an uncultivated language and possesses neither a literature nor its own alphabet. The speech of Dili, which is the capital city differs from the language of the interior as much in its vocabulary as in its structure and syntax.[5]

---

1 'There are five or six islands which have very good water and anchorages for shipping inhabited by poor Heathen; these islands are called Nacabar.' Duarte Barbosa, p. 374. [Hak. Soc. Longworth Dames's Transl., Vol. II, p. 181.] 'Francisco de Almeida on his way from India to Sumatra died of fever in the islands of Nicubar.' Fernão Pinto, Ch. XX. 'Returning to D. Paulo de Lima (who had been becalmed among the islands of Nicobar).' Fr. João dos Santos, II, p. 210.

2 See Aparício da Silva, *Diccionario de Portuguez-Tetum.* Rafael das Dores, *Diccionario Teto-Português.* Dr. Alberto Osório de Castro, *Flores de Coral, s.v. Timor.*

3 See Dr. Castro, *op. cit.*, p. 189.

4 It is spoken in Dili, Viqueque, Luca, Lachute, Alas, Suai, Monofahi, Berique, Dotic, Bibiçuçu, Samoro, Batugadi, Sanir, Balibó, Cova, Joanilo, Silacan, and Fialaran.

'Tetum is almost the *lingua franca* of this country, just as Galoli is among the people on the littoral to the east of Dilli.' Dr. Castro, p. 189.

5 'The dialect which is spoken in Delly, which is *Teto* or *Tetum*, is understood over all the island; nevertheless the Teto spoken in Lachute and in other parts is very different from that dialect.' José dos Santos Vaquinhas, *Timor*, in *Journal*, Geo. Soc. of Lisbon; 4th ser., p. 276.

Timor being a Portuguese possession and Teto, a very poor language, it is obvious that its vocabulary is laden with Portuguese terms, which are current in a lesser or greater degree, according to the extent of the contact of the peoples with European civilisation. I do not mention in this work all the Portuguese words that find a place in dictionaries of Teto or Galoli, many of which are entered evidently to make up for the want of the corresponding vernacular terms; but I am finding a place for such in their respective indices.

42. Galoli[1]

Galoli is the other principal language or dialect of Timor. With regard to it says Rev. Alves da Silva: 'It is the dialect most employed by the Christian population to the north-east of Timor, that part of Malaysia which is the most loyal and faithful to the Portuguese crown. In the language too of this part there is a noticeable difference though not quite so perceptible; thus it comes about that this dialect spoken in Manatuto though understood in Laleia and Vemasse, presents certain variations which are noticeable as far as in Laclo, although this latter place is almost two hours distant from the former.'

The influence of Portuguese on this language is analogous to that exercised on Teto. In the dictionary of this language there are fewer Portuguese words[2] to be found than in that of Teto.

43. Malagasy[3]

From its geographical position the island of Madagascar, 'the Island of St. Lorenzo' of the old Portuguese writers, belongs

---

[1] See Rev. Alves da Silva, *Noções da Grammatica Galóli; Diccionario Portuguez-Galóli*.

[2] There are no materials for the study of Uaima, Macaque and Midic.

[3] See Malzac, *Dictionnaire Français-Malgache*. Marre, *Vocabulaire des mots d'origine européenne*, etc.

to Africa; but its ethnic and linguistic affinities are with Asia.[1] It is on this account that Cust includes Malagasy, which is the language spoken in the island, in his '*Languages of the East Indies*'.[2] Its population is about two millions and a half and it is divided among numerous tribes which differ from one another in their physical appearance, the result of a mixture in a greater or smaller degree of the African with the Malay, Arab, or Indian.[3] But all speak a common language, which has ten dialects, of which the Hova is the chief and the one that is understood by the bulk of the population.[4] It has no peculiar character, and therefore commonly employs the Roman.

The affinity of Malagasy to the Malayo-Polynesian Language Family was observed four centuries ago and has now been confirmed by the investigations in modern times of Van der Tuuck. Marre, Marin, and W. E. Cousins.[5] But the roots of the words

---

1 'The names Madagascar and S. Lourenço are foreign. Among the native population no general name for the whole island has been found.' Rev. Luis Mariano, *Relação da jornada e descobrimento da ilha de S. Lourenço* (1613), in *Journal*, Geo. Soc. of Lisbon, 7th ser., p. 315.

2 'This island of San Lourenço, which writers call Madagascar ...... All this island is inhabited by peoples not as black as the negroes, nor as fair as the Mohammedans of all that coast. The presumption is that this island was conquered by the Jáos (Javanese) and that the inhabitants are a half breed people, the result of the fusion of the conquerors with the former natives of the country who must have been the Caffres (negroes) from the other side of the mainland.' Diogo do Couto, Dec. VII, IV, 5.

3 'The second Mohammedan king who reigned in Cambay and who was a great conqueror sent certain ships to the coast of Melinde ... these touched at the island of San Lourenço, and as they were unseaworthy, they remained there, and their crew helped to people some of the ports.' *Commentarios de Afonso de Albuquerque*, IV, Ch. 23.

4 'The language in use all over is Buque, ... and it is so uniform all over the island that the natives from the southernmost point understand it just as well as those from the northernmost; its vocabulary is poor, but on that account as easy to learn as to pronounce.' Rev. Mariano, *op. cit.*, p. 353.

5 'In the interior of the island, and other parts and the coasts, only Buque is spoken, which is the language of the natives, entirely different from the Caffre (negro) language, but very similar to Malay; this is almost a sure proof that the first settlers came from the ports of Malacca. *Id.*, p. 323.

are not bisyllabic as in the languages of the Archipelago. All the words end in a vowel, especially in *a* and *i*.

In its vocabulary there are to be found many exotic words chiefly English,[1] which are due to the intense Protestant missionary activity in the island, and French words which have been introduced, thanks to the influence of the Catholic religion and its missionary labours.

The Portuguese visited many times the ports of Madagascar, to which they gave names derived from the Calendar of the Saints; but they had no frequent or permanent relations of a political or commercial nature with the island. From Goa were despatched to it expeditions of a politico-religious kind, but without any serious result; and the missionary labours started by the Jesuits were of short duration and not very fruitful of results.[2] Among the Romanic words adopted in Malagasy, it is difficult to distinguish those which owe their existence to the mediate or direct influence of Portuguese, the presumption as a rule being in favour of French or English as the channels of entry.[3]

44. Pidgin-English[4]

In the coast cities of China is spoken a dialect of English which serves as a means of oral communication, like the corrupt Portuguese dialect in former days, between the natives and the

---

'In some of the bays of these islands (of Madagascar) they found some people who appeared to be Javanese; whence they came to see that the outskirts of that coast had been peopled by the Javanese because the inhabitants spoke their language.' Diogo do Couto, Dec. VII, viii, 1.

[1] Just as: book, glass, page, pencil, Christian, Christmas, monastery, catechist, Bible, angel.

[2] See Bocarro, Chh. 42, 108, 146, and 147; and Fr. João dos Santos, ii, Ch. 9.

[3] 'Having heard these matters and noticed some Portuguese words which are today in use among this people: *camisa* (shirt), *calção* (trouser), *romã* (pomegranate), *filho meu* (my son), *espingarda* (rifle) and similar others, they went on board the caravel on the 11th.' Rev. Mariano, p. 341.

[4] See Leland, *Pidgin-English Sing-Song*.

European and American foreigners, and sometimes even among the Chinese themselves who speak very different dialects.

'In its first and low form,' says Leland, 'as it is given in the vocabularies published for the use of servants, Pidgin is a very rude jargon, in which English words singularly mutilated, owing to the difficulty of expressing their sounds in written Chinese, are set forth according to the rules of the Chinese grammar. In fact, it is a translation, word by word, with little effort at inflection or conjugation, in view of the fact that such grammatical forms, as we understand them, do not exist in Chinese. The result of this, naturally, is that the vocabulary being very limited, a Chinaman learns Pidgin-English with no more difficulty than is presented by the acquisition of a few hundred words, whose pronunciation and grammar have been modified to accommodate themselves to his own language. In this it resembles exactly *posh an posh* or the corrupt Romany dialect spoken by the Gipsies in England in which Hindi-Persian words follow English grammatical structure.[1]

It is owing to the facility with which the Chinese learn this dialect and the good will of the foreigners to go and meet them half-way, that it has spread to such an incredible extent, thus preparing the ground to make English the language of the Pacific. And as the Chinaman learns more easily a Romanic language than pure English, it is probable that were it not for the Pidgin jargon, corrupt Portuguese would have formed the popular means of communication between the foreigners and the natives of China—the large number of Portuguese words which at present exist in Pidgin-English appears to prove it.'

The word *pidgin* is supposed to be a corruption of the English word *business*, but with a meaning much more extensive and varied. And as commerce is the one great bond between the

---

1 'Pitchin English (business English) is the commercial language of the ports of China; it is bad English with some Portuguese words, the grammatical construction being English.' J. H. Calado Crespo, *Cousas da China*, p. 16.

Chinese and the foreigners residing in the country, it is not to be wondered at that the term came to be applied to denote the language that was evolved for the purposes of trade.

There are those, however, who think that 'pidgin' is derived from the Portuguese 'occupação.'[1]

45. Japanese[2]

Students of languages are not agreed upon the genealogical classification of the language of Japan, the Yamato. Some try to trace an affinity between it and Aryan; others conclude that it has sprung from the Ural-Altaic stock, and that it is akin to the Korean, Manchu and Mongolean. There are again others who regard the Japanese language, just as much as the race itself, as a distinct one.

Morphologically, Japanese is agglutinative and polysyllabic. The ordinary colloquial language is very different from the written and the literary, in which are to be found many Chinese terms.[3] In its vocabulary are met with various Sanskrit, or rather, Pali words, introduced by Buddhism.[4]

---

1 In the Anglo-Chinese vocabulary there are many Hindustani and Anglo-Indian terms carried there principally by the English, such as: *bangee, bobbery, chop, pukkha, punkah, puttee, go-down, tiffin, Griffin.*

2 See *The Encyclopædia Britannica, La Grande Encyclopédie.* N. Murakámi, *The Influence of Early Intercourse.* Ladislau Batalha, *O Japão por dentro.* Wenceslau de Morais, in the *Journal* of the Geo. Soc. of Lisbon, 2nd ser., No. 6, and especially, Gonçalves Viana, *Palestras Filológicas.*

3 'The primitive language of Nippon, the *Yamato-Kotóba*, must have been necessarily very poor in vocables; and it appears certain that the earliest Japanese were completely ignorant of the use of writing. With the successive and growing intercourse of Japan with China, about the 3rd century of our era, *Yamato-Kotóba* began to be enriched with Chinese words, though such an alliance might now appear strange; it was then that the art of giving graphic form to an idea was started.' Wenceslau de Morais, *op. cit.*

4 Such as: *araghyo* from arghya (oblation), *arano* from aranya (forest), *biku* from bhiksu (monk), *butsû* from buddha (enlightened), *karancho* from krauñcha (heron), *daruma* from dharma (duty), *namae* from nāma (name), *shishi* from çisya (disciple), *shishō* from siṁha (lion).

The dialectical differences which are noticeable in different localities are of minor importance and do not stand comparison with those that are to be found in China. The dialect of the group of islands, known as Riukiu, deserves especial mention inasmuch as it preserves its archaic character. The speech of the Aino tribes of the island of Spezo is totally different from pure Japanese and is therefore not understood by the people of the other islands.

In their writing they generally employ Chinese ideographs, which run to about 3,000 in number. The proper Japanese script is syllabic made up of 47 syllables,[1] and is known as *Kana*, of which there are two varieties: the *Katakana* and *Hiragana*. Japanese is written in vertical columns from the right to the left. Its literature goes as far back as the 7th century.[2]

Portugal was the first European nation which came into contact with Japan and for a long period maintained commercial and missionary relations with it. It left, as in almost every other part, indelible traces of its language in the vocabulary of Japan most of which were due to the introduction of new objects and of a new religion. Some of the terms have acquired such citizen rights that it is difficult to trace their foreign origin. The ancient books of the Japanese abound, according to the testimony of Dr. Murakami, in religious terms of foreign origin and only a few of these have entered into the common speech of the people.[3]

---

1 The modification of some of these syllables raises the total number to seventy-three. See Ballhorn, *Alphabete orientalischer und occidentalischer Sprachen.*

2 'Fourteen kinds of letters distinguished not only in their form but in their peculiarity and meaning, the young fidalgos study in the monasteries of the Bonzos.' Lucena, *Historia da vida do Padre Francisco de Xavier*, Bk. VII, 5.

3 Dr. Murakámi, Director of the School for Foreign Languages in Tokio, was kind enough to send me a list of such terms which he had not published in his work to which I have referred above. In recent times many English words have been introduced as also words which, though not English, have found their way into the language through English, such as: *alcali, alcool, blanket, butter,*

46. Persian[1]

Persian has passed through various phases. The primitive Iranian had two principal dialects : Iranian of the West or ancient Persian, written in cuneiform characters, the most ancient inscriptions dating from the time of Darius ; and Iranian of the East, confirmed by Avest and written in an alphabet of Aramaic origin. The middle form of ancient Persian is preserved in the Pahlavi inscriptions, the earliest of which date as far back as the 3rd century of the Christian era. Literary Persian makes its appearance with the Mussulman dynasties in the 9th century. Modern Persian, especially the written language, is full of Arabic terms ; there is no word of this origin which has not or could not have a place in its vocabulary. Its alphabet is Arabic with slight modifications. But its structure remains Iranian.

Persian was in great vogue in India during the period of the Mahommedan domination; it was the language of the court, of the tribunals of justice, and of the official and literary world. The first digest of Hindu Law compiled under the orders of Warren Hastings—The Gentoo Code—was translated from the Sanskrit into Persian and from this rendered into English. Many of the English officials found themselves under the necessity, even during the last century, of knowing Persian[2]; and even at the present day there are schools where Persian is taught in various parts of the country. The treaties which the Portuguese entered into with Mahommedan sovereigns were recorded in Portuguese and in Persian.[3]

---

beer, brush, gallon, gas, glass, lace, race, panorama, piano, pin, pipe, pump, punch, matches, soda, yard.

[1] See *The Encyclopædia Britannica.* K. Brugmann, *Abrégé de Grammaire Comparative des Langues Indo-européennes.* A. Meillet, *Introduction à l'Étude comparative des Langues Indo-européennes.*

[2] See W. T. Tucker, *A Pocket Dictionary of English and Persian.*

[3] 'The articles of the treaty having been drawn up two documents were framed, one in Persian and the other in Portuguese, the former to be given to the Ambassador and the latter to remain in the State archives . . . Of this

47. Arabic

There are very many works treating of the Arabic influence on the Spanish languages but very few dealing with the influence of the Spanish languages on Arabic. The reason for this must certainly lie in the fact that the influence of the languages of the Iberic peninsula upon the language of the Mahommedan conquerors was neither so intense, nor lasting nor general. The most important work on this subject known to me is that of Simonet; but it does not appear to be a safe guide because many of the terms, which he sets down as having been taken over from Spain by the Arabs, had, one is inclined to suspect, a different origin and a limited range.

Arabic is the sacred language of the Mahommedans of India where there are schools in which it is taught. But very few Portuguese words must have been introduced into it by this way. Those that I have recorded in the present work are only such as belong to Eastern Arabic and not to that which is in use in Africa, which has many more. Even these do not offer, generally speaking, a sure clue to their Portuguese origin. Lexicographers refer many of them, as I have noted in various instances, to Greek, Latin, French, and Italian sources. Arabic and Persian, therefore, occupy in my work a secondary place.

48. Other Languages

Besides the languages already referred to, there are a few others whose vocabularies were not the direct object of my investigations: they are the Chinese, Jewish, Turkish, and the languages of the Philippines. The dictionaries of the other languages which I waded through, incidentally mentioned some Romanic words which are found in these vocabularies. But few of these are, for certain, of Portuguese origin as *leilão* and *padre* are in the Chinese language; the other Romanic words may

---

declaration on oath two deeds were drawn up, the one in Persian and the other in Portuguese.' Diogo do Couto, Dec. V, I, 12.

have had a different origin. Those that are to be found in Tagalo and Bisaio must have been introduced therein directly from the Spanish. Romanic words in the Turkish and Jewish languages are reproduced from the Glossary of Simonet. Subject to this reservation such terms will be found in the present work.

Andamanese: I examined two dictionaries of the unclassified languages of the Andaman Islands,[1] and did not come across any Portuguese word in either of them; this is because no foreign word has been included in them and thus the words *sabão* (soap), *mesa* (table), *tabaco* (tobacco), etc. have been omitted. As the Andamanese were uncivilized, it is to be presumed that some Portuguese words entered into their speech by way of Hindustani and English as has happened in analogous cases.[2]

XIV. *Alphabets and their Transliteration*[3]

It is now an accepted fact among Sanskritists, after the palæographic investigations of Dr. Bühler, that the art of writing was known in India in the 8th century B.C., although it was not then nor much afterwards employed for literary purposes. The characters are of Semitic origin and belong to the Phœnician type, similar to the Moabite, introduced by traders by way of Mesopotamia. The most ancient documents which we possess are the stone-inscriptions of the Emperor Asoka (3rd century B.C.) which give variants of the different forms of letters.

---

[1] *A Manual of the Andamanese Languages*, by M. V. Portman, London 1887. *Notes on the Languages of the South Andaman Group of Tribes*, by M. V. Portman, Calcutta 1898.

[2] 'The vessel was lost among the islands which they call the islands of *Andramū*, the inhabitants of which eat human flesh.' João de Barros, Dec. III, V, 3.

[3] See Beames, *Comparative Grammar of the Modern Aryan Languages of India*. Caldwell, *A Comparative Grammar of the Dravidian Languages*. Arthur Macdonell, *A History of Sanskrit Literature*. Friedrich Ballhorn, *Alphabete orientalischer und occidentalischer Sprachen*. G. Bühler, *On the Origin of the Indian Brahma Alphabet*.

The remodelling, the systematisation, and the adaptation of the Semitic characters to the Indo-European phonetics resulted in the alphabet which is called Brahmi and this in the 5th century. And it is from this that all the modern alphabets of India are derived, even the Dravidian, though these might appear so different at the present day. The most important of the derived alphabets is the *Nagari* (the city alphabet) or *Devanagri* (that of the city of God) in which are chiefly inscribed the literary monuments of the Sanskrit language and which in its written form dates as far back as the 8th century B.C.

The following languages follow Devanagri : Hindi, Nepali, Bihari, and Kashmiri ; Sindhi and Hindustani use this as well as the Arabic-Persian characters ; then Marathi, Konkani only partially, and Guzarati make use of this script. Punjabi, Bengali, Oriya, Assamese, Sinhalese, Telugu, Kanarese, with Tulu and Malayalam, have their peculiar characters, which differ from the Devanagri in their form but not phonetically or in their arrangement. Many of these languages, however, do not use all the Devanagri sounds, and there are some that have one or other especial sound or additional sounds and letters.

Among the Dravidian languages only the Tamil alphabet differs a great deal from the Nagri, as much owing to the want of many letters as by the addition of some consonants, and, even more, owing to the use of certain consonants to convey two or three different sounds.

The Arab-Persian characters are employed by Hindustani, Sindhi, with a special system of diacritical marks, Malay and Achinese.

Burmese, Tibetan, Siamese, Kambojan, Batta, Javanese, as well as Sundanese and Balinese and Madurese use their own characters, derived from the Aryan script, but a great deal modified. The alphabet of Bugui and Macassar have been co-ordinated according to the Devanagri system.

Garo, Khassi, Dayak, Nicobarese, Teto, Galoli, Malagasy, and to a partial extent, Konkani, Low Malay, and Sundanese, use the

Roman alphabet. Annamite, Tonkinese, and Japanese employ the Chinese ideographs.[1]

The Congress of Orientalists, which took place in 1894 at Geneva, adopted as regards Devanagri a uniform system of transcription, which since then has been generally followed by Sanskritists. The same system can be, and it is desirable should be, used for the transliteration of other alphabets which have the same origin, with a especial notation which is easily understood for especial letters.

It is necessary, therefore, to understand, above all, the transliteration of the Devanagri alphabet and likewise those of Tamil and Arabic-Persian.

Transliteration of the Devanagri Alphabet.

Vowels	..	अ a, आ ā, इ i, ई ī, उ u, ऊ ū, ऋ ṛ, ॠ ṝ,				
		ऌ ḷ, ए e, ऐ ai, ओ o, औ au				
Gutturals	..	क ka	ख kha	ग ga	घ gha	ङ ṅa
Palatals	..	च ca	छ cha	ज ja	झ jha	ञ ña
Cerebrals	..	ट ta	ठ tha	ड da	ढ dha	ण ṇa
Dentals	..	त ta	थ tha	द da	ध dha	न na
Labials	..	प pa	फ pha	ब ba	भ bha	म ma
Semi-vowels	..	य ya	र ra	ल la	व va	
Sibilants	..	श śa (palatal), ष ṣa (cerebral), स sa (dental)				
Aspirates	..	ह ha : ं anusvara ṁ ; ः visarga ḥ				

Remarks

I. *A* has the sound of a neutral vowel or small *a*. In Konkani and in Bengali it approximates to *ŏ* short. *A*, *i*, *u*, *ṛ*, *ḷ* are short (=*ă*, *ĭ*, *ŭ*, *ṛ̆*, *ḷ*); *ā*, *ī*, *ū* *ṝ*, are long. The vowels, *ṛ*, *ṝ*, *ḷ* are especial to Sanskrit vocables. *E* and *o* are regarded as diphthongs in Sanskrit (originally *ăi* and *ău*) and as such are long and closed (=*ê*, *ô*).

---

[1] The Rev. J. Knowles maintains that 'the alphabets of the Indian Empire reach the total of fifty—a greater number than those of the languages of the world, ancient and modern taken together.'

II. In the Dravidian and in some of the Neo-Aryan languages *e* and *o* are short and long. I represent them as ē and ō when long and unstressed. Sinhalese has in addition *e* diphthong (=æ), short and long, much palatalised. I transliterate it generally as ẹ and ẹ̄, or better, as e̤ and ē̤. Konkani has *e* and *o* open and closed; I represent them when necessary by *é* and *ó* when open and accented, and by *ê* and *ô* when closed. The Dravidian languages have many terminations ending in *u* very short, which it is usual to represent by ụ or u̥. Grammarians, according to Caldwell, give to such a quarter of the length of a long vowel.

III. Many of the Neo-Aryan languages do not pronounce the short *a* at the end of a word and frequently also not when it occurs in the middle of a word, although they write the consonant whole (without the *virāma*) as though the vowel was a part of it. Thus they write राम Rāma, but pronounce it Rām. In such cases I drop the *a* in transliteration.

IV. The Dravidian and many of the Neo-Aryan languages have the sound as well as the letter ळ *ḷa* cerebral, which in Sanskrit is only to be met with in Vedic writings.

V. Konkani, Marathi, and Telugu have two letters with two distinct sounds each of them, without any graphic sign to distinguish the phonetic changes; the normal (before *e* and *i*) *ch* explosive (like the italian *c* before *e* and *i*) and *ts* almost equivalent to *zz* in Italian; *j* explosive (as in English) and *z* (or *dz*).[1] I have marked the difference when transcribing such sounds.

VI. For very especial and weighty reasons I have made the following alterations in the rules for the transliteration mentioned above: *ch, chh,* I represent by *c, ch*; *x* (palatal) by *ç* (or *ś*) and *ṣ*; I have employed *n*, as a rule, not only to convey the sound of the nasal dental consonant, but also the guttural *ṅ* and the palatal *ñ*. All the nasals, when they figure in the middle of a word and unaccompanied by a vowel, are commonly represented

[1] Beames calls *ts* and *dz* 'non-assimilated palatals'.

in Neo-Aryan script by a full point (*anusvāra*) placed over the preceding letter like the dot in Portuguese; and they are distinguished phonetically by the consonant which follows as in Konkani: *aṁg* for *aṅg*, *vāṁjh* for *vāñjh*, *phāṁṭ* for *phāṇṭ*, *dāṁt* for *dant*, *xiṁpī* for *ximpī*.

VII. In almost all the polysyllabic languages the accent falls on the ultimate syllable if it be long and on the penultimate, long or short, if the ultimate be short. But in Sinhalese the accent can precede the penultimate, even though it be short as in annắsiya=pineapple.[1] I have pointed out the exceptions by the acute accent when the vowel is long, by an accent and the short sign when the vowel is short.

Transliteration of the Tamil Alphabet[2]

அ a	எ e	க் k	த் t	ல் l
ஆ ā	ஏ ē	ங் ṅ	ந் n	வ் v
இ i	ஒ o	ச் ch	ப் p	ழ் ḻ (or ḷ)
ஈ ī	ஓ ō	ஞ் ñ	ம் m	ள் ḷ
உ u	ஐ ai (or ei)	ட் ḍ	ய் y	ற் ṟ
ஊ ū	ஔ au	ண் ṇ	ர் r	ன் n

Letters for Sanskrit sounds: ஷ் sh, ஸ் s, ஹ் h, ஃ ḥ.

Remarks.

I. The Dravidian alphabet is also syllabic; a dot on the consonant, equivalent to the Sanskrit *virāma*, is an indication of the absence of the short *a* which accompanies it.

II. Tamil has no aspirate sounds, nor especial letters for soft consonants; one and the same character serves to mark both the sounds.

---

[1] Such Sinhalese words as have the accent on the anti-penultimate syllable have the stress on the fourth syllable, including the suffix *ya* or *-va*; *kámaraya* from câmara (chamber), *púkuruva* from púcaro (cup), *víduruva* from vidro (glass).

[2] See Caldwell, *op. cit.*, Percival, *Tamil-English Dictionary*.

III. *K*, *ch*, *ṭ*, *t*, *p*, being medial and simple, that is, when not double, sound as *g*, *j* (very little used in vernacular words), *ḍ*, *d*, *b*. *Çh* initial, and even intervocalic, is represented at times by the unstressed *x* or the Sanskrit *ś* or *ç*; the same is also used to mark the sibilant dental *s*. I transcribe *ch*, *j*, and *s*, but not *x* which is not much used. The *d* intervocalic in Tamil and Malayalam is very soft like *th* in English in than, that. I am not differentiating it from simple *d*, nor does Caldwell make a difference between them. In foreign words there occur high sounding initial syllables.

IV. The Tamil rule regarding sonorous medials is likewise observed in Malayalam, but with distinct letters, except *k* medial which sounds like *g* weak, almost like *h*, and is transliterated by a special sign which I omit.

V. The consonants peculiar to this language are *ḻ*, *ṛ*, *n*˙ The first which also occurs in Malayalam 'is pronounced differently in different districts,' says Caldwell. According to this writer the normal sound of this resembles the English *r* in farm, more liquid and post-palatal. According to Percival it is a mixture of *r*, *l*, and of the French *j*. Telugu substitutes it by *ḍ* cerebral and modern Kanarese by *ḷ* cerebral.

VI. The *ṛ* hard, at present used in Tamil and Malayalam, has a sound which is midway between the cerebrals *ḍ* and *ḷ* as in the English *crack*.

VII. *N*, the last letter of the alphabet, is not differentiated phonetically from the *n* dental; it has, on this account, no discriminating mark.

VIII. Some of the vowels shade off into different sounds before certain consonants which I find unnecessary to describe. The diphthong *ai* occurs but rarely.[1]

---

[1] The Dravidian languages generally retain the tonic accent of Portuguese words in the syllable on which it falls.

Transliteration of the Arabic-Persian-Hindustani Alphabet [1]

ا a (etc.)	چ ch	ذ dh	ش sh	غ gh	م m
ب b	ج j	ر r	ص ṣ	ف f	ن n
پ p	ح ḥ	ڑ ṛ	ض ẓ (ḍ)	ق q	ه h
ت t	خ kh	ز z	ط t̤	ک k	و v (w)
ٹ ṭ	د d	ژ zh	ظ z̤	گ g	ی y
ث th	ڈ ḍ	س s	ع ʻ	ل l	

Remarks

I. Many of the above-mentioned letters take different forms when they are at the beginning, middle or at the end of a word. I do not describe them because they do not affect the transliteration.

II. The letters *th*, *ḥ*, *ṣ*, *ẓ*, (*ḍ*), *t̤*, *z̤*, ʻ, *q*, are peculiar to Arabic. *Kh*, *dh*, *z*, *gh*, are common both to Arabic and Persian. The letter *zh* is peculiar to Persian. *P*, *ch*, *g*, are common to Persian and Hindustani. The cerebrals *ṭ*, *ḍ*, *ṛ*, are peculiar to Hindustani.

III. Some of the Arabic letters have a different sound in Persian and Hindustani as : *th*=*s* ; *dh*=*z* ; *ḍ*=Hindust. *z* ; *t̤*, *z̤*= Hindust. *t*, *z*.

IV. The Congress of Orientalists, referred to above, likewise standardised the transliteration of the Arabic alphabet, and this I am following, showing however, a preference for such variations as are left to option. I am substituting *ḍ* for *ẓ* to avoid confusion with the Hindustani *ḍ*, and *w* for *v* to maintain harmony with the transliteration from the Devanagri alphabet.

V. As Simonet and other authors adopt various methods of transcription which they do not always explain, I am making use of different Arabic words employed by them without adhering strictly or even uniformly to the method of the Congress.

---

[1] See Duncan Forbes, *A Grammar of the Hindustani Language*. David Lopes, *Textos de Aljamia Portuguesa*.

VI. Malay does not use in its vernacular speech the following Arabic letters : *th, h, kh, z, sh, ṣ, ḍ, ṭ, ẓ, ', gh, f,* and employs the following in addition to those which it has from the Arabic : *ch, ng, p, g, ñ,* or *ny.*

VII. Dutch writers in accordance with the genius of their language transliterate the letters *ch, j,* and *ñ* from Malay and the other languages of the Archipelago by *tj, dj,* and *nj,* and these they pronounce exactly as in Devanagri. '*Ch* is always pronounced as *ch* in church'. Swettenham. 'Or like the Spanish word *muchacho*'. Favre. '*J* ought to be pronounced as in jury, justice, jew'. Rigg. '*Ñ* is pronounced as *gn* in *agneau*; it is the Spanish *ñ*'. Favre.[1]

---

[1] 'The Dutch language does not contain this sound (*ch*), and it is consequently represented by them by *tj*, which does not convey the sound even according to the Dutch use of letters, as *j* with them has the power of the English *y*. It rather conveys the force of the French letters so applied.' Rigg.

BIBLIOGRAPHY

Albuquerque, Afonso de. *Cartas*, 3 vols. Lisbon, 1884.

Alwis, Rev. C. *The Sinhalese Hand-book.* Colombo, 1880.

Amarakoça. *Diccionário sânscrito do 5.° século.* Bombay Ed., 1890.

A Polyglot Vocabulary, English, German, Canarese, Tulu, and Malayalam. Mangalore, 1880.

Archivo Portuguez Oriental, 5 vols. and 2 supplements, edited by J. H. da Cunha Rivara. Nova-Goa, 1857 and after.

Barbosa, Duarte. *Livro.* In *Collecção de Noticias.*

Barros, Joao de. *Decadas da Asia*, Lisbon, 1638.

Barua, Hemchandra. *An Etymological Dictionary of the Assamese Language.* Calcutta, 1900.

Beames, John. *Outlines of Indian Philology.* London, 1868.

Comparative Grammar of the Modern Aryan Languages of India. London, 1872.

Bell, C. A. *Manual of Colloquial Tibetan.* Calcutta, 1905.

Belot, P. J. B. *Vocabulaire Arabe-Français.* Beyrouth, 1899.

Petit Dictionnaire Français-Arabe, Beyrouth, 1900.

Behare, M. B. *An Etymological Gujarati-English Dictionary.* Ahmedabad, 1904.

Bergé, Adolphe. *Dictionnaire Persan-Français.* Paris, 1868.

Bikker, Dr. A. J. W. *Malay, Achinese, French,* and *English Dictionary.* London, 1882.

Bluteau, Rev. D. Rafael. *Vocabulario Portuguez e Latino.* Lisbon, 1712–1728.

Bocarro, António. *Decada XIII da Historia da India.* Lisbon, 1876.

Livro das Plantas das Fortalezas da India. (MS. in the Library of Evora) published by Cunha Rivara in the *Chronista de Tissuary.*

Boletim da Sociedade de Geografia de Lisboa (*Journals of the Geographical Society of Lisbon*).

Botelho, Simão. *Tombo do Estado da India.* In *Subsidios, q.v.*

Brooks, William. *An Oriya and English Dictionary.* Cuttack, 1875.

Brown, Charles Philip. *A Dictionary of Mixed Telugu.* Madras, 1854.

Caldwell, Rev. Robert. *A Comparative Grammar of the Dravidian or South Indian Family of Languages.* London, 1875.

Camoens, Luis de. *Os Lusiadas.* Lisbon, 1905.

Campbell, A. D. *A Dictionary of the Teloogoo Language.* Madras, 1821.

Candy, Thomas. *A Dictionary English and Maráthí.* Bombay, 1873.

Cardinal Saraiva, D. Francisco de S. Luís. Complete works, 10 vols. Especially: *The Glossary of Portuguese words derived from Oriental and African Languages excepting Arabic*. Lisbon, 1818.

Cardim, Rev. Antônio Francisco. *Batalhas da Companhia de Jesus*. Lisbon, 1894.

Carter, Charles. *An English and Sinhalese Dictionary*. Colombo, 1889.

Castanheda, Fernão Lopes de. *Historia do Discobrimento e Conquista da India*. Lisbon, 1833.

Castro, Alberto Osório de. *Flores de Coral*. Dilli, 1908.

Castro, João de. *Roteiro de Lisboa a Goa*. Lisbon, 1882.

Ceylon. *Glossary of Native, Foreign and Anglicised Words*. Colombo, 1904.

Chronica dos Reys de Bisnaga, edited by David Lopes, Lisbon, 1897.

Clough, Rev. R. *A Dictionary of the Singhalese and English Languages*. Colombo, 1830.

Collecção de Noticias para a Historia e Geographia das Nações Ultramarinas. Lisbon, 1812–1841.

Commentarios de Afonso Dalboquerque. Lisbon, 1897.

Conde de Ficalho. *Garcia da Orta e o seu Tempo*. Lisbon, 1886. See Orta.

Conquista do Reyno de Pegú. In an Appendix to the *Peregrinação* by F. M. Pinto.

Costa, Bernardo Francisco da. *Manual pratico do agricultor indiano*. Lisbon, 1872.

Coutinho, Lopo de Sousa. *Historia do cerco de Diu*. Lisbon, 1890.

Couto, Diogo do. *Decadas da Asia*. Lisbon, 1602 and after.

Dialogo do Soldado pratico. Lisbon, 1790.

Craven, Rev. T. *The Popular Dictionary English and Hindustani, and Hindustani and English*. Lucknow, 1889.

The English and Hindi Dictionary. Lucknow, 1896.

The Gem Dictionary in English and Roman-Urdu. Lucknow, 1897.

Crawfurd, John. *Malay Dictionary*. London, 1852.

Crepin, P. *Nouveau Vocabulaire Français-tonkinois et Tonkinois-français*. Paris, 1900.

Crespo, Joaquim Heliodoro Calado. *Cousas da China*. Lisbon, 1898.

Cunha, Gerson da. *The Origin of Bombay*. Bombay, 1900.

Cust, Robert N. *A Sketch of the Modern Languages of the East Indies*. London, 1879.

Dalgado, D. G. *Classificação botanica das plantas e drogas descriptas nos 'Colloquios da India'* by Garcia d'Orta. Bombay, 1894.

Flora de Goa e Savantvadi. Lisbon, 1898.

Dalgado, Sebastião Rodolfo. *Diccionario Konkant-Portuguez.* Bombay, 1893.

Dialecto Indo-Portuguez de Ceylão. Lisbon, 1900.

Diccionario Português-Konkanī. Lisbon, 1905.

Devic, Marcel. *Dictionnaire Étymologique des mots d' origine orientale.* In a supplement to the Dictionary of Littré.

Dias, J. *Lijst van Atjehsche Woorden.* In a Dutch Review of which I possess only a few pages without the title-page.

Diccionario Contemporaneo da Lingua Portugueza. Lisbon, 1881.

Diccionario Portuguez-Concani, composed by an Italian Missionary. Nova-Goa, 1868.

Dores, Rafael das. *Diccionario Teto-Português.* Lisbon, 1907.

Dozy, R. *Glossaire des mots espagnols et portugais dérivés de l'arabe.* Leyde, 1869.

D'Rozario, P. S. *A Dictionary of English, Bángáli and Hindustani.* Calcutta, 1837.

Eck, R. van. *Eerste Proeve vaneen Balineesch-Hollandsch Woordenbock.* Utrecht, 1876.

Edaljí, Shapurjí. *A Dictionary, Gujarati and English.* Bombay, 1868.

Elmslie, William Jackson. *A Vocabulary of the Kashmiri Language.* London, 1872.

Encyclopœdia Britannica. Edinburgh, 1875.

Engelmann, W. H. *Glossaire,* etc. Leyde, 1861.

English-Garo Dictionary by members of the Garo Mission. Shillong, 1905.

Erédia, Manuel Godinho de. *Declaraçam de Malaca e India Meridional com o Cathay.* Brussels, 1881.

Favre, Abbé P. *Dictionnaire Javanais-Français.* Vienne, 1870.

Dictionnaire Malais-Français. Vienne, 1875.

Grammaire de la Langue Malaise.

Ferguson, Donald. *Letters from Portuguese Captives in Canton.* Bombay, 1902.

Figueiredo, Cândido de. *Novo Diccionario da Lingua-Portuguêsa.* Lisbon, 1899.

Fokker, A. A. *O Elemento Português na lingua Malaia.* In the *Revista Lusitana,* Vol. VII, I.

Gois, Damião de. *Chronica d'el-Rey D. Manuel.* Lisbon, 1909.

Gomes, Francisco Luis. *Os Brahamanes.* Lisbon, 1909.

Goshal, Bojendra Nath. *A Dictionary of the Bengalee Language.* Calcutta, 1890.

Gouveia, Rev. António de. *Jornada do Arcebispo de Goa.* Coimbra, 1606.

Grierson, George. *Linguistic Survey of India.*

The Languages of India. Calcutta, 1903.

The Languages of India, and the Census of 1901. In *Asiatic Quarterly Review*, April, 1904.

Gubernatis, Angelo. *Storia dei Viaggiatori italiani alle Indie Orientali.* Livorno, 1875.

Gumdert, Rev. H. *A Malayalam and English Dictionary.* Mangalore, 1872.

Haex, David. *Dictionarium Malaio-Latinum et Latino-Malaicum.* Romae, 1631.

Hardeland, Aug. *Dajaksch-Deutsches Wörterbuch.* Amsterdam, 1859.

Hepburn, J. C. *Japanese-English and English-Japanese Dictionary.* Tokyo, 1907.

Heyligers, J. C. Th. *Traces de portugais dan les principales langues des Indes Orientales Néerlandaises.* La Haye, 1889.

Historia tragico-maritima, compiled by Henrique Gomes de Brito. 12 vols. Lisbon, 1904–1909.

Hobson-Jobson. Vid. Yule and Burnell.

Hoernle and Grierson. *A Comparative Dictionary of the Bihari Language.* Calcutta, 1885–1889. Incomplete work.

Hunter, W. W. *A Comparative Dictionary of the Languages of India and High Asia.* London, 1868.

Java. Information for Travellers. Batavia, 1913.

Joustra, M. *Karo-Bataksch Woordenboek.* Leyden, 1907.

Kazimirski, A de Biberstein. *Dictionnaire Arabe-français.* Paris, 1860.

Kloguen, Dinis L. Cottineau de. *An Historical Sketch of Goa*, translated by M. V. de Abreu. Nova-Goa, 1858.

Lajonquière, M. C Lunet de. *Dictionnaire Français-Siamois.* Paris, 1904.

Lal, Ram Narain. *The Student's Practical Dictionary English-Hindi.* Allahabad, 1908.

Lala, Guni. *Anglo-Nagari Dictionary.* Dinapore, 1887.

Langen, H. F. H. *Woordenboek der Atjehsche Taal.* S. Gravenhage, 1889.

Laquenan, Monsignor F. R. *Du Brahmanisme et de ses rapports avec le judaisme et le christianisme.* Pondicherry, 1884.

Latham, C. *Elements of Comparative Philology.*

Le Gouz de la Boullaye, François. *Les Voyages et observations.* Paris, 1653.

Leland, Charles. *Pidgin-English Sing-Song.* London, 1903.

Lembranças das Cousas da India. In *Subsidios.*

Littré, E. *Dictionnaire de la Langue Française.* Paris, 1885.

Lopes, Tomé. *Navegação ás Indias Orientaes.* In the Collection of Ramúsio, translated by the Academy of Sciences, Lisbon, in the '*Collepão de Noticias*'.

Lucena, Rev. João de. *Historia da Vida do Padre Francisco de Xavier.* Lisbon, 1600.

Macdonell, Arthur. *A History of Sanskrit Literature.* London, 1905.

Maffei, Angelus Francis Xavier. *An English-Konkani Dictionary.* Mangalore, 1883.

Malzac, P. *Dictionnaire Français-malgache.* Paris, 1899.

Man, Edward Horace. *A Nicobarese Vocabulary.* London, 1888.

Männer, Rev. A. *Tulu-English Dictionary.* Mangalore, 1886.

English-Tulu Dictionary. Mangalore, 1888.

Marre, Aristide. *Notice sur la langue portugaise dans l'Inde française et en Malaisie.* In *Annales de l'Eatrême Orient*, Vol. III, No. 36. Paris, 1881.

Vocabulaire des mots d'origine européenne présentement usités dans la langue malgache. Chalon-sur-Saone, 1909.

Marsden, W. *Dictionary of the Malayan Language*, 1812.

A Grammar of the Malay Language.

Memoirs of a Malay Family. London, 1830.

Matthes, R. F. *Makassaarsch-Hollandsch Woordenboek.* Amsterdam, 1859.

Boegineesch-Hollandsch Woordenboek. Amsterdam, 1874.

Supplement of het Boegineesch-Hollandsch Woordenboek. Amsterdam, 1889.

Mendis and Rev. T. Moscrop, B.A. *A Sinhalese-English Dictionary.* Colombo, 1899.

Michell, C. B. *A Siamese-English Dictionary.* Bankok, 1892.

Molesworth, J. T. *A Dictionary Maráthí and English.* Bombay, 1857.

Morais, António de Silva. *Diccionario da Lingua Portugueza.* Lisbon, 1844.

Morais, Wenceslau de. *Day-Nippon.* Lisbon, 1897.

Moura, M. *Vocabulaire Français-Cambodgian et Cambodgian-Français.* Paris, 1878.

Murakami, N. *The influence of early intercourse with Europe on the Japanese Language.* Tokio, 1906.

Nicholson, Rev. James. *A Pocket Dictionary of the English and Sinhalese Languages.* Colombo, 1895.

Nunes, António. *Lyvro dos Pesos da Ymdia e asi Medidas e Moedas.* In *Subsidios.*

O Chronista de Tissuary. An Historical Review, edited by Cunha Rivara. Nova Goa, 1866–1869.

O Gabinete Litterario das Fontainhas. A Review edited by Filipe Néri Xavier. Nova-Goa, 1846–1848.

Oppert, Gustav. *On the classification of Languages.* Madras, 1869.

Orta, Garcia da. *Colloquios dos simples e drogas da India.* The edition with notes by Conde de Ficalho. Lisbon, 1891.

O Ultramar. A periodical published at Margão, Goa.

Palmer, C. H. *A Concise Dictionary English-Persian.* London, 1883.

Patel, L. G. *A Pocket Gujarati-English Dictionary.* Ahmedabad, 1892.

Patel, N. H. *The English-Gujarati Dictionary.* Ahmedabad, 1895.

Patel, Withalrau Vyasand Thankerbhai. *The Student's Standard English-Gujarati Dictionary.* Ahmedabad, 1896.

Paul, Bulloram. *An enlarged English to Bengali Dictionary.* Calcutta, 1888.

Percival, Rev. P. *Tamil-English Dictionary.* Madras, 1877.

A Dictionary English and Tamil. Madras, 1893.

Pinto, Fernão Mendes. *Peregrinação.* Lisbon, 1725.

Portman, M. V. *A Manual of the Andamanese Languages.* London, 1887.

Notes on the Languages of the South Andaman Group of Tribes. Calcutta, 1898.

Pyrard, Francisco de Laval. *Viagem.* The Translation of J. H. da Cunha Rivara. Nova-Goa, 1858.

Ramúsio, G. Battista. *Delle Navigationi et Viaggi.* 3 vols. Venetia, 1563, 1565, 1583.

Rebêlo, Gabriel. *Informação das cousas de Maluco.* In *Collecção de Noticias.*

Reeve, Rev. W. *A Dictionary Canarese and English.* Bangalore, 1858.

Ressurreição, Fr. Clemente da. *Tratado de Agricultura*—In the works of B. F. da Costa.

Ribeiro, João. *Fatalidade historica da ilha de Ceilão.* In *Collecção de Noticias.*

Rheede, H. *Hortus Indicus Malabaricus.* Amstelod, 1686.

Rigg, Jonathan. *A Dictionary of the Sunda Language.* Batavia, 1862.

Rivara, Joaquim Heliodoro da Cunha. See *Archivo, O Chronista* and Pyrard.

Roberts, Rev. H. *An Anglo-Khassi Dictionary.* Calcutta, 1878.

Roteiro da Viagem de Vasco da Gama. Lisbon, 1838.

Sakuna, N. *An Intermediate Japanese-English Dictionary.* Tokio, 1904.

Sankaranarayana, P. *A Smaller English-Telugu Dictionary*. Madras, 1894.

Santos, Fr. João dos. *Ethiopia Oriental*. Lisbon, 1892.

S. Bernardino Fr. Gaspar de. *Itinerario da India por terra até este reino de Portugal*. Lisbon, 1611.

Schuchardt, Hugo. *Kreolische Studien IX. Ueber das Malaio-portugiesische von Batavia und Tugu*. Wien, 1891.

Beiträge zur Kenntnis des kreolischen Romanisch, V.

Sen, Ram Comul. *A Dictionary in English and Bengalee*. Serampore, 1834.

Shakespear, John. *A Dictionary Hindustani and English*. London, 1817.

Shellabear, W. G. *Malay-English Vocabulary*. Singapore, 1912.

Shirt, Rev. G. *A Sindhi-English Dictionary*. Kurrachee, 1879.

Silva, Rev. Manuel Maria Alves da. *Dicionario Portuguez-Galóli*. Macao, 1905.

Silva, Rev. Sebastião Maria Apparicio da. *Diccionario de Portuguez-Tetum*. Macao, 1889.

Simonet, D. Francisco. *Glosário de Voces Ibéricas y Latinas usadas entre los Mosárabes*. Madrid, 1899.

Singh, Gulab. *The Punjábí Dictionary*. Lahore, 1895.

Singh, Nissor. *Khassi-English Dictionary*. Shillong, 1906.

Sloan, W. H. A *Practical Method of the Burmese Language*. Rangoon, 1901.

Small, George. *A Laskari Dictionary in English and Hindustani*. London, 1882.

Soares, Joaquim Pedro Celestino. *Bosquejo das Possessões Portuguezas no Oriente*. Lisbon, 1851.

Sousa, Fr. João de. *Vestigios da Lingoa Arabica em Portugal*. Lisbon, 1830.

Sousa, Fr. Luís de. *Historia de S. Domingos*. Lisbon, 1767.

Stack, George. *A Dictionary English and Sindhy*. Bombay, 1849.

Starkey, Captain. *A Dictionary English and Panjabee*. Calcutta, 1849.

Stolz, C. *School-Dictionary English and Malayalam*. Mangalore, 1870.

A Malayalam and English School-Dictionary. Mangalore, 1870.

Subsidios para a Historia da India Portuguesa, comprising the books of Simão Botelho and Antonio Nunes, and *Lembranças das Cousas da India*. Lisbon, 1868.

Swettenham, Frank A. *Vocabulary of the English and Malay Languages*. Vol. I, *English-Malay*. Singapore, 1885. Vol. II, *Malay-English*. Leyden, 1910.

Sykes, J. *English and Bengali Dictionary.* Calcutta, 1874.

Taberd, J. L. *Dictionarium Latino-Anamiticum.* Serampore, 1838.

Tavernier, Jean Baptiste. *Les six voyages en Turquie, en Perse, et aux Indes.* Rouen, 1712.

Tennent, Sir James Emerson. *Ceylon, an Account of the Island.* London, 1860.

Tenreiro, Antonio. *Itinerario.* Appended to *Peregrinação* by F. M. Pinto.

Tucker, William Thornhill. *A Pocket Dictionary of English and Persian.* London, 1801.

Turnbull, Rev. A. *Nepali Grammar and Vocabulary.* Darjeeling, 1904.

Vallot, P. G. *Petit Dictionnaire Annamite-français.* Hanoi, 1904.

Viana, A. R. Gonçalves. *Vocabulário Malaio, derivado do português.* In *Revista Lusitana,* Vol. VIII, I.

Classificação summaria das linguas. In *Mappa Dialectologico do continente português* by J. Leite de Vasconcellos. Lisbon, 1897.

Apostilas aos dicionários portugueses. Lisbon, 1906.

Palestras filológicas. Lisbon, 1910.

Vieira, Fr. Domingos. *Grande Diccionario Português.* Porto, 1871.

Viterbo, Fr. Joaquim de Santa Rosa de. *Elucidario das palavras, termos e frases.* Lisbon, 1798.

Ward, Mrs. S. R. *Brief Vocabulary in English and Assamese.* Sibsaugar, 1867.

Webster. *Complete Dictionary of the English Language.* London, 1884.

Whitworth, George Clifford. *An Anglo-Indian Dictionary.* London, 1885.

Wilkinson, R. J. *An abridged Malay-English Dictionary.* Kuala Lumpur, 1908.

Williams, Monier. *A Sanskrit-English Dictionary.* Oxford, 1899.

Wilson, H. H. *A Glossary of Judicial and Revenue Terms of British India.* London, 1855.

Xavier, Filipe Néri. *Collecção de Bandos das Novas Conquistas.* 2 vols. Pangim, 1840–1850.

Yule and Burnell (Henry Yule and Arthur Burnell). *Hobson-Jobson, being a Glossary of Anglo-Indian colloquial words and phrases.* London, 1886.

Ziegler, Rev. F. *A School Dictionary English and Canarese.* Mangalore, 1889.

OPINION OF SENHOR A. R. GONÇALVES VIANA ON THE WORK IN MANUSCRIPT, 'INFLUENCE OF PORTUGUESE VOCABLES ON ASIATIC LANGUAGES', OF DR. SEBASTIÃO RODOLFO DALGADO.

Monsignor Sebastião Rodolfo Dalgado presents to our Academy a study very comprehensive in its extent which, I am not sure whether any other scholar, Portuguese or for that matter of any other nationality, could have satisfactorily accomplished.

The subject of this laborious work is the examination specific and systematic of Portuguese words adopted in a great number of Asiatic languages spoken by peoples with whom we have been in more or less intimate and direct contact. In respect of time this contact has been extended from the 15th century to the present day, and in respect of extent has covered the zone right from Ceylon to Japan. This work represents specialisation in a field of linguistic study for which its worthy author had not the benefit of an earlier model. He had therefore, in the carrying out of his objective, himself to evolve a new method adapted to an exposition at once clear and convincing. The truth is that uptil now, orientalists, by which I mean those who make a scientific study of these questions, have preferred to devote their time to investigate the origin of exotic vocables of varying provenance which have made their entry into European languages, and not to examine the influence which these latter have exercised over the vernaculars of the other parts of the world.

The author fully equipped for his task by continuous study and by a thorough assimilation of the exact laws of comparative philology, shows in every detail of his work a knowledge of scientific literature pertinent to his subject and a conscientious grasp of those facts which help effectively to make good his thesis, viz. the considerable influence of Portuguese civilisation in its various manifestations over indigenous civilisation, whether stationary or progressive. So large, in fact, is the number of Portuguese words adopted in so many languages distinct in their genius, seeing that they belong to diverse families and possessing the most varied grammatical structures, that we cannot help inferring that excluding the Greeks and the Romans perhaps no other people, unless they be the Arabs, succeeded in spreading a part of its vocabulary through so many diverse language fields, and this without affecting the integrity of these languages, no matter whether the words found an entry into these tongues through the spoken word or through written compositions, above all liturgical.

With regard to the grouping of the vernacular languages, the learned and worthy orientalist follows the system employed by the renowned English glotologist Robert Cust, well-known for his model of a book—'The Modern Languages of the East Indies,' not to speak of other works. I am of the opinion that he acted well in doing this, notwithstanding that the classification and its characteristics are not in complete agreement with the theories of the celebrated philologist, the late Frederick Müller, some of which are perhaps antiquated while others are too personal, and in spite of differing from the most recent doctrines and theories put forward by Finck with regard to grammatical structures which has reduced from a morphological standpoint to eight types all the languages known in the five continents of the world.

I hold that in deciding to follow Cust the choice was most happy in relation, at least, to the Asiatic languages, which was the sole field of the author's investigations.

I have already mentioned that Monsignor Dalgado, in the absence of any existing model for his work or of one even resembling it to guide him, had to set up a method entirely new. In fact, if we put aside some of the studies of Dr. Hugo Schuchardt on the Portuguese dialects in Asia, one of Aristides Marre and two of mine regarding Malay, the first of which was published in

1896 in the memorial volume 'Mélanges Charles de Harlez', and the second in the eighth volume of the 'Revista Lusitana' (1903-1905), preceded by an incomplete investigation of Dr. A. A. Fokker and also of Dr. Murakámi, which aims at tracing the various Portuguese or Spanish words still to be found in the Japanese of to-day, all the other languages of India, those of the Far East, of the south of Asia and of Polynesia had to be examined with reference to the question in hand, the absorption of Portuguese terms in these vernacular tongues.

The author does not expound the phonetic laws to which each of the languages conformed in accepting the Portuguese words and fusing them into their own vocabulary, as I attempted to do in the case of words in Malay, a task easy enough, considering the phonetic simplicity of the family of languages, to which Portuguese words had no difficulty in conforming.

On the other hand, a study of all the changes which these words had to undergo in the idioms of the other linguistic families would require arduous and sustained labour if it were to come within the four corners of the work which I am here surveying. Meanwhile the learned writer has pointed out in a concise manner some of the principal changes and among them the most notable is that which has reference to the elimination of the initial atonic syllable which immediately precedes a tonic syllable in a polysyllabic word, specially if the initial syllable should be a vowel, but also, in some cases if it should be a consonant. This phenomenon is well-known and is frequently to be met with when words of one language make their way into another, and if the transmission should be consequent on the result of hearing the spoken word.

This valuable study which has been entrusted to me for examination is preceded by an introduction which, looked at from whatever point of view is of very great interest. In it the author discloses his extensive learning in this very important branch of knowledge. This introduction is elaborated out with such art, as to make an appeal as much to the specialist as to the ordinary reader keen on being informed, so clear and delightful is his exposition, its strictly scientific character however, being in no way affected by his extraordinary conciseness both of treatment and expression.

In the whole work the author has employed Portuguese vernacular idioms with the most meticulous care and has avoided the use of even pardonable neologisms or words that betray their foreign descent ; the unique exception is the case of certain ethnic names, such as *khmer*, *cashmirês*, which in my opinion could have been reduced to our systems of orthography and written as *cmer*, *caxemirês* like the others to which the author skilfully gave a Portuguese guise. The result in consequence is, that he has imparted an atmosphere truly national to the whole of his work, which because of its worth and originality does much honour to our scientific attainments in a field of human knowledge, which unfortunately among us has but few scholars of eminence though it must be said that these are held everywhere in great respect and regard.

It is on this account that the work, as I have said, is of the greatest interest, not only to us Portuguese, as testifying to our enduring interest, in distant nations and peoples with whom we had been and are in contact, but as much also for those outside Portugal, who with great honour and distinction give themselves up to linguistic studies in their multifarious aspects.

I feel certain that the publication of this monumental study will receive the approbation and applause of scholars of all nations dedicated to this branch of learning, and from the public in general, and that it will redound to the glory of our country, to the well-merited honour of our Academy, and above all to the credit of him who with the greatest selflessness and dedication, a spirit truly scientific, and burning patriotism, took upon himself to carry out in an exemplary manner a work so well conceived and so useful and withal so difficult and one which belongs to a field of knowledge which till now has scarcely been explored.

In view of all these reasons I am of the opinion that the

masterly study of which I have just finished making a succinct analysis satisfies all the requirements necessary to have its publication sanctioned at the cost of the Academy of Sciences, Lisbon and I feel sure that its publication will enhance the reputation which our Academy has ever earned and upheld.

Academy of Sciences, Lisbon, April 11*th* 1912.

Joaquim Teófilo Braga.
Henrique Lopes de Mendonça.
Francisco Teixeira de Queiroz.
José Duarte Ramalho Ortigão.
José Leite de Vasconcelos.
Aniceto dos Reis Gonçalves Viana.

ALPHABETICAL LIST OF THE LANGUAGES AND DIALECTS OF THE VOCABULARY

Achinese or Atjeh
Anglo-Indian
Annamite or Annamese
Arabic
Assamese
Balinese
Batavian
Batta or Batak
Bengali
Bugui
Burmese
Chinese
Dayak
Galoli
Garo
Gujarati
Hindi
Hindustani
Indo-French
Japanese
Javanese
Kambojan
Kanarese
Kashmiri
Khassi
Konkani
Laskhari-Hindustani
Macassar
Madurese
Malagasy
Malay
Malayalam
Marathi
Molucan
Nepali
Nicobarese
Oriya
Panjabi
Persian
Pidgin-English
Rabbinical
Siamese
Sindhi
Sinhalese
Sundanese
Tamil
Telugu
Teto
Tibetan
Tonkinese
Tulu
Turkish

ORDER OF THE LANGUAGES ABBREVIATED IN THE VOCABULARY

Konk.	.. Konkani	Siam.	.. Siamese
Mar.	.. Marathi	Ann.	.. Annamite
Guj.	.. Gujarati	Tonk.	.. Tonkinese
Hindi	.. Hindi	Mal.	.. Malay
Hindust.	.. Hindustani	Ach.	.. Achinese
L-Hindust.	.. Laskari-Hindustani	Batt.	.. Batta
		Sund.	.. Sundanese
Nep.	.. Nepali	Jav.	.. Javanese
Or.	.. Oriya	Mad.	.. Madurese
Beng.	.. Bengali	Bal.	.. Balinese
Ass.	.. Assamese	Day.	.. Dayak
Sindh.	.. Sindhi	Mac.	.. Macassar
Panj.	.. Panjabi	Bug.	.. Bugui
Kash.	.. Kashmiri	Batav.	.. Batavian
Sinh.	.. Sinhalese	Mol.	.. Molucan
Tam.	.. Tamil	Nic.	.. Nicobarese
Malayal.	.. Malayalam	Tet.	.. Teto
Tel.	.. Telugu	Gal.	.. Galoli
Kan.	.. Kanarese	Malg.	.. Malagasy
Tul.	.. Tulu	Pid.-Engl.	.. Pidgin-English
Anglo-Ind.	.. Anglo-Indian	Chin.	.. Chinese
Indo-Fr.	.. Indo-French	Jap.	.. Japanese
Gar.	.. Garo	Pers.	.. Persian
Bur.	.. Burmese	Ar.	.. Arabic.
Tib.	.. Tibetan	Rab.	.. Rabbinical
Khas.	.. Khassi	Turk.	.. Turkish
Kam.	.. Kambojan		

ABBREVIATIONS

Ach.	Achinese
adj.	adjective
adv.	adverb
Ann.	Annamite
Ar., Arab.	Arabic
Bal.	Balinese
Batav.	Batavian
Batt.	Batta
Beng.	Bengali
bk.	book
Bur.	Burmese
Bot.	Botanical
Bug.	Bugui
Cf. (*confer*)	Compare
ch.	chapter
Chin.	Chinese
conj.	conjunction
Day.	Dayak
Dravid.	Dravidian
Engl.	English
ed.	editor
et. seq.	and the following
ex.	example
f., fem.	feminine
fig.	figuratively
Fr.	French
Gal.	Galoli
Gar.	Garo
Geo. Soc.	Geographical Society
Gr.	Greek
Guj.	Gujarati
Hak. Soc.	Hakylut Society
Hindust.	Hindustani.
Hol.	Holland
Id. (*idem*)	the same
Indo-Engl.	Indo-English
Indo-Fr.	Indo-French
interj.	interjection
Jap.	Japanese
Jav.	Javanese
Kash.	Kashmiri
Khas.	Khassi
L. Hindust.	Laskari-Hindustani
Lat.	Latin
m., masc.	masculine
Mac.	Macassar
Mad.	Madurese
Mal.	Malay
Malayal.	Malayalam
Malg.	Malagasy
Mol.	Moluccas
n., neut.	neuter
naut.	nautical
Nep.	Nepali
Nic.	Nicobarese
obsol.	obsolete
op. cit.	opere citato
Or.	Oriya
p.	page
Panj.	Panjabi
Pers.	Persian
Pid-Engl.	Pidgin-English
pl.	plural
pop.	popular
Port.	Portuguese

prep.	..	preposition	Tam.	..	Tamil
q. v. (*quod vide*)		which see	Tel.	..	Telugu
Rab.	..	Rabinnical	Tet.	..	Teto
Rev.	..	Reverend	Tonk.	..	Tonkinese
Sansk.	..	Sanskrit	Tul.	..	Tulu
ser.	..	series	v.	..	verb
Sindh.	..	Sindhi	v. int.	..	verb, intransitive
s. v.	..	*sub voce*			
t.	..	term	v. trans.	..	verb transitive
transl.	..	translation	vid. (*vide*)	..	see

PORTUGUESE VOCABLES
IN
ASIATIC LANGUAGES.

A

Abada (old Port. 'rhinoceros, female rhinoceros'[1]). Anglo-Ind. *abada* (obs.)—|Indo-Fr. *abada*|.

The origin of the word is doubtful. Two derivations are put forward: the Arabic *ābida*, 'a wild animal'; and the Malay *bādaq*, (the *q* scarcely pronounced), 'a rhinoceros.' The latter appears more probable. There is no mention of the term in Portugal before the sixteenth century and the early Portuguese chroniclers mention it as an Indian or Malay word, and also use the form *bada*[2]. Duarte Barbosa and João de Barros employ the Indian term *ganda*, instead of *abada*.[1] The proper term for a rhinoceros in Arabic-Persian is *karkaddan*.

[1] "The rhinoceros, which are the abadas." Fr. Gaspar de S. Bernardino, *Itinerario da India*, I, p. 79.

[2] "Many bring from the 'Cape of Currents' to Moçambique skins of tigers and of other big game, and from the same place come horns which they wish to say are equal to those of the Abada of Malacca." P. Monclaio (1569), in *Jour. Geo. Soc. Lisb.*, 4th ser., p. 547.

"Rhinoceros or **Badas**." João de Lucena, *Historia da Vida do Padre Francisco de Xavier*, Bk. X, ch. 18.

[1] "He (The King of Guzerate) sent a *Ganda* ('rhinoceros') to the King our Lord, as they told him he would be pleased with it." Duarte Barbosa, *Livro*, ed. of the Academy of Sciences, Lisbon, p. 263. [Hak. Soc., ed. Longworth Dames, Vol. I, p. 124. Lord Stanley of Alderley who was the first to translate and edit Barbosa for the Hakluyt Society thought the *ganda* of this passage meant "a woman of the Gond tribe." Col. Henry Yule in *Hobson-Jobson* (*s. v.* ganda) remarks that this annotation of Sir Stanley is "a marvel in the way of error."]

"A big animal......with a horn right above the nose, two spans long, thick at the base and pointed at the end; the inhabitants of Cambay whence this creature came call it *Ganda:* and the Greeks, and Latins Rhinoceros." João de Barros, Dec. II, x, 1

[The meaning and origin of this word has been fruitful of much discussion. Yule and Burnell (*Hobson-Jobson, s. v.* abada) observe that "more than one authority makes it the female rhinoceros, and in the dictionaries (Portuguese) the word is feminine." Crooke in the 1903 ed. quotes, in support of the above view, a suggestion of W. W. Skeat that "the female was the more dangerous animal, or the one most frequently met with, as is certainly the case with the crocodile." The plain fact of the matter is that in Portuguese the gender of a substantive is one thing and the sex another. *Abada* is a feminine substantive in Portuguese like many such ending in *a*: *zêbra, girafa, gazela,* and denotes the species as also the female. The use of the word by the old Portuguese writers is perfectly consistent with this view.

Some hold that, if the original of the word is the Malay *bādaq*, the elimination of the final consonant has to be accounted for. But Portuguese has *calamba* ('aloes wood') from Mal. *calambaq*, and *pucho* ('the costus of the ancients, the fragrant root of the *Saussurea Xappe*') from Mal. *puchuq*. Again, the initial *a* of *abada* though not found in the Malay original may have been due to the agglutination of the Portuguese article *a*, an instance of which we have in the English 'alligator' from the Spanish *el* or *al lagarto*, or what is more likely it may be a case of prosthesis such as we have in the Portuguese words *alacre* ('lac'), *alanterna* ('lantern'), *atambor* ('tambour'). See Dalgado's *Contribuições etc.*, and *Glossario Luso—As. s. v. abada, calamba,* and *pucho,* also *Hobson-Jobson s. v.* calambac, and putchock.]

Abafado (*subst.*, 'a dish of stew'; in the Port. dialects of the East *bafado*). Konk. *bāphád.*—Beng. *bāphādú*. Cf. *temperado.*

Abano (old Port. and Indo-Port. *avano*,[1] 'a fan'). Sinh.

---

1 "With the King of Cananor there came two pages......carrying large **avanos** made of peacock feathers with which they were fanning him." Gaspar Correia, *Lendas da India*, I, p. 171.

avánaya, *avánē*, *aváne;* vern. terms *pavanpata*, *pavan-atta*, *vatā-pata*.

Many of the Sinhalese nouns, and especially those derived from foreign sources, which are of the neuter gender, as are all those which denote inanimate objects, take the suffix *-ya*,—or *-va*, if they end in *-u*, —as: *gúṇaya* ('quality') from the Sansk. *guṇa ; tálaya* ('tone') from the Sansk. *tāla; garádaya* ('railing') from the Port. *grade ; sīnuva* ('bell') from the Port. *sino ; bébaduva* ('drunkard') from the Port. *bêbado*. In the middle of a word *-ya* contracts itself usually in ē long: *janélaya*, *janélē* (pl. *janéla*) from the Port. *janela* ('a window'); *kamísaya*, *kamísē* (pl. *kamísa*) from the Port. *camisa* ('a shirt').

Ábita (*naut.*, bitts; fixed wooden or iron pin for fastening the cable). L.-Hindust. *abít*, *habít*.—Mal. *abit* (Aristide Marre).

Abóbora (*Cucurbita Pepo*; a gourd, a pumpkin). Konk. *bhobḷó ; bobr* (us. in Salsete, a district of Goa). *Bhobḷí*, the plant.—Mar. *bhopḷá*, *bhoṁpḷá*. *Bhopḷí*, *bhoṁpḷí*, the plant.—Jap. *bóbura*.—Ar. *bobra*, *bubra*, according to Simonet.[1]

In Konkani, *bhobḷó* is used figuratively of 'a man who is fat and lacking muscle.' In Konkani, as well as in Marathi, the term is used to denote the body of certain stringed instruments, because it is generally made of the gourd hollowed out, as of the *viṇá*, 'the Indian lyre,' the *satar*, 'the guitar,' the *nāgsúr*, 'bagpipe.'

With regard to the *bh* aspirate, cf. *cruz*, *camisa*, *buraco*. The loss of the initial *a* is not abnormal, as can be seen in the Indo-Port. *bobra*; cf. *acafelar*. The substitution of the cerebral *ḷ* for *r* may have resulted from the word having found its way into the speech of the common people, or may also be due to the fact that there is a tendency towards such a change both in Konkani and Marathi. The nasalisation of the first syllable in Marathi (*bhõ*) has parallels in *píṁp*

---

1 Dr. Hugo Schuchardt (*Kreolische Studien*, ix) says that in the Malay spoken in Timor *bobera* is *Cucurbita Melopepo* ('the musk melon'); but Teto and Galoli dictionaries do not mention the word.

from the Port. *pipa* ('barrel'), *phiṅt* from the Port. *fita* ('ribbon').

The etymology of the word *abóbora*, which is used only in the Iberic Peninsula—and then not in the whole of it—has not till now been definitely established by lexicographers. The Portuguese dictionary, *Contemporaneo*, says its derivation is uncertain; Dr. Adolfo Coelho is of the opinion that it is from *aboborar*, 'to turn soft like over ripe fruit'; Cândido de Figueiredo derives it from Low Latin *apopres*, which does not find a mention in the *Glossarium* of Du Cange; Francisco Simonet asserts that it is from the Hispano-Latin or Iberic *apopores*, mentioned by St. Isidore, Bk. XVII, ch. 10, as equivalent to the *cucurbita*.

If the word was taken over from Portugal, as I believe it was,[1] and introduced into the Konkan country and into Japan, at the same time as the plant, whose place of origin says Dr. D. G. Dalgado in his *Flora of Goa and Savantvadi* is uncertain, it is remarkable that it should have given rise in Marathi to so many figurative compounds, with different meanings, enumerated by Molesworth, who does not, however, say what the origin of the word is. These are: *bhoṁpḷá-devatá*, "a tom-boy, a hoyden." *Bhoṁplá-suti* (*adj.*), "coarse, gross, rude, rough, disorderly, slovenly." *Bhoṁpḷí-kharbúz*, "a species of musk melon." *Bhoṁpḷyá-rôg*, "corpulency, obesity."

There are vernacular terms for the other varieties of the pumpkin: *dudhí*, *konkṇó dudhí*, *mahāró dudhí*, *kāḷó dudhí*, *kuṁvāḷó*, in Konkani; *kovhāḷá*, *kuśmaṇḍ*, *kāśí-phaḷ*, *dudhyá*, *kāḷá dudhyá*, *devḍan-*

1 "They brought many aboboras and cucumbers." *Roteiro da Viagem de Vasco da Gama*, 2nd. ed., p. 92.

"*Brinjelas*, lemons, abobaras,..... which articles none may sell in retail except the farmer of this excise, or some one who has his permission." Simão Botelho, *Tombo do Estado da India*, p. 49.

"Melons, aboboras of Portugal and of Guinea, water melons and *combalengas*." Gabriel Rebelo, *Informação das Cousas de Maluco*, in *Collecção de Noticias para a Historia e Geographia das Nações Ultramarinas*, Vol. XII, p. 172. [*Combalenga* is a species of pumpkin.]

gar, in Marathi; *tónasu*, *kabocha* (=Kamboja), in Japanese.[1]

In the Portuguese dialects in Asia, *abobora* is corrupted into *bóbra*, *bobr*.

Abril (April). Konk. *Ābríl*. —Tet., Gal. *Abril*.—Mal. *April* (Marre). See *Agosto*.

Acabar (to finish). Konk. *kabár-karuṅk*, *kabár-zavuṅk*. —Beng. *kābár* (*subst.*), the last day of the month. In Hindustani *mājkabár*. See *mês* [also *Hobson-Jobson*, *s. v.* mascabar.]

In the Indo-Portuguese dialect the initial *a* of *acabar* becomes eliminated, whence the form *cabá*.

Acafelar (to plaster; Indo-Port. has the form *caflá*). Konk. *kāphlār-karuṅk*; vern. term *chunó-kas kāḍhuṅk*.—Guj. *kaphlád* (us. as a subst. meaning 'plaster, lime').—Sinh. *kapaláruvä*.[2]—Malayal. *kabalarikka* ('to bind stones or bricks with a mixture of lime, sand and water') us. in Southern Malabar.[3]—Mal. *kápor* (us. as a subst.).[4]

Konkani adds *karuṅk* ('to do' or 'to make') to the transitive verbs in Portuguese and *zāvuṅk* ('to become') to the intransitive. The exception is the Konkani form *pintāruṅk*, 'to paint', from the Port. *pintar* ('to paint'). The change of *f* into *p* is normal in Sinhalese which has no corresponding sound, *ph* being *p* aspirate, as in Sanskrit; cf. *adufa*. In Malayalam, as well as in Tamil, the surd intervocalic consonant (*k*, *t*, *p*) becomes resonant (*g*, *d*, *b*).

Açafrão (saffron; Indo-Port. employs the forms *safrão*, *safran*). Guj. *jāphran*.—Siam. *fárān*.—Jap. *safuran*.[5]

Acêrca (*prep.*, about, concerning). Mal. *acerca* (Haex).

Haex does not, as a rule

---

1 "*Kabocha* (pumpkins) must have been introduced from Cambodia." Murakámi.

2 In Sinhalese,—*vá* is the infinitive termination.

3 *Ikka* is the termination of the infinitive. Cf. *capar*.

4 "The tomb of the King of Cochin's mother was acafelada with lime and fragrant waters." Gaspar Correia, *Lendas*, III, p. 714.

5 "Manamotapa sent word that Diogo Simões should send him as presents açafrão from Portugal, soap, pottery....' Antonio Bocarro, Dec. XII, p. 588.

indicate the exact pronunciation of Portuguese words, taken over into Malay, nor does he employ any special diacritical marks. He says, "the words are entered here (in his dictionary) not as they are written or joined together, but as they are pronounced."

Achar (an Indo-Port. term used to signify 'fruits conserved in vinegar or salt,' equivalent to the English 'pickles'). Mar. *āchár*; vern. term *loṅchéṁ* (as in Konkani).—Hindi, Hindust. *achár*.—Or., Ass., Punj. *āchár*.—Sindh. *āchāru*; vern. names *āthāṇó*, *sāndhaṇó*.—Sinh. *achchár*.—Anglo-Ind. *achar*.—Indo-Fr. *achar*, *achars*.—Mal. *áchar*.—Tet., Gal *achár*, *asár*; vern. term *budú*.

The word has its origin in the Persian *achār*; it was probably met with by the Portuguese in the Malay Peninsula and introduced by them into the other languages, directly or indirectly. The authors of *Hobson-Jobson* think it likely that Western Asiatics got it originally from the Latin *acetaria*.

It is worthy of note that the term did not find its way into Konkani, although current in the Portuguese dialect of Goa.[1]

Açoitar (to whip). Mal. *açotar* (Haex).

In Konkani *sait* is used in the sense of 'a whip,' and *saitár-kāḍhuṅk* is 'to whip.'

Acudir (to aid, to assist). Mal. *cudir* (Haex).—Tet., Gal. *kudir*.

Adem (a duck). Malayal. *ádi*.—Tet. *rádè*.

Adeus (adieu). Konk. *ādês*; the vern. term in vogue among the Hindus is *Rām-Rām*, and *salám* among the Mohammedans. *Ādês karuṅk*, 'to bow in token of salutation.'—Tet., Gal. *adeus*; vern. term *báôna*.[2]

---

[1] "When it (*Semecarpus anacardium*) is green they make a conserve of it with salt (which they call **achar**), and this they sell in the market, as we do olives." Garcia da Orta, *Coloquios dos Simples e Drogas da India*, Col. v. [ed. Sir Clements Markham, p. 33]. "**Achar**, appetizing curry, and conserves in salt." Dr. A. O. de Castro, *Flores de Coral*, p. 137.

[2] From *Ram-Ram* Gonçalves Viana derives the Portuguese *ramerrão* ['onomatopoeic sound suggesting routine or every day affair']. See *Apostilas aos Dicionários Portugueses*. The same writer admits in *Palestras Filológicas* that "it is possible that this curious word may have come

Adro (church-yard). Konk. *ádr.*—Tamil *ádru.*

Adufa (lattice, shutter; in the Port. dialect of Goa *adufo* is also used). Konk. *ādúph.*—Sinh. *adŭppuva, adīp-puva.*

The word is used to denote the window shutters commonly fitted with the shells of the mollusc *bhing*, and, therefore, called in Konkani *bhingaṭyô* or *bhingāṭyó.*[1]

Advogado (lawyer). Kon. *ādvogád* (the term more in vogue in this sense is *letrád*): vern. term *vakil* (l. us. in Goa).—Tet., Gal. *advogádu*; vern. term *sori.*

Afonsa (the name of a variety of the mango-fruit, also known as the 'Alphonso mango'). Konk. *āphoṅs, āphoṅsāchó āṁbó.*—Mar. *aphôs.*—Guj. *aphús.*—Anglo-Ind. *afoos.*

The art of mango-grafting was introduced into India by the Portuguese, and the varieties of the grafted trees and their fruit are differentiated by Portuguese names, which are, sometimes, converted into the feminine form. See *Carreira, Colaça, Peres.*[2]

Agosto (the month of August). Konk. *Āgôst.*—?Bihari has *Agast* (which probably owes its origin to the English 'August,' in the same way as does *Oktubar* or *Oktobar*).—Sinh. *Agôstu.*—Mal. *Agôstu Agústu.*—Tel., Gal.—*Agôstu.*

In Goa, as well as in Timor, the Portuguese names of the

originally from the chorus of some song, which became very popular among the people."

[1] | "The house in which he lived was storied and very beautiful, with handsome windows and adufas, and it all looked like a toy." Fr. Gaspar da Cruz, *Tractado da China*, ch. 13. |

[2] Other varieties with Portuguese names, which are in vogue only in Goa, are: *Bispo, Costa, Doirada, Dom Bernardo, Dom Filipe, Fernandina, Ferrão, Malagesta, Monserrate, Papel Branco, Rebêlo, Reinol, Salgada, Salgadinha, Santo António, Sacratina, Temuda* (in Konkani, *Chimbúd*), *Xavier, Bem-curada, Mal-Curada,* etc. [The manner in which Portuguese names of different varieties of the mango are disfigured, almost beyond recognition, may be seen from the following quotation taken from a description of a 'Mango Show' held in Bombay which appeared in the *Times of India,* 14th May, 1928. "Mr. Bodke's silver medals were for Mankulas, Mushrad........Real Pyree........" 'Mankulas,' 'Mushrad,' and 'Pyree are, no doubt, the Portuguese *Mal-curada, Monseratte,* and *Peres.*]

months are in use; outside Goa (in Kanara, Savantvadi, Malvan) and in other languages, English names of the months are adopted. Indian months are lunar and do not coincide with the European months. Some of the Malay names, like *Júlu*, *Mársu*, testify very clearly to their Portuguese source; the origin of others is doubtful, as of *Jun*, *Octuber*.

In Sinhalese, *Mártu*, *Júni*, *Júli*, are evidently from the Dutch, *Maart*, *Junnij*, *Julij*. The names of the other months may be either Dutch or English.

Agradecer (to thank). Mal. *agradecer* (Haex).—Tet., Gal. *agradéci*.

Água benta ('Holy water'). Konk. *āg-bént*; more commonly used is *ālmét*.—Beng. *ag-bent*.—Mal. *aguabenta* (Haex). [In Konkani the form *alménť* is also met with.]

In the Indo-Portuguese dialects *água* is contracted into *águ* or *ag*, and *bento* into *bent*. In *almét*, *l* takes the place of *g* and *m* of *b*, with the absorption of the nasal following.

The Hindus call their sacred water by such names as *tírth*, *gaṅgá*, *gaṅgodak*. The Christians could have used the term *pavitr udak*, in the same way as in Teto they speak of *bé saráni*, 'water Nazarene or Christian, i.e., Holy.'

[**Aguila, Aquila** (the name of an aromatic wood, *Aquilaria Agallocha*, Roxb. or of *Aloexyllum Agallochum*, grown in Cochin China and at one time highly prized in Europe). Anglo-Ind. *eagle-wood*.—Indo-Fr. *bois d'aigle*.[1]

---

[1] ["There (in Champa, coast of Cochin China) also grows abundance of aloes-wood which the Indians call **Aguila** *Calambua*. Barbosa, *The Book*, ed. Longworth Dames, Vol. II, p. 209.]

["In Ceylon there is a wood with a scent (which we call **aguila** *brava*), as we have many another wood with a scent; and at one time that wood used to be exported to Bengala under the name of **aguila** *brava*; but since then the Bengalas have grown more knowing, and buy it no longer...." Garcia da Orta, Coll. xxx; ed. Markham p. 254.]

["A big bon-fire of sandal-wood, **Aaquila**, and other aromatic woods." Damião de Góis, *Chronica de D. Manuel*, II, ch. 6.]

["From the **bois d' aigle**, which is more or less perfect, according as it is more or less resinous." Raynal, *Histoire*, II, p. 41, cit. in *Glossario*.]

["The **eagle-wood**, a tree yield-

The etymon is the Malayal. *agil*, from Hindi *agar*, Sansk. *aguru* (lit. 'not weighty; light') or *agaru*, which gave *gaháru* or *gáru* in Malay. The Portuguese converted the Mayalal. *agil* into *águila* which again some of the older writers corrupted into *áquila*, which in Anglo-Indian and Indo-Fr. was mistranslated respectively into *eagle-wood* and *bois d'aigle*. (See *Hobson-Jobson*, *s. v.* eagle-wood, and *Gloss. Luso-Asiatico*, *s.v. águila, áquila*, also Garcia da Orta, Coll. xxx)].

Aia ('dry-nurse'). Konk., Mar., Guj., Hindust., Sinh. *āyá*.—Or., Beng., Ass. *āiyá*.—Tel. *āyá*.—Tul *áya*.—Anglo-Ind. *ayah*.—Khas. *aiah*.—Mal. *áya*,[1] | 'Indian wet-nurse.' See *ama*. |

Simonet finds a remarkable similarity between *aia* (Basque *zaya*) and the Arabic-Persian *dāya*, 'midwife, a nurse.' In the Indo-Portuguese of Goa *daia* is used in the sense of 'a midwife'; the same also is the case in Teto.

The adoption of the word, *aia*, must be attributed to the fact that there was no corresponding term current, which was as simple as this.[2]

Ajoelhar (to kneel; the archaic form of the word is *ageolhar*). Mal. *ingeolar* (Haex), *injiolar*.

The etymon of *ingiolar* is evidently *engeolhar*, which, if it is not another archaic Portuguese form, must have been derived from *em geolhos* ('on knees') used, since the sixteenth century, in the bastard varieties of the Portuguese language

---

ing *uggur* oil, is also much sought for its fragrant wood, which is carried to Silhet, where it is broken and distilled". Hooker, cit. in *Hobson-Jobson*.]

["The fragrant wood call 'aloes' in Proverbs, VII, 17, etc., was the *Aquillaria Agallocha*, the Hebrew word for which *ahalim* or *ahaloth*, is evidently derived from the Tamil-Malayalâm form of the word, *aghil*, than from the Sanskrit *agaru*, though both are ultimately identical." Caldwell, *Comparative Grammar*, p. 92 (1875), cit. in *Glossario*.]

1 "The other day, early in the morning, the aya who had the care of her, went to the place to look for her." Fernão Pinto, *Peregrinações*, ch. cxcix.

2 *Ayál* in Tamil is a vernacular term; it means 'mother, wet nurse, maternal grandmother.'

current in the East.[1] The modern Portuguese dialect of Malacca has *injabel, injubel,* 'on one's knees, to kneel'; that of Singapore: *injilhá* 'to kneel'; of Ceylon: *injoelho, injivelho, injevejo, injivejo* (*adv.*), 'on one's knees, having knelt'; that of Damaun: *injoelh*, 'on one's knees, having knelt'; of Bombay: *injvelh*, 'on one's knees' (*pusá injevelh*, 'to kneel'); of Macau: *dizelo*, from *de joelhos*, 'on one's knees.'[2]

Bengali has *injuvel, enjíl*, 'knee', used by the Christians. *Enjil deon* 'to kneel.'

Ajudante (assistant, adjutant). Konk. *ājudáṅt* (us. in a restricted sense).—Mal. *ajudán.*

Ajudar (to assist, to help). Konk. *ājudár-karuṅk* (especially in the sense of 'serving Mass'); vern. terms *ādhár divuṅk, hát divuṅk.*—Tet., Gal. *aidúda.*

In Teto and Galoli there does not exist the sound *j*; on this account the Portuguese *j* is replaced by *d*; thus we have: *kreda* from Port. *igreja* ('church'), *duiz* from Port. *juiz* ('judge'), *kaidú* from *caju* (*Anacardium occidentale*).

Alar (to haul). L.-Hindust. *ālá* (us. only in the imperative form).

Alâmpada (a lamp in a church). Beng. *ālamp* (in use among the Christians). See *lâmpada.*

Alavanca (hand spike used as lever for moving heavy bodies). Konk. *lavaṅg*; from this has arisen the expression *lavaṅgáṁ pārayó ulauṅk*, which is figuratively equivalent to uttering high-sounding words, or undertaking a work beyond one's scope or powers.—Sinh. *alavánguva.*—Tam. *alavángu.*—Mal. *alabanka, albanka.*—Gal. *lavanka.*[3]

In Konkani the term is only used of the big hand-spike;

---

[1] "He stood em giolhos ('on his knees') with his hands raised aloft." João de Barros, Dec. II,x,3.

[2] Cf. *impé* ('to be on one's leg'), *impedo, impido* ('being on one's leg') in the Portuguese dialect of Ceylon; *impé*, in that of Cochin; and *empido*, in that of Macau.

[3] "The Governor ordered the factor Gaspar Paes to get ready plenty of lime, timber, mattocks, alavancas, pickaxes, mortar-pans, baskets, barrows for the fortress." Gaspar Correia *Lendas*, III, p. 619.

for the smaller one the vernacular term *pāray* is used.

Albacora (a large sea-fish of the tunny genus). Anglo-Ind. *albacore.* See *Hobson-Jobson.*[1]

[Yule is inclined to believe that the Port. word '*albecora*', from its form, is almost certainly Arabic, though Dozy is unable to trace it in Arabic dictionaries. The *O. E. D.* derives it from Ar. *al -bukr,* 'a young camel, a heifer.' Gray in his edition of *Pyrard* (Hak. Soc.) thinks it is probably *el-bakra*, 'the cow-(fish)', according to the common practice of naming marine animals after those of the land. There are some also who derive it from the Port. *alva* ('white') and *cor* ('colour'), but the consensus of opinion is in favour of the *O. E. D.*'s view. The *albecora* is the *Thynnus albacora,* Lowe.]

Alcatifa (a carpet). Konk. *ālkātíph*; vern. terms *tivāsí, satraṅgi.*—Mal. *alcatifa* (Haex).—Tet. *alkatifa, lakatifa.*—Gal. *alkatifa.*

The Portuguese word is derived from the Arabic *al-qatif.*[2]

Alcatrão (tar). Konk. *ál-katrámv* (l. us.); vern. terms *kíl, ḍāmar* or *ḍām̐bar.*—Beng. *ālkatrá.*—Garo *alkatra.*[3]

The original of the Portuguese vocable is the Arabic *al-qatrān*; but Bengali received the word directly from the Portuguese and passed it on to Garo; this is clear, because languages more influenced by Arabic than Bengali have not got it, and also because the word retains the definite article (*al*) which words that are derived directly from the Arabic drop, as for example: *jeb,* from Arabic *al-jeb* ('pocket'). Cf. *arrátel.*

Alcatraz (*zool.*, the great sea-bird, *Diomedia exulans*, L.).

---

1 "With his fish-hook to catch the fish which the sailors call **Albecóras,** which are of the size and appearance of the tunny. João de Barros, Dec. III, iii, 1.

2 "Here (in Diu) they bring from India many large alcatifas." Duarte Barbosa, *Livro*, p. 275. [Hak. Soc., ed. Longworth Dames Vol. I, p. 129]. "The ground all carpeted with big alcatifas." Bocarro, Dec. XIII, p. 390.

3 "Ordering that the walls be covered with many barrels of **alcatrão.**" Diogo do Couto, Dec. VI, iii, 10.

Anglo-Ind. *albatross*.—Indo-Fr. *albatros*. See *Hobson-Jobson*.[1]

Alcoviteira (a procuress). Mal. *alcobitera* (Haex). [The literal meaning of *alcoviteira* is 'messenger of love,' but it has degenerated into signifying 'a procuress'.]

Alcunha (nick-name). Konk. *ālkúṅh*; vern. terms *kul-náṁv*, *aḍ-náṁv*.—Mal. *alcunia* (Haex).

Aldeia (a village). Anglo-Ind. *aldea* (l. us.).—Indo-Fr. *aldée*.[2]

Alerta (alert). Konk. *āleṭó*.—Gal. *alerta*.

Alfaiate (a tailor). Konk. *ālphyád*; vern. name *darjí*.—Mal. *alfiate* (Haex).—Tet. *alfayáti*; vern. term *badain súku*. The Port. dialect of Malacca has *alfiáti*.

Alfândega (custom-house). Konk. *ālphánd*; vern. terms *māṇḍví*, *ḍobí*, *ghuḍí*. | Anglo-Ind. *alfandica* (obs.). See *Hobson-Jobson*.—Indo-Fr. *alfandegue*. | —Tet., Gal. *alfándega*.

Alféloa (a sweetmeat). Jap. *aruheiru*, *aruheilō*.

Alferes (an ensign; a commissioned officer of the lowest grade in infantry). Konk. *ālphér*.—Mal. *alpéres*.—Jav. *alpérès* (l. us.).—Bug. *lapér-esè*.—Tet., Gal. *alféris*.

The wife of an *alferes* is called *ālpherṇ* in Konkani.[1]

Alfinete (a pin) Konk. *ālphinêt*; vern. term *tāṅchní* (l. us. in Goa).—Hindi *ālpín*. *Pin*, which appears to be English, is also used.—Hindust. *ālpín*, *alpín*, *alpin*.—Beng. *ālpinêt*, *ālpín*.—Ass. *álpin*; the vern. term is *gonj*.—Sinh. *alpenê-tiya*, *alpêntiya*.—Tamil *alpinêti* (l. us.).—Mal. *alpineto* (Haex), *pinéti*, *piníti*, *penéti*.—Sund.,

---

[1] "On this day we saw in the morning **alcatrazes** and *garjaos*, which is the surest sign that we were nearing land." D. João de Castro, *Roteiro de Lisboa a Goa*, p. 227. [*Garjao* or, as it is more commonly written, *garajao* is a sea-bird found near the coast of Guinea; *Sterna fluvialis*.]

[2] "And at present between Damaon and Bassein there are so few Hindu inhabitants that most of the **aldées** are not under cultivation" (1653). Le Gouz de la Boullaye, *Voyages*.

[1] "As the Polynesian languages have neither *f* nor *ph* nor *v*, in adopting foreign words where these letters occur, they replace them by *p* or *l*." Dr. Heyligers.

Jav., Mac. *paníti.*—Bug. *panniti.*—Tet., Gal., *alfinêti*; vern. term *kusan-kik.*[1]

Algarismo (Arabic cipher). Konk. *ālgārijṁ* (us. in the Goa schools).—Mac., Bug. *lagarísi.*

Algoz (the public executioner). Konk. *ālgôz* (us. also in a metaphorical sense); vern. terms *kasáb, máṅg, phāsídár.*—Mal. *algójo, algója, algújo, algúju.*—Jav. *legójo.*—Mac., Bug. *alahója.*

Aljofar (seed-pearl). Anglo-Ind. *aljofar.*[2]

Almadia (a canoe, a small boat). Malayal. *olamári, ōlamári.*[3]

[According to Dozy (*Glossaire, s. v. almadia*) it is the Ar. *al-má dīya*, which appears to be a word derived from a Berber dialect. The meaning of this word was 'a ferry-boat' and it continues to denote 'a small boat' or 'canoe.' The meaning 'raft' given by Dozy is not found in Portuguese. Dalgado (*Glossario Luso-As., s. v. almadia*) is of the opinion that at the time of the Portuguese discoveries the word was in vogue in the south of Africa and that from there it was carried to India and found its way into Malayalam].

Almoçar (to breakfast). Beng. *almusár.*—Mal. *almursar* (Haex).—Tet., Gal. *almúsa, almósa.*

Almôço (breakfast). Konk. *ālmús*; vern. term *nāstó* (l. us. in Goa). *Almús karuṅk*, which literally rendered gives 'to make breakfast', is used in the sense of 'to breakfast'.—Sinh. *almúsu, almúsuva*; vern. term *udaya-kẹma* or *udē-kẹma* ('lit. morning-meal'). *Almúsuva-kánanā*, to breakfast.—Tet., Gal. *almúsa.*

The Hindus have their first meal at mid-day and call it *jevan*; the Christians (of Goa) take in the morning rice-gruel, '*péz.*' New terms coined from Sanskrit are *nyāhārí, pratarann, pratarbhojan.*

---

1 In Konkani the *f* sound is preserved. If the form mentioned by Haex is correct, the first syllable must have dropped out with time. In Javanese there was a metathesis of *a*, softened into *e*.

2 "All of them were loading themselves with the booty, which they took from the houses, consisting of gold, silver, aljofar," Diogo do Couto, Dec. VI, iv, 2.

3 "Almadias in which some negroes were going a fishing were sighted." João de Barros, Dec. I,i,9.

Almôndega (ball of meat). Tamil *almond* (us. in a restricted sense).—Tet., Gal. *almónik*.

Portuguese names of many dainties and sweetmeats are current, even to this day, in different parts of India among the Christian populations, but these do not find a place in dictionaries.

Altar (altar). Konk., Beng. *āltár*; vern. term *vedí*.—Tamil *altár*; vern. terms *pídam*, *balipídam*, *vēdikei*.—Tet., Gal. *altar*. The term is in use only among the Christians.[1]

Alva (alb, an ecclesiastical vestment). Konk. *álv*.—Beng. *álva*.—Tamil *alvei*.—Tet., Gal. *álva*.[2]

Alvorada (the dawn; also aubade or music played at the dawn of day before one's door). Konk. *ālvorád* (in the sense of 'aubade').—Tet. *alvorada*; vern. term *rai-nakei*.

[1] Some friends, missionaries in Madras, supplied me with lists of Portuguese words introduced into Tamil, many of which are not to be met with in the dictionaries, because they are not in common use.

[2] The names of vestments and vessels used in Catholic religious services are generally of Portuguese origin.

Ama (wet-nurse). Konk., Mar., Guj., Hindust., Sinh., Kan., Tul. *āmá*. (in Mar. also *amá*).—Anglo-Ind. *amah* (Withworth derives it from the Mar., *āmá*, 'the breast').—|Mal. *amah*, 'Chinese nurse'|—Pid.-Engl. *amah*.[1]

The Neo-Aryan terms are: *dúdh ditalí*, *dūdhkārīṇ*, *thānkārīṇ*, *dhātrí*. These are little used, because mothers in the East, as a rule, nurse their own children.[2]

Amancebado (one who lives with a mistress). Tamil *masuvádu*. The Port. dialect of Ceylon has *masabado*.

The term must have been introduced as a euphemism, like *alcoviteira* in Malay.

Amantilhos (*naut*., lifts; ropes pertaining to the arms of all yards, their object being to make the yards hang higher or lower). L.-Hindust. *mantēlá*, *mantelá*, *mantel*, *matelá*.

[1] "The **amahs** accompanying the children who go there to play." Calado Crespo, *Cousas da China*, p. 20.

"And they have **amas** who bring up their sons and daughters." Diogo do Couto, Dec. VII, x, 11.

[2] The Dravidian *amma*, 'mother,' is a vernacular word.

Amargosa (*Melia Azadirachta*; the neem tree). Anglo-Ind. *margosa.*—Indo-Fr. *margosier.*

Margosa is also used in the Indo-Port. dialect of Bombay; in that of Ceylon, *margoso* is used as equivalent to *amargoso*, 'bitter.'[1]

Amarra (*naut.*, cable). L.-Hindust. *hamár, már.*—Tamil *amár, amarkkayiṟu* (lit. *amarra-cairo*); the vern. terms are *kayiṟu, kambakam, tában, sambhan.*—Tel. *amáru, amárutádu.* See *cairo.*

In Tamil, as in Malayalam, the initial consonant of the second part of the compound is doubled, as happens in Italian, for example, in *acciocchè.*

Ambar (amber; especially ambergris). Konk., Mar., Hindi, Hindust., Beng., Tamil, Ach., Sund., Jav., *ambar.*—Sindh., *ambāru.* — Malayal., Mal. *ambar, amber.*—Mac., Bug. *ámbarā.*

Perhaps the word was imported directly from Arabic. The Indian names for amber, as a rule, are: *tṛṇamaṇi, tṛṇagrāhí.*[1]

Amen (Amen). Konk. *āmén*; vern terms *asém̃ zām̃v, tathast* (arch.), *svasti* (Sansk., l. us.).—Beng., Sinh., Kan., *ámen.*—? Hindi, Hindust., *āmín*, (perhaps from Arabic).—? Mal., Ach., Sund., Jav., Mac., Bug. *amin.*—Tet., Gal. *ámen.*—Jap. *amen*; vern. term *shikari.*

Amêndoa (an almond). Konk. *āménd, āmén,* (neut., *āmênd*, fem., almond-tree); vern. term *bādám* (from Ara-

---

1 "It was admitted officially in the *Pharmacopoeia* of India, being known in pharmaceutical language as *margosa* (the bark *cortex margosae*), which is clearly derived from the Portuguese word *amargosa.*" Conde de Ficalho in '*Coloquios de Garcia d' Orta*, Col. xl. [*Amargosa* in Portuguese means 'bitter' and describes the principal characteristic of the tree. In this connection it is useful to remember the very old Indian proverb to which Yule refers (*Hobson-Jobson, s.v.* margosa): "You cannot sweeten the *nim* tree though you water it with syrup and ghee."]

1 "The Arabs call it **ambar**, and the Latins *ambarum*, according to the Latin variation and usage; such other nations and languages, as I am acquainted with, give it the same name, or one with very slight variation." Orta, Col. iii. [In a note to *ambar*, in his translation of the *Colloquies*, Markham (p. 20) remarks, "*Amber* in Arabic means 'perfume,' and the word is applied to our Ambergris, while Amber, they call *inkitriun.*"]

bic).— ? Jap. *améndō*, *amméntō*.

Dr. Murakàmi gives to the Japanese *amendō* the meaning of 'almond'. But Hepburn who mentions the word says that it means 'a kind of peach,' and for almond he gives the following Japanese equivalents: *hanankyō*, *banankyō*. Sakuna does not mention the word.[1]

Amora (mulberry). Konk. *āmór*; vern. term *tút*.—Malayal. *amár*.—Tet., Gal. *amora*.

Amostra (a sample, pattern). Konk. *āmostr*.—Tet., Gal. *amostra*; vern. term *banáti*. See *mostra*.

Amura (*naut*., tack; rope for securing corner of some sails). L.-Hindust. *mūrá*.

Ananás (the pine-apple). Konk. *ānanés* (neut.; *ānanês*, fem., the plant), *ānás* (us. in Kanara).—Mar. *ananás*, *ananas* (the fruit is masc. or neut.; the plant is fem.)—Guj. *anenás*, *annas*.—Hindi, Hindust. *ananás*.—Or. *anáras*.—Sindh. *anānásu*.—Sinh. *annási*, *anaṇsi*, *annásiya*.—Tamil *aṇṇási*.—Malayal. *ananás*.—Tel. *anānásu*, *anásu*, *anás-paṇṭu*, *anāsavanasa-paṇṭu* (*paṇṭu*=fruit).—Kan. *ananásu*.—Anglo-Ind. *ananas* (more us. 'pine-apple').—Indo-Fr. *ananas*.—Gar. *anaros*; vern. term *terik sagil*.—[Bur, *nan-na-si*.]—Kamb. *manŏs*.—Mal. *ananas*, *anas*, *nānas*, *ninas*.—Ach. *ánas*, *anus*.—Batt. *kanas*. Sund. *danas*, *ganas*, *kanas*.—Jav. *nanas*.—Mad. *lanas*.—Bal. *manas*.—Batav. *honas*.—Day. *kanas*.—Tet. *ananaz*, *nánas*.—Gal. *ananaz*.——Malag. *mananasy*.—[Ar.-Pers. *aainunnās*.][1]

Anannási (Hindust.), *ānārasi* (Beng.) *adj*., 'having the shape of a pine-apple,' "made like a pine-apple" (Shakespear).

It is an American word (the Peruvian *nanas*, according to Candido de Figueiredo, but, according to Yule and Burnell, the Brazilian *nana* or *nanas*), introduced by the Portuguese

---

[1] The Sinhalese *amandel* is from Dutch.

[1] "You will have to write about this fruit called ananaz, because it is certainly the king of fruits as regards taste, and more so as regards its flavour." Orta, Col. lviii. [ed. Markham, p. 468.]

into the East together with the plant.[1]

[" The Spaniards called it *Pinas* because of its resemblance to the pine-cone, but the Portuguese adapted to their own tongue its Brazilian name *Nanas* and called it *Ananas*, a word which in some form or other has accompanied the plant throughout the world...There are no names for it in any of the classical languages of Europe, Asia, Arabia or Egypt." Sir George Watt, *The Commercial Products of India*, *s.v. Ananas sativa.* The same writer in *A Dictionary of the Economic Products of India* (1889), Vol. I, p. 236, says: " It was introduced by the Portuguese into Bengal in 1594." He does not cite any authorities, however, for this date. From the *Memoirs of the Emperor Jahangueir* (trans. Major David Price, Calcutta, 1904, p. 22), it is evident that the pine-apple was introduced much earlier into India. " I shall mention one (fruit) in particular, the *ananauss* (pine-apple), being among the most delicious of those reared in the island of the *Frengueis* (Portuguese); of which fruit this same garden has been known in a season to have produced nearly one hundred thousand." The garden referred to is the Gûlaf-shaun garden laid out by the Emperor Baber in Agra. For references to the pine-apple in Abul Fazl's *Aini Akbari* see *Hobson-Jobson*, *s.v.*]

The change of the first *n* in some of the Malasian languages must be attributed to dissimilation.

According to Männer, the Tulu name for the fruit is *parengi-pela-káyi*, which literally rendered gives 'Portuguese-fruit-jack.'

The word *farangi* or *firingi* is a Persian corruption of 'Frank' and is used to denote 'a European' in general, 'a Portuguese' in particular, and in a more restricted sense 'an Indo-Portuguese'; in Konkani, Sinhalese and Tamil, the word exclusively denotes a 'Portuguese'.[1] And as the

[1] Webster in his Dictionary derives it from Malay.

[1] " And when he heard this he said that such man could be no other than

Portuguese professed Christianity and were keen on the spread of their religion, *farangi* became a synonym for 'Christian.'[1]

In the Dravidian languages the word is also used to mean a 'cannon or a piece of ordnance.' Tam., Malayal. *perangi*; Tel., *pirangi*, *phirangi*, *phiringi*; Kan., Tul. *pirangi*, *phirangi*. In Kambojan *parĕang* means 'a European' and *parĕang-sês* from Port. *francês*, 'a Frenchman.' In Persian, *Firangistan* is the name for Europe.

Ancora (anchor). Sinh. *ánkara*, *ankáraya*; vern. term *nĕgurama*.—Mal. *jang-kar* (Bikkers), *dyankar*; the vern. terms are *saú*, *lábu*.—Pers., Ar. *anjar*, *anjara*.

Francos, for by this name they call us in these parts." *Roteiro da Viagem de Vasco da Gama*, 1838, p. 99.

"Pointing out that since the Portuguese—**Frangues**, as they call them —were so powerful, it would be no wonder if they would enter this port (Jeddah) and destroy the House of Mafoma." Duarte Barbosa, *Livro*, p. 248. [Hak. Soc., ed. Longworth Dames, Vol. I, p. 48.]

[1] "And letters which spoke of **franque**, which means Christian." Gaspar Correia, II, p. 344.

Dr. Hugo Schuchardt connects *dyankar* with the English 'the anchor.'[1]

***Andor** ('palanquin,' or 'a litter').[2] Konk. *āndôr*, *āndôl*.—Hindust. *handolá*.—Beng. *āndôla*.—Sinh. *andôreva* ("a Kandyan litter," Clough).—Malayal. *aṇḍólam*.—Kan. *andaṇa*. — Kodagu (Dravidian language) *andala*.—Tet. *andor*.[3]

What is the etymon of *andor* and its original meaning? the word is not a very old one in Portugal; it is used to signify 'an ornamented contrivance consisting of a square board with four arms, one at each end, on which images of the saints

[1] The word *laṅgar* or *naṅgar*, which is to be met with in the Indian languages, whether Aryan or Dravidian (and in Persian, *langar*), also in the sense of 'a plough,' comes from the Sanskrit *lāṅgala*.

[2] "Vasco de Gama was carried in **andores**, which are like litters (*leytos dandas*) except that they are uncovered and almost without any back, so low are the sides." Castanheda, I, 16.

[3] "I hereby order all pundits and Hindu physicians not to ride through this city (of Goa) or the suburbs thereof on horseback, nor in **andores** and palanquins." Proclamation of the Governor of Goa, 15th December, 1574.

are borne in processions.' (Cândido de Figueiredo). Portuguese lexicographers either do not give the etymology of the word or, some of the more modern ones when they do give it, say that it comes from *andar* ('to walk'), or from *andas* [*subst.*, 'a litter,' a portable vehicle much like the Indian '*dandy*']; there are others, like João de Sousa, who derive it from the Persian *andol* or *andul*, or, rather, *handūl*, and describe it as 'portable vehicle used in India' (Bluteau).

Bluteau gives under separate heads, without pointing out the etymology, both the Indian and the Portuguese meanings of the word. He says: "*Andor* among us is a contrivance with four arms, etc." Solano with much reason combines both the meanings: "It is a species of portable vehicle (*andas*) on which men are borne or the images of the gods in Asia, or the image of Christ, or the saints among the Catholics, in their processions."

Fifteenth century writers, like the author of the *Roteiro da Viagem de Vasco da Gama*, Duarte Barbosa, Castanheda, João de Barros,[1] Gaspar Correia, Damião de Góes, regard the term as new and foreign, and explain it by referring it to the Portuguese *andas*.[2]

Andor occurs as a foreign word in an Arabic book of the eleventh century (*Kitāb 'Ajāīb-al-Hind*), from the French translation of which Yule quotes in *Hobson-Jobson*): "Le même m'a conté qu'à Serandib (Ceylon), les rois et ceux qui se portent à la façon des rois, se font porter dans les **handoul**

---

[1] "Receiving the message of the Camorij, Vasco da Gama landed with a dozen followers and was received by a noble person whom they call *Catual* who was accompanied by two hundred men on foot, besides others for transporting him on their shoulders in an **andor**: because, in all that land of Malabar, they do not employ draught animals. One of the **andores** was also offered to Vasco de Gama for him to travel in." João de Barros, Dec I, iv, 8.

[2] Cristóvão Vieira (1534) employs the word *andor* without explaining it; many others who lived in the Orient likewise do not explain it. "The lesser mandarins who are unable to use an **andor** have a horse." *Letters from Portuguese Captives in Canton*, ed. Donald Ferguson, p. 79.

(*handūl*) qui est semblable à une litière, soutenue sur les épaules de quelques piétons." ["The same person has told me that in Ceylon, the kings and those who go about in the manner of kings are carried in *handouls*, which resemble a litter, borne upon the shoulders of some carriers."]

Shakespear derives the Hindust. *hanḍolá*, not from Arabic or Persian, but from the Sansk. *hindola*,[1] "a swing, a swinging cradle or hammock; a swing or ornamented litter in which are borne the images of Krishna during the Swinging-Festival."

From this it can be concluded that *andor* went to Portugal from India where it was used in a restricted sense.[2] See *palanquim*.

[The author, who makes a further exhaustive exposition of the various meanings of *andor*, its origin, and the difference between it and such other vehicles as *machila* (Anglo-Ind. 'muncheel') and *palanquim*, in his *Contribuições etc.*, and the *Glossario*, published subsequent to the present work, is definitely of the opinion that the Portuguese borrowed the word from India and in the form *aṇḍola* which it has in Malayalam, for it was in Malabar that they first heard it used. *Aṇḍola*, in its passage to Portuguese, would normally take the form *andor*. Cf. the Port. form *Moghor* from the Pers. *Mughal*.]

Anel (*naut.*, a piece of rope that fastens the oars to the thole-pins; also a piece of cable used in fastening the anchor). L.-Hindust. *ānila*.

Anil (indigo). Anglo-Ind. *anile, neel* (obs., the term now used is 'indigo').—Indo-Fr. *anil, anir*.

The original of the Port. *anil* is the Ar. *al-nil*, from the Sansk. *nīlī*, Neo-Aryan *níl*, *nil̤*.[1]

---

1 Konk. *hinduló*, *hindló*; Mar. *hindolá*, *hindulá*; Hindi *hindolá*.

2 "The **andores** are to-day uncommon and they are used exclusively by Hindu high priests, and in pagodas, under the name of *palqui*. The use of these, like that of the Umbrella and the Torch, was conceded by the Government in return for services rendered to the State." *O Gabinete Litterario das Fontainhas* (Pangim), III, p. 155.

1 "The *anil* is so called by Arabs and Turks, and in all languages, but only in

Animal (an animal). Konk. *animál* (l. us. and then only figuratively).—Tet. *animal*; vern. term *ulár*.—Gal. *animar*; vern. term *binátan*.

?**Anis** (the anise plant; also aniseed). Hindust. *anīsún*; vern. term *saunf*, *bādyán*.—Mac., Bug., *ánīsi*; vern. terms *áda*, *ádassa*.—Siam. *áni*.

Probably, Hindustani received the word from the Greek *anison*, Latin *anisum*, through Persian or Arabic, as the form seems to indicate. With regard to Macassar, the Dutch also have the form *anijs*. Michell derives the Siamese *áni* from the English 'aniseed.'

Aniversário (anniversary). Konk. *āniversár* (l. us.); vern. term *varsāchó dís*.—Tet. *aniversáryu*; vern. term *halutinan*.

Anjo (an angel). Konk. *ánj* (in use among the Christians); vern. terms *devdút* (l. us. among the Christians), and *bhaḍvó*. *Ánj-burgém*, an infant child.—Malayal., Tet., Gal. *ánju*.—Jap. *anjo*.

Ano (year). Tel. *áno* (in the sense of 'the year of our Lord'). Must have been introduced through the contracts of the Portuguese with the people of Vijayanagar or by way of treaties. Gal. *ánu*.

Anona (*bot.*, *Anona reticulata*. L., bullock's heart) Konk. *ānón* (neut.; *ānôn*, fem., the tree).—Beng. *lona*.—Sinh. *anōná*; vern. term *anôda*. *geḍiya*.—Malayal. *anona* (Rheede).[1]—Indo-Fr. *anone*.—Mal. *anónā* (Bikkers), *nóna*.—Sund. *nóna* (*Anona squamosa*).[2]

In the Island of Madeira it is also called *nona*. In Marathi it is given the name of *Ramphal*, 'Rama's fruit.'[3] See *ata*.

In Bengali, *n* and *l* are often

Guzarate, where it is made, it is called *gali*, but is now called *nil*." Garcia da Orta, Col. vii. [ed. Markham, p. 51.] "The sailors on board came across some bales of anil." Couto, Dec. VII, viii, 1.

[1] It is also called *parengichakka*, 'Portuguese jack-fruit.'

[2] "There is also another almost similar to the preceding (custard-apple tree) as regard its fruit, which is called **anoneira**; its fruit is bigger, but rougher and less savoury, its kernel harder, and its rind reddish in colour." Fr. Clemente da Ressurreição, in *Agricultor Indiano*, of B. F. da Costa, Vol. II, p. 339

[3] John Crawfurd, in his Malay Dictionary, confounds *nona* or *buah*-

interchangeable and there are instances of such cases: *lebú* from Sansk. *nimbuka*, 'lime'; *naṅgara*, from Sansk. *lāṅgala*, 'anchor."[1]

Apa ('cake, usually, of rice-flour, patted flat with the hand').[2] Anglo-Ind. *ap* (in vogue in the Bombay Presidency, and in the Indo-Port. dialect of Bombay), *hopper* (in Southern India).—Tet., Gal. *apa*, *apas*.—? Siam. *ahbam* —? Mal., Ach. *apam*.—? Day. *apam*, *abam*.—Mac., Bug. *ápang*.

The word is of Dravidian origin (Tamil *appam*), introduced, in all probability, directly into Siamese and Malay. It is in general use in Indo-Portuguese, whence it found its way, together with some other words, to Timor.

Apontar ('to aim with a rifle'). Konk. *āpontár-karuṅk*; vern. term *zokuṅk*.—Mal. *pontar*. See *fitar*.

Apóstolo (an apostle). Konk. *āpóstl*.—Beng. *āpostôl*.—Tamil *appostolamam*,—Malayal. *apōstalañ*. *Apōstal-atvam*, apostleship.—Kan. *apōstalánū*. *Apōstalatanu*, apostleship. *Apōstalara*, apostolic.—Tulu *apóstale*. *Apōstalatana*, apostleship—? Malag. *apostoly*; perhaps from the English 'apostle.'

| **Aqui** (*adv.*, here). Chin. *aki*, 'foreigner.'—"At Amoy, the Chinese used to call out after foreigners **Akee**! **Akee**! a tradition from the Portuguese *Aqui!* 'Here!'" *Hobson-Jobson*, *s.v.* I—say. |

[It is interesting to note how, sometimes, a mere trivi-

---

nona ('the bullock's heart fruit') with the other word *nona* (see *dona*), and gives it the meaning "virginal fruit."

[1] Likewise in the Portuguese word *laranja* the *l* is in place of *n*: Arabic-Persian *naranj*, Sansk. *nāranja*.

Spanish has *naranja* and *naranjo*. [For a very interesting discussion as to whether the *ata* (*q.v.*) and the *anona* were indigenous, or imported into India from the New World, see *Hobson-Jobson*, *s.v.* custard-apple.]

[2] "Cakes made of rice-flour and coconut-oil which all the people of the Orient eat." Bluteau.

"Cakes of wheaten flour which the Malabars call **apas**." Castanheda, I, 15.

"Vegetable, **apas**, and *fogueos*, all these brought in an income of three thousand and odd *pardaos*. João de Barros, Déc II, v, 2. [*Fogueo* is a tax formerly levied in Goa, either on each hearth or house.]

"The income from **apas** and from cheese." Simão Botelho. *Tombo*, p. 53.

ality is responsible for providing a name or a sobriquet. Thus Yule says that the Chinese mob used to call the English soldiers *A'says* or *Isays* from the frequency of this apostrophe ('I—say') in their mouths. To this Crooke adds: "The French gamins, it is said, do the same at Boulogne." From a quotation furnished by Crooke it appears that about 1863 Indian Sepoys in China were invariably called 'Achas' because *Acha* or good was the constantly recurring answer of a Sepoy when spoken to.]

Araca, arraca, orraca, urraca ('distilled spirit from the sap of coconut-palm, or molasses, or rice').[1] Konk. *urrák*; vern. terms *pachak, pachkó saró*.—Anglo-Ind. *arrack, rack*.—Indo-Fr. *arack, rak*.—Malag. *laraka*; vern. term *tuaka* (from Malay).

The word is derived from the Arabic *'araq*, 'perspiration, exudation, distilled spirit.'

Arame (wire). Konk. *ārám*; vern. terms *sarí, tantí, tár*.—Tet. *arámi*; vern. term *kábati*.

Arcediago (archdeacon). Konk. *arsedyág*.—Ar. *arshidiak* (Simonet).

Arco ('the arch of a building'). Konk. *árk* (also used of 'the bow of a violin'); vern. terms *kamáṇ, gaj*.—Mar. *ark*.—Sinh. *arékkuva*.—Tul. *árka árkų* (in both meanings).—Mal. *árku* (of a paper kite).

Areca (betel-nut). Anglo-Ind. *areca* ('betel-nut' is more current). Indo-Fr. *arec, arèque, arequier*.

The original of the word is

[1] "The excise on the **orraquas** made from palm-trees, of which there are three sorts, to wit: *çura* (toddy), which is as it is drawn; **orraqua**, which is *çura* once boiled; *xarao* which is boiled twice or thrice over and is stronger than **orraqua**" Simão Botelho, *Tombo*, p. 50.

"They have two kinds of coco palms, one kind they keep for the nuts and the other for *çura* which is *vino mosto*; and this when it has been distilled they call **orraqua**." Garcia da Orta, Col. xvi. [*Vino mosto* is the newly pressed juice from the grapes before fermentation. Sir Clements Markham (p. 140) translates it 'rough wine.']

"They strain and mix it with **Araqua** to make it ardent and durable." Gabriel Rebêlo, *Informações das Cousas de Maluco*, p. 170.

"This shop of **Orracas**, which are wines made from the jaggery (*jagra*, *q.v*) of palm trees." Diogo do Couto Dec. V, ix, 5.

the Malayalam *aḍekkā*[1] [which according to Bishop Caldwell is made up of *adai*, 'close arrangement of the cluster,' and *kay*, 'nut.']

Argamassa (mortar, stucco). Konk. *ārgāmás*; vern. term *gilāvó*.—Indo-Fr. *argamasse*.[2]

Argola (a large iron ring). Konk. *ārgól*; vern. term *vāḷó*, *āṅkḍó*, *kaḍí*.—Tet., Gal. *argola*.

Argolinha (an ear-ring). Konk. *ārgolinh*; vern. terms *āṅkḍó*, *āṅkḍí*.—Tet., Gal. *argolinha*.[3]

Armada (a fleet of war-vessels). Mar. *ārmár*, *armár*, *ārmar*, *armar*. It also signifies 'a war-vessel'. *Armārí*, *ārmarí*, *armarí* (*adj.*), relating to an armada or to a war-vessel. *Armāri śipāí*, a soldier of the armada.—Guj. *armár*, *ārmá*.—Mal., Tet., Gal. *armada*.

In Marathi the final unstressed *a* being silent, *d* assimilated itself to *r*. Again, there was oscillation between the *ā* long and the *a* short.[1]

Armário (cup-board; the archaic form of this word, which is even now in use among the people in Portugal, is *almario*; it is the result of dissimilation). Konk. *ālmár*; vern. term *chauk*.—Mar., Guj. *armārí*.—Hindi, Beng. *ālmārí*, *almārí*.—Hindust. *almārí*.—Ass. *ālmārí*; *ālmāirá* (from Anglo-Ind.).—Punj. *almāri* ('a stand, a chest of drawers').—Sinh. *almāriya*.—Tam. *alumári*.—Malayal. *āḷmárı*.—Tel. *almár*, *almára*.—Kan. *almārí*, *almáru*.—Tulu *almārí*, *almêru*.—Anglo-Ind. *almirah*, *almyra*.—Gar. *almari*.—Khas. *almari* ('chest of drawers').—Mal. *almaria* (Castro), *almári*,

1 "These bear a fruit as large as walnuts which they call **Areca**, which they eat with the betel-leaf." Duarte Barbosa, p. 347. [Hak. Soc., ed. Longworth Dames, Vol. II, p. 92.]

"In Malabar they call it *pac*; and the Nairs (who are the knights) call it **areca**, whence the Portuguese have taken the name." Garcia da Orta, Col. xxii. [ed. Markham, p. 193.]

2 "The mosque was a very large and beautiful edifice, the greater part of it being built of timber finely carved, and the upper part of **argamassa**." *Commentarios de A. de Albuquerque*, Part I, ch. 24. [Hak. Soc. Vol. I, p. 82.]

3 "And in the ears **argolinhas** of gold." Gaspar Correia, I, p. 32.

1 It is natural to suppose that the term was in use in former times in Goa, but at present there are no traces of it.

lamári, lemári.—Ach., Mac., Bug. *lamári.*—Sund. *almári* — Jav., Mad. *lamári, lemári.*—Tet., Gal. *armári.* In High Javanese (Krômôdusun) *lanantun*, " on the analogy of other words which are truly Javanese." Dr. Heyligers.

Armario is also used, in some of the languages, in the sense of 'a writing desk, a escritoire', as: in Bengali *likhibar ālmāri*; in Hindi *likhine ki almāri* or *mej.* In Sinhalese *pot almáriya* is 'a book stand.'

Aroma (aroma; the adjectival form in Portuguese is *aromatico.*) Mal. *arúm.*—Mad. *arom.*—Jav. *arum, rum.*[1]

Gonçalves Viana throws doubts on the Portuguese provenance.

Arraigada (*naut.*, ropes used in fixing the mast). L.-Hindust. *rikáda.*

Arrátel (a pound weight). Konk. *rát.*—Mar., Guj., Hindust. *ratal.*—Sinh. *ráttala.*—Tamil *aráttal.*—Malayal. *rattal.*—Kan. *rátalu.*—Tul. *rátalu, rátelu.*—Anglo-Ind. *rattle, rottle.*—Indo-Fr. *arratel.*

The etymon is the Arabic *raṭl* or *riṭl*, which, in its turn, is supposed to be derived from the Greek *litra.* See *Hobson-Jobson.* It appears that the word, in some of the languages at least, has proceeded directly from the Portuguese. The corresponding vernacular term is *ser.*[1]

Arrear (*naut.*, to ease off a rope, to lower). L.-Hindust. *ariyá.*—Tul. *áriya.* —Mal. *aría.* It is generally used as an imperative. In L.-Hindust. *ariya-kurná* is 'to lower'.[2]

Arroio (a little stream of water, a brook). The identical Portuguese form is used in Malay and Indo-Fr. "The word *Arroyo*, which has been adopted by the French from the Malay of Cochin-China, is a genuine Portuguese word." (Castro).

---

1 "In this last-named language (Javanese), the words *pôrô arum*, 'the sweet, the fragrant,' are used as an elegant phrase to denote the fair sex." Dr. Heyligers.

1 "Forty ceres make a maund, and twenty maunds one *bahar.*" *Lembranças das Cousas da India*, p. 39 [*Bahar* is Ar. *bahār*, or Sansk. *bhāra*, a load, and is a weight of about 400 lbs.]

2 "I shall never forget the word *árriá*! which is heard all over the seas of India." Dr. A. O. de Castro.

? **Arroz** (rice) Mal. *árus* (perhaps from the Ar. *aruzz*); vern. terms *padi* ('rice in husk'), *bras*.

Arruda (*Ruta graveolens*; the rue herb) Malayal. *arúda*. —Mal. *arrúda*, *arúda*.—Bug. *arúda*.

Arsenal (arsenal). Konk., Tet., Gal. *ārsenál*.

Arte (art; skill). Konk. *árt*; vern. terms *vidyá*, *kaḷá*; *ghāḍāmôḍ*.—Tet. *árti*; vern. term *badáin*.

A saber (to wit). Mal. *a saber* (Haex).

Asna (a rafter). Jap. *azna* (obs.).

Assado (*subst.*, roast-meat). Konk. *āsád*.—Tamil *asádu*.

Assar (to roast). Mal. *assar* (Haex).

Assistir (to attend). Konk. *āsistír-zāvuṅk*; vern. terms *āsuṅk*, *pāvuṅk*.—Tet., Gal. *assísti*.

Astrólogo (astrologer). Mac., Bug. *isitāraluga* (Matthes).

Ata (*bot.*, *Anona squamosa*, L.; custard-apple). Konk. *át* (the fruit is neuter, but the name of the plant, which is the same as that of the fruit, is feminine).—Hindi, Hindust. *át*, *ātá*.—Or. *át*—Beng. *ātá*.—Ass. *átlas*.—Sinh., Tam. *āttá*.—Malayal. *átta*; *ata-maram* (Rheede; *maram* = tree), *ātta-chchakka* (lit. *ata-jaca*); *muḷḷātta-chchakka*, bullock's heart (*muḷḷa* = thorn).[1]

The question of the place of origin and of the etymology of *ata* and *anona*, names often used promiscuously and, there-

---

[1] In Marathi and Gujarati *Sitá-phal*, 'Sita's fruit,' in Sindhi *Sita-phalu*, in Kanarese *Site-phala*. In Tamil simply *sittá*; also *aninuna*, perhaps for *anona*. In Hindustani it is called *sharifa*, [and in Pers. *sharifah* and *kāj*.]

"There is to be found likewise another tree in the land with the name of **ateira** ('the custard-apple tree'), the fruit of which is similar to the small pine; it contains a white kernel which is very savoury and sufficiently hot (*quente*)." Fr. Clemente da Ressurreição in *Agricultor indiano*, of B. F. da Costa, Vol. II, p. 337. ['Hot' is evidently used of the custard-apple in the same way in which Garcia da Orta often speaks of plants and drugs as being hot and dry, cold and moist. Even at the present day in India, there is a general belief that some fruits and vegetables are 'hot' and others 'cold.' Sir George Birdwood's explanation is that in practice 'hot' or 'cold' drugs are those which either promote or repress aphrodisia. (See Garcia da Orta, *Simples and Drugs of India*, ed. Markham, Introduction, p. xv.]

fore leading to confusion, is a very intricate one; these names are used quite spontaneously in various parts of India, as is also the case with *caju* and *goiaba* (*q.v.*).

Among the sculptures of Bharhut, among the engravings at Muttra, and among the mural paintings at Ajanta, there is a fruit represented which is very like the custard-apple, but of an uncommon bigness. General Cunningham identifies it with the *Anona squamosa*, and traces its Indian name *át* or *ātá* to the Sansk. *ātrapya*, and maintains that the Portuguese in introducing the fruit into India were merely bringing coals to Newcastle.

[To this Watt (*A Dict. of the Econ. Prod. of India*, Vol. II, p. 260) says that the representations referred to by General Cunningham might be associated with a large number of plants; they may prove to be conventional representations of the jack-fruit tree or some other allied plant: they are not unlike the flower-heads of the sacred *kadamba* or *Anthocephalus*. He also remarks that the Bengali names *nona* and *ata* are so much opposed to the custard-apple tree being indigenous to India as are the names *Rámphal* and *Sitáphal* in favour of that idea. He maintains that people of India have adopted pre-existing names for introduced plants, and that there is no evidence to shew that this is not the case with the vernacular names given to the custard-apple.]

But Max Müller doubts the existence of such a word as *ātrapya* in real Sanskrit; Yule and Burnell suggest that Sanskrit names have been invented for many objects which were unknown till recent centuries. Relying on the authority of the Dutch botanist Rheede[1] and of a Manilla vocabulary, these writers presume that the *ata* and its name came to India from Mexico by way of the Philippines, whilst the *anona* and its name came to India from Hispaniola by way of the Cape of Good

1 This author says that in Malabar the custard-apple is sometimes called *manil-jaca*, 'the jack-fruit of Manilla,' and the bullock's heart, *parengi-jaca*, 'Portuguese jack-fruit.'

Hope. See *Hobson-Jobson*, *s.v.* custard-apple.

It is, however, necessary to note that if the *Anona squamosa* entered by way of the Philippines, it did not carry with it its name of *ata*, because the Malayan languages do not give it that name, but call it *nona*, and it may well be that *ate* or *atte* of the Manilla vocabulary is of modern introduction. The plant is also a native of Brasil, where it is likewise called *ata* or *ateira*.

Atalaia (a watch-tower; also a boat used for patrolling). Sinh. *aṭṭálaya*.[1]

The doubling of the consonants is very common in Sinhalese, as also in Malayalam and in Tamil; but the cerebralisation of *ṭṭ*, as in this case, is uncommon.

[The Portuguese dictionaries give 'watch-tower' as the meaning of *atalaya*. According to Dozy (*Glossaire etc.*), it is the Ar. *at-talāyi'* plural of *at-tali'a*, originally meaning 'watchmen or sentinels'. He makes no mention of its being used to denote a boat, a meaning which the word has in the old Portuguese writers on India, who frequently employ the term to describe a boat used for patrolling and watching the coast, and sometimes also of a boat equipped for fighting. Dalgado (*Glossario*) says it is not easy to make out whether the Portuguese carried to India the term which they had received from the Arabs, or adopted it from some of the Indian languages. From the way in which it is employed by the old Portuguese writers, he is inclined to take the latter view. But he does not know of any vessel in India with a similar name and object unless it be *aṭālī*, from the Sansk. *aṭṭāla* or *aṭṭāli* (*kā*), which means 'the top-storey of a house, tower or observation-post,' and is current in Gujarati, Marathi and Hindustani. It is but natural that a patrol-boat should have an elevated place from which to carry on observations.]

Atenção (attention). Konk. *atensáṁv* (l. us.); vern. term *chitt*, *chatráy*.—Tet. *atensã*; vern. term *rôna*.

---

[1] "Having always in the field large number of guards and attalayas." Diogo do Couto, Dec. VI, viii, 8.

Atrevido (bold, daring). Konk. *ātrevíd*; vern. terms *tíd*, *mastó*, *tavṇás*.—Tet. *atrevídu*; vern. term *áti*.

Ave Maria ('Hail Mary'). Konk. *āvémari*.—Beng. *āvemārí*. [In Konk. the form *aimorí* is more in use; both, however, are used to denote the Angelus, the opening words of which are 'Hail Mary.']

Avêsso (the wrong side). L.-Hindust. *ābês*.—Mal. *avés* (Marre).

Avisar (to warn). Konk. *āvizár-karuṅk* (l. us.); vern. terms *kaḷauṅk*, *gamauṅk*, *khabar divuṅk*.—Tet. *avíza*; vern. term *hanôrin*.

Aviso (warning). Konk. *āvíz*; vern. terms *kaḷauṇí*, *gamauṇí*, *zāṇauṇí*.—Tet. *auídu*.—Gal. *avízu*.

In Teto, *v* becomes vocalised.

Avó (grandmother). Beng. *āvó* (us. among the Christians of Hoshanabad).

Az (ace in cards). Konk. *áz*.—Mac., Bug. *ássā*.

Almost all the terms in card-games, in the Konkani in use among the Christians, are derived from Portuguese. Macassar and Bugi have also many of them. See *rei*, *sota*, *espadilha*, *manilha*, *codilho*, *basto*.

Azagaia (an African javelin or spear). Anglo-Ind. *assegay*.—Mal. *asegay*; vern. term *tombak*.

The original of the word is the Berber *zagaya*.[1]

["The Portuguese *azagaia*, which had been adopted both in Spain and Portugal from the Berber *zaghāya*, brought into the Peninsula by the Moors, was carried by them to Africa, and applied to the throwing-spears of the Zulus and other Bantu races comprised under the name Cafres, *i.e.*, Kāfirs or Heathen, given them by the Arabs....."Assegai" is now naturalised in S. Africa." Longworth Dames's note in *The Book of Duarte Barbosa*, Vol. I, p. 10].

Azeitona (olive). Konk. *āzetón*. *Azetin*, the olive-tree.—Tet. *azeitona*.

Azul (blue). Konk. *āzúl*; vern. terms *āsmāní*, *niḷó*.—Tet. *ajul*.

[1] They (the Cafres) also carry azagaias in their hands; and others carry bows and arrows of middle size." Duarte Barbosa, p. 234. [Hak. Soc., ed. Longworth Dames, Vol. 1, p. 10.]

B

Bacalhau (cod-fish). Konk. *bākālhāṁv* (also us. of cod-liver oil); vern. term *tāṭó*.—Tet. *bakalhau*.

Bacia or bacio (in the sense of 'a dinner-plate'). Konk. *basí, baśí*.—Mar. *basí, bāsí, bāśí*.—Guj. *basí*.—Tam., Tel., Kan., Tul. *bási*.—Malayal. *vássi*.—Mal. *bási* (*basil*, according to Castro).—Ach. *bási, besoi*.—Sund. *bási* ("a large dish for joint; a large bowl," Rigg).—Jav. *bási, bési*.—Tet., Gal. *basía*.—Malag. *basi*.[1]

S before *e* and *i* becomes palatalized in Konkani and Marathi. In Malayalam *v* takes the place of *b*. Cf. *bateria*.

There is another word with the very same meaning—*básan*: in Konk., Mar., Guj., Hindi, Hindust., Or., Beng., Ass., Punj., Sinh., Mal. (*bájan*), Sund. (*bájan, vájan*), Jav. (*vájan*), Anglo-Ind. (*bassan*)—whose origin *Hobson-Jobson* also attributes to *bacia*. But there is *bhājana* in Sanskrit with the very same meaning.[1]

?Bafo (vapour). Konk., Guj., Hindust. *báph*.—Mar. *váph*.—Hindi, Punj. *bháph*.—Nep. *báf*.—Or. *bháp, bhámp*.—Beng. *bháp*.—Ass. *báp*.—Sindh. *bápha*.[2]

---

1 "And with Timoja and Cojebequi......there came many people with kettle-drums and trumpets of the country, beating **bacias** ('metal pans') and drums, as is their custom." Gaspar Correia, *Lendas da India*, II, p 77.

"**Bacios** ('plates') and other dishes which are made of metal." António Nunes, *Livro dos Pesos da Ymdia*, p. 38.

"A gentleman of noble decent.... was carrying in a large silver **bacio** the *pareas* ('tribute') of the King of Quiloa (to the King of Portugal)." João de Barros, Dec. I, vi, 7.

"Fifteen to twenty scores of earthen ware, and as many scores of **bacios** to eat from, and half a dozen **bacios** *de agua* ('wash basins')" (1585). *Archivo Portuguez-Oriental*, Fasc. 5, p. 1021.

1 See Hugo Schuchardt, *Beiträge*, etc., p. 511.

2 "The betel-leaf is eaten all over India, because it produces good **Bafo**." Castanheda, I, ch. 16. [Bafo is evidently used here in the sense of 'aroma' or 'taste.']

"There is a species of rice called *pulot*, which when boiled only in **baffo** ('in steam'), sticks to the hands and is so moist that it looks as though it had been cooked in butter." Garcia da Orta, Col. lviii [ed. Markham, p. 460.]

The etymology of the Portuguese word is uncertain. In Spanish *vaho* corresponds to *bafo.* "F. Diez believes that it may be an onomatopoeic word, but since its plausible etymon has not yet been discovered, and although imitative words are as a rule suspect, when they are not mere interjections, we shall, in the absence of a better derivation, accept provisionally the opinion of the unsurpassed founder of Romanic philology." Gonçalves Viana, *Apostilas aos Dicionários Portugueses.*

Molesworth derives the Marathi word from the Sansk. *bāṣpa* or *vāṣpa*, 'tear, vapour.' Shakespear does the same with regard to the Hindustani term. It seems that in the Portuguese word we have a case of parallelism, as in *chapa* ('stamp or mark'), *tanque* ('tank'), *varanda* ('verandah').[1]

Bailadeira (dancing-girl). Indo-Fr., Anglo-Ind. *bayadère.* In English the compounds 'dancing-girl' or 'nautch-girl' are more in use. See Gonçalves Viana, *Palestras Filológicas.*[1] [Tavernier uses the form *baladine,* which Crooke says is from the Port. *bailadeira.* See *Travels in India* (ed. Ball, Ox. Univ. Press), Vol. I, p. 71.]

Bailar (to dance). Mal. *bála* —Sund. *bálla,* a dance. *Main bálla,* to dance.

At times the final *r* of Portuguese verbs is dropped. Cf. *emprestar, tomar.* In the Asio-Port. dialects also, there is the form *bala.*

Bainhar (to hem). Konk. *bāṅhar-karuṅk*; vern. term *metuṅk.*—Tet., Gal. *banha* (also us. as a subst. to mean 'a hem', or 'selvedge').

---

1 Notice the identity of meaning and the close resemblance of sound of the Sanskrit *vāṣpa,* whose root is not known, and of the Latin *vapor.*

1 "Beating pans and drums, according to their custom, and in front **bailadeiras** and buffoons." Gaspar Correia, II, p. 77.

"There used to come to the parade-ground many **bailadeiras** with their musical instruments by means of which they earn their livelihood." *Id.,* II, p. 363.

"The **bailadeira** dances in the public square, sings in the temple, and sells her body at her house." F. L. Gomes, *Os Brahamanes,* p. 184. [For the different names of dancing-girls in the different parts of India see *Hobson-Jobson, s.v.* dancing-girl.]

Baioneta (bayonet). Konk. *bāynêt.*—Sinh. *bayinêttiya, bayinêttuva.*—Tet., Gal. *baionêta.* —? Mal. *gaganet.*

Gonçalves Viana declines to accept that the Malay word is Portuguese in origin.

Baixa (decrease, fall). Konk. *báyś.*—Tet. *baiśa.*

?**Baixel** (in the sense of 'an Arab barge'). Konk. *bagló.*—Mar., Guj. *baglá, bagalá.*—Tel. *bagalé. Bagalé-báyi,* 'mouth of the *bagale,*' a glutton. —Anglo-Ind. *buggalow.*—Ar. *baqalá.*

Yule and Burnell think it very probable that the term was in use in India before the arrival there of the Portuguese, and had been carried thither by the Arabs.

There is another variant probable or possible of the Portuguese word, but designating another kind of vessel: Konk. *bazró.*—Mar., Beng. *bajrá.*—Hindust. *bajrá, bujrá.* —Anglo-Ind. *budgerow.*

[Yule says: "In Correa (c. 1561) *bajel* or *baxel* occurs in the form *pajer*, pl. *pajeres* (*j* and *x* being interchangeable in Sp. and Port. See *Lendas*, I, 2, pp. 592, 619, etc.)". But Dalgado is of the opinion that, if *pajer* is not a mere phonetic variant of *paguel*, 'a cargo boat formerly used in Southern India,' then it may have come from *bajrā*, used in Marathi, Bengali and Hindustani, to designate another kind of sea-vessel; and this term would be pronounced *pajara* or *pachara* in the Dravidian country. See *Glossario, s. v. paguel.*]

Balão (in the sense of 'a species of rowing vessel'). Sinh. *balama.*—Malayal. *balam.* —Anglo-Ind. *balam, baloon, balloon.*[1]— | Mal. *báloq* |.

The primary word is the Guj. *baliyan*; *balyāṁv* in Mar.-Konkani. Bengali has *baulia.*

---

[1] "With five *lancharas* (*q. v.*) and a dozen **balões** he came looking for me." Fernão Pinto, ch. xv.

"He gave orders to enter the creeks which surround the city even by means of **balões**, which are small vessels." João de Barros, Dec. II, ix, 3.

"D. Estevão de Gama sent Simão Sodré with eight **balões** (which are a species of light vessels)." *Id.* Dec. IV, ix, 12.

"Dom Estevão sent Pero Barriga and Jorge d'Alvarenga, in **balões**, to go along the river to see what they could find there." Gaspar Correia, III, p. 627.

[In his *Glossario Luso-As.*, the author expresses his doubts regarding the Gujarati origin which he had ascribed to the word in the present work. The word under various forms is found in several languages all over India. Marathi has *balyāṁv*, Gujarati, *baliyan*, Bengali, *baulia* (used chiefly in Chatigão), Malay, *balang*, the meaning of which does not square with that of *balão*. He thinks it very probable that the birth-place of the Portuguese *balão* was Malabar and that its original is the Tamil-Malayalam *vaḷḷam*, "a canoe hollowed out from the trunk of a tree" (Percival); and this is the primary meaning of the word. It is not unlikely that the Malays received the word, like other names of boats such as *parau* and *kapal*, from the people of Southern India, before the arrival of the Portuguese. Fryer uses the English variant of the word, viz., 'balloon,' in the sense of a 'Barge of State'. See *East India and Persia* (Hak. Soc.), I, p. 182. It is evidently in this very meaning that the word is used in Siam for the *O.E.D.* describes it as "a Siamese state-barge, upwards of a hundred feet long, and richly decorated".]

Balchão ('a species of caviare'). Konk. *balchāṁv*.—Beng., Tam. *balcham*.—Anglo-Ind. *balachong*, *blachong*.

From the Malay *balāchán*, it was introduced by the Portuguese, and employed in the Portuguese dialects of Asia[1].

Balde (a bucket). Konk., Mar., Guj. *bāldí*.—Beng., Hindust., L.-Hindust. *bāldí*, *bāltí*.—Sinh. *báldiya*, *báliya*.—Tam. *báldi*.—Tel. *baldí*, *bādlí*. Tul. *báldi*.—Anglo-Ind. *balty*.—Gar. *balti*, *baltin*.—Mal., Tet., Gal. *báldi*.

The etymology of *balde* is not clear. The Portuguese dictionary, *Contemporaneo*, derives it from Low Latin *batellus*, and Cândido de Figueiredo associates it, in a doubtful manner, with *baldo* ('unprovided, penniless'). Gasper Correia regards the word as new and assigns to it an Indian origin.

---

[1] "Besides this the *bilimbins* (*q. v.*) are useful in the preparation of appetising balchão." B. F. da Costa, *Agricultor Indiano*, II, p. 216.

"All this our men will see for themselves in the port of Cananor, in which there are very large vessels, which the Captains will send their men to see, so that they might give an account of everything they had seen when they go to Portugal; on these ships there are no pumps, only some pails made of thick cow's hide, tanned in such a way, that they last long, and with these they bale the water out by hand; these pails they call **baldes** (I, p. 123).

"Luis de Mello de Mendoça set out with his companions to help at the **baldes**, with which they began to bale out the water" (1546). Diogo de Couto, Dec. VI., iii, 3.

Indian dictionary-writers give the Portuguese word as the original: "Balty, s. H. *bālti*, 'a bucket', is the Portuguese *balde*". *Hobson-Jobson.*

Bálsamo (balsam, ointment) Konk. *bálsm̃.*—Hindust. *balsán.*—? Mal. *balasan* (Ar.) ? Mac., Bug. *balasáng.*—Jap. *bársan, bārusamo.*—Ar. *bálsam, balsám, bolasán, bolsán.*

Baluarte (bulwark). Mal. *baluvárdi.*—Jav. *baluvárti, balovárti, balúrti.*

Bambu (*bot., Bambusa vulgaris*; bamboo). Anglo-Ind. *bamboo*, [*bambou*].—Indo-Fr. *bambou.*[1]

The origin of the word is very obscure. Marsden mentions it as a pure Malay word; but the common name for it is *buluh.* Crawfurd considers it to be a term that belongs to the west coast of Sumatra. Wilson regards it as coming from the Kanarese, and Reeve mentions it as such; but the usual terms are *biduru* (Tulu *beḍuru*) and *gala.* It appears to me that the most probable source of the word is the Marathi *bāmbú* (the same in Gujarati), which is the generic and common name of the plant.

The form *mambu,* which occurs in the Portuguese chroniclers, might have been

---

[1] "They regarded death as certain either from the blows of **Bambús** (lit. 'from scourges of bamboos'), or from perpetual captivity in the prisons of Cantom." Lucena, Bk. X, ch. 26.

"He wished to reduce the weight by taking away from the *canga* (*q. v.*) a **bambu.**" A. F. Cardim, p. 199.

really in use then in the Konkan, as the authors of *Hobson-Jobson* suppose, and the present day Konkani term *mán* ('bamboo') would then represent the contraction of the word; or it might be due to dissimilation in the mouth of the Portuguese.[1] Inversely, *Bombaim* is due to the assimilation of *Mombaim*, a form employed by Barbosa, Botelho, Garcia: the vernacular name is *Mumbai*, a corruption of *Mumbadevi*, 'the Goddess Mumba'. See Gerson da Cunha, *The Origin of Bombay*.

[The earlier Portuguese writers of the sixteenth century speak of the bamboo by the generic name of '*cana*' or '*cana de India*. Barbosa (1516) refers to "some *canas* in India which are as thick as a man's leg". Cit. in *Glossario*.']

1 "The people where it grows call it *sacar-mambum*, which means 'sugar of *mambum*'; because the Indians of the place where it grows called the canes of that plant *mambu*." Garcia da Orta, Col. ii. [ed. Markham, p. 410. *Bambu* in Goa is also 'a measure of length,' and the early Portuguese writers when referring to it in connection with China mean 'a scourge of bamboos'. (See citation above from Lucena).]

Banana (the fruit of *Musa Sapientum*, L., plantain). Anglo-Ind. *banana* (l. us.)—Indo-Fr. *banane*, *bananier*.[1]

The Portuguese called the bananas, by analogy, 'the figs of India', and as *figos* they are known over the whole range of Asio-Portuguese dialects, which also employ *figueira*, 'the banana-tree', and *figueiral*, 'a plantation of the banana-tree,' and in Goa also *bananeira* ('the banana-tree'). Tomé Lopes, who sailed for India in 1502, compares bananas with figs: "A species of figos long and big like small cucumbers, which is one of the most savoury fruits that can be had in the world".[2] Cf. the German *Paradiesfeige*.[3]

1 "There is in China such an abundance of mangoes, *carambolas* (*q.v.*), jack-fruit, water melons, bananas, and all Indian fruits." Lucena, Bk. X, ch. 18.

2 *Navegação das Indias Orientaes*, in the Collection of Ramusio, translated by the Lisbon Academy of Sciences, ch. vi.

"Another fruit which is like *figos* ('figs') and has a fine taste." *Roteiro de Vasco da Gama*, p. 60.

3 "In Mombassa there are many kinds of limes, pomegranates, Indian *figos*, and all kinds of vegetables."

It is not known for certain when and by whom the word 'banana' was introduced into India, which, according to Garcia da Orta, came from Guinea. "They also have figs in Guinea, where they call them **bananas**."[1] It appears that the term made its entry (through the Portuguese ?) in the seventeenth century as being more appropriate, or, rather, to mark the difference between the fruit of the *Musa paradisiaca* and of the *Musa sapientum*, now reduced to only one species.[1]

Anglo-India employs generally the term 'plantain', which is a corruption of the Spanish *plantano*, another name for the 'banana.' See *goiaba*.

[Mocquet, *Voyages* (ed. 1645), calls 'bananas' *fiques de platane.* Watt (*The Commercial Products of India*) says: "The name 'banana' is very seldom used by the English in India, though it is universal in the fruit-shops of England. In India all kinds are indiscriminately called plantains." Yule quotes Robertson Smith, the great Arabic scholar, who points out that the coincidence of the name 'banana' with the Ar. *banān*, 'fingers or toes', and *banāna*, 'a single finger or toe',

Duarte Barbosa, *Livro* p. 239. [Hak. Soc., ed. Longworth Dames, Vol. I, p. 21].

"**Bannanes** which the Portuguese call Indian figs." Pyrard de Laval, *Voyage*, 1615. [Hak. Soc. Vol. I, p. 113.]

"He ordered cooked rice to be served out there, and this they served upon the green leaves of the *figueira* ('the banana-tree'), which are broad like a sheet of paper." Gaspar Correia, I, 17.

1 "It is possible that there is reason for this; it can safely be said that the word is not Asiatic in origin, and it also does not appear to be American." Conde de Ficalho, Col. xxii.

"But it is the commonest fruit which is to be found everywhere all the year round, and in great abundance, not only in these Indies (West), but also in our India, and all over Guinea and Brazil, where it exists, and where we saw more and better species than these, and where they call them *plantanos*, and in our India *figos*, and in Brazil **bananas**." Padre Gabriel Afonso, in *Historia tragico-maritima*, Vol. VI, p. 50.

1 "Books distinguish between the *Musa sapientum* or plantain, and the *Musa paradisiaca*; but it is hard to understand where the line is supposed to be drawn." *Hobson-Jobson.*

can scarcely be accidental. The fruit grew in Palestine before the Crusades; and, though it is known in literature as *mauz*, it would not follow from this that it was not somewhere popularly known as 'fingers'. He thinks it possible that the Arabs, through whom probably the fruit found its way to W. Africa, may have transmitted a name like this. To this Dalgado says that it is hardly credible that the word should have crossed over from Arabia to West Africa without leaving any trace of itself in the languages of the East Coast. See *Glossario*, Vol. I, p. 90.]

Banco (wooden seat, bench). Konk., Mar., Guj., L.-Hindust., Beng. *bánk.*—Sinh. *bánkuva.*—Tam. *bánku.*—Tel. *bankatí.*—Tul., Mal., Sund., Jav. *bánku.* —Ach. *banké.*—Mad., Day. *banko.*—Tet., Gal. *bánku*—Jap. *banko.*— | Turk. *bánqa* | .

In Konkani, Teto and Galoli, the term is also used of 'a commercial bank'. The other Indian languages adopt the English 'bank'.

Banda (side; also an ornamental band round the waist). Konk. *bánd*; vern. terms *kuś, bagal*; *kamarband.*—Tet. *banda*; vern. term *kalum.*

Bandeira (flag.) Konk. *bandér*; vern. terms *bāvṭó, dhajá.*—Mal.,[1] Batt., Sund., Bal. *bandéra.*—Jav. *bandéró, gandéró*[2].—Day. *bandéra. Habandéra,* to carry the flag. *Mandéra,* to hoist the flag.—Mac., Bug. *bandéra. Pabandéra,* a flagstaff (*pa* is a prefix). —Tet., Gal. *bandeira*; vern. term *sair.*—Ar. *bandeira, bandera, bandira, bandaira.*— | Turk. *bándara*; vern. terms *báyraq, sánjaq.* |

Bandeja (a tray). Konk. *bandêj*; vern. term *táṭ vāṭí.*—Sinh. *bandêsiya.*—Anglo-Ind. *bandejah* (l.us.).—Mal. *bandeja, bandeya*; vern. terms *tálan, tarana.*—Mac., Tet., Gal. *bandeja.*[3]

Bando (in the sense of 'a

1 "*Bandêr* or *Bandêrra,* flag (*tiang-bander,* flag-mast)." A. O. de Castro, *Flores de Coral.*

2 "In Javanese the substitution of a labial by a guttural is very frequent." Heyligers.

3 "We placed the letter and books in a gilt **bandeja** from China, and with the **bandeja** in hand we made four profound bows." A. F. Cardim, p. 80.

proclamation'). Konk. *bánd*; vern. terms *ḍāṅgoró*, *dāṇḍoró*. —Tet., Gal. *bándu*.

Bandola (a shoulder-belt). Mal., Mac., Bug. *bandóla*, *bandála*.—Ach. *bandála*.

[**Banean, Banian** (a Jain trader, and especially of the Province of Gujarat or Cambay). Anglo-Ind. *Banyan*.[1]

The word was adopted from Guj. *vāṇiyo*, sing., *vaṇiyā*, pl. (which form appears to be the immediate source of the Port. word), which itself comes from the Sansk. *vaṇiɟ*, 'a trader', and *vaṇiɟ-jana*, 'a tradesman'. Yule thinks that it is probable that the Portuguese found the word already in use by the Arab traders. Among the humours of philology might be mentioned P. F. Vincenzo Maria's (1672) explanation that the Portuguese called the Hindu traders of Gujarat *Bagnani*, "because of the frequency and superstition with which they washed themselves throughout the day". *Bagnáre* in Italian means 'to bathe'. The early European travellers applied the term to the followers of the Hindu religion generally. The old Portuguese writers, with the exception of da Orta, say that "all the *baneanes* follow the doctrine of Pythagoras", whereas the truth is that Pythagoras drew a large part of his doctrine from India. There is a third sense in which the term is or was used in Calcutta, viz., of an Indian broker who is generally attached to European business houses in India.

One compound in which,

[1] ["And in this kingdom (of Guzerate) there is another sort of Heathen whom they call **Baneanes**, who are great merchants and traders ......This people eats neither flesh nor fish, nor anything subject to death; they slay nothing, nor are they willing even to see the slaughter of any animal......" Duarte Barbosa, *The Book*, ed. Longworth Dames, Vol. I, p. 110.]

["......the **Banianes** of Cambaia which observe Pythagoras lawe......" Linschoten, *Voyage* (Hak. Soc.), Vol. I, p. 223.]

["The **baniani** are a certain class of Hindus who eat neither flesh nor fish, and consume grain, vegetables, milk, and a great deal of butter...... If the talk is of business, they give a ready answer, and are such strong arithmeticians that in the shortest time they can make any sort of calculation, never making a mistake of a single figure. They hold it a sin to kill any animal." Manucci, *Storia do Magor*, I, pp. 155-156.]

'banyan' figures is the 'Banyan-tree' (*Ficus Indica*), called in Hindi *baṛ*, and in Guj. *vaḍ*. "The Franks call it the tree of the Banians, because, in places where there are any of these trees, the idolaters sit under them and cook there. They reverence them specially, and generally build their pagodas either under or close to one of the great trees." (Tavernier, *Travels in India*, Ox. Univ. Press, Vol. II, p. 155.) Another more modern compound is "banian-hospital", which is the equivalent for what is commonly known as *pinjrapole*, derived, according to Crooke, from *pinjra*, a cage, and *pola*, the sacred bull released in the name of Śiva.

The form *bunya* used in Anglo-Indian homes to describe the dealer in ghee and grain is borrowed directly from Hindi and not from Portuguese.]

Bangue (' the dried leaves of *Canabis sativa* '). Anglo-Ind. *bangue, bang*.—Indo-Fr. *bangue*.—Pid-Engl. *bangee*.[1]

The source word is the Neo-Aryan *bhāṅg* from the Sansk. *bhaṅgā*. [Crooke (*Hobson-Jobson, s. v.* bang) remarks that though the word is usually derived from the Sansk. *bhaṇga*, 'breaking', Burton derives both it and the Ar. *banj* from the old Coptic *Nibanj*, "meaning a preparation of hemp; and here it is easy to recognise the Homeric *Nepenthe*".]

Baptismo (baptism: the old and popular form of the Port. word is *bautismo*). Konk. *bāvtijm*.—Beng. *bāvtijmá*.—Sinh. *bavtísmaya*.—? Mar. *baptismá*.—? Guj. *baptijhma*.—?Hindi, Hindust. *baptismá*.—?Tel. *baptismam*.—Malag. *batisa*—? Jap. *baputesuma*.

The appearance of *p* in

"And I will now satisfy you respecting the nature of **bangue**, viz. the plant and the seed." Garcia da Orta, Col. viii. [ed. Markham, p. 53.]

"In all this land of the Kaffirs (*Cafres*) a certain herb is grown which the Kaffirs cultivate and which they call **bangue**; it has the appearance of coriander run to seed." João dos Santos, *Ethiopia Oriental*, Vol. I, p. 88.

"Oh Manamotapa **bangueiro**! (which is to say drunk, because he used to eat certain herbs which they call **bangue**, the effect of which is to intoxicate). Bocarro, Dec. xiii, p. 560.

[1] "And the revenue from opium and **bangue**." Simão Botelho, *Tombo*, p. 53

some of the words seems to indicate that their source is English.

Baptizar (to baptise). Sinh. *bavtisár karaṇavā* (lit. 'to make to baptize'). In Konkani the common expression is *bāvtijm divuṅk*, 'to give baptism'.

Baralhar (to shuffle cards). Konk. *bārālhár karuṅk.*—Tet. *barálha*; vern. term *kákul*.

Baralho (a pack of cards). Konk. *bārálh.*—? Mar., Guj., Pers. (according to Molesworth) *barát.*—? Tel. *baredo*. In Marathi and Persian it means 'one of the suits of cards, sequence of cards'.

The origin of the Portuguese word is uncertain. Spanish has *baraja*. Hindi and Hindustani, more allied to Persian, do not use *barát*. *Ganjiphá*, used in the Indian languages for 'a pack of cards', is of Persian origin.

Barba (beard). Mal. *barba* (Haex); vern. term *jángut*.

Barcaça (a big bark or boat). Konk., Guj. *bārkas.*—Malayal. *varkkas.*—Ar. *barkús.*[1]

Barqueta (a small bark). Mar. *barkatá*. "A small barque or boat, the same as *barkín* or *barquinha*." Molesworth.

Barquinha (a small boat). Mar. *barkíṇ*. "A little barque or boat of a particular description. *Barkuṇí* (current in the Malwán-pránt). A small kind of hoḍí or planked boat." Molesworth.[1]

Barracas (a rude shelter, hut, tent). Tel. *bārkásu*; *barkásu*.

Barriga (belly). Mol. *bariga*, camphor of medium quality.[2] See *cabeca* and *pé*.

---

[1] "He boarded a big **barcaça**." Diogo de Couto, Dec. VI, iv, 5.

"But the men of the **barcaças** and galleys, which now here, now there were firing their guns." *Id.*, Dec. VIII, i, 35.

[1] "He himself carried....Dom André in the **barquinha** to the shore." Bocarro, Dec. XIII, p. 485.

[2] Garcia da Orta says (Col. xii): "The Hindus, Banians, and Moors, who buy this article, divide it into four kinds, viz., *Cabeca* ('head'), *peito* ('breast'), *pernas* ('legs') and *pé* ('foot')." And Conde de Ficalho makes the following comment: "Rumphius (*Herbarium Amboinense*) also describes the qualities according to which it is classified: big pieces, each approximately as big as a nail, they call *Cabessa*, which he says means 'head'; grains or very thin layers are called *Barriga*, or 'stomach'; and the kind in the form of powder or in very

It is probable that the terms had been in use in other parts of Insulindia and that they are now obsolete.[1]

Barrete (birreta, square cap worn by a priest). Konk. *barrêt*.—Tet., Gal. *barreti*.

?**Barrica** (cask) Malag. *barika*.

Barril (barrel, cask). Konk. *barl*,—Tet., Gal. *barril*.—Ar. *barmíl*, *bermil*, *birmíl*, *baramíl*, *varil*.— | Turk. *váríl* | .[2]

In other languages they use *pipa* for 'barrel.'

Barrote (beam, joist). Guj. *bārotiuṁ*.

Basta (*verb*, stop, it is enough). Konk. *bást* (l. us.); vern. term *puró*.—? Mar., Hindust., Sindh., Khas., Pers. *bas*.—? Anglo-Ind. *bus*.—Mal. *basta* (Haex).

Indian dictionary-writers give the word a Persian origin. [Yule does the same.]

Bastão (staff, cane). Konk. *bastáṁv* (l. us.); vern. terms *bét*, *betó*, *betkāṭhí*.—Sinh. *bastámu*.

Bastarda ('a species of old canon'). Bug. *bisatirída*.

?**Bastião** (bastion). Mal. *bartion* (Haex).

Basto (the ace of clubs). Mac., Bug. *basáttu*. See *az*.

Bata (an extra allowance made to soldiers or public officers). Anglo-Ind. *batta*, ration, foodstuffs; allowance, gratuity.

The word is Indian, and the corresponding Portuguese term employed by the old Portuguese writers is *mantimento* ('subsistence money' or 'allowance').[1] Simão Botelho says

minute grains is called *Pees*, which means 'feet'."

[1] The early Portuguese writers also speak of *coral de perna* ('coral of the leg-kind'). "He sent in a box a *quintal* [118 lbs.] of *coral de perna* to be wrought." "And a box of *coral de perna*, the best that was to be had." Gaspar Correia, I, pp. 89 and 101.

[2] "Rumecan went all over his army ......taking measures which seemed to him necessary......ordering that the walls be covered with many **barris** (the pl. of *barril*) of tar." Diogo de Couto, Dec. VII. iii, 10.

[1] "And there are six artisans, blacksmiths, who work in the smithy for two *pardaos* a month, in addition to their **mantimento** ('allowance') of rice, fish, fuel, as aforesaid." Simão Botelho, p. 237.

"All those who served in Malacca, whether by sea or land, were to be paid six months' salary in advance, and also were to receive monthly two

(p. 237): "And for two *farazes* ('porters') two *pardaus* each per month, and four tangas for *bata*." The editor of Botelho's *Tombo do Estado da India*, Rodrigo Felner, remarks that *bata* appears to stand for *bate*, i.e., 'paddy', or 'rice in the husk'. But there is no error in the text; because *bate* is itself a corruption of *bata*, (*a*), Marathi-Konkani *bhát* Kanarese *bhatta*.[1] But the author does not use the word in this sense, but in that of 'ration', as is seen from the text and the item that follows: "And for the chief gunner, thirty eight thousand nine hundred and twenty reis per year, inclusive of *mantimento*." In this case, *bata* is the same as the Hindust. *bhata*, *bhatta*, or *bhātá*; Mar. *bhatta bhātá*, or *bhātéṁ*; Konk. *bhātéṁ*.

Reeve says that *bhatta* is a Kanarese corruption of a Sansk. word, which cannot be other than *bhakta*, 'food' in general, and 'cooked rice' in particular, which is the principal diet of the Indian people.[1] In this last acceptation *bhát* (masc.) is current in Hindustani and Marathi; but in Konkani it is less used than *śit*; in Sinhalese *bhakta*, *batta*, and *bat*.

With the lapse of time *bhát* (neut.) came to be the prevailing name in Marathi and Konkani of 'rice in the husk' and of the 'rice-plant' itself, supplanting other terms like *sáḷ*, *dhán*; it then passed into Kanarese and was found side by side with the vernacular *nĕllu*.[2]

Naturally, *bhát* in its twofold meaning, of 'cooked rice' and 'rice in the husk', did not take long to designate, first, 'ration of cooked rice', then, 'uncooked rice' or 'money to buy the allowance of uncooked rice', and finally, 'food-stuffs, allowances, gratuities'. And to denote these

cruzados towards mantimento, cash in hand." Gaspar Correia, II, p. 267.

[1] Cf. the Portuguese *cate* or (*cato*) from *káta* ('catechu'), *bétele* from *vettila* ('betel-leaf').

[1] "In Calicut there is little rice, which is the chief *mantimento* ('staple food'), as wheat is among us." Castanheda I, ch. 73.

[2] *Néli* is used in the Port. dialect of Malacca, and Cândido de Figueiredo mentions it as a term old and inedited.

secondary meanings, it assumed, in Marathi and Konkani, the specific form of *bhātēṁ*. See *Hobson-Jobson.*

[From a citation made by Dalgado in his *Glossario* (Appendix) from P. E. Pieris, *The Kingdom of Jafanapatam*, p. 4., it is perfectly clear that Simão Botelho, in the aforesaid work, used *bata* in the sense of 'allowance', and not in that of 'paddy'. "The Canarese sailors were allowed **batta** at five fanams a month and the *mocadaens* double that amount."]

Batalhão (battalion). Konk. *bātālhāṁv*; vern. term *palṭaṇ* (l. us.)—Tet., Gal. *batalhã, batayã.*

Batão ('difference in exchange' or 'agio'). Anglo-Ind. *batta.*

The original word is the Hindust. *baṭṭáu* (*baṭṭá, bāṭṭá*), whence Mar. *vaṭáv*, Konk., *vāṭáv.*[1]

Batata (potato—not sweet). Konk. *baṭāṭó*. *Baṭāṭín* is used of a certain medicinal bulb.—Mar. *baṭāṭá*; vern. term *ālú.*—Guj. *baṭāṭá.*—Sinh. *batála* ('the sweet potato', the other is called *artapal*, from Dutch). —Malayal. *batatas* ("sweet potato", Rheede); vern. term *kappaliḻangu.*—Kan. *baṭāṭé*; vern. term *uralagaḍḍe.*—Tul. *baṭāṭé, paṭāṭé.*—| 'Mal. *batattas* (according to Rumphius); the vern. term is *úbi castila* ('Castilian or Spanish yam'). | —Nic. *patáta* ('sweet potato'). —Malag. *batata.*

It is not probable that the Indian words owe their origin to the English 'potato', because, besides appearing without the initial syllable *pa*, they are to be found in the language-field which was more influenced by the Portuguese; the Konk. *baṭāṭín* is, undoubtedly, derived directly from the Port. *batatinha* (diminutive). With regard to the cerebral *ṭṭ*, cf. *atalaia, abóbora, sorte.*[1]

[1] "Besides this there is the **batão**, which is difference in exchange or agio." António Nunes, *Livro dos Pesos da Ymdia*, p. 40. [See *Hobson-Jobson s. v.* batta (b)].

[1] In the Portuguese in vogue in Goa they speak of *batata de Surrate* that is the potato which found its way to the Indian market through the English factory at Surat; Fr. Clemente da Ressurreição (1782) calls it *batata inglesa* ('English potato').

The sweet potato (*Convolvulus batatas*), native of America, was introduced into India by the Portuguese, together with its name in the place of origin, which some of the languages preserved, whilst others replaced it with vernacular ones. Subsequently, the English imported the ordinary potato (*Solanum tuberosum*), and this as Yule and Burnell observe robbed the former of its name. The Portuguese in India must have distinguished the one kind from the other by the names *batata doce* ('sweet potato'), and *batata de Surrate* ('Surat potato') or *Inglesa* ('English potato'); and the vernacular languages must have restricted the use of the name *batata* to one species or the other.

"There is another which produces tubers similar to the small English potatoes." (In *Agricultor Indiano*, of B. F. da Costa, II, p. 339.) In the island of St. Nicholas, Cape Verde, they also speak of *batata inglesa*. (See *Jour. Geo. Soc. Lisb.*, 3rd. ser., p. 354.) In the Island of Madeira, the sweet potato is called *batata*, and the other kind *semilha*. Spanish uses *batata* of the sweet-potato, and the kitchen variety it calls *patata*.

Bate ('rice in the husk'; also 'growing rice'). Anglo-Ind. *battee* or *batty*; formerly used in the south of India, now supplanted by *paddy*.

The source-word is the Marathi-Konkani *bhát*. See *bata*.[1]

The Anglo-Indian *paddy* is from the Malay *pádi*, Jav. *pári*, which Crawfurd identifies with *bate* and seems to think that the Malayo-Javanese word may have come from India with the Portuguese. But Yule and Burnell think "this is impossible, for the word *pārī*, more or less modified, exists in all the chief tongues of the Archipelago, and even in Madagascar, the connection of which last with the Malay regions certainly was long prior to the arrival of the Portuguese".

[1] "(At Baçaim) the *mura* (*q. v*) of batee, which is rice in the husk, contains three *candis*." António Nunes, *Livro dos Pesos*, p. 40.

"From this rice which they call bate, the kingdom is called *Batecalou*, which is interpreted as meaning 'the Kingdom of Rice'." João de Barros, Dec. III, ii, 1.

"In the fields (of Ceylon) there is plenty of rice, which they call **bate**." Lucena, Bk. II, ch. 18.

Bátega (a metal basin; here used in the sense of 'metal tray' or 'platter'). Konk. *bátk*; vern. terms *táṭ*, *vāṭi*, *vāṭéṁ*.—Tet. *bátik*.—? Tonk. *bāt*, porringer.—? Mal. *bátil*.—?Mac., Bug. *bátilı*.

In the sense of 'metal basin', the term is obsolete in Portugal, but is in vogue among the corrupt Portuguese dialects under the forms of *bática* and *bátic*. See *Elucidario* of Viterbo.[1]

[The derivation of *batega* is open to doubt says Dalgado (*Glossario*, *s. v.*). Old Portuguese writers sometimes explain the word when they use it, a proof that it was not much in vogue. The Ar. *bāṭya* is generally given as its original, but Dozy says that the insertion of *g* is singular and the etymology of the word is far from certain. It would be interesting to know if the word was in use in Portugal before the discovery of the sea route to India. The Indian *batica*, 'a plate', has been suggested as a possible source-word.]

1 "In this kingdom of Pegu there is no coined money, and what they use and employ as money are **bategas**, pans and other similar ware, made of metal." António Nunes, p. 38.

"Then they bring him ten **batygas**, which are plain latten or brass plates ......and they drink the water which is contained in other **bategas**." Gaspar Correia, III, p. 715.

"And food stuffs in **bategas** of silver." Damião de Góis, IV. ch. 10.

Bateira (a little bark or vessel). Jap. *battera*.

Batel (little boat). Konk., Guj., Sindh. *báteló*.—Mar. *batelá*.—Anglo-Ind. *batel*, *batelo*, *botella*, *botilla*. Whitworth also mentions the form *buteela*.—? Mal. *bahatra*.—? Mac., Bug. *batará*. Matthes points to the Sansk. *vahitra*[1] as the source word.

Bateria (battery; set of guns). Konk. *bāterí*.—Malayal. *vattéri*.—Tel. *battéri*, *phattéri*. Brown gives as the source *batĕrí* in Arabic characters, but does not say to which language it belongs.—Mal. *bateria*, *teria* ("to shout, to

1 "The **batel** having moved away from the land, they soon came to it in an *almadia* (*q. v.*)." *Id.*, I, ch. 38.

"Because the **batel** in which they were going required more draught." Bocarro, Dec. XIII, p. 392.

hawk", Haex).—Ar. *battariya*, ship's bridge.[1]

Baú (a trunk, box). Konk. *bāú*; vern. term *péṭ*.—Guj. *bāú*, *bávuṁ*.—Hindust. *bāolá*.—Gal. *baban baú*.[2]

?**Bazar** (a permanent market or street of shops). Mal. (*bazar*, according to Bikkers), Low Jav., Sund., Mad., Batt. *pásar*. — Mac. *pásarā*. — Bug. *pása*.—Tet., Gal. *básar*.

"From Persian *bāzār*, a permanent market or street of shops. The word has spread westward into Arabic, Turkish, and, in special senses, into European languages, and eastward into India, where it has generally been adopted into the vernaculars." *Hobson-Jobson*.

But Dr. Heyligers says that in the Malayan languages it was probably introduced by the Portuguese, who might have received it from the people of the Levant or from the Moors of the Iberic peninsula, "because it is not at all probable that before that time Persia had commercial relations with the Far East". But the Arabs and the Indians had such relations, and they must have been then employing the word. Dr. Schuchardt's conjecture is that the Malays received it from Southern India. "The people of Kling (Kalinga, on the Coromandel Coast) carried on a big trade with the Archipelago before the arrival of the Europeans." Rigg.[1]

João de Sousa observes that *bazar* is an old word in Portuguese but little known, and Simão Botelho (1554) explains what the bazar of Chaul is: 'The rent of the **bazar**, that is of the shops where things

1 "The other day they dealt with the manner of directing **bateria** against the fortress." Bocarro, Dec. XIII, p. 643.

2 "A small **baull** valued at a thousand and five hundred reis." (1601) A. Tomás Pires, in *Jour. Geo. Soc. Lisb.*, 16th ser., p. 724.

1 The old Portuguese writers when speaking of Malacca frequently mention *Quelins*, *mercadores Quelins* ('Quelin merchants') and the *Quelin* quarter of the City.

[*Quelin* is the Portuguese transliteration of *Kĕling*, the name applied in the Malay countries to the Tamil traders settled in those parts. The Anglo-Indian form is 'Kling'. "The name is a form of Kalinga, a very ancient name for the region known as the "Northern Circars". *Hobson-Jobson*.]

are sold by retail."[1] [Dalgado (*Contribuições*, p. 88) is convinced that the word found its way from India to Portugal and was not introduced there by the Arabs.]

Bazaruco (a coin formerly current at Goa and on the Western Coast). Anglo-Ind. *budgrook*. In the Indo-Port. dialect of Bombay *budruc* signifies 'money in general'.[2]

The derivation of the word is uncertain. See *Hobson-Jobson*.

[Linschoten (Hak. Soc., Vol. II, p. 143) says: "Bezar in the Indian speech signifieth a market or place where all victuailes are kept and solde, and for the same cause they call the smallest money Bazarucos, as if they woulde say market money." Burnell, in a note, remarks that the origin of the name is obscure, but the statement in the text is certainly wrong. But Gray, in his *Pyrard* (Hak. Soc., Vol. II, p. 68), edited four years later, thinks that "*basaruco*" is perhaps connected with "bazār". Crooke is not quite exact in stating (*Hobson-Jobson*) that Burnell and Gray are of one view regarding the origin of this difficult word.]

[*Leaes* (the plural form of *leal*) were small copper coins struck at Goa under the orders of Afonso de Albuquerque. The name is the Port. *leal* ('loyal') and was given, according to Castanheda (*Historia*, III, ch. 4), owing to the love of loyalty of the Portuguese. The *leaes* are the same as the *bazarucos* which were current under the Mohammedan rule in Goa and on the Western coast. The subject of Portuguese coinage in India offers many difficulties. Even in 1554 António Nunes, who compiled a book on the coins

---

1 "The Indians even more corruptly call it (the Bezoar stone) *pedra de bazar* which means 'stone of the market-place or fair'; for bazar means a place where they sell anything." Garcia da Orta, Col. xlv. [ed. Markham, p. 364.]

2 "Twenty-four *leaes* make one *barguanim*, which is equal to twenty four **bazarucos**." Simão Botelho, p. 46.

"The Governor ordered **bazaruqos** to be coined in Cochin, as they were in Goa, and also ordered that they should be current at the rate of fifty **bazarucos** for one *tanga*." Gaspar Correia, IV, p. 337.

and weights of India (*Lyvro dos Pesos da Ymdia e asi Medidas e Moedas*), says that monies exhibit such variations that it is impossible to write anything certain about them. To have an approximate idea of the coins mentioned either in the text or the citations, it will be useful to know that in the early sixteenth century, for purposes of account, a *tanga branca*, equivalent to 120 reis, was divided into 4 *barganins*, and each *barganim* into 24 *leaes*, and each *pardao* into 5 *tangas*. For *barganim* see *Hobson-Jobson, s. v.* bargany].

Beatilha (the name of a kind of muslin). Anglo-Ind. *betteela, beatelle.*—Mal. *bitila.*[1]

[Yule thinks that the Sp. or Port. *beatilla* or *beatilha*, 'a veil', is derived, according to Cobarruvias, from "certain *beatas*, who invented or used the like". *Beata* is a *religieuse*. Compare the modern English use of 'nun's veiling'. Crooke quotes from the *Madras Admin. Man. Gloss.* p. 233 to show that *beatilha* is the same as what is known at present under the name of 'organdi'.]

Bêbado (a drunkard). Konk. *bebdó*; vern. terms *sarekár* (which likewise signifies 'a liquor-seller'), *saró piyetaló, saró-lāglaló*, and similar others. *Bebdúl*, a sot. *Bebdikáy, bebdepaṇ*, drunkenness.—Sinh. *bêbaduva, bêbaduvu, bêbadda, bêbayiyā*; vern. terms *bímatkaráyā, bónayā, viri. Bêbedukáma*, drunkenness.

Beijoim, benjoim (a kind of incense, derived from the resin of the *Styrax benzoin*, Dryander, in Sumatra). Anglo-Ind. *benzoin, benjamin*. Indo-Fr. *benjoin.*[1] [See *Hobson-*

---

[1] "From Chaul and Dabul they bring thither great store of *beirames* and **beatilhas**." Duarte Barbosa, p. 275. [Hak. Soc., ed. Longworth Dames, Vol. I, p. 129. *Beirame* is a very fine cotton stuff—calico—in various colours, formerly produced in India. It is the Pers. *bairam, bairami.*]

"Very finely woven pieces of **beatilha** from Bengal." António Tenreiro, *Itinerario*, ch. xvii.

"There are other kinds of fabrics which are made near the suburbs of Masulipatan in the country of the King of Golconda, and these pieces are called **Betilles**." Tavernier, *Voyages* (1676), v, p. 201.

[1] "There is here much lac, and **beijoim** of two kinds, white and black." *Roteiro da Viagem de Vasco da Gama*, ed. 1838, p. 112.

"In the inland country **beijoim** is

Jobson s. v. benjamin. Yule says that it got from the Arab traders the name *lubān-Jāwī*, i.e., 'Java frankincense', corrupted in the Middle ages into the various European forms extant. According to D. G. Dalgado (*Classificação Botanica*, p. 5), Garcia da Orta was the first European to describe correctly the origin of this incense. He distinguishes three varieties of it: *amendoado* or that filled with sort of white almonds, which was considered very good; *preto* or black, which was less valuable; and the third, *beijoim de boninas* or 'flowery benzoin' (see note to citation below), which was worth ten times as much as the others. Their present trade names are respectively: Siam, Sumatra and Penang benzoin.]

found; it is the resin of a tree which the Moors call *Lobam*." Duarte Barbosa, p. 369. [Hak. Soc., ed. Longworth Dames, Vol. II, p. 164. *Lobam* is for *luban*, Pers. for 'frankincense.']

"The sweet-smelling **beijoim** which our men because of its sweet smell call **beijoim de boninas**." João de Barros, Dec. III, iii, 3 [*Bonina* in Port. is the name of a little and delicate flower. See cit. from da Orta above.]

Bem-ensinado (*adj.*, 'well-brought up') Mal. *bem-ensinado* (Haex). Cf. *mal-ensinado.*

Bem pode (ser.) (*adv.*, perhaps; might well be). Mal. *ben pode* (Haex).

Bênção (blessing). Konk. *bemsáṁv* (in use among the Christians); vern. terms *āśirvád*, *āśirvatsan.*—Beng. *bemsámv.*—Tet. *bénsa* (also in the sense of 'to bless'); vern. terms *díak saráni.*—Gal. *bensã*; vern. term *lálan.*

Bentinho (scapular). Konk. *bentín.*—Tet., Gal. *bentinh.*

Benzer (to bless). Konk, *benhár-karuṅk. Benhar* is also used as an adjective in the sense of 'blessed'.—Tam *venjan-pradu.*

Beringela (*bot.*, *Solanum Melongena*, L., 'the egg-plant'). Hindust. *berinjal*; vern. terms *bhaṇṭá, baigan, baingan.*—Anglo-Ind. *brinjaul.*—Mal. *berinjal*; | vern. term *térong.* | —Tet., Gal. *beringela*; vern. term *bumáran, pumáran.* [1]

[1] "To fetch more rice and beans cooked with **beringellas.**" Fernão Pinto, ch. cxix.

"There are (in Angola) cucumbers different from those of that place, but very good, and pumpkins and *mangus-*

The word is originally Sanskrit (*bhaṇṭāki*), brought to the Spanish Peninsula by the Arabs and carried by the Portuguese, with the vegetable from India, to Malacca. See *Hobson-Jobson*.

[Yule says that probably there is no word of the kind which has undergone such extraordinary variety of modifications, whilst retaining the same meaning, as this. "The Skt. is *bhaṇṭākī*, H. *bhāṇṭā*, *baigan*, *baingan*, P. *badingān*, *badilgān*, Ar. *badinjān*, Span. *alberengena*, *berengena*, Port. *beringela*, *bringiela*, **bringella**, Low Latin *melangolus*, *merangolus*, Ital. *melangola*, *melanzana*, *mela insana*, French *aubergine* (from *alberengena*), *melongène*, *merangène*, and provincially *belingéne*, *albergaine*, *albergine*, *albergame* ......It looks as if the Skt. word were the original of all. The H. *baingan* again seems to have been modified from the P. *badingān*, [or, as Platt asserts, direct from the Skt. *vanga*, *vangana*, 'the plant of Bengal',] and *baingan* also through the Ar. to have been the parent of the Span. *berengena*, and so of all the European names except the English 'egg-plant.' "]

Bétele, bétel, betle, betere, betre (*bot.*, the betel; the leaf of the *Piper betel*). Anglo-Ind. *betel.*—Indo-Fr. *bétel.*

From the Malayal. *veṭṭila*. "All the names which are not Portuguese are Malabar (Malayalam). For instance **betre**, *chuna*, which is lime; *mayanato*, which means washerman; *patamar*, a courier." Garcia da Orta, Col. lix.[1] [ed. Markham, p. 477. The Malayal. *veṭṭila* is itself a compound of *veṛu*. 'simple or mere,' and *ila*, 'leaf,' i.e., 'simple or mere leaf.' The Neo-Aryan languages also use

---

goas which are like **Berengelas**." P. Baltasar Afonso (1585) in *Jour. Geo. Soc. Lisb.*, 4th. ser., p. 376. [We have not been able to identify *manguegoas*. Portuguese dictionaries do not mention it.]

1 "This betele we call *folio Indio*, ('the Indian leaf'); it is as broad as the leaf of the plantain herb." Duarte Barbosa, p. 286 [Hak. Soc., ed. Longworth Dames, Vol. I, p. 168. The 'plantain herb' referred to is the *Plantago lanceolata*, the common plantain weed, and not the Indian plantain or banana.]

the name *pān*, 'leaf,' from which is derived *pawn* used by modern Anglo-Indians, and *pan-vêl*, 'the plant or creeper.' Where, as in Goa, *pān* is also the name for 'tobacco' (see under *tabaco*), the one is distinguished from the other, when necessary, by the terms: *khāvunchéṁ pān*, 'the leaf for eating,' and *oḍhchéṁ pān*, 'the leaf for smoking.']

Bezoar (bezoar stone). Jap. *basara*.

Bicho do mar (sea-slug or *holothuria*). Anglo-Ind. *beech-de-mer*.—Indo-Fr. *biche-de-mer.*[1]

Bife (beef). Konk. *bíph*.—Tam., Tet., Gal. *bíphi*.

It is possible that the word in Konkani and Tamil was introduced directly from English.

Bilimbim (*bot.*, the fruit of *Averrhoa bilimbi*, L.). Konk. *bilambí*, *bimblí* (the tree); *bilambéṁ*, *bimbléṁ* (the fruit). —Mar. *bilambí*, *bimblá* (the tree); *bimleṁ* (the fruit).—Hindust. *bilambú*.—Malayal. *vilimbi*, | *vilumba* | —Tul. *bilimbi*, *bimbali*, *bimbili*, *bimbuli*.—Anglo-Ind. *bilimbi*, *blimbee*.[1]

From the Malay *balimbing*, very probably introduced into India by the Portuguese.

Binóculo (binocular). Konk. *binokl*.—Tet. *binókulu*.

Biscoito (biscuit). Konk. *biskúṭ*.—Mar. *biskúṭ*.—Hindi *viskuṭ*.—Hindust., Beng. *biskuṭ*.—Sinh. *biskóttu*, *viskóttu*, *viskottuva*.—Tam. *viskaṅ*.—Tel. *biskotthu*.—Tul. *biskoṭu*. —Nic. *biskut*.—Tet. *biskóitu*. —Jap. *bisukóto*, *bisuko*.

It is possible that the cerebral *ṭ* in some of the words is due to the influence of the English 'biscuit,' which does not, of course, mean that they owe their origin to English (see *batata*). Biscuit was introduced by the Portuguese at the very beginning of their

[1] "**Bicho de mar**, "Holuthuria," the name which the Portuguese gave it and by which it is known, though some English writers speak of it as "sea-slugs." Calado Crespo, *Cousas da China*, p. 232.

[1] "It (*carambola*, *q. v.*) is called in Kanarese and in Deccani *camariz*(?), and in Malay **balimba**." Garcia da Orta, Col. xii. [ed. Markham, p. 98. *Camariz* is probably a corruption of Sansk. *karmara* or of *khamrak*, the name by which the fruit is known in Upper India.]

contact with India. In the *Lembranças das Cousas da India* there appears, among the "prices fetched by goods in Diu and their actual cost," "a *maund* of **biscuouto** 7 *fedeas.*" *Maund* and *fedeas* are Indian terms. And Castanheda says that Afonso de Albuquerque arranged with Meliquiaz (Malik Ayaz) in Diu "to have **bizcoyto** made there, so long as there was wheat," and that he left behind "for making the **bizcoyto** a new convert to Christianity called Andrade."[1]

The Achinese have *meskut*, which must have come from English, because Langen says that the word is specially used of Huntley and Palmer's biscuits.

Bispo (bishop). Konk. *bísp.* [*Bism̃* is more current.]—Beng. *bispa.*—Tam., Kan., Tet., Gal. *bíspu.*

Bissexto (leap-year). Konk. *bisêst* (l. us. and only in Goa).—Bug. *biséselu.*

[1] "The admiral-ship began to make water from the stern (in 1505), and of this they were not aware, because the water entered in the **biscouto** storeroom." Gaspar Correia, I, p. 535.

Boa tarde (good afternoon). Beng. *bovás tardiyá.*—Tet. *bôa tárdi.* They also use *bôa nóiti* ('good night').

Bobo (buffoon). Konk. *bob*; also *bob dekaméd* (from *bobo de comedia*, 'the clown of the comedy'); vern. terms *bhāṇḍó, bhorpí.*—Tet., Gal. *bôbu*; vern. term *loré.*

Bocal (mouth-piece). Konk. *bukál*; vern. terms *kánṭh, tonḍ.*—? Mal. *bókar* (box, casket).—Ar. *buqál.*

Boceta (box, casket). Konk. *busét*; vern. terms *peṭúl, ḍabó.*—Mal. *boetta* (Haex), *bosséta.*[1]

Boi ('a palanquin bearer; one who carries an umbrella, a menial'). Anglo-Ind. *boy.*

Neo-Aryan languages *bhôi*, Dravidian *bôyi.*

In the sense of 'servant, or personal attendant,' 'boy' is English.

Bói is no longer in use in the Portuguese of Goa; the form that enjoys a currency is

[1] "Make search in their chests and **boetas** ('boxes')." Gaspar Correia, II, p. 299. "And they found in a **bueta** a book in which he had written many things about India." *Id.*, IV, p. 18.

"They were bringing, in a **boceta** of gold...." Lucena, Bk. II, ch. 23.

boiá, which is the vocative singular and the nominative plural in Konkani, *bhoyá*.[1]

[The Portuguese used *moco* ('boy') in the same way as the English did 'boy' for 'a servant.' As Yule and the *O. E. D.* remark, 'boy' came to be especially used for 'slave-boy,' and was applied to slaves of any age. "In 'Pigeon English' also 'servant' is *Boy*, whilst 'boy' in our ordinary sense is discriminated as '*smallo-boy*!'"]

Boia (buoy). Guj. *bôyu bôyuṁ*.—L.-Hindust. *boyá*.—Beng. *bayá*.—Mal. *bóya*.[2]

Boião (pot, generally, of clay or porcelain). Konk. *buyáṁv*; vern. term *barṇí*.—Hindust. *boyam*.—Beng., Ass. *bhoyám*. Sinh. *bujāma*.—Tul. *biyam, bíyamu*.—Khas. *buiam*. — ?Mal., Day. *búyong*.

The Portuguese dictionary, *Contemporaneo*, and also that of Cândido de Figueiredo derive *boião* from *bojo* ('belly, swell, paunch'). Gonçalves Viana, relying on a passage of Diogo do Couto, cited by Morais,[1] regards the term as originally Asiatic, belonging either to Malay or some of the monosyllabic languages of Indo-China. Fernão Pinto employs the word without explaining it: "Satins, damasks, and three big-sized **boyões** containing musk" (Ch. 55). Whatever be the origin of the word, there can be no doubt that in India the term was introduced by the Portuguese.

Bola (a ball). Konk. *ból*;

---

1 "They hired for work, by means of tickets, almost all the **boias** in the market square." *O Ultramar*, of 15th July, 1912.

"Shaded by *sombreiros* (*q. v.*), which are carried by men whom they call **boys**." Castanheda, I, ch. 16.

"And the said captain has three **bóys** for carrying water, and one umbrella **boy**." Simão Botelho, p. 206.

"And there are men who carry this umbrella so dexterously to ward off the sun, that even though their master should go on his horse at a trot, the sun does not touch any part of his body, and such men are called in India **boy**." João de Barros, Dec. III, x, 9.

2 "Untied the cable of the **boya**." Diogo do Couto, Dec. VIII, i, 8.

1 "In a **boião** from Pegu rice was cooked." [This is the same as what at one time was known as *martaban*, or Pegu jar, a glazed pottery famous all over the East and exported from Martaban. See *Hobson-Jobson s. v.* martaban, and Barbosa, ed. Longworth Dames, Vol. II, p. 158*n*.]

vern. terms *guḷó, cheṇḍú.*—Sinh. *bólaya*; vern. terms *golaya, panduva, tandukaya.*—Mal., Sund., Jav., Mad., *bóla*. *Meja-bola* (lit. 'a table of balls'), a billiard table.—Malag. *bolina*.

Bolacha (sweet-biscuit) Konk. *bulách* (more in use is *biskut*).—Tet. *bolacha*.

Bolina (*naut*., bow-line). L.-Hindust. *bulin*. *Bulin ká kunhiyán* or *kunhyá* (=Port. *cunha*, 'wedge'), cringle. *Bulin ká pám* or *paó*, bridle of the bow-line.—Mal. *bulín*.

Bolinho (a small cake). Konk. *bolính* (in use among the Christians).—Beng. *bolinos*, small cakes which are blessed and distributed on the feast-day of St. Nicholas Tolentine in the Portuguese Churches in Bengal.

Bôlo (cake). Konk. *ból*.—Tam., Mac., Tet., Gal. *bólu*.—? Ach. *bói*—Jap. *bóru*.[1]

Bôlsa ('purse'). Konk. *bóls, bolas*.—Mal. *bolsa* (Haex).—Tet., Gal. *bolsa*.

In the ecclesiastical sense of 'burse for the corporal,' it is used in different other languages.

Bomba ('a water-pump'). Konk. *bómb*.—Mar. *bamb*.—Guj. *bamb, bambó*.—L.-Hindust. *bambá, bumbá*.—Beng. *bomá* (by assimilation).—Sinh. *bómbaya*.—Tel. *bombásu, bombása* (from *bombas*, the pl. of *bomba*).—Kan. *bámbu*.—Anglo-Ind. *bumba*.—Mal., Tet., Gal. *bomba*.[1]

In *pomba*, which is another Malayan form, it appears that there is the influence of the Dutch *pomp* or the English 'pump.' Macassar has *pompa*, which Matthes derives from Dutch.

Bomba ('bomb-shell'). Konk. *bómb*; vern. term *kulpí-guló*.—Hindust. *bam ká gulá* (lit. 'shot of the bomb').—Ass. *boma-gola* (lit. 'bomb-shot').—Mac. *bong*, which Matthes derives from the Dutch *bom*.—Tet., Gal. *bomba*.—? Malag. *bomba, bumba*.[2]

---

[1] Two **bolos** of millet and *nachiniṁ* to each person. Diogo do Couto, Dec. V, vii, 9. [*Nachiniṁ* is a very tiny cereal, *Eleusine Coracana*.]

[1] "They rather found every time that the water was increasing because neither **bombas** nor barrels could exhaust it." Diogo do Couto, Dec. VII, v, 2.

[2] "The rest passing through those

Bom dia (good day). Konk. *boṁ dí* (l. us.).—Beng. *Devus boms diyá.* Also *Devus boms nouti* ('good night').—Tet. *bom dia.*

Bombardeiro (bombardier). Mal. *bombardero* (Haex).

Boné (cap, also the cap of an infantry soldier). Konk. *bonéṁ* (sometimes used of 'a hat').—Gal. *boné.*

Boneca (a doll). Sinh. *bônikka*; vern. term *ṛeka-ḍaya.*—Mal. *bonéka, boníka.*—Sund. *bonéka.*—Jav. *bonékô.*—Tet., Gal. *bonéka*; vern. term *babata.*

Bonito (a species of the tunny fish, *Thynnus pelamys*, Day). Anglo-Ind. *bonito.*—Indo-Fr. *bonite.*[1]

clouds of great shot, and arrows, and the flames of **bombas**" Diogo do Couto, Dec VII, ii, 9.

1 "They used to store dry fish which they call *moxama*, which is the loin of the **bonitos** which they dry in the sun, because in the Maldive Islands there is no salt." Gaspar Correa, p. 341.

"From the saw-fishes and **bonitos** which are caught on this coast, the King of Ormuz derives a big revenue." *Id.*, I, p. 792.

"There were also big ones, such as **bonitos** and *albacoras.*" Pyrard *Viagem*, I, p. 8. [Hak. Soc. Vol. I, p. 9.]

Fr. João de Sousa derives it from the Ar. *bainito*, which appears to be the Portuguese adjective *bonito* ('delicious') used as a noun.

Bonzo ('a Buddhist priest in Japan or in China').—Anglo-Ind., Indo-Fr. *bonze.*[1]

The word is of Japanese origin, *bózu* or *bónzu*, first mentioned by Jorge Álvares, and, a little after, by St. Francis Xavier in his letters. It appears that *bónzu* is traceable to the Sanskrit *vandya*, 'venerable', applied to the Buddhist clergy in Nepali, in the form *bandhya*, and in

["From the stomach of the great sperm whales bonitos and albicores have been taken." *Illustrated London News*, Nov. 26, 1927, p. 948.]

1 "Three **Bonzos** who were there (they are their priests)." Fernão Pinto, ch. xc.

"They (the Emperors of Japan) confirm their **Bonzos**, who are the chiefs of their religion. Diogo do Couto, Dec. V, viii, 12.

"**Bonzos** is the name common to the ministers who are appointed to the worship of the gods *Camis.*" Lucena, VII, ch. 8. [*Camis* is the plural form of the Japanese *Kami*, the name of the divinities of the Shinto religion; these are illustrious men deified whose number is said to total about eight millions]

Tibetan in that of *bandhe* or *bande*. See *talapão*.[1]

? **Bórax** (borax). Guj. *borás*.

Bordo (board; ship's side). Konk., Mar. *boḍad*; vern. term *báṇ*.—Guj. *buḍḍu*.—L.-Hindust. *būrdú*.—Tel. *boḍa*.—Tul. *bórdu*.—Mal. *bórdo*, *bórdu*. Mac. *boroló*, *baroló*.—Bug. *baraló*.

Borla (tassel on a biretta or cap). Konk. *bórl*; vern. term *goṇḍó*.—Tet *borla*.

Bôrra ('lees of wine'). Konk. *bôrr*; vern. term *múr*, *rôḍ*.—Sinh. *bora*; vern. term *roḍi*, *kẹlata*.

Sinhalese has no double *r*. Cf. *burro*, *fôrro*.

Bota (boot). Konk. *bót*.—Tet. *bota*.

Bota-fora (the act of launching a vessel; used familiarly also of bidding farewell to a traveller by accompanying him up to the place of departure). Mal. *botafóra*, *botapóra*, *batapóra*, coin to go into a money-box.

[1] "From Japan the Portuguese brought with them the following names:—*biombo* (*bióbu* or *biómbu*), screen, *bonzo* (*bóuzu* or *bônzu*), a religious person." Gonçalves Viana, *Palestras Filológicas*.

Botão (button). Konk. *butáṁv*.—Mar. *butāvéṁ*; vern. term *guṇḍí*.—Hindust. *bótám*; vern. term *tukmá*—Beng. *botam*.—Sinh. *bottama*.—Tam. *bótan*.—Tel. *butaum*, *bottam*.—Gar. *butam*.—Khas. *budam*.—Mal. *bútan*, *bótam*; vern. term *kanching*.—Tet., Gal. *butã*.—Jap. *bútan*, *bótan*. *Hazari-bútan*, an ornamental button.

Hepburn derives the Japanese *bótan* from the English 'button.' *Botton*, another Sinhalese form, betrays its English origin.

? **Bote** (boat). Konk., Mar. *bôt*.—Siam *bote*.—Mal. *bot*.

In Konkani, as in Marathi, *ág-bôt* (lit. 'fire-vessel') signifies 'a steamship.' The cerebral *ṭ* leads one to suspect that the original of the word is the English 'boat,' pronounced in the same way as the Port. *bote*. As Malay and Siamese have no cerebral *ṭ*, it is also possible that *bote* and *bot* are derived from the same English source.

Bóto in Japanese has also the same origin, which is testified to by the expression *boto-reisu* = 'boat-race.'

? **Botelha** ('bottle'). Konk.

botl: vern. term *maḍtel*.—Hindi, Or. *botal*.—Hindust. *botal*, *bottal*.—Beng. *botal*, *botol*.—Punj. *bodal*.—Sinh. *bótale*, *bótalaya*.—Gar. *botal*.—Khas. *butol*.—Mal. *bótol*, *bótul*.—Batt., Sund., Bal. *botol*.—Mac. *bótelõ*.—Tet. *bótel*.—Gal. *bótir*.

It is not quite clear whether the source-word is the Portuguese *botelha* or the English 'bottle,' though, it is true, in none of the languages mentioned above there appears the *ṭ* cerebral, which corresponds to the English *t*. Matthes derives the Macassar word from *botelha*. Dutch has *bottel*, and African Arabic *botelya* and *butelya*.[1]

Bāṭli, in Marathi and Gujarati, is evidently from English. Sindhi has *buti*. The Port. dialect of Macau has *botle*, and that of Ceylon, *botle*, *botel*, and *bottal*. In Kanarese, *baṭṭalu* signifies 'a cup, a small vessel,' and is regarded as a vernacular term by W. Reeve. The Persian *butri* is, without doubt, a corruption of 'bottle.'[2]

[1] The difficulty is to ascertain whether the word *botelha* was used in Portugal in the 16th and 17th centuries.

[2] "Three **botelhas** of Venetian glass valued at three *tostoes*" (1613) A. Tómas Pires, *Materiaes*, etc., in *Jour. Geo. Soc. Lisb.*, 16th ser., p. 746. [A *tostão* was a Port. silver coin valued at six pence three farthings sterling.]

Botica (a retail shop). Konk. *butik* (us. in the sense of an 'apothecary's shop').—Anglo-Ind. *boutique* (a common word in Madras and Ceylon for a small shop, or booth).[1]

Botiqueiro (a shop or stall-keeper). Anglo-Ind. *botickeer*. The Konk. *butkár* is a corruption of *boticario*, 'apothecary.'

Botiqueiro is no longer used in Portugal but is current in the Indo-Portuguese dialects in the sense of 'a stall-holder or shop-keeper.'[2] See Bluteau.

Bouba (buboe). Mal. *boba* (Haex).—Tet., Gal. *bôba*.

Braça (a measure of extent;

[1] "And the revenue from the other **buticas**, where are sold silks, camlets, cloth from Portugal, porcelain, and other knick-knacks" Simão Botelho, p. 51.

"The people of the land used to fit up **boticas**, in which they used to sell food-stuffs in great plenty" Gaspar Correia, I, p. 624.

[2] "The **botiqueiros** will not keep their shops open on feast-days, unless after the mass of the terce." Decree of the Council of Goa in 1567.

"Also a **botiqueiro** called Lounddó was arrested." *O Ultramar*, 12th February, 1912.

naut., a fathom). Konk., L.-Hindust. *brás, barás.*[1]

[In Guj. and Mar. *brás*, 'a measure for a heap of stones,' is from the same source. In both these languages the word is also used to denote one hundred cubic feet. In Goa a *brás* is a little over fifty cubic feet or, to be very exact, fifty-six and a quarter cubic feet.]

Braçal ('a species of bracelet'). Konk. *barsál.*—Sinh. *barasel̤.*

In Konk. *bar–* for *bra–* is normal.

[**Branco** (*adj.*, white; in the pl. form, *Brancos* is used of 'whites' or 'Europeans'). Anglo-Ind. *blanks.*[2]]

Brandal (*naut.*, swifters, shrouds). L.-Hindust. *brándal, brāndál, barándal, baranda.*

Brava (the palmyra tree or *Borassus flabellifer*). Anglo-Ind. *brab* (us. as a noun). Cf. *amargosa* and *pintado.*

[*Bravo, adj.*, in Port. means 'wild,' and the Portuguese spoke of this palm as 'wild,' whence the English corruption.]

? **Bruça** ('clothes-brush'). Konk. *burús.*—Guj. *barás.*—Malayal. *buruss.*— | Tel. *barusu* | .—Gar. *burus.*—Mal. *brús, berus.*—Malag. *burusi.*

It appears that the English 'brush' ought to be accepted as the original of these words. The dictionary of Cândido de Figueiredo mentions *bruça* as a word no longer in use and synonymous with *brossa* ('brush'). Other dictionary-writers do not mention it. The Dutch at the Cape have *bras.*

Bucha ('cork'). Mar. *búz.*—Guj., L.-Hindust. *búch.*—Sindh. *bunji*; vern. term *ḍaṭo.*—Punj. *bujá, bujjá, bujjí*; vern. term *gaṭṭá.*—Malayal. *burchcha.*—Tul. *búchi, búchu.*—? Bur. *bú-zo.*

Búfalo (buffalo). Anglo-Ind. *buffalo.*[1]

---

[1] "The piece of wall was thirty **braças** long." Diogo do Couto, Dec. VI, viii, 7.

[2] [1718.—The Heathens.... too shy to venture into the churches of the **Blanks** (so they call the Christians), since these were generally adorned with fine cloths and all manner of proud apparel."—Ziegenbalg and Plutscho, *Propagation of the Gospel*, etc. Pt. I., 3rd ed., p. 70. cit. in *Hobson-Jobson, s. v.* blanks.]

[1] "The quilted coats (*laudeis*) were furnished with iron plates and **bufaro** horn." Damião de Góis, *Chronica del-Rey D. Manuel*, II, 39. [*Laudel*,

[The form most used by the early Portuguese writers is *bufara*. It is interesting to note that at an early period of the English connection with India the name 'buffalo' was given erroneously to the common Indian ox and the true Indian domestic buffalo was spoken of as the 'water buffalo.' See *Hobson-Jobson*.]

Bula (bull, a papal edict). Konk. *búl*.—Tet., Gal. *bula*.

Bule (tea-pot). Konk. *búl*. —Sinh. *búliya*.—Tam. *bulei*.— Tet. *búli*; vern. term *dardón*.

The origin of the Portuguese word is not a matter of certainty. Gonçalves Viana derives it from the Malay *buli*, 'flask,' or 'small bottle.' Rigg says that *búli-búli* in Sundanese is "a covered cup ordinarily used to keep oil." In Konkani, *bul* also stands for a porcelain snuff-box shaped like a small flask.[1]

Buraco (a hole). Konk. *burák*; vern. terms *bíḷ*, *biḷúk*, *vivar*, *bhoṅk*, *bhontó*, *dompḷó*.— Mar., Guj., *burákh*.—Kan. *biráku*, *biríku*, *birúku*.

The reason why the Portuguese word was adopted is not known. Persian and Hindustani have *surakh* with the same meaning; I do not know whether it has any etymological relation with the Portuguese *buraco*. The Portuguese dictionary, *Contemporaneo*, derives it from the Latin *foraculum*, and Cândido de Figueiredo from High German *bora*. Gonçalves Viana is of the opinion that the former suggestion is the more probable one and, in support of his view, refers to *furaco* met with in some of the Portuguese dialects.

---

pl. *laudeis*, in the sense of 'quilted coat' is a Portuguese word and used by them before their arrival in India. It is supposed to be the Latin *lodix*. Sewell's suggestion (*A Forgotten Empire*, pp. 268 and 276) that it is the Kanarese *lodu*, 'a stuffed cloth or cushion,' is without foundation.]

["There is also much cattle, **bufaras**, cows, bulls, and other live stock." *Chronica de Bisnaga*, p. 82.]

["They brought for sale some big cuts of **bufaros** and other game, with which all that land is plentifully provided." Manuel Perestrelo, *Hist. Tragico-maritima*, I, p. 116.]

[1] "It was a sort of mania in Siam to collect **bules**, just as in other parts they collect stamps, monograms, etc." H. Prostes, in *Jour. Geo. Soc. Lisb.*, 4th. ser., p. 399.

? **Burrico** (ass-colt). Malag. *borika, boriki.*

Burro (an ass). Konk. *búṛr* (us. in a fig. sense; in the ordinary sense, *gadhuṁ*); vern. term *gaddhá.*—Sinh. *búruva, búrẹva ;* vern. terms *koṭaluvá, koṭalivá, garddabhayá. Búrẹ* is used in the sense of 'asinine.'

Why should the Portuguese word have found an entry into Sinhalese? Perhaps owing to its frequent use in the figurative sense, which was also the very reason for its introduction into Konkani.

C

? **Cá** (abbreviated form of *aqui*, here). Mal. *ca* (Haex).

Cabaia (a long tunic with wide sleeves used in the East). Konk., Tam. *kabáy* (a kind of tunic).—Mar. *kabáy, kabāī.*—Sinh. *kabáya* (coat).—Mal., Sund., Jav., Tet., Gal. *kabáya.*—Mac., Bug. *kobáyā.* In the Indo-Portuguese dialect of Ceylon *cabaya, cabai, cuobai* are used in the sense of 'a coat.'[1]

From the Pers.-Ar. *qabá* (adopted in Hindustani), 'a vesture,' introduced into India by the Portuguese, according to Yule and Burnell. Matthes derives it from the Persian *qabay.*[1]

[1] "He (the Sultan of Moçambique) used to be wrapped up in a **cabaia** of white cotton cloth, which is a tight fitting garment." Castanheda, Bk I, ch. 6

"A garment which they call **cabaya,** which the Moors commonly use in those parts; it has long sleeves, is provided with a cincture, and is open in front with one flap over another in the manner of the dress of the Venetians." João de Barros, Dec. II, iv. 2.

"**Cabaya** is a garment such as the *pelote* is among us." Gaspar Correia, I, p. 14. [*Pelote* in Portuguese is the name of a robe with broad flaps, used in former times.]

"They brought to the King a costly **cabaya,** which he with his own hands put on the Governor, and this was the highest honour which he could bestow on him according to their usages." *Id.*, III, p. 620.

"The **Kabaia** is a kind of white dressing-gown made of cambric and furnished with lace. The complete outfit of a Malay woman is called *Sarang-Kabaia.*" Albert Osório de Castro, p. 145.

[1] In an analogous meaning the word *quimão*, from the Japanese *kimono,* was used formerly in Konkani, but at the present day the term is used only of a bodice worn by girls. "Dressed in a purple *quimão* in the manner of a long loose robe, embroidered with pearls." Fernão Pinto, ch. cxxii.

[Gray in his notes to *Pyrard* (Hak. Soc. Vol. I, 372) seems to think that quotations from Correa, and Albuquerque (*Commentaries*) point to the existence of *cabaia* in Eastern parlance prior to the Portuguese arrival, and to its being previously unknown to the Portuguese. "*Cabaya* is a garment such as a *pelote* is with us" (Correa, in Stanley's *Three Voyages*, p. 132); "*Cabayas*, or native dresses of silk" (Alb., *Comm.*, IV, 95). He also observes that "*Kabáya* is still a common word in Ceylon for a coat or jacket, worn by a European or native."]

Cabeça (the head of a top). Mal. *kembesa.*—Mol. *cabessa* (=*kabesa*), used of the best quality of camphor. See *barriga.*

Cabide (a clothes-rack). Konk. *kābíd.*, vern. term *ôṇ*, *dānḍí.*—Tet., Gal. *kabídi.*

Cabo (in the sense of 'hilt or handle'). Malayal. *kábu;* vern. term *píḍi.*

[*Cabo* in Portuguese also means 'a corporal in the army.'] As a military title, the term is employed in Konkani, Teto, and Galoli.

Cabouco (in the sense of 'laterite'). Sinh. *kabuka.*—Anglo-Ind. *cabook.*

["Mr. Fergusson says that the Ceylon term *cabook* is a corruption of the Port. *pedras de cavouco*, 'quarry-stones,' the last word being by a misapprehension applied to the stones themselves." Crooke in *Hobson-Jobson*, *s.v.* cabook. The ordinary meaning of *cabouco* in Port. is 'ditch, quarry.']

In Konkani *konker* is used in the same sense as the Port. *cabouqueiro*, 'a quarryman.'

Caboz (a kind of fish belonging to the order *Gobius*). Mal. *kabos* (Schuchardt).[1]

Cabra (she-goat). Nic. *kápre*, sheep. *Koán-kápre*, lamb. *Ok-kápre*, the fleece of the sheep. *Anha-kápre*, sheep's mutton.

The Nicobarese very likely became acquainted with the sheep (and perhaps the goat) through the Portuguese, who

1 ["Owing to the inundations of rivers two other species are carried across to these lands, but these are not so common as the Gobius, in Malay *Cabus*." Rumphius, *Herb. Amboinense*, VIII, ch. 30].

also gave the name *Cabra* to one of the small islands, which in the vernacular is called *Komváña.* In Indo-Port. *cabra* includes also 'sheep.' The Nicobarese *mé*, 'she-goat,' is onomatopoetic and, perhaps, of recent date.

Caçar (to hunt). Mal. *kajar.*

In Konkani the form *kás* is used in the sense of 'game.' *Kas maruṅk* [lit. 'game to kill'] is 'to go out in pursuit of game.'

Caçarola (casserole; a heat-proof earthenware vessel). Mal. *kasrol* (Marre).

Cacau (cacao). Konk. *kākáv.*—Tet., Gal. *kakau.*

Cadeira (chair). Konk. *kadēr* (l. us.), *kadêl*; vern. terms are *kurśi*, *chaváy*, as in Marathi, but little used.—Beng. *kaderá*, *kadārá.*—Sindh. *kadela*, *gadela.*—Tam. *kadêra* (l. us.); vern. term *píḍam.*—Malayal. *kasêla.*—Mal., Mac., Bug. *kadéra.*—Nic. *katére. Katére-ol-lál*, sofa.—Tet., Gal. *kadeira.*

Cadernal (*naut.*, luff-tackle). L.-Hindust. *katarnál.*

? Café (coffee). Konk. *kāphó* (plant and the whole berry; pl. *kāphé*); *kāphí* ('coffee ground or prepared into a beverage').—Mar., Guj., Or. *kāphí.*—Beng. Ass. *káphi.*—Sinh. *kópi.*—Tam. *káppi*, *kóppi.*—Malayal. *kāppi*, *kāppi-kkuru.*—Tel. *kápi.*—Kan., Tul. *káphi.*—Gar. *kapi.*—Bur. *kap-phe.*—Khas. *kaphi.*—Kamb. *cafê.*—Siam. *kafē*, *khåofe.*—Ann., Tonk. *cà-phe.*—Mal., Sund., Mac., Bug. *kópi.*—Day. *kúpi.*—Tet., Gal., Malag. *kafé.*— | Chin. *kiá-fe* |.

It is not known by what way the term found its way into India. The first syllable of the Indian term for it (*ka-*) is identical with that of the Portuguese, and the second (*-phi* or *-pi*) with that of the English or Dutch (*coffee*, *koffij*). But Turkish also has *kaphe. Hobson-Jobson* gives no citation from any early Portuguese writer on this point. The use of coffee had already been introduced into Arabia in the fifteenth century.

["The history of the introduction of coffee into India is very obscure. Most writers agree that it was brought to Mysore some two centuries ago by a Muhammadan pilgrim named Baba Budan, who, on his return from Mecca, brought seven seeds with him. This tradition is so universally believed in, by the inhabitants of the greater part of South India, that there seems every chance of its being founded on fact. ....In Ceylon it is believed coffee was introduced by the Arabs prior to the Portuguese invasion of that island." Watt, *The Commercial Products of India*, p. 367.]

But in 1782 Fr. Clemente da Ressurreição, in his *Treatise on the Agriculture* (of Goa),[1] says: "There is another plant which could yield a safe and growing income to the owner of a plantation (provided its cultivation was increased), and it is the **café** (the coffee plant) because of the high esteem and relish in which it is held among the European and Muslim peoples. From its berry is prepared a very exquisite beverage, stimulating, promoting digestion, and nutritive, though it is attended with evil effects to the nerves if taken in excess; these injurious effects are mitigated by mixing milk with it, as is done in Europe and all over Turkey."

The term is derived generally from the Arabic *qahua*, which originally meant 'wine' and which was afterwards employed to denote the 'infusion of coffee.' *Bunn*, in Arabic, is the name given to the plant and the berry. Both these terms have been adopted by some of the Indian languages.

It is, nevertheless, not unlikely that the real origin of the word is to be found in the geographical name *Kaffa*, in Abyssinia, which is the primitive habitat of the plant.

[Sir George Watt (*The Commercial Products of India*), however, says: "The names given to the plant, its fruits.. ....are mostly derived from either of two words: "*kahwah*," an Arabic term that originally denoted "wine," and "*bun*," the Abyssinian name for the coffee plant or its beans. From these we have *cahua*, *kawa*, *chaube*, *kapi*, *câve*, *kava*, *café*, coffee, and *caféier*; also *boun*, *bun*, *ban*,

[1] Published by Bernardo Francisco da Costa in his *Manual pratico do agricultor indiano*, Vol. II.

ben, bunu, buncha. The earliest Arabic writers, however, used the Abyssinian name by itself or in combination: thus Avicenna (11th century) calls it *buncho*, and Rhases *bunco*. It was by them viewed as a medicinal plant and one very possibly that came from Abyssinia, so that the appearance of the Arabic name *kahwah* may with safety be accepted as marking the progress into the final development as a beverage."]

Cafre (in the sense of 'negro'). Konk. *khāpri*. Beng. *kāphiri*. – – Ass.—*káphri*.—Tam., Malayal., Tel. *káppiri*. —Kan. *káphri*.— Tul. *kápri, kapiri* — Anglo-Ind. *caffre, caffer, caffree*,—Bur. *kap-pa-li*. —Mal. *kápri, káfris*. — Ach. *kafíri*. — Day. *kápir*. | *Nona kápri* is *Anona reticulata*. |

In Konkani, *khāpurḍó* (a diminutive form) is 'a little negro'; *khāparlẽm* (neut.), 'a negress,' and, *khāparpaṇ*, 'coarseness, barbarousness.' In Indo-Portuguese *cafrona* means 'a negress'.

The word is derived from the Arabic *káfir*, 'infidel, unbeliever.' In some of the languages this sense is retained.[1] With regard to the *kh* aspirate in Konkani, cf. *camisa, cruz*.

Cairel (narrow gold lace). Malayal. *karal*.

Cairo (the fibre of the coconut husk). Anglo-Ind. *coir*.—Indo-Fr. *caire*.

[Yule seems to be of the opinion that the Anglo-Indian form *coir* was introduced by the English in the 18th century. Crooke refers to the *O.E.D.* which gives 'coire' in 1697; 'coir' in 1779. 'Coir' was less likely to have been used by the Portuguese because

[1] "Beyond this country lies the great kingdom of Benametapa which belongs to the Heathen whom the Moors call Cafres." Duarte Barbosa, p. 234. [Hak. Soc., ed. Longworth Dames, Vol. I, p. 9. The origin of Benametapa or Monomotapa is uncertain In some Bantu languages it means 'Lord of the Mountain.']

"And by another name which is common they also call them **Cafres**, which is to say people without law, a name which they give to every heathen idolater; this name of **Cafres** is applied among us to the many slaves which we have from this people." João de Barros, Dec. I, viii. 3.

"Among us, the **Cafres** are the Heathens from Cafraria." Fr. João da Sousa. ['Cafraria' is the land of the Cafres, or 'Kaffirs,' a very large tract in the southernmost part of Africa.]

coiro in their language is 'leather'. See *Hobson-Jobson*, *s.v.* coir.]

The word is the Malayal, *kāyāṟu*, 'rope made out of the fibre'.[1] [The fibre is called in Malayal. *jaggari.*]

Caixa (a coin).—Anglo-Ind. *cash.*[2]

The word is the Dravidian *kásu*, derived from the Sanskrit *karsha*, 'a weight of silver or gold'.[3] ["From the Tam. form *kāsu*, or perhaps from some Konkani form which we have not traced, the Portuguese seem to have made *caixa*, whence the English *cash.*" *Hobson-Jobson.*]

Caju (*bot., Anacardium Occidentale*). Konk. *kāzu ; kaz* (the name of the plant but, in certain parts, also of the fruit). *Kājel*, a spirit distilled from the juice of the fruit.—Mar. *kāzú* (plant, fruit, and nut); *kāzūgoḷá* (us. in the Konkan), fruit.—Guj. *káju*, *kájuṁ* (neut.; 'the sugared nut' is masc.)—Beng. *kājú.*—Sindh. *kházu*, *kházo*, the nut.—Sinh. *kaju*, *kajju ; kaju-geha*, the plant.—Tam. *káju-paḷam ; káju-maram*, the plant.—Malayal. *kaśu.*, *káśu-máṟu.*—Anglo-Ind. *cashew.*—Mal. *káju*, *gájus.* —Sund; *káju*; vern. term *jambu méde.*—Tet., Gal. *kajús*, *kaidú.*— | Chin. *kiá-tsú.* |

["The Tamil name (for *caju*) is, *e.g.*, Mundiri, referring to the form of the nut, and "kājū" is only found in Dravidian dialects (*e.g.*, Malayâlam) influenced by the Portuguese.

1 "From the first outside rind which covers it (the coco-nut) is made **cairo** ..after they have soaked, beaten and spun it in the manner of fibre from flax." João de Barros, Dec. III, iii, 7.

"The first outside rind is very woolly and from it is made **cairo**, so called by the Malabars (in Malayalam) and by us." Garcia da Orta, Col. xvi [ed. Markham, p. 141].

"From the outer rind of these coconuts, which they call **cairo**, ropes are made." Fr. João dos Santos, *Ethiopia Oriental*, I. p. 299.

2 According to António Nunes, one **caixa** of the Moluccas was worth 3/10 of a *rial* and that of Sunda, 3/5. [The *rial* is a Portuguese coin equal to $\frac{27}{100}$ *d.* The plural form of the word is *reis* and accounts were kept in Bombay in rupees and *reis* down at least to November 1834. Twenty five *reis* then made an anna. See *Hobson-Jobson*, *s.v* reas, rees.]

3 "It is a copper coin of the size of our *ceitijs*.... which they call **caixas**." João de Barros, Dec III, v, 5.

"They have the head shaved for only one copper coin which they call **caixa**." Gaspar Correia, IV. p. 301.

The Malays have a name ("Būwa frangi", Flax., p. 64), which shows that it is not indigenous in the Archipelago, though they also use "kaju". Burnell in *Linschoten* (Hak. Soc.), Vol. II, p. 27.

The evolution of a new form *cadju* in Anglo-Indian vocabulary is evidenced by the following passage taken from *The Times of India*, June 23, 1928: "The story of a leper living among the beasts of the jungle and subsisting entirely on fruit is being used to support the claim that the Cadju fruit (*Anacardium Occidentale*) is a cure for the disease."]

The suffix-*s* in Malay and in Teto and Galoli are due to the Portuguese plural form, *cajus*, as in *meias* ('socks'), *uvas* ('grapes'), *tiras* ('strips of cloth'), *apas* ('rice-cakes').

The word is Brazilian: *acaju*. The cashew-tree is one of the most useful plants introduced by the Portuguese into India and is now perfectly naturalised.[1]

[1] "Spirit distilled from cane and from caju has enormous sale in the crown lands." Caldas Xavier, in *Jour. Geo. Soc. Lisb.*, 2nd ser., p. 485.

[Garcia da Orta does not mention the tree in his *Colloquies* (1563), but Christoval Acosta does in his *Tractado* etc. (1578). Linschoten writing about 1590 speaks of them as being in great numbers all over India.]

Calabaça (calabash). Anglo-Ind. *calabash*, the dry rind of a gourd used as a bottle or float.

[The Portuguese word is itself derived from the Arabic *garah*, 'a gourd', and *aibasah*, 'dry'.]

Calafate (a caulker). Hindi *kālapatti*.—Hindust. *kalpatti*, *kalápatiyá*—Or. *kalāpātí*.—Beng. *kālāpātí*.—Sinh. *galapatti*(*-kara ṇavā*, 'to caulk').—Tam. *kalappar-radī*, to caulk;

See Conde de Ficalho in the *Colloquies* of Garcia da Orta, Vol. I, p. 67. [In the passage referred to above Conde de Ficalho expresses surprise that da Orta makes no mention of the *caju tree*, which, a few years later, was described by Acosta (1578) and by Linschoten. From this he concludes that the interval between the publication of the *Colloquies* (1563) and Acosta's *Tractado de las Drogas y Medecinas de las Indias Orientales* (1578) marks the period when the tree must have been introduced into India from America.]

kalapparradippal, a caulker.—Tel. *kalapati.*—Anglo-Ind. *calputtee.*—Ma. *kalépet*, | *kalpát.* | —Ar. *qālāfat*, *qalfat*, *qāllaf.*[1]

The Portuguese dictionary, *Contemporaneo*, derives the Portuguese word from the Italian *calafattare.* Fr. João de Sousa and Devic refer it to Arabic. Dozy and Jal have doubts about this derivation and prefer that from the Latin *calefacere.* Yule and Burnell favour the Arabic origin, but admit that the word in the Indian languages owes it origin to Portuguese.

[**Calaim** (tin). Anglo-Ind. *kalay.*—Indo-Fr. *calin.*[2]

The original is the Ar *qal'aī*, which has been adopted by the Indian languages, and which probably is related to the Malay *kālang*, the name for tin, and which, according to Yule, may have been the true origin of the word before us. Some Arab geographers derive the word from a place called *Qalah* or *Qaleh*, which was certainly somewhere about the coast of Malacca, which even to-day is famous for its tin-mines. In Malay *Nagri-Kālang*, 'Tin-Country,' is the ancient name for the State of Selangor. See *Hobson-Jobson*.

The old Portuguese chroniclers also give the name *calaim* to a coin made of tin current in Malacca.]

Calçado (*subst.*, foot-wear; boots). Konk. *kālsád.*—Mal., Ach., Batt., Sund., Jav. *kásut.* —Mac. *kásu.*—Ar. (popular) *kalsat*, socks (Simonet).[1]

---

1 "The Governor Jorge Cabral placed Dom João Lobo in charge of the **calafates.**" Diogo do Couto, Dec. VI, viii, 5.

2 ["Tin, which the people of the country call **Calem.**" Castanheda, III, 213.]

["The *baar* of **calaim** is in every respect like that of cinnamon." António Nunes, *Lyvro dos Pesos*, p. 6.]

["They hold in great esteem tin, or **Calaim**, and it is valued among them (the people of Madagascar) as much as silver, for women's ornaments." Diogo do Couto, Dec. VII, iv, 5, cited in *Glossario.*]

["Each **calaim** was worth, according to an appointed law, eleven *reis* and four *ceitils.*" *Commentaries of Afonso Dalbuquerque*, Hak. Soc., III, p. 78.]

["He (The Governor of Malacca) gave them (Portuguese prisoners) ten thousand **calains** worth of Cambayan stuffs." *Id*, p. 45. Birch, the translator of the *Commentaries*, erroneously remarks that "*Calaim* signifies a very fine kind of Indian copper."]

1 "By *kāsut* is meant the 'surtout'

Calção (in the sense of 'trousers'). Konk. *kālsáṁv*, *kalsáṁv*. *Moḷvéṁ kalsáṁv*, breeches or 'shorts'.—Sinh. *kalisama*, *kalasama*.—Tam. *kāl-chaṭṭei* (lit. 'puts on trousers').—Malayal. *kāl-chchaṭṭa*. —? Malag. *kalisanina* (perhaps from the Fr. *caleçon*).—Jap. *karusan*. In Galoli *kálsa*, trousers.[1]

Calção, properly speaking, signifies in Portuguese 'breeches,' but in Indo-Portuguese it is used in the sense of 'trousers'.

It appears that *kaus*, 'shoe', of the languages of the Malay Archipelago, is not derived from the Port. *calça* which formerly meant, according to Viterbo, 'sock or stocking',[2] nor from the Dutch *kous*, 'sock'. It makes its appearance already in the first quarter of the seventeenth century. "*Caous* (pronounced *kaus*), sock; *caous sa-paris*, a pair of socks" (Haex). Swettenham and Favre attribute it to an Arabic origin; but in Arabic there is no such word. Rigg says that in Sundanese *kaus* signifies, at the present day, 'sock' and admits it is from Dutch. The same is the opinion of Hardeland in respect of Dayak, and of Matthes with reference to the Macassar *káusu* and Bugui *káusu & koso*. Langen doubtfully gives '*kaus*' as corresponding to the Achinese *kaus*. It is quite possible that *kaus* is the abbreviation of *kásut*, from *calçado*, 'shoes', which in Macassar loses the *t*, or it may subsequently have felt the influence of Dutch.

Caldeirão (a boiler, a large kettle). Sing. *kaldérama*, *kaldarama*.

Caldo (broth). Konk. *káld*. —Beng. *kāldó* (in use among

of a Malay shoe, which is a kind of sandals or leather soles fastened by means of laces." Favre.

1 "Calsoens, hats, shoes, to be distributed there among the soldiers" Diogo de Couto, Dec. VI, vi. 6.

2 "One night with calça ('breeches') loaded with sand, they give him such calçadas ('basting'), that it is reported he died of it Document of 1458, quoted by Viterbo. [Linschoten (Hak. Soc. Vol. I, p. 195) describes how the Portingals "use long bagges full of sand, wherewith they will breake each others limmes, and make them lame." Burnell in a note to this says that "this is a common method of torture in S. India at the present time, and is originally Indian."]

the Christians).—Sinh. *kálduva.* —Mal., Sund., Jav., Mad. *káldu*, *káldo.*

Calibre (caliber, the diameter of the mouth of a gun). Bug., *lívarā.*

The first syllable is dropped as in *dílu*, which is from the Portuguese *codilho*, 'codille, a term in a game of cards'.

Cális (a chalice). Konk. *káls* —Beng., Tam., Tet., Gal. *kális.*—Ann. *calicê ;* vern. term *chén thánh* (lit. 'sacred cup'). —Jap. *karisu.*[1]

Calmaria (a calm at sea). L.-Hindust. *kalmariyá*, *karmariyá. Karmariyá paḍná*, to be becalmed.[2]

[**Calumba** (*Jateorhiza palmata*, Miers). Anglo-Ind. *columbo root*,[3] *calumba root.*

The plant is a native of East Africa and its roots are largely exported to India from Mozambique because of their medicinal properties. *Kalumba* is the name by which it is called by the natives in Africa. The *O.E.D.* derives it from Colombo, the capital of Ceylon, from a false notion that it was supplied from thence.]

Cama (a bed). Konk. *kám ;* vern. terms *báz*, *khāṭlém ; ānthrún-pāṅghrún*, *sêj.*—Mal. *camma* (Haex).—Tet., Gal. *kama ;* vern. term *phátik.*

Câmara (a room). Konk. *kámr*, *kámbr ;* in the sense of a 'room', the term is little used in Goa, but it is current in the sense of 'a municipality' (*câmara municipal*). There is a popular saying, *kāmbrāchyá kustár kalvantám nāchtát*, 'the dancing girls perform at the cost of the municipality',[which is another way of saying 'to enjoy at another's cost,' or, as it would be expressed in English, 'the municipality pays the piper, but some one else calls the tune.']—Hindi *kam'rá.*—Hindust. *kāmará*, *kamará*, *kamera*, *kam'ra* (more used). It also means 'a cabin in a ship'. *Khāne ka kamrá*, dining-room.—Or. *kam'rá.*—Sing. *kámaraya*, *kámarê.*—Tel. *kāmará*, *kāmerá*, *kamrá*, *kāmiri ; kamelá* ('the

---

[1] "Altar-stones, calices and other things." Diogo do Couto, Dec. VII, i, 2.

[2] "On the way met with many calmarias." Diogo do Couto, Dec. VI, ix, 4.

[3] [" Calumba, a root. . . . is an excellent remedy against tertian fever, stomach-ache. . . . ." Fra Paolino, *Viaggio* (1786), p. 363.]

round-top of a ship's mast').—Anglo-Ind. *cumra*.—Khas. *kam'ra*.—Mal. (*kámĕrá*, Wilkinson), Bat., Sund., Jav., Mad. *kámar*.—Bug. *kamáli*.[1]—Tet., Gal. *kámara*.— | Turk. *qámara*. | —Rab. *kamarón*.[2]

Dr. Hugo Schuchardt refuses to accept the Portuguese origin for the Mal. *kámar*, as also for *musik* ('music') and *pistol* ('pistol'), and prefers instead the Dutch *kamer*, *musiek*, *pistool*, as the originals of the Malay forms. He lays down that "the criterion for distinguishing one from the other is principally the termination which these words have in Malay: if it is vocalic, the immediate source of the word is Portuguese; if consonantal, then it is Dutch". And Gonçalves Viana observes that "these two laws to which Dr. Schuchardt refers are of the greatest importance".

It appears that the above criterion is not after all very safe, because there are other words the Portuguese origin of which is unquestioned which have a consonantal ending, that is, after losing the vowel termination of the parent word, as for example: *karpus* from Port. *carapuça* ('a kind of cap protecting one from cold'), *martil* from *martelo* ('a hammer'), *gargalet* from *gorgoleta* ('water-jug'), *bulin* from *bolina* ('bow-line'), *prum* from *prumo* ('a plummet').

In respect of *kamer* and *musik*, it may be said that the especial reason for the elimination of their last syllable is the necessity of getting rid of words accented on the ante-penultimate syllable, in view of the fact that the Malayo-Polynesian languages have no proparoxytones. If it can be established that *mármar* ('marble') is derived from the Port. *mármore*, then we have another instance in proof of our view. Perhaps, *almári* or *lamári* from the Port. *armario* ('cupboard'), obey the same law.[1]

Camarada (a comrade).

[1] Matthes derives this term from the Port. *cama* ('a bed'), and mentions the compound *kamáli—levuranna*, "*iemand's slaap-kamer*, bed-room."

[2] "Withdrawing with him to a camara, he spoke to him these words." Diogo do Couto, Dec. VII, i. 9.

[1] The Malayo-Portuguese dialect of Túgu has *cámber*.

Konk. *kāmbrád;* vern. terms *sāṅgāli, saṁvgaḍi, gaḍi.*—Tet. *kamarada;* vern. term *bêlu.* In the Portuguese dialect of Ceylon, *cambrado.*

Camisa (a shirt). Konk. *kamís, khamís.*—Mar. *kamíz, khamís.*—Guj. *khamis.*—Hindi *qamiz.*—Hindust. *qamis, qamij.* —Beng. *kamíj.*—Sinh. *kamíse, kamísaya, kamíseya* —Tam. *kamísei.*—Malayal. *kamís, kamísu, kammísu.*—Tel. *kamísu, kamsu.*—Kan. *kamísu.* —Tul. *kamísụ.*—Anglo-Ind. *cameeze.*—Gar. *kamij.*—Mal., Ach. *kamíja, kaméja.*—Sund., Day. *kaméja.*—Jav., Mad. *kaméjô.*—Tet., Gal. *kamiza.*— ? Ar., Pers. *qamís.*[1]

Loma kamísaya (lit. 'a woollen shirt'), a singlet or an undervest, in Sinhalese; in Konkani, *khamśi* is used of a 'child's frock'.

St. Jerome is the first European writer to mention *camisia* in *The Epistle to Fabiola.*[2] Càndido de Figueiredo derives the Port. vocable from "Low Latin *camisia*, the origin of which is uncertain". Fr. João de Sousa assigns to it an Arabic origin.[1] [Skeat derives *camisa* from Celt and says that the Arabic *qamiṣ* is from Latin. The *O.E.D.* is of the view that the Ar. *qamiṣ*, 'a tunic', is from the Lat. *camisia* of St. Jerome.]

The initial *q* of Hindi and Hindustani and, perhaps, the *kh* of Marathi and Gujarati, indicate the direct source or influence to be Arabic. The initial *k* becomes sometimes

1 "Vasco de Gama received him very kindly and ordered **camisas** to be given to him." Castanheda, I, ch. 25.

2 Simonet says that it is also used by Festus and derives it from the Latin-Spanish *cama.*

1 "Faria wishes to regard it as a Punic word; but it is without a doubt Arabic; on this account it occurs more than once in the Alcoran in the chapter on Joseph."

"Although the name of this garment may have come to us through the Arabs, it is necessary to search for its earliest origin. The Arabic word is derived from the Sanskrit *kschumá* (*kschaumi*), linen, *kshaumas*, made of linen; the garment has received this name from the material from which it is made." Engelmann, *Glossaire.*

"These Moors of Ormuz go about in very fine long white cotton **camisas** of very fine texture." Duarte Barbosa, p. 261. [The translation by Longworth Dames in the Hak. Soc.'s ed. does not square with this version and is the result apparently of some variation in the texts. See Vol. I, p. 79.]

aspirated in Konkani. Cf. *cruz*.

Camisola (an undervest, a singlet). Konk. *kāmizól* (a lady's chemise).—Tet. *kamizola*.

Campainha (a bell). Konk. *kāṁpín* ; vern. term *ghānṭlí*.—Tet., Gal. *kampainha*.

Campo (a field). Konk. *kámp* (in the sense of 'the plot of land fronting a church over which processions pass').—Mar., Hindust. *kampú*, field of battle.—Anglo-Ind. *campoo*, a camp.—? Mal., Sund., Jav., Mad., Mac. *kampong, kampung*, a village protected by an enclosure of hedges or bamboo.—Tet., Gal. *kámpu*, vern. term *klés*.[1]

Some philologists regard *kampong* as a vernacular term of the Malayan languages, and not of Portuguese origin. Yule puts up a strong case in favour of the Malay *kampong* being the original of the Anglo-Indian 'compound', but he admits the possibility of the Malay word itself being "originally a corruption of the Port. *campo*, taking the meaning first of *camp*, and thence of an enclosed area." See *Hobson-Jobson*, *s.v.* campoo and compound.

[Crooke, in *Hobson-Jobson* *s.v.* campo, refers to Whiteway's note that both Castanheda (Bk. VI, ch. ci, p. 217) and Barros (see below) speak of a ward of Malacca as **Campu** *China*, which de Eredia (1613) calls **Campon** *China*, and he thinks this last name may supply a link between *Campoo* and *Kampung*.]

?Cana da Índia (Indian cane). Bur. *kyane*.

[*Cana da Índia* was also called *Cana de Bengala* and is the *Arundinaria Wightiana*, Ness, or *Bambusa arundo*, Dalz. and Gibs., which grows in Bengal and from which were obtained walking sticks highly prized in early Portuguese days. But besides the meaning of 'walking stick' it also implied a staff of office, principally a sort of baton, used by military officers. The term and its different acceptations have been discussed at length in Dalgado's *Contribuiçoes*, *q.v.*]

[1] "And by land he threw up works half a league from Malacca, in that part which is called **Campochina.**" João de Barros, Dec. III, x, 3.

Canada (a measure in Portugal containing three English pints). Sinh. *kanáde* (pl. *kanáda*).[1]

Canal (canal). Konk *kānál* (us. only in Goa).—Tel. *kanáli*.

Brown assumes that *kanálī* is from French.

Canapé (a couch). Konk. *kānāpó* (pl. *kānāpé*).—Sinh. *kanáppuva*.—Tet., Gal. *kanapé* | Turk. *qànapé*. |

Canário (a canary-bird). Konk. *kānár*.—Jap. *kanáriya*.[2]

? **Candelabro** (a candelabrum; a large, branched, candle stick). Sinh. *kandalăruva*. In the Port. dialect of Ceylon: *candelar, candelér*. Probably from the Dutch *kandelaar*.

? **Candil** (in the old acceptation of 'a lamp', now obsolete). Guj. *kandil*, a glass lamp.—Hindi, Hindust. *qandil*.—Kan. *kandíla*.—Mal. *kandíl*.—Ach. *khandél*.—Jap. *kantera*, a hand lamp.

[1] According to António Nunes (*Livro dos Pesos da India*, p 34), *canada* was in use in Cochin; but dictionaries do not mention the word.

[2] "Specially certain (birds) which they call *inhapures*, which resemble very much **canarios** in colour and song." João dos Santos, *Ethiopia Oriental*, I. p. 134.

In all probability the word is imported directly from the Arabic *qandil*.

The origin of the Japanese term is doubtful; perhaps it is from the English 'candle', notwithstanding the difference in meaning. Gonçalves Viana believes that it is from the Spanish *candela*, 'a candle'.

Canela (the shin bone). Konk. *kānél*, the shin of a cow.—Tet. *kanela*, the bark of the cinnamon tree.

Canequim (a thick cotton fabric formerly made in India). Jap. *kanekim*.[1]

[1] "A white, quilted, robe made of **canequim.**" *Espolio de Balthazar Jorge* (1549), in *Jour. Geo. Soc. Lisb.*, 4th ser., p. 290.

"**Canequis**, *bofetas, beyrames, sabagagis*." Diogo do Couto, Dec. IV, l. 7.

[The above are names of different cotton fabrics which were formerly woven in India and exported to Europe. It is very true what Yule and Burnell observe that it is most difficult to draw intelligible distinction between the various kinds of cotton fabrics which under a variety of names were formerly exported to Europe. *Bofetas* is the same as the Anglo-Ind. *baftas*, a kind of calico made especially at Broach (see *Hobson-Jobson*, *s.v.* bafta); for *beyrames* see under **beatilha**. *Sabagagis* is mentioned as one of the text-

[The original of the word is the Marathi *khaṇkī*.]

? **Canga** (an ox-yoke). Mal., Jav., *kang*, bridle—[Anglo-Ind., *cangue.*] — Pid.-Engl. *cango*, "a species of chair or litter suspended from a pole and carried by two men". Leland.

Swettenham regards *kang* as a vernacular Javanese term, and not without reason, because of the difference in meaning between it and the Portuguese word and, secondly, because the Javanese word has no vowel ending, which normally words in Malay borrowed from the Portuguese retain. See *câmara*.

Leland says that *cango* is a Japanese word; but the dictionaries which I have consulted do not give it the meaning which he says it has. These are the meanings which they give: "Chinese words; attending to the sick; safe custody; rigorous imprisonment." Hepburn.

Leland and Yule notice another vocable with the same meaning, *viz.*, *cangue*, which Joaquim Crespo describes in *Cousas da China* as follows:

"The *canga* is a weighty square board, 80 centimetres wide and 5 thick, having a hole in the centre wherein the neck of the delinquent is held fast and locked."

There is, according to Yule, a genuine Chinese word noted in a dictionary of the eleventh century under the form *kang-giai* (in modern Mandarin speech *hyang-hiai*). From *kanggiai* is derived the Canton form *k'ang-ka*, 'to wear the *canga* ', and probably the Annamite *gang*.[1] He thinks it probable that the Portuguese took the word from one of these latter forms and associated it with their own *canga*, 'an ox-yoke', or 'porter's yoke for carrying burdens'. But Gonçalves Viana says that the Portuguese word *canga* implied "either from analogy of the

iles produced at Cambay; Dalgado (*Glossario*) says he cannot trace its etymology with any sense of certainty. It is no doubt the Ar. *sab'* ('seven') and *gaz* ('a yard'), *i.e.*, cloth sold seven yards to the rupee.]

"And from above one **canequim** spread out" António Bocarro, Dec. XIII, p. 538.

[1] In Siamese, *kha'ng* means 'to imprison'.

form or its use the board which is used in China for punishment." But there is no evidence that, in these meanings, *canga* was at that time in use in Portugal, nor has its origin, up to now, been investigated; the presumption is that it comes from *con(ju)gar* ('to join or unite').

Fernão Pinto calls the Chinese 'canga', *collar* ('a collar'). "Ordered us to be put into a narrow prison with fetters on our feet, manacles on our hands and collares on our necks." But Cardim in his *Batalhas da Companhia de Jesus* (1650) employs the term in its Chinese acceptation: "André was arrested for being a Christian and taken to the prison where they put round his neck a canga, which, as I have already said, is made of two thick pieces of wood in the shape of a ladder, and weighted more or less according to the crime of the offender."

[Crooke notes that the *O.E.D.*, on the authority of Professor Legge, rejects Yule's view (see above) and maintains that 'cangue' is from the Portuguese *canga*, 'a yoke'. Professor Giles is also entirely of the opinion that the word is from Portuguese and not from any Chinese term. As against all this, Dalgado, in his *Gonçalves Viana e a Lexicologia Portuguesa* published four years after the present work, inclines to the view that *canga*, in the acceptation of 'a wooden board worn round neck by Chinese criminals', is not from the Portuguese *canga*, 'a yoke for oxen', but has its origin in an Annamite word. His reason for this view are: (1) The earliest Portuguese chroniclers of India speak of this 'pillory of wood' as *colar*, and *tabua* ('board'). One of them who describes very minutely 'this instrument of torture' calls it by the Chinese name *kiahao*; none use the term *canga*. (2) the earliest reference to *canga*, in the Chinese acceptation, is in Cardim's *Batalhas* (see above), but before him, in 1635, António Bocarro refers to *ganga* in the same sense. "With his hands tied, they placed him in a boat and, accompanied by a bell, they took him with some speed along the whole fleet, and finally threw him into a sort of cage with a *ganga* round his neck" (in Pegu). Dalgado, therefore, is of the view that the source word of *canga* is not the Portuguese *canga* but the Annamite *gang*, which afterwards, following the laws of attraction, became transformed into *canga*. Cardim's reference to *canga* is also in connection with Anname. The Chinese name for this portable pillory is *kiā*. See Yule, *Cathay*, I, p. 179.]

Cânfora (camphor). Konk. *kámphr*; vern. term *kāphúr*, *kāpúr*, from the Sanskrit *karpûra*, which is the mediate source of the Portuguese word. —Tet., Gal. *kánfora*.

Canhão (a piece of ordnance: also a shirt-cuff). Konk. *kānhámv*. (in the sense of 'a cuff'). Tam. *canhão* (in the same sense).[1]—? Beng. *kāmán*, cannon.—Bug. *kanháo*, cannon.

Canivete (penknife). Konk. *kānvêt*; vern. term *chākú* (l. us.).—Tet., Gal. *kanivéti*.

Canja ('rice gruel'). Anglo-Ind. *conjee* (in the sense of 'rice gruel', and also in that of 'a medicinal drink made of rice decocted with spices and herbs').[1]—Indo-Fr. *cange*. In Konk. 'rice gruel' is called *péz*.

In Sanskrit and the modern Prakrits *kānjī* stands for 'water in which rice has been boiled and allowed to become acid', such as is used for starching by Indian washermen.[2] Yule says that the English received the term from the Portuguese; perhaps he says this because of the identity of meaning of the two words, though *congee* is nearer the Indian word.

---

[1] A friend writes to me that the word is pronounced in the same way as in Portuguese.

[1] "They give the patient rice water to drink with pepper and cummin seed which they call **canje**". Garcia da Orta, Col. xvii [ed. Markham, p 158].

"The Chinaman held his tongue, and immediately gave orders for a large supply of rice **canja** to be prepared, which was sufficient to enable all to recover from the hunger which every one felt." Bocarro, Dec. XIII, p. 168.

[2] "This word is improperly used by ladies and ayahs for gruel." Candy.

"Their white clothes are washed with water in which rice has been boiled, and thereby they become well starched." Gaspar Correia, p. 357.

[I cannot trace the reference for this statement of the author. In *Hobson-Jobson*, Yule connects the Anglo-Ind. 'conjee' with the Tamil *kanjī*, 'boilings'. It is true that in Sanskrit and the modern Prakrits, as has been said above, *kānji* signifies the usual starch of Indian washermen; but in Tamil *kañji* has both meanings: 'rice gruel', and 'starch', whereas in Malayalam the word is used only in the former sense, the latter being conveyed by the compound *kañjippaśa* = starch from 'congee'. From this it might be inferred that the Portuguese word was derived from Malayalam. See Dalgado, *Glossario*, and *Contribuições.*]

Cano (a pipe, a conduit). Konk. *kán;* vern. terms *naḷ*, *sārṇi.*—Sinh. *kánuva. Tubakka kánuva*, the barrel of a gun. —Tet., Gal. *kánu.*

Cantar (to sing, to chant). Konk. *kāntár-karuṅk. Kāntár* or *kantár* (subst., masc.), a song.—Mal. *kantar.*

Canto (in the sense of 'a corner'). Mal. *kántu.*

Capa (a cloak). Konk. *káp*, a cloak, an envelope for letters, a priest's cope, and a capot in a game of cards.—Beng., Tam., Malayal. *kāppa*, pluvial, long cloak used as ceremonial vestment.—Tel. *kappu*, a superscription.—Siam. *kāb*, cloak; vern. term *song muen.*—Mal. *capa* (Haex).—Mac., Bug., Tet., Gal. *kápa*, cloak.—Jap. *kappa. Ama-gappa*, rain-coat[1] —? Ar. *qabá*. See *cabaia.*

Capado (gelding, he-goat castrated). Sinh. *kappádu*, *kappádu-kala* (lit. 'made a gelding'). *Kappádu-karaṇavā*, to geld or castrate; vern. term *kara-ambanavā. Kappádu-kerima*, castration; vern. term *kara-ẹmbima.*—*Kappáduvā*, the animal that is castrated; a eunuch; vern. term *napuṁsakayā* (Sansk.) *Kappádu-kala kukulá*, a capon.—Gal. *kapádu.*

In Konkani *kapáṁv*, 'castrated', *kapáṁv-karuṅk*, 'to castrate', from the Port. *capão* ('a castrated cock'), are in use.[2]

---

[1] *K* intervocalic becomes *g* in Japanese, as in *ama-gasa*, from *ama* and *kasa*, 'rain-coat'; *ko-gatana*, from *ko* and *katana*, 'pen-knife'.

[2] *Kapanava*, 'to cut, to amputate', in Sinhalese, is a vernacular verb.

Capar (to castrate). Malayal. *kapparikka* (also used in the sense of 'castrated').—Tet., Gal. *kápa* (also in the sense of 'castrated').

Capaz (capable, clever). Konk. *kapáz*; vern. term *śakt, samarth, salav.*—Tet., Gal. *kapás;* vern. term *matének.*

Capela (in the sense of 'a chapel'). Konk. *kapél* (also 'a chaplet of flowers').—Tam. *kapelei.*—Tet., Gal. *kapéla.* [The Port. *capela* also signifies 'a garland or chaplet of flowers.']

Capitão (a captain). Konk. *kāpitáṁv*; *kopít* (also 'a chief or leader').—Guj. *kaptán, kapattán.*—Hindi, Hindust. *kaptán.*—Sinh. *kappita, kappeta.*—Malayal. *kappitán.*—Khas. *kaptan, koptan* (probably from the English 'captain').—Mal. *kapitán, kapítan.*—Ach., Sund., Jav., Day., Tet., Gal. *kapítan.*—Bug. *kapítan-móro* (=Port. *capitão mór*, 'chief captain').—Pid-Engl. *cab-tun.*—Jap. *kapitan*, 'a ship's captain; the leader of a company of workmen.'— | Turk. *qáptan*[1] | .

Capote (a cloak). Konk. *kāpôt.*—Bal. *kaput.*—Tet. *kapóti*; vern. term *pháru bóti.*—? Malag. *kapoti.*—Ar. *kabút, kabábit.*— | Turk. *qáput*[1] | .

? **Carabina** (carabine). Mar., Hindust., Punj. *karābín.*—Sindh. *karabínu.*—Mal. *karrebin* (Marre). *Karābiní*, carabineer, in Punjabi. In Marathi the vern. term is *dama.*— | Turk. *qàrabína* | .

Some Indian lexicographers

---

[1] "The very title of *capitão-mor* ('the chief-captain') which used to be given to the Portuguese governors passed into these languages (Malay, Javanese, Sundanese), which used it first to denote these and subsequently the governor-generals of the Dutch colonies. In Hitu, the chief part of the island of Amboyana, the title of *kapitan hitu* was borne for many centuries by the principal indigenous chief upon whom this title was conferred by António de Brito, Governor of the Molucas, at the beginning of the 16th century, as a reward for services rendered to the Portuguese." Heyligers.

"The song in Malay begins thus: **Capitão** *Dom Paulo ba poram de Pungor, anga dia malu, sita pa tau dar*" Rendered into English gives: "Captain Don Paulo fought in Pungor and preferred to die rather than yield a foot." Diogo do Couto, Dec. IV, viii, 11.

[1] "The hidalgos of that time did not repose their vanity in **capotes** ('cloaks') and breeches." Couto, Dec. VI, x, 8.

admit that the immediate source of the word is French. The term is a modern one in Portuguese.

Carambola (*bot.*, *Averrhoa carambola*). Anglo-Ind. *carambola.*—Indo-Fr. *carambole*, *carambolier.*

The source word is the Mar.-Konkani *karambal* [or *karmal* from the Sansk. *karmaraṅga*][1].

? **Caramelo** (a caramel, a sweetmeat). Jap. *karameiru*, *karumera*, *karumeira*, sugar-plum.

Gonçalves Viana is of the opinion that the source of the Japanese word is probably Spanish.

Carapuça (a cap; covering for the head). Mal. *karpús*, *karpúz.*—Sund., Batav. *karĕpus.*—Jav. *kárpus*, *krápus.*[2]

Caravela (small, light, fast ship). Anglo-Ind. *caravel*, *carvel.*

[The Port. dictionary, *Contemporaneo*, says that the derivation of the word is uncertain. Yule, because of the character of swiftness attributed to the *caravel*, suggests, but half-heartedly, the Turki *ḳarāwul*, 'a scout, an outpost, a vanguard', as the source word. The *O.E.D.* says that it is probably the diminutive of Sp. *caraba.*]

Cardamomo (cardamom). Sinh. *kardamúnga* ; vern. term *ensál.*[1]—Mal., Jav. *kardamon.* —Mac. *garididong.*—Bug. *garidimong* ; vern. term *kapulága.*

Caridade (charity). Konk. *kāridád* (l. us.) ; vern. terms *dharm*, *daya.*—Tet. *karidádi* ; vern. term *diák.*

Caril (curry). Anglo-Ind. *curry.*—Indo-Fr. *carry.*—Tet., Gal. *karíl.*

---

1 "Antonia, pluck from this tree some **carambola**, for this is how they are called in Malabar." Garcia da Orta, Col. xii [ed. Markham, p. 97. See also quotation under *bilimbim*].

"There is in China as great an abundance of **carambolas** as of mangoes." Lucena, *Historia*, Bk. X, ch. 18.

"Divers kinds of fruits, such as mangoes, jack-fruit, **carambolas.**" João dos Santos, *Ethiopia Oriental*, II, p. 270.

2 "And on the head over a coif of gold, a velvet **carapuça.**" João de Barros, Dec. II, x, 8.

"And on the head a round **carapuça** which did not cover the ears." Gaspar Correia, *Lendas*, I, 2.

1 "In Malabar it is called *etremilly*, and in Ceylon *ençal.*" Garcia da Orta, Col. xiii [ed. Markham, p. 100.].

Kari in Tamil, *kaḍhi* in Marathi and Konkani.[1]

[Either of these may be the source of the Portuguese word but presumably the latter. That the Port. word took to itself a final *l* is nothing strange; the phenomenon is observable in the Port. *candil*, a measure, from Mar. *kaṇḍī*; Tam. *kaṇḍi*.]

[**Carrane** (agent or factor; supercargo of a ship, in India). Anglo-Ind. *cranny*.[2] "In Bengal commonly used of a clerk writing English, and thence vulgarly applied generically to the East Indians, or half-caste class, from among whom English copyists are chiefly recruited." (*Hobson-Jobson*).

The Portuguese borrowed the term from the Malayal. *karana*, Hindust. *karāṇi*, which in its turn is the Sansk. *karan*, the present participle of *kar*, 'to do'.

Longworth Dames (in a note to *Canarins*, Duarte Barbosa, Vol. I, p. 62) opines that *Karānī*, as applied to the class of Eurasians, is the metathesis of *Canarim*. It is needless to say that such a view is entirely without any foundation, and that the two words are distinct in meaning and etymology. For the meaning of *Canarim* see under *Castiço*.]

Carreira (the name of a species of mango-tree and its fruit). Konk. *karél*.—Mar. *kurêl*. Cf. *Afonsa* and *Colaça*.

Carrêta (in the sense of 'carriage, cart'). Konk. *karét* (also used of 'a jagging-iron such as pastry cooks use'); vern. term *gāḍí*.—Sinh. *karette* (pl. *karatta*), *karéttiya*, *ka-răt-taya*, *karéttuva*; vern. term

---

1 "They also make dishes of fowl and flesh which they call **caril**." Garcia da Orta, Col. XVI [ed. Markham, p. 142].

2 ["You can safely send to the ships the factors and **carranes** of the place to whom all the ships will be shown." *Instruções de D. Manuel*, in *Alguns Documentos da Torre do Tombo* (1500), p. 98, cit. in *Glossario*.]

[*C* 1590.—"The **karránī** is a writer who keeps the accounts of the ship, and serves out the water to the passengers." *Āin* (c. 1590), ed. Blochmann, I, 280, cit. in *Hobson-Jobson*.]

["Doubt you not but it is too true, howsoever the **cranny** flatters you with better hopes." Danvers, *Letters*, I, 117, cit. by Crooke in *Hobson-Jobson*.]

["The **karanes** are the offspring of metizo and Indian unions, and are proud of their descent. De la Boullaye de Gouz, *Voyages, etc.*, p. 226.]

rathaya (Sansk.), *gela*. *Karetta-kárayā*, coachman. *Asvakarattaya* (lit., 'horse-carriage'), a coach, chaise. *Karattayen geṇayáma*, transport, freight.—Siam. *kra-tā*.—Mal. *karéta*, *keréta*, *kréta*, *kríta*. *Kreta api* (lit., 'cart of fire'), locomotive.—Batt., Sund. *karéta*, *kréta*.—Jav. *karéta*, *karétô*, *kréta*.—Mad. *karétó*.—Day., Mac., Bug. *karéta*.—Tet., Gal. *karreta*.

Carrêta, in the sense of a 'carriage', is also used in the Portuguese dialects of the East.[1]

In Arabic *karrus*, *kārusát* are used.

[1] "They (the women of Cambaya) go in horse-**caretas** ('carriages') entirely covered, so that nobody can say who travels within." Duarte Barbosa, p. 272. [Hak. Soc., ed. Longworth Dames, Vol. I, p. 121.]

"The **carretas** (of Surat) in which he and the Portuguese travelled were elaborately wrought and furnished with silk hangings." Gaspar Correia, II, p. 369.

"And from there came many **carretas** laden with this *uplot*." Garcia da Orta, Col. xvii [ed. Markham, p. 149. *Uplot* according to da Orta is the Gujarati name for the *Costus Arabicus*, the root of *Auklandia Costus*, Falconer. Dymock (*Mat. Med.*) mentions that the name is still in use in Gujarat in the form *ouplate*.]

[Wilson suggests a probable Portuguese origin for the Anglo-Indian 'hackery,' the common bullock-cart of Bengal, from *acarretar*, 'to convey in a cart'. To this Yule says, "It is possible that the mere Portuguese article and noun '*a carreta*' might have produced the Anglo-Indian *hackery*. But it is almost certain that the origin of the word is the Hindi *chhakra*, 'a two-wheeled cart'." See *Hobson-Jobson*, *s.v.* hackery.]

Carta (playing-card). Konk. *kārt*.—Mal. *kárta*, *kártu*.—Sund. *kártu* (also 'a geographical chart').—Jav. *kártu*.—Mad. *kértô*.—Mol. *kértu*, *kérto*.—Jap. *karuta*.

In Japanese the compound consonants (with the exception of *st*) of foreign words are separated by the intercalation of *u*: *Furansu* = France; *burashi* = brush; *daruma* = *dharma* (Sansk.). But *Kiristo* = Christ, by assimilation; *saberu* = sabre. Cf. *pistola*.

Malayalam has *chartta*, a writing, document; *chárttuka*, to execute a deed; *chárttupaṭi*, a catalogue; *chárttumuṛi*, a deed in writing.

Wilson, in his *Glossary*, thinks it probable that the word is of Portuguese origin. In which case, the change of the *c*, in the first syllable, to *ch* is to be expected.

?**Carta** or **cartaz** (in the sense of 'paper'). Siam *kra-dart.*—Kamb. *credas. Bier credas*, game of cards.—Mal., Sund., Jav. *kártas, kértas.*—Ach. *kértas.*—Day. *karátas, krátas.*—Mac. *karátasa.*—Bug. *karáttasă.*

"It is probable that it is one of these two words whose transformation gave rise to the Malay, Javanese, and Sundanese *kartas* or *kertas*, 'paper'. Although Arabic has the word *kratas*—otherwise *qartas*—(from the Greek *chartés*), *kartas* is not of Arabic origin, because in the Dutch Indies it is precisely the European and the Chinese paper that is called *kartas*." Heyligers. Michell also attributes a Portuguese origin to the Siamese word.

Notwithstanding these views, the Portuguese origin appears very improbable, especially, because of the divergence in the meaning of the word in Portuguese and the Eastern languages.

There is no evidence to show that the word *carta* had ever been employed in Portuguese to mean 'paper'. *Cartaz* was employed in India in the sense of 'a passport' or 'sailing-licence'; and in this meaning, it appears to be of Arabic origin. [The Ar. *qirtās*, 'paper, document.'] "Sailors from Coulão would send to Cochym for the certificate which they call **cartaz.**" Gaspar Correia (I, p. 298). "They had gone to Bassein to obtain a pass (which they call **cartazes**) from the captains." Diogo do Couto (Dec. IV, ix, 2)[1].

Cartucho (a cartridge). Konk. *kārtúś.*—Guj., Hindi, Hindust., Punj. *kārtús.*—Tel.

1 "Send me a **cartas** ('safe-conduct') in your own hand-writing for my *lancharas* and *jurupangos* to enable them to sail in safety in all weathers." Fernao Pinto, ch. xiii. [*Lancharas* and *jurupangos* are names of vessels mentioned in Portuguese histories of the 16th and 17th centuries. They are both supposed to be derived from Malay. See *Glossario*, and for *lanchara* also *Hobson-Jobson.*]

"He will give **cartazes** to the ships of Idalxa ('Adil Shah'), so that they may sail to all parts...The said factor to give **cartazes** to the vessels which might sail from the said port." Simão Botelho, pp. 43, 44.

kātarusu, kātanusu, ? kākitamu.—Gar., Khas. *kartus.*—Mac., Bug. *karatúsa.*—Tet., Gal. *kartús.*[1]

Tonkinese has *cát-tút*, which must be a corruption of the Fr. *cartouche.*

Casa (slit to receive fastening; a button-hole). Konk. *káz.*—Mar. *káj;* vern. terms *gunḍichém ghar, birḍem.*—Guj. *gája.*—Beng., Hindust. *káj.*—Tam. *káju. Bottam-hilu* (lit. 'a slit for the button') is the Sinhalese equivalent.

Casado (married). Sinh. *kasádaya, kasáda-beṇdíma*, marriage; vern. terms *viváha-beṇdíma, viváhaya* (Sansk.). *Kasáda-beṇdinavá*, to marry. *Kasáda-beṇdápu*, married.

Casar (in the sense of 'a Christian marriage'). Konk. *kāzár. Kāzár-karuṅk*, to give in marriage. *Kāzár-zavuṅk*, to marry. *Kāzró*, an ill-sorted marriage. It is also the name of the *nux vomica* tree. *Kâzāri*, married (to distinguish from a bachelor or a widower). *Kāzārāchó* (*kāzārāchí*, fem., *kāzārāchém*, neut.) marriageable, nubile.

Many Portuguese verbs are employed in Konkani as neuter substantives, as for instance: *pintár* from Port. *pintar*, 'to paint', is used in Konk. to mean 'a painting'; *razár* and *kumsár*, from Port. *rezar*, 'to pray' and *confessar*, 'to confess', are respectively used in Konk. in the sense of 'prayer' and 'confession.'[1]

Caso (a happening, an incident). Konk. *káz;* vern. terms *ghaḍṇí, gošṭ; parvá.*—Tet. *kásu.*

---

[1] "The *Condestabre* ('Captain-General') of Luis de Mello discharged a small cannon which he was carrying with stone **cartuxo** ('ball') in its muzzle." Diogo do Couto, Dec. VII, vi, 2.

"When they saw from this side that what was hoped for had been carried out, they began to get ready the arms and artillery and to prepare **cartuxos** and other requisites of war" (1604). In *Historia tragico-maritima* vii, p. 11.

"We fought until we had only two barrels of gun-powder and twenty-eight **cartuxos** left." *Ibid.*, IX, p. 9.

[1] As an exception to the rule I have hitherto followed, I am registering here the Portuguese word *casar*, though it has been adopted only by Konkani. I am doing this because of the various derivatives from the word which are in use in that language. There are various terms for marriage among the Hindus; *lagn, varád. vārdik, hātí, vavar, viváha.*

Casoar (a cassowary). Jap. *kasováru, kasvaruchō*.

The original of the Portuguese word is the Malay *kasuvári*.

Casta (caste). Konk. *kást*; vern. terms *zát*, *varṇ*.—Anglo-Ind., Indo-Fr. *caste*.—Mal. *kásta*.

In the Konkani of Goa the terms *kastist*, 'one who is keenly alive to caste distinctions,' and *kāstijm*, 'a strong caste sentiment', are met with. Both these terms are borrowed directly from the Portuguese spoken in Goa which has the forms *castista*, *castismo*.

Yule says that Duarte Barbosa (1516) does not apply the word *casta* to the divisions that obtain in Hindu society, but he calls these divisions so many *leis de gentios*, *i.e.*, 'laws' of the heathen. But this view is disproved by the following passage (p. 334): "There are, besides the divisions mentioned above, eleven others composed of the lower classes . . . which prevent one **casta** from mixing with another **casta**[1]." [Ed. Longworth Dames, Vol. II, p. 59.]

["**Caste**, the artificial divisions of society in India, first made known to us by the Portuguese, and described by them by the term *casta*, signifying breed, race, kind, which has been retained under the supposition that it was the native name." Wedgwood, *A Dictionary of English Etymology*. But a most fanciful derivation of the word is given by W. Hamilton, *Descr. of Hindostan*, I, 109, quoted by Crooke in *Hobson-Jobson*: 1820—"The Kayasthas (pronounced Kaists, hence the word **caste**) follow next.]

Castanha (a chestnut). Mal. *kestén*, a knock on the top-head in the game of tops. Ar. *kastána*, *kastánia*.—Turk. *kestáne*.

Castela (Castile, the name of one of the two kingdoms of Spain). Mal., | Bal. | *katéla*.[1]

[1] "As regards the **castas**, the greatest impediment to the conversion of the Hindus is the superstition which they maintain with regard to their **castas**; this prevents them from touching, communicating or mingling with others, in the same way as superiors will not mix with inferiors: members of one observance with those of another." Diogo do Couto, Dec. V. vi. 4.

[1] In *katéla* "the *s* is elided, and the

a species of potato.— | Jav. *katelo* (*idem*) | .—Mac. *kasatéla*, a potato.—Jap. *kastéra*, *kasutera*, a sponge-cake.

In one or the other of the above vocables another meaning is perhaps also implied. Cf. cambric, cashmere, etc. In Italian they speak of *pane di Spagna*, and Yule conjectures that the English term 'sponge cake' is a corruption of 'Spanish cake'.

Castiçal (candle-stick). Konk. *kāstisál*.—Tam. *kastisál*, *kastrisál*.—Tet. *kastisál*.

Castiço (a child of Portuguese parents, born in India). Anglo-Ind. *castees* (obs.).

According to Dr. Schuchardt, *casliços* are, among the Germans and the Dutch, the offspring of marriages between Europeans and mestizos. See *mestiço* and *topaz*.[1]

[The distinction between the pure Portuguese and their mixed descendants, as far as nomenclature is concerned, is succintly given by Teixeira Pinto, *Memorias sobre as Possessões Portuguezas*, p. 168, and will bear quoting: "The Portuguese, whether of Europe or Brazil, are at Goa called without distinction *Frangues* or *Fringuins* or *Reinões*: those born in India of pure Portuguese blood, **Castiços**, corresponding to the *Creoles* of America; half-castes are called *Mestiços*; children of native Christians are *Canarins*; those of Hindu parents are *Conkanos*." *Canarim*, correctly speaking, is a native of Kanara, but the Portuguese from the earliest times erroneously spoke of the people of Goa, who geographically are Konkani and ethnically Indo-Aryan, as *Canarim*. In modern times, and at the present day, the Goans regard the term and its application to them as offensive, just in the same way as Indians regard the term

word thus acquires the form usual with names of plants and parts of plants." Dr. Fokker.

[1] "Next are those born in India of Portuguese fathers and mothers and called **castiços**" (1616). Pyrard. *Viagem*, II, p. 32 [Hak. Soc. Vol. II, p. 38].

"The **Castissos** are those who are born of father and mother who are *reinols* ('European Portuguese'); this word is derived from *caste*; they are held in contempt by the *reinols*." Le Gouz de la Boullaye, *Voyages* (1643).

'natives' when used by Europeans to designate them.]

Castigar (to punish). Mal. *castigar* (Haex).

Castigo (punishment). Konk. *kāstíg* (l. us.); vern. term *khást*.—Tet., Gal. *kastígu*. vern. terms *úkum*, *báku*.

* **Castor** (beaver; also a beaver hat). Mal., Sund., Jav. *kastúri*, *kastóri*, musk, a civet cat.—Mac., Bug. *kasatúri*.

Gonçalves Viana regards the Portuguese origin of these words as certain. Dr. Heyligers is of the opinion that they are derived from Sanskrit. In fact, *kastūri*, in Sanskrit, means 'musk', and *kastūri-mṛga*, 'a civet cat'. And in this sense these terms are employed as vernacular all over India. In Goa, however, *castor*, even at the present day, is the name for the 'black silk top-hat'.

Catana (a large broad-sword). Tet., Gal. *katána*.—*Jap. *katana*.

Wenceslau Morais (*Day-Nippon*) gives *catana* as a Portuguese word, introduced among the Japanese. Cândido de Figueiredo is undecided as to whether it is derived from Japanese or Italian. Bluteau, Morais, and Dr. Adolfo Coelho regard it as of Japanese origin, and Gonçalves Viana (*Apostilas*) says that this view is unquestionable.[1]

In the Portuguese of Goa, *catana* is employed in the same meaning as the Konkani *koytó*, 'a large kitchen knife, or a wood-cutter's knife'.

Catanar, caçanar (a priest of the St. Thomas Christians of Malabar). Anglo-Ind. *cattanar*, *cassanar*.

The word is the Malayal. *kattanár* ('chief'), derived from the Sansk. *kartṛ*. The

---

[1] "There are no better armourers in the lands we have discovered, for these cut through our iron with their **catanas**, as though it were soft wood." Lucena, Bk. VII, ch. 6.

"Manuel Rodrigues....took a **catana** which he had with him and with it suddenly dealt the captain a terrible **catanada** ('blow with a broad sword')." A. Bocarro, Dec. XIII, p. 361. [*Catanada* is built up on the analogy of *facada* ('thrust with a knife') from Port. *faca*, a knife. Similarly from *cris*, the Port. form of the Malayo-Jav. *kĕres* or *kris*, a Malay dagger, they formed *crisada*, 'a thrust or blow with the *cris*'.]

"**Catanas**, bucklers, and other small arms without number" (in Tonquin). A. F. Cardim, *Batalhas da Companhia de Jesus*, p. 217.

term is not to be found in Portuguese dictionaries.[1]

[Dalgado (*Glossario, s.v. caçanar*) quotes Fr. Vincenzo Maria (*Viaggio* (1655)) and La Croze (*Histoire du Christianisme* (1724)) who derive *cassanar* from the Syriac *qasīs* ('priest') and the Malayalam *nāyar* ('Nair'), that is, 'priest of the Nair', or 'noble or Nair priest,' and thinks that this derivation of the word is not improbable. The word is not mentioned in the *O.E.D.*]

Catarro (a catarrh). Tet., Gal., Jap. *katáru.*

It might be that the Japanese term is not derived immediately from the Portuguese, but, like many others, is of modern importation.

? Catavento (a weather-cock; ventilator; also the space from the main mast to the stern of a ship which is occupied by the ship's officer who directs its course). L.-Hindust. *kátvāī.*

[In India, the Portuguese employed the word *catavento* to describe a sort of wheel with holes, set at the top of the houses, to draw in the air and refresh the house. "Al their houses (at Ormuz) are flat above, and in the toppes thereof they make holes to let the ayre come in, like those of Cayro, and they use certaine instruments like Waggins ('swings') with bellowes, to beare the people in, and to gather winde to coole them withall, which they call **Cattaventos.**" *Linschoten* (Hak. Soc.), Vol. 1, p. 51.]

Cate, cato, cáchu ('an extract from the wood of several species of Acacia'). Anglo-Ind. *catechu, cutch, caut.*—Indo-Fr. *caoutchouk.*

---

[1] "The Christians of St. Thomas call their priests **Caçanares.**" António do Gouveia, *Jornada do Arcebispo de Goa,* 1606, p. 28.

"With all their priests (whom they call **Cassanares**)." Diogo do Couto, Dec. VII, viii, 2.

"And it was owing to the Providence of our Lord, for it was the same route which was followed by the **Cacenar** whom the Bishop sent the year before...There I found the same *chatim* who had gone with the **Cacenar**" (1603). In *O Chronista de Tissuary,* III, p. 186. [*Chatim* in Port. is the same as the Anglo-Indian 'chetty', a member of any of the trading castes in Southern India, corresponding to the Bania of Northern and Western India. The word is the Malayal. *cheṭṭi* (See *Hobson-Jobson s v.* chetty.)

Cate is from the Marathi-Konkani *kat*, Sansk. *kvātha* or *kvatha*. *Káchu* is a Dravidian form.[1]

[The Anglo-Indian 'catechu' is a compound of *kát* and *káchu*.]

Catecismo (archaic form *catequismo*, a catechism). Konk. *kātesizm*, *katekízm*.—Beng. *kātekisma*.—Sinh. *katekísmaya*.[2]

Católico (a Catholic). Konk. *kātólk*.—Mar., Guj. *katholik*.—Hindi, Beng. *katholika*.—Sinh., Mal. *katólika*.—Tam., Malayal. *katólik*. –Tel. *kathóliku*.—Kan., Tul. *kathólika*.—Jap. *katorikku*.—Ar. *katholiki*.

It is possible that in some of the languages the word may have felt the influence of, or been derived from, English.

[**Catre** (a light bedstead, a folding bed). Anglo-Ind. *cot*.[3]

The etymon of *catre* is the Malayal. *kaṭṭil*, in the meaning of 'bed, sofa,' derived from the Sansk. *khaṭvā*, which gave *khāṭ* in Konkani and Marathi, and also the diminutive *khāṭlêṁ*, 'a cheap rough-hewn bed'. It is interesting to note that, just as the Malayal. *veṭṭila* assumed in Portuguese the forms *bétele*, *bétel*, *betle*, *bétere*, *betre*, so likewise *kaṭṭil* took the forms *catele*, *cátel*, *catle*, *cátere*, *catre*.

The Spanish Academy Dictionary mentions *catre* in the sense of 'a light bed-stead intended for one person only', and derives it from *cuatro*, 'four', with reference to its four legs. But the mere mention of such a word in the Spanish dictionary is no proof that it is a genuine Spanish word, for *coco*, *manga*, *palanquim*, *bazar* are also to be met with in Spanish dictionaries, and these are unmistakably Indian words which

1 "**Cate**, which here (Ormuz) is called **cacho**." António Nunes, *Livro dos Pessos*, p. 22. See Gonçalves Viana, *Apostilas*.

2 "It is for the (religious) brother to remain to help in Christian doctrine, **catecismo**, and the conversion of the infidels." Lucena, Bk, VI, ch. 3.

3 [As one entered the corridor (of the palace), he saw a **catre** hanging from two silver chains......*Chronica de Bisnaga* (1525), p. 120.]

["A **catre** valued at 8,000 reis." Tómas Pires, *Materiaes* (1548), in *Jour. Geo. Soc. Lisb.*, XVI. p. 703.]

["The better sort sleepe upon **cots**, or Beds two foot high, matted or done with girth-web" (1634). Sir T. Herbert, *Travels*, p. 149.]

had been taken over to the Iberic Peninsula by the Portuguese and were adopted not only by Spanish but also by other European languages.

Yule very properly remarks: "*Cot*, though well understood, is not in such prevalent European use as it formerly was, except as applied to barrack furniture, and among soldiers and their families. Words with this last characteristic have very frequently been introduced from the south. There are, however, both in north and south, vernacular words which may have led to the adoption of the term *cot* in their respective localities. In the north we have Hindi *khāṭ* and *khaṭwā*.....; in the south, Tam. and Malayal. *kaṭṭil*, a form adopted by the Portuguese."

The form *catre*, to judge from the quotations in the *Glossario*, was used as early as 1525, and acquired great currency in Portuguese. Besides the meanings of 'bedstead' and 'folding bed' noticed above, the word has been used in various other senses. In Port. India it is even at the present day used of a sort of hammock-litter or a palanquin. In the early Portuguese days it meant a throne, especially of the Malabar kings. For citations to support these acceptations see *Glossario*. Prof. S. H. Hodivala (Notes on *Hobson-Jobson*, *Indian Antiquary*, Vol. LVIII, 1929) quotes from Alberûnî's *India* (*c.* 1030) showing that *katt* was used in the sense of 'throne'. He also gives a fourteenth century quotation in which *khaṭ* is used of a 'bedstead'.

Cot was first used by Sir T. Herbert in his *Travels* (1634), according to the *O.E.D.*, and this, as well as the fact that the form *catre* would more easily than the Hindi *khāṭ* give 'cot', inclines us to the view that the Anglo-Indian word is the same as the Port. *catre*.]

Catur ('a small and swift Indian rowing vessel'). Anglo-Ind. and English *cutter*.[1]

---

1 "After some time as Simam Rranjel and a companion were returning to Cochin in a *paguer* of the Moors, they were captured by **caturis** from Calecut." A. de Albuquerque, *Cartas*, I, p. 29. [*Paguel, paguer, pagur, pajer*

The origin of the word is uncertain. Yule says that he has not been able to trace the name to any Indian source. Burton, who is cited by Yule, derives it from the Arabic *katīreh*, 'a small craft'. Fr. João de Santo António Moura derives it from the Persian *kātūr*, 'a small ship armed in time of war'. But it is not certain whether such terms exist in Arabic and Persian. It appears to me that the true origin of the word must be the Malayal. *kattiri* or the Neo-Aryan *kātar*, from the Sanskrit *kartarī*, 'a scissors'; literally 'a cutter', from the verb *kṛt*, 'to cut'. The craft whose distinguishing feature was its narrow shape, especially at the prow, which enabled it to cut through the water with ease, a fact noticed by the Portuguese chroniclers, might well earn the denomination *kātar*. This term is employed in various metaphorical senses: for instance, in Konkani, *kātar* is used to denote 'a cross piece of timber to hold fast larger beams, a pyramidical structure, an obelisk'. The word was current in Malabar and in the Konkan when the Portuguese arrived there; and if to-day it is not in use, it is because similar craft do not exist.

[The *O.E.D.* regards 'cutter' as an English word from 'to cut'; though this view does not agree with the author's which

---

are the different names by which a cargo vessel was known on the southern coast of India. Dalgado, in his *Glossario*, says that Malayalam dictionaries do not mention any word corresponding to it, and that it is not unlikely that it was already in use in the Malabar Coast at the time when the Portuguese arrived there in the form *pagala*, equivalent to the Marathi *baqalā*, which represents the Ar *baqalā*, and is the name commonly given on the Western Coast of India to Arab vessels of the old native form. It is not impossible that the Arabic *baqalā* is itself a corruption of the Spanish *bajel*, *baixel* or *bairel*. For the form *pajer* employed by Gaspar Correia, see *baixel*.]

"And twelve thousand reis from the **catur** or *fusta*" (*q.v.*). Simão Botelho, *Tombo*, p. 246.

"He entered a **catur** with only one page, intending thereby to disarm the covetuousness of the king which would have been roused if halberdeers had accompanied him." Lopo de Sousa Coutinho. *Hist. do Cerco de Diu*, p. 70.

"He dispatched a very swift **catur** with letters for Christovão de Sousa." Diogo do Couto, Dec. IV, i, 2.

would have 'cutter' indebted to the Port. *catur*, yet by analogy it helps to lend strength to the derivation proposed above for *catur*, namely, from a Sansk. word implying 'to cut'.]

Cavala (*Caranx caballus*; a species of horse-mackerel). Anglo-Ind. *cavally* (us. in Ceylon).

Gaspar Correia says (I, p. 71): "There was (in Calicut) a lot of fish like sardines, which they called **cavalinhas.**" The Portuguese called it by this name, not the people of Malabar, even as in Indo-Portuguese this fish is called *cavala*, because it resembles so much the small mackerel [1].

* **Cavalo** (a horse). Kamb. *capăl*, a ship. *Capal chŏmbăng*, a man-of-war. *Capăl phlúng*, a steamer. *Capăl kdong*, a sailing vessel.—Siam. *kampăn.*[2]—Mal., Ach., Batt., Sund., Jav., Mad., Bal., Day. *kápal*, a large ship; (in Batta there is an additional form *hopal*). *Kápal-ápi* (lit. 'fire horse'), a steamer. Cf. Mar., Konk. *ág-bôṭ.*—Mac. *káppalā.*—Bug. *kaválu*, a horse (vern. terms *titingang*, *anharang*); *káppalā*, a ship.

Yule and Burnell, following Marsden, say that the Malay word *kápal* was imported from Tam. *kappal*, 'a ship,' which is undoubtedly a vernacular term, for in the *Roteiro da Viagem de Vasco da Gama* there appears *capell* as the equivalent of the Port. *naoo* ('ship'). Haex mentions the word in the same identical form and with the same meaning (*cappal*, 'a ship'), but not as of Portuguese origin, and distinguishes it from *capalla*, 'head', which is from Sanskrit.

If the source of the word is really Portuguese, it is a matter for wonder that a foreign word should be employed in a sense so far-fetched, without being used in its proper meaning or one having any relation to it. But Dr. Heyligers bears witness to the fact that only in High Javanese "the true

[1] "These Moucois ('Mukkuvar') fishers (of Malabar) catch a large quantity of a sort of little fish which is no longer than the hand, and as broad as a little bream; the Portuguese call it **cavalla.**" Pyrard, *Viagem*, II, p. 328 [Hak. Soc., Vol. I, p. 388]. See *Hobson-Jobson*.

[2] The final *l* is pronounced *n* in Siamese. See *rial*.

meaning has been retained by the side" of the other. It is, however, possible, and very probable, that the word which means 'a big ship' has come to signify metaphorically in a poetical language, like High Javanese, a 'high horse', and not vice versa. W. W. Hunter mentions *kapal* as the vernacular name for the horse in *Krama* (High Javanese), and gives *járan* as its equivalent in *Ngoho* or Low Javanese [1]. Bugui makes a distinction between *kavâlu* and *kappala*.

Again, there is no satisfactory explanation as to why the Malays adopted the Portuguese *cavalo* when they had their own word *kúda*. The adoption of *kovelú* or *torvélu*, from Port. *coelho*, 'rabbit', in Malay and Javanese, and of *koélhu*, in Teto and Galoli, must be attributed to the fact that the animal was unknown among those people, owing to which there was no vernacular term for it. In the same way there is no especial name for the rabbit in India and it is, therefore, called by the same name as the 'hare'. "The Marathas make no distinction between the hare and the rabbit." Candy.

[1] *A Comparative Dictionary of the Languages* (Non-Aryan) *of India and High Asia.*

Cavilha (a wooden pin used in ship building; bolt). L.-Hindust. *kavíla*, *kabíla*.

Cear (to eat one's supper). Mal. *cear* (Haex).

Cemitério (a cemetery). Konk. *simitér*; vern. terms *masaṇ*, *pretbhumy* (the burning ground of the Hindus).—Beng. *semiterí*.—Tam., Kan., Tet., Gal. *semitéri*.

[**Centopeia** (many-footed crawling animal). Anglo-Ind. *centipede* [1].

The *O.E.D.* says that the forms *centipie*, *centapee*, in West Indies and among the early navigators were probably from Spanish.]

Cepilho (a plane used by joiners). Malayal. *chippuli*.—Tet. *sepilho*, *sebilo*.

Cêrco (a siege, also a fence). [Konk. *cêrk*, a fence.]—Mal. *cerco* (Haex).

[1] [1662.—"There is a kind of worm which the Portuguese call *un* **centopè**, and the Dutch also 'thousand-legs' (*tausend-bein*)."—T. Saal (1662), 68, cit. in *Hobson-Jobson*.]

Cerimónia (a ceremony). Konk. *sermón*; vern. terms *rít*, *kriyá*, *parvaḍ*.—Tet. *seremóni*: vern. term *knál*.

Ceroilas (drawers; sleeping pant). Konk. *serúl*.—Guj. *survál*, *suravála*.—Sinh. *saruválaya*, *sareválaya*.—Mal. *serával*, *servál*, *selúvar*, *selúar*.—Batt. *saravar*.—Sund. *serável*.—Jav. *seruval* Mac., Bug. *saluvára*.[1]

The Portuguese word comes from the Persian *shalvár*, through the medium of the Arabic *siruál*. In the group of Malayan languages it stands for 'trousers', as in Persian.

Cerveja (beer). Konk. *servêj*.—Tet. *serveja*.

Cevadeira (*naut.*, a sprit-sail). L.-Hindust. *sabdorá*, *subdhará*.

Chá (tea). Konk. *chá*, *cháv*.—Mar. *chahá*. — Guj. *chá*, *cháha*, *cháhe*.—Hindi, Hindust. *chá*, *cháh*, *cháy*, *cháe*.—Nep. *chiyá*. — Or., Beng. *chá*. — Assam. *cháh*, *chái*.—Sindh. *chá*, *cháhi*.—Punj. *chāhá*.—Kash. *chāí*.—Tam. *chá* (also *te*).—Malayal. *chá*, *cháya* (also *teyila*, lit. 'the tea-leaf'). — Kan., Tul. *chá*.—Anglo-Ind. *chaw* (l. us.).—Gar. *cha*.—Khas. *sha*.—Tib. *ch'a*; *sö-ch'a* (honorific name). *Ch'a-pa*, tea-slab.—Siam. *ša*.—Ann., Tonk. *chè* (also *tra*).—Nic., Tet., Gal. *chá*.—Pers. *chāí*.—Ar. *shāí*.—| Turk. *cháy* |.

Chahādán, *chahādāní* (Mar.), *chādāní* (Guj.), *chādán* (Hindust.), a tea-pot.

The Chinese ideograph which stands for the tea plant answers to two phonetic forms: *chhá* in the 'Mandarin dialect', and *té* in the dialect of Fuh-Kien. The first was adopted by Japan and by Indo-China, by Portugal, Greece, and Russia; and the second, by the other European nations, as also by the Malayo-Polynesian group of languages, and four Indian languages: Sinhalese and Telugu, Tamil, and Malayalam. The last two have also the other form.

It is not known for certain whether tea was known in India before the Portuguese arrival there, nor to what extent the propagation of the word is to be attributed to

[1] "Breeches, **ceroulas**, stockings from the knee downwards, with shoes having holes in their soles." António Tenreiro, *Itinerario*, ch. vi.

Portuguese influence, nor by what route the other form found its way to the Coromandel coast and made its entry into Ceylon. In the old Portuguese chroniclers there are not many references either to tea or coffee. The first mention of it, according to Gonçalves Viana (*Apostilas*), is made by Frei Gaspar da Cruz in his *Tratado da China* (1569): "Whatsoever person or persones come to any mans house of qualitee, hee hath a custome to offer him in a fine basket one Porcelane...with a kinde of drinke which they call **cha**, which is somewhat bitter, red, and medicinall, which they are wont to make with a certayne concoction of herbes." [See Da Cruz in *Purchas*, III, 180.] And João Lucena (1600) says: "The Japanese attach a value to the most trifling and ridiculous things, as are the stuffs used in preparing a decoction from the herb which is called **cha**." Bk. VII, ch. 4.

Mandelslo, quoted in *Hobson-Jobson*, says in 1638: "In our ordinary meetings (at Surat) which we had every day, we did not take anything but *Thé* (tea), *the use of which was very common all over India.*" But this ought to be understood in connection with the Europeans, their descendants, and some indigenous Christians; for, even to-day, the strictly orthodox Hindus abstain from tea, and Mussulmans prefer coffee.[1]

John Crawfurd alleges that the word *tea* in its various European forms came from the Malay *Te*. If it did not find its way into India through the same channel, which is little likely, Sinhalese must have received it from the Dutch *thee*, and Tamil and Telugu from the French *thé*. And, in this case, it is very likely that the other Indian languages received their various forms directly or indirect-

[1] "They hold in great esteem this herb which is called *Thé*, which comes from China and Japan, and that from the later country is the better of the two..At Goa, Batavia, and in all the Factories of the Indies, there is scarcely a European who does not take tea thrice or four times a day, and they are careful to save the leaf in order to turn it into a salad for the evening, with some oil, vinager and sugar" (1676). Tavernier, *Voyages*. V, p. 257.

ly from the Portuguese *chá*. It is noteworthy that Persian and Arabic have this same form, and it is not known when it was introduced into either of them.

[The *O.E.D.* says that the Portuguese brought (into Europe) the form *cha* (which is Cantonese as well as Mandarin) from Macao. The form *te* (*thé*) was brought into Europe by the Dutch, probably from the Malay at Bantam (if not from Formosa, where the Fuhkien or Amoy form was used). The original English pronunciation (*tē*), sometimes indicated by spelling *tāy*, is found in rhymes down to 1762, but the current (*tī*) is found already in the 17th century as can be seen from rhymes and the spelling *tee*. It also cites Meyer, *Konversations-Lexikon*, to show that the first mention of tea in Europe is due to the Portuguese in 1559 (under the name *cha*). It was first known in Europe about 1650–1655 and, according to Watt (*The Commercial Products of India*, p. 212), the first mention of tea-drinking in India is made by Mandelslo in the passage cited above.]

?**Chalupa** (a sloop). L.-Hindust. *salúp*. Perhaps it is from the Engl. 'sloop'.

Chamador (one who calls). Konk. *chāmādôr*, a subordinate church or temple official; it is used in this sense in Tamil, and probably also in some other Indian languages.

Chamalote (a sort of stuff partly made of silk and partly of camel's hair; a camlet). Mac., Bug., *chamalóti*.[1]

[*Chamolotes* is the same as 'camlets', so called because they were "supposed to have been made of camel's hair, owing to the mistaken notion that the Arabic *khaml* meant 'camel', but in reality were made of silk mixed with wool, and often with the hair of the Angora goat. The mixture of some other fibre, generally some sort of wool, with silk is common among Muhammadans, owing to their belief that silk is forbidden by their religion." Longworth Dames, from whose translation of

1 "The Mandarins received him with presents of **chamalotes** and velvets." Vasco Calvo (1536), in Donald Ferguson, *Letters from Portuguese Captives*, p. 101.

Barbosa (Hak. Soc. Vol. I, p. 120, n.) the above is taken, also says (see Vol. I, n. 3, p. 63) that *cambolim* is evidently identical with the old French and English *cameline*, a sort of brown cloth made of or supposed to be made of camel's hair, like *camlet*. But *cambolim* is only the Port. form of the Konkani *kambléṁ* (pl. *kamblīṁ*), from the Sansk. *kambala*, appearing in the Indian vernaculars in slightly varying forms ; it is the name of a coarse woollen cloth and has no affiliation with *cameline*.]

Chão (*adj*., planed, smooth) Sinh. *chán, chánnu*.

? **Chapa** (a seal, impression, stamp, or brand). Konk. *chháp* or *śáp* (masc.), seal, stamp ; punch, a seal-impression ; mould ; in the sense of 'type' used with the verbs *māruṅk, lāvuṅk* ('to affix'), *basuṅk* ('to set') ; (fem.) a sod of earth, a glebe (us. with the verbs. *kāḍhuṅk, māruṅk*). *Chhāp-kháṇ, chhāp-khāṇó* (*khāná* Hindust.), a printing or stamping press establishment. *Chhāp-yantr* (*yantra* Sansk.), printing machine. *Chhāpunk*, to print, to stamp ; to edit, to publish ; to mark, to seal ; to stamp with a marking-iron. *Chhāpṇí*, impression, sealing ; edition. *Chhāpkár ; chhāpkárí* (l. us.), printer, one who stamps with a die ; one who seals ; a compositor. *Chhāpí*, printed, stamped ; marked, sealed. *Chhāpó*, type ; a stamp ; seal ; mark. *Chhāpó* (pronounced by the common people *sopó*), a lead seal affixed to merchandise by the custom's office ; seal of a tax levied on the sale of commodities. *Chhāpekár* or *sopekár*, one who affixes the seal ; also used to denote the individual who is a farmer of the tax raised on the sale of goods.

Mar. *chháp* type ; stamp ; impression. *Chhāpkhāná* (m.) *chhapṇéṁ* (v.t.) *chhāpṇi* (f.), *chhāpári* (m.), *chhāpi* (adj.), *chhāpá* or *chhāppá* (m.) : for the meanings of these see above. *Chhāpíl, chhapímv*, "stamped, printed, marked-paper, cloth, coins. *Chhāpí-sulākhí* (adj.), one who bears a *chháp*, and a *sulákh*, *i.e.*, a particular stamp or mark and a hole for assaying—a rupee, etc. Much marked and punched (and thus of less weight and value)—a rupee, etc." Molesworth.[1]

Cháp, trigger. *Chāpí*, that which has a trigger (a rifle).

Guj. *chháp*, type; mark, seal; stamp, impression. *Chhāp-khánum*, press, typography, printing-machine. *Chhāpvum*, *chhāpávum*, to print, to publish. *Chhāpmārví*, to stamp, to mark. *Chhāpgár*, *chhāpnár*, printer. *Chhāpuí*, impression; cost of printing. *Chhāpāmaṇ*, *chhapāmaṇi*, *chhāpán*, cost of printing. *Chhápvum te*, publication, edition. *Chhāpvāni āvṛiti*, impression. *Chhāpêlum*, printed, stamped. *Chhāpu*, periodical, newspaper. *Chhāpô*, a mark; a periodical; a tax; a sudden attack.

Chámp, trigger of a gun.

Hind. *chhāpá*, impression, edition; the mark delineated by the Vaishnavas on their bodies. *Chhāpná*, to print. *Chhāpnevālá*, printer. *Chhāpāgar*, printing-press. *Chháp*, seal. *Chháp dená*, to seal.

[1] Molesworth derives *chháp* from Hindustani.

Hindust. *chháp*, seal; mark, impression. *Chhāpá*, edition; impression, mark; seal. *Chhāpkhāná*, a printing-press. *Chhāpáí*, edition, cost of printing. *Chhāpná*, to stamp, to print. *Chhāpāná*, *chhapāvāná*, to get or order to be printed. *Chhapná*, to be printed. *Chhāpvālá*, *chhāpevālá*, *chhāpnevālá*, *chhāpāvālá*, *chhepí*, printer.

Chámp, trigger of a gun.

L.-Hindust. *chápas*, pieces of wood used to strengthen a mast when it is racked, called in nautical language 'a fish'; vern. term *chappal*.

Nep. *chháp*, seal; stamp. *Chhápākhánā*, a printing-press. *Chhápnu*, to print.

Chámp, trigger of a gun.

Or. *chháp*, stamp, impression. *Chhāpá*, stamped, printed.

Beng. *cháp*, *chháp*, seal; printing-machine; a ridge of land, a mound of earth. *Chhāpā-yantra*, a printing-machine. *Chāpá-*, *chháp-*, *chhāpá karan*, to print. *Chhāpan*, printer. *Chhāpākár*, printer; one who stamps from a die. *Chhāpá* (*verb*), to get a thing printed; (f.) impression; (*adj.*) printed. *Chhāpán*, the act of getting a thing printed. *Chhāpākhāná*, a press.

Ass. *cháp*, a mark, impression; a press. *Chāpá*, any sort of press. *Chápi*, *chāpái*, to stamp, to print. *Chapá*, *chapalá*, stamped. *Chapkhāná*, a press, printing-office. *Chapá*, *chap* or *cháb mar*, to stamp, to print.

Sindh. *chhápa*, *chhāpô*, print. *Chápa*, a ridge left unploughed, sod. *Chhāpaṇu*, to print.

Chámpa, trigger of a gun.

Punj. *chháp*, seal; stamp; impression. *Mohar chháp*, the mark on a measure or weight that agrees with the standard; the customs-seal; the distinctive mark of the Vaishnavas; a judicial seal. *Chhapāi*, *chhapvāi*, impression; stamping; the cost of printing or stamping. *Chhāpṇá*, to print, to stamp. *Chhapṇá*, to be printed. *Chhapāuṇá*, *chhapvāuṇá*, to get a thing printed or stamped. *Chhāppá*, printing; edition; stamping.

Malayal. *chháppa*, mark; trigger. *Chhappiḍuka*, to seal. *Chhāppayiḍuka*, to cock the trigger.

Tel. *chhappá* (for *chāpá*), seal; stamp; impression.

Chhámp (for *chámpu*), trigger.

Kan. *chāpê*, stamp, print; impression; customs-mark. *Chāpisu*, to print; to stamp; to mark. *Chāpisuvara*, a printer.

Chhāppá, *tubákiya chápu*, trigger of a gun.

Tul. *chappi*, *chappe*, seal; stamp; mark. *Chhápu*, *chhappe*, a press. In the sense of 'a shop', it is derived from the English 'shop'. *Chhāpisuni*, to seal; to stamp; to print.

Chápu, trigger.

Anglo-Ind. *chop*.

Gar. *chapa*, impression.

Khas. *sháp*, seal; impression; to print.

Siam. *chabap*, copy, model.

Mal. *chap*, seal, die; stamp, impression; licence, passport. *Chapkan*, *tukang chap*, to seal; to stamp, to print. *Ber-chap*, *ter-chap*, sealed, printed. *Ber-chap-kan*, one who seals or stamps. *Menge-chap*, to print. *Men-chapkan*, to get a thing printed.

Pengechap-an, a press. *Membuluh-chap*, to affix a seal.

Ach., Batt. *chap.*—Sund. *chapa, echap.*—Jav. *echap.*—Bal. *hechap, chapchap.*—Day. *chap.*—Mac., Bug. *chá.*—Tet., Gal. *sapa.*

Pid.-Engl. *chop*, impression, inscription; label, card; a motto; characteristic. *First chop*, of superior quality.

As regards its etymology, *chapa* is one of the most intricate vocables in this book. Is it Portuguese or Indian in origin? Or, rather, are the two words etymologically distinct? Has one of them influenced the other in some of the meanings?

Yule and Burnell allege that "it has been thought possible (at least till the history should be more accurately traced) that it might be of Portuguese origin".

Gonçalves Viana in his *Vocabulário Malaio* remarks that "the Portuguese vocable has been explained by the Germanic root *klap*, and also by *plak*, equally Germanic.. It appears to me admissible that this word came from India." But in his *Apostilas* he maintains that "the most probable source of the word is the Germanic *klap* or *plak*; and he adds that "in the special sense of order, permission, ordinance, prescript" it *is* an Asiatic word and must be the Hindustani *c'āp*, 'stamp, seal'.[1]

Castanheda (1552) also regards the term as Asiatic, and explains its meaning: "He ordered that nobody should be allowed to enter the Island nor depart from it unless he carried his **chapa**, as was the practice before. And this **chapa** was, as it were, a seal except that it was open from one side to the other, and used red ochre for making the official impression."[2] And Bluteau traces the relationship between the Portuguese *chapado* and the Indian

[1] "The bonzes enter, they find every thing ready, they depart with a **chapa** or permit." Lucena, VII, ch. 20.

[2] But in the following passage he employs it in the European acceptation: "He ordered a raft to be made of ships' masts **chapados** ('covered') with many iron **chapas** ('plates')." Bk. 1, ch. 72. Cf. L.-Hindust *chápas*.

chapa: "*Homem chapado* is a man who is armed in the *chapa* of his virtue or his honest toil, etc. The expression is borrowed metaphorically from the *chapas* or plates of metal on which the kings of India caused their letters patent to be engraved."

Beames, Thomson, Fallon, and many other writers on Indian languages have no doubt at all that *chapa* is a pure Hindi term.

In the *Tombo do Estado da India* there is "a draft of the contract which the Governor Nuno da Cunha entered into with Nizamafe Zaman with respect to Cambay in the year 1537". In this are met with not only the substantive form *chapa*, but also the verb *chapar* and its participle *chapado*, all of them employed in their genuine Indian meaning: "Soon after in my presence he (Nizamafe Zaman) signed and swore on his koran (*moçafo*) to keep and to maintain and to fulfil this agreement in its entirety..... and he sealed it **(chapou)** with his seal **(chapa)**..." "And inasmuch as the coins were stamped **(chapada)** with the coining die (*sicca*), i.e., struck with their mark..." Diogo do Couto likewise says: "He [D. Manoel de Lima] granted to him [a servant] a firman inscribed in big and beautiful letters and **chapado** (sealed) with the **chapa** (seal) of his coat of arms. Dec. VI, vii, 7.[1]

It is worthy of note that in India the term *chapa* is met with only in the modern languages, with the exception, as far as I know, of Tamil and of Sinhalese, wherein it is not to be found. *Chāpa* in Sanskrit is the name of a bow. The introduction of the press has given the word new meanings and a greater denotation. Yule and Burnell are opposed to the view that *chap*, which is used in the Far East, is derived from the Chinese, and they maintain that it was carried there from India.

[1] Gaspar Correia, referring to Pedro de Covilhã, says: "Displaying a brass **chapa** ('plate') on which were engraved letters forming the name of His Majesty D. João and of Preste, in Chaldaic." Bk. III, p. 29.

As regards, the sematology of the word, the principal difference lies in the fact that in India we do not find *chapa* used in the sense of a 'metal-plate' (without inscription or engraving), for which there are special terms, like *pāṭí*, *tagaḍ* or *lagaḍ*, *patrém̃*. Likewise it is not used in the sense of 'a plain or flat piece of land'.

But there is one very notable coincidence, assuming there has been no transmission. Molesworth mentions *chhápo*, "a play among children", as a term used in the Marathi spoken in the Konkan; and Cândido de Figueiredo gives, among other meanings of *chapa*, that of "a kind of game among children". The Port. dictionary, *Contemporaneo*, explains, as also does Bluteau, the nature of the game of *chapa*, which consists in tossing up a coin and asking whether it is to be heads or tails, or cross or pile.[1]

[1] I have not been able to discover what is the nature of this children's game, which is said to be played in the Konkan.

It appears to me that *chámp* or *cháp* (with the *ch* mute), in the sense of 'a trigger of a gun' which is met with in several Indian languages, is derived from a different primary word, *chāmpná* in Hindustani, *chāpṇém̃* in Marathi, 'to press, to compress'. In Konkani the word for trigger is *kám̃v*.

To conclude, it is almost certain that *chapa* was not transmitted from Portugal to India. The argument which carries most weight is that *chháp* or *chhapá* is "a technical term used by the Vaishnavas to denote the sectarial marks (lotus, trident, etc.) which they delineate on their bodies" (Thompson, cit. in *Hobson-Jobson*); such a term could not be a foreign one, imported in modern times. The origin of the Portuguese word being itself enshrouded in uncertainty, it is not unlikely that it is Indian in origin, seeing that there is no evidence of its having been employed before the Portuguese conquests in the East. It is to be noted, however, that Duarte Barbosa (1516) employs *chapeado* in the sense in which it was used in Europe. "In front rides the Preste Joam in another waggon *chapeado* (plated) with gold, very richly attired...." P. 215. [Ed. Longworth Dames, Vol. I, 41.]

Chapéu (a hat). Konk., Mar., *chepéṁ*.—Mal. *chapéu chapíyu*.—Sund. *chapéo*.—Mac., Bug. *chapíyo*.—Nic. *śapéo*.[1]

Molesworth says: "*Chepem* n. R. (Rájápur) W. (Wari) (*chepṇem*). A low, flattish hat or cap. U̇sed esp. of the military hat or cap of the Sepoys and their officers." *Chepṇéṁ*, from which the author wrongly derives the word, signifies 'to flatten, to compress'.

In Konkani · *chepekár*, one who uses a hat; a hatter.

Chapinha (in the sense of 'a small metal-plate'). Malayal. *chappiññа*.— | Mal. *chaping*, "a metallic plate (used to cover the nudity of a very young female child)". Wilkinson. | — ? Siam. *cha' ping, ta' ping*.

Charamela (a bag-pipe). Konk. *chermél*.—Mac., Bug. *charaméle*.—Jap. *charumera, charumeru*; vern. term *rappa*.[1]

Charuto (cheroot) Tet., Gal. *sarútu*.

The primary source of this word, which has been adopted in so many Indian and Malayo-Polynesian languages, is the Tamil *churuṭṭu*, 'roll, twist, cheroot; to wrap or roll round' (Percival). "It is, therefore, evident," says Gonçalves Viana with much reason, "that from India, and not from Portugal, this term was passed on to Malay, as it was to English, and from this latter to Portuguese".[2]

Chave (a key). Konk.,

[1] "A chapeo ('hat') with purple silk nap." Gasper Correia, I, p. 534.

"On his head a black velvet chapeo." Diogo do Couto, Dec. VII, iv. 6.

[1] "With many charamelas, trumpets, etc." Diogo do Couto, Dec. VI, iv, 6.

[2] "The cherutos, as they constitute a distinct kind of merchandise, ought to be sent out in boxes, and pay a duty per thousand." F. N. Xavier, *Collecção de Bandos*, I, p. 200.

Mar. *chāví.*—Guj. *chhāví.*—Hindi *chābí.*—Hindust. *chāví*, *chābí*, *chābhí.*—L.-Hindust. *chāví*, *chābí*, (*naut.*, fid, *i.e.*, a conical wooden pin used in splicing).—Nep., Or. *chābí.*—Beng. *chābí*, *chábi*, *sābí.*—Ass. *chábi*, *sábi*. The Neo-Aryan terms are: *kilí*, *tālí*, *kunji*, *kunz.*—Tam. *sávi*; vern. terms, *tiŗappu*, *tiŗavukól.*—Tel. *sávi*, *chevi.*—Kan., Tul. *chávi.*—Anglo-Ind. *chabee.*—Gar. *chabi.*—Khas. *shabi.*—Tet. Gal. *chávi.*

In Konkani: *chāvyekar*, one in charge of the key; *chāvêr*, a bunch of keys. In the Portuguese spoken at Goa, *chaveiro* means 'a bunch of keys'.

| **Cheiro** (scent). Mol. *cheyro*, name of a plant, according to Rumphius[1]. |

Chícara (a tea-cup). Konk. *chíkr.*—Tet., Gal. *chíkara.*

[Vieyra does not mention *chicara* in his dictionary. Moraes (*Dicc. da Lingua Portugueza*) hazards the opinion that it is derived from the Hebrew *shigar*, a spirituous beverage; but the *Dicc. Contemporaneo*, more confidently, affiliates it to the Mexican *śicalli*. This fact is interesting, because the words for 'tea' and every thing associated with its service were borrowed by the Portuguese either from China or Malaya: *chávena* ('tea-cup') from Mal. *chávan* which is itself the Chin. *tch'a-van*; *pires* ('saucer') from the Mal. *pirim*, pl. *pirins*; *bule* ('tea-pot') from the Mal. *búli*. The Chinese equivalent of a 'tea-pot' is *tch'a-kuan* or *tch'a-h'u*.]

Chinela (a slipper). Konk. *chinel*. *Chinel-kárņ*, a woman who uses slippers.—Sinh. *chinélaya.*—Tam. *chinelei.*—Mal., Sund. *chinela.*—Jav. *chinélô*, *chanélô.*—Mad. *chinélô.*—Tet., Gal. *sinela.*[1]

[The Portuguese dictionaries, *Contemporaneo*, and that of Moraes Silva, do not give the derivation of *chinela*. Vieyra merely says it is an Arabic word. If this is so, it is per-

---

1 | "Its name in Latin is *Mentha crispa*; in Portuguese and Spanish **cheyro**...., by which name it is known in the Moluccas."—*Herb. Amboinense*, VIII, ch. 58. |

1 "Some **chinelas** of black velvet." Lucena, Bk. IX, ch. 5.

haps made up of the Ar. *ka-* ('like') and *n'ala* ('a shoe').]

? **Chiripos** (in the sense of 'wooden shoes'). Konk. *chirpáṁ* (neut. pl.); vern. term *khaḍhāvô*.—Tam. *cherippu*.—Malayal. *cherippu*. *Muṭṭu cherippu*, boots. *Oru vaka cherippu*, slippers.—Mal. *cherpu*.

The Port. dictionaries, *Contemporaneo*, and that of Cândido de Figueiredo, do not mention *chiripos*, perhaps, because the word is not now in use. Bluteau, Morais, Vieyra, João de Deus, and Dr. Adolfo Coelho say simply: "V. *tamancos* (wooden-shoes)". It appears to me that the word is of Dravidian origin carried by the Portuguese to Goa and Malacca. It is in use in the Portuguese spoken in India. Gabriel Rebelo says: "Some bring (in the Moluccas) wooden **chiripos**".[1]

[It is the Tam.-Malayal. *cherippu*, according to the *Glossario*.]

Chita (an Indo-Port. word; chintz, a printed cotton cloth). Konk. *chít*.—Sinh. *chitta*.—Indo-Fr. *chite*.—Mal., Mad. *chita*.—Sund. *chita*, *inchit*.—Jav. *chîtó*.—Day. *chita*, *sita*.—Mac., Bug. *chí*.—Tet., Gal. *sita*.

Bengali, Marathi, and Sindhi have *chhít*. The English 'chintz' is from the Hindustani *chinṭ*, from which is also derived the Persian *chít*. The source of the primary word is the Sanskrit *chitra*, 'speckled'.[1]

---

1 *Informação das Cousas de Maluco*, ed. Acad. of Sc., Lisb., p. 158.

Cândido de Figueiredo said, in reply to my enquiry, that he had not listed *chiripos* in his dictionary, probably because he had not found sufficient justification for doing so.

1 "All the **Chites** which are made within the Empire of the Great Mogul are printed and are of different degrees of beauty, according to the printing and the fineness of the cotton cloth" (1676). Tavernier, *Voyages*, III, p. 359 [Ox. Univ. Press ed. (1925), Vol. II, p. 4.]

"And I presented him with six stone-bottles of gin, six bottles of wine, a whole piece of **chita** printed with tree-branches, and a red coral necklace." A. J. de Castro (1845), in *Jour. Geo. Soc. Lisb.*, 2nd ser., p. 57.

The old Portuguese writers speak of the material as *pano pintado* ('painted or spotted cloth') and the term passed into Anglo-Indian speech. ["Though the word (*pintado*) was applied, we believe, to all printed goods, some of

Chocolate (chocolate). Konk. *chokolát.*—? Sinh. *sokalat.*—Tet., Gal. *chokoláti.*—*Tonk. *cù-lac.*— | Chin. *chi-kú-láh.* |

Chouriço (sausage). Konk. *chauris* (more used is *liṅgís* from Port. *linguiça.*—) Tet. *surisa.*

Chumbo (lead). Nic. *chumbo.*

The Nicobarese must have received the word directly from the Portuguese, like the names *cabra* ('goat') and *sal* ('salt'), because they are not employed in any other Asiatic language.

Chuname (Indo-Port. form adopted from the Gaurian languages; *chunambo* is the Indo-Port. form of the Dravidian word for 'lime'). "*Chuna* which is lime." Garcia da Orta, ed. Markham, p. 477.—Anglo-Ind. *chunam, chinam.*

The primary word is the Malayal. *chuṇṇámbu*, related to the Neo-Aryan *chuná*, Sansk. *chūrṇa*, 'powder'.[1]

the finer Indian chintzes were, at least in part, finished by hand-painting." *Hobson-Jobson.*]

1 With a number of pages, of whom one carries his (the ambassador of the King of Dealcan's) fan, another his silver casket full of betel, another a little box containing **chuname,** which is prepared lime." Pyrard, *Viagem*, II, p. 117 [Hak. Soc. Vol. II, p. 135].

"We asked your Lordship to pass orders that wood, tiles, and **chunambo** be given to us for the repairs." A. Bocarro, Dec. XIII, p. 736.

Cidade (a city). Konk. *sidád*; vern. terms *śahár, nagar, pur.*—Tam. *sīdári.*—Batav., Tet. *sidádi.*

Cidrão (citron). Sinh. *sideran, sidaran*; vern. term *maharaṭadehi.*

Cifra (a cipher). Konk. *síphr* (us. among the Christians); vern. terms *púz, śúnaya, bindu.*—Tet., Gal. *sifra.*

Of Arab origin, it passed on from Arabic to Persian, Hindi, and Hindustani.

Cigarro (cigarette). Konk. *sigár*; vern. term *viḍí.*—Tet. *sigáru* (more in use *canudo,* as in Indo-Port.).

Cinta (*naut.*, outward pieces of timber on a ship's sides on which men set their feet when they clamber up, wales).—Hindust. *sinta, sit.*

Cinto (girdle, belt). Mal. *cinto* (Haex).

| **Cintra** larangas de (Cintra oranges). Hindust., Pers. *sangtara*. See *Hobson-Jobson*, *s.v.* orange and sungtara | .

[Dalgado herein follows Yule who, as well as Dr. Hunter, favour the derivation of *Sangtarah* (of Babar) or *Santara*, as it is nowadays called, from Cintra, the city in Portugal famous for its oranges, from as early at least as the beginning of the fourteenth century. But Crooke points out that Col. Jarrett in his translation of the *Āīn-i-Akbarī* disputes the derivation of *Sangtarah* from *Cintra*, and is followed by Beveridge who is inclined to think that *Santra* is the Indian hill name of the fruit, of which *Sangtarah* is a corruption, and refers to a village at the foot of the Bhutan Hills called *Santrabārī*, because it had orange groves. Again, Watt (*The Comm. Products of India*, *s.v. C. Aurantium*) speaks of Bonavia who refers to four races of this fruit, the first of which is the *Süntara*, which word he regards as of Sanskrit origin and not a corruption of *Cintra*. He does not, however, mention the Sanskrit word from which it is evolved. The 'santara oranges' are the best in quality of those grown in India and may be distinguished by their yellow colour and loose skin or jacket.]

Cinturão (waist-band). Konk. *sinturáṁv*; vern. term. *kamarband*.—Tet. *sinturã*.

Cinzel (a stone cutter's chisel). Malayal. *chiññer* (=*chinnher*).

Cipai (indigenous soldier disciplined and dressed in the European style). Anglo-Ind. *sepoy*, *seapoy*. Indo-Fr. *cipaye*.[1]

From the Persian *sipāhí*, [from *aspa* (Sansk. *açva*), 'a horse'].

[The Pers. *sipāhí* bears generally the sense of 'a horse-soldier', for in early times horsemen formed the principal part of the army. The earliest Portuguese writers do not speak of *cipai* but of *lascarim* and *pião* in the same sense. The earliest

[1] "Orders were passed that other companies were to be formed, but these were to be of **sipaes.**" Cunha Rivara, *O Chronica de Tissuary*, I, p. 30.

use of the word, and that in the form *hispains*, is to be found in the *Itinerario* of Fr. Gaspar de S. Bernardino (1609), and is mentioned in the *Glossario*.]

Citação (citation, court summons). Konk. *sitsáṁv*. Sinh. *sitásiya*, *sitāsikerima*. *Setásiya karaṇavā*, to summon.—Mal. *sita*. *Surat sita*, the order of the summons.

Citar (to summon). Konk. *sitár-karuṅk*.—Mal., Ach., Sund., Bug. *sita*.—Mad. *nyíta*.

? **Coa** (liquid that is strained). Mal. *coa* (Haex), *kua*, sort of pea-soup. *Coa-anghar* (lit. 'juice of the grape'), wine.

Cobra, cobra de capelo (the venomous snake *Naja tripudians*). Anglo-Ind. *cobra*, *cobra de capello*, *cobra capella*. — Indo-Fr. *cobra-de capello*, *cobra-capello*.—Mal. *kobra*.[1]

[The following citation from P. Francisco de Sousa, *Oriente Conquistado* (1697), I, ii, 1, will help to explain why the Portuguese gave the venomous reptile this name: "This is called **cobra de capello**, because it has on its head a cartilaginous skin, which it unfolds and closes, and which when it spreads out looks like the hood of a friar, or more properly resembles a woman with false hair on her head sticking out on both sides of the face and wearing a wimple. It is a most ferocious creature, and when provoked to anger spreads its hood, rears itself up....and emits such poisonous puffs of breath that it kills chickens, fowls, and small four-

1 "There are some snakes which the Indians call Nurcas, and which we call **cobras de capelo**, because they erect a sort of hood over their heads." Duarte Barbosa, p. 344. [Hak. Soc., ed. Dames, Vol. II, p. 83. "*Murcas* is an emendation from Nurcas of the Portuguese text, in accordance with the forms in the Spanish version and in Ramusio." "It is the Malayal. *Mūrkhan*, 'a cobra', used in the term *Eṭṭaḍi mūrkham* 'eight paces cobra', because a man dies within eight paces of the spot where he is bitten"—(T.)]

"We saw here also a great number of **cobras de capello**, of the thickness of a man's thigh." Fernão Pinto, *Peregrinações*, ch. 14.

"There are many of these snakes which the common people call **cobras de capelo**, but called by us in Latin *regulus serpens*." Garcia da Orta, Col. xlii [ed. Markham, p. 336].

footed animals... The Hindus regard the *cobra* as sacred, and keep some in their temples..... An author in Rome, once happening to refer to the **cobra de capello,** heard a Portuguese who had returned from India describe it, and the Portuguese not being able to give another word for *capello*, the author was much puzzled as to whether it stood for 'hair' or 'hat', because the Italian *capello* denotes both these. As a result of this he had a cobra represented in one of his Latin books with more hair on its body than a bear, though there is not a trace of a hair on it, and with a hat on its head, with its tassels spread out. We laughed a great deal at the sight of this picture." Not less provocative of good humour is the derivation or mistranslation of the name of this snake cited by Crooke from Christopher Fryke (1700): "Another sort, which is called **Chapel snakes,** because they keep in Chapels or Churches, and sometimes in Houses." This description is obviously influenced by stories of the cobra being kept in temples, and also in private houses in India.]

Cobra manilla (the venomous snake *Bungarus caeruleus* or *Daboia Russellii*). Tel. *mañila-páyu* (*páyu* is 'snake'). —Anglo-Ind. *cobra manilla* or *minelle* (us. in South India). [In Ceylon called *polonga*.]

The source-word is the Marathi-Konkani *maṇêr*, from the Sansk. *maṇi*, 'a jewel'. The Telugu term appears to be an importation.[1]

[Molesworth in addition to *maner* also mentions the form *maṇyār*. The snake perhaps takes this name from the common belief of the people that it 'wears a precious jewel in its head'. A citation from

1 "There is yet another kind of snake even more venomous, which the Indians call Madalls. Such is their renown that they kill in the very act of biting, so that the person bitten cannot utter a single word, nor turn him round to die." Duarte Barbosa, p. 344 [Hak. Soc., Vol. II, p. 83. "No doubt in the MS. this word was written Mãdali, *i.e.*, Mandali, which is evidently the correct form". It is clearly the *Manḍali*, varieties of which are regarded as very venomous in Southern India.]

Lockyer (*An Account of the Trade in India*, etc., London, 1711, p. 276) in *Hobson-Jobson* provides one more popular explanation of the name: "The **Cobra Manilla** has its name from a way of Expression common among the *Nears* on the *Malabar* Coast, who speaking of a quick motion.. say, in a Phrase peculiar to themselves, *Before they can pull a Manilla from their Hands*. A Person bit with this Snake, dies immediately; or before one can take a *Manilla* off. A **Manilla** is a solid piece of Gold, of two or three ounces Weight, worn in a Ring round the Wrist." See *manilla*.]

Coche (a coach). Konk. *kôch*, palanquin.—? Guj., Hindi., Beng. *kôch*, sofa—? Sindh. *kôchu*, sofa—? Sinh. *kôssiya*.

Probably, like the Hindust. *kauch*, the above are derived from the English 'couch'. This appears plausible in view of the difference in meaning between the Portuguese word and those in the other languages mentioned above.

Cocheiro (coachman). Konk. *kochêr*; vern. term *gāḍīvālό*.—? Hindust. *kochbán* (perhaps from the English 'coachman').—Tet. *kochéiru*; vern. term *kuchata*.

? **Cochonilha** (cochineal). Mal. *kosnil* (Heyligers).[1]

Côco (the tree and nut *Cocos nucifera*; coco-nut). Anglo-Ind. *cocoa*, *cocoa-nut*, [*coker-nut*].—Indo-Fr. *coco*, *cocotier*.[2]

["The old Portuguese writers speak of the coco-nut palm by the generic name of *palmeira* and not as *coqueiro* ('coco-nut tree'), which is a modern term, even now not much used in Port. India. Foreign writers, who preceded the Portuguese, called the fruit *nux indica* or *noce d'*

1 "A cochonylha ('scarlet dyed') cloak valued at three thousand reis." A Tomás Pires, *Materiaes*, etc., in *Jour. Geo. Soc. Lisb.*, 16 ser., p. 715.

2 "The provision consisted of coquos." *Roteiro de Vasco da Gama* (1498-99), p 95.

"Nothing was found except **cocos** and jaggery." Castanheda, I, ch. 25.

With regard to the origin of the word *coco*, see Conde de Ficalho's ed. of Garcia da Orta, Col. xvi; Cândido Figueiredo, in the *Instituto* of Coimbra, Vol. XLVIII, p. 655, and Gonçalves Viana, *Apostilas*.

India, in imitation of the Arabs who called it *jauz-al-Hindī*. At the present time, the word *coco* is employed by all European languages.

With regard to the etymology of the word, a number of hypotheses have been suggested, not excepting that which assigns to it an Egyptian origin, *kuku*! But if we note what the old Portuguese writers, who are the most competent to speak on this matter, say, there can be no doubt about the origin of the word.

The author of the *Roteiro* (1498), referring to Mombasa, says: "The palms of this country bear a fruit as large as melons of which the kernel within is eaten and tastes like nutty galingale" (p. 28). And the same writer, when in India, says: "And the provisions consisted of **coquos** and four jars containing cakes of palm-sugar" (p. 94). It is, therefore, in Malabar that the companions of Vasco da Gama gave the name to the fruit, and certainly did not borrow it from the vernacular of the country which calls it *teṅgu*, nor from the modern Aryan languages which call it *nārel* or *nāral*, Sansk. *narikela*, Pers. *nargīl*. That they did not learn this name in the locality, but transferred it by way of analogy from one object to another, as they did in the case of *figo* and *pera* (*q.v.*), we know from Barros, da Orta, and others.

The source-word is, therefore, the Portuguese *coco*, which was formerly used, as it is even to-day in Castilian, in the sense of 'a bugbear, a grotesque face to frighten children with'. Bluteau gives a derivation which is the very reverse of this, but it indicates the meaning which *coco* had in Portugal: "*Coco* or *Coca*. We make use of these words to frighten children. because the inner shell of the *Coco* has on its outside surface three holes giving it the appearance of a skull." Dalgado, *Glossario*.

The passages from Barros and da Orta referred to in the above quotation are as follows: "Our people have given it the name of **coco**, a word applied by women to anything with which they try to frighten children; and this name has stuck, because nobody knew any other, though the proper name was, as the Malabars call it, *tenga*, or, as the Canarins call it, *narle*." Barros (1553), Dec. III, iii. 7.

"And we, the Portuguese, with reference to those three holes, gave it the name of **coquo**, for it has the appearance of the face of an ape or some other animal." Garcia da Orta, Col. LIII; ed. Markham, p. 139. But earlier Barbosa (1516), describing the coco-nut palm of Calecut, or rather of Malabar, says: "We call these fruits **quoquos**" (Lisb. Acad. ed.).

Linschoten (1596) says: "The Portingalls call this fruit (of the 'palme tree') **Coquo**, by reason of the three holes that are therein, like to a Munkie's head" (Hak. Soc., Vol. II, p. 43.). There is no doubt that herein the Dutchman is merely reproducing either da Orta (1563), or Acosta (*Tractado de las Drogas y Medecinas de las Indias Orientales*, 1578) who had borrowed largely from da Orta. But P. A. Tiele who edited the second volume of Linschoten for the Hak. Soc. in a note to *coquo* says that "the name 'coco' was first used by the Spaniards who found the tree in America". He gives no evidence for this statement which, after the thorough and convincing exposition of Dalgado, needs merely to be mentioned as one of the various suggestions that have been put forward to explain the name.

There is no unanimity of opinion with regard to the question as to what is the original home of the coco-nut palm. De Candolle ultimately inclined to the idea of an origin in the Indian Archipelago. Cook stoutly upholds an American origin. Wiesner (*Die Rohst. des Pflanzenr.*, 1903, II, 419) quotes authority for a dual nationality (American and Asiatic). But the general trend seems to be in favour of an Asiatic origin. See Watt, *The Commercial Products of India, s.v. Cocos nucifera.*]

Codilho (codille; a term at ombre when the game is won

against the player). Mac., Bug. *dílu*.

Côco do mar (the twin fruit of the *Lodoicea Seychellarum*;[1] 'the coco-nut of the Maldives,' according to Garcia da Orta). Anglo-Ind. *coco-de-mer*.—Indo-Fr. *coco de mer*.[2]

Coelho (rabbit). Mal. *kovélu, tarvélu*.—Jav. *tarvélu*.—Tet., Gal. *koêlhu*. See *cavalo*.[3]

Cofre (coffer; safe). Konk. *kophr*.—Tet., Gal. *kófri*.

Coifa (head-dress of women, skull-cap). Mal. *kofiah*, | *kópiah* |, *kúpia*, a birreta, the square cap worn by Roman Catholic priests.[1]

Coitado (miserable, to be pitied). Konk. *kuitád*; vern. term *bābḍó*.—Mal. *coitado* (Haex).

Colaça (the name of one variety of the mango). Konk., Mar. *kulás*. Cf. *Afonsa, Carreira*.

Colchão (mattress). Konk. *kulchámv*.—L.-Hindust. *kuñiyáñ*.—Sinh. *kulach-chama*.—Tet., Gal. *kulchã*.

Colchete (hook, clasp). Konk. *kulchêt*; vern. terms *kaḍí, āṅkḍí*.—Tet., Gal. *kulchêti*.

Colégio (college). Konk. *koléj*: vern. terms *pāṭhsáḷ, maṭh*.—Tet. *koléju*.—Jap. *koreijo*.

Cólera (*Cholera Morbus*). Guj. *kolerô*.—*Jap. *korera* (introd. in modern times). See *mordexim*.

[It is said that references to the disease, known to-day as 'cholera', are to be met with in the writings of the

---

1 "Wide forests there beneath Maldivia's tide
From with'ring air their wondrous fruitage hide.
The green hair'd Nereids tend the bow'ry dells,
Whose woudrous fruitage poison's rage expels."
Mickle's Tr. of the *Lusiad*, Bk. X, p. 348 (Bohn Lib).

2 "It is probable that G. da Orta was the first European who described this shape of the coco-nut, and that the Portuguese were the first to introduce it into Europe." Dr. D. G. Dalgado, *Classificação Botanica das Plantas e Drogas*, etc., p. 9.

3 "And two dozen of **coelhos** male and female for the King, to be kept in enclosures, because they are not to be had in Cambay." Diogo do Couto Dec. VII, iii, 1.

1 "And on the head over a coifa of gold, a velvet cap." João de Barros, Dec. II, x, 8.

Hindu physician Susruta. Whitelaw Ainslie (*Mat. Med.*, Vol. II, p. 531) gives various names by which the disease was known in the different parts of India: *Ennērum vāndie* in Tam., *Dānk-lugnā* in Deccani, *Chirdie rogum* in Sansk., *Vāntie* in Tel., *Nirtiripa* in Malayalam. This would indicate that the disease was widespread in India and certainly known in the zone in which the Portuguese influence was most felt. Garcia da Orta speaks of it as **collerica passio,** and Couto as **colera** (see *Hobson-Jobson*); one might, therefore, have expected that the foreign name for this disease would have found an entry into more of the Indian languages, especially in view of the extensive practice then enjoyed by Portuguese physicians. But the curious fact is that, far from this being the case, the Portuguese themselves borrowed the Konk.—Marathi *modśi*, the name for cholera, corrupted it into *mordexim* (*q.v.*) and passed it on to the English and the French in the form *mort-de-chien*, which was the name by which cholera was known to Europeans up to the end of the eighteenth century. Da Orta says that *morśi* was called *hachaiza* in Arabic. This Ar. name in the form *haizah* is still used in Hindustani to denote 'cholera'. Burnell (n. *Linschoten*, Hak. Soc., Vol. I, p. 235) says that the first European to mention this frightful disease was Garcia da Orta in 1563, but it was known long before in India under the Sanskrit name *vīsūcikā*, which does not however agree with the name given by Ainslie.]

Colete (a waistcoat). Konk. *kulêt.*—Tet. *kolêti.*

Colher (a spoon). Konk., Malayal., Tulu. *kulér.*

Coluna (a column). Konk. *kolún.* (l. us.); vern. term *khāmbó.*—Sinh. *kuluna, kulunna* (pl. *kulunu*); vern. terms *stambhaya* (Sansk.), *ṭemba.*

Comadre (the godmother in her relationship to the father and mother of a child who is christened). Konk. *kumár;* the term also signifies 'mistress, concubine'[1]. *Kumarki*, the relationship of a '*comadre*'.—Beng. *komādri*. —Tam. *kumádri*.

Comandante (a commander). Konk. *komāndánt*. Punj. *kumedan*.—Tel. *kumumdán*.—? Day. *kamandan*.—Tet. *komandánti*.—Ar. *qumandán*.[2]

Comando (command). Tel. *kómánu*.

Comedoria (ration; meat and drink allowed to one of the king's officers). Konk. *komedorí* (l. us.); vern. term *bhātém*.—Beng. *komedorí* (us. among the Christians).

Comenda (commendam; also a decoration). Konk. *komend*, decoration, medal.—Mal. *koménda*.[3]

Commendador (commander of orders of knighthood). Konk. *komendādôr*.—Mal., Jav. *komendadór*, *komendúr*, a title of certain civil officials. Cf. *mandador*. —Bug. *kamánderē* (from the Dutch *kommandeeren*, according to Matthes).

Compadre (the godfather in his relationship to the parents of a child who is christened). Konk. *kumpár*; also used in the sense of a 'clandestine lover'. Cf. *comadre*.—*Kumpārki*, the relationship of a '*compadre*.' —Beng. *kompādri*, godfather. —Tam. *kompádri*, godfather. —Tel. *kumbádri*.—Tul. *kumpádri*, *kumpari*, godfather.—Tet. *kompári*, *kombári*.

Compasso (a compass; also measure, time). Konk. *kumpás*.—? Guj., Hindust., Beng., Ass. *kampás*.—Tet. *kompásu*.—? Jap. *kompasu*.

Yule and Burnell are of the opinion that the Hindust. *kampās* is a corruption of the English 'compass'; the same may be said of the forms in the other languages, excepting Konkani and Teto. *Kumpas* in L.-Hindust. has certainly its origin in English, and the Malay *kampas*, in Dutch.

---

1 It appears that this word, in this acceptation, is related to the Sanskrit *kumārī*, 'young lady, maiden'.

2 In Kambojan, *comandang*, *general*, *amiral*, *compagni* ('association'), are of French origin.

3 "Specially in the Moluccas the word *kommenda* implies a contract of civil law which is absolutely the same as the *commodatum* of Roman law." Heyligers.

Compra (a purchase) Jap. *kompra.*

Dr. Murakámi associates *compra* with *compradoru*, and gives them the same meaning.

Comprador (in the sense of 'a purchaser; a house-steward'). Anglo-Ind. *compradore, compadore.*—Pid.-Engl. *compradore, compladore, kampat-to.*—Jap. *kompradoru.*

In India, the term is falling out of use; in China, it was used at one time, and is still used at times, to designate a commercial agent, the intermediary in business transactions between European and indigenous merchants. In this sense, *comprador* is also used in the French of Tonquin.[1]

["This word was formerly in use in Bengal, where it is now quite obsolete; but it is perhaps still remembered in Madras. In Madras the *compradore* is (or was) a kind of house-steward who keeps the household accounts, and purchases necessaries." *Hobson-Jobson.* The duties of the *compradore* were subsequently performed in Bengal by the 'banyan', now usually called 'sircar.']

Comungar (to receive communion). Konk. *kumgár* (also us. as a subst.).—Tet. *komúnga.*

Comunhão (Holy Com-

"And so Martim Afonso wrote to António da Silva, who kept his own counsel about the (threat of) war, because, during the delay caused by the exchange of messages, he was all the time buying and selling through his **compradores.**" Gaspar Correia, III, p. 562.

"The **comprador** ought to be a conscientious man, diligent, and intelligent in the matter of his duties" *Archivo-Portuguez Oriental*, Fasc. V, p. 1040.

["This inconvenience did not frighten them into settling the bargain; but it did frighten the sellers, and then all the Provinces, who could not understand the self-assurance of the **Compradores.**" Faria y Sousa, *Asia Portugueza*, III, p. 96.]

1 "After the war between China, England, and France, the institution of the "Hongs" or official agents, tradesmen intermediaries between the European and Chinese merchants, was abolished. They, therefore, got hold of some special indigenous agents to whom the Portuguese had given the name **compradores,** a designation which the other European nations adopted; they are the agents whom the business houses even to this day employ." Calado Crespo, *Cousas da China*, pp. 15-16.

munion). Konk. *komunháṁv.*—Beng., Tam., Kan. *komuniyāñ.*

Concêrto (agreement; concert). Konk. *konsért* (l. us.).—Mal. *concierto,* agreement, harmony (Haex).

Conde (knave in cards). Konk. *kond.*—Mac., Bug. *kóndi.*

Condenado (damned). Konk. *kondenád* (in use among the Christians).—Tet. *kondenádu.*

Confeito (comfit, sugarplum). Konk. *komphêt* (l. us.).—Tet. *konfeitu.*—Jap. *conféto* (Wenceslau de Morais), *kompeito, kompéto.*

Confessar (to confess). Konk. *kumsár,* confession. *Kumsár-karuṅk,* to hear confession; (fig.) to advise privately and insistently. *Kumsár-zāvuṅk,* to make one's confession.—Malayal. *kompasá-rikka,* to confess.—Tul. *kumusákụ,* consultation.—Tet., Gal. *konfésa,* to confess, confession.

The Tulu term is, both in respect of its form and meaning, an immediate adoption of the Konkani *kumsár.*

Confiança (confidence, trust). Konk. *koṁphyáṁs*; vern. terms *visvás, lagtí.*—Tet. *konfiansa*; vern. term *fiér.*

Confissão (confession). Beng., Tam., Kan. *komphisáñ.*—Jap. *kohisan.*

Confraria (brotherhood; a sodality). Konk. *komphrārí, komphr.*—Tet. *konfraría.*

Conselho (advice). Konk. *konselh* (l. us.); the vern. term is *budh.*—Mal. *conseillo* (Haex).—Tet., Gal. *consêlu.*

Consentir (to consent). Mal. *consentir* (Haex).—Tet. *konsénti*; vern. term *lérus.*

Consoada (a light supper as upon a fast day). Konk. *kuṅsvár.*—Beng. *konsuvādá.*

Cônsul (a consul). Konk., Tet., Gal. *kónsul.*—* Kamb., * Siam. *cŏngsul* (from French).—* Pid-Engl. *consu* (probably from English).[1]

---

[1] "One who was in service among them as *Xabandar,* an office which among us corresponds to the consules of nations." Barros, Dec. II, vi, 3.

[*Xabandar,* from Pers. *Shāh bandar,* lit. 'King of the Haven', Harbour-Master. This was the title of an officer at the ports all over the Indian seas, who was the chief authority with whom foreign traders and ship-masters had to transact. In the big

Conta (an account). Konk. *kont*; vern. terms *hiśób*, *lekh*, *lekhó*, *ganṭí*, *bábat*, *sankhyá*.—Mal. *kunta*; vern. term *kíra-kíra*.—Tet., Gal. *konta*: vern. term *rótus*.

Contas (beads of a rosary). Konk. *kont*; vern. terms *mālá*, *zapmālá*, *samarṇí*.—Sinh. *kôntaya*, *kontêya*; vern. terms *akśa*, *māláva*, *japa-māláva*. Malayal. *konta*.—Tet. *kontas*. —Jap. *kontasu*.[1]

Contente (contented). Mal. *contento* (Haex).—Tet. *kontenti*; vern. terms *sólok*, *mók*.

Contra (against). Konk. *kontr* (also in the sense of 'contrary, opposite'); vern. term *áḍ*.—Tet. *kontra*; vern. term *sákar*.

Contrato (a contract). Konk., Mar., Sinh. *kontrát* (also used in the sense of 'a business, a monopoly'); the Neo-Aryan terms are *kablát*, *karár*, *khaṇḍ*, *khotí*, *guttó*.—? Bug. *kóntarā* (from the Dutch *contract*, according to Matthes).—Tet., Gal. *kontrátu*.

In Konkani, *kontrat karuṅk* is 'to contract; to enjoy a monopoly; to do business, to traffic'; *kontrát ghevuṅk* is 'to secure a monopoly'.

Contra vontade (against one's wish, unwillingly). Konk. *kontrā vontád* (l. us.); vern. term *khuśê bháyr*.—Tet. *kontrāvontádi*; vern. term *hírus*.

Convite (invitation). Konk. *koṁvít*; vern. term *āpauṇéṁ*.—Tet. *konvíti*; vern. term *téne*.

? Copaiba (copaiba). Jap. *kapaibe*.

It perhaps made its entry through English.

Cópia (copy, transcript). Konk. *kóp*; vern terms *nakal*, *prat*. *Kop kāḍhuṅk*, *kopyár-*

---

commercial emporiums of the East, separate quarters of the city used to be occupied by merchants of distinct nationalities, each of which was under the control of an officer appointed by the King who was called *shabunder*, and who was, as a rule, of the same nationality as the merchants. In some ports, as in Malacca, there were in the early Portuguese days as many as five *shabunders*. The Persians still call their consuls *Shāh-bandar*. See *Hobson Jobson*, and *Glossario*.]

1 "Afonso d' Albuquerque with some **contas** in his hand, and behind him a page carrying a prayer-book, went to Church." Gaspar Correia I, p. 982.

"I distributed many **contas**, gilt crosses, medals, and other tokens." A. F. Cardim, p. 162.

karuṅk, to copy; vern. term *utruṅk*.—Tul. *koppi*.—Tet., Gal. *kópi* (also 'to copy'); vern. term *bonáti*.

Copo (a drinking cup). Konk. *kóp*.—Sinh. *kóppaya*, *kóppe*. *Loku kóppaya* (lit. 'a big cup'), a basin.—Malayal. *kóppa*.—Tel. *kōpá*.—Tul. *kópu*. —Ann. *cõc*.—Tonk. *cóc*.—Tet., Gal. *kópu*, *kóbu*.—Jap. *kóppu*; it also signifies 'a tea-cup', perhaps under the influence of the Dutch *kop* or of the English 'cup'; vern. term *ippai*.—Ar. *koba*.

In Konkani, *kóp* is used solely of 'a wine glass' and, figuratively, of 'wine'. The drinking glass is called *vidr* from Port. *vidro*, 'glass'. *Kóp ghevuṅk*, to drink a cup. *Kopíst*, a drunkard.

Copas (hearts in cards). Konk. *kopáṁ*.—Bug. *kópasã*.

Copra (the dried kernel of the coco-nut). Anglo-Ind. *coprah*.—Indo-Fr. *copre*.

The immediate source-word of the Indo-Portuguese word is the Malayal. *koppara*, from the Hindust. *khopṛa*. Sansk. *kharpara*.[1]

Côr (colour). Konk. *kôr*; vern. term *rang*.—Tet. *kôr*.[1]

Coração (heart). Konk. *kurãsáṁv*. a heart-shaped ornament. Mal. *korsang*, *krusang*, *krungsang*, "a sort of gold brooch which serves to fasten in front the dress of women". Favre.—Jav. *korsañ*.

Corda (cord). Konk. *kórd* (of musical instruments).—Malayal. *karaḍa*.

Cordame (cordage). L.-Hindust. *kurdamí*.

Cordão (silk rope, twist, or braid). Konk. *kordáṁv*.—Hindust. *kardhaní*.—L.-Hindust. *kurdam*.—Tam. *kordan*. —Malayal. *koḍudam*.— | Turk. *qordéla*. |

1 "They also dry the cocos after removing the rind and make them into dried pieces which they call **copra**." Garcia da Orta Col. xvi [ed. Markham, p. 142.].

"The kernel of the coco after it is dried and shrunken is called **copra**." Fr. João dos Santos, *Ethiopa Oriental*, I, p. 294.

"Their food is coco-nuts dried in the sun, which in India they commonly call **copra**." Diogo do Couto, Dec. IV, iv, 8.

1 "They do not use the word *cór* ('colour'), but only the quality of the colour, as: white colour they call *mútin*, and not *cór mútin*, etc." P Aparicio da Silva.

Corja (a mercantile term for 'a score'). Konk. *kórj*. Malayal. *kórja*, *kórchchu*.—Tul. *kórji*.—Anglo-Ind. *corge*, *coorge*.—Indo-Fr. *corge*, *courge*.[1]

It appears that the source-word is the Neo-Aryan *koḍí*. Wilson (*A Glossary of Judicial and Revenue Terms*) mentions the Telugu *khorjam* as the original, which Yule and Burnell presume to be a corruption of the trade word.

[*Corja* in Port. or *corje* in Anglo-Ind. is a very interesting word and its derivation is a source of considerable divergence of opinion. Dalgado, in his *Glossario*, modifies his views expressed herein and suggests that the Malayalam *kórchchu*, which means 'a threaded string' (like a string of pearls) or 'a bundle of thread', derived from the verb *kōrkk*, 'to thread', is the original of the Port. word *corja*; for the *ch* of Malayal. is represented by *j* in Port. and *vice versa*. The Port. *jagara* is from *chákkara*, and *jaca* from the Malayal. *chakka*; conversely the Malayal. *chenel* is the Port. *janela*, and *chudu* the Port. *jogo*. He is of the opinion that the term acquired great vogue in India, owing to its being synonymous with the Aryan *koḍī*, in the sense of 'a score', because it was usual for a great number of commercial articles to be sold 'by the score'. H. H. Wilson gives the Telugu *khorjam* as the source-word, but Yule and Burnell presume this to be a corruption of the trade word. And in fact, Brown in his Telugu dictionary observes that *korja* or *khorja* is a commercial term. Konkani has *korj* (side by side with *kôḍ*), Tulu *kōrji*, and Malayal. *kōrja*, which is evidence that they owe their origin to the

1 "These kinds of cloths are reckoned in **corjas**, for among them they count by scores, just as we do by dozens." Duarte Barbosa, p. 283 [Hak. Soc., ed. Dames, Vol. I, p. 161].

A **corja** of *cotonia* (*q v.*) costs one hundred and forty '*tangas*.' *Lembranças das Cousas da India*, p. 49.

"We speak of **corja** rubies, which is as much as to say they are sold in lots of twenty. Garcia da Orta, Col. xliv. [Markham renders this: "Such as we call score rubies because they are sold at twenty the *vintem*". There is an evident confusion between *vinte* ('twenty') and *vintem* ('a Portuguese coin worth about twenty *reis*.')]

Port. form. The Neo-Aryan languages have *koḍī*, admitted also in Tamil, to designate the number twenty; it is very much in vogue among the people who reckon in *kodis* or 'scores'. But the difficulty is to show the process of phonetic evolution which could give *corga* from *koḍī* or *koṛī*, in view of the fact that the normal representation of this word, in Portuguese, would be *cori* or *core* as *areca* is from *aḍeka*. Longworth Dames who has taken special pains to collect expert opinions on the origin of this word comes to the conclusion that, if the Dravidian origin is admitted as possible, the Malayal. form suggested by Dalgado seems more probable than the Kanarese *korji* put forward by Crooke in *Hobson-Jobson*, especially, as trade words are most likely to have come into use on the Malabar coast. He notes that Dr. G. P. Badger (*The Travels of Ludovico di Varthema*, Hak. Soc.) says that *koraja* is in use in the same sense among the Arabs of the Red Sea and Persian Gulf, but he did not consider it of Arabic origin. It is no doubt purely Indian, and must have been introduced into the Red Sea and Persian Gulf by the Portuguese and by Indian traders. See Longworth Dames, *The Book of Duarte Barbosa*, Vols. I and II, pp. 162 and 234 respectively; Dalgado's *Glossario*, and *Hobson-Jobson*, *s.v.*]

Cornaca (an elephant-driver). Anglo-Ind. *cornac*.

Probably from the Sinh. *kúrava-náyaka*, 'chief of the elephant-stud.'[1]

[The author, in his *Glossario*, says that the immediate source-word of the Portuguese *cornaca* is not the Sanskrit *karṇakin*, but the Sinhalese *kuruneka*, from which were also evolved the

---

[1] "The wife of a **Cornaca** (**Cornacas** are those who look after elephants)." Diogo do Couto, Dec. V, vii, 11.

"The **cornacas** are those who tame elephants and ride on them." João Ribeiro, *Fatalidade Historica da Ilha de Ceilão*, Bk. 1, ch. 10. "These animals go about in the forests in bands, and there is always among them one who is bigger and more feared than the others, who is called the *guarda-bando* ('the leader of the band'). *Id.*, I, ch. 17.

forms *kūrunāyak* and *kuruvanāyaka*. *Kūruva-nāyaka* is 'the chief of the *kūruva* or herd of elephants; tamer of elephants'. Among other citations, he gives one from P. E. Pieris, *Ceylon* (II, p. 67), which brings out the Sinhalese meaning very clearly: "They (the elephants) were then led away by the **Kurunayakas** whose duty it was to tame them, each animal being secured to four tame ones."]

? **Corno** (horn). Mal. *kurn*, | *kérnu*, 'a powder-horn'; | vern. term *tandoq*. | In Ar. also *karn* signifies 'horn'. |

Corneta (a cornet, trumpet). Konk. *kornêt*; vern. term *karṇó*, *kál*.—Tet., Gal. *korneta*.

Côro (choir). Konk. *kôr*.—Tet. *kôru*.

Coroa (crown). Konk. *kurôv*; vern. term *mukuṭ*, *táz*.—Tet., Gal. *koróa*.

In Konkani, the term is also used to signify 'the clerical tonsure', which the common people also speak of as *pharád* (fem.), from the Port. *frade*, 'a friar'.

Coronel (colonel). Konk. *kornél*.—Mar. *karnel*.—Guj., Hindi, *karnel*.—Hindust. *karnail*.—Beng. *karṇel*.—Sinh. *kórnel*.—Tul. *karnélu*.—Mal. *karnel*.—Bug. *koronéli*.—Tet., Gal. *koronel*.

[It may be that in some of the Indian languages the term found its way from English, and in Malay, from Dutch.

Corpinho ('a little doublet or bodice'). Mal. *kurpinyu*.

Corredor (a corridor). Konk. *kurredór*.—? Mal. *koridor*, a balcony, a verandah.

It is probable that the Malay term is of Dutch or English origin.

Corrente (*subst.*, a stream, current; also a chain). Konk. *kurrênt*, a chain; vern. term *sarpaḷí*.—Tet. *korrénti*, fetters for convicts; vern. term *bési*.

Cortesia (courtesy). Konk. *kortesí*, bow.—Tet. *kortezia*; vern. terms *úkur*, *kuát*.

Cortina (a curtain). Konk. *kurtín*; vern. term *paḍḍó*.—Guj. *kurtaní*.—Tet., Gal. *kortina*.

Corveta (*naut.*, a corvette, a war-vessel with one tier of guns). Konk. *kurvêt*.—Tet. *kurveta*.

Costa (coast). Mal. *kósta*, 'the Coromandel Coast'. *Sagu sa-Costa*, the sagu of the Coast (Haex). *Saputangang kosta*, or *supo etangang kosta*, a kerchief from the Coast (*lensu di costa*, in the Portuguese dialect). Sund. *kósta*. *Kain kosta* or simply *kosta*, a variety of printed fabric. *Char kosta* (lit. 'banana of the Coast'), a species of banana.[1]

In Anglo-Indian speech 'The Coast' had likewise the same restricted meaning.[2]

["This term in books of the 18th century means the Madras or Coromandel Coast and often the Madras Presidency." *Hobson-Jobson*, *s.v.* The Coast."]

1 "Here (in Malacca), live all sorts of rich (*grosos*) merchants, both Mohammedans and Hindus, many of them from Choromandel." Duarte Barbosa, p. 371. [Longworth Dames (Vol. II, p. 172) mistranslates *grosos mercadores* by "wholesale merchants"; the confusion is between *grosso, adj.*, 'rich', and *per grosso*, 'wholesale'].

2 "Great was the joy and gladness on all the **Costa** at the arrival of the great, and holy Father Francisco." Lucena, Bk. V, ch. 23. "Of the instructions and directions he gave on the **Costa** to the priests." *Id.*, ch. 25.

Costado (*naut.*, the side of a ship). L.-Hindust. *kustád*.

Costume (a custom). Konk. *kustum* (l. us.); vern. terms *samvay*, *vaz*, *chál*.—Mal. *costume* (Haex); vern. terms *ádat*, *resam*.—Tet. *kostúmi*.

Costura (*naut.*, the seams of a ship). L.-Hindust. *kasturá*.

Cotão (a sort of vest hanging to the knees). Konk. *kutáṁv*, tunic, dressing gown; a bodice.—Sinh. *kottama*, jacket.—Tam. *kuttán*, chemise.—? Mal., Mac., Bug. *kútang*, bodice, chemise.—? Sund. *kutang*, *kutung*.—? Jav. *kotang*.[1]

The question of the origin of this word, in the Asiatic languages, is not very clear. It may be the Port. *cotão* in the sense of 'garment for

1 "A species of under-shirt or close-fitting **cutão**" *O Gabinete Litterario das Fontainhas*.

"Francisco Barreto used to ride on a horse, one of those which had an escape from poison at Sena, always arrayed in a thick knitted **cottão**." P. Monclaio (1569), in *Jour. Geo. Soc. Lisb.*, 2nd ser., p. 550.

"**Cutão** or jacket of deep blue colour with scarlet cuffs." (part of the military uniform in Goa, 1828.) *Bosquejo das Possessões Portuguezas*, I, p. 81.

every day wear' (Morais). or an augmentative of *cota*, 'a vest of thick texture' (*Segundo Cerco de Diu*, from which Morais quotes). But it is also possible, if not probable, that the original word may be the Malay *kútong*, which is also used in the corrupt Portuguese dialect of Malacca, carried to India by the Portuguese together with the *baju*, another article of Malay dress. which is worn on the top of the *kutong*. This explanation would fit in better with the meanings of the Indian words, excepting that of 'dressing gown' in Konkani, which appears to agree with that of the augmentative *cotão*.

It is to be noted that *kútong*, in its turn, may be traced to the Persian *khaftán*, 'gown', since Fabre is of the opinion that *báju* has also its origin in the same language, although there is a difference in the meanings of the words: "*bazu*, the name of a garment used in bathing which is tied at the waist". There is another word in Persian, *kattán* or *kuttán*, which signifies 'a fabric made of linen'. According to Shakespear, *qaftán*, in Turkish. is "a robe of honour".

With regard to *baju*, the word belongs to the Portuguese vocabulary. Cândido de Figueiredo mentions it as a term current in Miranda, and the Portuguese dictionary, *Contemporaneo*, says that "the women's jackets, used in the province of Minho, are called by that name".

João de Sousa derives *baju* from the Arabic *badjú* and defines it as "a certain species of gown which was largely used by women, and which some women, even now. use in our provinces where they give it this name"; he quotes in support Damião de Góis: "The King of Calicut was dressed in a white *baju* of silk and gold, and was seated on a *catel*[1] [a sort of bed in

1 "The king was dressed in a **Baju** (which is like a short gown) of very fine cotton cloth, with many gold and pearl buttons; on his head he wore a velvet-cap adorned with precious stones and gold plates. This is the usual apparel of all the kings of Malabar, because no other person except they wear the **baju** and the cap." I, ch. 41.

Malabar]." Morais, who attributes to the word the same origin, says that it is "a garment which covers the body; it has short sleeves and a skirt up to the knees: in Asia, both men and women wear it; in Brazil, only the women, and some of them there call it *bajó*". Vieira mentions both forms *bajó* and *bajú*, and defines either as "an Asiatic garment in the form of a jacket"; in support he quotes Castanheda,[1] and observes that the term is "used in the popular songs of the Azores Islands". Bluteau has *baju* as a "word from India", and gives it the meaning of "a shirt covering half the body".

The author of *Chronica dos Reis de Bisnaga* gives the form *bajuris* and says that "they are like shirts with a skirt". The term is met with in the Port. dialect of Goa specially in connection with the phrase *pano-baju*, which is used of a certain style of female dress, to distinguish it from the *pano paló*, a style which is purely indigenous.[1]

Among the Indian languages Konkani alone recognises the word (*bãzú*), and employs it in the Malay acceptation. The Sinhalese women use the *baju*, but they call it *báchchiya*.[2]

The Arabic and Persian dictionaries which I have consulted do not mention *badju* or *bazu* in the sense of 'a gown' or anything like it, nor could the Arabic scholars whose assistance I sought help me to clear the point. But H. N. Van der Tuuk is of the opinion that the Persian *bāzū*, 'arm' (Sansk. *bāhu*), is the source of the word; that orig-

1 "The king of Ceylon was wearing a silk **bajo**, which is a garment like a jacket made of cotton cloth." "The kings of the Moluccas dress in the Malay manner and the **bajús** are of rich silk with gold buttons."

1 "The word is met with in connection with the dress of the Christian women of Damaun and Diu, and even in Goa, under the form *saráss*, signifying, unless I am mistaken, the *pano-baju* of the Brahmin Christian women of Salsete (in Goa)." Alberto de Castro, p. 172.

2 "They wear the *bajú* and a cloth which reaches right down to the soles of the feet, a style very staid and decorous." João Ribeiro, Bk. I, ch. xvi.

inally *bājū* was no other than "*een kleeding-stuk met armen*, a gown with arms", i.e., sleeves! Yule and Burnell hold it for certain that the source of the Anglo-Ind. *badjoe* or *bajoo*, 'the Malay jacket', is the Mal. *bājū*; and the authors whom they cite appear to confirm their opinion.[1] The term is met with in the principal languages of the Indian Archipelago, as for instance, Javanese, Batak, Dayak, Macassar, Bugui. [Linschoten (Hak. Soc. Vol. I, p. 206), speaking of "the maner and customes of Portingale and Mesticos women in India", says, "within the house they goe bare headed with a wastcoate called **Baju**, that from their shoulders covereth their navels, and is so fine that you may see, al their body through it...." Burnell who edited this volume explains the word thus: *Baju*, *i.e.*, Hind. *bāzū*, is "a kind of short shirt, reaching down to the hips, with very short (if any) sleeves; sometimes open at the upper part of the chest in front" (*Qanoon-e-Islam*, ed. 1863, p. xv.]

1 "Over this they wear the **badjoo**, which resembles a morning gown, open at the neck, but fastened close at the wrist, and half-way up the arm." Marsden.

"They wear above it a short-sleeved jacket, the *baju*, beautifully made, and often very tastefully decorated in fine needle-work." Bird.

Cotonia (a kind of piece-goods either of silk or mixed silk and cotton). Konk., Mar. *kutní*, striped cloth either of silk or cotton.—Anglo-Ind. *cuttanee*.[1]

The original word is the Arabic *quṭnía*; but Yule and Burnell suggest doubtfully the Persian *kuttán*, 'linen or cotton cloth'.

1 "With the awnings of the *fustas*, and some sails and **cotonias** which they had bought they prepared tents and shelters." Gaspar Correia, III, p. 617 See *corja*.

"**Cotonias** of cotton, *teadas*, and inferior cloth of other kinds." A. de Albuquerque, *Cartas*, Vol. I, p. 224. [*Teada* is used by the Portuguese chroniclers of India exclusively in the sense of 'whole piece of white cotton cloth'. See *Glossario*, p. 364.]

"With breeches of **cotonia** reaching half-way down the legs, a coat of mail, and a two-handed sword in hand." Diogo do Couto, Dec. VII, ii. 11.

"**Cotoni** of silk...**Cotoni** of silk and gold, and of silk and silver." Tavernier, *Voyages*, V, p. 202.

Couve (cabbage). Konk. *kôb.*—Mar. *kôb, kobí, koí*; vern. term *karam.*—Guj. *kobí*; *kobíj* (=*couves*, the pl. form). —Hindi *kobí, gobí, gobhí*; vern. term *karamu-kallá.*— Hindust. *kobí.*—Or. *kobi.*— Beng. *kobi, kobiśák, kopiśak* (*śak*=vegetable).—Sinh. *kóvi*; vern. terms *sudumul, góva, gova-geḍiya* (lit. 'fruit from Goa').—Tam. *kóvi.*—Malayal. *góvi, goviṇṇu.* Kan. *kōbisu.*— Tul. *góbi.*—Gar. *kóbi*; vern. term *mesumasa.*—Tib. *ko-pi*; vern. term *pe-chhe. Ko-pi metok,* cauliflower.—Khas. *kubi.*—Mal. *kóbis, kúbis.*—Jav. *koubis, kúbis.*—Mad. *kóbis.*— Tet., Gal. *kóbi.*

The compound hybrid *phúl-kobí* or *phúl-gobí* is the name of the cauliflower in almost all the Indian languages. In Malasia *kól* is more in use; it is derived from the Dutch *kool.*

Cova (pit, hole, grave). Mal. *koba* (a term used in some game).—Mac. *kova.*

Côvado (a cubit or ell). Konk. *kôbd.*—Anglo-Ind. *covid* (obs).—Tet., Gal., *kóvadu.*

This term was at one time very much in use in trade circles in India. Tavernier (1676) refers to it frequently and regards it as a vernacular term. "*Bofetas* measure 21 **cobits** when they are unbleached, but when bleached they are only 20 **cobits.**" (V. p. 200). [Ox. Univ. Press. ed. (1927), Vol. II, p. 6.]

[Tavernier gives further information of the 'cubit' in Bk. II, ch. xii: "The *cobit* is a measure for all goods which can be measured by the ell, of which there are different kinds, as we have different kinds of ells in Europe. It is divided into 24 *tassots.*" *Tassot* ought to be *tasū*, which is properly the breadth of the second and third fingers. *Bofeta*, in the former quotation, is the Pers. *bāfta* (past part.), 'woven', and is the name of a very fine calico, made specially at Broach.]

Cozido (*subst.*, boiled meat). Konk. *kuzíd.*—Tam. *kujíd.*

Cozinha (kitchen). Konk. *kuzín.*—Sinh. *kússiya.*—Tam. *kusini. Kusinik-káran,* a cook.—Tel. *kusini-kára, kusi-ni-vádu,* a cook.—Kan. *kuśi-ni.*—Tul. *kusinu, kusini,* *kusní. Kusnida*, culinary.—Malag. *kozina.*

***Crasso** (thick, gross). Mal., Sund., Jav. *kras, keras* (*adj.* and *adv.*), strong, vigorous; strongly, energetically. Haex and Swettenham also mention the form *dras.*

Dr. Heyligers admits the Portuguese origin; but it appears to me that his opinion is not well-founded. *Crasso* is a term used generally by the learned. See *grosso.*

?Cravado (stuck into, thrust into). Tam, Malayal. *karuváḍu*, salted fish.

The derivation, suggested by Gundert, is improbable because of the meaning of the word. *Karavala* is 'dried fish' in Sinhalese, and Percival says that the Tamil "*karuvāṭṭuváli* is the name of a bird whose tail is like that of a fish,—*Corvus Balicassius*".

[1] **Cravo** (*Caryophyllus aromaticus*, clove). Beng. *karábu.*—Sinh. *krábu, karábu;* vern. terms *lamange* (Sansk. *lavaṅga*), *dēvakusuma* (Sansk., lit. 'the flower of God'). *krábu-gaha*, the clove tree.—Tam. *karámbu, kirámbu*: vern. terms *lavangam, ilavangam.*—Malayal. *karámbu, karayábu, karappa.*—Siam. *kravhn*, cardamom.

Gundert says that *karappa* comes from the Ar. *qarfah.* But *qarfah* signifies 'bark, cinnamon', and *qaranful*, mentioned by Belot as vernacular, is the name of the clove, which it is also in Persian, in addition to *mēkheh* or *mekheh*, 'a small nail'. Shakespear, in his Hindustani dictionary, derives *qaranful* or *qaranphúl* from the Greek *karyóphyllon*, which is literally equivalent to 'the leaf of the walnut-tree'. Garcia da Orta, in Colloquy xxv, says: "Your Greeks did not speak of this *gariofilo*" [ed. Markham, p. 213].

[The primary meaning of the Port. *cravo*, from Lat. *clavus*, is 'a nail'; this name was, evidently, given to this spice because of the clove's resemblance to a small nail. Cloves in the early days of the Portuguese connection with the East were more in demand than other spices, and, to use the phrase of

Camoens, "clove-trees were bought with Portuguese blood". This is a way of saying that many Portuguese lost their lives in attempting to discover the islands in the Moluccas which grew clove-trees. Conde de Ficalho (*Colloquies de Garcia da Orta*, Vol. I, p. 368) thinks that the Gk. *garyophyllon* or, as da Orta writes it, *gariofilo* does not represent an original Greek word but the Hellenisation of some oriental name; he also believes that the Ar. *qaranfal* or *karumpfel* are likewise derived from the same oriental name. In the opinion of Dymock (*Mat. Med.*) all these names are derived from the Tam. *kirámbu*, and the Malay *karámpu;* because it was through the medium of these people that this spice penetrated into India, and afterwards came to be known to the Arabs and the Greeks.]

[2] **Cravo** (*Dianthus caryophyllatus*, a pink; from which it came to mean 'a flower-shaped ear-ornament'; in this latter meaning it has been adopted by the languages mentioned below). Konk. *karáb*. —Sinh. *krábuva, karábuva.*—Malayal. *krábuva.*—Mal. *krábu, kerábu.*—Ach. *kerábu.*—Sund. *karābu, kurābu. Karábu-ros* (lit. 'the ear-ornament-rose'), "very ornate ear-rings" (Rigg).—Mac., Bug., Tet., *karábu.*[1]

Crescer (to grow). Mal. *crescer* (Haex).

Criado (servant). Konk. *kryád* (us. both of a male and a female servant): vern. terms *chākar, rāvaylalo* (mas.); *rāvaylaleṁ*, woman servant.—Tet., Gal. *kriádu*; vern. terms *áta máne, klósan.*

Criar (to bring up). Mal. *crear* (Haex).—Gal. *kriar.*

Crisma (chrism; the sacrament of confirmation). Konk. *krízm.*—Beng. *krisma.* —Tam. *krismei.*—Tel. *krismu.* —Tet., Gal. *krisma.*—Jap. *kirismo.*

Cristão (a Christian). Konk. *kristáṁv.*—Beng. *kristáñ.*—Tam. *kiristavan.*—Malayal. *kiristānmár.*—Tel. *kristannú, kirastuvánu.*—Kan. *kiristánu.*—Kamb.

[1] "The ears are adorned with three pairs of cravos." *O Gabinete Litterario das Fontainhas.*

kristăng.—Siam. *khrĭstàng.*—Jap. *kirishtan, kirishitan.*

The other Indian languages have *kristi,* derived from 'Christ,' or *kristiyan,* from the English 'Christian.'

The Malayo-Polynesian languages have *Nasaráni* or *Saráni* from the Portuguese *Nazareno,* 'Nazarene.' It is worthy of note that Kambojan keeps the Portuguese form. Sinhalese, notwithstanding that Ceylon was twice christianised by the Portuguese, has adopted the English form *kristiyáni.*

Critica (criticism; censure). Konk. *kirít,* defamation. *Kirít māruṅk,* to defame.—Malayal. *krittikka,* to criticise.

Cruz (a cross). Konk. *khurís. Khurís kāḍhuṅk* (lit. 'to take the cross'), to make the sign of the cross. *Khursár kāḍhuṅk* (lit. 'to take upon the cross'), to torment, to cause great distress. *Khursár zaḍuṅk,* to nail to the cross. *Khursár māruṅk* (lit. 'to kill upon the cross'), to crucify. *Khurís karuṅk* (lit. 'to make the cross'), to make a mark, usually a cross, in lieu of signature. There is no vernacular term for a cross. *Chavó* signifies 'the cross of St. Andrew.'

Mar. *krús. Krusāchí niśāṇí* (lit. 'the sign of the cross'), cross-mark used for signature. *Krusár chaḍhavṇēṁ, -deṇēṁ* (lit. 'to raise, to give upon the cross'), to crucify. *Krusāverēl Khristāchi múrtti* (lit. 'an image of Christ upon the cross'), a crucifix.

Guj. *krus, krús. Krúspar jaḍhavavuṁ,* to crucify.

Hindi: *krús. Krús-, krussa-, krusíya pratimá,* a crucifix.

Hindust. *krús*; vern. term *salíb* (from Ar.).

Beng. *kruś. Kruśākṛiti, kruśākár,* cruciform. *Kruśe hata-kṛi* (lit. 'to make dead upon the cross'), to crucify.

Sinh. *kurúsiya, kuręsiya. Kuręsi surẹvama,* a crucifix. *Kuręsi ākára,* cross-shaped. *Kuręsiyé engasa-navá,* to crucify.

Tam. *kurus*; vern. term *siluvei. Kurusadi,* the big cross in the middle or the end of the church-yard, transept.

Malayal. *krúśu, kuriśa*

Krúšil tarekka, *krušikka*, to crucify. *Krušāróhaṇaní*, crucifixion.

Kan. *krúji*.—Tul. *krussu*, *kursu*, *krúji*.—Kamb. *crus*, *chhú crus*. *Chhu* is 'wood.'—Tet., Gal. *kruz*.—Jap. *kurusu*, *kurosu*.

Cuidado (care). Konk. *kuidád* (us. in Goa among the Christians).—Mal. *cuidado*, *cudado* (Haex).—Tet. *kuidádu*; vern. term *aládi-diak*.

Cuidar (to take care). Mal. *cudir* ('to take to heart, to have a care for.' Haex); perhaps from the Port. *acudir* ('to help, to succour').—Tet. *kúida*; vern. term *hanôin*.

Cunha (wedge). Konk. *kunh*, *kunj*; vern. terms *pāchārém̃*, *koyāḍúm̃*.—Hindust. *kuñya*, *kuñiyáñ*, *koniyá*. See *bolina*.—Sinh. *kúññaya*, *kúññeya*. *kúññē*.—Gal. *kunha*.—Pers. *kuhnah*, cork.

Cunhada (sister-in-law). Beng. *koindó*.—Mal. *cuniada* (Haex); vern. term *ipar parampuan*.

Cunhado (brother-in-law). Konk. *kunhád* ('sister's husband').—Beng. *koindú*.—Mal. *cuniado* (Haex); vern. term *ipar laki*.

Curar (to cure). Konk. *kurár-karuṅk*.—Malayal. *kura*, to cure leather.—Mal. *curar* (Haex).

Curral (a cattle pen, a paddock). Anglo-Ind. *corral* (us in Ceylon), 'an enclosure for the capture of wild elephants.'—? Kamb. *crol*; this may be a vern. term.

The word *curral* does not appear in the dictionaries of the Sinhalese or Tamil languages, nor is it in use at present, according to my information; nor do I know whether it is current in the Indo-Portuguese dialects in this sense. It must have become current in Ceylon during the sway of that island by the Dutch, who carried the word to Africa, in the form *kral*, 'a native village or settlement.' See Webster, *s.v.* kraal.

Conde de Ficalho (Colloquy xxi) says: "It appears that this method of hunting elephants was introduced or brought into general use in Ceylon by the Portuguese; the enclosure, which in India is called *keddah*, receives there the name of *korahl* or *corral*, which is evidently the Portuguese word *curral.*" But the method was known and practised before the sixteenth century, according to the testimony of Tomé Lopes, who sailed for India in 1502: "Ceylon has a large number of wild elephants, very big ones, whom they domesticate by building a big enclosure with a strong palisade, and a drawbridge between two trees, inside which they place a female elephant already domesticated." *Navegação ás Indias Orientaes*, in the Coll. of Ramusio, trans. Acad. of Sciences, Lisb., ch. xix.

Curva (*naut.*, the knees of a ship). L.-Hindust. *karvá.*

Cuspidor (arch. for *cuspideira*, a spittoon). Konk. *kuspidôr*; vern. terms *thukpáṭ, pikdāṇi.*—Anglo-Ind. *cuspadore* (obs.).[1]

Used in the same sense by Portuguese Indian dialects.

Custar (to cost). Konk. *kustár-zāvuṅk*, to be worth; to become difficult; vern. terms *láguṅk, paḍuṅk*; *puró zāvuṅk.*—Mar. *kust hoṇĕṁ.* to become aggrieved.—Tet. *kústa*, (also used in the sense of 'costly'): vern. term *tós.*

Molesworth does not give the etymology of the Marathi expression. In Konkani *kustar*, by itself, means 'at the cost of.'

D

Dado (in the sense of 'a die used in games of chance'). Konk. *dád*; vern. term *phāsó.*—Sinh. *dáduva. Dádu hinkaradímu*, a raffle.—? Siam. *tau*; vern. terms *pō, saká.*—Mal. *dádu, dudu. Dadu-dádu*, cannon shot.—Ach., Batt. *dádu.*—Sund. *dádu. Mata dádu*, a chess-board pattern. Jav. *dadu, ḍaḍu. Adadu*, to play with dice. *Andadu*, similar to dice.—Mac., Bug. *dádu.* See *jôgo.*

Phonetically, *dado* can give *tau* in Siamese. *D* initial is changed into *t. Cf. tipya* from Sansk. *divya*; *tavipa* from Sansk *dvípa*; *tasa* from Pali *dasa.* The *d* could easily be dropped in the process of monosyllabification. *Cf. mit* from English 'mister'; *Rut* from 'Russia'; *Phrik* from 'Africa';

---

[1] "There was there a cospidor of gold." Castanheda, I, ch. 17.

khrūt from Sansk. *garuḍa*. [But Chinese has also *tau-tiz*.']

Dama (in the sense of 'game of draughts'). Konk. *dám*.—Mal. *dam*.

Damasco (damask). Konk. *damásk*.—Mar. *dhumás*.—Guj. *dhumás*, *ḍumás*.—Beng. *damás*.—Tam., Kan. *damásu*.—Tul. *damása*.[1]

Dança (dance). Konk. *dáṁs* (more in use *nách*).—Mal. *dánsa*, *dánsu*. *Dánsah*, to dance.

Decreto (decree). Konk. *dekrét*; vern. term *śásan*. *hukum*, *pharmaṇ*.—Tet. *dekretu*.

Dedal (thimble). Konk. *didál*.—Sinh. *didálaya*, *didále*. —Malayal. *tiṭaḷ*. Also *thimbaḷa*, *tumbala*, from the English, 'thimble.'—Mal. *dídal*, *lídal*, *bídal*, *deidál*.—Sund. *bídal*.—Tet., Gal. *dedál*.

Degrau (a step). Konk. *degráv* (l. us.); vern. term *pāuṅḍó*, *sopaṇ*.—Tet. *degrau*; vern. term *héin*.

Desconfiar (to distrust). Konk. *diskoṁphyár-závuṅk* (l. us.); vern. term *dubhāvoṅk*.—Tet. *deskonfia*; vern. term *téan*.

Descontar (to discount). Konk. *diskontár-karuṅk*; vern. term *bád divuṅk*.—Tet. *deskónta*; vern. term *ha sái*.

Desgraça (disgrace, misfortune). Konk. *dizgrás*; vern. terms *nirbhág*, *hál*.—Tet. *desgrasa*; vern. term *óti*.

Desmorecer (us. for *esmorecer*, in the sense of 'to be discouraged'). Mal. *desmorecer*, "to be down hearted" (Haex).

[**Despachador** (in the sense of 'some sort of official, probably a customs-official.' The ordinary meaning of the word is 'one who is quick in the execution of any work; also a judge or an official of the Court'). Anglo-Ind. *dispatchadore*.[1] "This curious

---

[1] "Very good silk is produced here (in China) from which they make great store of **damasquo** cloths in colours." Duarte Barbosa, p. 382 [Hak. Soc., ed. Dames, Vol. II, p. 214].

"With six saddle-clothes of coloured **Damascos**." Diogo do Couto, Dec. VII, iii, 1.

[1] ["The 23 I was sent to the Under-**Dispatchadore**, who I found with my *Scrutore* before him. I having the *key*, he desired me to open it." *Bowyear's Journal at Cochin China*, in Dalrymple, *Oriental Repertory* (1791–97), I, 77, cit. in *Hobson-Jobson*.

Scrutore is, no doubt, the same as

word was apparently a name given by the Portuguese to certain officials in Cochin-China" (Hobson-Jobson).]

Despacho (official communication in answer to a petition). Konk. *despách.*—Tet., Gal. *despáchu.*

Despensa (a pantry). Konk. *dispeṁs.*—Mal. *dispén, spens, spen, sepén.*—*Túkan-sepén*, a steward.—Tet., Gal. *despénsa.*

Despesa (expense). Konk. *despêz*; vern. term *kharch.*—Tet. *despeza.*

Desprezar (to despise). Konk. *desprezár-karuṅk*; vern. terms *beparvá karuṅk, haḷuvā-ṭuṅk.* Tet. *despréza*; vern. term *heunai.*

Desterrar (to banish). Mal., Tet., Gal. *distérra.*

Deus (God). Beng. *Devus*; us. in such expressions as *Devus bons diyá* (lit. 'God good day'), *Devus bons noiti* (lit. 'God good night').—Mal. *Deos. Deos tuong* is used in the sense of 'God willing,' according to Haex.—Gal. *ámu Deus. Ámu*, from Port. *amo*, 'master,' stands for 'Lord.'—Nic. *Deuse. Menlúana Deuse*, a priest.—Pid-Engl. *Joss, Josh*, God, an idol. *Joss-house* (lit. 'house of God'), a church. *Joss-house-man*, a priest. *Joss-pidgin* (lit. 'business of God'), the bonze; the minister of God.—*Joss-stick* (lit. 'stick of God'), an odiferous stick lighted and allowed to burn before idols in temples.

"Before the Mohammedans there was no reckoning (in the Moluccas) of time, or of weights, or measures, and they lived without a belief in one God, or knowledge of any definite religion." João de Barros, Dec. III, v, 5.

"Formerly the Malays, having had no knowledge of God, did not use any term in speaking of Him. But with the lapse of years, having received Mohammedanism from the Arabs, they adopted, at the same time as their religion, the expression *Alla* and *Alla te Alla*, and this was done in the islands of Amboyna, Moluccas, etc. When the inhabitants were instructed by the Portuguese in the Catholic

---

escritoire or a writing desk with drawers. Yule says that 'dispatchadore' is met with only in the document quoted above.]

faith, they, in their turn, adopted the name 'Deus.'" (Haex).[1]

Devoção (devotion). Konk. *devosáṁv*, *devaspaṇ*; vern. terms *bhakti*, *bhakti-bháv*.—Tet., Gal. *devosã*.

In Konkani *devôt* (*adj.*) means 'a devout man;' *devót* (*subst. neut.*), 'a religious serenado during Lent;' this is spoken of as *devota* in the Portuguese dialect of Goa

Diabo (devil). Konk. *dyáb* (l. us. and only among the Christians).—Malayal. *diyáb*.—? Gar. *diabol*; perhaps from the Italian *diavolo*, introduced by the missionaries.—Tet. *diábu*.

Diamante (diamond) Konk. *dyamánt*; vern. term *vajr* (Sansk.).—Sinh. *diyamántiya*; vern. terms *vajraya*, *vadura* (the Elu form).—Tet., Gal. *diamánti*; vern. terms *phátuk laka*.

Dicionário (a dictionary). Konk. *disyonár*; vern. terms *koś śabdakoś*.—Tet. *disionári*.

[1] The word *dev* or *deva*, used in Konkani and other Indian languages, is derived directly from the Sanskrit *deva*.

Dinheiro (money). Mal., Tet., Gal., *diné*.[1]

"Afonso de Albuquerque coined two kinds: one he called **dinheiro**, and the other, which was equivalent to ten **dinheiros**, he called *soldo*, and

[1] *Dinár* (Achinese), *dinūrū* or *jíngara* (Macassar), *dinara*, *jínara*, *jingara* (Bugi), 'gold coin', are from the Arabic-Pers. *dīnár*, which is affiliated to the Lat. *denarius*. *Amarakośa*, a Sanskrit dictionary of the fifth century, mentions *dīnāra* as a synonym of *niśka*, 'a gold coin' But there are *dinares* of smaller value. "Two *fules* are worth one *dynare*, and twelve *dunares* one *tanga*." (*Tanga* is here used for the *larim*, a coin in use in the Persian Gulf). *Lembranças das Cousas da India*. "The *dīnār* in modern Persia is a very small imaginary coin, of which 10,000 make a *tomaum*" *Hobson-Jobson*.

[*Fule* is evidently the same as the Ar. *falas*, the name of a copper coin of very small value "The names of the Arabic pieces of money..are all taken from the coins of the Lower Roman Empire. Thus, the copper piece was called *fals* from *follis*; the silver *dirham* from *drachma*, and the gold *dīnūr* from *denarius*, which, though properly a silver coin, was used generally to denote coins of other metals, as the *denarius aeris* ('copper or bronze denarius'), and the *denarius auri*, or *aureus* ('gold denarius')" James Prinsep, in *Essays*, etc., cit. in *Hobson-Jobson*, *s.v.* dīnār. See also Dalgado, *Glossario*, *s v. faluz*.]

a third worth ten *soldos, bastardos.*" João de Barros, Dec. II. vi, 6.

["Lastly were struck (by Albuquerque, in Goa) copper coins called *dinheiros* and *leaes.* Now the word *dinheiros* (Lat. *denarii,* Fr. *deniers*) when used in the singular is a generic name for all kinds of money, and, although in this case it was used to designate a very small coin, it caused no little confusion, and consequently they agreed to call the *dinheiros cepayquas,* a word still in vogue in the Portuguese settlement of Macao in the form of *sapeca,* and the origin of which I have not yet been able to determine." J. G. da Cunha, *Indo-Portuguese Numismatics,* in *J.B.B.R.A.S.*, Vol. XIV. p. 271. *Cepayqua,* the origin of which presented difficulties to da Cunha, is, as he says, the same as the Macao *sapeca,* which is a Malay word composed of *sa,* 'one.' and *pāku,* 'hundred coins called *pichis* strung together.' The word is used by Albuquerque in his *Letters* before his conquest of Malacca, from which it is to be inferred that, as the result of commercial intercourse, the Malay term was known in India as a synonym for *cash* in the early sixteenth century. See *Glossario, s.v. sapeca.*]

Dispensa (dispensation). Konk. *dispeṁs*; vern. term *māphí.*—Tet. *dispensa.*

Dobrado (*adj.*, double). Konk. *dobrád*; vern. term *dupêṭ.*—L.-Hindust. *dubrál,* a double knot.—Tul. *dubrálu, dibrálu* (*subst.*), twice-distilled spirit.

In Konkani also *tibrád saró,* that is, 'thrice-distilled spirit,' is used. See *tresdobrado.*

Dôbro (*subst.*, double). Konk. *dôbr* (l. us.).—Mac., Bug. *dóbalō,* used in game of cards.

Doce (*subst.*, a sweet). Konk. *dôs.*—Sinh. *dôsi* (also us. in the sense of 'jelly or a preserve').—Tam. *dósei,* cake made of rice flour. *Dōseikkal,* a frying-pan.—Malayal. *dôś.*—Kan. *dôse,* cake, fritter.—Tul. *dôse,* cake made of rice flour. Tet. *dôsi*; vern. term *mídel.*

Dom (a title given to gentlemen and persons of position in Portugal and Spain). Konk.

Doṁ.—Sinh. *Don.*—Tet., Gal. *Dom.*[1]

Domingo (Sunday; literally 'the Lord's day'). Mal. *domingo, dumingo* (Haex), *domingo* (Castro), *míngo, míngu. Hári mingo* (lit. 'the day Sunday') is 'Sunday;' vern. terms *ahad* (Ar.), *hári-ahad. Sátu miṅgo* (lit. 'one Sunday') is 'a week;' vern. terms *sátu jema'at* (Ar.), *tújoh hári* (lit. 'seven days').—Sund., Mad. *mingo*, a week.—Jav. *míngu* (more us. *ahad*). *Mingon* (*adj.*), relating to Sunday.—Day. *mingo, mengo.*[2]—Jap. *domingo, domiigo.*

Dona (a title given to ladies of quality; lady, mistress of the house). Sinh. *nónā*, a lady, a European woman.—Mal. *dónia, nona, nónya, nyonya, noña* (=*nonha*), *ñóña* (=*nhonha*), a woman of European or Chinese descent, or a woman married to a European or Chinaman.—Ach. *nona*, the daughter of a European by a Chinese woman: a young lady. *Ñoña*, the wife of a European or a Chinaman; a married woman.—Sund. *nóna*, a young lady; *núnya*, a European or Chinese married woman.—Jav. *ñóña.*—Day. *ñoña*, a married woman, specially a European.—Mac., Bug. *nóna*, a young lady; *nhonha*, a married woman.—Batav. *ñóña* or *nyónya.*—Tet., Gal. *dona.*

Favre distinguishes between *nóña* and *nóna*, in respect of orthography and etymology, and gives as the meaning of *nóna*, without making mention of its derivation, "an unmarried woman, a damsel, daughter of a person of quality," and indicates the Portuguese *dona* or the Spanish *dueña* as the probable original of *nóña*.

Dr. Heiligers likewise suggests *dueña*.

---

[1] "The chiefs of the south and west perpetuate with pride the honorific title of **Don**, accorded to them by their first European conquerors." Tennent, *Ceylon* [ed. 1859, Vol. II, p. 70].

"At the present time many of the indigenous people have the title of **Dom**, though it is certain that in the beginning when government was first established this title was given only to the Chiefs for services rendered and as an honorific title, for which they even used to pay a tax." José dos Santos Vaquinhas, *Timor*, in *Jour. Geo. Soc. Lisb.*, 5th ser., p. 63.

[2] The first syllable is dropped, in order that it may become a dissyllabic word; this is in keeping with the genius of the Malayan language family.

Dr. Fokker says: "With regard to the origin of the word *ñoña*, which some pronounce *nôña* (a woman married to a European or a Chinaman), etymologists are not in agreement. It is more probable that the word comes from Chinese rather than from the Portuguese *senhora*, with the elision of the first syllable, as in *gareja* from '*igreja*.'"

Gonçalves Viana traces a connection between *senhora* and *nyóra*, *nyónya*, *nónya* and *nóna*, and indirectly conveys that there has been an evolutionary process involved; Dr. Schuchardt holds this origin as most certain and supports it with an intermediate form *nhonha*, used in Cape Verde.

But this does not appear to be so very certain. The word *nóna*, as an honorific praenomen and a title of reverence, is current in the Portuguese dialects of Ceylon, Cochin, Mahé, Bombay, Diu, Malacca and Singapore; and, in some of these, it has acquired the additional meaning of 'grandmother,' as *nono*, in the Portuguese dialect of Ceylon, exclusively means 'grandfather.' Now, in the Portuguese dialect of Malay and of the Cape Verde Islands, *dono* signifies 'grandfather' and *dona* 'grandmother,' and these are mentioned by Morais as archaic meanings of the word in Portuguese.[1]

The transition from *dona* to *nona* is much easier and more natural (by means of regressive assimilation) than from *senhora* (*sinhara*, *nhara*, *siara* in Portuguese dialects), which would have to be subjected to an extensive process of the aphesis of a syllable, the assimilation of a liquid and nasal palatal, and of single and double depalatalization. And the word *senhor* did not go through this process in Malay when it was transformed into *sínho* and *siyu*. Besides this,

1 "Do you know the reason? It is because **Dona** is a term which in the Portuguese dialect of the place means 'the name of the house,' and is used of children. And it is by this name they are called till they reach majority or till death........Now, if you wish to know what **Dona** means, I will tell you; it is equivalent in Portuguese to *avó* ('grandmother') and **Dono** to *avô* ('grandfather'). *Creolo da ilha de Santo Antão*, in *Jour. Geo. Soc. Lisb.*, 2nd ser., p. 131.

the influence of another word having the same sound, *nona* =*anona* (*q.v.*), not only with respect to phonetics, but equally so with regard to the diminutive sense that the word has acquired, is not impossible.

It is pertinent to note that the Malay variants are not in fact successive but synchronous, with difference in meaning, and that *dona* was employed formerly to signify 'a lady, a woman of quality,' and was used by itself without being prefixed to a name.[1] In this sense, the word is still in vogue in East Africa, where it is used of ladies of Portuguese descent.[2]

The palatalized forms *nonha* and *nhonha* do not necessarily imply their derivation from, or the influence of, *senhora*; they could have been the result of the evolution of *nona*, as can be seen in the Portuguese *vizinha* from Latin *vicina*, *ponha* from *poniat*, *nenhum* from *nem hum*, *ninho* from *nidum*, with the previous assimilation of *d*.

Cf. *pipínhu* (from *pepino*, a cucumber) in the Portuguese dialect of Malacca. Moreover, *nonha* (l. us.) in the Portuguese dialect of Ceylon, and *nhonha* in that of Macau have a diminutive meaning, and are probably diminutive forms.

On this account, I do not regard as improbable the derivation from *dona* and the contact of *dona* and *senhora* and their

[1] "The virtuous **Dona** beating her breast in sign of great surprise." Fernão Pinto, ch. xxxv.

"With the letters which His Majesty addressed to you, there goes a list of despatches, which are, by his Majesty's command, this year to be delivered to some **donas**, wives of hidalgos, and other persons who have served this State" (1597). *Archivo Port. Or.*, Fasc. 5th, p. 1493.

"This **Dona** was as yet young in age, but a very gentle woman." Diogo do Couto, Dec. V. x. 7.

[2] "**Dona**. Title given in East Africa to women of mixed (Portuguese and Negro) origin." A. C. de Paiva Raposo, *Dic. da lingua landina*, in *Jour. Geo. Soc. Lisb.* 8th ser., p. 59.

The title of one of Ismail Gracias's publications is *Uma* **Dona** *Portugueza na Côrte do Grão-Mogol.* [The *Dona Portugueza* is Dona Juliana da Costa who played an important rôle in the reign of Aurangzebe's successor, Bahadur Shah. She died about 1733. There are references to her, and there is also a portrait of her, in François Valentijn's *Oud en Niew Oost-Indien* (1724-26).]

mutual influence; and what appears to me also possible is the influence of *nona*=*anona* ('bullock's heart') and of *nina* =*menina* ('a girl'), which in the Portuguese of Macau makes its diminutive *nhinina*, according to J. F. Marques Pereira (*Ta-ssi-yang-kuo*, 1st series. Vol. 1, no. 1). See *senhor* and *senhora*.[1]

Dossel (canopy). Konk. *dosél*; vern. terms *sezó*, *māndvi*.—Tet. *dosel*.

Dourado (*adj.*, gilded) Konk. *daurád* (l. us.); vern. terms *bhāṅgār kāḍhlaló*.—Bug. *dorádu*.

Dourado (*subst.*, the name of a fish). Anglo-Ind. *dorado*. —Indo-Fr. *dorade*.

It is called *dourada* in the Portuguese of Goa. [It is the *Coryphaena hippurus*, Day, 'the gilt head,' the sea-bream, often called dolphin.]

Doutor (doctor; physician). Konk. *dotôr*; vern. terms *śāstrí*; *vaiz*.—? Mal. *dogtor*, which Fabre derives from Portuguese.—Bug. *dórtorō*, which Matthes derives from the Dutch *dokter*.—Tet., Gal. *dótôr*, physician; vern. term *badain*.

Doutrina (Christian doctrine). Konk. *dotín*, *dotôn*.—Tet., Gal. *dotrina*.

Durar (to last). Konk. *durár-zāvuṅk*; vern. terms are *taguṅk*. *zaguṅk*, *uruṅk*.—Mal. *durar*. "*Durar*, 'to last', there is no special word to express this, in Malay." Haex.—Tet., Gal. *dúra* (also used in the sense of 'duration'); vern. term *kléur*.

Dúzia (a dozen). Konk. *dúz*.—Tet., Gal. *dúzi*, *dúsi*.

E

Elefante (elephant). Konk. *elephánt*, an unbleached or white cotton shirting.—[Anglo-Ind. *elephanta*.]—? Nic. *lifanta*.—? Malag. *elifantu*.

In the Portuguese of Goa *elefante* is also the name of a white shirting; the elephant 'chop' or mark on the piece appears to have given rise to the name; there are other kinds with the 'camel' and 'deer' marks, but not so largely in demand as the former.

---

[1] Gonçalves Viana says that by *nhonha* language is meant "the corrupt Portuguese dialect spoken in Macau." *Apostilas*.

[Others call it *nhom*.]

It is quite possible that the original of the Nicobarese word is, as Man suggests, the English 'elephant.'

[In Anglo-Indian speech and writings one meets with the term 'Elephanta' in connection with showers of rain: elephantas or elephanta showers. Elephanta is, according to Yule, a name given originally by the Portuguese to violent storms occurring at the termination, though some travellers describe them as at the setting-in, of the Monsoon.[1] Crooke is of the opinion that "the Portuguese took the name from the Hindi *hattiyā*, Sansk. *hastā*, the 13th lunar Asterism, connected with *hastin*, an elephant, and hence sometimes called 'the sign of the elephant.'" But the Sansk. *hasta* means 'a hand,' and this is the name of the Nakshatra because of its supposed resemblance to a hand. In Marathi, too, *hasta* means 'a hand,' and the plural form of the word, *hastin*, is used to signify "the thirteenth lunar asterism, designated by a hand" (Molesworth). The thirteenth asterism has nothing to do with an elephant; and yet in popular speech and proverbial sayings, whether in the Deccan or Gujarat, this asterism is associated with the elephant: *Padel hathi tar padel bhinti* (Mar.), lit. 'if the elephant falls, then walls will begin to tumble', which is a way of saying that, if the 'Elephant Nakshatra' should send rain, there will be heavy downpours and houses will collapse; *Hāthyiā-nim sundh fari khari* (Guj.), 'the trunk of the elephant has verily turned,' by which it is intended to convey that torrents of rain have descended from the constellation *Hasta*. Etymologically it is not possible to connect the Sansk. *hasta*, directly, with *hāthiyó* (Guj.) or *hattī* (Mar.). These two forms could have come from *hastin*, an animal that uses one of its limbs as a hand, i.e., the elephant. But the difficulty is to show how the 'Hand Nakshatra' came to be trans-

1 ["The Mussoans are rude and boisterous in their departure, as well as at their coming in, which two seasons are called **Elephant** in India, and just before their breaking up, take their farewell for the most part in very ruggid huffing weather." Ovington, *A Voyage to Suratt*, O.U.P. p. 83.]

formed in the popular imagination into the 'Elephant Nakshatra.' We deliberately say 'popular imagination,' for, among the learned, the term used is not *hāthiyó* or *hattī* but *hasta.* The only plausible explanation, to some extent borne out by the quotation below from Thevenot, that we can offer, is that when the Sun enters *Hasta*, just about the end of the Monsoon, perhaps, the banking of immense dark clouds in the north-east created in the popular mind the picture of a herd of elephants assembling together, and the deep rumbling sounds, which accompany the thunderstorms, became associated with the trumpetings and terror-inspiring rage of these mighty beasts.[1] The name of this Nakshatra in Western Astronomy is *Corvus*, 'the Raven,' and this in itself is proof of how the imagination of different peoples can conjure up different pictures or forms from the same object.

Dr. S. K. Banerji, Metereologist, writing to *The Times of India*, 24th April, 1929, propounds, however, a novel theory with regard to the origin of the name 'elephantas.' This is what he says: "I do not propose to discuss the origin of the word 'elephantas,' as to whether the Portuguese got the word from the Nakshatra 'Hasti' (Elephant, one of the 27 Nakshatras in Hindi Astrology), but there appears to be no harm in calling these heat thunderstorms 'Elephantas,' for amongst the hills over which they are seen to develop from the Colaba observatory, the most well-known is the little island-hill 'Elephanta.'"

The observation that the thunderclouds form in the direction of the Elephanta Island is no new one,[1] but the

1 ["Especially in the Gulf of Cambay, there is such great danger for ships at the commencement of this month, because of a wind which blows towards it with great violence from the west, and which is always accompanied by heavy clouds which are called **Elefans**, because they have the appearance of these beasts, that shipwreck is almost inevitable." Thevenot, *Voyages*, III, p. 38.]

1 ["A tremendous burst of thunder and lightning, termed the **Elephanta.**. The heavy thunderbolts.... apparently form directly over the Island of

attempt to explain the term 'elephanta' by connecting it with the Elephanta Island is new. *A Ilha do Elephante*[1] ('The Island of the Elephant'), and not 'Elәphanta' (an Anglo-Indian transformation, feminine in form) was the name given by the Portuguese, in the early part of the sixteenth century, to the island which was then known, as it is even to this day, to its inhabitants and those of the surrounding country, as Ghārāpurī or, shortly, Purī. This name was given because of the life-size figure of an elephant, hewn from one single mass of trap-rock, which formerly stood in the south of the island, not far from the usual landing-place, and which, to save it from destruction, was removed in 1864-5 to the Victoria Gardens, Bombay, where it can still be seen. Dr. Banerjee's explanation appears to us untenable, first of all, because it is not to be presumed that the indigenous people, who to this day cling tenaciously to their own name for the island, viz., Ghārāpurī, and will not make use of the foreign name 'Elephanta,' could have introduced the latter term into their folk-lore and proverbial sayings. Again, the term 'elephanta' was used of the storms that were usual about the termination of the Monsoon in places far away from Bombay or the Island of Elephanta. Sir Thomas Roe when at the Moghul Emperor's Court at Ajmere experienced on the 20th August, 1616, "a storme of rayne called the **Oliphant,** vsuall at goeing out of the raynes" (*The Embassy of Sir Thomas Roe*, Hak. Soc. p. 247). And Fryer when sailing near Ceylon (1673) refers to these thunderstorms and definitely connects them with the '**Elephant Constellation**'.[1]

Elephanta." *Life in Bombay*, (1852), p. 194, in *O. E. D.*]

[1] ["This is called *Ilha do* **Alifante** because in a forest there is found a large **alifante** of stone, very similar to living specimens, in colour, size, and appearance." D. João de Castro, who visited the island in 1538, in *Rotéiro desde Goa até Dio*.]

[1] ["Not to deviate any longer, we are now winding about the *South-West* part of *Ceilon*; where we have the *Tail of the* **Elephant** full in our

There is a reference to 'the Elephant' in a quaint letter dated "Suratt, October the 31st, 1704." From "*Sir* N. Waite *and Council at* Surat *for the New Company*, to "Sir John Gayer, *knight, Generall* (for the) *Honble Old Company and* (Council)," quoted in Hedges' *Diary* (Hak. Soc., Vol. II, p. cccxlix)[1] which suggests further and interesting folklore —this time not Hindu but Christian—associated with the constellation.

What has 'St. Francisco' to do with 'the Elephant,' and which of the different saints that go by this name in the Roman Catholic Calendar is the one referred to here? Here is Sir Richard Temple's conjecture (*Indian Antiquary*, Vol. xxx, p. 395): "What these early Europeans were told was that the SW Monsoon "turned" during the asterism Hâthî, *i.e.*, in **September-October**, which is the fact. With the Elephant was clearly associated

mouths; a constellation by the *Portugals* called *Rabo del* Elephanto ('Tail of the Elephant'), known for the breaking up of the *Munsoons*, which is the last Flory this season makes, generally concluding with *September*, which goes out with dismal storms." *East India*, etc. Hak. Soc., Vol. I, p. 127. See also, Vol. II, p 94.]

[1] ["Is very plaine and evident to every impartiall man there's no other time if any Limitted to Sir Nicho: Waite goeing to Bombay then the 3 months allowed and appointed Sr Jno: Gayer, the one month afore the Turne of the Monsoon is a Espetiall ffavour and respect Singly to Sr Jno: Gayer without any coherance relating to Sr: Nicho: Waite, every one of us unwilling interfearing in said affaire expecting that you Gentlemen or the Deputy Governour and Councill for the United Trade at Bombay to have Notified the true Genuin Time and Turne of the Monsoone as held and Esteemed by the Portugueiz and other antient European and the severall inhabitants of India for the Queens Men of Warr Rashly comeing to this Barr alters not the Annuall Season that by accident may meet with Severe & Calme weather otherwise any Nation may assume an Almighty Power equally with Mr. Burniston and Aislabee.

"But it being notorious & Certified by all Europeans, Dutch, Ffrench, English, Portugueez, the Last under a Notary publick as well as the Moores Accountt, the turne of the Monsoone **St: Francisco or the Elephant** ends att or upon and not before the new moon in 7ber: which fell out this year to be the 18th Ulto: and the new moon the 17th Inst: or the 18th Inst: a full Callender month. . . "]

the term "**St. Francisco,**" alluding, I suppose, to the Saint's Day, either of St. Francis of Assisi, the founder of the Franciscans, 4th October, or of St. Francis Borgia, the third General of the Jesuits, 10th October." I am inclined to think that the odds are in favour of 'St. Francisco' being the Assisian, rather than the Jesuit General, for the earliest religious to come out to India were the Franciscans who were spread all over the East; they were very influential, and their convent in Goa was described by Pyrard (Hak. Soc., Vol. II, p. 53) as "the handsomest and richest in the world," and they were indefatigable in promoting everywhere the cult of their great founder. They must have helped to create the general belief in the minds of the Portuguese and the Indian Christians that after the feast-day of St. Francis of Assisi there were no more 'elephantas' to be feared and the fair season might safely be assumed to have begun. Even up to the present day there survives an analogous belief in Goa. It is, that the sand-bar, which blocks the mouth of the harbour of Goa from the beginning of the rains, disappears on the feast-day of St. Lawrence, the 10th of August, from which date it becomes possible for vessels to enter the port. Compare with this the Hindu belief associated with the festival of the *Nārelī Punimā*, which takes place on the 15th day of *Shravan*, usually sometime early in August, viz., that after this date it is safe for ships and boats to put out to sea. This popular belief is connected with the appearance in the sky at this time of the star *Agastya* ('Canopus'), named after the great Rishi of this name, one of whose feats was to drink up the ocean because it had offended him. I feel perfectly convinced that the Christian legends associating St. Francis and St. Lawrence with certain weather conditions in Western India are instances of the way in which the Roman Catholic Church has in all ages been ever ready to accept habits, customs, dress, and legends of the people to whom she preached the new faith, so long as they did not appear to conflict with her principles of faith and morals, and very often to adopt them by giving them a Christian setting or background. In India, as far as the bulk of the people is concerned, not only are weather conditions governed by the movements of the stars and constellations, but practically most of the events in their lives, even such questions as the propriety of eating particular fruits or foods at certain seasons. For instance, in the Konkan, the popular belief is that it is not wholesome to eat *ānvalās* (*Phyllantus emblica*), sugar-cane, or the fruit of the tamarind tree before the 12th day of the first half of *Kārtika* ('Pleiades'), on which day is commemorated the marriage of Krishna and the Tulsi plant; in Gujarat, the mango is believed to be unhealthy if eaten before Holi, i.e., the fifteenth day of *Fālguna*.

How keen the early administrators were on collecting and co-ordinating all kinds of information and traditions about weather conditions in India, no matter whether the reports were derived from friends or foes so long as they were trustworthy and they could help in rendering navigation safe, is also borne out by a reference given by Foster in his edition of Roe in connection with the quotation from him given above.[1]

There can be no doubt, from all that has been said above, that Anglo-India owes the name 'elephanta' to the Portuguese, but it is very strange that there are hardly any references to this term among the Portuguese chroniclers. Dalgado, in his

1 At a consultation held September 3rd, 1637 (I.O. Marine Records, Misc. i), mention was made of "The Gennerall reports of all or most of the Cheefe Portugall Gentlemen and fryers as well of this place (Bombay) as others near Aioyninge, That before the new Moone in September .... It was impossible for any shipp of Charge to gett Cleere of the Coast without apparent and eminent dainger (if Bound to the Southwards) By Reason they Constantly expect euery yeare at that Season an extraordinarie storm vpon the Coast, Called by them the Elophant, which Comes with such Vyolence and soe variable that noe Shipp or Vessell may pass without eminent dainger as aforesaid."

Glossario, says that he has met with only one reference to this word, and that, dated 1662.[1]]

Empatar (to make equal). Konk. *empātár-karuṅk* (l. us.); vern. term *bád karuṅk* or *divuṅk*.—Tet. *empáta*; vern. term *hatáu*.

Emplastro (a plaster). Konk. *emprás*; vern. term *lêp*. — ? Tel. *palástaru*.—?Kan. *palástar*; probably from the English 'plaster.'—Malag. *empelastra*.

Emprêgo (employment). Konk. *emprêg*; vern. term *chākrí*.—Tet. *emprêgu*; vern. term. *lákon*.

Emprestar (to lend). Konk. *emprestár-karuṅk* (l. us); vern. term *uśṇó divuṅk*.—Mal. *impústa*.—Tet. *emprésta*.

Enganar (to cheat). Mal. *enganar* (Haex); vern. term *típu*.

Engenho (skill, art; also an engine or machine). Mal. *inginio*, "a contrivance to raise up something, a pulley" (Haex).—Mol. *ingeniyo*.[1]

Achinese has *énjin*, from the English 'engine.'

Então (*adv*., then). Mal. *entaon* (Haex).—Tet. *antã*; vern. terms *aló*, *bá-sá*.

Entendimento (understanding). Mal. *entendimento* (Haex).

Entregar (to deliver). Konk. *entregár-karuṅk* (l. us.); vern. terms *divuṅk*, *samarpuṅk*.—Mal. *entregar* (Haex).—Tet. *entréga*; vern. terms *sára*, *lólo*.

Entrudo (Shrovetide; carnival). Konk. *intrúd*.—Beng. *entrudú*.—Tet. *entrúdu*.

? Enxerto (used in the sense of 'a grafted mango-tree'). Konk. *isáḍ*, *iśeḍ*.—Mar. *isáḍ*, *isāḍá*.

Molesworth derives the Marathi word from the

---

1 [1662.—"And because a big shower was threatening (towards the end of September) which they call an **ellefante**, they began to moor and secure both the ships." *Apud* Júlio Biker, *Collecção de Tratados*, III, p. 11.]

1 "There were (in Muscat) orchards, gardens, and palm-groves with wells for irrigation from which water was drawn by an **engenho** (contrivance) which made use of bullocks." *Commentarios de Afonso de Albuquerque*, I, ch. 24. [In the Hak. Soc.'s edition Vol. I, p 83, "*con engenho de bois*" is rendered 'by means of wooden engines'. The translator has confounded the Portuguese *bois* which is the pl. of *boi*, 'an ox', with the French *bois*, 'timber or wood']

Sansk. *īsā*, "the shaft of a car or the beam of a plough." In Konkani *gárph* (from the Port. *garfo*, 'graft') is also used of 'a grafted mango-tree'.

Era (Christian era). Mac. *héra*.

Ermida (hermitage with a chapel by its side). Konk. *irmít*.—Tet. *ermida*.

Ervilha (a species of *Dolichos*, Linn., a kind of French beans). Konk. *virvíl*.—Tet. *ervilha*.

Escada (stair-case). Konk. *iskád*; vern. terms *śiḍi* (l. us.), *nisaṇ*, ladder.—L.-Hindust. *iskát*. [Yule mentions *iskat* in *Hobson-Jobson* and gives 'ratlines' as its meaning; that is also its meaning in L.-Hindust.]

Escaler (a ship's boat; also a barge). Konk., Tet. *iskalér*.

Escândalo (scandal). Konk. *eskánd*.—Tet. *iskandálu*.

Escola (a school). Konk. *iskól*; vern. terms *sáḷ*, *pāṭhsáḷ*, *vidyāsáḷ*.—Sinh. *skólaya*, *iskóle*; vern. terms *pāṭhaśaláva*, *akśaraśaláva*, *akaru-maḍuva*. *Skólayê sahakáriya*, a school-fellow.—Tam. *iskolei*.—Mal. *skola*, *sakola*, *sekola*. *Sekula* (Favre) indicates the influence of Dutch, or of the English 'school'.—Sund. *iskola*.—Jav. *skólah* (*h*, in order to retain the sound of *a*, which otherwise would have become *ó*), to go to school. *Nyekolahakê*, *nyekolahaken* (causative verb), to send to school.—Mad. *sekóló*.—Tet., Gal. *escola*; vern. term *anôri*.

Escolta (a guard, an escort). Konk. *eskolt*; vern. terms *valāvó*, *balāvó*.—Tet., Gal. *eskolta*.

Escôva (brush). Konk. *eskôv*.—Tet., Gal. *eskôva*.

[**Escrito** (a note under one's hand; an attestation). Anglo-Ind. *scrito*, *screet*.[1]]

The *O.E.D.* mentions *scrite*, 'a writing, written document,' as an obsolete word with references that do not go beyond 1450.

---

[1] ["A Plummer dyeing there about the same tyme, the officers came to enquire his estate and beeing tould he was a seruant and a poore man were satisfied, yet with their brokers Scrito in testemony." *The Embassy of Sir Thomas Roe*, Hak. Soc., Vol I, p. 70.]

["This night the Officers, seeing I sent not, deliuered the Prisoners into my Procuradors power, and tooke his Screete for Sixtie *Rupias*." *Idem*, Vol. II, p. 446.]

Escritório (a writing-desk). Guj. *iskotaró*, [*iscotri*, *iscutri*. —Anglo-Ind. *screetore*, *scritoire*, *screwtore*.][1]

["The word (*iscotri* or *iscutri*), though of rare occurrence in good literary Marâṭhî, may occasionally be heard of used by old-world men and women of the middle classes as a colloquialism." Balcrushna V. Wassoodew, in *Indian Antiquary*, Vol. XXIX, p. 307. Sir Richard Temple (*op. cit.* p. 116) connects the Anglo-Indian names for the desk "with the English auctioneers' word **escritoir** for a fancy writing table (*bureau*), which is perhaps old French for **écritoire,** a horn or other receptacle for ink." The *O.E.D.* mentions several instances of the use of 'scrutoire' in the 17th and 18th centuries, and these not necessarily connected with India. *Iskotaró*, *iscotri*, etc., in Guj. and Mar., however, are undoubtedly of Portuguese origin, and the entry of the words in these languages can be accounted for by the Portuguese influence in Bombay, Bassein, and Damaun, it being scarcely credible that they could have derived them from English in which 'escritoire' has never been in ordinary use. Has the Port. *escritório*, in the archaic sense of 'writing-desk' (its present-day acceptation being 'an office-room'), in any way been responsible for the Anglo-Indian terms? Very old writing-desks believed to be of Chinese workmanship are still to be seen in many families in Goa preserved as heirlooms. The Portuguese must have had many of these pieces of furniture turned out in their settlements in India and

---

[1] [1669.—"(Goods imported into Achin) ffrom Siam Tinne, Coppar, China Wares, Rice and **Screetores** both plaine and lackared, etc."—MS. Account of India, by T.B., p. 158, cit. by R. C. Temple, in *Indian Antiquary*, Vol. XXIX, p. 116.]

["The Seamen, handing a small **Scritoire** into ye boat, in which were Gold Mohurs and Rupees to ye value of R. 2036 : 11 for account of ...., the said **Scritoire** dropt into the Sea, striking on ye Shipp's Side, broke y^{e} **Scritoire,** and the money dropt out into ye Sea". Hedges, *Diary*, Hak. Soc., Vol. I, p. 182.]

[1700.—"I have sent a Small Sandal **Screwtore** for a Pallakeen." *Letter* of *Cath: Nicks* in Hedges, *Diary*, Vol. II, p. cclx.]

imported others of superior craftsmanship from the Far East and thus familiarised the indigenous population both with the uses and name of this type of writing-desk.]

Escrivão (a scrivener, a recorder). Konk. *iskrivámv* (especially, 'the clerk or recorder of the village communities'), *sikirámv* (popular form); vern. terms *śeṇay*, *kārkúṇ*, *śrīkarṇí*.—Tam. *iskiriván*, clerk of a sodality.—Anglo-Ind. *scrivan* (obs.)[1]—Tet., Gal. *eskriván*.—Jap. *ishikiriban* (obs.).

Esmola (charity). Konk. *izmól* (us. among the Christians); vern. terms *bhík*, *dharm*.—Beng. *ejmolá*.—Mal. *ismola* (Haex), *samola*.—Tet. Gal. *esmola*.

Espada (a sword). Konk. *ispád*; vern. terms *tarvár*, *khaḍg*.—Hindi, Hindust., Beng., Punj. (also *aspát*) *ispát*, steel.—Mal. *spada* (Haex); vern. terms *pedang*, *sudang*.—Mac. *sapada* —Ar. *spáda*.—Rab. *espáthe*.

[The Portuguese are reputed to have introduced the straight cut and thrust swords into India, and these and others made in imitation of them were known as *Farhangí* or *Phirangí*.]

Espadilha (the ace of spades). Konk. *espādilh*.—Mac., Bug. *sapadila*. See *az*.

Espera (a sphere; also a piece of ordnance). Mal. *spera* ("fire-spitting machines," Haex).—Mol. *espera*, "a cannon, from the old word *espera* (from the Malay of the Moluccas," Castro)[1].

---

1 ["This is indeed the custome of Persia Merchants, to bring all to the King..., who takes his choice and deliuers the rest to his Nobilitie, his **Scriuanoes** writing to whom, and his Officer cutting price." *The Embassy of Sir T. Roe*, Hak. Soc., p. 416.]

["We continued at Tunis till our **Scrivan**, or purser, had made "Consolato" for yᵉ damage done yᵉ Shippe..." Hedges, *Diary*, Hak. Soc., Vol. I, p. 239.]

["The *Sinais* ('Shenvis') are more biass'd by Secular Offices, out of which are made their fighting Bishops, *Desies* ('Desais'), or Farmers of the King's Rents, *Pundits*,... Physicians, Accountants, **Scrivans**, and Interpreters" Fryer, *East India*, etc., Hak. Soc., Vol. II, p. 101. See also *ibidem*, p. 104.]

1 "They (the Turks) fired against him some **esperas**, the shots from which fell around the *Fusta* (*q.v.*)." Diogo do Couto, Dec. V, iii, 6. "There where three basilisks, and six **esperas**, which he entrusted to Beran Baxa." *Id.*, 7.

Esperança (hope). Konk. *esperáṁs* (l. us.); vern. term *bharvāṁsó.*—Jap. *superansa* (obs.)

Esperto (wide awake, smart). Konk. *eśpert*; vern. terms *huśár, śiḍúk, chatur.*—Tet. *espértu*; vern. terms *matének, badain.*

Espingarda (a gun, a rifle). Mal. *espingarda* (Haex), *istingarda,* | *istingar* |; vern. term *térkul. Bedil-espingarda* (Haex), a sort of big gun, a mortar.

Espirito (spirit). Sinh. *sprítuva*; vern. terms *átmaya, práṇaya.*—Tet. *ispirítu*; vern. term *klámar.*—Gal. *ispirítu*; vern. term *mánar.*

Espirito Santo (the Holy Ghost). Konk. *Sprit Sánt.*—Beng. *Spiritú Śāntú.*—Tam., Tel., Kan. *Spíritu Sántu.*—Ann. *Chúa śi-phiritô.*

Espoleta (a percussion cap). Konk. *ispilêt.*—Tet., Gal. *espoleta.*

Esponja (a sponge). Konk. *esponj.*—Hindi *ispanj.*—Hindust. *ispanj, isfanj.*—Beng. *spanj.*—Malayal. *spoñu.*—Tel. *spanji.*—Kan. *spanju.*—Ar. *espinkh, esfinkh, isfonkh, isfankh, safankh, sifankh, sufankh.*

The original word is Greek.

Essa (a cenotaph; an empty tomb set up in honour of the dead). Konk. *es*; vern. term *gar* (not in use among the Christians).—Tet., Gal. *esu.*

Estado (state, condition). Konk. *estád*: vern. terms *gat, bheś*; *dabāzó.*—Mar. *istád,* household furniture.—? Tel. *istuva, istuvu.* property.—Tet. *estádu,* government.

Molesworth and Wilson derive *istád* from the Ar. *isti'dád,* 'capacity, aptitude'; but they do not explain why only Marathi should have adopted it.

? Estala (stable; stall). Sinh. *stálaya, istálaya, istále.*—Sund. *istal.*

Also in the Portuguese dialect of Ceylon, *stella, stal.* Probably from the Dutch *stal.*

Estante (book-case, a desk). Konk. *estánt.*—Beng. *stāntí.*—Tam. *stántei.*

Esticar (to stretch, to extend). Sinh. *istrìkaya, istirikaya, strìkaya* (*subst.*), flat-iron for smoothing clothes. *Istirikayen madinavā,* to run the flat-iron.—Mal. *istríka,* flat-iron;

Tet., Gal. *estrika*, to smooth with a flat-iron, to starch.

The Portuguese dialect of Malacca has *estika*. See *estirar*.

Estingue (*naut.*, brails). L.-Hindust. *istingí*. *Istingí chāmpná*, to furl the sails.

Estirar (to extend: to stretch out). Mar. *istrí* (*subst.*), a flat-iron for smoothing linen; the act of passing the iron over. *Istrí karṇem*, to run the iron on the clothes. —Guj. *istrí*, *astrí*, *astarí* (*subst.* and *verb*), flat-iron; to pass the iron over.—Hindi, Hindust., Or., Beng., Ass., Punj., Malayal., Khas. *istrí*, flat-iron. —Sindh. *isitiri*, flat-iron.—Tel. *istiri*. the act of passing the iron over.—Kan., Tul. *istri*, to pass the iron over.

Swettenham says that the Malay *istríka* comes from the Hindustani and signifies literally 'the woman's work'. But neither Hindustani has *istríka* nor does *strīka* in Sanskrit mean 'woman's work'; but at the end of the compound possessive (*bahuvrīhi*) it means 'accompanied by a woman, he who has a wife, married.' *Strīkāryam* is what stands for 'work, woman's work'; it cannot, therefore, be the source word of *istríka*, because it is very generic, and because the washing of linen as a profession is done in India, since the remotest times (and, perhaps in modern times, also that of ironing clothes), more by men than by women. The form in use in the Portuguese spoken in India, *mainato*, 'washerman' (*q.v.*), is indicative that washing was done more by men than by women.

Shakespear, in his Hindustani dictionary, distinguishes between *istrí*, *istirí* or *strí*, Sanskrit, 'woman, female,' and *istrí*, 'flat-iron,' which he says is from Hindi. But Molesworth connects the Marathi *istrí* with the Sanskrit *strí*, through the intervention of Hindustani, without assigning any reason. And Wilson derives the Hindustani *istrí* from the Sanskrit verb. *stṛ*, 'to stretch out,' and mentions the compound *stri-vālá*, 'an ironing man, one who irons linen.'

It is very probable that the flat-iron (Konkani *phér* from Portuguese *ferro*, 'iron'), which has the same shape as the one used in Europe, and which is only employed by tailors and washermen, was not formerly known in India. I am of the opinion that the true originals of *istríka* and *istrí* are the Portuguese words *esticar* and *estirar*, which would have been used in the sense of 'running or passing the iron over'.[1]

Estivador (one employed in loading and unloading ships). Anglo-Ind. *stevedore*.

Estopa (oakum). L.-Hindust. *istap*, *istúb*.—[Anglo-Ind. *istoop*, oakum. "A marine term from Port. *estopa* (Roebuck).]—Ar. *usthubba*.

Estribo (stirrup). Konk. *estríb*: vern. term *rikābí*.—Tet., Gal, *estríbu*.

Estudar (to study). Konk. *estudár-karuṅk* (l. us.); vern. terms *śikuṅk*, *paṭhuṅk*.—Tet. *estúda*; vern. terms *hanôin*, *lóta*.

Estudo (study). Konk. *istúd*; vern. term *śikap*.—Tet. *estúdu*; vern. term *hanónun*.

Evangelho (gospel, evangel). Konk. *vānjel*.—Kan. *evanjélu*.—Tet., Gal. *evanjélhu*.

Hindustani. Oriya, Bengali, Malay and other languages of the Malay Archipelago have *injíl*, from Arabic-Persian.[1]

Exame (an examination). Konk. *ezám*; vern. terms *parīkśá* or *parikhyá*, *zhaḍtí*.—Tet., Gal. *ezámi*.

Excomunhão (excommunion). Konk. *eskomunháṁv*, *eskomunyáṁv*.—Tet., Gal. *eskomunhã*.

Exemplo (example). Konk. *ezempl*; vern. term *dekh*.—Tet, Gal. *ezémplu*.

Explicar (to explain). Konk. *esplikár-karuṅk*; vern. terms *samzāvuṅk*, *durāḷuṅk*, *arthuṅk*.—Tet. *esplíka*; vern. terms *hakláken*, *kátak*.—Gal. *splíka*.

F

Fadiga (used in the sense of 'gonorrhoea'). Mal. *fadiga* (Schuchardt). [The usual meaning of the Port. word is 'toil, anguish of mind.']

Falca (side-boards of a ship which are removed to take in the cargo). L.-Hindust. *fālká*.—Mal. *fálka* (Marre).

---

[1] C. Alwis (*The Sinhalese Hand-Book*) admits the Portuguese origin but does not mention the source-word.

[1] ["He then turned to me and said that he had nothing to say in reply to me, as those were all truths in our sacred **Anzir** (for so they name our blessed Gospel)" *Travels of Fray Sebastien Manrique* (1629–1643), Hak. Soc., Vol. II, 112. See also *idem*, Vol. I, pp. 37 and 101.]

Falcão (in the archaic sense of 'a species of cannon'). Bug. *palakko*.

[The ordinary meaning of the Port. word is 'falcon, the bird of prey'.]

Falso (false). Konk., Mar. *phál̥s*; vern. terms *laṭik*, *khoṭó* or *khoṭá*.—Mal., Sund. *pálsu*.—Mad. *pálsô*.—Tet. *fálsu*; vern. terms *lá*, *lós*, *bosôku*.

The term is used particularly in connection with coins and precious stones.

Faltar (to want, to need). Konk. *phāltár-zāvuňk*.—Beng. *phāltár* (in use among the Christians).—Tet. *fálta*; vern. term *múkiti*.

Falto (deficient, wanting). Konk. *phált*; vern. terms *uṇó*, *vikhaṇ*, *apúrṇ*.—Mar. *phāltu*, excessive.—Guj., Hindi, Hindust., Punj. *phállu*, excessive.—L.-Hindust. *phāltú*, *fāltú*, deficient, short; what is necessary to make up deficiency, superabundant.—Nep *fālṭo*, excessive.—Sindh. *phaliṭu*, exceeding.—Mal. *fáltu* (Marre).

? **Falua** (a barge). Mal. *báluq*.

The final *q* leads one to suspect a Spanish origin (*faluca*) or Arabic (*fulq*).

Fama (report). Konk. *phám*; vern. terms are *ḍág*, *khabar*, *nāmvrúp*.—Guj. *phám*, remembrance, memory.—Tet. *fáman*; vern. term *náran*.—Gal. *fáma*.

Fantasma (a phantom, a ghost). Mal. *fantasma*, *pantasma*.

Dr. Fokker says that it is little used; but it is mentioned by Haex.

Farol (a light-house). Konk. *pholér*. –Tet., Gal. *farol*.

Fastio (weariness, distaste). Mal *fastio* (Haex.)

Fatia (slice). Konk. *phātí*; vern. terms *kap*, *śir*, *pês*.—? Sinh. *petta* (pl. *peti*).

Favor (favour). Konk. *phāvôr* (l. us.); vern. term *upkár*. –Tet., Gal. *favor*.

Fazendeiro (*subst.*, a landholder). Konk. *phajendár* (l. us.).—Mar. *phajindár*; vern. terms *mālkár*, *vittkár*.—Anglo-Ind. *fazendar*. [*Fazendari* (*adj.*).]

[*Fazendeiro* is derived from the Port. word *fazenda*, which means 'an estate.' It is strange that the word does not find a place in *Hobson-Jobson*. Whitworth (*Anglo-Indian Dictionary*) says that "*Fazendar* is a superior landholder under the Portuguese government. He paid a small quit-rent, and levied from the cultivators a fixed proportion of the produce".]

Fé (faith). Konk. *phé-bhāvárth* (us. among the Christians). *Bhāvárth* is the vernacular synonym for 'faith.'—Gal. *fé*.

Fechar (in the sense of 'to solder'). Mal. *píjar*.—Batt. *píjer*.—Mac. *píjarā*, *píjā*.—Bug. *píja*.

Fecho (the bolt of a rifle). Mal. *píchu*.—Batt. *péchu*.

Feira (a fair). Konk. *phêr*; vern. terms *sánt*, *penṭh*.—Tet., Gal. *feira*; vern. term *bázar*.

[**Feitiço** (sorcery, charm). Konk. *phitís*; vern. terms *jādū*, *mañtar*; also *phitser* from the Port. *feiticeiro*, a sorcerer, a wizard; vern. terms *ghādi*, *jādūkār*.—Anglo-Ind. *fetish*.[1]

"The word is not Anglo-Indian; but it was at an early date applied by the Portuguese to the magical figures, etc., used by natives in Africa and India, and has thence been adopted into French and English" (*Hobson-Jobson*).]

Feitor (a factor). Konk. *pheytôr*.—? Anglo-Ind. *factor*.—Mal. *feitór*, *fetór*, *pētór*, | *petúr* |.—Sund., Jav. *pétor*.—Mac. *pétorō*.

Feitoria (factory). Konk. *pheytorí* —? Anglo-Ind. *factory*.

Yule and Burnell say: "Possibly the expressions *Factor*, *Factory*, may have been adopted from the Portuguese *Feitor*, *Feitoria*": | perhaps through the intervention of the Spanish *fator*, *fatoria*. |

Feriado (holiday) Konk. *pheryád*; vern. term *suṭí*.—Tet. *feriádu*; vern. term *kasala*.

Ferreiro (smith). Konk. *pherrêr*; vern. terms *lohár*,

[1] [1553.—"And as all the nation of this Ethiopia is much given to **feitiços** (sorceries) in which stands all their trust and faith....and to satisfy himself the more surely of the truth about his son, the King ordered a **feitiço**, which was used among them (in Congo). This **feitiço** being tied in a cloth was sent by a slave to one of his women, of whom he had a suspicion." Barros, Dec. I, iii, 10.]

["As we rowed by the Powder-Mills, we saw several the Holy Office had branded with the names of **Fetisceroes**, or Charmers, or in *English*, Wizards, released thence to work here." Fryer, *East India*, Hak. Soc., Vol. II, p. 24.]

kāmár, sāḷikár.—Mal. *ferrero* (Haex); vern. terms *pándei bési, túkan bési, kímpu besi.*

Festa (feast). Konk. *phest*; vern. terms *parab, uchav. Phestākár,* feaster.—Beng. *phestá.*—Mal. *festa, pesta, péstu.*—Sund. *pésta.*—Jav. *péstô, pistô. Pestan, pistan,* to feast.—Bug. *peseta.*—Tet., Gal. *festa*; vern. term *ksólok.*

Fiador (a surety; one that is bound for another). Konk., Tet., Gal. *phyādor.*

Fidalgo (one nobly descended, a hidalgo). Konk. *phidálg.*—Mar. *phidālkhôr.*—Mal. *fidalgo, hidalgo* (Haex).

Molesworth derives *phidālkhôr* from the onomatopoeic word *phid! phid!*, and gives as its meaning: "That swells and vapors, puffs and vaunts; a swaggerer or braggart; that giggles sillily."

Figura (figure). Konk. *phigúr* (us. in a lit. as also in a fig. sense); vern. terms *bāhulém, putḷí*; *song, yantr.*—Mal. *figura,* image, picture.—Tet., Gal. *figura,* image, effigy; vern. terms *hílas, ein.*

Filhó (fritter, pancake). Konk. *philhó,* [us. generally in the pl., *philhós.*]—Beng. *philó* (us. among the Christians).—Jap. *hiryúzu*

Finta (tax, imposition). Konk. *phínt* (l. us at present), vern. terms *danḍ, paṭṭí.*—Tet., Gal. *finta*

Fiscal (*subst.*, inspector, superintendent). Konk. *phiskál.*— [Tam. *pēškār*].—Mal. *piskal.*—Bug. *pasikála.*

Fita (ribbon). Konk., Mar., Guj. *phit, phínt.*—Hindi *phitá.*—Hindust. *fitá, fītá, phītá.*—Or., Beng., Ass. *phitá.*—Sindh. *phíta*—Punj. *fītá, fítah.*—Sinh. *pítta-paṭaya, pítta-paṭiya*—Malayal. *phiṭṭa, phiṭṭu,* lace.—Tel. *phíta, píta.*—Khas. *phita, fita.*—Mal. *fita, pita.*—Ach. *fítah, pita.*—Sund. *pita.*—Jav. *pitô.*—Mad. *péta.*—Bug. *píta.*—Tet., Gal. *fita*; vern. term *táli.* The Neo-Aryan terms are *nāḍí, nāḍó, dál, navár.*

Such languages as have no *f* sound find a substitute for it in *p.* The tonic *i* becomes nasalised in some of the Neo-Aryan languages, as for instance *piṅt,* 'bile', from the Sansk. *pitta.* Cf. *pipa.*

Fitar (to fix one's eyes upon; to hit). Mal. *pitar,* to aim at.

Fivela (shoe-buckle). Konk. *phivel.*—Tet. *fivela, fiela.*

[**Flamengo, flamenco,** or **framengo** (*Phoenicopterus*; the long-necked, long-legged scarlet-feathered bird). English and Anglo-Ind. *flamingo.*][1]

Flanela (flannel). Konk. *phlānel.*—Tet., Gal. *flanela.*— | ? Chin. *fáh-lán-jin* | .

Fogaça (a cake baked in embers). Anglo-Ind. *fogass* (us. in S. India).

[Yule describes it as being composed of minced radish with chillies, etc., used as a sort of curry, and eaten with rice.]

? **Foguete** (in the sense of 'Chinese cracker'). Konk. *phugaṭí.*—Mar. *phaṭkaḍí.*—Hindust. *phaṭakhá.*—Ass. *phaṭaká.*—Sindhi. *phaṭakô.*—Tam., Malayal. *paṭṭake.*—Tel., Kan., Tul. *phaṭóki.*[2]

It is used in the same sense in the Portuguese dialects of the East which distinguish it from the *foquete do ar*, 'a rocket', which in Portuguese is simply *foguete.*

It appears that the names of the cracker in the Indian languages, with the exception of the one in Konkani, are onomatopoeic (of *phaṭ*, 'a cracking explosive noise'); the cerebralisation of the Konkani name ought not to offer difficulty with regard to its Portuguese derivation. Cf. *tumor.*

Fôlha (in the sense of 'a sheet of paper'). Konk., Mar. (in Savantvadi) *phôl.*—Tul. *pulli.*

[*Fôlha*, in Port. also means 'leaf of a tree or of a book.']

Fonte (in the sense of 'a seton; a sore or ulcer which is the result of cauterisation'). Konk. *phônt. Phontyó*, one who has a discharging sore. *Phontló*, the pus which is discharged; (us. fig. in the sense of 'filth, impurity').—? Mar. *pot, pont, ponth.*

---

1 ["In this place (Bharoch)....in the moist ground we behold at a distance many Fowls, as big or bigger than Turkies, go up and down rather running than flying. They told us they were the same which the *Portugals* call *Paxaros Flamencos*, from their bright colour" Pietro Della Valle, *Travels*, Hak. Soc., Vol. I, p. 119. *Paxaros*=Port. *pássaros*, birds.]

2 "What threw most of them into confusion were the **foguettes** and fire bombs which the Turks used at the first onrush." João de Barros, Dec. IV, vii, 12.

"Discharging some shots and many **foguetes.**" Gaspar Correia, I, p. 165.

"He ordered the governor to make a signal to the armada by discharging three **foguetes.**" Diogo do Couto, Dec. VI, iv, 1.

Molesworth does not give the etymology of the Marathi words.

Forca (gibbet, gallows). Sinh. *pôrke* (pl. *pôrka*).

Fôrça (strength, force). Konk. *phôrs*; vern. terms *baḷ, tej, tráṇ*.—Mal. *forsa* (Haex), *parúsa*; vern. term *kakuátan*.—Tet., Gal. *forsa*; vern. term *biéti*.

Forma (in the sense of 'mould, appearance'). Konk. *pharm*; vern. terms *sâṅchó*, *sāṭhó*; *ākár, rúp, ākṛiti*.—Guj. *pharmô, phárm*, pattern, mould; plan, map; model.—Hindust. *farmá*, mould; configuration.—Beng. *pharmá, pharmmá*.—Punj. *farmá*.—Tet.—*fórma*.

In Konkani: *phormí* (*adj*.), having shape, printed. *Phormí kāgad*, printed paper. *Phormí letr*, print-type letter. *Ekphormāchó* (*genitive-adjective*), of the same form; of the same kind.

In Marathi: *ekpharmá* (*adj*.), "of one shape, size and general appearance—troops in array, letters of a writing, etc.; of one *form* more generally. *Ekpharmá*[1] (*subst*.), unity of form or of general appearance" (Molesworth).

1 *Ek* is from the Sansk. *eka*, 'one'.

Fôrno (oven). Konk. *pharn* (in Salsete), *kharn* (in Bardês);[1] it is also used to denote a receptacle in which are stored rice-husks and ashes.—Sinh. *pôrṇuva, pôraṇuva*;[2] vern. term *uduna*.—Malayal. *bôrmma*.—Mal. *fúrnu, fúrun*.—Tet., Gal. *fôrnu*.—? Pers. *foran*, furnace, boiler.—Ar. *forn, furn*.—Rab. *forni*.

Fôro (in the sense of 'quit-rent, or small rent payable by tenants to the lord of the manor'). Konk. *phôr*; vern. terms *śidáv, pat*.—Anglo-Ind. [*foro*,] *foras* (=Port. *foros*; us. in Bombay). *Foras lands*, lands subject to foro, 'a quit-rent'. *Forasdárs* are holders of 'foras lands.'[3]

1 In Bardês (a district of Goa) *kh* frequently takes the place of *f*: *khurí* from Port. *furia* ('fury'); *khursém* ('viper') for *phursém*; *khursat* ('leisure') for *phursat*.

2 *N* after *r* becomes a cerebral, just like other dentals.

3 "Especially that of the coco-nut groves of Chaul, and the **foros** which they had to pay" Bocarro, Dec. XIII, p. 352.

[1671.—"That in regard the Gen[ll] charges of the Island are great and doe far exceed the revenew,.... to the end that the sole burthen of y[e]

[Whitworth very briefly describes **Foras** as the name of the tenure on which the lands reclaimed from the sea, or inter-insular channels about the island of Bombay, used to be held before the settlement made by Act No. VI of 1851. These lands were reclaimed chiefly by the erection of vellards (see *valado*), and being originally very salt, they were let out at very low rents to induce people to cultivate them. In process of time they improved and became valuable, and it was a question much discussed in 1844 whether the foras quit-rent could be raised or not. For the way this question was decided, see *Hobson-Jobson. s. v.* Foras-Lands.

That philology and the correct derivation of words are not without their influence on legislation is seen in the manner in which this Port. term *fôro* was derived and interpreted by an eminent jurist like Sir Michael Westropp, a Chief Justice of Bombay, — an interpretation vitiated by the learned judge's ignorance of the Portuguese language: "*Foras* is derived from the Portuguese word *fora*, (Latin *foras*, from *foris*, a door) signifying *outside*. It here indicates the rent or revenue derived from outlying lands. The whole island of Bombay fell under that denomination when under Portuguese rule, being then a mere outlying dependency of Bassein. Subsequently the term *foras* was, for the most part, though perhaps not quite exclusively, limited to the new salt batty ground claimed from the sea, or other waste ground lying outside the fort, native town, and other the more ancient settled and cultivated grounds in the island, or to the quit-rent arising from that new salt batty ground and outlying ground. The quit-rent in Governor Aungier's convention called *foras* also bore the still older name of *pensio* (*pensão*, pen-

---

charge may not light on the Comp^d only, ... it seems reasonable that a Gen^ll tax or assesment be enordered on the respective Inhabitants over and above the present **foro**; wch is only a kind of quit-rent and very inconsiderable." Forrest, *Selections*, Home Series, Vol. I, p. 51.]

sion), and since that convention has been chiefly known by the name of *pension*. It was payable in respect of the ancient settled and cultivated ground only". *Bombay High Court Reports*, Vol. IV, 1866-67.

Dr. Gerson da Cunha (*The Origin of Bombay*, BBRAS. Vol. XX, Extra No., p. 228) has very lucidly and effectively pointed out the faults in the judge's derivations and the consequences they led to. "*Fôro* has no connection whatever with *fóra*, nor can the latter be derived from the Latin *foris* 'a door'. There are two *foris* in Latin, one a substantive and the other adverb. The first *foris* means 'a door,' and the second *forìs*, with a grave accent on *i* means outside. It is from the latter that the Portuguese *fóra* is derived, which means 'without,' 'abroad' or 'out of doors'......

"*Fôro* means a quit-rent payable by tenants to the King or the Lord of the Manor......It also means 'court or hall of justice.' If *fóro* is to be traced to a Latin origin, it is more appropriate to derive it from *forum*, a public place, where public affairs, like the payment of rents or tributos, were transacted. A Latin word more appropriate to *fôro* is *census*, meaning valuation of estates or rating of property, and not registry or roll of the citizens, just as *foral* corresponds to *liber censuum* or 'book of rates to be paid.' It is in this sense that the Portuguese term *pensão*, derived directly from the Latin *pensio* 'payment,' is taken...

"From the assumption that *fôro* was derived from *fóra*, and the latter from the Latin *foris* 'a door,' the eminent Bombay Judge concluded that this derivation plainly indicated that the rent or revenue was drawn from the outlying lands alone, and that the whole island of Bombay fell under that denomination when under the Portuguese rule, Bombay being then a mere outlying dependency of Bassein. And in order to justify this far-fetched derivation of the word *fôro* from *fóra*, he confined the quit-rent to the outlying ground, and to the island of

Bombay, as a mere outlying dependency of Bassein. But the fact generally known that *fôro* was imposed both on the inlying as well as on the outlying ground, and that it was not limited to Bombay, but was indifferently applied to Bassein, to Sálsette and to all other parts of that province, ought to have convinced him of the feebleness of his hypothesis." A male tenant who paid the quit-rent was spoken of as the *foreiro*, a female tenant as the *foreira* of the estate; thus, in 1727, D. Senhorinha de Souza e Tavora was the *foreira* of the village of Mazagon, and, in 1731 upon her demise, her grandson Martinho da Silveira de Menezes was entered in the records as the *foreiro* of the said village.

Another term intimately connected with *fôro* and frequently met with in a study of the old land tenures of Bombay is *aforamento*, which originally denoted the contract by which the grantor made a grant of a holding or estate to be held in possession and enjoyed by the grantee, either in perpetuity or for a specified period, upon his paying a certain annual *fôro* or quit-rent. In course of time the term came to denote the holding itself rather than the contract of the lease.

Forrar (to line; to cover). Konk. *phorrar-karuṅk.*—L.-Hindust. *pharal* (*karná*), to cover the cable.—Tet. *fóra.*

Fôrro (*subst.*, lining). Konk. *phorr.*—Guj. *phôr.*—Sinh. *pôru. Pôru redda*, cloth used for lining.

Forte (*adj.*, strong). Konk. *phórt*; vern. terms *baḷí*, *ghaṭṭ*, *nibar.*—Tet., Gal. *fórti*; vern. term *rósak.*

Fortuna (fortune). Konk. *phurtún*; vern. terms *naśib*, *lakṭó.*—Tet., Gal. *furtuna.*

Fraco (*adj.*, weak). Konk. *phrák*, *pharák*; vern. terms *aśakt* or *askat.*—Tet. *fráku*; vern. term *mámal.*—Gal. *fráku.*

In Konkani, from *phrák* are derived *pharkatáy* or *pharkajáy*, 'weakness.' *Fraquez* (from Port. *fraqueza*, 'weakness') is also used in the same sense.

Frade (a friar). Konk. *phrád*, *pharád.*—Tet. *frádi.*

In Konkani, *pharád*, as a substantive feminine, denotes

in common parlance the 'clerical tonsure.' See *coroa*.

Fragata (a frigate). Konk. *phargát*.—Mar. *phargád*.—Mal. *pragata*.—Bug. *parágata*.—Tet., Gal. *fragata*.— | Turk *firgatéyn*. |

Franga (a pullet, chicken). Mal. *franga* (Haex); vern. terms *áyam*, *ának áyam*, *áyam betína*.

Frasco (a flask). Konk. *phrásk* (l. us.); vern. terms *śiṁsó*, *kupó*.—Tet., Gal. *frásku*.—Jap. *furasuko* (perhaps from the Engl. 'flask'); vern. term *tokuri*.—Ar. of Egypt, *falaskiya*, *balaskiya*.

Frasqueira (a box or case for bottles). Konk. *phrāsker*.—Tet., Gal. *fraskeira*.

Frecha (an arrow, a shaft). Mal. *parecha*.

Freguesia (a parish). Konk. *phirgaz*.—[Anglo-Ind. *freguezia* (obs.)].—Tet., Gal. *frequezía*.

[Yule mentions the word in his *Glossary*, and says that "this Portuguese word for 'a parish' appears to have been formerly familiar in the West of India."]

Freio (a bridle). Konk. *phrey*; vern. term *lagam*.—Tet. *fréyu*.

Fresco (*adj*., cool, fresh). Konk. *phresk* (l. us.); vern. terms *thanḍ*, *śitaḷ*.—Mal. *parésku*.

[Fryer uses 'fresco' and 'frisco' as substantives in the sense of 'a cool wind'.[1]]

? **Fulano** (such a one). Konk. *phalāṇó*, *phulāṇó*.—Mar. *phalaṇá*.—Guj. *phaláṇuṁ*.—Hindust. *fulán*, *fulaná*.—Beng. *phalāṇá*.—Sindh. *phalānô*.—Punj. *phalāṇá*, *phalāṇí*, *phalāuṇá*.—Tel. *phulána*, *phaláni*.—Kan. *phaláni*.—Tul. *phaláne*.—Anglo-Ind. *falaun*.—Mal. *fulán*, *púlan*.

It appears that the word was imported directly from Arabic or through Persian. Gonçalves Viana remarks that "the true Portuguese form is *fuão*, *fulano* being Castilian."

Fundal ('lower extremity of a mast'). L.-Hindust. *fūndál*, *pūndál*. [*Fundal* in the above sense is not mentioned in most Portuguese dictionaries.]

---

[1] ["Near the Latitude of 30 deg. *South* we had a promising **Fresco.**" *East India*, etc., Hak Soc., Vol. I, p. 51.]

["Although in the Afternoon we had an humming **Frisco.**" *Idem*, p. 131.

Funil (a funnel). Konk. *phunel*; vern. term *turbāṇí* (l. us.).—L.-Hindust. *phannel, fannel*.—Beng. *phunnel*.—Sinh. *punílaya*; vern. term *kemiya*.—Kan. *phannále*; vern. term *lálike*.—Tet., Gal. *funíl*; vern. term *kakún mátan*.

Fusta (a foist, a pinnace). Mal. *fusta*.[1]

[The English 'foist' is not derived, as one might have supposed, from the Port. word which one meets with so frequently in the Portuguese chroniclers, but, according to the *O.E.D.*, from O. Fr. *fuste* adapted from the It. *fusta*, fem., originally a log, piece of timber, from Lat. *fustis*, 'a cudgel.' The earliest mention of the word is by Caxton in *Paris and Venus* (1485).]

[1] "They build other small boats for rowing, like *bargantins* or **fustas**." "Duarte Barbosa, *Livro*, p. 353 [Hak. Soc., Vol. II, p. 108. "The *atalayas* (*q.v.*) were shore boats often used for patrolling; the **fustas** made longer voyages, and were employed in the attack from Gujarāt on Lourenço D'Almeida's ships at Chaul." Longworth Dames, *Barbosa*, Vol. II, p. 236. *Bargantins* were light rowing boats, drawing little water and suitable for coast work, they had no resemblance to the modern brigantine].

? **Fuzil** (a steel with which to strike fire). Mal., Ach., Batt., Sund., Low-Jav., Mad., Bal. *bedíl*.—Day. *badil*.—Mac. *bádili*.—Bug. *bálili*.

Dr. Heyligers says that the interchange of *e* and *u* is frequent, and that *f* changing into *p*, the latter would easily be transformed into *b*, resulting in the form *bezil* or *besil*, the corruption of which would be *bedíl*.

G

Gage (*arch*., gift over and above wages; bye-profits, pledges.) Mal. *gade*, pledge; *gáji*, stipend. *Gádei*, *gádeikan*, to pawn.—Ach., Sund., Jav., Mac., Bug. *gáji*, stipend.[1]

? **Gago** (*adj*., stammering; us. also as a substantive). Konk. *gag* (*subst*.), stammer;

[1] "Two thousand cruzados on account of their salaries and **gagens** (perquisites)." Bocarro, p. 490 [Cruzado was a Portuguese piece of money so called because of the cross (*cruz*) on it, and worth about two shillings and a half.]

["The salaries, **gages**, and other interests of these as well as of the Fortresses were not only sufficient but even superfluous" Faria y Sousa, *Asia Portuguesa*, III, p. 578.]

vern. terms *luḍbepaṇ, totrepaṇ. choṅchrepaṇ* (derived from the adjectives *luḍbó, totró, choṅchró*). *Gág yevuṅk* (dative of the person), to have a stammer. *Gāgyó*, a stammerer. *Gāgyéṁ ulauṅk*, to speak stammeringly. *Gāgevuṅk*, to stammer.—Sund. *gágu*, stammer.—Mol., Batav. *gágu*.—Mac., Bug. *gága*, to stammer.—Ach. *gagab*, to stammer; to prattle. In Batta, *gagap* signifies, according to Joustra, "to follow a wrong way".—Mal. *gágap*, ? *kókok*.

Haex has *gagu*, 'to stammer', and *gagab, bergagab*, 'to prattle'. Dr. Schuchardt mentions the following Malay forms: *gegeb*, 'to stammer', *gagap, gagáp, gegáp* 'confused', and *gugup*, 'murmur'. And he observes that "in Batavia *gagu* is equivalent to dumb"; but, in the vocabulary of the Portuguese dialect of Malay, he gives "*oen-gagoe* (=*un gágu*) ein Stotterer (orang gagoe)". *Kriolische Studien*, ix.

Gonçalves Viana says: "The etymology of the Portuguese word *gago* is unknown: what Dr. Ad. Coelho gives us in his *Diccionario Etymologico*, viz., that it is from the Castilian *gago*, does not take us far, and besides this and the fact that it is little used in Castilian, it must be noted that in it the word has an entirely different meaning which corresponds more or less to 'a snuffler' rather than to 'a stammerer.' In the opinion of Cândido de Figueiredo, it is an onomatopoeic word. *Gago*, as a nickname or surname, appears very often in the old writers: Gabriel Gago in João de Barros. Fernão Gomes Gago in Gasper Correia, Diogo Gago in *Lembranças das Cousas da India*

Dr. Schuchardt maintains that *gágap*, because of its termination, is Malay and not of Portuguese origin; Gonçalves Viana eliminates it from his new list, revised and augmented, of Portuguese words introduced into Malay. But the reason alleged for this is not good as far as the form *gágu* in the other dialects is concerned. Matthes derives the Macassar *gága* from the Malay *gágap*.

It is not possible to explain why among the Indian languages Konkani alone should have *gág* ('stammer'), with some derivatives of the word, all in common use, and even more current than the vernacular terms. Onomatopoeia is improbable in the case, because onomatopoeic words of this kind are, as a rule, common to Konkani and Marathi. Might it have been imported from Portuguese or, rather, from Malay through the intervention of Portuguese ?

It is useful to note that in the Portuguese spoken in Goa the word *cacoethe* is used in the sense of 'stammering'. This term does not appear in the *Diccionario Contemporaneo*, nor in the dictionary of Cândido de Figueiredo; but it is mentioned by old lexicographers, like Morais, who says: "**Cacoethe** (from Lat. *cacoethes*; from Gk. *kakos* 'bad' and *êthos* 'custom'). V. *Cachexia*. Bad bodily habit, like twisting the body, or similar movements or ugly gesticulations. An evil habit."[1]

[1] "Cacoete——Although this term may appear more scientific than common place, yet we have many times heard it, in the province of Minho (Portugal), used by persons who are illiterate." Cardinal Saraiva, IX, p. 24.

Galão (gold-lace). Konk. *gālāṁv*; vern. term *zarpāṭí*.—Tel., *galan*.—Tet., Gal. *galã*.

Galé (galley). Mal. *galey*, *galay*.—Bug. *gále*.[1]

Can they have come from the Dutch *galei* ?

Galeão (galleon). Mal. *galyún*, | *galiong* | .—Ar. *galion*.[2]

Galeota ("a small galley with one mast and with 15 or 20 benches a side, and one oar to each bench"). Anglo-Ind. *gallevat*.—Ar. *galitha*.[3]

Fr. José de Moura says that *galiun* and *galiuta* are Turkish words.

[Sir J. Campbell (*Bombay Gazetteer*, XIII, 417) states that *galbat*, a form of *gallevat*, was in use in Bombay to denote large foreign vessels, such as

According to Marsden, *gágu*, in Malay, is the name of a small fish.

[1] "An armada of three hundred sail, in which there were **galés**, *lancharas* (*q. v.*), *bantins*." Diogo do Couto, Dec. VI, v, 1.

Bantim (pl. *bantins*) is a brigantine or a brig; the word is derived from the Malay *banting*, a two-masted trading vessel. See *Glossario*.

[2] "He gave a **Galeão** with plenty of munitions." Diogo do Couto, Dec. VI, viii, 5.

[3] "He chartered a beautiful **Galeota**." Diogo do Couto, Dec. VI, iii, 9.

English ships and steamers, and he refers *galbat* to *jalba*, a word for a small boat in the Red Sea. The correct Arabic form, however, is *jilba*, and it is met with among the early Portuguese chroniclers as *gelba* and *gelva* (*Glossario*, *s.v.*). Yule does not look with favour upon Campbell's derivation of *gallevat* and is more inclined to trace it directly to the Portuguese *galeota*. For the connection of *galeota* with 'galley' and the very remarkable etymological history of the latter, see *Hobson-Jobson* *s. v.* gallevat.]

Galeria (a gallery.) Konk. *gālerí*.—? Mal. *galari*, *galri*.—? Jav. *galadri*, *gladri*.—? Mad. *galdri*.

Gonçalves Viana thinks the Portuguese origin is unlikely in respect of the Malaysian words.

Galo (a cock). Mal. *gallo* (Haex); vern. terms *áyam jantam*, *áyam kambiri*.

The reason for the introduction of this word is not known; it is not mentioned in modern dictionaries.

Gamela (wooden bowl; porringer). Konk. *gamél*; vern. te suṃpardém, *karlém*.—Mar. *gamêl*, a mason's trough.—[Anglo-Ind. *ghamélla*].—? Malag. *gamela*.[1]

Molesworth also mentions *gabelem*, as used in the Konkan in the same sense.

Gancho (hook; hair-pin). Konk. *gánch*: vern. terms *āṅkḍó*, *phāsó*, *kél*.—Tam. *gánchu*, bolt.—Mal. *gánchu* (*subst.*), a hook; also used as an adj. in the sense of 'provided with a hook'. *Mug-gánchu*, to hook.—Turk. *cancha*, according to Simonet.

Ganho (profit). Konk. (*subst.*) *gáṅh*, gain; also used in the sense of 'interest on money'.—Mac. (*adj.*) *gánhu* (a term used in sport), gained, won.—Bug. *gánho* (the same as in Macassar).

? **Ganso** (a goose). [Burm. *ngan*].—Mal. *gánsa*, *gása*.—Batt. *kánsa*.—Sund. *gánsa*.—Day. *gása*.—Jap. *gan*, wild goose; *gacho*, domesticated

---

1 "Hoes, crow-bars, picks, **gamelas**." Gaspar Correia, III, p. 619. [" **Ghamellas**, Powrahs, Picks, Steel Bars, and all kinds of excavating tools" Advertisement in *The Times of India*, 8 October, 1929.]

goose.—Malag. *gisa*; vern. term, *vorombe*.[1]

"*Angsa* and *gangsa* are the usual words, in the whole of the Archipelago, for goose, and they are evidently from the Sanskrit *hansa*." Rigg.

? **Garça** (heron). Kamb. *cársa*, *crâsa*.—Siam. *kra-sá*, *ka-sá*.

Kambojan and Siamese have no *g*. Cf. Kambojan *casêt*.=Fr. *gazette*; Siam. *khru*=Sansk. *guru*. *khiri*= Sansk. *giri*.

It appears that *cársa*, *krasá* are corruptions of *gansa*, which is met with in the Malayo-Polynesian languages. Moura gives 'crane' as the meaning of *carsa*.

Garfo (a fork). Konk. *gárph* (more us. *kāṅṭó*, lit. 'a thorn').—Sinh. *gárpuva*, *gárp-puva*, *gerpuva*, *gáruppuva*.—Malayal. *kárpụ* (us. in Cochin).—Mal. *gár/u*, *gárpu*, | *kárpu* |.—Sund. *gárpu*.

[**Garopo** (a kind of sailing vessel from Malasia). Anglo-Ind. *grab*.[2]

The Portuguese word is from the Malay *gorap*, which, in its turn, is the Ar. *ghurāb*, 'a crow', 'a raven'. The Marathi *gurāb*, a sailing vessel, also owes its origin to the very same Ar. *ghurāb*.]

Gasto (expense). Konk. *gást* (l. us.); vern. terms *kharch*, *vech*. More in use is *gāstár-karuṅk*, 'to spend', concurrently with the vern. *kharchuṅk*, *sāruṅk*, 'to spend'.—Sinh. *gástuva*, honorarium, gratuity.

Gávea (top-sail). Guj., L.-Hindust. *gāví*.—Mal. *gávei*.—Ar. *gabia*.[1]

---

1 "Peacocks, **ganços**, ducks, and all domestic fowls." Lucena, Bk. X, ch. 18.

2 [1552. "The fleet consisted of twenty-four *lancharas*. And six of these were very big; these we call in their language **garopos**." Castanheda, *Historia*, III; ch. 151, cit. in *Glossario*.]

["It was found to be the fleet of Achem, of a hundred and more three-masted galleys and fifty **gurabos**." António Bocarro, Dec. XIII, p. 412.]

["On appearance of the *Desy's* **Grob** they (Seva Gi's men) retreated again". Fryer, *East India*, Hak. Soc., II, p. 6.]

["An old *English* Master of a **Grab**, or small Vessel, *George Toach*, has frequently reported this Story to me." Ovington, *A Voyage to Surat* (O.U.P.), 1929, p. 158.]

1 "They used to take many fire-spears and powder pots which they used to place on the **gaveas**." Gaspar Correia I, p. 512.

Gaveta (a drawer). Konk. *gavét*; vern. term *khaṇ*.—Tam. *gavêtei*.—Tet., Gal. *gavêta*.

Gaxeta (*naut.*, the lines that fasten the sails to the yards). L.-Hindust. *ghāset*, *ghaseth*, *ghānset*, *ghansit*.

Gelosia (a window-blind). Sinh. *jalúsi*.[1]

Genebra (gin, the spirit distilled from malt). Konk. *jenebr*.—Tet., Gal. *jenebra*.

General (*subst.*, a general). Konk. *jenerál*; *jernel* (from English); vern. terms, *senāpati*, *dalpati*.—Malayal. *janarál*.—Mal. *jendral*. *Jendrál laut* (*laut*=sea), general of the sea, admiral.—Ach. *jendral*.—Bug. *jinerála*. —Tet. *jeneral*.[2]

Gentio (gentile, a heathen; applied by the Portuguese in India to the Hindus in contradistinction to the *Mouros* or 'Moors', i.e., Mohammedans).[3] Konk. *jintú* (used in combination with *Konkṇó* of which it is a synonym, or as a depreciative); vern. terms *anbhāvārthi* (lit. 'an unbeliever'), *Konkno* (lit. 'a Konkani' or 'Konkan man.'). —Anglo-Ind. *gentoo*, pagan; Hindus;[1] Telugu-speaking Hindus and their language.[2]

---

1 "There were many windows projecting outside, with **gelozias**." Diogo do Couto, Dec. VI, iv, 7.

2 "The **general** sent one Bernardo de la Torre as the captain of a small galleon." Diogo do Couto, Dec. V, VIII, 10.

3 ["And before this kingdom of Guzerate fell into the hands of the Moors, a certain race of **Gentios** whom the Moors called *Resbutos* dwelt therein." Duarte Barbosa, ed. Dames, Vol. I, p. 109.]

["And in this kingdom there is another sort of **Gentio** whom they call *Baneanes*" *Idem*, p. 110.]

1 ["The Originall of this Petition (to Charles II) .... is signed by 225 of the principalest Inhabitants of this Island, vizt.

123: Christians and
84: **Gentules**
18: Moores.

Anglo-Portuguese Negotiations relating to Bombay 1660-1677 (O.U P.), by S. A. Khan, p. 453.]

["The late scarcity of provisions necessitating us to take some cows from the **Jentue** inhabitants to supply the fleet...." Forrest, *Selections*, Home Series, Vol. II, p. 31.]

["The **Gentues**, the *Portugal* Idiom for *Gentiles*, are the *Aborigines*, who enjoyed their freedom, till the *Moors* or *Scythian Tartars* ... undermining them, took advantage of their Civil Commotions." Fryer, *East India*, Hak. Soc., Vol. I, p. 81.]

2 [For citations of 'gentoo' in the acceptation of Telugu Hindus and Telugu language, see *Hobson-Jobson*.]

—Tet. *jentiu.*—Gal. *jentiu, sentiu.*

The word 'gentoo' is used at the present time only in Madras of the Telugu-speaking Hindus, and of their language. But formerly it had a very wide meaning; the first digest of Indian legislation, which was compiled under the orders of Warren Hastings and published in 1773, has the title *A Code of Gentoo Law.*

[According to Yule, the reason why the term became thus specifically applied to the Telugu people is probably because, when the Portuguese arrived, the Telugu monarchy of Vijayanagara was dominant over a great part of the Peninsula. The officials were chiefly of Telugu race, and thus the people of this race, as the most important section of the Hindus, were *par excellence* the 'Gentiles' and their language the 'Gentile language'. This appears to be a very plausible view, because of the intimate political and commercial relations that existed between the Portuguese in Goa and the Vijayanagar sovereigns.

Yule is led to believe that the English form 'Gentoo' did not come into general use till late in the 17th century, whilst Longworth Dames (Intro. *Duarte Barbosa*, p. lxiii) is of the opinion that in the 18th century 'Gentoo' was limited in its meaning to some of the lower castes in South India.

From *gentio*, the Portuguese formed *gentilico*[1] (*subst. masc.*) with the meaning 'language of the Hindus.' The word is used in the phrase *em gentilico* ('in the Hindu or vernacular language').]

Geração (generation). Konk. *jerasáṁv*; vern. terms *pīṇḍká, pilgí.*—Tet., Gal. *jerasã.*

Gergelim (the seed of *Sesamum indicum*). Mar., Hindust. *jinjalí* (trade name, according to *Hobson-Jobson*); vern. terms *til, tíl.*—Anglo-Ind. *gingeli, gingelly.*[2]

The word is of Arabic origin

---

[1] ["I had some notices published in **Gentilico**..." *Apud* Júlio Biker, *Collecção de Tratados*, viii, p. 174, in *Glossario.*]

[2] "They make much use of **gergelin** oil." Duarte Barbosa [Hak. Soc., ed. L. Dames, Vol. I. p. 13].

"Full of rice, oil, and **jerzilim.**" Bocarro, Dec. XIII, p. 478.

(*juljulán*). [Dr. Rice, quoted by Watt, derives it from the Arabic *chul-chulan*.]

[Botanists are of the opinion that sesamum is not a native of India, but was introduced into India, perhaps at a period prior to the Aryan invasion. "Indeed some of the Indian names given to it come from Arabic or Persian; few or none belong to the aboriginal languages of India....There is, moreover, no reason to doubt that the *tila* of the Sanskrit authors is the *til* of India to-day" (Watt, *The Comm. Prod. of India* (1908), p. 982). It is interesting to note how *tila*, which originally was the name of the seasum plant, came to assume the generic significance of oil (*taila*). Watt observes : "It is certainly very remarkable that few, if any, of the early European travellers in India, such as Garcia de Orta, Linschoten, etc. etc., make mention of this plant or its oil". In this he is mistaken, for Duarte Barbosa (1516), forty-seven years before the publication of da Orta's *Colloquies* (1563), and Castanheda (1552) refer to '*gergelin*' and its oil. References to it by later travellers and writers are legion.]

Gêsso (chalk). Konk. *jês*; vern. term *ṡeḍ*, *khêḍ*.—Ar. *chess*, *chiss*.

Globo (a spherical glass bowl used as a candle-holder). Konk. *glôb*, *galôb*.—Sinh. *golôva*.—Tam. *galobei*.

Sinhalese has *gôla* (Sansk.), 'globe in general, sphere,' which could give *gôlava*, but not *golôva*, where the *v* takes the place of *b*.

Goiaba (*Psidium guyava*). ? Tam. *goyá palam* (lit. 'guava fruit or Goa fruit'?). It is also called *pêrá*.—? Tel. *gōvā-panḍu* (*panḍu*=fruit).—? Anglo-Ind. *guava*.—? Indo-Fr. *gouave*, *goyave*, *goyavier*.— | Mal. *kuyávu* (Rumphius).—Mol. *guayáva*, *goyávu* (*idem*) | .— Nic. *koyanva*.—Tet., Gal. *koyabas*. —Malag. *guavy*. [In modern Arabic this fruit is called *juwáfa*, Arabicised from 'guava.' See *JRAS*, July, 1927, p. 560.]

Just as the Portuguese called bananas *figos* ('figs'), so likewise they gave the name *pera* ('pear') to the guava, when they introduced it into India; and just as subsequently the word *banana* made its way into India, so likewise did *goiaba* or *goiava*. But have *banana* and *goiaba*, as a matter of fact, been introduced from Portuguese into Anglo-India and Indo-French? It appears that the Tamil *goyá* and the Telugu *gōvā* are for 'Goa'. [An exact parallel of the Tam. and Tel. names is found in one of the Bengali names of the fruit *góaāchiphal*, which obviously means 'fruit from Goa'.] See *pera* and *banana*.[1]

[The guava tree is a native of South America now naturalised and largely cultivated throughout India. It was, in all probability, introduced into this country by the Portuguese.]

Gola (collar of a coat). Konk. *gól*; vern. term. *gaḷó*.—Tam. *golla*.

Goma (gum). Konk. *góm*; vern. terms *bôḷ*, *chik*.—Tet. *goma*.—Jap. *gomu* (perhaps from English). *Arabíya gomu*, gum Arabic.

Gorgoleta ("an earthen and narrow-mouthed vessel, out of which the water runs and gurgles"). Konk. *gurgulét*; vern. term *kuzó*.—Sinh. *gurulêttuva*.—Anglo-Ind. *goglet*, *guglet*.—Mal. *gargalét*, *bargalét*.—Mac., Bug. *guléta*.—Tet. *gorgoleta*, ? *gargó*; vern. term *dardón*.—Gal. *gorgoleta*.[1]

[The Portuguese word is itself derived from *gorja*, an archaic term, meaning 'throat', and the pitcher perhaps gets its name from the gurgling sound made in the throat when the water poured out of it into the mouth is drunk, as Indians do, without touching the spout with their lips. Linschoten (Hak. Soc., Vol. I, p. 207) and

---

1 Some of the Indian languages give the guava the name '*jambo*.'

[The Port form *goiaba* is derived from *guayaba* by which name the fruit was known in Brazil and from where it was introduced into India. The name *pera* ('pear'), which the Portuguese first gave it because of its resemblance to that fruit, has its counterpart in the Hindustani name for the guava, *āmrūd* (Pers.), which means 'a pear'. In Gujarat the fruit is also called *jam*, and *jāmrūd*, the latter, perhaps, a combination of *jam* and *amrūd*.]

1 "Because we threw among them many pots, and **gorgoletas** containing powder". João Ribeiro, *Fatalidade historica*, Bk. II, ch. 25.

Pyrard (Hak. Soc., Vol. II, p. 74) describe the way this water vessel had to be handled and the derision that followed its employment in an improper fashion.[1]]

Gôsto (taste, savour). Konk. *gôst*; vern. terms *rúch*, *svád*.—Gal. *gôstu*.

Governador (governor). Konk. *governãdor* (in popular speech '*rāzá*').—Malayal. *gōvernnador* (archaic; current *gavarnar*, from English).—Mal. *gubernadúr*, *gubernúr*, *gurnadúr*, *gurundúr*.—Bug. *goronádora*.

Govêrno (government). Konk. *govêrn*; vern. term *sarkár*.—Tet., Gal. *govêrnu*.

Graça (grace, indulgence; pleasantry, fun). Konk. *grás*, joke, jest; vern. terms *khebaḍ*, *cheśṭáy*.—Tet. *grasa*; vern. terms *díak*, *túlun* ('help').—Gal. *grasa*; vern. term *lálan* ('jest').—Jap. *garasa* [1].

Grade (grate, railing). Konk., Guj. *garád*.—Mar. *garád*, *garáz*, *garadá*.—Hindust., Beng. *garādiyá*.—Sinh. *garádiya*. *Garádi messa*, railing. *Garádi dammalada*, railed in. *Garādivata*, a palisade.—Tam. *garáde*, *girádi*.—Malayal. *girádi*, *grádi*, *grási*.—Siam. *kratū*.[2]—Mal. *grado* (Haex), *gerádi*. The Neo-Aryan term is *kaṭhḍó*.

Gralha (crow, rook). Mol. *graia* (Castro).

---

[1] [" When they (the Portuguese and Mestico women) drinke they have certaine pots made of blacke earth very fine and thin, and much like those that we use in Holland for flower pottes, having in the necke thereof a partition full of holes with a spout, (and these cruses are called **Gorgoletta**), to this end, that when they drinke, they may hold the potte on high, and touch it not with their mouthes, but the water running from the spout falleth into their mouthes, never spilling drop, which they doe for cleanlinesse, because no man should put it to his mouth, and when any man commeth newly out of Portingall, and then beginneth to drinke after their manner, because he is not used to that kinde of drinking, he spilleth it in his bosome, wherein they take great pleasure and laugh at him." Linschoten.]

[" The same way they have of cooling their Liquors, by a Wet Cloth wrapped about their **Gurgulets** and Jars, which are Vessels made of a porous kind of Earth; the best of *Mæcha*, reasonable good from *Goa*... " Fryer, *East India*, Hak. Soc., Vol. I, p. 125.]

[1] In Konkani, the equivalent for 'divine grace' is *kurpá*, from the Sansk. *krpá*.

[2] Cf. Siam. *khru*=Sansk. *guru*, 'master'; *thūt*=Sansk *dūta*, 'messenger'. See *garça*

Granada ('grenade, bomb'). Konk. *garnál, garnêl.*—Mar., Hindust. *garnál.*—Tul. *garnalu.*[1]

? **Granadeiro** (grenadier). Hindust. *garandil.*—Tel. *garandilu.*[2]

? **Grande** (big). Pid-Engl. *galanti, ka-lan-ti.*

It appears more probable that the source is Portuguese rather than English (from 'grand'). The change from *r* to *l* and from *d* to *t* is normal.

Grão (grain). Konk. *grámv* (weight).—Anglo-Ind. *gram,* the chick-pea, *Cicer arietinum,* Linn..[3]

["This word (gram) is properly the Portuguese *grão, i.e.* 'grain', but it has been specially appropriated to that kind of vetch (*Cicer arietinum,* L.) which is the most general grain- (rather pulse-) food of horses all over India, called in Hindustani *chanā.*" *Hobson-Jobson.* The Portuguese formerly called the above vetch *grão de cavalo* ('vetch for horses') and not merely *grão*; it is smaller than the kind grown in the Iberic Peninsula. At the time when the Portuguese took Goa they found that *mungo,* the Hindust. *muṅg* (*Phaseolus mungo*), was used there as horse-feed.]

Graxa (blacking for boots). Konk. *graś.*—Tet *gracha.*

Grosso (big, thick). Mal. *grosso,* dense, thick (Haex).

Grude (glue). Konk. *gurûd*; vern. terms *páṅk, chikaṭvaṇ*; *khaḷ.*—Tet. *grúdi*; vern. terms *reten, dámer.*

Guarda (guard). Konk. *guvárd.*—Mar. *gārdí, gāḍḍí. Gārdāi,* "insurrectionary tumult amongst foot-soldiers, and hence tumult, confusion, uproar, more generally" (Molesworth).—Guj. *gārdí, gaḍḍí.*—Hindust. *gārad.*—Khas. *garod, karod.*—

[1] "For only in this (company of grenadiers) consists our defence, and in the awe they inspire in them, the dread these barbarians have of the new **granadas** being something extraordinary" (1728). *O Chronista de Tissuary,* I, p. 52.

[2] "But, more than in any other part, in this province (of Bassein and Damaun) there is the need of a company of **granadeiros,** which ought never to withdraw from here except in case of necessity." *Ibid.*

[3] ["These serais are generally noble monuments of individual bounty, and were in ancient times liberally endowed, and furnished supplies of **gram,** milk .. to the traveller". Heber, *Narrative,* (1828), p. 303.]

Mal. *gárdu, gàrdu.*—Sund. *gárdu.*—Jav. *gárdu, gérdu, grédu.* —Tet., Gal. *guarda.*—Ar. *virdiyán* (from the Italian *guardia*, says *Belot*). In Javanese it is also employed as a verb, in the sense of 'to place guard'.

Molesworth observes that the word is met with in the most ancient Marathi documents and does not regard it as foreign; but he does not say whether the documents are anterior to the sixteenth century. He adds that it denotes especially the infantry soldier employed to guard the person of the Peshwa or other Raja. But Wilson derives it from the English 'guard' and remarks that it is obsolete. [It is well known that Portuguese military officers were employed in the Peshwa's armies, and it is, therefore, reasonable to suppose that *guarda* and other military terms such as *coronel, ronda, tronco* found their way through them into Marathi.]

Guardanapo (napkin; serviette). Konk. *guvārdānáp.*—Sinh. *gardenappa.*—Mal. *gardenappa* (Haex).

Gudão ('a warehouse for goods and stores'; it is an Indo-Port. word)[1]. Konk., Mar. *gudámv*; vern. terms *kaṭhí, kaṭhár, sānṭhó, ṭhevó.*—Hindust., Nep. *godám.*—Or. *gudáma.*—Beng. *gūdam.*—Ass. *gūdám.*—Sinh. *gudama.*—?Tam. *giḍangu.*—Malayal. *guḍḍam.* —? Tel. *gaḍangu, giḍḍingi.*—Kan., Tul. *gaḍangu.*—Anglo-Ind. *godown.*—Khas. *kudam.*—Day. *gudang* (nearer to the Port. form than to that of the original word).—Bug. *gúdang*, pantry in European houses, besides *gudong* which is the vernacular term for 'a warehouse.'

The word is the Malay *gadong* or *godong* | or *gudang*,

---

1 "**Gudões**, which are rooms almost underground as a protection against fire." João de Barros, Dec. II, vi, 3.

"Two **gudões** of the king which it was said were full of goods." *Id.*, 4.

"It will be stored in the **gudões** of the Customs Office." Filipe Néri Xavier, *Collecção de Bandos.*

["1615.—Was given me old ruined brick house or **godung**... the same goods to be locked up in the **gaddones**... the one half of the charges of building and purchasing a **godone** and houses." Foster, *Letters of the E.I.C.* Vol. III, pp. 109, 159, 181, in *Indian Antiquary*, Vol. XXX, p. 456.

Wilkinson, | disseminated by the Portuguese. Yule and Burnell, however, say that the word appears to have come primarily from the South of India, where in Telugu *giḍaṅgi*, in Tamil *kiḍaṅgu*, signify 'a place where goods lie,' from *kiḍu*, 'to lie'. It appears in Sinhalese also as *gudāma*. It is a fact that many common Malay and Javanese words are Tamil, or only to be explained by Tamil. Free intercourse between the Coromandel Coast and the Archipelago is very ancient, and when the Portuguese first appeared at Malacca they found there numerous settlers from S. India.

Guisado (*subst.*, ragout, stew). Konk. *gizád*; vern. terms *pakvan*.—Tet. *gizádu*.

Guitarra (guitar). Konk. *gitár;* vern. term *vīṇó*.—Sinh. *kittárama*.—Mal. *getéra*. Also found in the same form in the Port. dialect of Malacca.—Ar. *qitár*.

The original of the Arabic word is by some referred to Greek.

Guloso (gourmand). Mal. *galôjo*.

H

Hábita. See *ábita*.

Hábito (in the meaning of 'habit of a monk; soutane'). Beng. *ābdú* (us. among the Christians).—Jap. *abito* (obs.).

Harpa (harp). Konk. *árp*.—Bug. *arapa*, which Matthes derives from the Dutch *harp*.

Harmónio (harmonium). Konk., Tet. *ārmónyu*.

Herdar (to inherit). Konk. *erdár-karuṅk*.—Tet. *érda*; vern. term *hétan*.

Hissope (hyssop). Konk. *isóp*.—Beng. *isopa*.—? Sinh. *hisop* (perhaps from English). —Tam. *isopei*.

História (history). Konk. *istór*; vern. terms *kathá* or *kanthá*, *charitr*, *itihās*.—Mal., Jav., Mad. *setóri* (also used in the sense of 'a cabal, machination').—High-Jav. *setanton*.—Sund. *stóri*.—Tet., Gal. *istóri*. "anarchy, contention, controversy, debate, misunderstanding, disorder, discord, dispute, dissension, disturbance, rising, litigation, riot, scuffle, law-suit, wrangling, quarrel" (Raphael das Dores).[1]—? Malag. *hisitoria*.—Ar. *usthúra*.

---

[1] "Forbes claims that in the island

The Malayo-Polynesian meanings of the word are supported by old Portuguese writers. Francisco Vaz de Almada, referring to the boatswain of a ship, says: "He conducted himself in such a proud, uneducated, and unrestrained manner, that there was scarcely a person with whom he did not have ***historias*** ('quarrels')." (*Hist. tragico-marit.*, ix, p. 14.)

Honra (honour). Konk. *onr*; vern. terms *mán, iśím, ãbrú.*—Tet., Gal. *onra*; vern. term *díak.*

Hora (hour). Konk. *ór.*—? Sinh. *hôrã, hôrāva*; vern. terms *peya, kanisama.*—Mal. *hora* (Haex): vern. term *jam* (Pers.).—Tet., Gal. *ora.*—Malag. *ora.*

There is *horā* in Sanskrit, borrowed from Greek, little used in modern Prakrits, except in astronomical works and in a figurative sense. But the *h* aspirate of the Sinhalese word appears to indicate such an origin, perhaps by way of Pali, the sacred language of the Buddhists. In Malay, however, I believe it represents simply the imitation of the Portuguese word.

Awar in Marathi and Gujarati is obviously the English 'hour'.

The Neo-Aryan terms are *tás, ghāṇṭá*; *ghaḍí, ghaṭká* (of 24 minutes).

Horta (a garden, an orchard). Konk. *órt*; vern. terms *parsúṁ, bág.*—Malayal. *óḍam.*—Anglo-Ind. *oart* (us. in Western India), a coco-nut garden.[1]

Hortulana (*zool.*, a small

of Timor the word *istori* is employed as an adjective in the sense of 'bad'." Heyligers. My sources of information do not confirm this statement.

[1] "To cut down the **hortas** and coco-nut groves which the Portuguese had therein." Bocarro, Dec. XIII, p. 22.

["There is also a great number of *Palmero* or **orta**, like our orchards here (Goa), full of *cocos* trees planted close together....They are enclosed with walls, and, along with a house and pretty garden, are called **orta**, wherein they take their recreation with their families." Pyrard, Hak. Soc., Vol. II, p. 28.]

[1758.—"Oart Charney, situated at Bombay, containing 200 cocoanut trees, bearing fruit, let to the Bhandáris, for Rs. 627". *Materials towards a Statistical Account*, etc., Part III, pp. 439-440, in da Cunha's *The Origin of Bombay*, p. 223."]

lark, *Calandrella brachydactyla*, Temm., and also *Pyrrhalauda grisea*, Scopoli). Anglo-Ind., Indo-Fr. *ortolan*.

Littré derives *ortolan* from "old Fr. *hortelan*, a gardener." But the application of the term to Indian birds must be due to the Portuguese. [The name of the bird in Hindi is *bargel* or *bageri*.]

Hospital (hospital). Konk. *ospitál*; *ispaṭal* (influenced by English).—Sinh. *ispiritále*.—Malayal., Tel., Kan., Tul. *āspatri*.—Tet., Gal. *ispital*. — | Turk. *isspitálya*. |

Espertal and *espertel* are used in the Portuguese dialect of Ceylon. In Alentejo (Portugal) are found the forms: *espital*, *espitel*, *espritel*.[1]

Hóstia (host, consecrated wafer). Konk. *ôst*.—Beng. *ostí*.—Tam., Kan. *óstu*.—Tet., Gal. *óstia*.—Jap. *óstiya*.

I

Igreja (church). Konk. *igraz*, *igarz*.—Hindi *girjá*. *Baḍá girjá* (lit. 'a big church'), a cathedral.—Hindust. *girjá* (us. only in the north of India).[1]—Or. *girjá*.—Beng. *girjá*, *girjjá*. *Vaḍgirjá*, a cathedral. *Girjjāvishayak*, ecclesiastical.—Ass. *girjá*, Catholic worship. *Girjághar* (lit. 'house of the church'), a church.—Punj. *girjá*. The Neo-Aryan terms are *devúḷ*, *devasthan*, *devmandir*.—Tul. *igreje*.—Anglo-Ind. *girja*.—Garo *gilja*.—Khas. *kirja*.—Mal. *igresia* (Haex), *gréja*, *gríja*. *Búrung gréja*, a sparrow.—Sund. *gréja*, *gríja*. *Manúk gréja*, a sparrow.—Jav. *gréjô*, *gríjô*, *garínjô*.—Mad. *gréjô*, *grijô*.—Mac., Bug. *garéja*.—Mol. *gréja*.—Tet., Gal.

[1] "For the expenses of the espritall (hospital)." Simão Botelho, p. 23.

[1] [The following incident, quoted in *Hobson-Jobson* (*s.v.* girja), has an interest of its own, apart from the philological:—"It is related that a certain Maulví, celebrated for the power of his curses, was called upon by his fellow religionists to curse a certain church built by the English in close proximity to a *Masjid*. Anxious to stand well with them, and at the same time not to offend his English rulers, he got out of the difficulty by cursing the building thus:

'Gir jā ghar! Gir jā ghar! Gir jā!'
(*i.e.*) 'Fall down, house! Fall down, house! Fall down!' or simply
'Church-house! Church-house! Church!'" W. J. D'Gruyter, in *Panjab Notes and Queries*, II, 125.]

kréda.[1]—Jap. *ekirinjiya, ekirinji* (from the Latin *ecclesia*, according to Dr Murakámi). [The Port. *igreja* is itself a corruption of the Lat. *ecclesia.*]

Imagem (image). Konk. *imáz*; vern. terms *rūpkár, sūrkém, sarūpáy, múrti, bāhulí, putḷí.*—Mal. *imagem* (Haex).

Incenso (incense.) Beng. *insensú* (us. among the Christians).—Kan. *inséñsu* (us. among the Christians).—Mal. *incenso* (Haex).—Tet., Gal. *insénsu.*

Indiano (*adj.*, Indian). Sinh. *indiyánu. Indiyánu tinta*, Indian ink.—? Malag. *indiana.*

Indulgência (*eccles.*, an indulgence). Konk. *dulgeṁs.*—Tet. *indulgénsia.*

Inferno (hell). Konk. *iṁphern*; vern. terms *yam kanḍ, pātáḷ, narak.*—Tet. *inférnu*; vern. terms *rái kidun, rái ókos.*—Gal. *inférnu.*—Jap. *inferno, imberno.*

Inglês (arch. and pop. form, *ingrês*, English). Konk. *inglêz, ingrêz* (*subst.*), *ingrezí* (*adj.*).—Mar. *inglejí* (also *ingliś*, from 'English').—Guj. *angrêj, angrejí.*—Hindi, Hindust. *angrezí.*—Bihari *angrej, angrejí.*—Beng. *ingláj.*—Ass. *ingráji.*—Sinh. *ingrisi.*—Malayal. *ingirisu̥.*—Kamb. *áncgris.*—Mal., Sund. *ingris.*—Mac., Bug. *angarísi.*—Jap. *ingirisu.*[1]

Some of the above words might owe their origin directly to the term 'English'.

| **Inhame** (the name given to various species of *Dioscorea*). Anglo-Ind. *yam.*—Indo-Fr. *igname.*

It appears that the word is of American origin. |

[The author in his *Glossario* says that the Portuguese word is borrowed from a West African language, probably

[1] In the languages of Timor the initial *g* is changed at times into *k*: *kojabas* or *koabas*=*goiabas* ('guavas'). The same is the case in Khassi: *kudam*=*gudão* ('godown'). With regard to *d* taking the place of *j*, cf. *ajudar.*

[1] "They suffered in it many misfortunes, as much owing to bad times, as to robbers who were **ingreses**." Fr. João dos Santos, *Ethiop. Or.*, II, p. 170.

"The **ingrezes**, who were in the anchorage with a man-of-war and a pinnace, at once left the place." António Bocarro, Dec. XIII, p. 25.

[The English factory at Malda was called **Angrezábád** or Englishavad. See Hedges, *Diary*, Hak. Soc., Vol. I, p. 71.]

from Guinea, and this is also the view of Skeat (*Etymological Dictionary*, and *Notes on English Etymology*) who definitely mentions that the name of the tuber originally came from Benin, on the West African coast. This, he thinks, is settled by a passage in Hakluyt's *Voyages*, in which a voyage made by Master James Welsh in 1588 is described.[1] The *O. E. D.*, however, says that the ultimate origin is uncertain. For other derivations of the word, see Watt (*The Comm. Prod. of India* (1908), p. 496, *s. Dioscorea*.]

Injustiça (injustice). Konk. *injustís*; vern. terms *anít*, *anyáy*.—Tet. *injustisa*; vern. term *aáti*.

Inocência (innocence). Konk. *inoseṁs* (l. us.); vern. terms *anaparádh*, *nirmaḷpaṇ*, *nenṭepaṇ*.—Tet. *inosénsi*; vern. term *la sála*.

Instrumento (tool; musical instrument). Konk. *instrument*; vern. terms *āspáv*, *yantr*; *vāzantr*.—Tet. *instruméntu*.

Inteiro (entire, whole). Mal. *intero* (Haex), *intéru*, *enteiro*, *entéro*, *antéro*; vern. terms *sagolla*, *samuványa*.—Sund. *antéro*.—Jav. *antéro*. *Sa-antéro*, *soantéroné*, wholly entire.

Intenção (intention). Konk. *inteṁsáṁv*; vern. terms *man*, *yojan*, *bháv*.—Gal. *intensã*.

Irmão (brother). Konk. *irmáṁv*, elder brother; vern. terms *dādá*, *báb* (not used by the Christians of Goa); also used as an honorific suffix to names of persons older than the speaker, as for instance: *Anton-irmáṁv*, *Pedrú irmáṁv* (lit. 'Anthony brother, Peter brother').—Beng. *irmáñ* (us. among the Christians).—Jap. *iruman*, a friar. See *mana*.

J

Jaca (the tree called by botanists *Artocarpus integrifolia*, and its fruit). Anglo-

[1] ["Their (of the people of Benin) bread is a kind of roots; they call it inamia; and when it is well sodden I would leave our bread to eat of it; it is pleasant in eating, and light of digestion; the roote thereof is as bigge as a man's arme. Our men upon fish-dayes had rather eate the rootes with oyle and vinegar, then to eate good stockfish." Hakluyt, *Voyages* (1904), Vol. VI, p. 457.]

Ind. *jack.*—Indo-Fr. *jaque, jaquier.*[1]

The original word is the Malayalam *chakka.*[2] [In Tamil the tree is called *pila* or *pala.*]

Jagra (coarse sugar from cane juice or sap of various palms). Anglo-Ind. *jaggery, jagri.*—Indo-Fr. *jagra, jagara, jagre.*

The author of the *Roteiro da Viagem de Vasco da Gama* describes the article without giving it a name. "Four vessels containing some cheese-shaped cakes of palm-sugar."[1]

1 "Fruits of the country (Calecut), which are different from ours, but very savoury, and some of them are called **jacas**, and others mangoes, and a third kind figs." Castanheda, I, ch 16.

"There were many fruits of the country, such as durians and **jacas**, dainties when once you take to them." João de Barros, Dec. III, v, 7.

2 "They are called in Malavar **jacas.**" Garcia da Orta, Col. xxviii [ed. Markham, p. 235].

["A certaine fruite that in Malabar is called Iaca, in Canara and Gusurate, *Panar* and *Panasa*, by the Arabians, *Panax*, by the Persians, *Fanax*. This fruite groweth upon great trees, not out of the branches like other fruites, but out of the body of the tree, above the earth, and under the leaves." Linschoten, *Voyage*, Vol. II, p. 20. Burnell, in a note, remarks that the fruit only is called *chakka*, the tree is called *pilāva* in Malayalam.]

["**Jacke** trees, whose Fruitte groweth on the very body, stemme, or biggest braunches of the tree. There bee some thatt Wey Near 40 pound waight, and in my opinion is the biggest Fruit thatt groweth on trees, as I thincke the Cocotree bearest the biggest Nutte." Peter Mundy, *Travels*, Hak. Soc., Vol. I, p. 57.]

1 "Palm sugar, which they call **jagra.**" Duarte Barbosa, p. 274 (Hak. Soc., ed. L. Dames, Vol. I, p. 127).

Coco-nuts and **jagra**, which is produced from them, in the manner of sugar." João de Barros. Dec. III, iii, 7.

"And this sugar (from the palm) is called, in India, **jagra.**" João dos Santos, *Ethiopia Oriental*, I, p. 297.

["Here (in Chaul) is great traffike for all sortes of spices and drugges, silke, and cloth of silke, sandales,........ and much sugar which is made of the nutte called **Gagara.**" Fitch, in Foster's *Early Travels*, O U.P. (1921), p. 13.]

[They call it (wine) Raack (arrack), distilled from sugar and a spicie rinde of a tree, called Jagra. Terry, in Foster's *Early Travels*, p. 300.]

["Sugar and **Jaggaree** or Mulasso's made into Past." Fryer, *East India*, Hak. Soc., Vol. I, p. 251.]

["Arack is a liquor distilled Severall ways, as Some out of the graine called Rice, another Sort from the Jagaree or Very coarse Sugar." Bowrey, p. 77 *et seq.*]

The immediate source-word is the Malayalam *chakkarā* (cf. *jaca=chakka*), which is connected with the Sanskrit *śarkarā* through the intervention of the Neo-Aryan forms *śākar*, *sākar*, *sākhar*. Refined sugar goes by the name of *panchasára* in Malayalam.

[The quotations above from Fitch and Terry will show what confused notions they had about 'jagri' and the way it was prepared.]

Jalapa (jalap root). Konk. *zuláb.*—Kan., Tul. *julábu.*—Jap. *yarapa.* Perhaps imported directly from English in the last mentioned language.

The word *jalap* comes from *Xalapa*, a Mexican city.

In the sense of evacuation of the bowels in general and of a purgative: Mar., Guj., Beng. *juláb.*—Hindust., Ar. *juláb* or *julláb* (Port. *julepo*, julep).—Khas. *julap.* This is derived from the Pers. *gul.* 'rose' and *ab*, 'water'.

In Konkani, Kanarese, and Tulu there has probably been a shifting of meaning in consequence of the phonetic similarities of the two words.

Janela (window). Konk *zanél*; vern. term *khiḍkí* (l. us. in Goa).—? Hindust. *jhilmil.*—Beng. *jānālá*, *janālá.*—Ass. *jalangani.*—? Sindh. *jhirmirí.*—Sinh. *janélaya*, *janéle*; vern. terms *kavaluva*, *sīmedura*. *Janēlatiraya*, a window-curtain, a window-blind. Tam. *jānalá*, *jannal. Jannal-pinnal*, window-blind; (fig.) confused, intricate.—Malayal. *janel*, *chenel*, *chenárel*, *janavātil*; vern. terms *chálakam.*—Tel. *janalu.*—? Anglo-Ind. *jillmill*, Venetian shutters.—Mal. *janéla*, *janalá*, *jinelá*, *jandéla*, *jendéla*, *jindéla*; vern. term *tingkap.*—Sund. *jandéla.*—Jav. *jendélô*, *jindélô.*—Mad. *jindélô.*—Bal. *jendéla*, *gendéla.*—Mac., Bug. *jandéla.*—Tet. *janela*, *jinela.*—Gal. *janela.*

[With regard to the Anglo-Ind. *jill-mill*, Yule also makes an alternative suggestion that it might be the Hindi *jhilmilā* which seems to mean 'sparking', and to have been applied to some kind of gauze. Possibly this may have been used for blinds, and thence transferred to shutters. This is also, according to Crooke, the view of Platts (*A Dict. of Urdū, Classical Hindī, and English*).]

Jangada (a raft; two boats lashed together, with a planking laid across them). Tul. *jangálu, jangalu̥, jangáru̥.*—Anglo-Ind. *jangar.*

Cândido de Figueiredo derives *jangada* from *jangá* (*junga*, according to other dictionary-writers), "a small vessel worked by oars in former times." But Yule and Burnell give as its source the Tamil-Malayal *shangāḍam*, transcribed as *zángara* in the *Periplus Maris Erythrei*, of the first century. Konkani and Marathi also have *sāngaḍ* in the same sense, derived from the Sansk. *saṅghaṭṭa*, 'junction, union, cohesion', which is without a doubt related to *shaṅgáḍam.* Many of the old Portuguese writers regard the word as foreign.[1]

[1] "Vasco da Gama sailed with our men in two *almadias* ('canoes'), which were fastened together, forming, what in that country is called, a **jangada.**" Castanheda, I, ch. 16.

"They had constructed a **jangada** of pieces of wood, and of planks which were ready at hand, and fastened them with the ropes of the sails." Fernão Pinto, ch. clxxix.

"And Pulatecão got aboard a **jangada** which was made up of many small boats fastened together and boarded on top, enabling 800 well armed men to cross over." Gaspar Correia, Lendas, II, p 89.

They crossed the river in **jangadas** made of timber and branches of trees which a Jew had gone in advance to get ready." *Id.*, IV, p. 373.

["We therefore set out to look for a ford through the fierce current, but could find none, and so decided to make a **janguada** or raft of big logs firmly bound together with grass ropes." Manrique, *Travels*, Hak. Soc., Vol. I, p. 105. The editor Lt.-Col. Luard, hazards the opinion that *janguada* may be the Hindi word *chaughaḍa* or *changaḍa*, a raft made of bamboo frame supported on earthen pots, the Portuguese word being a corruption.]

[For the seven different acceptations in which *jangada* is employed by the old Portuguese writers, see *Glossario*, p. 482, and *Contribuições* etc., p. 138. Yule regards the term of particular interest as being one of the few Dravidian words, preserved in the remains of classical antiquity, occurring in the *Periplus*. But as the Malayalam *chaṅgāḍam* is, as has been noted above, affiliated to the Sansk. *saṅghaṭṭa*, (from the verb *saṅghaṭ*), it is scarcely correct to regard *jangada* as a purely Dravidian word.]

There is another word *jangada* [in Anglo-Ind. *jancada*], of Malabar origin, which denotes a guide in the Nair country who escorted and guarded travellers from one place to another.[1] See under *Naire*.

[This word too is from *shaṅgāḍam* and its application to the Nair guides is derived from the ideal of the moral bond, close and indissoluble, between the guide and his employer.]

Jantar (archaic form *gentar*; to dine). Mal. *sentar* (Haex).—Tet. *jantar*.

Jaqueta (jacket). Konk. *jākêt*.—L.-Hindust. *jāket*.—Jap. *jaketsu*. Hepburn mentions *chokki* as derived from the English 'jacket'.[2]

Jarra (a jar). Konk. *jár*; vern. terms *barṇí*, *kunḍí*.—Tet. *jara*; vern. term *tóos*.—Gal. *jara*.

Jaspe (jasper). Mal. *jaspe*, *jasbe*.

Dutch has *jaspis*.

Jejuar (to fast). Konk. *jinvár* (*subst.* m.), a fast. Cf. *jogar*, *casar*, *pintar*, *pagar*. The vern. terms are *upás* (starvation), *ekbhakt* (ecclesiastical fast). *Jinvár dharuṅk*, to fast.

The nasal of *jinvár* is due to the Goa-Portuguese word *jenjuar*. The *e* after *j* becomes sometimes softened into *i*. Cf. *gentio*. The second *j* was absorbed by the nasal and was the cause of the *u* being changed into the consonant *v*.

Jejum (a fast). Tet. *jinjum*, *dindum*.—Gal. *jinjum*, *jijum*, to fast.—Jap. *jejun* (arch.)

Jibão (doublet, a kind of waistcoat.) Konk. *zubáṁv*; vern. terms *jhubó*, *ḍagló*.—? Bug. *júmba*.—Jap. *jiban*, | *juban*, 'shirt' |[1]

---

[1] "A stranger requiring help in going from one part to another against robbers or highway men, when he comes across a Nair asks him to be his **jangada**, and for this service he gives him some money.... and, taking him as his **jangada**, goes perfectly secure....without anybody troubling him." Diogo do Couto, Dec. IV, vii, 14.

[2] "Men with gilt halberds wearing **jaquetas** of black velvet." Gaspar Correia, I, p. 533.

[1] "They wear a **gibão** of coloured satin." Castanheda, I, 91.

"A **jubão** of rose-coloured satin, very short, and lined with blue taffeta." Gaspar Correia, II, p. 371.

The source of the Portuguese word is the Arabic *jubba*, which passed directly into Hindustani and the other Indian languages. | Bluteau mentions the form *jubão*. |

Jogar (in the sense of 'a game of chance or game with stakes; a raffle.') Konk. *jugár* (us. outside Goa). *Jugár kheḷ*, game of chance with stakes. *Jugár-kheḷuṅk*, to gamble.—*Jugārí*, gambler. In Goa, the words *jôgo* and *jogador* are used in the above sense of gambling; vern. terms *duḍvānchó khêḷ*; *kheḷgaḍyó*.

Mar. *jugár*, *juvá*, *juvebājí*, *juvá kheḷṇeṁ*. *Jugár* or *juvá kheḷṇeṁ*, to gamble. *Jugārí*, *jugāryá*, *juvebáj*, gambler. *Jugārāchá* or *jugāryāchá*, *juvyāchá aḍḍá*, gaming-house.

Guj. *jugár*, *jugáru*, *juveṁ*, *juô*, game with stakes. *Jugáru áḍa*, *jugár* or *jugaṭ ramvuṁ*, to gamble. *Jugārí* *juvâkhor*, *jugāru āḍuvava*, a gambler. *Juvākhánuṁ*, a gaming-house.

Hindi *juá*, games of chance for money; vern. term *dyut*. *Juá khelná*, to gamble. *Juāri*, *juvāri*, *juanḍí*, a gambler.

Hindust. *juá*, game of chance; raffle. *Juá khelná*, to gamble. *Juākhāna*, a gaming-house. *Juārí*, *juābáj*, a gambler.

Nep. *juvá*, game of chance. *Juvá khelnu*, to gamble.

Or. *juá*, game of chance. *Juārú*, a gambler.

Beng. *juá*, *juvá-khelá*, *juá-khelá*, *juyá-khelá*, *jurá-khelá*, game of chance. *Juvá-khelá*, *juyá-khelá*, *jurá-khelá kṛi* (='to make'), to gamble. *Juá-chor*, trickster, cheat. *Juyāri*, *jurārí*, gambler.

Ass. *juá*, game of chance. *Jūá khelá*, to gamble.

Sindh. *juá*, game of chance. *Juá khelṇu*, to gamble. *Juá-khanô*, gaming-house. *Juāri*, gambler.

Punj. *jūá*, game of chance; dice. *Jūá kheḷná*, *jūá mārná*, to gamble. *Jue-khāná*, gaming-house. *Juārí*, *juāriá*, *juebáj*, a gambler. *Juebājí*, game of chance.

? Sinh. *súdu*, *súduva*, *súdu-keliya*, *súdu-kelima*, game of chance. *Súdu-kelinavā*, to gamble. *Súdu-maḍuva*, *súdu-gedara*, gaming-house. *Súdu-mêsaya*, gaming-table. *Súduvā*, *súdu-keliyā*, *súdu-kelinā*, gambler.

Tam. *jūá*, *jūdáṭṭam* (*áṭṭam*,

game in general,' like *khel* in Neo-Aryan languages), game of chance. *Judáḍi*, *jūdādikôn*, *juddan*, gambler. *Jūdádu*, *jūá-viḷaiyádu*, to gamble.

Malayal. *chūdu-kaḷi* (*kaḷi*, 'game in general'), *chūdádum*, game of chance. *Chūdāduka*, *chūdu-kaḷike*, to gamble. *Chūdáli*, *chūdukáran*, gambler.[1]

Tel. *jūādamu*, game. *Jūādamáḍu*, to gamble. *Jūádari*, gambler.

Kan. *jugáru*, *júju*, game of chance. *Jugáru áḍu*, *jūjáḍu* (*āḍu*, 'game in general'), to gamble. *Jūjugára*, *jugáru āḍuvava*, *jūjáḍuvava*, *jūjuṇega*, gambler. *Jūjuna paḍe*, set of players or gamblers. *Jūjuna kôli*, fighting-cock.

Tul. *jugárụ*, *jugārí*, *jugārigobbunáya*, gambler. *Jugārigobbuni*, to gamble.

Gar. *joa*, game of chance, *Joa kala*, to gamble.

Khas. *juvari*, game of chance; gambler.

Mal. *jógar*, game of draughts. *Ber-jógar*, to play with draughts; what is played with draughts. *Juvára*, expert in the game, especially, of cock-fighting. *Júdi*, game of dice, game of chance. *Ber-júdi*, to gamble; gambler.—Ach., Jav. *júdi*.—Batt. *júdi*, game of chance. *Erjúdi*, to play for money, to play with dice, to bet. *'Njudiken*, to lose in a game of chance. *Perjúdin*, gaming-house. Day. *judo*, lot, destiny. Mac., Bug. *júgarā*, to gamble.[1]

Tet. *júga*, *dúka*, *dôka*, *yôka*, to gamble, game of chance; vern. term *halimar*.—Gal. *júga*, to gamble, also game.

Molesworth derives the Marathi *juva* from the Hindust. *jūá*, which Shakespear derives from the Sansk. *yuga* (Lat.

[1] Malayalam does not retain, as a rule, the soft initial sounds of foreign vocables, and changes *y*, *j*, *d*, *b*, into *k*, *ch*, *t*, *p*.

[1] The game of *tabulas* ('backgammon') was introduced into India by the Portuguese. In Konkani: *túbl* is 'dice'. *Tablañcho khêl* is 'game of dice.' *Tablêr* is 'backgammon board.'

"He found Ruy Dias, seated in the forepart of the ship, playing **tauolas** with the Captain Jorge Fogaça" Gaspar Correia, II, p. 116. 'He was playing **tauolas** for heavy stakes which all of them used to win from him." *Id.*, p. 284. "Manoel Falcão ordered that they should go to him and play a game of **tauolas**, which they often used to do" (in the Moluccas). Diogo do Couto, Dec. IV, iv, 3.

jugum, 'a yoke'), which signifies 'a yoke', and also 'one of the ages of the world.' But Wilson, more plausibly, connects *juá* with the Sansk. *dyuta*, 'a game.' Reeve likewise attributes to Sanskrit the Kanarese words, but does not mention their source-word. Favre, following Newbranner Van der Tuuck, connects the Malay *júdi* with the Sansk. *yodhī*; but he does not explain how the word, in passing over to Malay, lost its meaning of 'warrior' and acquired that of 'game of dice and of chance', seeing that, phonetically, *yodhī* could give *júdi* just as *yoga*, 'union' (if not *yuga*), gave *júga*.

The verb *jogar*, according to the regular law, became changed in the Portuguese dialects of Asia into *jugá*, which, with the loss of the intervocalic *g*, became *juá* or *juvá*. Cf. Hindust. *jūá*, 'a yoke', from the Sansk. *yuga*; Mar. *juḷá*, 'twins', from the Sansk. *yugala*; Konk. *múi* (or *múy*), 'ant', from the Mar. *muṅgí*.

The *d* that is to be found in some of the languages may have been intercalated in order to remove the biatus, or makes its appearance because of the influence of *jugador*, or of the Sansk. *dyuta*, 'a game of chance', the intervocalic *t* being changed into *d*. Cf. Konk. *kāpaḍ*, 'a *saree*, or cloth which constitutes the main part of a woman's dress', from the Sansk. *karpaṭa*; *máḍ*, 'coco-nut palm', from *mahātāla*: *cheḍó*, 'boy,' from *cheṭa*.

It is, however, a matter for wonder that the Portuguese word should have penetrated so thoroughly into so many languages (in many of them, as is to be expected, mediately), and produced so many forms.

Games of chance, especially those of dice, have, in India, been indulged in from Vedic times, as is evidenced by: 'The Lament of the Gambler' (*Rigveda*, x, 34)[1]; the disastrous contest of Yudhisthira; and the celebrated episode of

[1] J. Muir translates the first strophe as follows (*Original Sanskrit Texts*):

These dice that roll upon the board
To me intense delight afford.
Sweet Soma-juice has not more power
To lure me in an evil hour.

Nala, one of the oldest and most beautiful in the *Mahābhārata*. The *Yajurveda* ironically calls confirmed gamblers 'pillars of the gaming-house', *sabhāsthanu*. Sir Arthur Macdonell observes that the principal social recreation of men in Vedic times, when they came together, was the game of dice, which were made from the nuts of [the Vibhīdaka tree] *Terminalia bellerica*. The moralists of that age held dice, wine, and wrath as the principal causes of sin. And Manu prohibits gaming, even as a pastime, and desires that the king should mete out to the gambler corporal punishment.

It is probable that the Portuguese introduced new games, and that either they or their descendants popularised the game of dice, which had fallen into disuse, thanks to civil and religious legislation. The word *dado* ('dice') has been adopted in Konkani, Sinhalese, Malay, Javanese, and Sundanese.[1]

The Sansk. *dyuta* could also have been corrupted into *júda* or *júdi*. Cf. Konk. *uzó* 'fire', from Prakrit *vijju*, Sansk. *vidyut*, which also gave *viz*, 'lightning-bolt', in Marathi and Konkani. And *Bisnágar* or *Bisnaga*, of the old Portuguese chroniclers, is a corruption of *Vijayanagara* ('City of Victory') or of *Vidyānagara* ('City of Wisdom'), both names being applied to the capital of Narsinga.

It appears that the Sinhalese *súdu* is in place of *júdu* in the other languages and is derived from the Portuguese word. The Malayal. *chúdu* does not present great difficulty. Cf. *chenel*, *chenarel* from Port. *janela* ('a window'), side by side with *janel*. Cf. also the Port. *jaca* from the Malayal. *chakka*: *jagra*, from the Malayal. *chakkara*, Sansk. *śarkarā*.

| **Joia** (jewel). Anglo-Ind. *joy*. "This seems from the quotation to have been used on the west coast for 'jewel'"[1] *Hobson-Jobson*. |

[1] See Lucena, Bk. III, ch. 12.

[1] [1810—"The vanity of parents sometimes leads them to dress their children, even while infants, in this manner, which affords a temptation

Jornal (in the meaning of 'newspaper'). Konk. *jornal*; *phol* is also used, from the Port. *folha* ('a sheet of paper'); vern. term *vartamánpatr.*—Tet. *jornál.*

Juiz (judge). Konk. *juyíz*; vern. terms *mansubīdár*, *nītidár.*—Tet. *juiz*, *duiz.*—Gal. *juiz*, *juis*, *duis.*

Julho (July). Konk. *Júlh.*—Mal. *Julu.*—Tet., Gal. *Julho.*

Junho (June). Konk. *Júnh.*—? Mal. *Jun.*—Tet., Gal. *Junho.*

Favre derives *Jun* from the English 'June'; but Marre prefers the Portuguese provenance.

Juramento (oath). Konk. *jurāment*; vern. terms *pramáṇ*, *śapúth.*—Tet., Gal. *juraméntu*, *duraméntu.*

Jurar (to take an oath). Konk. *jurár-zavuṅk*; vern. terms *pramáṇ* or *śapúth divuṅk.*—Tet. Gal. *júra*, to take an oath, oath.

Juro (interest on money). Konk. *júr*; *jurí* (us. in Kanara); vern. terms *kalāntar*, *váḍh*, *vyáz.*—Tet., Gal., *júru*; vern. term *dánik.*

Justiça (justice). Konk. *justís* (us. only in Goa); vern. terms *nít*, *nyáy.*—Tet., Gal. *justisa.*

Justo (just). Konk. *júst* (*adj.* and *adv.*); vern. terms *sārkó*, *sāmkó*, *barābar*, *ṭhík.*—Mal. *lústo*; vern. terms *ādil* (from Ar.), *pátul*, *hárus.*

It appears that *lústo* passed through an intermediate form **dústo*. Cf. *lidal*, *didal*, from Portuguese *dedal*, 'a thimble'.

L

Laço (tie, knot). Konk. *lás* (l. us.); vern. terms *phás*, *kaṭ.*—Tet. *lásu*; vern. term *fafóati.*

Lacre (a resinous incrustation on certain trees produced by the lac insect). [Anglo-Ind. and Eng. *lacre*, *lacquer*, *lacker.*[1]]—Mac. *lakári*; | *alkári*, according to Wilkinson. |

..... to murder these helpless creatures for the sake of their ornaments or toys." *Maria Graham*, 3, in *Hobson-Jobson.*]

[1] [" Between these (havens) is one called Martaban whither come many ships. . . and obtain cargoes. . for the most part of laquar . . . this the Indians and Persians call laquar *Martabam*, "Martaban lac." Barbosa, ed. Dames, Vol. II, p. 158.]

[" From whence I went the same

[The Port. *lacre* and its other variants *laca*, and *alacre* is the Sansk. *lākṣā* or *rākṣā* which became in Prakrit *lakkha* and in Hindi *lākh* from which the Anglo-Ind. 'lac' is apparently derived. No form with the *r*, as there is in Portuguese, can be traced in any Indian language, and we must therefore conclude that the Portuguese form is directly responsible for the above English and Anglo-Indian words.

Garcia da Orta (Col. XXIX) was perhaps the first European who critically examined and described lac in India, and Watt (*The Comm. Prod. of India*, p. 1054) says that he gives the properties and uses of both the dye and the resin in such detail that the passage may be quoted as from the pen of a 20th instead of 16th century writer.]

Ladainha (litany). Konk. *ladín*.—Tet., Gal. *ladainha*.

Lagarto (alligator). Anglo-Ind. *alligator*.—Mal. *lagárti*.[1]

[The Port. word, which is the same as the Spanish, is itself a corruption of the Lat. *lacerta*, 'a lizard.' The prefix *al* or *el* bespeaks Spanish influence. The early European writers, both Portuguese and English, used the terms 'alligator' and 'crocodile' promiscuously; often, when they describe the alligator, they refer to it as being very much like the crocodile of the Nile.]

---

day to a *Moorman* that cuts all sorts of Stones, except Diamonds, with a certain Wheel made of **Lacre.**" Fryer, *East India*, Hak. Soc., Vol. I, p. 284.]

1 "There are also in this kingdom (of Cananor) in some of the big rivers, very large **lagartos** which devour men." Duarte Barbosa, p. 344 [Hak. Soc., Vol. II, p. 83. Longworth Dames translates *lagartos* as lizards (which is etymologically correct) but notes that the word refers to crocodiles. For the various forms which this word took in the writings of the old chroniclers, see *Hobson-Jobson*.]

"All along this River there were a great many **lagartos**, which might more properly be called Serpents." Fernão Pinto, *Peregrinação*, ch. xiv [in Cogan's tr. 17].

"Very big **largartos** which in form and nature are just the crocodiles of the Nile." João de Barros, Dec. I, iii, 8.

"In which there are so many **lagartos** that, at times, they overturn little boats and get hold of the passengers." Gaspar Correia, II.

["In this place I have seen very great **allgartos** (which we call in English crocodiles), seven yards long." Master Antonie Knivet, in *Purchas*, iv. 1228, cit. in *Hobson-Jobson*.]

Lais (yard arm in a ship). L.-Hindust. *lás*.

| **Lâmina** (thin metal plate; also picture painted on copper). Konk. *lámn*, framed picture.—Mal. *lamina*. |

Lâmpada (lamp). Konk. *lámpt* (especially the sanctuary lamp).—Hindust. *lamp* (probably from English.)—? Sinh. *lámpuva*; vern. term *pána*.—Mal., Sund. *lámpu, lámpo*.—? Ach. *lampo*.—? Batt. *lámpu*.—Tet., Gal. *lámpa*.[1]

Dr. Fokker attributes—and it seems on good grounds—the Malasian terms to the Dutch *lamp*.[2] The Japanese *rampu* is, I believe, derived from English.

Lampião (a lantern). Konk. *lāṁpyáṁv*.—Tet., Gal. *lampiã*.

Lança (a lance). Sinh. *lắnsaya*, *lanse*; vern. terms *sellaya*, *hellaya*.—Gal. *lansa*.

[In Pyrard's *Dictionary of Some words of the Maldive Language* (Hak. Soc., Vol. II, pt. II, p. 414) occurs *lancia* as meaning 'lance'; its modern equivalent is *lonsi*; both terms are undoubtedly of Port. origin.]

Lanceta (a lancet). Konk. *lāṁsét*.—Jap. *ranseta*.

Lancha (a launch). Konk. *lánch* (us. in Goa).—Guj. *lancha* (us. in Damaun).—Mal. *láncha*.

["Launch is a name for a boat picked up by Portuguese sailors in the East (it is probably of Malay origin), and handed on by them to Spanish sailors, from whom it was borrowed into English." Logan Pearsall Smith, *Words and Idioms* (1925), p. 17. This view is based on the *O.E.D.* which opines that launch is probably derived from Malay. Cândido Figueiredo, in the *Novo Diccionario*, refers it to Castilian *lancha*. Gonçalves Viana, an acknowledged authority on the influence of Portuguese on Malay vocabulary, does not dispute in his *Apostilas* Figueiredo's derivation of the word.

1 "With their altars, frontals, canopies, and lampadas always lighted." Lucena, Bk. VI, ch. 6.

2 "The loss of the final syllable of *lámpada* I would explain in the last extremity by reference to its derivation, seeing that it is impossible to admit in Malay a combination of three consonants like *mpd*; nevertheless it is more natural to expect that the source word is the Dutch *lamp*." Gonçalves Viana.

Spanish dictionaries trace *lancha* to Lat. *planca*. Wilkinson (*Malay Eng. Dict.*) derives the Malay *lancha* from Portuguese. On the other hand, the Portuguese dictionaries of Lacerda, Morais, and of Eduardo Faria, are inclined to connect the Port. word with the East. The *Diccionario Contemporaneo*, at present regarded as most authoritative, however, says that the derivation of the word is uncertain. The early Portuguese writers speak of *lanchara* (the correct Malay form is *lancharan*, 'a swift ship of war, a kind of Malay cruiser'), *lanchuem* ('a light and small Chinese vessel'), and also *lantea* ('a large oared barge or cargo boat'), and it is not surprising if the Portuguese lexicographers were led to assume that *lancha* was either a contraction or transformation of one of these terms. Yule says that he cannot identify *lantea*, but Dalgado (*Glossario*) seems to think it is the Malay *lantey* 'a storey or raised place,' which the *lantea* would be sure to have. Malay owes her names for several kinds of ships, not to speak of many naval and sea-faring terms, to Portuguese. See *fragata, fusta, galé, galeão.*]

[**Lanchara** (a small swift oar-boat mentioned by Portuguese chroniclers of the 16th and 17th centuries). Anglo-Ind. *lanchara.*

The original of the Port. word is the Malay *lancharan*. 'rapid, swift.' Wilkinson has *pĕrahu lancharan*, 'swift vessel.' See *O.E.D.*]

Lanchão (a lighter, barge). Mal. *lanchong*, | *lanchang.* |

Lançol (a bed-sheet). Sinh. *lansóluva.*—Tet., Gal. *lensol.*

[The form *lançol* is not to be found in the Port. dictionary *Contemporaneo*; the more usual form is *lençol.*]

[**Lanha** (coco-nut when it is not quite ripe and, therefore, tender and soft). Anglo-Ind. *lanho lagne, lanha* (obs.).[1]

---

[1] ["When this Coquo is green it is called **Elevi** in Malayalam, and here in Goa **lanha**" Orta, Col. XVI. ed. Markham, p. 140.]

["As I was taking leave of the King, he caused to be presented to me, . . . and delivered to my Servants to carry home, four **Lagné**. (so they in *India*, especially the *Portugals*, call the Indian Nuts before they be ripe, when,

The Port. form is the Tamil-Malayalam *iḷanir*, 'milk of a tender coco-nut,' from *iḷanir-kkay*, *ila* = 'tender,' *nīr* = 'water,' and *kay* = 'fruit.' In Malayalam *iḷanīr* is also 'the tender coco-nut.' Tender coco-nuts were much in use in the old Portuguese fleets because of the abundance of sweet and refreshing water they contained. They are even to-day sold in large numbers in Bombay, on the Esplanade and on Chowpatty. *Lanha* is not in *Hobson-Jobson*, but an allusion is made to it in a note on p. 874, under 'Sura'. There, Yule conjectures that it might be Tam. *lanha*, but Dalgado (*Glossario*, note *s.v.*) says that there is no such word in that language. The word is not in the *O.E.D.*]

Lanterna (a lantern.) Konk. *lāntern.*—Beng. *lantará.*—Sinh. *lanteruma, lanterema.*—Tam., Malayal. *lántar.* —Tel. *lántaru, lándaru.*—Kan. *lántaru.*—Tul. *lándaru.*—Khas. *linten* (perhaps from English).—Mal. *lantérna, lantéra.*—Sund., Mac., Bug. *lantéra.*—Jav., Mad. *lantérô.*

Lápis (pencil; crayon). Konk. *láps*; vern. term *chím.*—Tet., Gal. *lápis.*

Largo (broad, wide, open). L.-Hindust. *largá. Largá bulin rākhná*, to sail full, to gain the offing.

Lascarim (in the sense of 'an Indian soldier'). ? Konk. *laśkarí.*—Anglo-Ind. *lascar.*[1]

The source-word is the

instead of Pulp, they contain a sweet refreshing water which is drunk for delight." Della Valle, *Travels*, Hak. Soc., Vol. II, p. 336.]

["But first he (the King of Calecut) caused many bunches of Indian Figs and **Lagne** to be brought and presented to us." *Idem*, p. 375.]

["Sometimes they gather the cocoa fruit before it comes to perfect maturity, and then it is called '**Lanho**'". Mandelslo quoted by Grey, editor of Della Valle, in note to passage on p. 336 given above.]

["When grown (the coco-nuts) to the size of twenty-eight up to thirty inches round, and as much in length, they are called **lanha**. The nut is then full of a sweet water, a drink of which is very refreshing." Manucci, *Travels*, ed. Irvine, Vol. III, p. 186.]

[1] "A thousand **lasquarys** on foot....**Lasquarys** on horseback." *Lembranças das Cousas da India*, p. 37.

"That in the said Kingdom there should be no class of fighting men, called **lascarins**, except in the service of the King." Simão Botelho *Tombo*, p. 83.

Persian *lashkarí* from *lashkar*, 'an army'.

[Yule remarks: "The word *lascár* or *láscár* (both these pronunciations are in vogue) appears to have been corrupted, through the Portuguese use of *lashkarī* in the forms *lasquarin*, *lascari*, etc., either by the Portuguese themselves, or by the Dutch and English who took up the word from them, and from these *laskār* has passed back again into native use in this corrupt shape." The early Portuguese writers distinguished between *lascar* and *lascarim*. The former they used in the sense of 'an Indian seaman or marine', perhaps, because in the Indian languages *laśkar* was used as a collective noun to denote 'the entire crew'.[1] The later they used in the sense of 'a land soldier', now designated by the term 'sepoy'. There is one other meaning given by them to *lascar* when the term is used with reference to Bengal, viz., that of 'a governor of a city'.[1] In this meaning there appears to be a latent suggestion that *lascar* or *lascari* is employed to denote 'the commander of an army', much in the same way as the Sansk. *senapati*, which literally means 'lord of the army,' is used. See *Glossario*.

[1] ["With the exception of some who go out in their own vessels or in those of His Majesty as masters and pilots, the entire crew of the ships consists of Mohammedans who are called **Laschéres**." Lucena, *Life of St. Francis*, Bk. IV, ch. 1.]

["Where the Portuguese are well received, they associate with the natives and join in their voyages; yet all the mariners and pilots are Indians, either Gentiles or Mahometans. All these seamen are called **Lascar**, and the soldiers **Lascarits**." Pyrard de Laval, Hak. Soc., Vol. I. p. 438.]

[1] ["Within the gates he (the King of Bengal) employs eunuchs who in course of time come to occupy important positions and become governors of cities who in the language of the country are called **lascares**." Castanheda, IV, 37, cit. in *Glossario*.]

["When the governor (of Chatigão), who is called **Lascar**, heard of this..." Damião de Góis, *Chronica de D. Manuel*, IV, ch. 27, cit. in Glossario.]

["On its (a parley) being granted they told us, on behalf of their **Lascōr**, or Captain General, to have no misgivings as their King had no wish to break or violate the treaties made with the Portuguese of the City of Ugulim." Manrique, *Travels*, Hak. Soc., Vol. I, p. 15.]

Manrique (*Travels*, ed. Col. Luard) employs a compound form **Lascourusil**[1] which the editor surmises might be a corruption of *laśkar-aswār*. *Lascarin* or *Lascoreen*, in the sense of a 'soldier,' is still current in Ceylon where the Portuguese influence was very intense.[2] Gray (Pyrard, *Travels*, Hak. Soc., Vol. I, p. 438, *n.*) says it means 'a native gunner', or 'a trooper of the Governor's native bodyguard'.]

Lata (tin; tin-box). Konk. *lát*; more in use is *pholinh*, derived from the Portuguese *fôlha*, a sheet.—Tet., Gal. *lata*.

Lázaro (a lazar; a leper). Sinh. *lásuru*. *Láduru*, leprosy.[3]

Ladru for 'Lazarus' (proper name) is used in Konkani.

Lebre (hare). Nic. *lévere*. See *cabra*.

1 ["First came the **Lascorusil**, that is the captain of the cavalry escort and of the eunuch swordsmen." Hak. Soc., Vol. I, p. 373.]

2 ["A large open boat formed the van, containing his Excellency's guard or **lascoreens**." Cordiner, *Ceylon*, 170, in *O. E. D.*]

3 "To the lazaros he would himself give the most Holy Communion." Lucena, Bk. II, ch. 2.

Lei (law). Konk. *ley*; vern. terms *nyáy*, *kāydó*, *nem*.—Tet. *lei*; vern. term *lia fúan*.—Gal. *lei*; vern. term *limúsan*.

Leilão (auction sale). Konk. *leylámv*; vern. term *pāvṇí*.—Mar. *lilámv*, *lilám*, *nilám*.—Guj. *lilám*, *nilám*.—Hindi *nilám*, *nīlám*.—Hindust., Or. *nīlám*.—Nep. *līlám*.—Beng. *nilám*, *nīlám*, *nilāmá*.—Ass. *lilám*.—Sindh. *nilámu*, *nīlámu*.—Punj. *lalám*, *nilám*.—Tam. *élam*.[1]—Malayal. *lelam*, *élam*.—Tel. *lélām*, *yálam*, *yalam*, *yélamu*.—Kan. *leylam*, *lilámu*, *yálam*, *yélamu*.—Tul. *leilámu*, *yelamu*, *yélamu*.—Anglo-Ind. *leelam*, *neelam*.—Gar. *ilam*.—Bur. *lay-lan*.—Khas. *lilam*, *nilam*. *Die lilam*, to sell at an auction.—Siam. *leláng*.—Mal. *lélan*, *lélon*, *lélong*.—Ach., Batt., Sund., Jav., Mac., Bug., *lélang*.—Day. *lelang*.—Tet., Gal. *leilã*, *lelã*.—Chinese of Canton *yélong*.—Amoy *lélang*.—Swatow *loylang*.

Leylāmkár (Konk.), *lilámv-karṇārá*, *lilám-vālá*, [*lilamdar*, *lilamvdar*.] (Mar.), *lilám-karnár* (Guj.), *nīlám-karná*,

1 See *lenço*, and the note to it.

nīlam-vālá (Hindi, Hindust.), *nīlangar* (Hindi), *nīlám-kari-vālá* (Beng.), *yālamgára*, *yálam-hākuvara* (Kan.), an auctioneer. *Vālá* (Hindi-Hindust.) means 'agent, man of', and is equivalent to the Portuguese suffix-*dor* and —*eiro*.

Lalāmí, bought at an auction sale (Punj.). *Yalam-chīṭu*, a lottery ticket. *Yalam-vīguṭa*, to sell by auction (Telugu). *Nglélong*, *ngleng-lang*, to place in an auction. *Ngligan gaké*, *neglē langaken*, to put up for sale, to sell (Jav.).

With regard to the change of *l* into *n*, cf. *nimbú* and *limbú* ('lemon'), *nāngar* and *lāngar* ('anchor'), *nāchár* and *lāchár* ('indigent, wretched'); and the Portuguese *laranja* from the Ar. *nāranj*, Spanish *naranja*.[1]

Cândido de Figueiredo says that the origin of *leilão* is uncertain. Brown gives as its probable derivation the Arabic *al-i'lam*, "proclamation, advertisement, notice, placard", which, according to Belot, signifies "to stamp, to distinguish with a sign."

Auction-sales took place very largely among the Portuguese, when one of them died or was transferred from one place to another. The Dutch traveller Linschoten (1598) is a witness to the fact that even the effects of a Viceroy were disposed of by auction. There were in the city of Goa signboards with the following inscription "The auction-sale which is held every morning in the *Rua Direita* ('The Straight Street') of Goa."[1]

[1] This was also the case in the following: *lembrar* < *nembrar*, < Latin *memorare*

[*Lembrar* in Port., and *memorare* in Latin = 'to remember'.]

[1] "Gil Fernandes de Carvalho received them and soon had them set up in the market place (of Cochin) where they hold **leilões**" ('auctions'). Diogo do Couto, Dec. VI, x, 9.

[The following is the passage in Linschoten (Hak. Soc., I, 184) referred to above; "In Goa there is holden a daylie assemblie, as wel of the Citizens and Inhabitants, as of all nations throughout India, and of the countries bordering on the same, which is like the méeting upon the burse in Andwarpe, yet differeth much from that, for that hether in Goa there come as well Gentlemen, as marchants, and there are all kindes of Indian commodities to sell, so that in a

Lenço (a handkerchief). Konk. *lens*; vern. term *rumál*, *urmál* (l. us. in this meaning in Goa).—Sinh. *lémsuva*; vern. terms *redikaḍá*, *indulkaḍá*.—Tam. *ilansi*.[1]—Malayal. *lanchi*. *lenji*.—Tul. *lésu*, *lesu*.—Mol. *lénsu*.—Nic. *lenše*.—Tet., Gal. *lénsu*.

Ler (to read). Mol. *lês* (Schuchardt).—Tet. *lê*.

In the Portuguese dialect of Ceylon *les* is used for '*ler*'.

Lestes (ready). Sinh. *lésti*, *léstiya*. *Lésti-karaṇavā*, to get ready, to prepare.

Lesto (light, brisk, ready). Mal. *listro* (Schuchardt).

Letra (alphabetic letter; also bill of exchange). Konk. *létr*; vern. terms *akšar* or *akher*; *hunḍí* (a commercial bill).—Tet., Gal. *letra*. *Letra konta*, an arithmetical number.

Levantar (to raise; to lift). Mal. *levantar*, "to rebel, to raise one's self" (Haex).[1]

Lião (lion). Malayal. *léyam*, sign of the Zodiac (Gundert).—Mal. *liao*; mentioned in an unpublished vocabulary of the Malay language; vern. term *singa* (from Hindust.).—Tet. *lião*.

Lição (lesson). Konk.

manner it is like a Faire. This méeting is only before Noone, everie day in the yeare, except Sondayes and holie dayes: it beginneth in ye morning at 7, and continueth till 9, but not in the heate of the day, nor after Noone, in the principal stréete of Citie, named the straight stréete, and is called the **Leylon**, which is as much to say, as an outroop . . . There are also Arabian horses, all kinde of spices and dryed drugges, swéet gummes, and such like things, fine and costly coverlets, and many curious things, out of Cambaia, Sinde, Bengala, China, etc. . . . And when any man dieth, all his goods are brought thether and sold to the last pennieworth, in the same outroop, who soever they be, ye although they were the Viceroyes' goods: and this is done to doe right and justice unto Orphanes and widdows, and that it may be sold with the first ('at the dearest'). . . . The like assemblie is holden in all places of India where the Portingales inhabite." In the original edition there is a very interesting and vivid copper-plate illustration of the market place and an auction sale in the 'Straight Street' in the city of Goa.]

[1] "No old Dravidian word can commence with *l* or *r*. Hence *rājā*, a king, becomes commonly *erāsá*, *lōka*, *ulagam*." Caldwell.

[1] "With this army he (the King of Benametapa) goes about subduing kings who have risen (*que se* **levantaom**) or would rise (**alevantar**) against their lord." Duarte Barbosa, p. 235 [Hak. Soc., ed. Dames, Vol. I, p. 13].

lisáṁv; vern. terms *páṭh*, *dhaḍá*.—Tet., Gal. *lisã*; vern. term *hanánun*.

Licença (permission). Konk. *liseṁs*; vern. term *rajá*.—Mal. *licensa* (Haex).—Tet., Gal. *lisensa*.

Lima (*bot.*, the fruit of the small *Citrus medica*). Anglo-Ind. *lime*.

[The Portuguese word is itself derived from the Ar. *līma*. Yule believes that 'lime' probably came into English from the Portuguese in India, but the *O.E.D.* says that the English word is an adaptation of Fr. *lime* = modern Port. *limo*. This is evidently a mistake, for *limo* in Port. is a plant of the *algae* family which has no connection with that of the *citrus*.]

Limão (*bot.*, *Citrus medica*, var. *Limonum*, Hooker; lemon). Konk. *limbó*, *nimbó*, *nimbú*.—Mar. *limbú*, *nimbú*.—Guj. *limbu*, *límbu*.—Hindi *nībú*.—Hindust. *līmú*, *lemú*, *nīmbú*.—Or. *lemu*, *nemu*, *nimu*.—Beng. *lebu*.—Ass. *nemú*.—Sindh. *līmô*.—*Līmāí*, *limãõ* (*adj.*), that which has the colour of lemon.—Punj. *nimbú*.—Tel. *nimma*.—Kan. *limbe*, *nimbe*.—Tul. *limbe*.—? Siam. *mănao*.—Mal *limon* (Haex), *liman*, *limán*, *limún*.—Sund. *limó*.—Day. *liman*.—Mac., Bug. *lémo*.— | Turk. *līmón*.[1] |

Limbí, *nimbí* (Konk.); *limbúṇ*, *nimbúṇ*, *limbuṇí*, *nimbuṇí*, *limboṇí*, *nimboṇí* (Mar.); *limbuḍí* (Guj.), the lemon-tree.

The Portuguese word comes from the Arabic *leimún*, or *limún* (Pers. *līmú*), which, in its turn, comes from India, Sansk. *nimbūka*. It appears that from this last are derived almost all the Indian forms, the *n* being changed into *l*.

[Mr. Skeat writes: "The Malay form is *liman*, 'a lime, lemon, or orange'. The Port. *limão* may possibly come from this Malay form. I feel sure that *limau*, which in some dialects is *limar*, is an indigenous word which was transferred to Europe." The *Ency. Brit.* (14th ed.) says that the lemon which seems to have been unknown to the ancient Greeks and Romans was introduced by the Arabs into Spain

1 "Figs, oranges, limões, cucumbers." Gaspar Correia, I, p. 505.

between the 12th and 13th centuries. In 1494 the fruit was cultivated in the Azores, even then subject to Portugal. After all this evidence, it is scarcely credible that the Portuguese should have derived *limão* from Malay. The *O.E.D.* traces 'lemon' to the Arabic *leimûn*; there is, therefore, all the more reason for assuming that the Portuguese also derived the word from the same source.

But is *leimun* an Arabic word and is it correct to hold the view generally accepted that the lemon is indigenous to Arabia? Or is it more correct to hold with V. Hehn, quoted by Yule, that the fruit and its name *leimun* are of Indian origin? It would appear to us that the citations furnished by Prof. S. H. Hodivala (*Notes on Hobson-Jobson* in *The Indian Antiquary*, Vol. LVIII, 1929) go to prove conclusively that the Arabs became acquainted with the lemon only in the 10th century and it was then known in Sindh as *laimun*.[1]]

[1] [c. 951. "The land of Manṣûra (in Sindh) also produces a fruit of the size of the apple, which is called *Laimún* and is exceedingly sour." *Kitabu-l-aqâlim* of Istakhri, Tr. in Elliot and Dowson, *History of India*, I, 27.]

[See also Ibn Hankal, *Ashkâlu-l-bilâd* (c. 976). *Ibid.*, p, 35.]

Lingua (an interpreter). Anglo-Ind. *linguist* (obs.).[1]

Even at the present day there is an official in Goa who is called the *lingua do estado*, i.e., 'the official interpreter'.

Linguiça (thin sausage). Konk. *lingís*.—Hindi, Hindust. *langūchá*; vern. term *kulmá*.—Sinh. *linguyis, lingus*.

Lista (roll; list). Konk. *líst*; vern. terms *paṭṭi, śivḍí, patrak, kharḍó*.—Malayal.

[1] "Ready to listen to all that the **lingua** was recapitulating to them." João de Barros, Dec. I, iii, 2.

"To a **lingua** of the factory at Goa two *pardaus* (*q.v.*) monthly." Simão Botelho, *Tombo da India*, p. 63.

"And as **lingua** there was one Antonio de Noronha." Antonio Tenreiro, *Itinerario*, ch. ii.

["He commaunded all his owne people out of the roome leaving none but Mr. Wight, John Tucker, **linguist**, and myselfe." *The English Factories in India (1618–1621)*, ed. Foster, p. 73.]

["He (the President of the Bombay Council) has his Chaplains, Physician, Chyrurgeons, and Domesticks; his **Linguist** and Mint-Master." Fryer, *East India*, Hak. Soc., Vol. I, p. 178.]

líst.—Tul. *lístu, listu.*— | Mal. *lis.* | —Tet., Gal. *lista.*

Gundert refers the Malayalam word to the English 'list'.

Livrar (to deliver, to set free). Konk. *livrár-karuṅk* (l. us.); vern. term *vāṭāvuṅk.*—Tet. *lívra*; vern. term *sôri.*

Livre (free). Konk. *lívr* (l. us.); vern. terms *svādhín, súṭ, súḍ.*—Tet. *lívri*; vern. term *isín-leéti.*

Livro (a book). Konk. *lívr*; vern. terms *pustak, granth.*—Mal. *libro* (Haex); vern. term *kitáb* (Ar.); *buku* also is used from the Dutch *boek* or the English 'book'.—Nic. *lébare,* book, letter, paper.—*Anét-lébare.* pen, pencil. *Penśiva-anet-lébare,* ink. *Karra-lébare,* to read. *Et-et-lébare,* to write [1]. —Tet., Gal. *lívru.*

Loba (soutane). Konk. *lôb.*—Tam. *lobei.*[2]

[1] In Nicobarese, the compound consonant is done away with either as the result of extension or *suarabacti* (cf. *lévare* from Port. *lebre,* 'hare') and the final *o* is replaced by *e* (cf. *lenśe,* from Port. *lenço,* 'handkerchief').

[2] "The priest was carrying with him one **loba** of black camlet." Fernão Pinto, ch. ccix.

Loiça (plates, dishes). Konk. *loys.*—Tet., Gal. *loisa.*

Loja (ground-room; shop). Konk. *loz*; vern. terms *koṭhí, koṭhár, mánḍ, pasró, āngaḍ.*—Indo-Fr. *loje.*—Mal., Jav., Mac., Bug. *lóji,* warehouses, big shops, fortresses.

Matthes derives *lógi* from the Dutch *loge,* "a hut, room, cabin"; but the meanings of *lóji* are more like those of the Portuguese than of the Dutch word.[1]

[? **Lorcha** (a small kind of trading vessel used in China). Anglo-Ind. *lorcha.*[2]

"To spread over the bed of Nuno da Cunha, a coverlet of velvety crimson satin, and he to wear an open **loba** of camlet." João de Barros, Dec. iv, viii, 5.

[1] "He (D. Fernando) was ordered to be placed in the **logea** of the tower of Banastarim in a very small house." Gaspar Correia, *Lendas,* II, p. 319. "All the people used to retire to the **logias** of the towers, in which they found themselves very crowded." *Id.,* p. 899.

[2] ["In this ill-fated storm two junks were lost, and one **lorcha,** or *lanteá,* in which more than hundred persons perished." F. M. Pinto, *Peregrinação,* ch. 62, cit. in *Glossario.*]

["The **lorcha** 'Arrow'. employed in the river trade between Canton and the mouth of the river, commanded by an English captain and flying

"Giles explains it as having a hull of European build, but the masts and sails Chinese fashion, generally with a European skipper and a Chinese crew. The word is said to have been introduced by the Portuguese from S. America (*Giles*, 81). But Pinto's passage (*Peregrinacão* (1540), ch. xlii, Cogan's tr., p. 50, cit. in *Hobson-Jobson*) shows how early the word was used in the China seas, a fact which throws doubt on that view." The *O.E.D.* quotes Cobden, *Speeches* (1878), 370: "A vessel called a **lorcha** which is a name derived from the Portuguese settlement at Macao..." Dalgado (*Glossario*) thinks it quite possible that **lorcha** is a corruption of *long-chuen*, a description of which he quotes from T. B. du Halde (*Description Géographique*, etc., 1735, I, p. 189): "For this feast small barks, long and narrow, all gilt are got ready; they carry at one end the figure of a dragon and, on this account, they are called *Long tchuen*." Crooke quotes a suggestion that *lorcha* may be the Port. *lancha*, the English 'launch'.]

Lotaria (lottery). Konk. *loterí*.—Sinh. *lottareya*, *lotaruyiya*. See *sorte*.

Louvado (in the sense of 'an expert, an arbitrator'). Konk. *lovád*.—Mar., Guj. *lavád*. The Neo-Aryan terms are *panchātkár*, *panchāīdár*, *madyasth*, *madesth*, *ākārí*, *āmín*.—Anglo-Ind. *lawad*.[1]

Lavādí (*subst.*), the office of an arbitrator; (*adj.*) relating to an arbitrator or an arbitration. *Lavādīchá nivāḍá*, opinion of an umpire, arbitration. *Lavādí-hūkumnāmá*, arbitration deed (Mar.).

Lavādí, opinion of an arbitrator, arbitration. *Lavádíchu kāvó*, arbitration (Guj).

['Lawad' as an Anglo-Indian term is not mentioned by Yule and Burnell, but finds a place in Whitworth's

an English flag, had been boarded by a party of Mandarims and their escort while at anchor near Dutch Folly." Boulger. *History of China*, 1884, iii. 396, cit. in *Hobson-Jobson*.]

1 "For they were agreed about having their case settled by **louvados** ('arbitrators')." João de Barros, Dec. III. i, 9.

Anglo-Indian Dictionary which assigns it to Marathi. Besides giving it the meaning of 'an arbiter' and 'an umpire,' the author says it is the name of some arbitration courts lately established in Poona and some other districts to decide civil claims without the expense of resorting to the courts established by government. As arbitration courts are, at the present time, claiming an unusual amount of interest, it is, we trust, not irrelevant to describe the constitution of the 'Lawad Courts': "A set of rules has been framed defining the constitution and function of the courts. The members are drawn for the most part from the class of pleaders, traders, and retired government officials. They agree to serve as arbiters in turn for a week at a time. They receive no remuneration. The arrangements of the court are in the hands of a secretary, who, in each week, chooses two members to act as umpires. Each court has a staff of clerks and messengers. To meet this expense fees are charged. But these are very moderate, amounting to not more than one-third of the cost in the ordinary subordinate civil courts" (*Bombay Administration Report for 1876-77*, in Whitworth).

Luminárias (illumination on occasions of public rejoicing). Konk. *lumináḍ*; vern. terms *dīpāvali*, *dīpochav*.—Tet., Gal. *lumínári*.

Luto (mourning). Konk. *lút* (l. us.); vern. terms *duḥkh*, *kāḷěṁ*.—Tet. *lútu*.

Luva (glove). Konk. *lúv*.—Tet., Gal. *lúva*.

M

Maçã (apple). Sinh. *masan*.

[**Macaréu** (the name given to dangerous tides and to the phenomenon of the bore or tidal wave in certain seas and rivers). Anglo-Ind. *macareo*.[1]—? French *macrée*,

1 ["Sailing from these ports is very dangerous for keeled ships, because being at the top of the tide the water here runs so far in the gulf that, in a very short space of time, four or five leagues are left bare, more in some places and less in others, and when there is a flowing tide it flows so strongly that they say a man running at full speed cannot escape it."

mascaret (used for the bore in the Seine).

This is what the author has to say about this curious word in his *Glossario*: "The origin of this word is not quite clear. It is generally supposed to be the Sansk. *makara*, the name of a mythological monster, and also of the zodiacal sign Capricorn. This designation would not be at all inapt if the monster were regarded as the author of the phenomenon.

"But none of the Indian languages actually employs the term *makara* to denote the phenomena referred to. There are other names employed to do this, like *Ghora* ('The Horse') in Gujarati, *Meṇḍha* ('The Ram') in Hindi, and it is, therefore, not unlikely that formerly in some part of India *makara*, which ordinarily means 'a crocodile,' had been used to designate this phenomena.

"Yule, however, throws doubt on this explanation because French has *macrée* and *mascaret*, in addition to *barre*, evidently the same as the English 'bore'. But there is no evidence to show that these words have existed prior to the Portuguese discoveries in the East, because no authorities earlier than the sixteenth century are quoted. The etymology of these words is unknown. Littré does not suggest any which appears plausible. He does not give reasons for the diversity of forms or for their existence side by side with *barre*, which is supposed to be older. Nor is there any explanation to show how it is that the French word crossed over to India, if, to judge from the accounts

---

Duarte Barbosa, ed. Dames, Vol. I, p. 138.]

["I was advised by the people of the place to unload the ships, so that they might be light when the flood tide came, for they would be destroyed if they were laden and had to meet the full force of the **macareo.**" Castanheda, *Historia*, VIII, ch. 107, in *Glossario.*]

["The sea-coast in some parts of this kingdom (of Cambay) extends over two and three leagues, and with the flood tide there comes a wind with such suddenness that a man, no matter with what speed he runs, cannot save himself from the **macareo.**" Damião de Góis, *Chronica de D. Manuel*, III, ch. 64.]

of the Portuguese chroniclers, the phenomenon and its name were unknown in Portugal.

"Gonçalves Viana (in *Palestras Filológicas*) has pointed out most clearly that, phonetically or morphologically, neither *macrée* nor *mascaret* could be converted into *macaréu*, and he came to the conclusion that "the three vocables, *mascaret*, *macrée*, and *macaréu* are independent of each other, and that their formal and phonic coincidences are merely fortuitous."

"I am almost convinced, however, that the French changed the Port. *macaréu*, first, into the form *macrée*, and, afterwards, into the more cultured *mascaret*, in the same way as they changed the Portuguese *pateca* (*q.v.*) into *pastèque*; *mordexim* (*q.v.*) into *mort-de-chien*; *bicho do mar* (*q.v.*) into *biche-de-mer*; *pau de águila* (see *aguila*) into *bois d'aigle*. Jancigny[1] would not have used in 1854 *maquerie*, if the other forms had been well-known in his time.

". . . . The explanation that I would offer with regard to this term is that the people of Cambay might have told the Portuguese, eager to know the cause of this strange happening, that it was due to the *makaró* (the vulgar form in Gujarat) who came to devour ships and men, for in popular tales similar performances are ascribed to the monster."

Though the name, in the vernacular form *magur*, is given to the crocodile, the *Makara*, the fabulous sea-serpent, the vehicle of Varuna, the god of the ocean, is represented in sculpture with the head and forelegs of an antelope, and the body and tail of a fish. If the forelegs of the antelope are intended to connote speed, and the tail of the fish the marine character of the monster, might not the bore, the special feature of which is the rapidity of its approach, have appropriately

[1] ["The mouth (of the Setang, in Burma) is obstructed by banks of sand, and the maquerie (bore) is so terrible, that the navigation of this river is wholly impossible for large ships and difficult for smaller ones." Jancigny, *Indo-Chine*, p. 295, in *Glossario*.]

suggested to the popular imagination the picture of this monster? Longworth Dames (in *Duarte Barbosa*, Vol. I, p. 138) has collected the more important references to the bore or *macaréu* in the Gulf of Cambay from as early as the *Periplus* down to Forbes in his *Rās Mālā*. Heber (in his *Journal of a Narrative*, 1828, Vol. I, p. 81) describes a bore on the Ganges.]

Machila ('a sort of a hammock-litter used as a substitute for palanquin'). Konk. *māchíl, māñchíl.*—Tul. *manchilu.*—Anglo-Ind. *muncheel, manjeel* (us. on the Malabar coast).—Tet. *machila.*[1]

The original word is the Malayal. *manjil*, from the Sansk. *mañcha.* The word has been introduced into Portuguese Africa.

[1] "Because of the Caffres (of Manamotapa) having run away from him, for these used to carry him on their shoulders in an *andor* (*q.v.*), which they call **manchira.**" Bocarro, Dec. xiii, p. 552.

"The only species of conveyance used by the rich are the palanquins, or rather covered **machilas.**" Cottineau de Kloguen, *Bosquejo hist. de Goa*, p. 163.

[The author's subsequent investigations appear to have led him to quite the opposite view, viz., that the word was an importation into India from Africa. This is what he says in the *Glossario*: "As regards its etymology, Konkani has *māchīl* or *māñchīl*, which passed into Tulu in the form *māñchilu*; but it is not a vernacular word. Yule and Burnell derive the Anglo-Indian *muncheel* or *manjeel* from the Malayalam *mañjīl*, which in its turn is from the Sansk. *mañcha*, 'bed, platform'. *Mañjīl* is not to be met with in all dictionaries which, however, mention *mañcham* and *mañchakam*. Wilson does not insert it in his *Glossary of Indian Terms* by the side of *doli* and *palki*. Of the authorities cited in *Hobson-Jobson* only one refers to Malabar, and is dated 1819. Moreover, it is not clear how the Sansk. *mañcha*, which passed into almost all the Neo-Aryan languages *ipsis literis*, assumed only in Malayalam the form *mañjīl* and a very peculiar meaning, synonymous with *andor* (*q.v.*) and 'palanquin,' which terms are also to be found in the same language, in addition to another, viz., *dayaman*.

"If Portuguese colonial history were to be examined, it will be found that *machira*, as the name of a textile and of a species of litter, is very old in West Africa, where it is still in vogue in the vernacular languages in both these senses. It is, therefore, logical to conclude from this that the term was brought into India from Africa where it was applied to a litter different from the *andor*".

Machira in West Africa is used in the sense of (1) 'a litter,' and (2) 'of a thick cotton-sheet woven in the country'.[1] The latter, which is the earlier acceptation, gradually developed into the former, as the earliest means of transport was a piece of canvas, the two ends of which were tied to a pole. In course of time, this crude kind of hammock-litter developed into the more comfortable *machilla* or Anglo-Indian 'muncheel'. Vieyra mentions *machira* and gives it the meaning of 'a sort of cloke or upper garment worn by the Caffres,' presumably the same as the hand-spun textile mentioned above.

Whitworth says that 'manchial' is a Portuguese corruption of Hindust. *manzil*, which he describes thus: "A stage, a station; thence the Goanese word *manchial*, a litter. Also a house, a palace." This is an instance of the perils attendant on discovering etymologies by paying more regard to the sound or form of words rather than to what is known to-day as 'semantics,' the study of the meanings of words.]

Madeira (wood, timber). Konk. *madér*; vern. terms

1 [1569.—"All of them generally go about clothed in cloths of cotton, not closely woven, which I have seen made near Sena and which are called *machiras*."—P. Monclaio, in *Jour. Geo. Soc. Lisb.*, 2nd ser., p. 543, cit. in *Contribuições* etc., p. 71.]

[1609.—"The dress of the King (Quiteve) and of the other men is a thin piece of cotton or silk cloth..and another much larger of cotton which the Kaffirs weave and which they call *machiras*."—Fr. João dos Santos, *Ethiopia Oriental*, I, p. 82, in *Contribuições*.]

ãṅkúḍ; *rukháḍ*, *mop* (us. in Kanara).—Tel. *mádiri*, teak wood: vern. term *másu*.

Madre (mother; nun). Konk. *mádr*, nun.—Tel. *mādá*; the term is used of the Virgin Mary: *mādá-kavilu*, the church of the 'Mother'.—Tul. *mátri*, nun. *Mátri-maṭha*, convent of nuns. *Maṭha* is Sanskrit for 'convent.'

Madrinha (god-mother). Konk. *madan*, *madín*.—Beng. *madí*.—Mal. *matiri*.

Mãe (mother). Konk. *mãy* (us. among the Christians).—Mal. *mai*; vern. terms *ibu*, *ma* or *maq*.

In Konkani: *māvśí-mãy* (lit. 'aunt-mother'), *mãy-tí* (lit. 'mother-aunt'), maternal aunt. *Vhaḍlí mãy* (lit. 'great mother'), the wife of the uncle who is older than the father. *Dhākṭí-mãy* (lit. 'small mother'), the wife of the youngest uncle. Some of the Portuguese dialects of India have *mãe-tia*, in the sense of 'paternal aunt.' See *pai*.

The Konkani *máy* is from the Sansk. *mātā*: it is used in ecclesiastical idiom. *Mãy* (or *māṁy*) for 'mother-in-law' is not from Portuguese; it is the feminine of *máṁv*, 'father-in-law.'

Mainato ("one who is a washer of clothes" (da Orta). [Indo-Fr. *mainate*.—Mal. *mĕnátu*.]—Ach. *menátu*.—Sund. *minátu*.—Jav. *manátu*, *nenátu*.—Mol. *mainato*.[1]

[1] 'There is (in Malabar) another Heathen caste which they call **Mainatos**, whose occupation is to wash clothes for the *Kings*, *Bramenes*, and *Nayres*." Duarte Barbosa, p. 334 [Hak. Soc., Vol. II, p. 58. Longworth Dames thinks that the sect or caste referred to is the Vannathān, the fullest account of which is found in Thurston's *Castes and Tribes of Southern India*, VII, p. 389; also in *Cochin Tribes and Castes*, II, p. 115, and in the *Malabar Gazetteer*, p. 121].

"Men who wash clothes whom they call **Mainatos**." João de Barros, Dec. III, iv, 4.

"And the revenue from the **mainatos**, which arises from the fact that no one can take washing, that is, work as a **mainato**, except by arrangement with the revenue farmer." Simão Botelho, *Tombo*, p. 53.

"In this enclosed ground live all the **maynatos** who do the washing for the whole city (of Pequim)." Fernão Pinto, ch. cv.

["The Portuguese have had it (the water spring called *Banguenin*) enclosed with walls....; while lower down are large reservoirs, where most of the men and women come to bleach the linen; these folks are called **Menates**." Pyrard, Hak. Soc., Vol. II, p. 71.]

The word is derived from the Malayal. *maṉṉaṭṭán*, fem. *maṉṉaṭṭi*. It is used in Asio-Portuguese. There is a place in Macau which is called *Tanque dos Mainatos* ('The Washermen's Tank.')

[The Portuguese carried the name *mainato* to Ceylon and applied it to the washermen there, so that Pieris (*Ceylon*, I, p. 513) says: "The word *mainato* is used among the Washer caste even in remote villages of the seven Korales, as a proper name."

Mainel (hand rail of stairs). Konk. *māynel*.—? Sund. *panel*. Rigg believes that *panel* is the Dutch *paneel*, 'panel,' but the meaning of the word is very different.

Major (major; an army officer). Konk. *mājor*, *māṅjor*.—Tel. *mayóru*. Brown derives it from French.

Mala (in the sense of 'a bag'). Konk. *mál* (l. us.); vern. terms *potém*, *boksém*.—? Sinh. *malla*; vern. terms *pasumbiya*, *kurapasiya*, *maḍissalaya*.—Tet. *mala*.

Malcriado (uncivil, badly educated). Konk. *mālkryád*; vern. term *amaryādi*, *váytoló*.—Tet., Gal. *malkriádu*; vern. term *óin kabóbil*.

Maldição (curse, malediction). Konk. *māldisáṁv*; vern. terms *śap*, *śiráp*.—Beng. *māldisán*.—Mal. *maldiçaon* (Haex).—Tet. Gal. *maldisã*, *malisã*.

Mal-ensinado (rude, badly brought up). Mal. *mal ensinado* (Haex).[1]

| **Malhado** or **Molhado** ('an article in the Anglo-Indian menu'). Anglo-Ind. *maladoo* or *manadoo*, "cold meat such as chicken or mutton, cut into slices or pounded up and re-cooked in batter." See *Hobson-Jobson*, *s.v.* maladoo. |

[Prof. S. H. Hodivala (*Notes on Hobson-Jobson*) suggests that it is not necessary to go

---

["The Menates will bring you your shirt and a pair of drawers, very white and cleaned with soap, for two bousuruques." *Id.* p. 72, Gray derives *menates* from the Malayal. *maināttu*, a washerman.]

Gundert mentions the form *mānátti* with the meaning 'foreign washerman.'

---

1 "He became so overbearing, mal-ensinado, and free, that there were few persons with whom he had no quarrels." Francisco Vaz de Almada, in *Hist. tragico-marit.*, ix, p. 14.

to the Portuguese *malhado*, 'beaten up,' to explain the origin of the Anglo-Indian *maladoo*, for "*malîda* is a very well known preparation in Musalman cookery, and is made of flower, sugar, almonds, pistachios, etc., thoroughly kneaded or pounded, beaten up and baked and fried in *ghî*. The word is derived from the Pers. *mâlîdan*, to rub, grind, crush or pound." This suggestion seems to be perfectly sound, for the meanings that Portuguese dictionaries give to *malhado* cannot by any stretch of imagination be made to include a culinary preparation.]

Malícia (malice). Konk. *mālís*; vern. terms *kusḍáy*, *kapaṭ*.—Tet. *malísi*; vern. terms *láran áti*.

Mama (breast, pap). Konk. *mám* (in the language of young children).—Mar. *máma*.

Molesworth says that it is an onomatopoeic term.

Mamã (mamma). Konk. *māmáṁ* (us. by some of the Christians of Goa).—Mol. *maman*.— | Chin. *má-má*. |

Mana (sister). Konk. *māṇá*, eldest sister (us. among the Christians of Goa); vern. terms *bāí*, *bái* (l. us. in Goa in this sense). Beng. *maná* (us. in Hoshnabad among the Christians).

The term used of a male, corresponding to *māṇá*, in Konkani is *irmamv*, 'eldest brother'. It was believed that the Portuguese terms, besides being simple, carried more distinction about them, and hence their adoption.

Maná (manna, the heavenly food: also a medicine). Konk. *māná*.—Hindust. *man*. —Beng. *maná*.—Tel. *manná*. —Kan. *manu*.—Tul. *manna*. —Mac., Malag., Jap. *mana*.[1]

The Portuguese origin of the word is not incontestable, except in the case of Konkani.

[**Manchua** (a single masted vessel employed in the coasting trade of Malabar). Anglo-Ind. *manchua*.[2]

---

1 "The first taste of that celestial maná used to make one feel very much superior to everything." Lucena, Bk. VI, 12.

2 ["A very great fleet of junks, lancharas, balloons, **manchuas**, which are rowing boats, big and small." Castanheda, *Historia*, II, ch. 114.]

["When the viceroy or the archbishop goes anywhither by water, they are accompanied by an infinite

The original of the Port. word is the Tam.-Malayal. manji. The Portuguese carried the word with them to different parts of Asia, and also used it of vessels other than those used in the Malabar trade. At Goa, for instance, it was used to designate a gondola, rowed however, and not pushed.

Sir Richard Temple in a note on the passage from Mundy quoted below says: "The term *manchua* has apparently been transferred to the Far East by the Portuguese to represent the Cantonese term, *man-shün*, a sea-going trading vessel."

Yule also lists *muchwa* in *Hobson-Jobson*, and assigns it to Marathi *machwā*, Hindust. *machuā*, *machwā*, and gives it the meaning of 'a kind of boat or barge in use about Bombay.' There can scarcely be any doubt that etymologically *manchua* and *muchwa* are the same words and have a common origin.]

Mandador (one who commands). Mal., Jav., Mad. *mandôr*, *mandúr*, head of a body of artizans, overseer,

---

number of **manchoues** of lords. On board of these is excellent music of cornets-à-bouquin, hautbois, and other instruments; all the great lords have the same." Pyrard de Laval, Hak. Soc., Vol. II, p. 90.]

["**Manchooas** or small vessells of recreation, used by the Portugalls here (Macao), as allsoe att Goa, pretty handsome things resembling little Frigatts, Many curiously carved, guilded and painted, with little beake heads". Mundy, *Travels*, Hak. Soc., Vol. III, pt. i, p. 205. There is an illustration of the 'manchoa' on Pl. XII in the book.]

[1686.—"We sent out ye R^t^ Honourable Companys **Munchua** to cruise after those shipps." Forrest, *Selections*, Home Series, Vol. I, p. 154.]

["Entring with us into one of those boats which they called **Maneive**, going with twenty, or four and twenty, Oars, onely, differing from the Almadies in that the **Maneive** have a large cover'd room in the poop, sever'd from the banks of rowers, and are greater than the Almadies, which have no such room, we pass'd out of the Port". Pietro della Valle, *Travels*, Hak. Soc., Vol. II, p. 211. *Maneive* appears to be a misprint for *manceive*. On p. 217, the same vessel is called **mancina**, and both forms are used for 'manchua'.]

["I commanded the Shibbars and **Manchuas** to keepe a little a head of me." Hedges, *Diary*, Hak. Soc., Vol. II, clxxxiv. in *Hobson-Jobson*.]

["Boat (**machwás**) hire per day, from 10*s*. to 16*s*." (in Bombay), Hunter, *The Imperial Gazetteer*, VIII, p. 268.]

inspector.—Batt., Day. *mandúr*.—Sund. *mandôr*.—Anglo-Ind. *mandadore*.[1]

Mandar (to order). Konk. *māndár-karuṅk* (l. us.).—L.-Hindust. *madár*, command, order.

Mandarim (a Chinese official). Anglo-Ind., Indo-Fr. *mandarin*.[2]

Etymologically, *mandarim* has nothing to do with *mandar* ('to command'); it is a corruption of the Neo-Aryan (from Sansk.) *mantri*, 'a counsellor, a minister of state,' [*māntari*, in Malay]. The change of *t* into *d* and the dissolution of the compound consonant *tr* may be due to the influence of *mandar* or, preferably, to that of some language of Insulindia. Cf. Bug. *manătari*=*mantrī*. Gaspar Correia says: "He who brought in seven heads of enemies was made a knight and they called him **manderym,** which is their name for Knight". *Lendas*, II, p. 808. And in another passage: "Soon after the Queen (of Ternate) and her **Mandarijs** were sent to complain to the new captain." III, p. 371.[1]

[In *Hobson-Jobson* will be found a number of quotations in support of the 'old and persistent mistake' made by otherwise unimpeachable authorities that *mandarim* is formed from the Port. *mandar*, 'to command'. Even Wedgwood (*A Dict. of Eng. Etym.*), in the first edition, explains and derives the word thus: "A Chinese officer, a name first made known to us

---

[1] "Each of which Tribes have a **Mandadore,** or Superintendent." Fryer, in *Hobson-Jobson* [Hak. Soc., Vol. I, p. 175].

[2] "Three hundred **Mandarijs,** who are what the hidalgos are among us." João de Barros, Dec. III, iii, 2.

"He had met (in Siam) a **Mandarim** (they there call their Civil Magistrates by this name, which they have derived from the Chins)." Diogo do Couto, Dec. V, vi, 1. "Being in China as Ambassador, he whipped a **Mandarim** (they are those who administer justice, which among those heathens is treated with great reverence)". *Id.*, Dec. V, viii, 12.

[1] The nasalization of the final *i* is the rule in the case of words which have passed from oriental languages into Portuguese. Cf. *lascarim*, *mordexim*, *palanquim*. But João de Barros and some others write *mandarijs*, as well as *Çomorij*, *Cochij*, *Comorij*, *chatijs*, for *mandarí*, *Çamorí*, *Cochí*, *Comorí*, *chatís*.

by the Portuguese, and like the Indian *caste*, erroneously supposed to be a native term. From Portuguese, *mandar*, to hold authority, command, govern, etc." Wedgwood is right in saying that the word was first made known by the Portuguese, but wrong in his etymology which he corrected in later editions. The Portuguese chroniclers do not employ the word with reference to ministers of state in India, but to official dignitaries in China, Malasia, and Annam.]

? **Mandil** (coarse cloth, apron). Mal. *mandil* (l. us.).[1]

Perhaps received directly from Arabic.

[*Mandil* in Arabic is the Arab's head-dress; from this it came to acquire the meaning of 'a cap'.]

Manga (*Mangifera indica*). Anglo-Ind. *mango.*—Indo-Fr. *mangue*, *manguier.*—Malag. *manga.*— | Chin. *máng-koo.*[2] |

The etymon of the word is the Tamil *mānkáy*, which is, properly speaking, the name of the fruit when green, which when ripe is called *mampaḷam*. Both the words have been introduced into Malay: *manga* in Malacca, Singapore, and Sunda, and *memplam* in Penang, Achem, and Batta.

In Konkani, *māngád* is 'a conserve made from mangoes'.

[Crooke in *Hobson-Jobson* quotes W. W. Skeat's opinion: "The modern standard Malay word is *mangga*, from which the Port. form was probably taken." But Malayal. has *maṅga*, and it is more probable that the Portuguese who borrowed so many words from the Malabar country, with which they first came into contact, carried the word to Malacca and gave it to Malay. Yule very properly says: "The word has sometimes been supposed to be

---

1 "A **mandil** very finely woven, a quilted coat of silk with breeches to match." Castanheda, II, ch. 13.

2 "Some are called *jacas* (jack-fruit), others **mangas**, and others again figs." Castanheda, I, ch. 16.

"Betel, areca, jack-fruit, green ginger, oranges, limes, figs, coir, **manguas**, citrons." Simão Botelho, p. 48.

"The clove-trees always take a year's rest just as the olive-trees do in our Europe, and the **mangueiras** ('mango-trees') do in India." Diogo do Couto, Dec. IV, vii, 9.

Malay; but it was in fact introduced into the Archipelago, along with the fruit itself, from S. India......The close approximation of the Malay *mangka* to the Portuguese form might suggest that the latter name was derived from Malacca. But we see *manga* already used by Varthema, who, according to Garcia, never really went beyond Malabar."

The cultivation of the mango, especially in the western parts of India, owes a great deal to the Portuguese and to the religious orders in Goa, particularly the Jesuits, who had, as a rule, extensive orchards around their monasteries. Owing to their efforts, the Goa mango acquired a great reputation which is attested to by Bernier (1663), Fryer (1673), Hamilton (1727), and other travellers (see below).[1] But da Orta tells us in his *Colloquies* (1563) that in his time the mangoes of Ormuz

[1] ["The mangoes of Goa are reputed to be the best in the world, due to the care which the Jesuits took in grafting, for the very best mango-tree which has not been grafted will produce a fruit ill-flavoured and ordinary." *Annaes Maritimos* (1842), p. 270.]

["*Ambas*, or **Mangues**, are in season during two months in summer, and are plentiful and cheap (at Delhi); but those grown at *Delhi* are indifferent. The best come from *Bengale*, *Golkonda*, and *Goa*, and these are indeed excellent. I do not know any sweetmeat more agreeable." Bernier, *Travels*, ed. Constable and Smith (1916), p. 249.]

["I may mention that the best mangoes grow in the island of Goa. They have special names, which are as follows: mangoes of *Niculao Affonso*, *Malaiasses* (? of Malacca) *Carreira branca* (white Carreira), of *Carreira vermelha* (red Carreira), of *Conde*, of *Joani Parreira*, *Babia* (large and round), of *Araup*, of *Porta*, of *Secreta*, of *Mainato*, of *Our Lady*, of *Agua de Lupe*. These are again divided into varieties, with special colour, scent and flavour. I have eaten many that had the taste of the peaches, plums, pears, and apples of Europe." Niccolao Manucci, *Storia do Mogor*, ed. Irvine, Vol. III, p. 180.]

["In Goa the gentlemen are very particular about having good kinds of this fruit (mango). They give them special names, taken from the first person to have good mangoes of that kind." *Idem*, Vol. II, p. 169.]

["The **Mango** (of Goa) which they have improved in all its kinds to the utmost Perfection...are the best and largest in *India*, most like a Pear-Plum, but three times as big, grow on a Tree nearest a Plum-Tree; the Fruit when Green scents like Turpentine, and pickled are the

were the most celebrated; that those of Gujarat were also very good, especially some called 'Gujaratas', which, though not large, had very fine fragrance and taste and a very small stone; that those of Balaghat were both large and toothsome, the author having seen two that weighed four pounds and a half (Markham, p. 286, incorrectly says 'two pounds and a half'); and that those of Bengal, Pegu, and Malacca were also good. From this it would follow that the mango in Goa must have been brought to a state of perfection during the hundred years which followed the publication of the *Colloquies*. Da Orta himself had a celebrated mango-tree in his island of Bombay which used to yield two crops, one in December, and the other at the end of May. He admits that though the second crop surpassed the earlier in fragrance and taste, the later was just as remarkable for coming out of season (Coll. XXXIV). Sir George Birdwood, writing to the *Bombay Saturday Review*, 28th July, 1886, refers to a similar phenomenon in the case of a mango-tree which belonged to one Mr. Hough, in Colaba, Bombay.]

best *Achars* to provoke an Appetite; when Ripe, the Apples of Hisperides are but Fables to them; for Taste, the Nectarine, Peach, and Apricot fall short." Fryer, *East India*, Hak. Soc., Vol. II, p. 84.]

["The *Goa* **mango** is reckoned the largest and most delicious to the Taste of any in the world, and, I may add, the wholesomest and best tasted of any Fruit in the World." A. Hamilton, *A New Account* etc., (1727), Vol. I, p. 255.]

Mangação (mockery, scoffing). Konk. *mãngãsáṁv*; vern. terms *khebaḍáṁ*, *maskaryô*.—Tet. *mangasã*.

[**Mangas de veludo** (lit. 'velvet-sleeves'; the name given to a kind of sea-mews found near the Cape of Good Hope). Anglo-Ind. *Mangas de velludo*, *Manga Voluchoes*, *Mangafaleudos* (obs.).[1]

[1] ["**Mangas de valeudo**, a kind of sea-mews, being white all over the bodies and having black wings." Mandelso, *Voyages and Travels*, E.T., (1669), p. 248.]

["The **Manga Voluchoes**, another Sea Fowl that keeps thereabouts." Ovington, *A Voyage to Surat*, O.U.P., p. 279.]

["Gaining upon the *East* with a slow

The birds were called 'velvet-sleeves' by the Portuguese because "they have wings of the coulor of velvet and boweth them as a man boweth his elbow." Various references to this bird are collected in Pyrard de Laval, Hak. Soc., Vol. I, p. 21, n.]

Mangelim (a small weight used in the S. of India and in Ceylon for weighing precious stones, equivalent more or less to a carat). Anglo-Ind., Indo-Fr. *mangelin*.[1]

It is the Tamil *manjáḍi*, Telugu, *manjáli*. See *Hobson-Jobson*.

[*Mangelim* in Portuguese is also the name of the seed of the *Adenanthera pavonina*, because it was used as the measure for the weight referred to above. In the *Glossario* there are many quotations illustrating the use of this word.]

pace, we met....**Mangofaleudos.**" Fryer, *East India*, Hak. Soc., Vol. I, p. 51.]

[1] "Each **mangelim** weighs 8 grains of rice." António Nunes, *Livro dos Pesos*, p. 35.

"One of these **mangelins** is equal to two carats of ours". Damião de Góis, *Chronica de D. Manuel*, II, 6.

Mangostão (mangosteen, the fruit of the *Garcinia mangostana*). Konk. *maṅgustáṁv.*—Anglo-Ind. *mangosteen.*—Indo-Fr. *mangostan, mangonstan.*[1]

The source-word is the Malayo-Javanese *manggistan, manggis*.

[The *Garcinia purpurea*, Roxb., is called in Konk. *bhirâṇḍ*, which the Portuguese converted into *brindão*. *Brindão* is not a Port. word, nor one invented by the Portuguese, as is believed by Ficalho and other writers.]

Mangual (a flail). Konk. *maṅgil.*—Tul. *mungáru̥, mungaru̥.*

[1] "What I have learnt about the **mangostães** is that it is one of the most delicious fruits in this land." Garcia da Orta, Col. xxxviii [ed. Markham, p. 322].

"The whole of Siam abounds with rice and fruits, the principal of which are called mangues, durions, and **mangoustans.**" Tavernier, *Voyages*, IV, p. 197 [ed. Ball, O.U.P., Vol. II, p. 225].

["The peerless **Mangosteen** of Malacca, the delicacy of which we can imagine to resemble that of perfumed snow, has been successfully cultivated in the gardens of Caltura and Colombo." Tennent, *Ceylon*, I, p. 120.]

Manguço, mangusto (*Herpestes mungos*, Blanford; 'ichneumon'). Anglo-Ind. *mungoose.*—Indo-Fr. *mangouste.*[1]

From the Marathi-Konkani *mungús* or *mungas*, Sansk. *aṅgūsha*. [Yule derives it from Telugu, *mangīsu*, or *mungīsa*; Crooke says that Platts very doubtfully derives it from Sansk. *makshu*, 'moving quickly'. In Ar. it is *bint' 'arūs*, 'daughter of the bridegroom,' in Egypt *kitt* or *katt Farāūn*, 'Pharaoh's cat' (Burton, *Ar. Nights*, II, 369).]

[Da Orta (Col. XLII, ed. Markham, p. 336) describes unmistakably the Indian mungoose, but does not give it that name, but calls it *quil* or *quirpele*. From this it must be concluded either that *manguso* or *mongus* had not then acquired much currency in the Konkan, or that the creature had been first described or pointed out to the naturalist by one who had known it in the Tamil country, and who, therefore, gave it the names it has in that language. "*Kīri*, *kīripillei*, the Tamil name of the mongoose," says Prof. H. Kern (Linschoten, Hak. Soc., Vol. II, p. 104, *n.*). Da Orta refers to the mungoose in connection with his interesting dissertation on *Pao de Cobra*, or 'Snakewood'. This is what he says: "In the island of Ceylon, where there are many good fruits, forests, and beasts for the chase, there are yet many of those serpents vulgarly called *cobras de capello*.... Against these God has given this *Pao de Cobra*. It is found to be good against snake bites because in that island there are small beasts like ferrets which they call *quil*. Others call them *quirpele*. They often fight with these serpents. When one of them knows that it must fight with them, or fears that it may have to, it bites off a piece of this root

1 "There is a kind of vermin which they call **mongûs**, creatures somewhat different from the ferrets." João Ribeiro, *Fatalidade hist.*, Bk. I, ch. xx.

"Its Telugu name is *mangisu*, from which is derived *mongús* (as João Ribeiro writes it), and the mungoose of Anglo-India, the *mangouste* of the French, and other forms." Conde de Ficalho, Col. xlii, [p. 188.]

and rubs its paws over it, or rather rubs its paws which are wet with the juice over its head and body and over those parts which he knows the cobra is likely to bite when it springs. It then fights with the cobra, biting and scratching it until it is dead. If it does not succeed in killing the cobra, or if the snake should prove more powerful than its antagonist, the *quil* or *quirpele* again rubs itself against the root and returns to the combat, and at last conquers and kills its enemy. From this the Chingalas took an example, and saw that this root would be good against the bites of cobras. The Portuguese believed the good things that the people of the country said about the root and in time they gained some experience about it founded on reason.... Many Portuguese keep these mungoose in their houses, tamed and domesticated, to kill the rats, and to fight the *cobras de capello*, which the *Yogis* bring who seek for charity.... Of this snakewood there are three kinds in Ceylon..."

Deadly combats between the cobra and the mungoose, like those between the Egyptian 'ichneumon,' who also belongs to the *Herpestes* family, and the asp, go back to a very remote antiquity. They are mentioned in the *Atharva Veda*, in *Panchatantra*, and *Hitopadeśa.* But is there any warrant for the belief that the mungoose secures immunity from the snake's poison by means of certain roots or herbs? In the opinion of a competent investigator and observer like Blandford, the naturalist, the frequent triumphs of the mungoose over the cobra are the result of the former's bristly coat into which the fangs of the snake can only penetrate with difficulty, the hardness of its skin, and, above all, its cunning and dexterity in warding off the attack of the cobra and its patience in waiting for an opportunity to seize the cobra by its occiput, thereby rendering its poisonous fangs harmless. The claims of snake charmers to immunity, because of this very snakewood or root which they allege they carry about their person, are equally unfounded. Their secret of success, even when they handle cobras whose fangs have not been removed, appears to consist in their energetic decisiveness of manner and in the rapidity of their movements which completely dominate the reptile. That their pretences to immunity are hollow is proved by numerous reported instances of snake charmers succumbing very quickly to the bite of a cobra, especially when, trusting to their own devices, they will not avail themselves of scientific remedies.

What are the 'snakewoods' to which da Orta refers? One of these, which he says is called in Ceylon *rannetul*, has been definitely identified with the *Rauwolfia serpentina*, Benth., and Ficalho believes that it is the *chātrākī* mentioned in *Amarakośa* as one of the herbs used as an antidote by the *nakula* or the mungoose. The others are supposed to be the *Strychnos colubrina*, Linn., and the *Hemidesmus indicus*, R. Brown, or *Asclepias pseudosarsa*, Roxb..]

Manha (bad habit, distemper). Konk. *mánz*; vern. terms *khôd*, *avguṇ*.—Tet. *manha*; vern. term *kaba-kaba*.

Manilha (a term used in a game of cards; seven points of a suit). Konk. *mānilh*—Mac., Bug. *maníla*.

Manilha (bracelet). Anglo-Ind. [*moneloes*, bracelets,] *manilla-man*, 'an itinerant dealer in gems'.

Yule and Burnell say that *manilla-man*, in this sense, is a hybrid from Telugu *manelā vādu* and the English 'man' with a mixture of the Portuguese *manilha*.[1] But Brown derives *manéla-vānḍlu* from the geographical name

---

[1] "And Diogo d' Azambuja sent the grain which had been seized to the factor that he might fetch *lambeis* ('coarse stripped woollen cloths'), **manilhas**, basins and other things." João de Barros, Dec. I. iii, 2.

["The Women (in Goa), both White and Black, are kept recluse, vailed abroad; within doors, the Richer of any Quality are hung with Jewels, and Rosaries of Gold and Silver many times double; **Moneloes** of Gold about their Arms..." Fryer, *East India*, Hak. Soc., Vol. II, p. 27.]

[*Moneiloes* is used by Ovington (O.U.P., p. 294) and *Moneela* by Bowrey (Hak. Soc., p. 5) for the city of Manila.]

Manila. The man who sells glass bangles or bracelets is called '*manilheiro*' in Goa, and he goes from door to door crying his wares. It is, however, possible that *manilla* derives its origin from *maṇeri*, which in Marathi and Konkani is the name of 'a vendor of jewels,' Sansk. *maṇikāra*. [See *cobra manila*.]

Mano (brother). Konk. *mán*; it is prefixed to the first name in certain families: [*man Antonio, man João,* and corresponds to the Gujarati *bhai*, which however is used as a suffix: Vithalbhai, Jashbhai.] — Beng. *mānú* (us. among the Christians in Dacca).

Manteiga (butter). Mal. Sund., Mac., Bug. *mantéga.*—Ach. *mentíga.*—Jav. *mantégô.* —Mad. *mentégô.*—Tet., Gal. *mantéga*; vern. term *bókur.*—Jap. *manteka*, which, according to Gonçalves Viana, is from Spanish.[1]

Manto (mantle). Konk. *mánt* (us. among the Christians).—Jap. *manto.*

[1] "The natives of the Malay Islands neither drink milk nor make butter. The same is said of Chinese." Marsden, *Memoirs of a Malay Family*, p. 10.

Mão ('a measure of content and of weight'). Anglo-Ind. *maune* (arch.), *maund* (modern).[1]

The origin of the Portuguese word is Neo-Aryan: Hindustani-Bengali *man*, which Shakespear derives from the Arabic *mann*; Marathi-Konkani *maṇ*, which Molesworth derives from the Sansk. *māna*, the root of which is *mā*, 'to measure,' or from Arabic.

Professor Sayce (*Principles*

[1] "Maos, of which twenty go to the *candil*, which, as I have said, weighs a *bahar*, that is four *quintals*." Duarte Barbosa [Hak. Soc., ed. Dames, Vol. I, p. 157. At the end of the Appendix to his book, Barbosa has provided a comparative table of weights and measures of Portugal and India in his time (the beginning of the 16th century), from which and from other information interspersed in his book Dames arrives at the following table:—

14 ounces	=	1 (old) arratel.
128 old arratels	=	1 (old) quintal.
4 (old) quintals	=	1 bahar.
20 mãos	=	1 candil.

The new *arratel* contains 16 ounces.]

"The **mão** of oil is equal to twelve *canadas* (in Goa)." António Nunes, p. 31. [A *canada* is a Portuguese measure = three English pints.]

"Forty seers one **mão**, and twenty **mãos** one *bahar*." *Lembranças das Cousas da India*, [p. 39].

of Comparative Philology) and Dr. Haupt (*Die Sumerisch-akkadische Sprache*) attribute to the word *mana* an Accadian origin. Yule and Burnell observe that in any case it was the Babylonian name for the eightieth part of a talent, whence it passed, with other Babylonian weights and measures, almost all over the ancient world: Egyptian *men* or *mna*, Coptic *emna* or *amna*, Hebrew *māneh*, Greek *mna*, Roman *mina*; and through the medium of the Arabs, Spanish-Portuguese *almena*, old French *almène*,[1] [for a weight of about 20 lbs. (Marcel Devic)].

The authors of *Hobson-Jobson* also say: "The introduction of the word into India may have occurred during the extensive commerce of the Arabs with that country during the 8th and 9th centuries; possibly at an earlier date".

In the *Rigveda* (VIII, 67, 2) there appears the word *manā*, which has given rise to heated discussion among orientalists. Is it a genuine Aryan word or of Semitic origin? What is its true meaning?[1]

François Lenormant and some other writers regard the terms as identical, and adduce this fact, among other arguments, in proof of the very ancient relations that must have existed between India and Babylon, and also to point out traces of Babylonian influence on the Vedic poems.[2]

Max Müller (*India, What can it teach us?*) and other Sanskritists deny the Babylonian origin and the influence of the Semitic civilization upon ancient India; but there is no unanimity in their interpretation of the word.

[The recent excavations at Harappa in the Punjab and Mohenjo-Daro in Sindh have revealed the existence of an Indus Valley civilisation and culture which shows close

[1] Cândido de Figueiredo defines *almena* as "Indian weight equivalent approximately to one kilogramme," and gives as its source-word the Arabic *al-mena*.

[1] *Manā* is neither to be confounded with *māna* quoted above, nor with its homonym in the *Rigveda*, which signifies 'zeal, ardour, anger, envy.'

[2] See Cristóvão Pinto, *India Prehistorica*.

resemblance with those of early Sumer and Babylonia These discoveries indicate the existence of great cities with traces of luxury and refinement which suggest affinities with the Sumerian, or even an earlier, culture, Sir John Marshall going so far as to put their standard of life higher than anything contemporary in Mesopotamia or Egypt.]

The strophe is addressed to the god Indra, and is as follows: *Á naḥ bhara vyáñjanam gām áçvam abhyáñjanam.*

Sáchā manā hiraṇyáyā.

The first part is translated: "Bring us a jewel, a cow, a horse, an ornament." The difficulty hinges on the second part which has been variously rendered. Grassman: *Zugleich mit goldenen Gerāth* (=jointly with a vessel of gold). Ludwig: *Zusammt mit goldenen Zierrath* (=together with an ornament of gold). Zimmer: *Und eine Manâ gold* (=and a *maná* of gold).[1]

Max Müller impugnes the rendering with the instrumental case, because the preposition *sachā* never governs such a case, and referring *manā* to the Sansk. *maṇi*, Lat. *monile*, translates the verse: "*Give us* also two golden armlets". "To suppose," says he, "that the Vedic poets should have adopted only this word and only this measure from the Babylonians would be opposed to all the rules of historical criterion. The word *manā* never more appears again in all Sanskrit literature, no other Babylonian weight is ever mentioned in all Sanskrit literature and it is not probable that a poet who asks for a cow and a horse, should ask at the same time for a foreign measure of weight, that is, about 60 guineas."

Griffith follows this mode of rendering, but in place of the 'bracelets' he has 'rings.')[1]

[The Portuguese converted *man* into *mão*, of which the

---

[1] Langlois translates the stanza as follows: "Give us some cows, horses, perfumes, and ornaments of gold".

[1] The St. Petersburgh Dictionary defines *manā*: "Ein bestimmtes Geräth oder Gewicht." And Capeller: "A certain vessel or weight of gold."

English made *maune*, and so probably by the influence of the old English word *maund*, "a kind of great Basket or Hamper, containing eight Bales, or two Fats," the modern word was derived. *Mão* in Portuguese means 'hand' and some of the older travellers like Linschoten, misled by this meaning of *mão*, rendered it as equivalent to 'hand'. The values of the 'maund' as weight vary greatly in different parts of the country. The standard maund in British India is 40 *sers*, each *ser* being equal to 80 *tolas* or rupee-weights. See *Hobson-Jobson*.]

| **Máquina** (machine). Konk. *mákn*; vern. term *yantr*.—Turk. *mákina*. |

Marca (mark, stamp). Konk. *márk* (l. us.); vern. terms *khúṇ*, *kurú*, *chihném̐*, *niśāṇém̐*, *sopó*.—L.-Hindust. *mārká*—Mal., Tet. *márka*.—? Malag. *marika*.

Marchar (to march). Konk. *mārchár-zāvuṅk*.—Tet., Gal. *márcha*.

Março (month of March). Konk. *Márs*.—Mal., Tet., Gal. *Márṣu*. See *Agosto*.

? **Marear** (to work a ship). Sinh. *mariyá* (*subst.*), sailor, mariner; vern. terms *nāvikayá*, *nẹvkārayá*, *nẹvīyá*.

In Konkani, *mareação* signifies 'sagacity, astuteness.'

Marfim (ivory). Konk. *mārphim̐*; vern. term *hattyāchó dánt* (lit. 'elephant's tooth')—Tet., Gal. *marfim*.

Maria (Mary). Tel. *Mariyansu-át* (lit. 'Mary's game'). Brown is of the opinion that the word is of Portuguese origin.

Marmelo (quince). Jap. *maruméru*.

? **Marmore** (marble). Konk. *mārmar*.—Guj., Hindi, Hindust., Beng., Punj., Mal. *marmar*. *Marmarí* (in the Aryan languages), marbly.—Pers. *marmar*.—Ar. *marmar*, *marmer*.

The Portuguese origin can be contested. The original word is the Greek *marmoros*. From Persian *sangmarmar* (*sang*=stone) are derived directly: Konk., Mar. *sangmarmar*: Hindi, Punj. *sangmarmar*; Sindh. *sangimarmaru*; Kan. *sangamaravarí*, *sangamára*.

Marquesota (a sort of

mantle). Mal. *marcadjota* (=*markajóta*), "a gown, a woman's dress" (Haex).

Cândido de Figueiredo mentions the word thus: "**Marquesota,** f., a species of Indian root; (arch.) mantle, which was worn round the neck. (From *marquês* ?)".[1]

Marrafa (curled hair on the brow). Konk. *mārráph*; the vern. term is *pākhāḍí*.—Gal. *marrafa*; the vern. term is *garerom*.

Martelo (hammer, mallet). Konk. *martél* (us. in Salsete (Goa) and in Kanara); vern. terms *kuḍṭí*, *kuḍṭó* (mallet); *tutyó*, *hātāḷó* (iron hammer).—Hindi *martaul*; vern. terms *hathanḍá*, *ghan*, *mongrí*.—Hindust. *mārtil*, *mārtol*, *martol*, *martaul*.—Nep. *mārtaul*.—Beng. *mārtel*.—Anglo-Ind. *martil*, *martol*.—Mal. *martello* (Haex), *mártel mártil*.—Mol. *martélo*, *martélu*.—Tet., Gal. *martélu*.

Mártir (a martyr). Konk. *mārtír*.—Kamb., Tet., Gal. *mārtir*.—Japanese *maruchiru* (arch.).[1]

Martirio (martyrdom). Jap. *maruchiriyo* (arch.).

Mas (*conj*., but). Sund. *mása*.—Tet., Gal. *mas*.

Máscara (a mask). Mal. *maskára*.[2]

Mas que (*conj*., but, that). Mal. *máski*, *míski*.—Jav. *máski*, *méski*.—Tet. *maskê*.—Pid-Engl. *maskee*, *mashkee*, *ma-sze-ki*, be it so, all the same, it does not matter; never mind; it is alright, perfectly; just, correct. "This word is used in a very irregular manner. It is not Chinese, its equivalent in Mandarin being *pvo-yow-cheen*." Leland.

Masqui (Port. dialect of Macau), *masque* (Port. dialect of Ceylon), 'but, for all that, even'. In these meanings it is met with in the Portuguese classics. "Contae, **mas que** me deixem congelado".

---

1 "The gay fashioned breeches (*imperiaes*) of silk, **mercasotas**, and scarlet cloaks, were no longer met with at feasts, and in royal progresses." Diogo do Couto, *Dialogo do Soldado Pratico*, p. 38.

1 *T* intervocalic sounds like *ch* in Japanese (marutiru=*maruchiru*).

2 "The most dignified styles are not entirely free from these kinds of words such as *tempo* ('time'), *senhor* ('sir'), **mascara**." W. Marsden, *A Grammar of Malay Language*.

"Por Deos, **mas que** me fundam, **mas que** me confundam, eu hei de tanger sempre a verdade." D. Francisco de Melo. *Dialogos Apologaes.*[1]

Mastro (ship's mast). Hindi, Hindust., Punj., Ass. *mastúl.*—Or., Beng. *mástul.* —Khas. *mastul.*[2]

Matador (a term used in a game of cards). Bug. *matadóro.*

? **Matar** (to kill). Mal., Jav. *máti*, to die.—*maténi*, to kill.—Batt., Mac., Bug. *máte*, death.—Day. *matei.*—Malag. *mati.*

Dr. Heyligers thinks that the derivation from Portuguese is probable. On the contrary, it is very probable, if not quite certain, that the word is a vernacular one, perhaps derived, as Crawfurd believes, from the Sanskrit *mṛti*, 'death'. Favre suggests that it may be of Semitic origin, *mant*, 'death,' in Arabic. Malagassy must have received the word directly from the Malayan languages, much before Portuguese, or perhaps even Arabic, influence was felt in Malaysia. The term was current in the time of Fernão Pinto who writes (ch. 177: "*Cahio morto, sem dizer mais que somente*: **Quita mate,** *ay que me matou*" ("He fell dead, without saying anything but this: **Quita mate,** i.e., who is it that has killed me").

Matalote (sailor, seaman). Mal. *matelote* (Haex).

Matraca (a wooden rattle). Konk. *mātrák*; vern. terms *phaṭphaṭéṁ, khaṭkaṭéṁ.*—Tet. *matraka*; vern. term *di krarika.*

Medalha (medal). Konk. *medálh*; vern. term *ārlúk.*—Tet. *medalha.*

[**Medida** (a measure). Anglo-Ind. *medeeda* (obs.); also *memeeda* (*meia*, 'half,' and *medida*).[1]]

---

[1] "It is supposed that it may be the corruption or ellipsis of a Portuguese expression, but nothing satisfactory has been suggested." *Hobson-Jobson.* [See Crooke's quotation from Mr Skeat in *Hobson-Jobson, s.v.* maskee.]

[2] It would appear as though the *l* stands for *r* which is transposed, *mastur*; but the old Port. form is *masto.*

---

[1] ["*Dry measures are these,* viz., Teman is 40 Memeeda's. Medeeda is 3 Pints *English.* By this Medeeda

Medula (bone marrow). Sinh. *midulu*; vern. term *ẹtamola*.

Meia, meias (sock, hose). Konk. *mey.*—Sinh. *mês. Koṭa-mês*, socks. *Aṭ-mês* (lit.: 'hand socks'), gloves.—Tam. *mey-jóḍu* (lit.: 'a pair of socks'), *kal-mês* (lit.: 'feet socks'). *Kai-mês* (lit.: 'hand socks'), gloves.—Tel. *mējóḍu, mējóḷḷu.* —Kan., Tul. *mējóḍu.*—Tet. *meias.*—Gal. *meia.*

Meirinho (in the sense of 'a sacristan, a sacristan's assistant'). Konk. *mirní*; *miraṇ* (us. in Kanara).—Tam. *miriñ.*—Tul. *mírne.*—| Indo-Fr. *merigne.* |—Mal. *meriniyu.* —Sund., Mac., Bug. *marínio.*—Mol. *marinjo,* harbour-master. Dr. Heyligers derives it from *marinho* (*adj.* 'marine').—Tet., Gal. *mirínhu.*

Meirinho was formerly, in Portugal, a judicial official corresponding to the present day bailiff. In the colonies every fortress and every city had its '*meirinho*'. See *O Tombo do Estado da India*, *passim.*[1] In India, the parish priests had, besides the sacristan, an official whose business was to look after the spiritual interests of the parish, to whom they naturally gave the title of *meirinho.*[2] At the present day the '*meirinhos*' of Goa correspond, in their duties, to the summoners in Europe; they have also, because they have not enough

they sell Oil, Butter, and Liquids." Ovington, *Voyage to Surat*, O.U.P., p. 269.]

1 "The Captain-in-Chief ordered the sailors to land and also his **meirinho** of the fleet with an *Ouvidor* ('magistrate') whom he had on board, that they might keep an eye on the people and prevent mischief.' Gaspar Correia, I, p. 165.

["We were then landed, and a miserable sight we were, all naked, save only for the covering of a mere rag of cotton. We were forthwith taken in charge by a Portuguese sergeant, whom they call a **Merigne**, who was accompanied by seven or eight slaves, Christian Caffres of Mozambique, each with his halbert or partisan". Pyrard, Hak. Soc., Vol. I, p. 427.]

2 "The **meirinhos**, and the very parents are very careless, and will continue to be so, in the matter of reporting to you births." *Instructions of S. Francis Xavier*, in Lucena, Bk. V, ch. 25.

"In each of these villages (of Goa) there is a **meirinho** whose duty it is to give religious instruction." João de Santos, *Ethiop. Or.*, II, p. 97.

to do, to assist the sacristans. Outside Goa, *meirinho* is synonymous with sacristan. In the Archipelago, however, it retains its original meaning, more or less modified. In Madagascar, for example, according to Matthes, the term is used of the European Civil Magistrate—'*Europesche schout*'.[1]

Melão (melon). Tel. *meláma.*

Mercê (favour, benefit). Konk. *mersél,* land held as a grant for service rendered.—Tet. *mersê*; vern. term *díak.*

Merecer (to merit). Mal. *merecer* (Haex).—Tet. *meréci* (also used in the sense of 'merit').

Mês (month). Hindust. *mājkabár*, "(corruption of the Port. *mês* [month] and *acabar* [to end]) the last day of the month". Shakespear. Wilson mentions *kābār,* in Bengali, as the name of the last day of the month and *kābārī* (*adj.*), "relating to the last day of the month, due or payable on this day (salary, rent, etc.)."

In Konkani, *kabár* is very much used as equivalent to the Portuguese *acabar* ('to end').

[Brown suggests, as the etymon of *majkabar*, the Hindust. *mās-ke-ba'ad*, 'after a month'. Crooke, on the other hand, observes that, according to Platts, it is more probably a corruption of Hindust. *māsik-war* or *mās-kā-wār*. But Prof. S. H. Hodivala (*Notes on Hobson-Jobson*) suggests that, "if 'Mascabar' is an Indo-Portuguese word for the last day of the month, it must be a corruption, not of *mâs-kâ-bâr*,.... but of *amâs-ka-bâr*. 'Amâs,' from Sans. *amāvasya*, is commonly used for the last day of the month. If 'Mascabar' means 'monthly statement or account', it must stand for *mâsik-vâr*, as Platts says".]

Mesa (table). Konk. *méz.*—Mar., Guj., Nep., Or., Beng., Ass. *mej.*—Hindi *mez, menz, mench. Dhalvān-mez*, writing-desk.—Hindust. *mej, mez.*—

[1] "**Meirinho.** A superintendent of police under the Portuguese government of Bassein in the sixteenth and seventeenth centuries". Whitworth.

Sindh. *meza*, *mezu*.—Punj. *mez* (also us. of 'a bench').—Kash. *mez*.—Sinh. *mêsaya*, *mêse*. *Lihina-mêsaya*, writing-table, a case for pen and ink. *Sayilod-mêsaya*, side-board. *Sayilod* is corruption of the English 'side-board.'—Tam. *mesei*.—Malayal. *meśa*, *més*.—Tel. *méja*. *Méjar*, a big table.—Kan. *méju* (also us. in the sense of 'ration', owing to confusion with the English 'mess').—Tul. *méji*.—Mal. *meja*, *méza*, *mésa*.—Ach., Batt., Sund. *méja*.—Jav., Mad. *méjô*. *Méjah túlis* (Mal.), *meja súrat* (Ach.), writing-desk.—Day. *méja*.—Mac., Bug. *méjan*.—Tet., Gal. *meza*.—Nic. *menśa*.—Pers. *mez*, *miz*.—Ar. *mez*.— | Turk. *massa*. |

Molesworth derives the Marathi word from Persian and gives the following compounds as Persian words: *mej-bán*, *mej-ván*, *mej-mán*, a guest, also a host. *Mej-bānkí* or *mej-vānkí*, *mej-mānkí* or *mej-mānī*, hospitality.

Guj. *mej-bán*, *mej-mán*, guest; host. *Mej-bānī*, feasting, banquet; hospitality.

Hindust. *mej-bán*, guest; host. *Mej-bāni*, feasting, hospitality.[1]

Sindh. *mizimánu*, *mizmánu*, *mihmánu*, guest. *Mizimānī*, hospitality.

Punj. *majmán*, *mahmán*, *mamán*, guest; son-in-law. *Mamānī*, feast. *Mijmán*, guest. *Mijmānanī*, a female guest. *Mijmānī*, feast.

?**Mesquinho** ('poor, miserable'). Mar. *miskin*, *miskīl*.—Hindust. *miskín*.—Punj. *mas-kín*. *Maskinī*, humility.—Malayal. *miskín*, *maskín*.—Mal. *meskin*, *miskin*.—Sund., Jav., Bal. *miskin*.—Mac., Bug. *misĕkin*.[2]

The term appears to have been directly imported from Arabic.

?**Mesquita** (a mosque). Anglo-Ind. *mosque*, [*muskeell*, *musqueet* (obs.).]—Mal. Ach.,

1 Shakespear also attributes the Hindustani words to Persian.

2 "Those inhabitants are fishermen, a **mezquinha** folk, for this is how they speak in India of people who are of low descent and poor." Castanheda, I, ch. 13.

"Robbers who were Moors used to rove on the seas plundering the **mesquinhos**." Gaspar Correia, IV, p. 83.

Jav., Mad. *misigit*, *mesigit*, *masigit*.—Mac., Bug. *masigi*.[1]

Dr. Schuchardt derives *misigit* from Portuguese, although the word in its origin is the Arabic *masjid*.

[Yule believes that the probable course which *masjid* took in getting evolved into the Anglo-Indian *mosque* is as follows: (1) in Span. *mezquita*, Port. *mesquita*; (2) Ital. *meschita*, *moschea*; French (old) *mosquete*, *mosquée*; (3) Eng. *mosque*. This is more or less also the view of the *O.E.D.*

Sir George Oxinden, in a letter from Surat, dated 28th January, 1663, addressed to the Directors of the East India Company, says: "Hearing they ('Sevagy's men') had taken their randavous in a **Muskeett** or Moore Church...." (Forrest, *Selections*, Home Series, Vol. I, p. 25). The influence of the Portuguese word on *muskeett* appears to be unmistakable.

Duarte Barbosa uses *mesquita* of a Hindu shrine[1]; and owing to a similar confusion Faria-y-Sousa speaks of a 'Pagoda of Mecca.']

Mestiço (a half-caste). Konk. *mistís*. It is also used as an adjective: *mistís bonchurḍí*, the bulbul, or the eastern song-thrush, *Ixos jocosus*.—Hindust. *mastisa*.—Anglo-Ind. *mustees*, *mestiz*, *mastisa*, [*mustechees*.]—Indo-Fr. *métis*.[2]

---

1 "There is a big **misquita** with many columns and verandas, in every respect very beautiful." Gaspar Correia, IV, p. 173.

1 ["The *Bramenes* and also the *Baneanes* marry one wife only.. At their weddings they have great festivities which continue for many days. ..On the day appointed for their reception the bride and bridegroom are seated on a dais; they are covered with gold and gems and jewels, and in front of them they have a **mesquita** with an idol covered with flowers with many oil-lamps burning around it." Hak. Soc., ed. Dames, Vol. I, p. 116.]

2 "After this victory (at Diu) the Governor gave orders that all the **mestiços** who were there should be inscribed in the Book, and that pay and subsistence should be assigned to them." Gaspar Correia, IV, p. 574.

"The least esteemed are the offspring of a Portuguese father and an Indian mother, or vice versa, and these are called **Metices**, that is, **Metifs**, or mixed" Pyrard, *Viagem*, Vol. II, p. 32 [Hak. Soc., Vol. II, p. 38.]

["It's alsoe of very ill consequence that your Covenant Servants should

[Tavernier uses the forms *mestif*, *mestive*, and *mestice*.] See *castiço* and *topaz*.

[Fryer speaks of this class also as *Misteradoes*[1].]

intermarry with any of the people of the Country or those of mixed Race or **Mustechees.**" Hedges, *Diary*, Hak. Soc., Vol. II, p. ccix.]

"The **Métissos** (at Goa) are of several sorts, but very much despised by the *reinols* and the *castissos*, because they have inherited a little black blood from their ancestors." Le Gouz de la Boullaye, *Voyages*, ed 1657, p. 226. [*Reinol*, pl. *reinoes*, from Port. *reino*, the kingdom of Portugal, was the name by which the European Portuguese were distinguished from those born in India of Portuguese parents and who were called *castissos* (*q. v.*). In the early seventeenth century, *reinol* was used in much the same sense as 'griffin' was in Anglo-Indian vocabulary. "When they are newly arrived in the Indies, they are called *Raignolles*, that is to say, "men of the kingdom," and the older hands mock them until they have made one or two voyages with them, and have learned the manners and customs of the Indies: this name sticks to them until the fleet arrives the year following". Pyrard, *Voyage*, Hak. Soc., Vol. II, p. 123. A. Hamilton (*New Acct. of the East Indies* (1727), I, 248) speaks of this class as "the *Reynolds* or *European Fidalgoes*."]

[1] ["Beyond the Outworks live a few *Portugals* **Mustezoes or Misteradoes.**" *East India*, Hak Soc., Vol. I, p. 148.]

Mestre (master). Konk. *mestír*, a teacher; *mestírṇ*, a lady teacher; vern. terms *šeṇay*, *pantojí*, *paṇḍit*. *Mestīrpaṇ*, teachership, the teaching profession. *Mest*, master of some craft; artist; an honorific appellation given to artisans.

The phonetic difference between *mestír* and *mest* arises from the fact that the former is employed by itself, whereas the latter is generally prefixed to the name of some person.

Mar. *mestarí*, *mest*, "honorific distinction of goldsmiths or carpenters, or masons, or the chief armourer: also of the man, if a Portuguese, who makes bread in a bakery. Applied frequently to a superintendent in general. Used more, by an excess of courtesy, of Portuguese servants, especially cooks." Molesworth.[1]

Guj. *mīstrí*, *mistarí*, mason. *Vaḍô mistarí* (lit. 'the great mason'), an architect. Hindust. *mistrí*, a skilled artisan, foreman.—L.-Hindust.

[1] By 'Portuguese' the author means the inhabitants of Goa.

mistri, a carpenter.—Beng. *ráj-mistrí* (*ráj* is Persian for 'mason'), a mason or bricklayer. *Lohár mistrí* (lit. 'iron-master'), a blacksmith.—Ass. *mistrí*, carpenter.—Punj. *mastarí*, the official head. *Mistarí-khānā*, workshop.—Malayal. *mestarí*, craftsman.—Tel. *mestrí*, *mestarí*, a foreman.—Kan., Tul. *mestre*, carpenter, stone-cutter, mason.—Anglo-Ind. *maistry*, *mistry*, *mistery*, a master-workman, a foreman, and in W. and S. India also 'a cook, a tailor.'—Gar. *mistri*, mason.—Khas. *raj-misteri*, mason.—?Mal. |*mĕstĕri*|, *mester* (perhaps from the Dutch *meester*).—Tet., Gal. *méstri*.

Some dictionary-writers give as the etymon the English *mister* or the French *maistre*.

Milagre (miracle). Konk. *milágr*; vern. terms *acharyéṁ*, *naval*, *vismit*, *adbhut*.—Mal. *milagro* (Haex).—Tet., Gal. *milágri*.

In the Marathi of the Konkan and in the Hindustani of the south, *milāgrí*, by extension of meaning, sometimes stands for an image of the Blessed Virgin Mary, at other times for any Roman Catholic church, because in India there are many churches dedicated to 'Our Lady of Miracles.'

Milho (maize; Indian corn). Mol. *milo*, *mīlu*.

Militar (*subst.*, soldier). Konk. *militár*; vern. term *sipáy*, *laskarí*.—Tet. *militár*.

Ministro (minister). Konk. *minístr*; vern. terms *munyārí*, *mantrí*, *pradhán*.—Tet. *minístru*.

Minuto (a minute). Konk. *minút*; vern. term *ghaḍí* (not exactly corresponding).—?Guj. *miniṭ* (as in English).—Kamb. *minŭt*.—Tet., Gal. *minútu*.

Missa (*eccles.*, mass). Konk. *mis*. *Misāchó pādrí* (lit. 'priest of the mass'), priest.[1]—Kan. *mīsayágavu* (lit. 'sacrifice of the mass').—Tul. *mīsyyága*.—Kamb. *missa*.—Siam. *misá*.—Ann. *lê missa*; vern. term *lê*.—Mal. *misa*.—Tet., Gal. *misa*.— | Chin. *misáh*; vern. term *tá-tsián*. |

Missal (*eccles.*, a missal). Konk., Tam., Tet., Gal. *misál*.

---

1 Cf. *Clerigo de missa* ('clergy of the mass'). João de Barros, Dec. I, iii, 5. [It is almost the exact equivalent of the Konkani expression 'priest of the mass'.]

Missão (mission). Konk. *misáṁv.*—Beng., Tam. *misán.* —Tet., Gal. *misã.*

Missionário (missionary). Konk., Beng., Tam, Kan. *misiyonár.*

Mister (arch. form *mester*; need, function). Mal. *mester*, *místi*, necessity.— | Mol., | Ach. *miski na*, indispensable. *Míski teka*, to be compelled.—Sund. *místi.*—Jav. *pĕsti* or *pasti*, | certain, doubtless. |

In the Portuguese dialects, *mistê* signifies : 'it is necessary, it is proper, it ought to be.'

Mistério (mystery). Konk. *mistér*; vern. term *gúḍh.*—Tet. *mistéri.*

| **Moda** (fashion). Konk. *mód*; vern. term *chál.*—Turk. *móda.* |

| **Modêlo** (model). Konk. *modêl*; vern. term *namuno.*—Turk. *mòdèl.* |

Môlho (sauce, gravy). Kon. *môl*, pickled fish.—? Tam. *molei*, a kind of curry. —[Anglo-Ind. *moley*].

Yule says that the Tamil word is a corruption of 'Malay'; the dish being simply a bad imitation of one used by the Malays. [There is a recipe for preparing 'moley' in the *Indian Cookery* (The Army and Navy Co-operative Society Ltd., Bombay).

Monção (monsoon). Konk. *monsáṁv.*—Anglo-Ind. *monsoon.*—Indo-Fr. *mousson.*—Siam. *monsúm.*[1]

The source-word is the Arabic *mausim*, 'season of the year'

[Yule says : "Dictionaries (except Dr. Badger's) do not apparently give the Arabic word *mausim* the technical sense of *monsoon.* But there can be no doubt that it had that sense among the Arab pilots from whom the Portuguese adopted the word...... Though **monção** is general with the Portuguese writers of the 16th century, the historian Diogo de Couto always writes **moução**, and it is possible that the *n* came in, as in some

1 "Every **monçam** ten or fifteen of these ships used to sail for the Red Sea" Duarte Barbosa, p. 341 [Hak. Soc., ed. Dames, Vol. II, p. 77].

"We also speak of **monções**, which are the seasons there for making sea voyages" João de Barros, Dec. III, iv, 7.

"There they had to remain for a long time because of the absence of the **moução**" (throughout spelt thus). Diogo do Couto, Dec. V, x, 6.

other cases, by a habitual misreading of the written *u* for *n*. Linschoten in Dutch (1596) has **monssoyn** and **monssoen.** It thus appears probable that we get our *monsoon* from the Dutch." Skeat traces 'monsoon' from Ital. *monsone*. But the *O.E.D.*, with more reason, states that it is adopted from Dutch, *monsooen—soyn*, which, in its turn, was adopted from the Port. *monção* in the 16th century. At the present time, both according to Anglo-Indian and Indo-Portuguese usage, 'monsoon,' or *monção* means 'the season of the rains,' which, as a rule, lasts for four months and is a period during which sailing vessels do not put out to sea. We also speak of 'the monsoon having burst,' which is another way of saying that the rains have begun. The 'rainy season' was also called *inverno* ('winter') by the Portuguese, and this practice was followed by the other European nations and lasted right up to the eighteenth century. '*Inverno*' is even to-day used of the 'rainy season' in the Portuguese possessions in India. See quotation from Correia under *mordexim*: also *Hobson-Jobson, s.v.* winter.]

| **Morcego** (bat or flying fox). Mal. *morsego*, according to Rhumpius. "The fruit is eagerly eaten by bats. In Malay the tree is called *Caju* **Morsego**; in Latin *Arbor Vespertilionum*" ('Flying fox tree'). |

Mordexim ('a name for cholera up to the end of the 18th century'). Indo-Fr., Anglo-Ind. *morte-de-chien* (obs.)[1]

---

[1] "This 'winter' (of 1543) they had in Goa a fatal illness which the inhabitants call **moryxy.**" Gaspar Correia, IV. p. 288. [For 'winter' see *monção* above.]

"Our name for the disease is *colerica passio*, the Indians call it *morxi*; and we corrupt the word into **mordexi**". Garcia da Orta, Col. xvii (ed. Markham, p. 104).—"In our century the old names **mordexim** and *mort-de-chien* have gone out of use, having been, as a rule, replaced by the word *cholera*." Conde de Ficalho.

["The ordinary diseases of this country (Goa) are **mort-de-chien** (cholera)—that is, colic of the bowels with vomiting and laxity—and this complaint is the death of many. The best remedy is to burn with a red-hot iron the middle of the heel until the

The Portuguese word represents the Marathi-Konkani *moḍśi*, which, even at the present time, is the term used of indigestion, especially in the case of children. [See *colera*.]

[The Marathi-Konkani word is from *moḍṇeṁ* or *moḍoṅk*, 'to break up, to sink, to collapse'. Dalgado (*Glossario*) thinks it very probable that in former times this term, which is used of indigestion, was employed, by a kind of euphemism, to denote cholera, it being regarded as inauspicious in India to mention the fell disease by its proper name. There is a great deal to be said in favour of this view as, even at the present day among the common people, it is regarded as unlucky to speak of a man as having been 'bitten by a snake,' but it is believed to be more favourable to his recovery if he is described as having been 'scratched by a thorn.' Yule observes that the Gujarati forms of *moḍśi* appear to be *moṛchi* or *moṛachi*. To this Dalgado says that Gujarati has no *ṛ*, and *moṛchi* cannot be traced back to *mōḍśī*. Portuguese has no *ḍ* cerebral, and the sound which comes nearest to it is *r*, as is seen in the case of *areca* from *aḍekka*. The Portuguese writers of the 16th century had very fine ears and they noticed that their *morxi* did not represent the exact transcription of *moḍśi* which is trisyllabic, the *a* of the second syllable (*ḍa*) being very silent or almost mute, and, therefore, very naturally added *de* to *r*, and in this way evolved the transcription *mordexi*, which after prolonged use became *mordexim* and existed side by side with the correct transcription *morxi*. During two centuries and more this word (*mordexim*) was employed by the Portuguese—and by all the Europeans who travelled to India—to designate cholera: at times written *mordicin* by the Italians, as by Carletti: other times *mordisin* by the French, as by Pyrard; sometimes *mordexi* by those who wrote in Latin, as by Bontius. Subsequently, the French thought of

heat is felt, and by this the pain is allayed and the discharge and vomiting stopped." Manucci, *Storia do Mogor*, ed. Irvine, Vol. II, p. 169.]

giving the word a meaning, and, combining the sound of the word with the horrors of death from the disease, called the malady *mort-de-chien*. In the *Lettres Edifiantes* for the year 1702 there occurs the following phrase, which helps to fix the time of the adoption of the new name: "This great indigestion which is called in India **Mordechin**, and which some of us French have called **Mort-de-Chien**" ('Dog's Death'). Although ridiculed, this name was adopted, not only in French works, but also in books written in other languages, and there was even an Englishman who literally translated the name thus: "The extraordinary distempers of this country are the *Cholick*, and what they call *Dog's Disease*, which is cured by burning the heel of the patient with a hot iron." See Ficalho, *Colloquies da Orta*, Vol. I, p. 275. The opinion of the 'Englishman' quoted above is taken from *Acct. of the I. of Bourbon*, in La Roque's *Voyage to Arabia the Happy*, etc., E.T. London, 1726, p. 155, cit. in *Hobson-Jobson*. The history of the various transformations through which this interesting word has passed would be incomplete if we did not refer to Anderson (*English in Western India*, etc., p. 62) who by a curious metathesis having changed *chien* into *Chine* and, therefore, *mort de chien* into *mort de Chine* ('Chinese death') says: "The disease which was prevalent in the country, and especially fatal in Bombay, was called by the Portuguese practitioners of medicine 'the Chinese death,' or colic."]

| **Moreia** (a fish). Mal. *morea*; according to Rhumpius, the word is used by the Malays to denote various plants by a kind of analogy. See *Herbarium Amboinense* VII, ch. 35. |

Morrão (a match used by gunners; piece of cord designed to burn at uniform rate for firing cannon) Konk. *muram*.—Mal. *murañ*.[1]

Mosquito (mosquito). Anglo-Ind. *mosquito*, *moskito*. [Fryer uses the forms *muskeeto*,

---

[1] "All the provisions, fuel, timber, murrões." Diogo do Couto, Dec., VI, i, 6.

mosquito, and *musquito*].[1] —Pid-Eng. *muskito, skeeta.*

[*Mosquito* is the diminutive of the Port. *mosca*, 'a fly', and its earliest use, connected with South America, more especially Brazil, was to denote not the gnat so much dreaded to-day, but a very common and troublesome insect in those parts, described at some length by Moraes Silva in his Dictionary. Barbosa (1516) uses the word in this latter acceptation. "And in their houses they (the *Baneanes*) sup by daylight, for neither by night nor by day will they light a lamp, by reason of certain **mosquitos** which perish in the flame thereof" (Hak. Soc., ed. Dames, Vol. I, p. 112). The restricted use of the word to denote the species of gnat we now know by that name is of a later date.]

Mostarda (mustard). Konk. *mustárd.*—Mal. *mostárdi, mustárdi,* | *moster* | (perhaps from the Dutch *mostard*); vern. term *ṣasávi.*—Tet, Gal. *mustarda*; vern. term *sasábi.*

In Konkani, the use of the term is limited to mustard prepared for use at table; otherwise the word *sāṅsvāṁ* is used.

[**Mosteiro** (? a big gun). Anglo-Ind. *mustira.*[1]

"Mustira is probably a corruption of the Portuguese word Mosteiro, which means a big gun." Forrest *Selections*, (Home Series), Vol. I, p. 27, n. In the Portuguese dictionaries which I have consulted I do not find this meaning of the word: it means a 'monastery or convent.']

Mostra (sample, pattern). Konk. *mostr*; vern. term *namunó.*—Sinh. *móstraya, móstaraya, mostra, mastare*; vern. terms *adıśaya, nidarśanaya.*—Tel. *mustaru̥, mūstaru̥.*—Anglo-Ind. *muster.*[2] See *amostra.*

---

1 ["Swarms of Ants, **Muskeetoes**, Flies, and stinking *Chints*." Fryer, *East India*, Hak. Soc., Vol. I, p. 100. See also Vol. I, p. 231, and Vol. II, pp. 99 and 191.]

1 ["They (the Dutch) having now lately sent a sloupe fro' Mallacca with a **Mustira** Portugall in her. Forrest, *Selections*. Might *mustira* perhaps not be a misreading of *mustiza* (*mestiço*, *q. v.*) ?]

2 ["Even amongst the English (in Ceylon), the number of Portuguese

[Yule says that *muster* is current in China, as well as in India. For citations see *Hobson-Jobson.*]

Mouro (used of 'a Mohammedan').[1] Konk. *Moir.*—Anglo-Ind. *Moor*, *Moorman.* —Sund. *Móri. Kápas móri* (lit. 'Moorish cotton'), a species of cotton.—Pid-Engl. *Molo-man.*[2]

[All Mohammedans without exception were called by the Portuguese *Mouros* or Moors: this name of their nearest Moslem neighbours and one time conquerors was extended by them to all the followers of Islam, and from the Portuguese the use of this term, as synonymous with Mohammedan, passed to the Dutch and the English. The use of the term in its comprehensive sense is well brought out by Barbosa (ed. Dames, Vol. 1, p. 119): "The **Mouros** of this kingdom (Cambaya) are fair in complexion, and the more part of them are foreigners from many lands, *scilicet* Turks, Mamalukes, Arabs, Persians, Coraçones, and Targimões (Turcomans); others come from the great kingdom of Dely, and others of the land itself."

Yule says that the use of the word *Moor* for Mohammedan died out pretty well among educated Europeans in the Bengal Presidency in the beginning of the last century, or even earlier, but probably held its ground longer among the British

---

terms in daily use is remarkable. The grounds attached to a house are its "compound," *campinho*; .... a tradesman is shown a "**muster,**" *mostra* or pattern." Tennent, *Ceylon*, Vol. II, p. 70, n. 2]

"Wee were lodged in an upper Chamber and not permitted soe much as to looke out of our doores, much lesse either to see anie goods (saveinge the **musters** or the waight of them)." In Mundy, *Travels*, Hak. Soc., Vol. III, pt. ii, p. 480.]

1 "He had in his company six hundred **Mouros** Guzarates, and Malavares." Fernão Pinto, ch. xxvii.

"In token of disparagement they call the Christians of those parts *Franques*, just as we incorrectly call them **Mouros.**" João de Barros, Dec. IV, iv, 16.

"I regard this word **mouro** in the acceptation in which the Portuguese of old regarded it, viz., as a synonym of Mohammedan, as denoting belief but not race." Conde de Ficalho, *Garcia da Orta e o seu tempo*, p. 112.

2 The change of *r* into *l* in Pidgin-English is normal.

soldiery, whilst *Moorish*, as an adjective, continued to be used up to a later date. In Ceylon, the Straits, and the Dutch colonies, the term *Moorman* for a Musalman is still in common use, and the word is still employed by the servants of Madras officers in speaking of a certain class of Mohammedans. *Moro* is still applied at Manila to the Mussulman Malays. Not only in Portuguese India, but wherever Portuguese is spoken in Asia to-day, the Mohammedan is called *Mouro*. The French in India have also adopted the use of this term in the same sense.]

Moutão (the block in a ship through which the ropes run). L.-Hindust. *mutám*. *motám*, *matám*.

Muita mercê (many thanks). Bong. *muita mercê*; a stereotyped expression used by the Christians in the Dacca district in raising toasts; it has nothing to do with its real significance and is used in a sense corresponding to 'your health'.

Mulato (one who is the offspring of a European and a negro). Konk. *mulát*.—Tul. *mulatta*.[1]

In Konkani, the term is also used as an adjective and is applied to fowls and chickens with frizzled feathers: *mulát kombí*, *mulát pil* [*kombí* = hen; *píl* = chicken].

[Mulatto means 'young mule', the offspring of a stallion and she-ass, hence, one of mixed race. The word is analogous to *mestiço*, *q.v.*]

Mulher, (arch. form *molher*, woman). Mal. *molér*; vern. terms *prempúan*, *betína*.

Multa (fine, penalty). Konk. *múlt*, vern. term *daṇḍ*.—Tet., Gal. *multa*.

Munição (in the sense of 'small shot'). Konk. *munisáṁv*; vern. term *chharró* (l. us.).—Sinh. *mūnissama* (pl. *mūnisan*); vern. terms *muṇḍa*, *uṇḍa*. *Mūnisan paṭiya*, shot-belt. Mal. *manisan*.—Ach.

---

1 "A **mulato** named João Leite dying in Bengal." Diogo do Couto, Dec. VI, vii. 3.

"Those born of a Portuguese father and a Caffre, or African negro mother, are called **Mulastres** ('Mulattos'), and are held in like consideration with the Metifs ('mesticos')." Pyrard, *Viagem*, II, p. 32 [Hak. Soc., Vol. II, p. 38].

menisan or *melisan*.—Tet., Gal. *munisã*; vern. term *kmuna*.

In Malay and Achinese, the term is used, by analogy, of 'comfits.'

Mura ("an ancient measure of Portuguese India corresponding to 735 litres," Cândido de Figueiredo). Anglo-Ind. *moorah*.

It appears that the source-word is the Marathi *muḍá* (Konk. *muḍó*), "rice made up in a circular package being fastened by wisps of straw," which, however, does not actually contain the quantity mentioned by António Nunes: "The **mura** of *batee* (*q.v.*) contains three candis."[1]

[Garcia da Orta who wrote about twenty years after Nunes says that a candy is 522 *arrateis* (pounds). Crooke quotes from the *Madras Glossary*: **Mooda**, Malayal *mūtā*, from *mūtū*, 'to cover'. "a fastening package; especially the packages in a circular form, like a Dutch cheese, fastened with wisps of straw, in which rice is made up in Malabar and Canara."]

Música (music). Konk. *múzg*, [also a musician]; vern. terms *gāyan*, *vāzap*.—Hindust. *mūsikí*, *mūsīqí*. *Mūsīqīdán* (*subst.*), a musician.—Mal. *músik*.—Tet., Gal. *músika*.—Pers. *mūsīqí*.—Ar. *musika*, *muzika*, *musikay*. *Musikí*, a musician. *Musikārí*, musical.—Malag. *mozika*.

Dr. Schuchardt prefers the Dutch *musick* as the original of the Malay word. See *câmara*.

N

Nababo (nawab). Anglo-Ind. *nabob*, [Indo-Fr. *nabab*]. From the Hindustani *nawāb*, plural of the Arabic *nāyib*, 'a deputy', [and, therefore, applied to a Viceroy or Governor-General under the Moghuls as the representative of the Emperor, e.g., the Nawab of Oudh, Nawab of Surat].[1]

[The Anglo-Indian 'Nabob',

---

[1] "And (to be given) in the form of *bate* ('paddy') two hundred and forty-three **muras**." Simao Botelho, *Tombo*, p. 163.

[1] "There was in Surat as **Nababo** a certain Persian Mohammedan (*Mouro Parsio*)...." Bocarro, Dec. XIII, p. 354.

in the sense of 'a deputy or delegate of the supreme chief', was directly taken from the Port. *nababo*. But in the Anglo-Indian vocabulary of the 18th century the name was also sarcastically employed to denote an Anglo-Indian who returned to England with an immense fortune from the East and affected a luxurious style of living. The Portuguese in the 17th century referred to a countryman of theirs in similar circumstances as *Indiatico*,[1] just as in a later age they spoke of one who returned to Portugal after enriching himself in Brazil as *Brasileiro*, and the Spaniards called one of themselves who returned to Spain after making his fortune in South America *Mejicano*.]

"By virtue of the gift made by the Moghul Prince Idail Moindikan, confirmed by the **Nababo** of Anata." *O Chron. de Tissuary*, I, 324

["As the Kingdom of Angelim was under the control of the **Nababo** the Prince was much disturbed by this message." Manrique, *Travels*, Hak. Soc, Vol. I, p. 23.]

1 ["An *Indiatico* boards a ship in Goa with plenty of money and arrives here (Brasil) or in Lisbon without a *bazaruco* (*q.v.*)." *Xavier Dormindo* (1694), in Dalgado's *Gonçalves Viana e a Lex. Port.* etc., p. 112.]

Naique (a captain of indigenous soldiers; a headman). Anglo-Ind. *naique*, *naik*.—Indo-Fr. *naïque*.

The source-word is the Neo-Aryan *náyak* or *náyk*, from the Sanskrit *nāyaka*. 'leader, director, chief'. [Its exact equivalent is the Latin *dux*.] It is also the title of some kings,[1] and a title of honour among certain classes. [It was the title of the petty dynasties that arose in S. India on the downfall of the Hindu empire of Vijayanagar in the 16th century.] In Konkani it is the name of a catchpole or bailiff.

Naique in Indo-Portuguese had various meanings: captain or chief of indigenous soldiers, ordinarily called *piães*; a headman; an Indian inspector or supervisor.[2]

1 "This **Ventapanaique** had become, in these times, very powerful, and had conquered and made himself the overlord of all the neighbouring chiefs." Bocarro, Dec. XIII, p. 471.

2 "He sent also a **Nayque** with twenty Abyssinians, who came to protect us from robbers, and to provide us with supplies." Fernão Pinto, ch. iv.

Naire ('name of the ruling caste in Malabar'). Anglo-Ind. *nair*.—Indo-Fr. *naïre*.[1]

It is the Malayal. *náyar*, derived from the Sansk. *nāyaka*, 'chief, leader.'

[" Another derivation is from *Nāga*, " a snake, or man of serpent descent ", and some possibility is lent to this by the fact....that every Nāyar family still holds the serpent

"To guard against these he established some people of the same island of the Canarese Hindus (*gentios*) with their **Naiques**, who are the captains of the footmen and of the horsemen, according to the custom of the land." Barros, Dec. II, v, 8.

" And in this wise about the salaries of the captains as of the **naiques** and *peães*" ('sepoys'). Simão Botelho, p. 72

"The footmen of the land having broken off with their **naiques**, who are their captains...." Gaspar Correia, II, p. 512.

" Among the Hindus, *Rao* means king and **Naique** means a Captain; when these Kings (the Mohammedan sovereigns of the Bahmani Kingdom) take a Hindu into their service, and do not wish to give any very great title, they add the title **Naique** to his name, as Salva Naique, Acem Naique...." Garcia da Orta, Col. X. [ed. Markham, p 72, omits parts of this passage.]

" But he assumed, out of very great humility, the title **Naique** which means captain or leader." Diogo do Couto, Dec. VI, v, 5.

["Captaine Weddell, then allsoe our Comaunder, wrote a lettre by him to the **Naigue**, or King of the country." Peter Mundy, *Travels*, Hak. Soc., Vol. III, pt. 1. p. 72.]

" Its common Anglo-Indian application is to the non-commissioned officer of Sepoys who corresponds to a corporal " *Hobson-Jobson*.

[Hyder Ali of Mysore was proud of being called Hyder Naik; this is interesting because Napoleon's soldiers after the crossing of the bridge of Lodi dubbed their leader '*caporal*' and even afterwards he came to be affectionately known as '*le petit caporal*.']

1 " In this land of Malabar there is another caste of people who are called **Nayres**, and among them are noblemen who have no other duty than to serve in war." Barbosa, p. 235 [Hak. Soc, ed. Dames, Vol. II, p. 38] "These men are called **Nayres** only from the time when they come forth for war." *Idem*, p. 327 [Hak. Soc., Vol. II, p. 45].

"This name **Naire**, although one may be of the same blood, cannot be assumed until such time as one is an armed knight, and as such enjoys the privileges of his rank." João de Barros, Dec. I, ix, 3.

"In this country of Malabar the class of hidalgos is called **Naires**, which means 'Men of War.' Gaspar Correia, I, p. 75.

"The **Naires** who are the Knights." Garcia da Orta, Col. XXII [ed. Markham, p. 193. For a description of Knighthood among the Nairs, see Barbosa, Hak. Soc., Vol. II, p. 45 *et seq.*].

sacred. It is possible that the Naga was at one time the totem of the tribe." Longworth Dames in Barbosa, Vol. II, p. 38, n.

Malabar being the country where the Portuguese first landed, fought many hard fights, and exercised considerable political and commercial influence, it is not to be wondered at that their chroniclers like Barbosa, Barros, Castanheda, and others should have devoted especial attention to this ruling caste in Malabar, and to the usages and customs, dress, bravery, and the knightly organisation of its members.

But, in the 16th and 17th centuries, the Portuguese also used *nair* in the very same sense in which they afterwards used *cornaca* (*q. v.*), viz., that of 'a mahout or elephant-driver', and the reason for this becomes obvious from the quotation below from Pyrard.[1]]

[1] [" When the elephant had to eat, its master (called **Naire** in Malabar, and in the Deccan *Piluane*) said that he had not got a good cauldron to boil the rice. . . ." Garcia da Orta, ed. Markham, p. 180.]

[" Throughout all the Malabar country, and even in the realm of Dealcan or Decan, I have remarked that only the **Nairs** tame and train this animal; and at Calecut I have seen little **Nair** boys caressing little elephants, and leading them hither and thither, and so becoming familiar with them. Only **Nairs** control them, give them their food, and lead them about the town or elsewhere, and none others would dare to come near them Led by his **Nair**, no animal is more docile or tractable. Pyrard, *Voyage*, Hak. Soc., Vol. II, p. 344.]

Não (*adv.*, not). Pid-Engl. *na* (l. us).

In the Portuguese dialects of Asia *nã* is current.

Natal (Christmas). Konk. *natál*.—Mar. *nātál*, *natāḷém*.—Guj., Beng. *nātál*.—Sinh., Tam. *nattal*.—Kan. *natálu*.—Kamb. *bŏn natal* (*bŏn*= feast).—Mal. *natal*.—Tet., Gal. *natál*.[1]

In British India, *Kissmiss*, from the Engl. 'Christmas', and *bará din*, 'great day', are also used.

? Naulo (freight or fare). Konk., Mar. *nôr*. *Norí* (Mar., *adj.*), hired or chartered.—Hindust. *naul*, *nuval*. *Naul ká mál*, cargo.

Shakespear says that the

[1] With regard to *l* cerebral in Marathi, cf. *bhompla* from *abobora* ('pumpkin').

Hindustani terms are of Arabic origin, and Belot says that the Arabic *naulún* comes from Greek.

Navalha (razor; a clasp knife). Malayal. *naváli*.

Negar (to deny). Konk. *negár-zāvuṅk, negár-vachuṅk*; vern. terms *nám mhaṇuṅk, nākāruṅk*.—Gal. *néga*.

Negociar (to trade). Mal. *negociar* (Haex).

Negro (negro). Anglo-Ind. *nigger*.

["It is an old brutality of the Englishman in India to apply this title to the natives....The use originated, however, doubtless in following the old Portuguese use of *negros* for "the blacks," with no malice prepense, without any intended confusion between Africans and Asiatics." Yule in *Hobson-Jobson*. The Portuguese never used the terms *negro* or *preto* ('black') of Asiatics, but only of Africans. Manrique uses the word *negros*, and the editor, Col. Luard, very correctly points out that he never uses it of Indians.[1] But very curiously he uses *cala*[1] (which is the same as Hindust. *kala*, and the equivalent of the Port. *negro*) to distinguish the Indian from the white European.]

Nem (*adv.*, neither). Mal. *nen* (Haex).—Tet. *nem*.

[**Nipa** (the name of a palm found chiefly in Malasia—*Nipa fruticans*; also of a fermented beverage prepared from the sap of the tree). Anglo-Ind. *neep, nipa*.[2]

[1] ["However, I sent the letter to him, and, as soon as he had read it, he (Bartolome Gonsales Tibao) rose from his bed....and getting into a Doli carried by four *negros*, came straight to see me." Manrique, *Travels*, Hak. Soc., Vol. I, p. 92.]

[1] ["They informed him that we were four Franguis, two assiles, and two **calas**, for these are the terms they employ to distinguish the Portuguese or white Christians, and those of the country of a dark or brown complexion." *Idem*, Vol. I, p. 408. *Assiles* means pure-bred Europeans from Hindust. *asali*, 'of pure breed'.]

[2] ["There are two other species of trees, one called **Nipa** and the other *Tuaca*; both provide bread, wine, and vinegar just as the Sagu-palm does..." João de Barros, Dec. III, v, 5, in *Glossario*.]

["They (the Banians) do not drink wine, nor vinegar, nor **ninpa**, nor orraca ('arrack'), nor wine of raisins." Garcia da Orta, Col. xxxiv, ed. Markham, p. 290.]

["The wine of Malacca properly

The word is the Malay *nīpah*. The Portuguese appropriated the term *nipa* to the spirit from this palm (subsequently extending it to arrack prepared from any Asiatic palm), and called the tree itself *nipeira*, on the analogy of *mangueira* ('the mango tree'), *jaqueira* ('the jack-fruit tree'), *pereira* ('the pear or guava tree').

Yule thinks that there can be little doubt that the slang word 'nip', for a small dram of spirits, is adopted from *nipa*. But the *O.E.D.* says that 'nip' is apparently an abbreviation of 'nipperkin', a 'half-pint of ale, a small quantity of spirits, usually less than a glass', and that the connection of 'to nip' with the Dutch and German *nippen*, 'to sip' is evidently accidental.]

Nota (mark, sign). Konk. *nót*; vern. terms *khûṇ*, *chihnén*, *lakheṇ*.—Tet., Gal. *nota*; vern. term *hanôin*.

Noticia (news, knowledge). Konk. *notís* (l. us.): vern. terms *khabar*, *gazāl*. *vārttá*.—Tet., Gal. *notísi*; vern. term *lia*.

Novena (*eccles.*, nine days devotion). Konk. *novén*.—Beng. *novená*.—Tam. *novenei*.—Tel. *novéna*.—Kan. *novénu*.

Número (number). Konk. *numr*, *numbr*; vern. terms

---

speaking is that which is called **Nypa**, obtained from **Nypeiras** or wild palms from marshy tracts." Godinho de Erédia, *Declaraçam de Malaca*, fl. 6, in *Glossario*.]

["Arack is a liquor distilled Severall ways, as Some out of the graine called Rice, another Sort from the Jagaree or Very course Sugar, with Some drugs, another Sort there is that is distilled from **Neep** toddy and that is called **Nipa** de Goa, but the weakest of these is much Stronger than any Wine of the Grape." Bowrey, *The Countries Round the Bay of Bengal 1669 to 1679*, Hak. Soc., p. 77 *seq.*]

["The same water (*Sura* or toddy from the 'Cocus') standing but one houre in the sunne, is very good viniger, and in India they have none other. This Sura beeing distilled, is called Fula, or **Nipe**, and is as excellent aqua vitae, as any is made in Dort (Dordrecht, a town in Holland) of their best rennish wine, but this is of the finest kinde of distillation." Linschoten, *Voyage*, Hak. Soc., Vol. II, p. 48.]

[At *Nerule* (in Goa) is made the best *Arach* or **Nepa** *de Goa*, with which the *English* on this Coast make that enervating Liquor called *Paunch* (which is *Indostan* for Five) from Five Ingredients." Fryer, *East India*, Hak. Soc., Vol. II, p. 28.]

áṅk, saṅkhyá, gaṇ, gaṇti.—? Sinh. *nómare, nommaraya* (perhaps from the English 'number').—? Bug. *nómoro*; probably from the Dutch *nommer.*—Tet., Gal. *númeru*; vern. term *súra.*

O

Obrigação (obligation). Konk. *obrigāsáṁv* (l. us.); vern. terms *kāydó, karm, kartúb.*—Mal. *obrigacion* (Haex), which has the Castilian form.—Tet. *obrigasā̃.*

Obrigado (obliged). Konk. *obrigád.*—Tet. *obrigádu.*

Obrigar (to oblige). Konk. *obrigár-karuṅk*; vern. terms *baḷ karuṅk, oḍhuṅk.*—Tet. *obríga*; vern. terms *hódi, biíti.*

Ocasião (occasion). Konk. *kājáṁv*; vern. term *saṁ-yoga.*—Tet. *okaziā̃*; vern. terms *phátin, léeti.*

Oco (hollow, empty). Sinh. *boku*; probably through the intervention of * *woku.*—Gal. *óku.*

Óculos (pair of spectacles). Konk. *okl*; vern. term *chālís-patr* (l. us. in Goa).—Tet. *ókulu, óku.*

? **Ocupação** (business). Pid.-Engl. *pidgin.* Extensively used in the sense of 'business, office, duty'.

"Probably the Chinese pronunciation of the word *business* (*Pi-tsin*), according to others, of the Portuguese word *ocupação.*" Leland.

Ofender (to offend). Konk. *ophendêr-karuṅk* (l. us.); vern. terms *akmán karuṅk, aprādhuṅk.*—Tet. *ofender*; vern. term *tólok.*

Oferecer (to offer). Konk. *ophereser-karuṅk* (l. us.); vern. terms *divuṅk, bheṭ karuṅk.*—Tet. *ofereser*; vern. term *fó.*

Oficial (*subst.*, official). Konk., Tet., Gal. *ophisyál.*

Ofício (office). Konk., Tam. *ophís.*—Tet., Gal. *ofísiu.*

In Tamil it is employed only in the ecclesiastical sense of 'office for the dead.'

Ola ("a leaf of the palm which we call *olla*", Orta).[1] Anglo-Ind. *ollah.*

---

[1] ["In the Maldiva Islands they build a kind of vessel which with its nails, its sails, and its cordage is all made of the palm (coco); with its fronds (which they call **olla** in Malabar) they cover houses and ships." Garcia da Orta, Col. xvii, ed. Markham, p. 140. Markham entirely misreads and misinterprets the passage; he reads *dos ramos* ('from

The word is of Dravidian origin, Malayal. *óla*, Tam. *ólei*, and does not only mean 'a palm-leaf,'[1] but also 'the leaf prepared for writing on,'[2] and 'a written order on the leaf'[3].

[Besides the above meanings there is one in which the term is used by Portuguese chroniclers, viz., that of gold or copper-plate, in imitation of the palm-leaf strip, with an inscription.[1]

Barbosa gives a very full account of the royal scribes of Calicut and of their manner of writing on palm-leaves[2].]

---

the branches') as *dois ramos* ('two branches') and arrives at a version which is meaningless.]

1 "All the rest of the town of (Calicut) was built of wood and thatched with a kind of palm-leaf which they call **ola**". João de Barros, Dec. I, iv, 7.

["It (the Town of Bombaim) is a full Mile in length, the Houses are low, and Thatched with **Oleas** of the Cocoo-Trees." Fryer, *East India*, Vol. I, p. 172.]

["The greater number of houses in the city (of Arakan) are made of bambus, which....are strong canes often of great thickness. These cane houses are covered in with palm-leaves, intertwined, known as **Olas**". (The palm referred to here is the *Nipa fruticans*, and not the coco-nut palm as in the preceding quotations.) Manrique, *Travels*, Hak. Soc., Vol. I, 208.]

2 "They are accustomed to prepare their **olas**, which are palm-leaves, which they use for writing-paper, scratching it with an iron point." Gaspar Correia, I, p. 212.

3 "He sent his **ola** of thanks to the inhabitants of São Thomé". Gaspar Correia, IV, p. 132.

"He wrote an **ola** to Modeliar, in which he informed him that he was in the camp, as he had said he would be" João Ribeiro, *Fatalidade hist.*, Bk. II, ch. x.

[In the last two quotations *ola* is used in the sense of 'a letter.']

1 ["All this he ordered to be inscribed on **ollas** of copper." Fr. António de Gouveia, *Jornada do Arcebispo* (1602), fls. 4 and 5, in *Glossario*.]

["He sent a Comptroller of the Revenue, the most important personage in his Kingdom, with fifty horses, and the **ola** of gold, which is a thin sheet like a thin plate of gold." *Conquista de Pegu* (1617), ch. 13, in *Glossario*.]

2 ["The King of Calicut continually keeps a multitude of writers in his palace who sit in a corner far from him; they write upon a raised platform...They write on long and stiff palm-leaves, with an iron style without ink; they make their letters in incised strokes, like ours, and the straight lines as we do. Each of these men carries with him whithersoever he goes a sheaf of these written leaves under his arm, and the iron style in his hand...." Hak. Soc., ed. Dames, Vol. II, p. 18. This is how writing on palm-leaves is still done in Malabar

Óleo (oil). Konk. *ól* (especially used of Holy Oil or of medicinal oils); vern. terms *tel*; *pavitr tel*; *oktí tel.*—Beng. *ól*, Holy Oil.

Onça (ounce). Konk. *oṁs.*—Jap. *onsu*; perhaps from the English 'ounce'.

Opa (long loose robe). Konk. *óp.*—Beng. *opá.*—Tam., Tet., Gal. *ópa.*[1]

and in Ceylon, where even to-day, when certain important documents have to be written, the *Ola* or palm-leaf is preferred to paper, in view of the former's durability and the indelible nature of the writing on it.]

["The books of the Singhalese are formed to-day, as they have been for ages past, of **olas** or strips taken from the young leaves of the Talpat palm, cut before they have acquired the dark shade and strong texture which belong to the full grown frond." Tennent, *Ceylon* I, p. 512.]

["Caps, fans, and umbrellas are all provided from the same inexhaustible source (the palmyra palm), and strips of the finer leaves steeped in milk to render them elastic, and smoothed by pressure so as to enable them to be written on with a stile, serve for their books and correspondence; and are kept, duly stamped, at the cutcheries to be used instead of parchment for deeds and legal documents." *Idem*, Vol. II, p. 527.]

1 "He ordered big **opas** to be made from rich brocades." Diogo do Couto, Dec. VII, i, 11.

Oração (prayer). Konk. *orãsáṁv*; vern. terms *māgṇeṁ*, *prārthan.*—Tet., Gal. *orasã.*—Jap. *orashyo*, from Latin *oratio*, according to Dr. Murakámi.

Ordem (order). Konk. *ord*; vern. terms *niróp*, *hukum*, *pharmaṇ*; *kram*, *mānḍāvaḷ.*—Mal. *órdi*, *úrdi*, *rúdi*, | *ródi.* |—Jav. *úrdi.*—Bug. *ródi.*—Tet. *órdi.*

Órgão (organ, in the sense of 'musical instrument'). Konk. *orgáṁ*; *org* (more us.). —Mar. *org*, *ork.*—Hindust. *argan*, *arghanúm.*—Beng., Tam. *orgán.*—Sinh. *orgalaya*, *orgale.* —Mal. *organ*, *orgam*, *organon.* —Tet., Gal. *órgão.*—Jap. *orogan.*—Ar. *arganún*, *argan*, *organ*, *orgon.*[1]

Shakespear derives the Hindustani vocables from Greek, through Arabic.

Ourives (goldsmith). Mal. *orivis* (Haex); vern. term

1 "He was carrying in a skiff some **orgãos** on which they were playing." Castanheda, I, p. 91.

"With all that was necessary they came well furnished from the Kingdom (of Portugal), with **orgãos** and a beautiful picture of Our Lady of Piety." Gaspar Correia, I, p. 687.

pande-mas, lit., 'craftsman of gold'.

[**Ouvidor** (lit., an auditor; one hearing cases, a magistrate). Anglo-Ind. *ovidore.*[1]

Whitworth (*Anglo-Indian Dictionary*) says that 'ovidor' is "the title of a magistrate under the Portuguese government of Bassein." This is but a part statement of a fact, for the Portuguese had *ouvidores* not only in Bassein but in all their important settlements in the East.]

P

Paciência (patience). Konk. *pasyeṁs* (l. us.); vern. terms are *sosṇáy, sosṇikáy, usarpat.*—Tet. *pasiénsi.*

Padeiro (baker). Konk. *padêr*; vern. term *unḍekár* (l. us.). *Pader-kháṇ*, bakery.—Guj. *pader*, in *pader-khánuṁ*. *Khán* and *khánuṁ* are from Hindust. *khāná*, 'establishment, workshop'. See *pão.*

In Konkani at times *pharn* or *kharn*, from the Portuguese *forno* ('oven'), are used for 'a bakery'.

Padre (in the sense of 'priest, clergyman, missionary, parish priest, pastor') Konk., Mar., Guj., Hindi Hindust., Beng., Khas. *pādrí*—*Pādrīpaṇ* (Konk.), the state or condition of a priest.—Sinh *pádiri, pádeli* (followed by the usual *unnánse*, 'reverend').—Tam., Malayal. *pádiri; pādriyár* (honorific).—Tel. *pádiri.*—Kan. *pádri, pádari.*—Tul *pádri, pádre.*—Anglo-Ind *padre, padri* (especially 'Catholic priest').—Siam. *bāt.*[1]—Mal., Sund., Tet., Gal. *pádri.*—Pid.-Engl., Chin. *pa-ti-li, pa-te-le.*—Jap. *báteren.*[2]

The clergy: *pādri-lok.* Konk., Mar., Guj.; *pādri-log*, Hindi; *pādrí-lok, pādrí-log*, Hindust.; *pâdilivare*, Sinh.;

---

1 ["After they had asked us questions of one sort and another, the captain ordered the Merigne to take us to the **Oydor** *de Cidade* (City Magistrate) as being robbers and his proper game." Pyrard, *Voyage*, Hak. Soc., Vol. I, 428.]

["On this the **Oyodores** and most of the Councillors assembled." Manrique, *Travels*, Hak. Soc., Vol. II, p. 40.]

1 For *b* in place of *p*, cf. *bāb*=Sansk. *pāpa*, ('sin'); for *t* in place of *dr*, cf. *intha*=Sansk. *indra* ('the god Indra').

2 *P* initial is little used in Japanese. The dissolution of the compound consonant is the rule. Cf. *vidro.*

pádri-gaḷu, Kan.; *pádreḷu*, Tul. *Lok* or *log* is from the Sansk. *loka*, 'persons, people.'

Pradhán pādri, a prelate. *Rum ká pradhán pādri*, the Roman Pontiff, the Pope. Hindi.

Baṛá-pādrí (lit. 'the great padre'), Father Superior.[1] *Sardár-pādrí*, the bishop. *Láṭ-pādrí* (also us. in Hindi and Khassi), bishop, archbishop. *Láṭ* is the corruption of the English 'lord'. *Rum ká sardár pādri*, the Pope. *Pādri ká muhalla*, a parish. *Sardár pādri ká taaluga*, a diocese. *Sardár pādri ká maqam*, Cathedral Church. Hindustani.

In Madras the name *Padrigudi* is met with, and in Bengal *Padriśibpur*, names of missions belonging to the Portuguese *Padroado*[1] [*q.v.*].

1 ["**Padre Giu**" (which corresponds to Reverend Sir in our language), "do you wish that we should proceed more severely against the Siguidar?" Manrique, *Travels*, Hak. Soc., Vol. I, p 425. *Padre Giu*=*Pādre-ji*, the affix *ji* being honorific. Siguidar=Pers *shiqdar*, a revenue officer]

["The Captain-major replied that among infidels it was essential that such demonstrations should be made in order that they should appreciate the position held by members of our Religious orders and by Priests and respect them. The more so in this case, since the news that the **boro Padre**, which is to say great Priest, was arriving had spread throughout the whole country. This name was applied by the pagans to the Priors of our Residencies in those Principalities, to whom the Bishops of San Tomé or Meliapor usually delegated the power to inspect and generally officiate in the territory lying within their spiritual jurisdiction." *Idem*, Vol. I, p. 162. *Boro padre*=Hindust. *Baḍa Padre*, 'Great Father.']

1 "**Padri** is used by all classes for a Christian Minister." Candy.

"And it is sometimes applied also to Brahmans or other religious persons." Whitworth.

"I have already mentioned in the *Journal of Rom. Phil.* 6 xiii, 510, that this word (*padre*) is also applied to protestant clergymen and even also to heathen priests." Schuchardt, *Kreol. Stud.*, ix.

"In Malay the word *padri* signifies a Catholic priest. However, in 1820 in the island of Sumatra, during an insurrection against the Dutch which has grown into a desperate struggle for more than twenty years, the chiefs, priests, and Mohammedan pilgrims, and the partisans of a very fanatical religious sect, have assumed the name *padri*, and from this time this name has been given to all the insurgents" Heyligers.

A Hindu landowner of Pernêm (Goa), in the course of conversation carried on in Konkani, once mentioned to me that his son, whom he introduced to me, was being taught Marathi by a

[Yule points out a peculiarity in the use of the term 'padre' in India among the Portuguese. It was a singularity of their practice at Goa, as noticed by P. della Valle,[1] to give the title of *Padre* to secular priests, whereas in Italy this was reserved to the *religiosi* or regulars. In Portugal itself the use was the same as in Italy; but, as the first ecclesiastics who went to India were monks, the name apparently became general among the Portuguese there for all priests.

Thomas Bowrey (*A Geographical Account of Countries Round the Bay of Bengal 1669 to 1679*) employs all three names: Priests, 'Patrees', and Fathers.[1]

Though the term was originally introduced by the Portuguese to describe their priests, it still does duty in India for a chaplain or minister of any Christian denomination.]

---

padre mestre ('a priest-teacher'). When I expressed my surprise at this, I was told that the boy's teacher was a layman but he was referred to deferentially by the same style and title by which the priest who taught in the Government school of the place was addressed.

["Many families of Braminys dayly leaving yᵉ Portuguezes territories and repaire hither (Bombay) frighted by yᵉ **Padrees**, who upon yᵉ death of any person forces all his children to be Christians." Forrest, *Selections* (Home Series), Vol. I, p. 120.]

[1] ["The *Portugals* call Secular Priests, Fathers, as we do the Religious, or Monasticks." Della Valle, *Travels*, Hak. Soc., Vol. I, p. 142.]

["I went into yᵉ City of Diarbikeer to visit yᵉ French **Padres** of yᵉ Order of St. Francis, who received and entertained me with great civility and respect." Hedges, *Diary*, Hak. Soc., Vol. I, p. 232.]

[1] ["Many of them (Parjars= (Pariahs) of Choromandel) nowadays are yearly converted to the Christian faith by the Portugal Priests and Jesuites." p. 41.]

["I have Seen many of the like Sort in Other places of India and Persia; but, however, the Portugal **Patrees**, whose dependence is meerly upon telling faire tales..." p. 50.]

["The Portugueses haveinge collected a good Summ of moneys (in Bengala) to the End they might build a very large and decent Church, they now make preparation to begin the worke. Haveinge provided Stone, brick, lime, timber, they pull downe the Old one, and begin the new foundation, but ere one fourth finished the Moors, by Order of theire Governour stopped the worke, commandinge the workmen Upon paine of imprisonment not to proceede, to the great griefe of the Fathers, and alias." p. 194]

Padrinho (god-father). Konk. *padan*, *padin*.—Beng. *pādú*.

Padroado ('the right of patronage called in English 'Advowson' granted by the Popes to Portuguese sovereigns over Roman Catholic Churches in the East, and especially over those in India). Konk. *pādrovád*.—Beng. *pādrovādú*. —Tam. *padrovádu*.—[Anglo-Ind. *padroado*.[1]]

[The frequent and tense misunderstandings and disputes between those Roman Catholics in Bombay, Calcutta, Madras, and other places in the East, who owed obedience to Bishops nominated by the Portuguese sovereign, called the Padroadists, and those others, who were under the spiritual jurisdiction of prelates appointed by the Congregation of the Propagation of the Faith in Rome, called the Propagandists, especially in the last two decades of the 19th century, were responsible for the introduction of this term into Anglo-Indian vocabulary. The 'Padroado Question' was then a familiar topic of conversation and of controversy in newspapers and pamphlets. The Portuguese word is derived from the Lat. *patrocinium*, 'patronage'.]

[**Padroadista** (a term coined in Indo-Portuguese to denote one who is under the spiritual jurisdiction of Bishops nominated by Portugal, or one who defends the right of the Portuguese nation to ecclesiastical patronage in British India). Konk. *pādroādist*.—Anglo-Ind. *padroadist*.[1]

A parallel formation was that of the term *Propagandista* (*q.v.*).]

Paga ('salary, payment'). **Pagar** ('to pay', used as a

1 ["With the abolition of the **Padroado** and the enjoyment of freedom from State trammels the Catholic Church will prosper in India..." *The Padroado Question* (1885), Examiner Press, Bombay.]

1 ["When all this is done, let India be divided into as many dioceses as will be required, let their endowment be legally secured....; then the new clergy may become the proprietors of all the Colleges, Schools, Churches... and in fact of all that is now held and done by the present clergy under the Vicars Apostolic in British India. That will then be the beginning of the realization of the loftiest dreams of the most eager **Padroadists**." *The Padroado Question*.]

subst.). Konk. *pág.*—Mar. *pág*, *pagár*. *Pagārí*, stipendiary. *Baiṭhápagár*, superannuation, pension.—Guj. *pagár*. *Pagár āpvó*, *pagár karvó*, to pay. *Pagár āpvó joyó*, payable, *Pagár lenár*. one receiving salary.—Hindust. *pagár* (us. only in the Bombay Presidency; in other parts, *talab*).—Sindh. *pagháru*. —? Kan. *pagadi*, tax, customs-duty.—Tul. *pagaru* (also us. in the sense of 'hire, rent').—Anglo-Ind. (in Bombay) *pagár*.[1] The Neo-Aryan terms are *muśaró*, *mazurí*, *vetan*, *phārīkpaṇ*, *talab*.

In Marathi there is another vocable, *pág* (fem.), which signifies "the duty paid by a vessel when it leaves port." I believe that it is derived from the Portuguese word, though Molesworth does not say so.

Página (page of a book). Konk. *pázn*, *paséṁ* (through a middle form **pásn*).—Guj. *pásuṁ*.—Sindh. *pāsô*.—The Neo-Aryan terms are *pán*, *puṭṭó*, *varakh*, *patr*, *patró*.

Pagode (in the sense of 'idol, temple, coin'[1]). Anglo-Ind. *pagoda*.—Indo-Fr. *pagode*, *pagodin*.—Tet. *pagódi*.[2]

---

[1] "This word is commonly adopted in the vernaculars for monthly salary." Whitworth.

[1] [The order in the original is "temple, idol, coin", which has been altered as above to fit in with the results of the author's latter investigations. A similar alteration was inevitable in the order and arrangement of the citations.]

[2] 1.—Pagode meaning 'an idol'.

[1525.—"And after the Brahmins had completed their ceremonies and sacrifices, they told the King that it was time for him to advance for the **Pagodes** had given him a sign of victory." *Chronica de Bisnaga*, p. 29.]

(When King Crisnarao was astonished to find that all the work done by day in making a water tank was undone at night) "he ordered all his wise men and wizards to be called together, and asked them what they thought of the phenomenon; whereupon they said that their **pagodes** were not pleased with the work......" *Idem*, p 56.]

["In this House of Victory the King has a house built of cloth with its door made fast in which he keeps a **pagode**, an idol...." *Idem*, p. 102.]

"Very often the devil is in them, but they regard him as one of their gods, or **pagodes**, for this is the name they give him" Castanheda. Bk. I, ch. 14.

"Saying that they all had offended their **pagodes** in not having offered sacrifices and gifts which had been promised to them." João de Barros, Dec. I, iv, 18.

"Swearing besides by his **pagodes**, which are their idols and which they

Half a dozen etymologies are suggested for this word, among them the Persian *but-kadah*, 'idol temple', and the

---

worship for gods." Gaspar Correia, I, p. 119.

["And they have their idols standing in the woods, which they call **Pagodes.**" Ralph Fitch, in *Early Travels in India* (1921), O.U.P., p. 15.]

["And the red sandal is also used on **pagodes** or idols" Orta, Col. xlix; ed. Markham, p 394. Markham's rendering is faulty, because he ignores entirely 'or idols', which gives *pagodes* the meaning of 'temples'.]

["It is a most grave offence against Divine Majesty....to light lamps before **pagodes**, or in places dedicated to them, to anoint them with oil, sandal, and other things, to place flowers on them...." *The First Provincial Council* (1567), in *Archivo Port. Or.*, Fasc. IV, p. 13.]

"Especially with the Bonzes, who had the house full of images of **pagodes.**" P. Sabatino de Ursis (1611), *Matheus Ricci.*

["Sevagee Raja....has vowed to his **pagod,** never to sheath his sword till he has reached Dilly, and shutt up Orangsha in it." Hedges, *Diary*, Hak. Soc., Vol. II, p. cccxxvi.]

B.—Pagode meaning 'a temple'.

"In their [of the Nairs of Malabar] temples, which are called **Pagodes,** they perform many enchantments and witchcrafts." Duarte Barbosa, *Livro*, p. 333 [ed. Dames, Vol. II, p. 57].

["In this city of Goa, and all over India, there are an infinity of ancient buildings of the Gentiles, and in a small island near this, called Dinari (Divari), the Portuguese, in order to build the city, have destroyed an ancient temple called **Pagode,** which was built with marvellous art, and with ancient figures wrought to the greatest perfection in a certain black stone, some of which remain standing, ruined and shattered, because these Portuguese care nothing about them. If I can come by one of these shattered images I will send it to your Lordship, that you may perceive how much in old times sculpture was esteemed in every part of the world." *Letter of Andrea Corsali to Giuliano de Medici*, in *Ramusio*, I. f. 177, cit. in *Hobson-Jobson.*]

[These **pagodes** are houses in which they conduct their worship, and have their idols, which are of different forms, viz., of men, women, bulls, monkeys, and there are others in which there is nothing besides a round stone which they adore." *Chronica de Bisnaga*, p. 84.]

"It is a **pagode** which is the house of prayers to their idols, which has been set apart for this purpose." Castanheda, *Historia*, I, 14.

"The buildings of their **pagodes,** which are their churches." Gaspar Correia, *Lendas*, I, p. 181.

"All that **pagode** in which we notice many wonderful things." Diogo do Couto, Dec., IV, iv. 7.

"On the other side (of Adam's Peak) is the **Pagode,** which is their Church." *Fatalidade hist.*, Bk. 1, ch. 23

["A **Pagode** or China Church. Wee went to a **Pagode** of theirs, a reasonable handsome building and well

Sanskrit, *bhagavatī*, 'a goddess', as especially applied to Durgā or Kālī. The latter has more reasons in its favour.

tyled." Peter Mundy, *Travels*, Hak. Soc., Vol. III, pt. i, p. 190.]

["At the present time they (the walls of Chitor city) are so dilapidated and ruinous that it is only here and there that one sees fragments of its past grandeur, for, besides other buildings, there still stand sumptuous and most magnificent **Pagodas** or Temples to Pagan and false Gods, as well as many other structures and private houses." Manrique, *Travels*, Hak. Soc., Vol. II, p. 284.]

["Overagainst where she (a great Junk of the Moors) rode, a fair **Pagod** or Temple of the *Gentus*, beleaguer'd with a Grove of Trees.... cast a Lustre bright and splendid, the Sun reverberating against its refulgent Spire, which was crowned with a Globe white as Alabaster, of the same tincture with the whole." Fryer, *East India*, Hak. Soc., Vol. I, p. 74.]

["It seems that some yeares if not ages since, I suppose about the time of the Moores first Conquests, they were severe against the Idolatry of the Hindooes, and sett a Poll Tax upon all the Family of Indians, which as I said made many of them turne Moores, nor was any **Pagod** or Idolatrous Temple of the Hindooes suffered to stand except the Hindooes at their owne charge made a place for Prayer for the Mahometans adjoyning to the very walls of it, and if they did soe, then they might build new **Pagods**, but since those times, especially during the Raignes of Jangeer and Sha-Jehaun, the Hindooes were not at all molested in the exercise of their Religion, but were in ffavour and Preferred to the great and Meane offices of the Kingdome soe well as the Moors" *Letter from Surat*, in Hedges, *Diary*, Hak. Soc., Vol. II, p. cccix.]

["The Party soe misdemeaneinge him selfe [by losing his caste], whether he be rich or poore, (Except he intends to live in perpetuall ignominie) must take his travaile to the great **Pagod** Jno. Gernact [Jagannāth]." Bowrey, *The Countries*, etc., Hak. Soc., p. 12 This temple of Jagannāth was also known as the 'White Pagoda'.]

"Decr. 23d. We sailed in sight of the **Black Pagoda** and the **White Pagoda**. The latter is that place called Juggernat, to which the Hindues from all parts of India come on pilgrimages". Streynsham Master's *Journal*, in Hedges, *Diary*, Hak. Soc., Vol. II, p. ccxxxviii.

C.—Pagode meaning 'a coin.'

"Which coins, the **Pagodes**, were formerly called *pardáo d'ouro* (see under *pardao*) and each was worth 360 reis" Francisco Pais, *Tombo Geral*, fol. 84.

"With a sum of gold **pagodes**, a coin of the upper country (Balagate), each of which is worth 500 *reis*" Diogo do Couto, Dec., VII, i, 11.

"There were many chetties, who are merchants, who spoke of candys of gold **pagodes**, which is a coin resembling lupine-seed, which has the figure of the **pagode** of these gentiles, and each one of which is worth more than four hundred reis." Diogo do

The word *bhagavatī*, in its passage to the Dravidian languages, ought in the mouth of the people to be transformed into *pagódi*, in accordance with phonetic laws. In fact, this form *pogŏdi* or *pavódi* is used in Coorg, with reference to Kālī, the goddess very popular in Southern India. Gundert mentions the Malayal. *pagódi* as the name of the temple of Durgā, from which he derives the Portuguese *pagode*; but Burnell maintains the contrary, and regards the Portuguese word as the original of the Malayalam. The name of the divinity would easily be extended to the temple, if not by the indigenous population, at any rate by foreigners, Arabs or Portuguese. There is, for instance, the term *milagre* ('miracle'), which the Marathas of the Konkan and the Mussulmans of South India sometimes use in referring to

---

Couto, *Dial. do Soldado Pratico*, p. 156.

["The Coin current here (Mechlapatan) is a **Pagod**, 8*s*.; *Dollar*, 4*s*. 6*d*.; *Rupee*, 2*s* 3*d*.; *Cash*, 1*d*.¼; a *Cash* ¼." Fryer, *East India*, Vol. I, p. 96. Crooke in a note to this word says that accounts at Madras, down to 1815, were kept in pagodas, fanams, and cash. 80 cash=1 single fanam; 42 single fanams=1 pagoda. In the above named year the rupee was made the standard coin.]

["Noe man is admitted to marry (in Choromandel), Unlesse he can purchase moneys to the Value of 20 or 25 **pagods**, a Coine very Current here, which moneys the Male must bestowe upon the Parents of her he purposeth to be his Wife, to gaine their consent." Bowrey, *The Countries* etc., Hak. Soc., p. 30.]

["*Currant Coynes in this Kingdome*" Fort St. Georg's, vizt.

	lb. s. d.
New **Pagods** here coyned passe att the Kingdome over all the Rate of ..	00 08 00
Pullicatt	
The **Pagod** Valueth	00 08 06
Golcondah	
The Old **Pagod** Valueth	00 12 00
Porto Novo and Trincombar	
The **Pagod** there Coyned Valueth but	00 06 00

Idem, pp 114 and 115.]

["You say likewise you think it not reasonable, that you should pay more money then was paid to the Black Merchants, and that at Nine Shillings a **Pagoda**....What sort of Idiot must that be to Lend you a **Pagoda** at Nine Shillings, when at Bottomry at that time could have had Thirteen and Sixpence, and Diamonds Security? or to have bought them, would have made from Sixteen Shillings to Twenty Shillings a **Pagoda**?" *From* T. Pitt *and* Council *of* Fort St. George *to the Court of Directors* etc., in Hedges, *Diary*, Hak. Soc., Vol. III, p. civ.]

an image of the Virgin Mary, and, at other times, a Catholic Church, because in those parts of the country there are many churches dedicated to Our Lady of Miracles. The third meaning, in which the word is used, is that of money; the origin of this, in the speech of the Portuguese, is in all probability due to the image of *bhagavatī* or other divinity which was stamped on one side of the coin. See *Hobson-Jobson*, and Gonçalves Viana, *Apostilas*.

In Portugal, *pagode* is more used in the figurative sense of 'feasting and revelry'; but such a meaning is unknown in India. The natural explanation for this appears to be that this meaning was suggested by the feasts of the pagodas which are very pompous, and at times extravagant, especially to the eyes of a foreigner.[1]

[The author has dealt at great length with the origin of this word in his *Contribuições*, etc., (1916), and his *Glossario*, Vol. ii (1921). As his investigations therein, subsequent to those set forth in this work, throw new light on the origin of this intricate word, we present a résumé of them here. For good and various reasons he rejects the suggestions which would give it a Chinese, Portuguese or Persian origin, and definitely states that it appears to him that the original of *pagode* is the Sansk. term *Bhagavatī*, 'Durgā or Kālī'. *Bhagavatī* in the process of its transition from Sansk. to the Dravidian languages, in accordance with the usual phonetic laws, must become *Pagawadi* or *Pagôdi*. With regard to the initial *p* for *bh*, we have Tamil *pāṇḍam* for the Sansk. *bhaṇḍam*, 'an earthen vessel'; *Pirama* for Sansk. *Brahma*; *baspam* or *parpam* for Sansk. *bhasman*, 'ashes'. With regard to *d* for *t* intervocalic, we have in Malayalam: *pradi* ('copy') for Sansk. *prati*, *sammadi* ('consensus') for Sansk. *sammati*, *apakaḍam* ('accident') for Sansk. *apaghāta*. It remains to justify the change of—*ava* to *o*. In

1 "The boys used to laugh whilst recounting the **pāgode** held last evening at the house of a half-caste maiden." *Garcia da Orta e o seu tempo*, p. 177. [For earlier references to the word, in this acceptation, see *Glossario*.]

this connection it must be noted that, whether the indigenous form was *pagàwadi* or *pagudi*, they would both sound to the ears of a stranger as *pagôdi*. The Indian *v* is a semi-vowel, equivalent to the English *w*, which with the short *ă* preceding it would sound like *au* (as happens generally in Konkani) and would absorb the vowel following. Of such cases we have instances in the Tamil *Paramechchuran*, from Sansk. *Parameçvara*, 'the Supreme Lord'; in the Neo-Aryan *sona* or *sonem̐*, from Sansk. *suvarṇa*, 'gold', in Dravidian *honā* or *hūn*. Moreover, the form *pagodi* exists in some of the Dravidian regions. In Coorg the people, according to Kittel, give to Kālī the title *Pagŏdi* or *Pavodi*. Gundert mentions in his dictionary the Malayal. *pagôdi* (but writes it *pakôti*, according to the character of the language) as a synonym of *Bhagavatī* Durgā, from which he derives the Port. *pagode*. It is of no use to allege that *bhagavat* or *bhagavatī* is in no Indian language the name of 'a temple', and that it is in this sense of a temple that '*pagode*' is generally employed, for it is not necessary to suppose, as Yule and other etymologists do, that the acceptation of 'temple' is the first and the most important one.

Historically, there is nothing to justify the view that in Portuguese the meaning of 'temple' must have priority over other acceptations. It is true that Barbosa and Corselli in 1516 use it in that sense, but there is very good reason for this. The Portuguese had the word *idolo* to denote 'the images of pagan cult'; it was a word very much used in that age. In an age of great religious fervour, such as the sixteenth century was, it would have been regarded as profanation to speak of the *casas dos falsos deuses* ('houses of the false gods') as temples or churches. Hence they were put to the necessity of employing *pagode* in that sense. In *Chronica de Bisnaga* (1525–1535) *pagode*, though used frequently in the sense of 'a temple', is employed five times in that of 'an idol' and not once as the name of 'a gold coin'. Duarte Barbosa who, according to Gaspar Correia, spoke 'the Malabar language' better than a native, says that only the prayer houses of a special caste, the *Cuiavens*, (supposed by Longworth Dames to be the potter caste called *Kusavan*) were called *pagodes*. The reason for this is, they were dedicated to Bhagavatī, which name, in the mouth of the people, would become *Pagôdi*, and this is precisely the meaning that Gundert gives to *Pagôdi* in Malayalam. From all this it is evident that the Portuguese took over the word as well as its two-fold acceptation from Dravidian sources and, in all probability, extended the use of the term to the gold coin *varāha* or *hūn*, because it bore on it the figure of Bhagavatī or some other divinity.

According to Sir Walter Elliot, "the village divinity throughout the south is always a form of *Durga*, or, as she is commonly called, simply '*Devi*' (or *Bhagavati*, 'the goddess') ....In like manner a figure of *Durga* is found on most of the gold *Huns*, (*i.e.*, *pagoda* coins) current in the Dakhan, and a foreigner inquiring what such a coin was, or rather what was stamped upon it, would be told it was 'the goddess', *i.e.*, it was '*Bhagavati*'." (*Hobson-Jobson*).

The Jesuit, Fr. Francisco de Sousa, the author of *Oriente Conquistado* (1710), who had spent years in India and who, therefore, can be trusted to know what he is speaking about, says: "*Pagode* among the Portuguese in India signifies an idol, and a temple, and also a certain gold coin." The order in which he mentions these acceptations point to the chronological development or evolution of the various meanings of the word, all of which hinge on the primary one of 'idol'.

Though the Portuguese used *pagode* at first to denote a Hindu temple, in course of time, the term came to be used also of Buddhist and Mohammedan places of worship. Peter Mundy (*Travels*, 1608-1667) uses the term of a Chinese-Buddhist temple, which is otherwise generally called by Portuguese and other European travellers 'varela' (from Malay *barhāla*, 'an idol'), and Faria-y-Sousa (1674) speaks of a 'Pagoda of Mecca' (*Hobson-Jobson*). There is a similar confusion in Barbosa in one passage in which he calls a Hindu shrine a *mesquita*, i.e., 'a mosque.' (See under *mesquita*.)

The **pagode** or **pagode de ouro** ('gold pagode') as it was sometimes called, was current in S. India, and was originally equal to about 360 to 400 *reis*, but later on was worth as much as 12 *xerafins* (*q.v.*) or 1,200 *reis*. The quotations above from Bowrey and Hedges will show how the rate of exchange of this coin kept on constantly shifting.

Before concluding, it would be useful to review the different etymologies of 'pagoda' that have been offered and to give reasons for their rejection.

1. The Chinese words *pao-t'ah*, 'precious pile', and *poh-kuh-t'ah*, 'white-bones-pile'. This does not find favour at present with scholars of Chinese language and culture. Yule very properly says that anything can be made out of Chinese monosyllables in the way of etymology.

2. The Portuguese *pagão* ('pagan'), which Yule thinks may have helped to facilitate the Portuguese adoption of *pagoda*. But *pagão* into *pagode* would be a very singular mutilation of the Portuguese word in order to describe objects so very different. Again, the term *pagão* occurs but rarely among the early Portuguese writers, who use the word *gentio* (*q.v.*) in this sense.

3. The Sinhalese *dágoba*, 'Buddhist sanctuary'. It was believed that the transposition of the syllables of this word gives *pagode*; this is not so, it gives *bágoda*. But *dágoba* was not in use in Ceylon in the time of Duarte Barbosa (1516), nor had the Portuguese then any intimate contact with that island. The Portuguese first came to be acquainted with Buddhist temples and monasteries in Indo-China which they then called *bralas* (from the Malay *barhāla*), which afterwards became corrupted into *varelas*.

4. The Persian *but-kadah*, 'idol-temple', proposed by

Ovington, Littré, Devic, and Burnell. But phonetically *but-kadah* or *but-kedah* differs a great deal from *pagode*, and semantically does not offer reasons for all the acceptations of the word. Moreover, it is necessary to assume that the Portuguese received the term from the Mohammedans. See Dalgado, *Contribuicões*, etc., p. 161 *seqq.*]

Pai (father). Konk. *páy*, the appellation generally used of a father among the Christians of Goa (*bābá*, in Kanara; *dādá* among the Hindus); vern. term *báp*; *bāpúy*.—Kamb. *pay*. Used in the sense of 'Pope', among the Christians. —Mal. *pay* (Haex): vern. term *bápa*.

In Konkani: *páy-tiv* (=*pai-tio* of the Port. dialects), paternal uncle, uncle on the father's side; *vhaḍló-páy* (lit. 'big father'), the paternal uncle who is older than the father; *dhākṭó-páy* (lit. 'small father'), the youngest uncle. See *mãe*.

Palanca (a defence made of large stakes). L.-Hindust. *palang*.

[Vieyra also mentions *palanco*, and gives as its meaning "(in a ship) one of the halliards so called." Might this word not be the original of the L.-Hindust. term?]

Palangana (a flat dish) Konk. *palgaṇ*.—Sinh. *palangana*, *palangánama*, a dish.—Tam. *píngān*, porcelain, a dish.—Malayal. *piññánam* *Chinappiññánam*, porcelain.—Tel. *pingáni*, *pīngáni*.—Kan. *pingáni*.—Tul. *pingana*, *pingani*, *pingáni*, porcelain.—Mal. *pingan*, *pinggan*, a dish.—Ach., Batt., Sund., Jav., Day. Batav., Tagalo, Bisaio (the last two languages belong to the Philippine Islands and are of the Polynesian family), *pingan* —Bal. *palúngan*; *pingan*, a hollow dish, a tureen.—Bug. *pínjan*.—Mac. *pinjen*.[1]

Pingaṇ or *pinjan* are perhaps not derived from *palangana*. Shakespear derives the Hindust. *finján*, 'a porcelain plate,' from the Persian.

Palanquim ('a litter carried on a pole'). Anglo-Ind. *palanquin*, *palankeen*.—

[1] "Another pallangnana made in a different style." A. Tomás Pires, *Materiaes*, etc., in *Jour. Geo. Soc. Lisb.*, 16th series, p. 716.

Indo-Fr. *palanquin*.—? Mal., Jav. *pelánki*, *plánki*; vern. terms *kremun*, *tandu*, *joli*, *usongon*.—Malag. *palankina*.[1]

The Neo-Aryan word is *pālkí*, from the Sanskrit *paryaṅka*. Yule and Burnell say that the nasal of the second syllable of *palanquim* may be explained by the influence of the Spanish *palanca*. But Malayalam has *pallankí*, which Gundert men-

---

1 "He takes twenty five or thirty women from those who are his greatest favourites and each one of them goes in her own **pallamque** which are like *andas* ('litters')." *Chronica de Bisnaga* (1535), p. 61.

"The King of Bisnagá also comes to this feast, and comes with the greatest possible pomp, bringing with him as many as ten thousand horse, and two hundred thousand foot-soldiers, and hundred, and two hundred women attached to his person, who come in **palanquyns** and litters locked with key, in a way that they might not be seen by any one, but that they might see everything through a fine silver net...." Gasper Correia, *Lendas*, IV, p. 302. [The page number in the original is 460 which is a slip.]

"No person of whatever quality or condition shall go in a **palanquim** without my express permission, except those who are more than seventy years old." *Letter Patent of the Viceroy Mathias de Albuquerque*, dated 22 June, 1591.

"The Governor used to go in a **palanquim**." Diogo do Couto, Dec. VI, v, 10. "He maintained that no public woman should go in a **palanquim** unless it was uncovered." *Id.*, Dec. VII, i, 12.

["November 27 (1615).—In much weaknes, beeing Carried in a **Pallankie**..... November 28.—I hastened away in my **Palenkie**....and soe rested in my **Palenkie**." Sir T. Roe, *Embassy*, Hak. Soc., p. 100.]

["Portugall Weomen Scantt (in Goa), The generality Mestizaes, apparelled after this country Manner.. The better sort have store of Jewells and are Carried in covered **Palanqueenes**." Peter Mundy, Hak Soc., Vol. III, pt. i, p. 63. The form of the palanquin in use at Goa can be seen from Linschoten's illustrations in the original edition: "Portuguese gentleman in palankin", and "Portuguese lady in open palankin."]

["Att Night, about the 7th or 8th houre, and from that to the 12th, the Bridegroom and bride are carried in a **Palanchino**, through all the principle Streets of the towne attended with many Lamps and Torches, dancinge women, with all Sorts of the Countrey musick...." Bowrey, Hak. Soc., p. 30. Bowrey gives an illustration of a *palanchino* on p. 86 which the editor, Sir Richard Temple, believes to be not of the palanquin of to-day but of what is known in the Madras Presidency as 'muncheel' (*q.v.*).]

[There are a large number of variant forms of Palanquin cited in *The Indian Antiquary*, Vol. XXX, p. 398.]

tions as a corruption (*tadbhāva*) of the Sanskrit word. Could the Portuguese have carried the word to Malacca or did they receive it thence?

[The author has devoted considerable attention and space to this word in his *Contribuições*, etc. (p. 73), wherein he suggests an answer to the query he puts in this book. He accepts that the Port. *palanquim* is derived ultimately from the Sansk. *paryaṅka* or *palyaṅka*, 'a bed', but maintains that there is no need whatever to suggest, as Yule does, that the Port. or Sp. *palanque* or *palanca* ('a pole used to carry loads on the shoulders of two bearers') had any influence in determining the form *palanquim*, especially as regards the nasalisation of the second syllable. He says the Sansk. *paryaṅka* or *palyaṅka* is represented in Pali by *pallaṅko*, and in the Indo-Aryan languages such as Mar., Konk., Guj., (which also has *paryaṅka*) by *palaṅg* ('bed, sofa'). In the sense of 'litter', it is met with in all Indian languages, Aryan or Dravidian, under the forms *pālkī*, *pālkhī*, *pālgī*, *pallakki*, *pallakku*, *pallakkiya*; and in Malayo-Javanese, *pĕlángki*, *plángki* or *paláng-king*.

The Port. *palanquim*, which in this form passed into the other European languages, is no doubt of Indian origin, but how are we to account for the two nasals *pala(n)ki(m)*? The nasal termination is easily explained by the well-known phenomenon in which the tonic *i* of the Indian languages becomes nasalised in passing over into Portuguese, as in *chatim*, *lascarim*, *mandarim*, *Samorim*, *Cochim*. The difficulty is to account for the medial nasal. If the Pali *pallanko* were accepted as the immediate source of the Port. word, the difficulty disappears; but Pali was scarcely ever a spoken language. Again, Sinhalese, which has been most influenced by Pali, has *pallak-ki(ya)*. If it were possible to fix the birth place of the Port. vocable in Insulandia, the Malayo-Jav. *palángki*, or, as Williamson has it, *palangking*, might be regarded as the source-word. But the vernacularity of the Malay word is open to doubt, nor is there evidence to show that it was current in those parts before the Portuguese arrival: again there are indigenous synonyms for palanquin, viz., *kremun*, *tandu*, *usongon*; *joli* which is Indian.

The form usually employed in Malayalam is *pallakku*, as in Tamil, or *pallakki*, as in Kanarese. But Gundert registers *pallaṅkī*, which appears to have the savour of Portuguese influence. But Tulu has *palleṅki*, side by side with *pallaki*, which squares neither with the Malayalan *pallanki*, nor the Port. *palanquim*, but with the English 'palanquin.' Moreover, the influence of Tulu on Portuguese is nil. It is extraordinary that none of the Indian languages should have preserved the original nasal which is found in *palang*, 'bed', of which *pālkī* or *pallaki* have all the appearances of being diminutives, in the sense of 'a couch or little bed.' Normally, the diminutive should have been *palaṅgī* or *pallaṅkī*. And in fact, Hindustani, Marathi and Gujarati have *palaṅgḍī*, as a diminutive used depreciatively, in the sense of 'a small and ordinary bed.'

But Shakespear does not derive the Hindust. *pālkī*, as he does *palang*, immediately from the Sansk. *palyaṅka*, but from the Hindi *pālakī*. Now, Hindi has also side by side with it the form *nālakī*, which appears to be due to the transposition of the medial nasal. From which it may be conjectured that the denasalization took place in Hindi and from it was transmitted to the other Indian languages.

The elimination of the nasal may also be explained by the law of least resistance, in view of the fact that the *a* which follows the *l* is surd in some of the Aryan languages and silent in others. The Sansk. *maṁsa*, 'flesh', becomes in Konk. and colloquial Mar. *mās*. For the same reason, the Sansk. *ānanda* is pronounced in Konk. *anad*, 'glory'.

Even if it were taken for granted that the *n* of the Portuguese word was not etymological, it is not necessary to have recourse to *palanque* or *palanca* to account for it. It may have developed of itself without outside influence, as has happened in the Port. words *fiandeiro*, 'spinner,' from *fiar*, 'to spin,' and *lavandeira*, 'washer-woman', from *lavar*, 'to wash', or in the Japanese words *bōzu*, 'priest', changed into *bonzu*, and *byobu*, 'screen', into *biombo*.]

Palhota (a thatched-house). Indo-Fr. *paillote*.

Pálio (pallium, pall). Konk. *pál*.—Tam. *pálli*.—Gal. *páliu*.

Palmatória (ferule). Konk. *pālmatór*.—Guj. *pālmantri*.—Tet., Gal. *palmatória*.

Palmeira (the fan-palm; *Borassus flabelliformis*). Anglo-Ind. *palmyra*.[1]

In Indo-Portuguese, *palmeira*, without qualification,

---

[1] [1505.—**Palmeiras** are trees yielding many fruits, and without receiving any aid furnish wine, vinegar, water, oil, sugar, and fuel". *Jour. Geo. Soc. Lisb.*, XVII, p. 366, cit. in *Glossario*. This is the earliest reference to *palmeira* in the sense of 'coco-nut tree'.]

[(In Muscat) "there are orchards, gardens, and *palmeiras*, with wells for watering them by means of a contrivance worked by oxen." *Commentaries of Afonso Dalboquerque*, Hak. Soc., I, 83. With regard to the translation see foot-note to '*engenho*' on p. 146. *Palmeiras* is used here of the date-palms.]

[1569.—"There are many **palmeiras bravas**, but they are not put to account (in Africa) as they are in India." P. Monclaio, in *Jour. Geo. Soc. Lisb.*, IV, p. 346, cit. in *Glossario*. This is the earliest reference there to *palmeira brava*.]

["The tenth of November we arrived at Chaul...Here is great traffike for all sortes of spices and drugges, silke, cloth of silke, sandales, elephants teeth, and much China worke, and much sugar which is made of the nutte called Gagara. The tree is called the **palmer**, which is the profitablest tree in the worlde. It doth alwayes beare fruit, and doth yeeld wine, oyle, sugar, vineger, cordes, coles...." Ralph Fitch (1583-91), in *Early Travels in India* (O.U.P.), p. 13.]

["Their houses (of the people of Ceylon) are very little, made of the branches of the **palmer** or coco-tree, and covered with the leaves of the same tree." *Idem*, p. 44. In the above, in fact throughout his narrative, Fitch uses 'palmer' of the coco-nut tree]

["Hence to Variaw 20 c., a goodly countrey and fertile, full of villages, abounding with wild date trees, which generally are plentifull by the sea-side in most places; whence they draw a liquor called tarrie, or sure, as also from another wild coco-tree called **tarrie.**" William Finch, in *Early Travels in India*, O.U.P., 175. 'Tari' is Anglo-Ind. toddy, the same as 'sure'=Sansc. *sura*; 'the wild coco-tree called tarrie' is the *Borassus flabelliformis*, called in

is the name of 'the coco-nut palm'. "With oil from the coco-nut which is the fruit of the *palmeira.*" Garcia da Orta, Col. LIII [ed. Markham, p. 423, in which is omitted the clause 'which is the fruit of the palmeira'].

[The Portuguese word *palmeira* has always stood for the various species of the palm family: in Portugal it stands for the *Phœnix dactilifera*, and in India for the *Cocos nucifera* (Ficalho, *Colloquies*, etc., Vol. I, 232). In fact, the Portuguese chroniclers invariably employ *palmeira* to denote the coco-nut palm and when they wish to refer to the fan-palm or the *Borassus flabelliformis*, from the leaves of which strips for writing on are prepared, speak of it as *palmeira brava* (*q.v.*).

Yule in *Hobson-Jobson*, (*s.v.*)

Guj. and Mar *tád*: it is not yet called *palmeira* or *palmyra.*]

["The **Palme** tree on whose leaves they here write with Iron bodkins." Peter Mundy, *Travels*, Hak. Soc., Vol. I, 78. Mundy refers to the *Borassus flabelliformis*, which, perhaps in his time was not yet called *palmeira.*]

["At the foot of this mountaine, for some miles, in Circuit, I have knowne delicate Groves and Gardens, fountains very pleasant to the Eye,... the Groves consisting of Mangoe and **Palmero**, Palmito and Coco nut trees, which are now quite demolished by the forces and Order of the Golcondah Kinge." Bowrey, *The Countries*, etc., Hak. Soc., p. 46. 'Palmero' in the above quotation, is, undoubtedly, the 'fan-palm'. 'Palmito' is here the wild date-palm, *Phœnix sylvestris*, which is very common in Gujarat. But the name is given to various varieties of the dwarf fan-palm. 'Palmito' in Portuguese is also the name by which the 'cabbage' or the edible heart at the end of the stem of a palm, whence the leaves spring, is called. "It is the eye of the coco-nut or its heart and the unexpanded mass of the very fine leaves that is called **palmito** and....it somewhat resembles in taste white and very tender chestnuts....But he who eats a *palmito* eats a coco-nut tree for it presently dries up; and the older the coco-nut tree the better is the *palmito.*" Garcia da Orta, Col. XVI, ed. Markham, p. 144. Markham has completely misunderstood the original, and his rendering of it, it must regretfully be confessed, makes no sense.]

["It has been said with truth that a native of Jaffna, if he be contented with ordinary doors and mud walls, may build an entire house (as he wants neither doors nor iron work), with walls, roof, and covering from the **Palmyra** palm. From this same tree he may draw his wine, make his oil, kindle his fire, carry his water, store his food, cook his repast, and sweeten it, if he pleases; in fact, live from day to day dependant on his **palmyra** alone." Tennent, *Ceylon*, Vol. I, p 111]

palmyra, quotes from Orta: "There are many **palmeiras** in the Island of Ceylon" (Col. XV), to support his view that the word stands for the *Borassus flabelliformis*, and to show that this palm was called by the Portuguese *par excellence*, *palmeira* or 'the palm-tree.' But in this he is mistaken, for, in almost all the places where the word occurs in the *Colloquies*, it is used to signify the 'coco-nut palm.' When Orta refers to Ceylon as being full of palms, he is merely stating a fact, viz., that in that island are to be found several varieties of the palm. He is using the term in the generic sense in which it was employed in Portugal. Here is Sir Emerson Tennent's evidence on this point: "But the family of trees which, from their singularity as well as their beauty, most attract the eye of the traveller in the forests of Ceylon, are the palms, which occur in rich profusion....; more than ten or twelve (species of the palm) are indigenous to the island" (*Ceylon*, I, 109).

In Indo-Portuguese *palmar* and *palmeiral* are used in the same sense in which the Anglo-Indian 'oart' is used in Bombay and its suburbs, to denote a plantation or grove of coco-nut trees.]

Pâmpano (a fish: *Stromateus sinensis*, *S. cenereus*, *S. niger*). Konk. *pámpl.* ? *pāmplít*; vern. terms *sarangó*, *sarangúl*.—? Mar. *pāpliṣṭ*; vern. term *sargá*.—Anglo-Ind. *pamplee* (*arch.*) *pamplet*, [*paumphlet*] (*arch.*), *pomfret*.—Indo-Fr. *pample*. Portuguese dialects of Malacca and Dutch *pampel*.[1]

[1] "And the fish found in that Mediterranean is very dainty shad, doradoes, *rubios*, and good mullets and saw-fish and **pampanos**" Godinho de Erédia, *Declaraçam de Malaca*, (1613), fol. 33. [*Rubios* is not found in dictionaries, it is perhaps a corruption of *ruivos* the Port. name for the roach.]

["Fish in India is verie plentifull, and some very pleasant and sweete. The best fish is called Mordexiin, **Pampano**, and Tatiingo." Linschoten, *Voyage*, Hak. Soc., Vol. II, p. 11.]

"The adjacent seas abound in Sharks, Saw fish, **Pampanos**, *Esmargaes*, Doradoes, etc." F. N. Xavier, *O. Gab. Litt.*, I, p. 32.

[1703.—"Here (in Pulo Condore) are in great plenty very fine Spanish Mackerell, Soles, Turbits, Mullets, Bonitas, Albacores, Daulphins, **Paumphlets**, and diverse sorts of Rock

Cândido de Figueiredo mentions *pâmpano* ('fish') as a term hitherto inedited and gives it as the synonym of *pampo*. Vieyra says that "it is a fish shaped like a boar-spear." I do not know whether the word is in vogue in Portugal. The Indian fish resembles a vine-leaf, from which it derives its name.

The words *pāmpliṭ* and *pāpliśṭ* appear to have as their direct source the Anglo-Ind. 'pamplet'.

[*Pampano* in Portuguese means primarily 'a vine-leaf'. The *O.E.D.* derives 'pomfret' from the Port. *pampo* (see above), French *pample*, and surmises that a diminutive *pamplet* may have become *pamphlet*, *pomphlet*, and finally *pomfret*]

Pangaio (a two-masted barge with lateen sails common in East Africa and in India). Konk. *pangáy*.—Malayal. *pangáyar*.—Kan , Tul. *pangayu*. | Mal. *pengaiu*. |

The word is of African origin. Almost all the old Portuguese writers suggest the same source.[1] P. Vítor Cortois mentions *pangaya* in his *Portuguese-Cafre-Teto Dictionary*.

[Yule and Burnell register the word under the forms 'pangara, pangaia', and give citations in support of these and other forms, including the Port. *pangaio*.]

? Pantalona (pantaloons; trousers). Mal., Sund. *telana*, *tjalana*, *tjilona*.—Jav., Mad. *tjelônô*.—Bal. *chelana*.—Bug. *chalána*.

Dr. Heyligers explains that the first syllable dropped out because it was regarded as an indifferent prefix, as happens with vernacular words. Gonçalves Viana has doubts as regards the word *pantalona*

fish..." From *Letter of Allen Catchpole*, in Hedges, *Diary*, Hak. Soc., Vol. II, p cccxxxiv.]

1 "Francisco Barreto left for the coast with the largest number of people in his *fusta* (*q.v.*) and **pangaios** and came to the city of Quiloa." P. Monclaio (1569), in *Jour. Geo. Soc. Lisb.*, 4th ser., p. 497.

"The **pangayos** of Moçambique should halt at Calimane, as Sena was very unhealthy." M. Godinho Cardoso (1585), in *Hist. tragico-marit.*, IV, p. 73

"It was a rough sea, and lifted the vessel (which on this coast is called **pangaio**). Fr. João dos Santos (1609), *Ethiop. Or.*, II, p. 191.

existing in the Portuguese of the seventeenth century. Dr. Schuchardt says that *telana* has nothing to do with *pantalona*. If *tjalana* stands for *chalana*, as seems likely, the word must be of Indian origin, viz., the Hindustani *cholná*, 'trousers, breeches', adopted in Marathi, Konkani, Kanarese, and Tulu.

Pão (bread, loaf). Konk *páṁv*; the vern. word *unḍo* is more in use in some parts.—Guj. *páuṁ*, *páṁu* (=*pãu*). *Paṁ-vāló*, baker.—Hindi *pav-roṭí*.—Hindust. *páṁv-roṭí*, *pao roṭí*. *Roṭí* means 'a hand-made flour cake'.—Sinh. *páṅ* (=*pã*), *páṅ*, *páṅ-geḍiya*. "*Geḍiya*, anything round, globular, fruit, abcess." Alwis. The vern. terms are *roṭi*, *púpa*. *Páṅ-petta*, a slice of bread. *Páṅ-piṭosa*, crust. *Páṅ-kuḍu*, the crumb or soft inner part of bread. *Karakarapu-pán*, *kara-kala-pānpetta*, bread-toast. *Páṅ-kárayā*, *páṅ-pulussamá*, baker; vern. term *apupika*. *Páṅ-pulussana ge* (lit. 'the house for baking bread'), a bakery.—? Tib. *pá-le*; *sh'e-pa* (honorific).—Kamb. *nŏm păng* (lit. 'cake bread').—Siam. *khànŏm păng*. *Khanŏm păng hĕng*, biscuit. Michell derives *păng* from the French *pain*.—Ann. *bánh*, *bánh mì*.—Tonk. *bánh*. *Bánh sũ'a* (lit. 'bread of milk'), cheese. *Bánh lễ* (lit. 'bread of the Mass'), sacred wafer. *Bánh ngot*, cake. Annamese and Tonkinese have no initial *p*.—Mal. *paon*, | *paung* |.—Tet., Gal. *pă*.—Jap. *pan*. *Pan-ya*, bakery; baker.— | ? Chin. *mien-páu*.[1] |

[Sir Richard Temple, in a note to "paying outt their gold and silver (in Macao and in China) by waightt, cutting itt outt in small peeces", in Peter Mundy, *Travels*, Hak. Soc., Vol. III, pt. i, p. 309, quotes Magaillans, p. 136: "The pieces of Gold and Silver are not Coyn'd,

1 "For a bag of rice which is the common food of all those who were then living in Goa, because at present the greater number of our men already use kneaded **pam**, as in Portugal, of wheat which comes from abroad...." João de Barros, Dec. II, vi, 9.

"No **pão** was to be had (in Cochin) because there was no wheat to be had there except in the country of the Moors." Gaspar Correia, I, p. 624.

"Japan grows rice...and wheat of which, however, they do not prepare pao." Lucena, *Hist. da Vida*, Bk. VII, ch. I.

but cast into Lingots in the form of a small Boat, which at Macao are called **Paes** [Port. *Pães*] or Loaves of Gold or Silver." This is a meaning of *pão* which I do not find mentioned in the Portuguese dictionaries I have consulted.]

[1]**Papa** (in the meaning of 'the Pope'). Konk. *páp-sāheb*. *Sāheb* is 'Lord'.—Mar. *páp*. *Pāpāchá adhikár*, papacy.—Beng. *pāpá*.—Sinh. *pap-unnánse*. *Unnanse* is a term of respect: 'reverend, venerable'.—Tam. *páppa*, *páppu*., *páppanavar* (more respectful).—Malayal. *páppà*.—Tel. *pápa*.—Kan. *pápu*.—Kamb. *santa pap*.—Mal. *sánto pápa*.—Tet., Gal. *pápa*.—Malag. *papa*.—Ar. *bābá*. *Bābāvi*, papal. The other languages of India employ the English form 'pope'.

[2]**Papa** (poultice). Konk. *páp*.—Sinh. *páppa*.—Jap. *pappu*.

Papá (papa, daddy). Konk. *pāpá* (l. us. and only among the Christians of Goa).—Mar. *pāpá*.—Mal. *papa* (Schuchardt).—Bug. *pápang*.—Mol. *papá* (Castro).—? Malag. *papa*.—| Chin. *pá-pá*. |

Molesworth thinks that the Marathi *pāpá* is a variant of the vernacular *báp* formed by children.

Papaia (*bot.*, *Carica papaya*, Linn., the papaw tree and its fruit). Konk. *papáy* (the tree and fruit).—Mar. *popáy*, *popayá*, *phopai*.—[Guj. *papaiya*, *bapaiyo*.]—Hindi, Hindust., Beng. *papayá*.—Tam. *pappai*.—Malayal. *pappáyam*.—Tul. *pappáya*, *pappayá*.—Anglo-Ind. *papaya*, *papaw*.—Indo-Fr. *papaye*.—Mal. *papáya*, *peppáya*, *pápua*.—Nic. *popai*.—Malag. *papai*.

It is an American term,[1] used in Cuba, probably introduced by the Portuguese together with the plant, as the Kanarese name *parangi-haṇṇu* ('Frank or Portuguese fruit') seems to indicate. Linschoten (1597) thinks that it came from the Philippines to Malacca and from thence to India. In Siamese

---

1 "There is another fruit **papayas** (in San Domingo) which in Brazil we call *mamões*, and they could well be called melons from their appearance" (1596). Gaspar Afonso, in *Hist. tragico marit.*, VI, p. 49.

"There is another tree called **papaeira** which produces fruit which goes by the name of *mamões* in America, and of **papaias** here." Fr. Clemente da Ressurreição, II, p. 391.

it is called *lùk ma-la-ko*, 'the fruit of Malacca', [and in Burmese *himbawthi*, which means 'fruit brought by sea-going vessels']. See *Hobson-Jobson*, *Apostilas* of Gonçalves Viana, [and also Skeat, *Notes on English Etymology*].

[The Portuguese introduced the 'papaya' into Africa and Asia. In Africa, it is reported to be very common in the Portuguese possessions, specially in Cape Verde Islands and in Angola. It must have been brought to India towards the close of the sixteenth century, for Linschoten (1597)[1] mentions it as one of the fruits of India and gives a very accurate description of the tree, but it is not referred to either by Orta (1563) or in the *Āīn-i-Akbarī* (c.1590). In 1656 it was figured and described by Boym (*Flora Sinensis*, pl. A) as an Indian plant introduced into China, so that it must be regarded as another instance of the rapid dispersion of new plants after the discovery of America.[1]

There can be no question about the home of this species being America, and it is, therefore, all the more curious to find American dictionaries referring its name to Asiatic sources. The *Century Dictionary* says: "*Papaya*, a name of Malabar origin. .. also written *pawpaw*". Webster referred it to Malay, but in the 1890 and subsequent editions he refers it to "the West Indies". According to Oviedo (1535), *papaya* is the name used in Cuba. Littré (see *papayer*) gives the Caribbean form as *ababai*. The *O.E.D.* derives the word from Carib, but is at a loss to indicate the immediate source of the English forms *papa*, *papaw*, and *pawpaw*. Sir Richard Temple (*Indian Antiquary*, Vol. XXX, p. 552) says that "in the Madras Presidency it is known as 'poppoy' and usually so spelt in accounts and letters". 'Poppoy' could give

---

1 ["There is also a frute that came out of the Spanish Indies, brought from Ye Philippinas or Lusons to Malacca, & from thence to India, it is called **Papaios**, and is very like a Mellon, as bigge as a mans fist, and will not grow, but alwaies two together, that is male and female..." Hak. Soc., Vol. II, p. 35.]

1 [Watt, *Comm. Prod. of India*, (1908), p. 269.]

'pawpaw', but how to account for the other forms? Sir T. Herbert (1630) speaks of 'pappaes',[1] and Peter Mundy (in 1636) of 'papaes',[2] but Fryer (1673) uses the word 'papaw',[3] which, it might safely be concluded, must have come into vogue after Peter Mundy's time.]

In Brazil the plant has another name—*mamoeiro*, from *mama*, 'pap', because of the fruit's resemblance to woman's breasts.

Papuses ('a sort of sandals'). Sinh. *pápus*. Also used in the Portuguese dialect of Ceylon, *papús*, boot, shoes. —Tel. *pāpásum*.—Kan. *papósu*.—Tul. *pápasu*, *pāpásu*.

It is derived from the Persian *pā-push*, 'footwear'. See Gonçalves Viana, *Apostilas*.

[The Arabs who have no *p* converted *pāpush* into *bābūsh*, which went over to France and became *babouches*, 'slippers', to return to Portugal in the new form *babuche*, which is etymologically not as correct as the older *papus*, pl. *papuses*.]

Par (pair). Konk. *par*; vern. terms *zôḍ*, *zoḍó*, *zoḍí*, *zuṅvlí*. —Mal. *paris* (from the Port. plural form *pares*). *Caus-sa paris*, a pair of shoes (Haex); vern. terms *jodo*, *klamin*.

Para (*prep.*, for). Mal. *para* (Haex).—Tet. *para*; vern. term *ató*.

Parabêm (congratulation). Konk. *parbém*.—Tet., Gal. *parabem*.

Paraiso (Paradise). Jap. *paraizo* (*arch.*).

[**Parau, paró** (a small vessel used in war or trade, compared by European writers to the galley or foist). Anglo-Ind. *prow*, *parao*, *praw*, etc.[1]

1 ["**Pappaes**, Cocoes, and Plantains, all sweet and delicious..." Ed. 1665, p. 350, in *Hobson-Jobson*.]

2 ["For to my Knowlidg it (Cocotree) affoardes Meat, Drink..., and good Cordage Made of the outtward rinde of the Nutte, which in Clusters grow outt att the toppe on a sprigge, as Doe allsoe the **Papaes** in a Manner, the tree Differing in leaves and height." Hak. Soc., Vol. III, pt. i, p. 58.]

3 ["Here (in Johanna Town) the flourishing **Papaw** (in Taste like our Melons, and as big, but growing on a Tree leafed like our Fig-tree), Citrons ...contend to indulge the Taste." Hak. Soc., Vol. I, p 64.]

1 ["1504.—He was bringing with him many men and lxx or lxxx **paraaos** each with ii mortars." *Letters* of A. de Albuquerque, III, p. 259, in *Glossario*.]

The *O.E.D.* connects the Anglo-Ind. forms with the Malay *p(á)rā(h)ū*, 'a boat, a rowing vessel', and says that the forms *prow* and *proa* are assimilated to the Eng. 'prow' and its Port. equivalent *proa*. Yule assigns to the word in European use a double origin: the Malayal. *pāṟu*, and the Malay *prāū* or *prāhū*. Dalgado (*Glossario*) maintains that the Port. derived their forms from the Dravidian *paḍavu*, and that the Malasian forms owe their origin to the Dravidian term. He is of the view that Yule's theory of a double origin is untenable, because, as he points out, *pāṟu* could not give the Port. *parau* or *paró*, and because the term was already known to the Portuguese before their conquest of Malacca. Both the forms could, however, be derived from *paḍavu*. See *piroga*, and, for citations, *Ind. Antiq.*, Vol. XXX, p. 161.

[1508.—" One night he made reprisal on **paraos** carrying water." A. de Albuquerque, *Letters*, I, p. 13.]

[(In Achein) "they goe from place to place and house to house in **prowes** or boates." Mundy, *Travels*, Hak. Soc., Vol. III, pt. i, p. 132.]

[" In the Morning they came and told me there was English on board there **Prues.**" In *Letter* d. 1705, in Hedges, *Diary*, Vol. II, p. cccxxxviii.]

[" They (the 'Saleeter Piratts')... have theire men of warre **Prows** in Upon the Maine of the Malay Shore." Bowrey, p. 238.]

There are illustrations of 'prowes' at Achein and at Madagascar in Mundy, *Travels* (Vol. III, Pl. viii and xviii), and one of "Men of warre prows" in Bowrey (Hak. Soc. ed., Pl. xviii). For a description of 'Flying Procs', see Dampier, Vol. II, p. 131.]

Parceiro (partner). Konk. *pārsêr*, *padsêr*; vern. terms *goḍó*, *saṁvgoḍó*.—Mal. *parséru*, *parséro*.—Jav. *bersérô*, *besérô*. In the last two languages it is used as a verb in the sense of 'associating one's self'.—Mac., Bug. *paraséro*.[1]

[Pardáo (*arch.*), **Pardau** (the name among the Portuguese of a gold coin from the mints of Indian Rajas in Western India, which entered

[1] "I hold it proper that the said rent-farmer and his **parceiros** should let out and collect all the rent of the said lands which were assigned for the service of the Pagodas" (1545). *Archivo Port. Or.*, fasc. 5. p. 182.

largely into the early currency of Goa and the name of which afterwards attached to a silver coin of their own coinage). Anglo-Ind. *pardao*, *pardaw*, *perdao*, etc.[1]

There were two kinds of *pardaus*: the *pardau de ouro* ('gold pardao') of the value of 6 *tangas* or 360 *reis*, and the *pardau de prata* ('silver pardao') worth 5 *tangas* or 300 *reis*. The former issued by Indian Rajas were already in circulation in Western India in the time of Albuquerque, and were known in the vernaculars as *varāha* or *varā*, the Sansk. name for 'the boar', one of the incarnations of Vishnu, whose effigy they carried. The Sansk. *pratāpa*, 'majesty, splendour,' was the legend on some of these coins, and referred to the sovereign who had ordered the coins to be struck; this *pratāpa* would be corrupted by the people into *partāp*, or *pardāp*, and would become transformed in the mouth of the Portuguese very naturally

---

[1] ["All this merchandize (in the city of Vijayanagar) is bought and sold by **pardaos**....gold coin....made in certain towns of this kingdom....The coin is round in form and is made with a die. Some of them have on one side Indian letters and on the other two figures, of a man and a woman, and others have only letters on one side" Barbosa, Hak. Soc., ed. Dames, Vol. 1, p. 203 *sqq*. See editor's note]

["And if there is any one who does not know what a **pardao** is, let him know that it is a round gold coin, which is not struck all over India, but only in this kingdom (of Vijayanagar); it has on one side two figures, and on the other the name of the king who had ordered the coins to be struck.. ....,it is a coin which circulates all over India, and each **pardao**, as I have said, is worth 360 reis." *Chronica de Bisnaga*, p 116.]

["The principall and commonest money is called **Pardaus Xeraphiins**, and is silver, but very base, and is coyned in Goa....There is also a kinde of reckoning of money which is called Tangas, not that there is any such coined, but are so named onely in telling, five Tangas is one **Pardaw** or Xeraphin badde money. Linschoten, Vol. I, Hak. Soc., p. 241. In the passage that follows the above citation, Linschoten gives a very complete account of the Goa currency in his time.]

["Their (Goa) Coin

1 *Vintin*..............15 *Budgeroocks*

1 *Tango*.............. 5 *Vintins*

1 *Xerephin* or **Pardoa**..5 *Tangos*." A. Hamilton, *East Indies* (1727 ed.), Vol. II, in *Table* at end.]

[See quotations bearing on 'Pardao' in *Indian Antiquary*, Vol. xxvii, p. 251.]

into *pardáo* or *pardao*. The *pardaus* which were most and longest current in Goa were those which had been struck by the Vijayanagar sovereigns, because of the intimate political and commercial relations that then subsisted between Goa and the Vijayanagar court. Silver pardaos began to be coined in Goa towards the middle of the 16th century and are distinguished from the gold ones in as much as the former are referred to as *pardau de tangas* or *pardau de larins* or *de xerafim*. When the gold pardao went out of circulation, the silver pardao was worth 6 *tangas* or half a rupee, and the *pardau de cobre* ('copper pardao'), or more correctly the *xerafim*, 5 *tangas* or 300 *reis*. Yule says that at the close of the 16th century the gold pardao was worth 4*s*. 2*d*. to 4*s*. 6*d*., but that by the first half of the eighteenth century the pardao had dwindled in value to 10½*d*. See *Hobson-Jobson*, *Glossario*, and Gerson da Cunha, *Contributions to the Study of Indo-Port. Numismatics*.]

Parent (parent). Konk. *pārent* (l. us.).—Mal. *parente* (Haex).—Tet. *parénti*.

Parte (part, a share). Konk. *párt*; vern. terms *kuṭkó*, *vānṭó*; *kúḷ*; *vādí*, *vādyó*.—Tet. *párti*; vern. terms *báluku*, *bálem*.

Páscoa (Passover, Easter). Konk. *Pásk*.—Beng. *Pāskuvá*.—Sinh. *Páskuva*. *Pásku*, Paschal. *Pásku kálaya*, Paschal time.—Tam. *Paská*.—Tel., Kan. *Páska*.—Kamb. *bŏn pās* (lit. 'Feast Paschal').—Tet. *Páskua*.

Pasquim (pasquinade, lampoon). Mal. *paskil*, *paskvil* (Heyligers). As a verb, it means 'to scold'.[1]

[1] "They used to treat Pero Fernandes as **pasquim** of Rome used to be; some of them writing to the King, all they wished to, in the name of Pero Fernandes." Diogo do Couto, Dec. VI, iv, 5. [*Pasquim* in Port., *Pasquino* or *Pasquillo* in Italian, was the name popularly given to a mutilated statue disinterred in Rome in 1501 and set up there. On St. Mark's Day, it became the practice to restore temporarily and dress up this torso to represent some historical or mythological personage of antiquity on which occasion it was customary to salute *Pasquino* in Latin verses which were usually posted or placed on the statue; the verses, in course of time, tended to become satirical; hence the term 'pasquinade', applied to satires and lampoons, political, ecclesiastical, etc]

Passador (*naut.*, a marlinespike). L.-Hindust. *pāsādor.*

Passaporte (passport). Konk. *pāsāport.*—? Sinh. *pāspórtuva* (perhaps from the English 'passport').—*Ar. bāsāburth.*— | Turk. *pàssàpòrta.* |

Passar (to pass). Konk. *pāsár-zāvuṅk* (*verb intrans.*), *pāsár-kāruṅk* (*verb trans.*)—Mar. *pasár* (*adj.*), passed, elapsed; e.g.: *áṭh pasár*, eight (hours) having elapsed.—Guj. *pasár thavuṁ* (*verb. intrans.*) *passar karvuṁ* (*verb trans.*), to pass an examination; to advance; to thrust forward; to drive away. *Pasárvuṁ*, to pass; to enter; to be admitted; to make one's escape, to run away.—Mac. *pásu* (from the 1st person present, *passo*), to pass in a game of cards.

In Gujarati there is another word *pasárvum*, from the Sansk. *prasar.* In *pás thavuṁ*, 'to pass', *pás* is from the English 'pass.'

Passe (pass, permission). Konk. *pás.*—? Sund. *pás* (probably from Dutch).—Tet., Gal. *pássi.*

Passear (to walk). Mar. *pasár* (*subst.*), "giving a few turns for exercise; walking up and down, like a sentinel on watch." Molesworth.—Mal. *pasiyar*, to walk; walking. *Pasiyar-an*, place for walking.—Batt. *pasar*, a wide street.—Jav. *pesiyar*, *besiyar*. *Radiman pasiyaran*, walking alley.

In Konkani, the expressions used are: *pāsey karuṅk* or *māruṅk*, *pāseyek vachuṅk* ('to go out for a walk').

Passo (step, pace, passage; a picture or image representing the Passion of Christ). Konk. *páz* (through the intervention of *pás*), a highway, quay.—Mar. *páz*, a narrow passage in a mountain or between two mountains.—Guj. *páj*, quay, bridge.

In Konkani, *pás*, masc., is 'the representation in a church of the passion of Jesus Christ.'

Pastel (pie, pastry). Konk. *pāstel.*—Mal. *pastel*, *pastil.*—Sund. *pastel.*

Pataca (a dollar). Konk. *pāták.*—Malayal. *pattāká.*—Anglo-Ind. *pataca.*—Tet., Gal. *pataka.*[1]

---

1 "Throughout India patacas and half patacas are current, and these

The word is of Arabic origin, *bāṭāqa*, or, according to Gonçalves Viana, Spanish.

['Pataca' is not found in the *O.E.D.* which mentions 'patacaoon' as an augmentative of *pataca*. Yule, too, like Dalgado is inclined to accept the Arabic *abūṭāḳa* or corruptly *bāṭāḳa*, the name given to certain coins of this kind with a scutcheon on the reverse, the term meaning 'father of window,' the scutcheon being taken for such an object, as the original of the Portuguese and Spanish *pataca*. But they do not appear to take into account the following considerations: The Ar. *bāṭāḳa* would not become in Port. and Sp. *pataca*, but remain *bāṭāḳa* for both Port. and Sp. possess a *b* sound, but if the original word was *pataca*, it would in passing over into Arabic become *bāṭāḳa*, for Ar. has no *p* sound, and the change of *p* into Ar. *b* is the rule when words are taken over into Ar. from other languages. See *papuses* and *pateca*. *Pataca* was originally used of a S. American silver coin, and the name was certainly carried from Spain to America, and, in the absence of any more convincing etymology, it might be safer to regard the term as Spanish. Littré, however, connects it with an old Fr. word *patard*, 'a kind of coin.']

Patacão (a coin). Anglo-Ind. *putacoon*.[1]

go from Portugal." João dos Santos, *Ethiop. Or.*, II, p. 276.

"The Captain General or the Admiral (of Ceylon) used on these occasions to promise each of them a pataca by way of encouragement." João Ribeiro, *Fatalidade hist.*, Bk. I, ch xvi.

1 "Some very good things he did in India, he minted **patacões** of silver, which was the best coin there was in India, and which, because of its purity, was current in all the foreign kingdoms." Diogo do Couto, Dec. VII, i, 6.

"With hundred thousand *Madrafaris*, each one of which is worth two silver larins which came to be equal to fifty thousand **patacões**." *Id.*, Dec. VII, ii, 3. [*Madrafaris* is obviously a variant of *Madrafaxão* which appears in old Portuguese works as the name of a gold and also of a silver coin of Gujarat: it is a corruption of the vernacular 'Muzaffar shahi,' Muzaffar Shah having being the grandson of Bahadur Shah of Guzerat. The gold coin weighed 200 grains, and the silver one 7 *Larin* is a kind of money formerly in use on the Persian Gulf, west coast of India and the Maldive Islands. It derived its name from Lar on the Persian Gulf where it was coined. It was a little rod of silver, a finger's length, bent double unequally.]

Patacho (a pinnace; a two masted sailing vessel). Malayal. *pattáchu* (Gundert.)

Patamar ('a courier', Orta; a letter-carrier; a kind of lateen rigged ship). Anglo-Ind. *pattamar*, *patimar*.[1]—Indo-Fr. *patemar*, *patmar*.

According to Yule and Burnell, the word in both acceptations is the Konkani *path-már*, 'a courier', at present not used in the first sense, and in the second, which is more modern, usually employed in the form of *pātmārí*. [The Konk. *path-már* is lit. equivalent to 'kill-road or road-killer'. In this sense it is not used at present; they are sent by your **Pattamars**, except the Company pay all the charges of their own and other people's Letters, which is most unconscionable." From *Court's Letter* to Fort St. George, 6th march, 1694-5, in Hedges, *Diary*, Vol. II, p cxix].

1 "The news of which disaster soon became known through **patamares**, who are men that make big journeys by land." João de Barros, Dec. I, viii, 9.

"He soon despatched **Patamares** (who are couriers) by land to San Thomé." Diogo do Couto, Dec. V, v. 6.

"He wrote that he would get into a small vessel, one of those which are called **patamares**, and cross the bay." Lucena, Bk. III, ch. 7.

["Even if no ship were to go from this coast this year, but only a **Patamar** (i.e. a small vessel) I would confidently sail in it, placing all my trust in God." St. Francis Xavier, in *Missões de Jesuitas no Oriente* by Câmara Manuel, cit in *Glossario*.]

["Presentlye after this, there came a **pattamar** with letters from Agra, certifyinge us of the death of Mr. Caninge." Nicholas Withington (1612-16), in Foster, *Early Travels in India*, p. 202.]

["You will tell us there is great Difference between East India and England, which is true; but peradventure upon due Consideration they may find a way to make something of this and carry the Company's Letters cheaper, safer, and speedyer then now

["Running on Foot, which belongs to the **Pattamars**, the only Foot-posts of this Country, who run so many Courses (*kos*, a measure of distance) every Morning, or else Dance so many hours to a Tune called the **Patamars** Tune." Fryer, *East India*, Hak. Soc., Vol. I, p. 278 *sqq*.]

["Just as the time was approaching for my departure to Cochim (from Goa), a Courier (called **Patamar** in these parts) was received from Bengala." Manrique, *Travels*, Hak. Soc., Vol. II, p. 6.]

["And not being satisfied with our evading his (Sir Gervase Lucas's) discourse about their building fortifications, hee sent the **Pattamarr** that brought his letters wth his Broker home to our howse to justifie it." Forrest, *Selections* (Home Series), Vol. I, p. 216.]

perhaps, *pathmár* is merely a variant of *vātmár* which is used in the same sense even to-day. There are instances in Konk. of the change of *v* into *p*.]

Garcia da Orta derives it from Malayalam [Col. on Betel, etc.] which Charles Brown admits but only as regards its meaning of 'a sailing vessel'. Molesworth derives the Marathi *pātemārí*, 'a native craft', from the Hindust. *pātimārí*, 'courier', but Hindustani dictionaries do not mention any such word.

["The principal difficulty consists in knowing where it was that the Portuguese first received the word. Hindust. and Mar. have *patta*, 'tidings, information', which with the addition of the suffix *vār* or *mār* could have given *patamar*, 'the bearer of tidings'. It is also worthy of note that Duarte Barbosa, speaking of Gujarat, says that among the Brahmins "there are others of low degree who act as messengers and go safely everywhere without molestation from any, even during war or from highwaymen; these men they call *Pateles*". Now, *patel*, besides denoting the headman of a village, is in Gujarat also borne as a name by certain sub-divisions of castes, and by the Ahīrs and Bhoyars it is used as a title. Longworth Dames observes (Vol. I, p. 117): "It is probable that some men of these castes acted as messengers for the Brahmans in Barbosa's time". *Patel*, with an affix, *var*, for instance, or in Malayalam *ar*, could be transformed into *patamar*." Dalgado, in *Glossario*, s.v. *patamar*.]

Patarata (affectation; boasting). Konk. *pātrál*; vern. terms *baḍáy*, *tāvdārkí*.—Mal. *patrás*, *patráz*. *Patrāsí*, *patrājí*. boasting, boaster.—Tet. *patarata*; vern. terms *lôkô*, *bósok*.[1]

In Konkani, there is also the form *pātrātêr* meaning 'boaster'.

Pateca (*arch.* for 'watermelon').[2] Sinh. *patágaya*, *pat-*

[1] "We (Portuguese) either lett the word patarata in Malay or borrowed it from that language." Dr. Albert de Castro.

[2] Fr. João de Sousa mentions the form *bateca*.

"In respect of fruits it (the city of Cairo) is not very rich, except for patecas, which are like melons, but not as savoury." António Tenreiro, *Itinerario*, ch. xlii.

takka geḍiya.—Tam. *pattaká, vattakei.*—Malayal. *vattakka.*—Tel. *batéka.*— | Indo-Fr. *pastèque.*— | ? Siam *tëng.*—Mol. *pateka, bateka.*—Tet., Gal. *pateka*; vern. term *babuar.*

The Port. word is from the Arabic *baṭṭīkh* or *biṭṭīkh.*

Pato (gander; drake). Konk. *pát*, drake; vern. terms *háṁs, rājháṁs.*—Or., Beng. *pátihaṁs.*—Ass. *pāti-hámh.*—Sinh. *pāttayá. Pātti*, goose.—Tam. *vattu.*—Malayal. *páttu*, drake —Tel. *bátu̥. Fedda bátu̥* (lit. 'big drake'), gander.—Kan. *bátu.*—Tul. *battu̥.*—Siam. *pet. Pet pã*, wild duck.—Tet., Gal. *pátu.*

"The melon of India, which we (the Portuguese) here call **pateca**". Garcia da Orta [Col. xxxvi]. "Melons of India or **patecas** which must be what to-day we call *melancias* [water-melon or *Cucurbita Citrullus*, Linn." Conde de Ficalho, *Coloquios*, Vol. II, p. 144. [Ficalho, who is surprised that Orta should speak of the *pateca* as though it were unknown in Portugal, identifies it with the *melancia*, which he says was cultivated from immemorial times in the Mediterranean basin, and must, therefore, have been also cultivated in Spain and Portugal. To this Dalgado, in his *Gonçalves Viana e a Lexicologia Portuguesa*, says:

"Inspite of Ficalho's opinion to the contrary, it can be seen from António Tenreiro, from Garcia da Orta, and others that the water-melon was then little cultivated in the Iberic peninsula. The name which the Portuguese gave to the fruit in India is *pateca*, from the Ar. *baṭṭikh*, which they probably heard used by the Arab traders in Malabar. As *pateca*, the fruit is even to-day known in the Portuguese speech current in Asia. Frei João dos Santos, however, speaks of the *melancia* ('water-melon') as a fruit, very common, in his time [1608], and it is, therefore, not improbable that the Portuguese who had sampled the fruit in India, had either introduced it into Portugal or extended its cultivation there, and that the popular form *balancia* was a corruption of the cultivated term *melancia*. Notwithstanding the fact that the Spaniards had *sandia*, a term received, according to Dozy, from the Ar. *sindīya*, and derived from Sindh in India, it cannot be said that they had given the fruit to the Portuguese, because, had they done so, its name would have accompanied it, and in Portuguese there is no word for it corresponding to *sandia*. According to the testimony of Pyrard de Laval, Bernier, and Tavernier, the fruit was also unknown to the French, their word for it *pastèque* being a corruption of *pateca* and imported from India."]

"Melons, pumpkins from Portugal and from Guinea, **patecas**, *combalengas* and *biringelas.*" Gabriel Rebelo, *Informação*, p. 172 [*Combalenga* is a species of Indian pumpkin. *Biringela* is the same as *beringela, q.v.*].

"They ate nothing but the bran of the millet and the rind of **patecas**, which are like our water-melons." João dos Santos, *Ethiop, Or.*, II, p. 182.

The original of the Port. word appears to be the Ar. *bat*, 'drake, gander' (*batak* is the diminutive), also used in Persian and Hindustani.[1] It may be that *batu* has been derived directly from *bat*. The old Portuguese writers use *adem* for *pato*.[2]

[Gonçalves Viana is not disposed to accept the Arabic origin for *pato* and for the following reason: The change of *b* into *p*. In the Bulgar language the gander is called *pátek* or *pátok*, which is a derived form and presupposes the existence of an earlier one, *pat*; it is possible that the Ar. *bat* came to be written that way because of the absence of *p* in that language. In Persian the drake is also called *bat*, and it is probable that the Arabs imported either from Persia, Armenia or India the word which belongs to the stock of Aryan and not Semitic languages. In Armenia, too, it is called *pat*, or *bad*, according as the dialect which uses the word belongs to Europe or Asia.]

Patrono (in the sense of 'patron-saint'). Konk. *pātron.*—Tet., Gal. *patrónu*.

?**Patrulha** (military patrol). Mal., Jav., Mad. *patrol* (Heyligers).—Batt. *pataróli*.

Patrol appears to be Dutch. The Portuguese term introduced in these languages is *ronda*, *q.v.*

?**Patuleia** (a mob, rabble). Mal. *patuley*, race, tribe.

Did the word go from Portugal or did it come to Portugal from Malacca? The Portuguese dictionaries do not give the derivation of *patuleia*. Gonçalves Viana, however, presumes that it is *patulé* in the sense of 'rustic'.

It might have been brought from Asia by the Spanish gipsies and introduced into Castilian which employs it in the sense of 'irregular troops'.

Pau (piece of timber). Mal. *páu*, shaft.

Paulista (a Jesuit). Konk.

---

1 Gonçalves Viana disputes the Arabic origin of the word.

2 "In the breeding of **adens** some break the egg and bring out the duckling which they then rear for the market." F. Pinto, ch. xcvii.

"Peacocks, ganders, **adens**, and all domestic fowls." Lucena, Bk. X, ch. 18.

Pāvlist (l. us. at present).—Anglo-Ind. *Paulist* (obs.).[1]

Many legends of a mythic character are current in Goa in respect of the old Paulists.[2]

[The Jesuits were so called in Goa from the famous College of St. Paul (consecrated on the 25th January, 1542, the day of the conversion of St. Paul) which they had there, and the name spread all over India with the extension of the missionary work of the order.

The Church of St. Paul, completed in 1602, was the seat of the Jesuit College at Macao; this church, according to the testimony of Père Alexandre de Rhodes (*Voyages et Missions*, ed. 1884, p. 56, in Peter Mundy, *Travels*, Hak. Soc., Vol. III, pt. I, p. 163, n. 2.), was the most magnificent that he had seen, with the exception of St. Peter's at Rome, and from this Church and College the Jesuits in China derived the appellation 'Paulists', of which they appear to have been quite proud [1]

Yule says that the Jesuits "are still called Paolotti in Italy, especially by those who don't like them".]

Pavão (peacock). Mal. *pavam.*

Peão (foot-man, foot-soldier, messenger). Konk. *pyáṁv* (us. in Salsete).—Sinh. *piyon.*—Anglo-Ind. *peon.*[2]

---

1 The news I have is that Don Antonio goes to Śhagardy with his household and the *RR. PP.* **Paulistas** will look out for him with all zeal expecting that we will be sure to go with him" (1682). *O Chron. de Tissuary*, I, p. 318 [*RR.* is a plural form, abbreviation of 'Reverend' and *PP* of *Padres* ('Fathers or Priests'.]

[See also quotations from Tavernier and Pietro della Valle in *Hobson-Jobson.*]

2 "It was in the possession of the Jesuits (commonly called **Paulistas** with reference to the College of St. Paul)." *O Gabinete Litterario das Fontainhas.*

1 ["Jesuitts calling themselves **Paulists** and wherefore.

"As the Church (in Macao) is Named St. Paules, soe Doe they stile themselves **Paulists**, as Paules Disciples in imitating or Following him in his Function, For as hee was Cheiffe in conversion of the gentiles in those Daies, Soe Doe they attribute thatt office More peculier to themselves in converting the heathen off these tymes." Mundy, *Travels*, Hak. Soc, Vol. III, pt. i, pp. 163 and 164.]

2 "The Samorim ordered the **pião** to carry the letter and strictly forbade him to say anything about having seen it." Gaspar Correia, I, p. 421.

[Whitworth gives 'peon' as a corruption of Hindust. *piyada*, 'a foot-soldier'. He is wrong. The Port. word is the Lat. *pedanus*, though ultimately *peon* and *piyada* are akin in root.]

Peça (piece, piece of cloth). Konk. *pés*; vern. terms *nag*, *ḍāgiṇó*, *tākó*.—Tet. *pesa*.

In Konkani, *peṣa* is also the name of 'a piece of gold jewellery'.

[**Pedraria** (in the sense of 'precious stones') Anglo-Ind. *pedareea*, *pedaeria* (obs.)[1]—not in *Hobson-Jobson* nor in the *O.E.D.*]

Pedreiro (stone-mason). Konk. *pidrêr*, *pidrêl*; vern. terms, *gam̃vḍó*, *chirekāntí*.—Mar. *pidrêl*; vern. terms *gaunḍí*, *gavanḍyá*, *ráj*.—Sinh. *pedaréruvā*, *pedaréreṿā*; vern. terms *galvaḍuvá* (lit: 'a worker in stones').—Malayal. *peridéri*.[1]

[**Pedreiro, pederero** ("a small piece of ordnance, mostly used in ships to fire stones, nails, broken iron, or cartridge shot on an enemy attempting to board. It is managed by a swivel." Vieyra). Anglo-Ind. *pattarero*, *pateraro*, *petarero*, *paterero*[2].

"He placed a guard of **plains** from the place, so that the enemy might not enter once again through the villages." Diogo do Couto, Dec. V, vii, 3.

["But he (Caninge) had a tedious.. journey of yt,...beeinge sett on by the ennemye on the waye, whoe shott him through the bellye with an arrowe... and killed and hurte manye of his **pyonns**". Nicholas Withington (1612-16), in Foster, *Early Travels*, p. 200.]

[[1] "Aboute the tyme that I was in Synda, the Boloches tooke a boate wherin were seven Itallians and one Portungale fryer, which fought with them and were slayne everye man; only the Portungale escaped alive, whoe beeinge verye fatt, they ripped upp his bellye and searched whether there were anye gould or **pedareea** in his guts". Nicholas Withington, in Foster, *Early Travels*, O.U.P, p. 220.]

["**Pedaeria** various". Foster, *The Eng. Fact. 1618-1621*, p. 62.]

[1] With regard to the change of *r* into *l*, cf. *kadél*, from Port. *cadeira* ('chair'), *kontrél*, from Port. *cantareira* ('a wall cup-board'), in Konkani.

[2] ["Hee likewise in the generall letter to the Radja &c. gave positive Orders that each of the 3 Sea Ports Shold build and fitt out to Sea 2 men of warre Prows, each to carry 10 gunns and **Pattareros**, and well manned and fitted with Small arms." Bowrey, Hak. Soc, p 254.]

["11th March, 1683. This morning.. we weighed anchor . and being got up with Kegaria, we went on shore .. and landed at an old ruined Castle with

Pyrard uses the French form *perrier*[1] and Manucci the term *petrechos*[2] to denote the identical kind of mortar or swivel-gun. The Anglo-Indian forms are not in *Hobson-Jobson* nor in the *O.E.D.*]

? **Pegar** (to join; to stick; to take hold of). Mal. *pĕgaṅ* (also used in the sense of 'knit, tied, stuck to anything').—Jav. *pegen.*

According to Dr. Schuchardt, it is a vernacular term.

mud walls and thatched. We saw one small Iron Gun mounted and an Iron **Pateraro.**" Hedges, *Diary*, Hak. Soc., Vol. I, pp. 66 & 67.]

["Camels of War with **Patereroes**, on their Saddles, marched with a Pace laborious to the Guiders." Fryer, *East India*, etc., Hak. Soc., Vol. I, p. 271.]

["Camels that carry **Petereros.**" *Idem*, Vol. II, p. 112.]

1 ["We gave them a mainsail, of which they stood in need, and in exchange they gave us two perriers, or small iron cannon." Pyrard, *Voyage*, Hak. Soc., Vol. I, p. 23. See Gray's note on 'perrier.']

2 ["Their armament was of small pieces, swivel guns and *petrechos* of bronze, of which the muzzles whence the ball issues were fashioned into shapes of animals—tigers, lions, dogs, elephants, and crocodiles." Manucci, *Storia do Mogor*, ed. Irvine, Vol. II, p. 100. See also note in Vol. IV, p. 430.]

Peito (breast, chest). Konk. *pêt*; vern. term *harḍêṁ*—Mal. *peito* (Haex); vern. term *dada.*

Pelouro (a ball, a great shot). ? Beng. *pilurí.*—? Siam. *pliuĕk.*—Mal. *pelúru, pélor, pilóru, pílor.*—Ach. *pilor*—Batt. *pélur, pinúru.*—Sund., Mad. *pélor.*—Mac., Bug. *pilúru.*[1]

Bulloram Paul gives the Bengali *piluri* as equivalent to the English 'pillory'.

Pena (in the sense of 'pain; punishment'). Konk. *pén*; vern. terms *duḥkh, khant*; *danḍ.*—Mal. *pena*, a fine (Haex); vern. term *denda.*

Pena ('quill, writing-pen'). Konk. *pén.*—Mar. *pên.*—Guj. *pên. Sīsapên* (lit. 'lead pen'), pencil.—Beng. *pená*; the vern. Neo-Aryan terms are *kalam, lekhné.*—Sinh. *pe̤na pene, taṭu-pe̤na* (lit. 'wing feather'). *Pe̤napihiya*, pen-knife.—Tam. *péna pennei. Pene-katti*, pen-knife.—Malayal. *péna. Penak-katti*, pen-knife.—Tel. *pĕná.*—

1 "From your magazines help me with **pelouros** and gunpowder, of which I am at present in great need". *Letter from the King of Bata*, in F. Pinto, ch. xiii.

Kan. *pénu*. *Sīsapénu*, pencil.—Tul. *penu̥*, *pénu̥*.—Mal., Tet., Gal. *péna*.

Kalam, from the Greek *kálamos* (already introduced into Sanskrit, *kalama*, and also adopted in Arabic, *qalam*), is generally used in the Indian and Malay languages.[1] Even to-day, in different parts, the style, or a small rod with pointed end for scratching letters, is used for writing. *Pen*, in Japanese, appears to be from English, as *pin* is, because they end in a consonant.

Penacho (plume or bunch of feathers). Mac., Bug. *pináchu*.

Peneira (a sieve). Sinh. *penéraya*, *penēréya* (pl. *penéra*); vern. terms *chálanaya*, *śataponaya*.

Penhor (pledge, pawn). Konk. *pinhor*. *Pinhor davruṅk*, to pawn; vern. terms *gāháṇ*, *tāraṇ*, *aḍav*.—Mal. *panjar*, earnest-money.—Sund., Jav. *panjer*.

Penitência (penitence). Konk. *penitems*, *pinṭems*; vern. terms *prājit*, *pirājit*.—Tet. *peniténsi*.

Pepino (cucumber). Sinh. *pipiññā* (=*pipinha*); vern. terms *kẹkiri*, *tiyambar*.—| Mal. *pepinio*, according to Rumphius. |

Pera (for 'guava', *Psidium guayava*). Konk. *pér* (neut.); *pêr* ('the guava-tree', fem.).—Mar. *perú*; vern. term *jámb* (properly *Eugenia jambos*).—Guj. *per*, *perum*; vern. terms *jam*, *jamphal*.—Beng *perú*, *piyará*.—Sinh. *péra*.—Tam. *pērá* (also *gōyá palam* (lit. 'the guava fruit or the Goa-fruit'?).—Malayal *pērá* (the tree), *pērakká*, *pérakka*.—Kan. *pérlamara* (the tree), *pérla haṇṇu* (the fruit).—Tul. *péranggáyi*.[1]

Amrút or *amrúd* is the name

[1] Gonçalves Viana points out that the term is Semitic in origin.

[1] "Oranges, pomegranates, myrabalans, Indian **peras** which do not resemble ours." Pyrard. *Viagem* I, p. 338 [Hak. Soc., Vol. I, p. 399].

"Of Indian fruits there are many, **pera**, figs, *jangoma*, pine-apple, all in abundance, especially in Luabo." Fr. António da Conceição, in *O Chron. de Tissuary*, II, p. 42. [*Jangoma* is the fruit of the *Flacourtia cataphracta*.]

"There is another tree seen in the Island called **pereira**, which bears a fruit resembling the guava of America." Fr. Clemente da Ressurreição, II, p. 338.

of the 'guava' in Hindustani, and *amrud* is the name of the 'pear' in Persian. In Hindustani and Bengali it is also spoken of as the *saphari am* (lit. the 'journey mango' or, rather, 'foreign mango', see *Hobson-Jobson, s.v.* ananas), corrupted into *supārí ám*, 'areca-mango'.

In Burma, the guava is called *ma-la-kah-thi*, 'the Malacca-fruit', and the guava-tree *ma-la-kah-bin*. Siamese has *lùk fárăng*, 'fruit European', and *tŏn fárăng*, 'tree-foreign' (*fárăng*=Frank).

The plant is indigenous to America and was introduced into India by the Portuguese, who, owing to its similarity, called the fruit *pera*, ('pear'), just in the same way as they called the fruit of the banana-tree *figo* ('fig').

In Africa also the term *pera* is used to denote the 'guava'.

In Konkani, *perad* (from *perada* in the Portuguese dialect of Goa) is a conserve prepared from guavas. See *goiaba*.

[A. Siddiqi (in *JRAS*, July, 1927, p. 560) says: "It is only in Urdú and also in certain other Indian languages that the name *amrut* is applied to *guava*. The reason is quite clear: *guava* became perfectly naturalised in India, where pear never thrived. The resemblance in shape and colour of guava to pear obviously led to the adoption of *amruth* for "guava"—most probably by the Persians or Moghuls naturalised in Northern India. In the South-Indian Urdú a "guava" is جام probably on account of its resemblance to a pear-shaped bowl".

Marathi and Gujarati use *jamb* and *jam* for the 'guava', perhaps because the shape of the latter is similar to that of the *Eugenia jambos* (Hindi *gulab-jāman*, 'rose-jāman'), which in its turn is in form like an apple or a pear.]

Percha (*naut.*, rails of the head, the outward planks between the beak-head and the keel of a ship). L.-Hindust. *perchá*.

Perdão (pardon). Konk. *perdámv* (l. us.); vern. terms *bogsaṇém*, *māphí*.—Tet. *perdã*.

Perdição (perdition). Konk. *pirdisámv*; vern. terms *naś*, *satyanáś.*—Tet. *perdisã*; vern. term *lákon.*

Perdido (lost). Konk. *perdíd*, a person gone astray; vern. terms *hogaḍlaló, avdisá lãglaló.*—Tet. *perdídu*; vern. term *lákon.*

Peres ('a variety of mango'). Anglo-Ind. *peirie.*—Konk., Mar., Guj., *payrí* (through the influence of the English word). See *Afonsa*, [and notes to *Manga*].

[For the way Portuguese names have been mutilated in Western India, see *Ind. Antiq.*, Vols. XIX, p. 442 and XXIII, p. 76.]

Permissão (permission). Mal. *permísi*, [perhaps from Dutch.]

Pertenças (appurtenances). Anglo-Ind. *pertenças*, in Bombay. "It (foras) occurs in old grants of the local government especially in the phrase *foras* and **pertenças**, the latter also Port., dependencies, appurtenances." Wilson, [*Glossary*, p. 577].

Peru (popular form *perum*, turkey). Konk. *perúṁ.*—Hindi, Hindust., Or., Beng., Ass., Punj. *perú.*—Khas. *perú, pirú.*

Gonçalves Viana calls into question the derivation of the fowl's name from the South American state of Peru, because, says he, it is not a native of Peru, but probably of Mexico, and also because the Spaniards, who must have given the word to the Portuguese, call the bird *pavo*, 'peacock', or *pavo común*, 'the common peacock', and not *peru*, and he adds, "for the present the origin of the bird and its name in Portuguese is an enigma". But Diogo do Couto calls the birds *galinhas de Peru*, 'Peru hens': "And all along that route (from Abyssinia) they had been eating many *gallinhas* **do Perú**, partridges, wild cows, stags, doves, turtle doves" *Decadas*, VII, iv, 6.

"There are many pelicans, which are as large as a big **gallo do Peru**" ('Peru cock'). Fr. João dos Santos, *Ethiop. Or.* I, p. 135.

The French *coq d'Inde*, the German *Calecutische Hahn*, the Dutch *Kalkoen* (from Calicut), the Arabic *Dajáj Hindi*, the Turkish *Hind Tánugu* would point to an Indian origin; but the bird is not a native of India, and its name *peru* is an exotic. The word does not exist in Marathi and Gujarati. Hindustani has, side by side with *peru*, *šutra-murgh* (lit. 'camel-cock, ostrich') and *fíl-murgh* (lit. 'elephant-cock') from Persian. The Dravidian languages describe the bird by means of various compounds, some of which assign to it a foreign origin.

[The view generally accepted that the domestic fowl all over the world had been derived from a bird met with it in its wild state in India had very likely a great deal to do with assigning the turkey also to India. That the turkey was an exotic and introduced into India by the Portuguese is borne out by the description of the bird from the pen of the Emperor Jahāngīr given below.[1] The turkey, domesticated by the people of Mexico and Peru, was introduced into Europe by the Spaniards, soon after the discovery of Mexico.]

Pés (feet). Mol. *pees* (=*pés*), camphor of an inferior quality. See *barriga* and *cabeça*.

Peste (plague). Konk. *pest*; vern. terms *mārí, marí, marík, piḍá*.—Tet., Gal. *péstí*.

---

[1] ["On the 16th Farwardîn [3 April, 1612 A.D.] Muqarrab Khân brought from Goa certain "rarities he met with in that port... Among these were some animals that were very strange and wonderful, such as I had never seen, and up to this time no one had known their names... One of these animals in body is larger than a peahen and smaller than a peacock. When it is in heat and displays itself, it spreads out its feathers like a peacock and dances about. Its beak and legs are like those of a cock. Its head and neck and the part under the throat are every minute of a different colour. When it is in heat it is quite red...and after a while it becomes white in the same places and looks like cotton... Two pieces of flesh it has on its head like the comb of a cock. A strange thing is this, that when it is in heat the aforesaid piece of flesh hangs down to the length of a span from the top of its head like an elephant's trunk, and again when he raises it up, it appears on its head like the horn of a rhinoceros, to the extent of two finger-breadths. Round its eyes it is always of a turquoise colour, and does not change. Its feathers appear to be of various colours, differing from the colours of the peacock's feathers" *Túzuk-i-Jahângîrí*, Tr. Rogers and Beveridge, I, 215-6. 'Aligarh Text, 104, last line, in Hodivala, *Notes on Hobson-Jobson*, in *Ind. Antiq.*, Vol. LVIII.]

? **Petardo** (petard). Mal. *pétas*, *petásan*.—Siam. *pa-thăt*.

Pia (stone trough; font). Konk. *pí*.—Beng., Tam. *piyá*. —Tet., Gal. *pia*.

Picadeira (a mason's pick-axe). Konk., Mar., *pikándar*.

Picão (sort of pick-axe with two sharp points used by stone-cutters). Konk. *pikáṁv*.—Mar. *pikáṁv*, ? *pikás*.—? Guj. *tíkam*.—Sinh. *pikama*; *piká-siya* (from the English 'pick-axe' ?).—Malayal. *pikkam*.—Tul. *pikkasu*, *pikkásu* (perhaps from English).[1]

Picota ('a pump-brake'). Anglo-Ind. *picotta*, *picottah* (us. in S. India), "a machine for raising water, which consists of a long lever or yard, pivotted on an upright post, weighted on the short arm and bearing a line and bucket on the long arm".[1]

The term must be well-known, because Percival, in his Tamil-English Dictionary. gives 'picotta' as the equivalent of the Tamil *tulá*, and 'the arms of a picotta' of *tulam*.

Pilar (*subst.*, a pillar, beam).

---

[1] "And so they used to carry *bancos pinchados*, *marões*, **picões**, gunpowder, and other materials." João de Barros, Dec. II, vii, 9. [*Banco pinchado* is a contrivance which had the appearance of a bench (*banco*) and was used formerly in battering down (*pinchar*) walls. *Marões* from *marram* is a sort of hammer used by bombardiers.]

"The Captain sent him a hundred men with mattocks, and another hundred with **picões**, and a third hundred with baskets and bowls." Gaspar Correia. III, p. 617.

[1] "They take a great ox-cart and set up therein a tall **picota** like those used in Castille for drawing water from wells." Duarte Barbosa, *Livro*, p. 304 [Hak. Soc., ed. Longworth Dames, Vol. I, p. 221. Mr. Dames (p. 220) says that this water lift was no doubt a contrivance like the *shadūf* used in Egypt, and introduced into Spain by the Arabs. It consists of a leather bag or a bucket which hangs from the end of the long arm of a bamboo crane, while the short arm is weighted with a heavy stone and so nearly balanced that a slight pressure will raise the long arm into the air.]

"The place in which the King orders justice to be administered to wrong doers is the **picota**." Gaspar Correia IV, p. 151. [This is another acceptation of *picota*. The dictionaries give 'a species of a pillory' as one of the meanings of the word, and it is apparently used here in that sense. In *Hobson-Jobson*, *s.v.* picottah, there is a quotation also from Correia, in which the word has the meaning of a 'pillory'. Yule says that the *picota* or ship's pump at sea was also used as a 'pillory' which explains its use by Correia in that sense.]

Mad. *pélar.*—Jav. *pilar. Milar,* "to crack along the whole length" (Heyligers).

The change of *p* into *m* is normal in the formation of Javanese words.

Piloto (pilot). Konk. *pilôt*; vern. term *sukāṇeṁkár.*—Tet. *pilôtu.*

Pimentos (*Capsicum grossum*, Roxb.). Camb. *metis.*

With regard to the dropping of the first syllable, cf. *Sês* = *Francês* ('Frenchman').

[? **Pinaca** (the residue that remains after oil has been expressed from seeds or coconuts; the word is current in Asio-Portuguese). Anglo-Ind. *poonac.*[1]

The Port. form shows the influence of Konk. *pinãk* (Sansk. *piṇyāka*): the Anglo-Indian form appears to be directly taken from the Tamil *punnakku* (Whitworth gives it as *pinnakku*) or the Sinh. *punakku* and not influenced by Portuguese dialects, though *pinaca* occurs much earlier than *poonac* in the writings of European travellers. The word is not mentioned in *Hobson-Jobson*, but is found in the *O.E.D.*]

Pinchar (to push, to thrust). Mal. *pícha*, to fling or throw down.

Used in the same sense in the Portuguese dialects in Asia.

[**Pinda** (*Arachis hypogaea*, ground-nut). Anglo-Ind. *pindar.*[1] Not in *Hobson-Jobson.*

The Portuguese word is an adaptation of *mpinda* used in Congo. The *O.E.D.* says that

---

1 [1786.—"What is left after the oil is expressed from coco-nut is **Pinàca**, which is useful for fattening pigs, ducks, and hens." Fra Paolino, *Viaggio*, p. 116, in *Glossario.*]

["The following are only a few of the countless uses of this invaluable tree (the palm): . . . The *oil*, for rheumatism, for anointing the hair, for soap, for candles, for light; and the **poonak**, or refuse of the nut after expressing the oil, for cattle and poultry." Tennent, *Ceylon* (1859), Vol. I, p. 109, n.]

1 ["Sometimes they (the common people of Surat) Feast with a little Fish, and that with a few **Pindars** is esteemed a splendid Banquet. These **Pindars** are sown under ground and grow there without sprouting above the surface, the Cod in which they are Inclosed is an Inch long, like that of our Pease and Beans. .. Some of these I brought for *England*, which were sown in the Bishop of *London's* Garden, but whether they will thrive in this Climate is yet uncertain." Ovington, *Voyage to Surat*, O.U.P., p. 50.]

this name for the nut was carried by negroes to America, and that the name for the ground- or pea-nut in the West Indies and Southern United States is 'pindar'. But which is the original home of this nut? De Candolle inclines to the view that it is a native of Brazil and that it was carried from there to Africa and Asia by the Portuguese. But there are serious difficulties in the way of accepting this view; the most important of which is that the dispersion of this plant over a very large part of Africa and the extensive zones in which it is and was cultivated cannot be easily accounted for by assuming that the plant was introduced into Africa after 1500. Burton (*Lake Regions*, II, 52) referring to a region situated on the borders of Tanganika says "*U-Karanga* signifies etymologically the land of ground-nuts." Now there are those who identify 'U-karanga' with the land of Mocarangas or —Ba-caranga—which as a province of the grand empire of Monomatapa was known to Fr. João dos Santos. If, therefore, the etymology suggested by Burton is reliable, it becomes very difficult to believe that a plant introduced into Africa after 1500 should by 1580 or 1590 have given its name to a vast region in the interior of the continent.

There are equally great difficulties in assuming that the plant is a native of Africa and was therefrom introduced into America.

There are a series of names by which this plant was known to the Portuguese. Some like the following appear to be of Brazilian origin: *manobi*, *mundubi*, *mendobi*, *mendobim*, *mendoim*, *amendoim*; others clearly African in origin: *mancarra* in Guinea and Cape Verde Islands; *mpinda* on the Congo Coast; *ginguba* in Angola; *karonga* in Swahili on the east coast.

The more probable view seems to be to regard it as indigenous both to America and to Africa. See Ficalho, *Plantas Uteis da Africa Portugueza*, p. 133 *seq.*, where the question has been discussed at length. Watt, however, is of opinion that the home of the plant is Brazil.

The ground-nut is another of the long list of plants introduced into India in recent times. In India it is known by different names in different localities; some of these are perhaps evidence of successive and independent efforts to introduce it into India. "It may have come from China to Bengal (hence the name *Chini-badam*); from Manila to South India (*Manila-kotai*), and from Africa and very possibly direct from Brazil as well, to Western India." Watt, *The Comm. Prod. of Ind.*, (1908), p. 74. In Konkani it is known as *Mosmichim biknam* ('Mozambique nuts') which attests to its introduction into Goa from Africa.]

[? **Pingue** (*adj.*, fat). Anglo-Ind. *penguin*, the general name of birds of the family *Spheniscidae*.

Yule says that 'penguin' may be from the Port. *pingue*, 'fat', but this conjecture is not accepted by the *O.E.D.* which also rejects, after due analysis and examination, all other derivations till now put forward and maintains that the origin of the word is obscure. The *Novo Diccionário* derives Port. *penguim* from Fr. *pingouin*. Pyrard mentions "numbers of birds called **pinguy**, which lay there (in the Maldive Islands) their eggs and young, and in quantities so prodigious that one could not.... plant one's foot without touching their eggs or young". But the editor (Hak. Soc., Vol. I, p. 97) says that there are no penguins at the Maldives and that the author is describing probably *manchots*.]

Pinho (pine-wood). Konk. *pinh.*—Malayal. *piññа* (=*pinha*). *Piññapeṭṭi*, pine-wood box.

Pintada (*Melagris numida*, Linn., Guinea-fowl; "the fowl of India or Angola"). Konk. *pintālgém*.—Anglo-Ind. *pintado*.—Indo-Fr. *pintade*.[1]

[The *Novo Diccionário* says that *pintada* in the above meaning is fem. of *pintado*, 'speckled'.]

---

1 "Everywhere on this island (of Saint Helena) there are many wild goats, many wild **pintadas**, very beautiful and big." João dos Santos, *Ethiop. Or.*, II, p. 379.

"The interior of the island [of Fogo in Cape Verde Islands] abounds with

Pintado (painted or spotted cloth). Anglo-Ind. *pintado* (obs.), chintz.[1] [See *salpicado*.]

---

game; **pintadas** (which they call Guinea-fowls), quails, and mountain goats" *Jour. Geo. Soc. Lisb.*, 5th series, p. 385. [Fryer (*East India and Persia*, Vol. I, Hak. Soc., p. 51) speaks of meeting "with those feathered Harbingers of the Cape, as **Pintado** Birds, etc.", and the editor identifies them with the "Cape pigeon or Pintado (Port *pintado*, "painted") Petrel, *Daption Capensis*", and also says in *Hobson-Jobson* (*s.v.*) that the word is more commonly applied to the Cape pigeon].

["**Pintados** is a Fowle well knowne and Much Noted by Seamen in these partts: Found no where butt aboutt Cape Bona-esperanza allthough seene sometymes 4 or 500 leagues off ot it to the Northward and Southward off itt aboutt the biggnesse of Pidgeons." Mundy, *Travels*, Hak. Soc., Vol III, pt. II, p. 359.]

[1] "And so there are (in Gujarat) also other **pintados** ('coloured clothes') of diverse kinds." Duarte Barbosa, p 282 [Hak. Soc., ed. Dames, Vol. I, p. 154]

"Here (in Paleacate) are made great abundance of cotton **pintados**." *Id.*, p. 360 [Hak. Soc., ed. Dames, Vol. II, p. 132].

"They use to make payment in **pintados** from Cambaya." Gaspar Correia, II, p. 41.

"Four bales of tapestry and **pintados**." *Id.* III, p. 51.

["For these remooue all like princes,

Pintar (to paint). Konk. *pintár-karuṅk*, *pintāruṅk* (an exceptional formation from the substantive *pintár*, 'painting').—Sinh. *pintárę-karaṇavā*.—Malayal. *pintāṛiká*.—Gal. *pintar*.

Pintura (painting). Konk. *pintúr*; *pintár* (from the Port. verb.); vern. terms *chitr*, *nakśó*, *pratirúp*.—Sinh. *pintáruva*, *pintárēma*, *pintūraya*; vern. terms *sitiyama*.—Malayal. *pintárani*.

Pipa (a cask; also a barrel). Konk. *píp* (also *pimp*, in Kanara).—Mar. *píp*, *pimp*.—Guj. *píp*.—Hindi, Hindust., Nep., Punj. *pīpá*.—Beng. *pipá*, *pipe*, *pimpa*.—Sindh. *pípa*.—Sinh. *píppaya*, *píppe*. *Píppa-vaḍuvá*, a cooper.—Tam. *píppā*.—Malayal. *píppa*.—Tel.

---

with seuerall shiftes of tents that goe before, compassed in with Pales of **Pintadoes**, which are ready euer two dayes for them." Sir Thomas Roe, *Embassy*, Hak. Soc., Vol. II, p. 275.]

["They (the 'Gentues') are generally a very Subtile and Cunninge Sort of men, Especially in the way of merchandizeing, also Very ingenuos in workinge Cotton Cloth or Silks, **pantados**." Bowrey, Hak. Soc., p. 9.]

["There was not One peece of **Pintadoe**, or any other Paintings." *Id.*, p. 9, n.]

pípaya.—Kan. *pípe*, *pipái*, *pīpáyi*.—Tul. *pipa*, *pīpáya*, *pipáyi*.—Gar., Khas., Mal., Ach., Mac., Nic., Malag. *pípa*.—Siam. *píb*; vern. term *thắng*.—| Chin. *pí-pá-tung* |.[1]

There is another word *pipa* in Malay, Madurese and Galoli (*pipô* in Javanese), which comes from the English 'pipe' and signifies a 'tobacco pipe'.

Pires (saucer). Konk. *pír*.—Hindust. *pirich*; vern. terms *taštarí*, *thālí* (as in Hindi).—Beng. *pirij*.—Ass. *piris*.—Sinh. *pírissya*.—Tam. *píris*.—Khas. *phiris*.—? Mal., Ach., Sund., Jav., Bal., Day., Mac., Bug. *piring*.—Tet., Gal. *píris*.

The Portuguese dialect of Malacca has *pirin*, and Cape Dutch *pierentje*.[2]

Kacha-piring, *picha piring* (lit. 'broken-plate'), in Sundanese, is the name of *Gardenia florida*.

Rigg says: "*Piring*, plate, big plate such as is used by Europeans. The small Chinese plates which are used by the natives are called *pinggan*." But Swettenham on the contrary in his English-Malay dictionary gives: Saucer, *piring*; Plate, *pinggan*. Favre gives to both words the meaning of "*soucoupe* ('saucer'), *assiette* ('plate')". Bikkers mentions *piring*, 'plate'; and *piring teh* (lit. 'plate for tea'), 'saucer'. | Wilkinson gives it the meanings of 'plate, saucer'. |

The word *pires* appears to be originally a Malay word, adopted by the Portuguese and taken to India together with the word *chá*. But the termination *es* or *is* offers some difficulty, because *piring* ought normally to give *pirim*. Per-

---

1 "For a Portuguese not to wish to pay for the transport of a **pipa** of wine!" Damião de Góis, *Chron. de D. Manuel*, IV, ch. 18.

"He handed over the cooper's workshop to Francisco de Mello Pereira, so that he might get him to turn out barrels, large wooden bowls, **pipas**." Diogo do Couto, Dec. VI, viii, 5.

2 "A dozen **pyres** from India, of ordinary quality, each valued at 80 *reis*" (1613). A. Tomás Pires, *Materiaes*, in *Jour. Geo. Soc. Lisb.*, 16th ser., p. 745.

"A **pires** of silver, gilded over." *Ibid.*, p. 754.

"He (the King of Annam) sent three big trays, japanned and gilt, round, two spans high, full of many dishes; each of these trays contained many **pires**, forming a sort of a mound, in which there were all sorts of eatables.' A. F. Cardim (1649), *Batalhas*, p. 80.

haps *pires* is the plural of **pirim* and stands for **pirins*. Its derivation from the Hindustani *pirich* is improbable, for it has the appearance of an exotic and is not mentioned by Shakespear in 1817.

[In the *Glossario*, the author says that it appears to him that the Hindust. *pirich*, the Beng. *pirij*, and the Sinh. *pirissiya* are adaptations of the Port. *pires*. The vern. terms in Hindustani, as also in Hindi, are *taśtari*, *thali*. The word is not mentioned by Shakespear in 1817; on the other hand it is to be met with in almost all the Malasian languages in the form *piring*, 'a little plate.' From this it might be inferred that it was in Malasia that the Portuguese first received the word, and from there introduced it into India. Again, Cândido Figueiredo mentions *pire* as a cant term and gives it the meaning of a 'plate.' To this Dalgado says that it is not improbable that the word in this form, modified by Portuguese influence, was imported by gipsies from the Malay *piring*, 'small plate.' It might be mentioned that Portuguese is the only one of all the European languages which uses *pires* in the sense of 'saucer,' and this in itself is proof that the word is of non-European origin. With regard to the borrowing of names for tea and everything connected with its service, see *chicara*.]

[? **Piroga** (a long canoe or dug out used by the American Indians).—Anglo-Ind. *porgo*, *purgo*, *purga*, *pork* (obs.).[1]

---

[1] ["Here in Bengala they have every day in one place or other a great market which they call Chandeau, and they have many great boats which they call **Pericose**, wherewithall they go from place to place and buy rice and many other things". Ralph Fitch (1583-91), in Foster, *Early Travels in India* (1921), p. 26. Foster says that 'pericose' is the 'porgos' or 'purgoos' of later writers, and that the word is possibly a corruption of the Port. *barca*; if this is so, it is the earliest reference to this word.]

["Immediately on receiving this information, the Father Vicar de la Vara ordered a **porca** to be got ready. This kind of rowing boat is almost as common in those parts (Kingdom of Angelim or Hijli) as dinguos and balones . . . The **porca** was manned with strong rowers . . " Manrique, *Travels*, Hak. Soc., Vol. I, p 24.]

["*Severall Sorts of boats that Use the Rivers, whose Shapes are as here followeth.* . . . .

'Porgo' in this sense is not found in the *O.E.D.* Yule says that 'porgo' most probably represents Port. *peragua*. Port. dictionaries mention no such word, but it is evident that Yule is referring to Port. *piroga* (Span. *piragua*, Fr. *pirogue*). Skeat lists it among Carib-bean words (*Notes* on *Eng. Etym.* (1901), p. 349), but Marcel Devic (Supplement to Littré) connects the Fr. *pirogue* with Malay *prāhū* which, according to Yule, is responsible for Anglo-Ind. *prow*, *parao*, etc., (See *parao*). Sir Richard Temple (*Ind. Antiq.*, Vol. XXX, p. 161) is of the opinion that 'purgoo or porgo' is probably an obsolete Anglo-Indian corruption of an Indian corruption of the Portuguese term *barco*, *barca*, terms which were used for any kind of sailing boat by the early Portuguese visitors to the East.[1]

"The purgoo then was a **barge (barca)** confused with the **bark (barco)**, just as the sail-less barge and the sailing bark have been confused in the West" (*op. cit.*, p. 162).

There is a description of a 'purgoo' in Bowrey (p. 228)

A **Purgoo**. These Use for the most part between Hugly and Pyplo and Ballasore. With these boats they carry goods into the Roads On board English and Dutch &c., Ships". Bowrey, Hak. Soc., p. 228. See also editor's note for other references in which the word is spelt 'Porgo', 'Porgoo', 'Porkoe', and 'Porka'.]

["*January* 30 (1683).—The *Thomas* arrived with ye 28 Bales of Silk taken out of the **Purga**, and was dispatched for Hugly ye same night". Hedges, *Diary*, Vol. I, p. 65.]

["Will send aboard with all expedition both goods and provisions—'some by the pynnace, others by **porks**'". Foster, *The English Factories 1634–1636*, p. 51.]

---

1 ["Into the Island ot Çuaquem they imported many spices from India, and there they embarked in *geluas* (which are a kind of barques (*barcos*), like *caravelas*, which ply in the Straits), and were carried to Coçaer . . . and there (Canà) they took passage in barges (*barcas*), and in a few days' time reached Cairo". *Comm. of A. Albuquerque*, Hak. Soc., Vol. II, p. 230.]

[1504.—"All the *paraaos* and *catures* left and many other small barks (*barcos*) which are called *tones*." *Letters of A. Albuquerque*, Lisbon, III, p. 261.]

[1560.—"All the people went in small boats (*bateis*); and the King in his barks (*barcos*) which are of fine workmanship and which are called *tones*". Gaspar Correia, *Lendas*, I, p. 378, in *Glossario*.]

and also an illustration (Pl. XIII) which most certainly does not look like an American Indian canoe.]

Pistola (a pistol). Konk., Guj. *pístol*.—Mar. *pistol*, *pistúl*.—Hindust. *pistol*, *pistaul*.—Beng. *pistol*.—Sindh. *pistola*.—Punj. *pistaul*.—Sinh. *pistólaya*, *pistóle*.—Tel. *pistólu*.—Kan., Tul. *pistúlu*.—Gar., Mal. *pistol*.—Ach. *mestol*. Cf. *meskut* =*biscoito* ('biscuit').—Batt. *pestúl*.—Sund. *péstol*.—Nic., Tet., Gal. *pistola*.—Jap. *pistoru*, *pisutoru*.— | Turk. *píshtow*.[1] |

Some dictionaries give as the source-word the English 'pistol' or the Dutch *pistool*. Dr. Schuchardt refers the Malay word to Dutch.

Poa (*naut*., bridle of the bow-line). L.-Hindust. *páo*.

Pobre (poor). Konk. *pobre* (l. us.). *Pobrāṅchéṁ ghar*, asylum for the poor.—Beng. *pobrí* (*subst*.). Properly speaking, it denotes 'the servant of the church' (such as a bell-ringer, grave-digger, etc.), who must formerly have been selected from amongst the poor.

Pobreza (poverty). Mal. *pavresa* (Haex).

Poial ("a raised platform on which people sit, usually under the verandah or on either side of the door of the house"). Konk. *puyál*.—Tel. *payal*, *payálu*.—Anglo-Ind. *pial*.—Indo-Fr. *poyal*.[1]

[The Port. word is itself derived from the Lat. *podium*, 'a projecting base, a balcony'. Yule says it corresponds to the N. India *chabūtra*.]

? **Policia** (police). Konk., Guj., Hindust. *polis*.—Tel. *polísu*.—Kan. *pólis*. The forms in some of the vernaculars, perhaps, owe their origin to English.

Poltrona (arm chair, as a rule, stuffed). Konk. *pultran*.—? Mal. *pātarána*.

Gonçalves Viana throws doubt on the Portuguese origin with reference to the Malay word.

[The Port. word is the It. *poltrona*, the feminine of

[1] "The arms which could be employed in this post were blunderbusses and pistolas." João Ribeiro, *Fatalidade hist*., Bk. II, ch. xxiv.

[1] "There were large seats like poyaes built of earth, very well made." Gaspar Correia, I, p. 87.

poltrone, in the sense of 'a lazy fellow'. *Poltrona* in It. is also 'a large chair, with arms, and almost always cushioned'—the very seat for an idler. Cf. the English 'easy-chair'.]

Polvorinho (powder-flask). Konk. *polvorính*; vern. term *tośdán*.—Tet. *polvorínhu*.

Pomba (dove). Mal. *pomba, pombaq, pamba, pambaq*; vernacular term *parapāti*.—Tet., Gal. *pomba*.

? **Pompa** (pomp). Mal., Sund. *pompa*.—Jav., | Mad. | *pómpô*.

Dr. Heyligers, who mentions the word and assigns to it a Portuguese origin, gives it the French meaning *pompe*, which may stand as much for 'pomp' as for 'pump'. In the former meaning, it may be derived from Portuguese; but in the second, undoubtably, from the Dutch *pomp* or the English 'pump'. Malay has *bomba* and *pomba* in this sense. | Wilkinson derives the word from Dutch and gives it the meaning of 'pump'. | See *bomba*.

Ponta (peak, tip). Konk. *pont*.—? Mar. *pot*; vern. terms *taḍ, tembí, agr, damas, śiṅg, suṅk, poṅkh, pālamv, padar* (according to different senses).—L.-Hindust. *pont, pontá, puntá*, promontory; *pontá*, the end of a rope. *Ponte ká phutín*, or *putín*, thick knot of the ropes of the sails. *Puntá chhoṛ dená*, to double a cape at sea.—Ach. *ponton*.

Molesworth derives *pot* from the Persian *póta* or *móṭa*.

Ponto (point, stitch, dot). Konk. *pónt*.—Bug. *póntu* (in a game of cards).—Tet., Gal. *póntu*.

Por (*prep.*, for). Mal. *por*, *for*.

Porcelana (porcelain, chinaware). Konk. *phuslán*. a porringer; vern. term *kāṁsó*.—Sinh. *pusalana, kusláua*, cup, beaker.

Persulana has the same meaning as *tigella*, 'a porringer', in the Portuguese of Goa. Gonçalves Viana says (*Palestras Filológicas*) that "the old Portuguese chroniclers regarded the term porcelana as synonymous with *chávena* ('tea-cup')".[1]

[1] Fernão Pinto invariably uses *perçolana* for *porcelana*.

"They were ready to give me in Balagate a **porcelana** for 200 *pardaos*." Garcia da Orta, Col. xliv.

[The Port. word comes from the Italian *porcellana*, which in mediæval times was the name given to the molluscs called *Cypraeidae*, or 'Venus shells', or in India 'cowries'. The word is adapted from the It. *porcella*, diminutive of *porco*, which is the same as the Latin *porcus*, 'a hog', and was applied to these shells because of their strong resemblance to the body and back of a pig. The enamel of these shells was used

---

"**Porcelana** is here used in the sense of a cup; it was customary to use it in that sense in that age." Conde de Ficalho [*Coloquios*, Vol. II, p. 221].

"Fifteen to twenty scores of **porcelanas** and as many more of plates." (1585). *Archivo Port. Or.*, fasc. 5th, p. 1021.

["'They make here (in China) great store of **porcelain**, which is good merchandize everywhere. This they make from the shells of fish ground fine, from eggshells and the white of eggs and other materials. From these they make a paste which they place under the ground "for a certain time." This among them is held to be a valuable property and treasure, for the nearer the time approaches for working it the greater is its value." Barbosa, Hak. Soc., ed. Dames, Vol. II, pp. 213 and 214. See also editor's note.]

"The earthen Pots, **Porcelains** ('Cuppes') and vessels that are made there (China), are not to bee numbred, which are yearely carried into India, Portingall, Nova Spaignia . . . . These Pots and **Porcelains** ('Cups') are made . . . of a certaine earth that is verie hard, which is beaten smal and then layed to stéepe in Cesterns of stone full of water." Linschoten, *Voyage*, Hak. Soc., Vol. I, pp. 129 and 130.]

["The heathenish Indians that dwell in Goa are verie rich Marchants, and . . . . . not onely sell all kindes of Silkes, Sattins, Damaskes, and curious works of **Porselyne** from China and other places, but . . . Silke . . ." *Id.*, p. 228.]

["When the Portugals go from Macao in China to Japan, they carry much white silke, golde, muske, and **porcelanes** and they bring from thence nothing but silver" Ralph Fitch, in Foster, *Early Travels* (1921), p. 41.]

["A chiefe citie of trade in his (Tartar) territorie is Yar Chaun (Yārkhand), whence comes much silke, **purslane**, muske, and rheubarb." William Finch, in *op. cit.*, p. 169.]

[References to the term 'porcelain,' in its various forms from English and Dutch writers have been given, because it is not easy to say for certain whether their use of this word (in use in Europe from about the 14th century), especially in reference to the Portuguese trade in this article, and in its acceptation of 'a tea cup', which is peculiar to Portuguese, was not influenced by the currency which the Portuguese term must have at one time acquired in India and the Far East.]

in the Middle Ages in lining ornamental pottery and especially cups. From this the word came to signify in Portugal the cup itself, and finally to denote the material out of which cups are made, and this is the meaning which it generally has today.]

Porco (pig). Malayal, *pórkku* (l. us.) ; vern. terms *panni*, *súkaram*.

The motive for the introduction of this word into Malayalam is not known; perhaps it was the same as brought about the adoption of *burro* ('ass') in Sinhalese.

Por força (by force). Mal. *par forsa, per forsa* (Haex).

| **Portugal** (Portugal). Pers. *purtughál*, orange; vern. terms *naránj, nárang*.—Turk. *pòrtugál*.

Italians also call the orange *portogallo*, but it is not known whether they transmitted the name to the Turks and the Persians, or whether the latter received it from some other source. See *Hobson-Jobson*, *s.v.* orange. |

[Yule thinks that, though it is scarcely right to suppose that the Portuguese first brought the sweet orange into Europe from China, credit must be given to them for the cultivation and propagation of the fruit in Portugal, especially, in Cintra; for thus only can one account for the persistence with which the name of *Portugals* has adhered to the fruit in question. "The familiar name of the large sweet orange in Sicily and Italy is *portogallo*, and nothing else; in Greece *portogalea*, in Albanian *protokale*, among the Kurds *portōghāl*; whilst even colloquial Arabic has *burtūḳān*."]

Português (a Portuguese). Konk. *Portuguêz*; vern. term *phirangí* (from the Persian).—Tet. *Portugêz*.

[Whitworth says that Portuguese is a term "applied in India not only to immigrants from Portugal, but also to the community of mixed Portuguese and Indian descent permanently settled in India. The latter are in western India called also Goanese." It is true that the 'Goanese' not only in western but also other parts of India are spoken of as 'Portuguese', but the implication that they are of mixed Portuguese and Indian descent is certainly not correct. The inhabitants of Goa with very few exceptions are pure Indians and have no vestige of Portuguese blood. Albuquerque's well-known policy of encouraging the Portuguese to marry women of the country has, perhaps, given currency to the belief that the Christian inhabitants of Goa who affect European ways of dress and have Portuguese names are the descendants of these marriages. This is far from the truth. The descendants of these and similar alliances during the centuries of Portuguese connection with the East are known as *mestiços* or half-breeds and form a social stratum distinct from that of the Christian natives who are converts from Hinduism. These latter would regard it as a very great offence to be referred to as being of mixed descent.

Some of the Christian inhabitants of Goa who emigrate to British India in search of their livelihood describe themselves as Portuguese. They do this because they believe that such a designation gives them a better social status and provides opportunities for more lucrative employment; also because they think that Portuguese constitutional law which recognises the political and social equality of the colonials with the citizens of Portugal gives them also a right to describe themselves as Portuguese. There are others who desire to stress their own individuality and race and to demonstrate their regard for their own country and its history and call themselves Goans—not Goanese;[1] the latter term has come to be regarded among them as containing a sneer. Others again who are alive to the confusion that results from Indians calling themselves Portuguese try to get over the difficulty by a sort of compromise and call themselves Indo-Portuguese or Goa-Portuguese. Thus in Bombay there used to exist two institutions belonging

[1] ["The growth of Goan communities in British India has been very marked and remarkable during late years.....The Goans have their school and Institute in Poona, societies in Bhusawal and Harda and a Hall and Association in Karachi—the outcome of much self-sacrifice and patriotism." *Boletim Indiano*, No. 1, p. 8.]

to these emigrants from Goa one of which was called the '*Gremio Português*' and the other '*União Goana*', whereas in Calcutta they have a review called 'The Indo-Portuguese Review' and in Karachi their principal centre of social life is known as 'The Goa-Portuguese Association.'

In their early connection with Goa the Portuguese referred to its inhabitants as *Canarins*, but as this term, like 'Goanese' in British India, came to be regarded as conveying an offensive connotation, they at the present time speak of the people of Goa as *Goeses* and not *Goanos*.

The Portuguese policy of intermarriages had been fruitful in a fairly large Luso-Indian population which was to be found in the principal centres of Portuguese trade in India: Calcutta, Madras, Cochin, etc. These mixed descendants were at one time proud of their Portuguese extraction and names, spoke a dialect of Portuguese, and described themselves as 'Portuguese', but during the closing decades of the last century, with the recognition of the Eurasian or Anglo-Indian community as deserving of especial consideration at the hands of the British Indian Government, the Luso-Indians were not slow to identify themselves with the Anglo-Indians with the hope of bettering their prospects. They gave up Portuguese speech, altered their Portuguese surnames, intermarried with Anglo-Indians, and, in fact, did everything that they thought necessary to draw a veil over their past history. When English factors or travellers speak of the 'Black Portuguese'[1] or *Kala Firingis*, they are probably referring to those Portuguese half-breeds who were found in most of the important cities in the East and, perhaps in some cases, to Indian converts to Christianity who

[1] ["The inhabitants (of the Island Junkzelone) are Siams, about 2,000 soules, and about 200 or 300 black Christians, who call themselves Portoguese ....The black Portogues would be sure to joyn with any European that settles there." *Ind. Antiq.*, Vol. LX, July 1931, p. 103.]

["I would send the Cala Franguis, by which term they indicate the coloured Christians who accompany and serve the Portuguese." Manrique, *Travels*, Hak. Soc., Vol. II, p. 228.]

adopted Portuguese style of dress. (See *mestiço* and *topaz*.)

Whilst on th subject it is interesting to record that the indigenous Christian inhabitants of Bombay, Salsete and Bassein, who nowadays call themselves 'East Indians' and who were referred to by the Portuguese as '*Norteiros*' (see note to *Sul*), spoke of themselves in the sixties and seventies of the last century either as 'Portuguese' or 'Native Portuguese' [1].]

Porteiro (porter). Konk. *portêr*.—Mal. *portero*, especially the door-keeper of the courts of justice.

Posta ('post, post-office'). Konk. *pôst*; vern. term is *ḍâṅk* (l. us.). *Postā-kár*, postman.—? Ar. *būsaṭa* (from Italian, according to Belot).

Posta ('a slice'). Konk. *pôst*; vern. terms *kapó*, *ravó*.—Gal. *posta*.— | Turk. *póssta*. |

Pôsto (office, employment). Konk. *pôst*; vern. terms *darzó*, *adhikár*.—Tet. *pôstu*.

[**Povo** (inhabitants, common people, parishioners). Konk. *pov*. (l. us.); vern. terms *lak*, *prajá*, *rayt*.—Anglo-Ind. *povo* (obs.).[1]

---

[1] ["The **Native Portuguese** community of Bombay, and its condition. - Ever since we have been in a position to judge for ourselves, we have been at a loss to comprehend by what anomaly, or fatality, an important section of the community in this city, we mean the Native Christians, denominated the *Portuguese*...have been treated with such disregard and indifference as to be reduced to utter insignificance both in the eyes of our rulers and the people at large." *O Patriota*, July 1, 1871, p. 9.]

["Our gratuitous adversaries, the Goanese sojourners, have taken it into their heads to charge the Bombay **Native Portuguese**, and especially the Editor of this Periodical...with envy and hatred towards them." *Idem*, Dec., 1874, p. 45.]

[1] ["And under these the names of one hundred and twenty of the eminents of the **Povo** in behalf of the whole **Povo** of the Isle" (of Bombay). *Articles of agreement made and entered into between the Right Honorable Gerald Aungier, Governor of Bombay, &c., and the people of this Island, on the 16th July, 1674*, in Forrest, *Selections*, Vol. II, p. 387.]

["Whereas . . . the contract made between the Governor or Honourable Company and the **Povo** was unjust.. ..the Governor summoned all the **Povo** to meet at a General Assembly ....whereupon the **Povo** in general said they never exclaimed against the said contract..." *Id., loc. cit.*]

["To His Sacred Majesty of great Britain. The Humble Petition of the

'Povo' in its Anglo-Ind. usage is not mentioned in *Hobson-Jobson* nor in the *O.E.D.*]

Praga (plague). Malayal. *prakuka, pirākuka*, to curse.—Tet. *praga*.

Pranch ('scaffolding for masons'). Konk., Guj. *paránch*.—Mar. *parānchí*; vern. terms *māḷá, pahāḍ*.—L.-Hindust. *parānchá*, raft; platform.—Sinh. *palanchiya*; vern. term *messa*.—Tet. *paranja, paranju*.—Tul. *parenji, pareji*. — | Mal. *paránja*. |

Prata (silver). Mal. *práda, paráda*, a thin plate of metal; silver-plating, gilding; silvered; gilt. *Ber-práda*, silvered, gilt. *Mam-rada*, to gild; to silver.—Sund., Day. *práda, paráda*, thin metal sheet, gold foil.—Bal. *práda*, gilding; gold foil; painting.—Mac., Bug. *paráda*, to gild; gilding; to paint, painter.—Nic. *paráta*, pewter, zinc.

Paráda-Makáo (Bug.), silver from Macau; tinsel. *Bátu-paráda*, marble. *Búnga-paráda, Bixa orellana*, Linn.

Prato (plate; dish). Konk. *parát*, dish of food; viand.—Mar. *parát*.—Hindi, Hindust. *parát, parātí*, big dish, a tray.—Kan., Tul. *paráta*.

Prazer (*verb*, to please). Mal. *paresser* (Haex).

Preço (price). Konk. *prês*; vern terms *mol, kimat, dar, dhāraṇ*.—Tet. *présu*; vern. term *fólin*.—Gal. *prêsu*; vern. term *hélin*.

Pregão (ban, proclamation). Konk. *pergáṁv*; vern. terms *ḍāṅgoró, dāṅḍoró*.—Guj. *pegám*, message.—Sinh. *peragama*, bans of marriage.[1]

Prego (hairpin, nail). Konk. *preg*, a gold ornament

Povo of the Island of Bombaim" (c. 1663). Khan, *Bombay (1660–1677)*, O.U.P. p. 453.]

["It (the Island of Elephanta) may be Ten Miles round, inhabited by the **Povo**, or Poor." Fryer, *East India*, Vol. I, p. 195.]

[(In Goa) "the *Segnioros* minding nothing less than Merchandizing, and the **Povo** imploying their Fish-hooks and knitting-needles to get a Livelihood." *Id.*, Vol. II, p. 21.]

---

[1] "He ordered the Magistrate to go to all the ships with **pregões**." Gaspar Correia, I, p. 556.

"The Governor ordered **pregões** to be made throughout Gogolá." Diogo do Couto, Dec. IV, v, 5.

["The persons who conduct the auction-sales are called **Pregonneurs** (*Pregoeiros*) or criers." Pyrard, *Voyage*, Hak. Soc., Vol. II, p. 65.]

shaped like a hairpin.—Hindust. *preg*, *pareg*.—L.-Hindust. *prek*.—Beng. *perek*.—Khas. *prek*, nail fork.—Mal. *prego* (Haex).—Tet., Gal. *pregos*; vern. term *kúsan*.

Pregoação (preaching). Mal. *pregoaçaon* (Haex).

Pregoar (to proclaim). Mal. *pregoar*, to proclaim; to preach (Haex).[1]

In the Port. dialect of Ceylon *pregoá* is used in the meaning of 'to preach'.

Preparar (to prepare). Konk. *prepārár-karuṅk*; vern. term *tayár karuṅk*, *sanzauṅk*.—Tet. *prepára*; vern. term *hálu*, *haloti*.

Presente (*subst.*, a present, a gift). Konk. *prezent*; vern. term *sāguvát*.—Mal. *persén*.—Tet. *prezénti*.

In Konkani the term is also used as an adjective.

Presidente (president). Konk. *pirzent*, one who celebrates a church feast. Used in the same sense also in Tamil and Malayalam.—Tet. *prezidénti*.

[1] "And they were soon proclaimed (**se pregoaram**) throughout the entirety of Goa with much festivity." Diogo do Couto, Dec. VI, v, 4.

Preso (imprisoned). Konk. *prêz*.—Guj. *parej*. In Konkani *prêz karuṅk*, and in Guj. *parej karvuṁ*, means 'to arrest; to imprison'.

Prima (a female cousin). Konk. *prim*; vern. terms are *bāpal-bahíṇ*, *chultí-bahíṇ*; *āyte-bahíṇ*; *mavśí-bahíṇ*.—Mal. *prima* (Haex).—Gal. *prima*; vern. term *liar*.

Primo (a male cousin), Konk. *prim*; vern. terms *bandhu* or *bandh*; *bāpal-bháv*, *chultó-bháv*; *āyte-bháv*; *māme-bháv*; *mavśí-bháv*.—Mal. *primo* (Haex).

Processo (judicial process). Konk. *prosés*; vern. terms *khaṭló*, *vyavahár*.—Tet., Gal. *proséssu*.

Procissão (procession). Konk. *pursáṁv*; vern. terms *dinḍí*, *jātrá* (us. among the Hindus).—Tet., Gal. *prosisã*.

Procuração (power of attorney). Konk. *prokurāsáṁv*; vern. terms *adhikár*, *sattyá*.—Tet., Gal. *prokurasã*.

Procurador (an attorney, proxy). Konk., Tet., Gal. *prokurādor*.—[Anglo-Ind. *procurador* (obs.)[1].]

[1] ["This night the Officers, seeing I sent not, deliuered the Prisoners into

[The Anglo-Indian word is found neither in *Hobson-Jobson* nor in the *O.E.D.*]

Profeta (prophet). Konk. *prophet.*—Sinh. *prophétaya.*

Promessa (promise). Konk. *promés* (l. us.); the vern. terms *bhāsāvṇí, bolí; āngvaṇ.*—Tet. *promesa.*

Pronto (ready). Konk. *promt*; vern. terms *tayár, ruzú.*—Tet. *próntu*: vern. terms *tók.*

[**Propagandista** (a missionary or convert of the Roman Catholic congregation of the Propagation of the Faith).—Anglo-Ind. *propagandist.*[1]

In India this term was generally used in opposition to 'padroadist' (*q.v.*).]

Proposta (proposal). Konk. *propost* (l. us.); vern. terms *bolṇéṁ, vachan.*—Tet. *proposta*; vern. term *lia.*

Próprio (one's own, proper). Konk. *propr*; vern. terms *āpṇāchó, khāsgí*; *āpaṇach.*—Tet. *própi*; vern. term *lólun, rásik.*

Protesto (protest). Konk. *portést*; vern. term *nākár.*—Tet. *protéstu.*

Prova (proof). Konk. *prov* (us. only among the educated classes), *puráv*—Mar. *puráv, purāvá.*—Guj. *purāvó.* The Neo-Aryan terms are *dākhló, pramāṇ.*—Tel. *puroya.*

Molesworth gives as the original of the Marathi word the Sanskrit *pur*, confounding the meanings of the various derivatives.

Provar (to prove). Konk. *provár-karuṅk.*—Guj. *purvár* (*adj.*), proved. *Purvar karvuṁ*, to prove. *Purvārí* (*subst.*), proof.

Proveito (profit, advantage). Mal. *proveito* (Haex)

Provisor (provisor; holder of a provision; a Bishop's Vicar-general). Konk. *provisor.* Beng. *provijor.*

Prumo (lead, plumb). Konk. *purím*; vern. terms *aḷambó, lamb*; *buḍíd, ṭháv.*

---

my **Procuradors** power." Sir T. Roe, *Embassy*, Hak. Soc., p. 446.]

["To receiue justice from our **Procurador** *Generall.*" *Id.*, p 509.]

[1] ["Let the **Propagandists** bring forth statistics....and show the conversions they have effected in India." *Plain Facts Plainly Told* (Bombay, 1885) by R M. P., p. 59.]

["The Padroado party aimed a blow at the **Propagandists.**" E. R. Hull, *Bombay Mission History* (Bombay, 1927), p. 290.]

—L.-Hindust. *prum*.—Mal. *prum*, *parum*.

Gundert derives the Malayalam *olumbu* from the Portuguese *plumbo*; but it appears that the word is affiliated to the Sanskrit *avalamba*.

Púcaro (an earthen cup). Konk. *púkr*; vern. terms are *mogh*, *guḷam*.—Sinh. *púkuruva*, *púkiraya*.—[Anglo-Ind. *puckery* (rare and obs.).]—Gal. *púkāru*.[1]

[The Anglo-Ind. form is not mentioned in *Hobson-Jobson* nor in the *O.E.D.*]

Púlpito (a pulpit). Konk. *pulpút*; vern. terms *manch* (l. us.), *sadar* (us. in Salsete). | Tam., Kan. *pulpitu*.—Mal. *pulpito* (Haex).—Tet., Gal. *púlpitu*.

Purga (purgative). Konk. *púrg*; vern. term *bhāyrí*.—Tet., Gal. *purga*.

Purgatório (purgatory). Konk. *purgator*.—Beng. *purgātorí*.—Sinh. *purgatóriya*.—Tet., Gal. *purgatóri*.

Q

Quanto (how much). Mal. *quanto* (Haex).

Quanto mais (how much more). Mal. *quanto mas* (Haex).

Quaresma (popular form *coresma*, Lent). Konk. *korejm*.—Beng. *korjmu*.—Tam. *karesmai*.—Tet., Gal. *koresma*.

Quartel (military barrack). Konk. *kartel*. The word is also used to signify 'contribution or tax paid every quarter.'—Tet. *kartel*; also signifies 'arrested, to arrest'.

Quarto (*subst.*, quarter; apartment). Konk. *kvárt*, room, apartment, also used of 'the fourth part of a piece of paper', or 'the quarters of an hour'.—Tet. *kuártu*, apartment.

Queijo (cheese). Konk. *kêj*.

1 "There are houses where they sell at the door water in many **pucaros** and earthen vessels, as they do along the riverside in Lisbon." Gaspar Correia, I, p. 815.

"An earthenware **pucaro**." Lucena, *Historia da Vida*, Bk. VII, ch. 4.

["The Water is preserved in Jarrs, and drank out of **Puckeries**, that keep it cooler than any where else." Fryer, *East India*, Hak. Soc., Vol II, p. 163. Crooke, who edited Fryer, could not give a satisfactory explanation of the word. I have not found the word used by any English traveller other than Fryer.]

["Earthern Jars for Water, and **Puckeries**, which are porous Vessels to keep their Liquor Cool." *Id.*, Vol. III, p. 135.]

—Sinh. *kéju.*—Mal. *kéju, kíju.* —Sund. *kíju.*—Jav., Mad., Mac., Bug. *kéju.*—Tet., Gal. *keiju.*

Querubim (a cherub). Konk. *kerubím.*—Hindust., Beng. *kārūbim.*—Malayal. *kheruba.*—Tul. *kerubi.*—Bug. *karūbiyúna.*—Jap. *kerubin, kerubu.*—Pers. *karūbí.*—Ar. *kirub.*

The word is of Hebraic origin. In some of the above languages it must have found its way without the intervention of Portuguese.

[**Queve** (a Portuguese form of the Cantonese *kan-pan*, 'an attendant, an interpreter', used in the sense of 'a broker or go-between').—Anglo-Ind., *keby.*[1]

The citation below from Mundy is the only passage in which we have come across this word. The Portuguese form is not mentioned in the *Glossario*, neither is 'keby' found in *Hobson-Jobson* nor in the *O.E.D.*]

Quintal (garden adjoining a house). Beng. *kintál.*—Batav. *kintal*, "the interior of a house". Favre.—Tet. *kintal*, a garden.[1]

Quita-sol (not now in use; literally it means 'bar-sun'; it was used in the sense of 'a sun-shade'). Anglo-Ind. *kittysol, kitsol*[2] (obs.). *Kittysol-boy*, the carrier of the sun-shade. See *bói.*

---

1 ["The Portuguese, at the instance of the **Queves** or merchants of the province of Canton...then moved to the island of Macan" (Macao). Manrique, *Travels*, Hak. Soc., Vol. II, p. 69.]

["18*th August*, 1637. On the morrow, haveinge procured a petition to be formally drawne by the meanes of the said Noretty (who after shalbe styled our **Keby** or Broker), they were called ashore." Mundy, *Travels*, Hak. Soc., Vol. III, pt. i, p. 209.]

["Silver we desire shall be delivered in presence of the **Queves.**" *Idem*, p. 211.]

1 "They soon went to the **quintal** of their houses." Diogo do Couto, Dec. VII, vii, 3.

2 ["Of **kittasoles** of state, for to shaddow him (the Moghul Emperor), there bee twentie." Williams Hawkins, (1608–13), in Foster, *Early Travels in India*, p. 103.]

["Costly Palanquines and ritche **quitasoles**" (in "Eecarce" (Ikkeri)). Mundy, *Travels*, Hak. Soc., Vol. III, pt. i, p. 86.]

[There is an illustration of "A **quitasoll** held over him ('a Mandareene'), if hee bee in the sonne: Scarce any withoutt them as they passe to and Fro" in Mundy, Vol. III, pt. 1, pl. xiii.]

["Sumbareros or **Catysols** are here (in 'Choromandel') very Usefull and necessarie....beinge rather more Convenient then the other but not soe fashionable or Honourable by reason any man whatever that will goe to the

The Spaniards even to this day call a sun-shade *quita-sol.*

R

Rábão ('radish'). Sinh. *rábu*; vern. term *mulaka.*

Rabeca (a fiddle). Konk. *rebek.*—Mar. *rabak* (also *rabáb*). —Malayal. *rabekka.*—Kan. *rabaku.*—Tet., Gal. *rabeka.*

Gonçalves Viana has doubts as to the Arabic *rabáb* being the source of the Portuguese *rabeca* [*Apostilas*, II, p. 325]. *Rabáb* is adopted in Persian, Hindustani, Gujarati and also in Marathi.

The names of European musical instruments and their accessories are, in Konkani, almost all Portuguese.

Charge of it, which is noe great Matter, may have one or more **Catysols** to attend him, but not a Roundell Unlesse he be in a Credible Office, and then noe more than one Unlesse he be a Governour or One of the Councell." Bowrey, *Countries Round the Bay of Bengal*, Hak. Soc., p. 86. There is an illustration of 'a roundel' in the book, Pl. VII. The use of umbrellas was the subject of sumptuary legislation both on the part of the Portuguese and the East India Company.]

["**Kitesall** or Barabulla Trees." Yule, *Early Charts, etc., of the Húglí River*, in Hedges, *Diary*, Hak. Soc., Vol. III, p. ccvii. In 1701 ed. of chart called *Parrasoll* Trees. See also *Ind. Antiq.*, Vol. XXX, p. 347.]

Ração (ration; allowance). Konk. *rāsám̐v.* It is especially used in connection with the allowance of liquor which is given to workmen.—L.-Hindust. *resan.*—Mal. *ranson.*—Jav. *rasan, ransan. Ngransommi*, to give ration. In the verbal form, the initial *r* is preceded by *ng.* —Tet., Gal. *resã*; vern. term *sáhi.*[1]

It is but proper to note that Dutch has *rantsoen.*

[**Ráia** (the ray fish, popularly also called skate). Anglo-Ind. *raia*[2] (obs.).]

The quotation below is the only passage where we have come across the use of this form in Anglo-Indian writings.

[**Ramada** (a shelter made of boughs; in Portuguese India, a temporary shed erected generally for marriage festivities, the roof and sides of which are covered over with coco-nut fronds the leaflets of which are braided into mats). Tam. *ramade*, according to Manucci (ed. Irvine, Vol. III, p. 339): "Seven days

[1] "And coming to himself, he found the shepherd by him with a **reção** of milk." Diogo do Couto, Dec. VI, v, 5.

[2] ["We have thornbacks here with severall other sorts of the **Raia** kind." Hedges, *Diary*, Vol. II, p. cccxxxiv.]

afterwards a sort of four-cornered tent was erected, called by these people **ramade**".

Irvine is evidently on the wrong track when he tries to explain the word thus: "The word used might be *aramanai*, 'royal palace', or *aṛaimanai*, 'single-room house'. Or can it have any connexion with *Rām-kelā*, a name for the plantain-tree? (see 'Madras Manual of Administration,' iii. 687). Plantain trees are used in erecting the *pandal*".]

Ramo (branch, bough). Sinh. *rámuva*, moulding, picture.—Mal. *ramo* (Haex).

In the Portuguese dialect of Ceylon, *ramo* also signifies 'a framed picture'.

It may be that in this sense *ramo* is a corruption of *lâmina*, used in Konkani as *lámn*. In Konkani *ram* is the name of 'the palm-leaf blessed on Palm-Sunday'. Cândido de Figueiredo says that *lâmina*, in the sense of 'frame, picture', is used in Miranda, Trás-os-Montes.[1] Dutch has *raam* in the sense of 'a frame'.

1 "A **lamina** of the birth of Our Lord". Cardim, p. 44.

Rancho (a group of men assembled for a journey or for marching; also the food that is served out to a company of soldiers or sailors). Konk. *ránch*.—Sinh. *ránchuva*, class of people (Eng. 'rank'); vern. terms *peḷa*, *peḷiya*.

?**Raso** (even, level). Mal. *rata*.—Jav. *rôtô*.

Dr. Heyligers attributes the change of *s* into *t* to the law of repulsion, that is, to the pre-existing vocable *rasa* or *rôsô* from the Sansk. *rasa*, 'taste, sentiment'.

From *rôtô* is formed in High Javanese *radin*, whence *radiman*, 'level plain; a street'. See *passear*.

Raxa (arch., 'a species of thick cloth'). Jap. *rasha*.[1]

Razão (reason). Konk. *razáṁv*. But *serezámv*=*sem-razão*, without reason; vern. terms *kārāṇ*, *prastáv*, *pramáṇ*.—Tet., Gal. *rezã*.

Recado (message, compliments). Konk. *rekád*.—[Anglo-Ind. *recado*, *recarders* (obs.)].—

1 "A cloak of **raixa** and a sheep-skin coat valued at two thousand *reis*" (1548). A. Thomás Pires, *Materiaes*, etc., in *Jour. Geo. Soc. Lisb.*, 16th ser., p. 706.

Mal. *recado* (Haex).—Tet., Gal. *rekádu*.

[Pyrard speaking of the pages that used to accompany in Goa the Portuguese lords and gentlemen says: "Their service only is to attend their masters and to carry messages, which they call **Recates**". Gray commenting on this term makes the following surmise: "Unless Dr. Murray and his coadjutors can give earlier authority, I venture to think we have here the original of our modern phrase "kind regards"".[1] The earliest citation in the *O.E.D.* of 'regard' in the sense of 'token or evidence of esteem or affection' is dated 1747, and of 'regards' in epistolary expressions of goodwill 1775. The Dictionary lists the Anglo-Indian forms *recado*, *recarders*, etc., but does not support Gray's conjecture; it derives the English 'regard' from French.

There can be no doubt, however, that the Portuguese *recado*, 'a message or errand', pl. *recados*, 'compliments or greetings' must have acquired considerable vogue among Anglo-Indians in the 17th century, to judge from the citations below.[1]]

Recheio (stuffing, in cookery). Konk. *rechey*.—Mal. *richá*, *richya*, a species of capsicum; vern. terms *chábi*, *chábey*, *lada china*.

Recibo (receipt). Konk. *resíb*; vern. term *pāvtí*.—Guj., Hindi, Hindust., Or., Sindh., Punj. *rasíd*.—Ass. *rachita*.—Malayal. *raśidu*, *rasdi*.—Tel. *raśidu*.—Kan. *rasídi*, *raśídi*, *raśidu*.—Tul. *rasídi*.—Anglo-Ind. *raseed*.—Mal. *resít*.—Tet., Gal. *resíbu*.—Pers. *rasíd*.

Yule and Burnell regard *raseed* or *rasid* as a corruption of the English 'receipt' through the influence of the Persian *rasída*, 'arrived', viz., an acknowledgment that a thing has 'come to hand'.

Rêde (a net). Konk. *rêd*

---

[1] [Hak. Soc., Vol. II, p. 80.]

[1] ["Pray give my **recadoes** to Pedro O Lavera..." Letter dated 13th Oct., 1663, in Bowrey, *Travels*, Hak. Soc., p. 75].

["Four Mile off *Bandora* (we) were stopp'd by the Kindness of the *Padre*-Superior, whose Mandate, whereever we came caused them to send his **Recarders** (a Term of Congratulation, as we say, *Our Service*) with the Presents of the best Fruits and Wines, and whatever we wanted." Fryer, *East India*, Vol. I, p. 184.]

(more in use is the vern. *jāḷí*).—Mal. *rede* (Haex); vern. term *jála* (Sansk.).—Tet. *rédi*; vern. terms *kháhoti*, *láhoti*.

Reformado (*subst.*, a person superannuated or pensioned off). Konk. *rephormád*.—Tet. *reformádu*.

Regalo (rejoicing; entertainment). Mal. *regalas*, "a sumptuous banquet" (Haex).

Registo (a register). Konk. *rejíst* (also us. of a small religious picture); the vern. terms are *paṭṭí*, *śivḍí*.—Tet. *rejístu*.

Regra (rule, example). Konk. *regr*; vern. terms *oḷ*, *regh*; *nem*.—Tet., Gal. *regra*.

Rei (king). Konk. *rey* (king in cards). Mac., Bug., *réi* (king in cards).—Nic. *deṁ*. *Deṁ-en-kána* (lit. 'wife of the king'), queen.

Man derives *deṁ* (=*dẽ*) from the Port. *rei* and, I believe, with reason, notwithstanding the phonetic divergency. *R* initial and medial can be changed into *d*; cf. *dai*=*rai*, 'leaf', *kaḍú* =*karú*, 'wide, large,' *lará* < Malay *láda*, 'pepper'. The Nicobarese have not got the diphthong *ei*, and the nasalisation is explained by the tendency of their language.

[**Reinol** (one born in the kingdom (*reino*), i.e., Portugal; a term used by the Portuguese in India to distinguish the European Portuguese from the country-born (see *castiço*). Konk. *reināl*.—Anglo-Ind. *reinol*, *reynolds*, *reynol* (obs.).[1]

The Anglo-Indian forms are not mentioned in the *O.E.D.*

Yule says that at a later date the word appears to have been applied to Portuguese deserters

---

[1] ["When they are newly arrived in the Indies, they are called **Raignolles**, that is to say, "men of the Kingdom", and the older hands mock them until they have made one or two voyages with them, and have learned the manners and customs of the Indies." Pyrard, *Voyages*, Hak. Soc., Vol. II, p. 123. *Reinol* in the above sense has the same meaning as the Anglo-Indian 'griffin,' or 'Johnny Newcome'.]

["He (the *Topass* chaplain) is only there for the better catching of the poor '**renols**'; who departing this life, leave the chaplain as their testamentary executor." Manucci, ed. Irvine, Vol. III, p. 283.]

[There are many *Gentows* dwell in the City (of Goa).., they are tolerated because they are generally more industrious than the *Christians*.., but the mercantil Part of them are very subject to the Insults of the **Reynolds** or *European Fidalgoes*, who will often buy their Goods, and never pay for them." A. Hamilton, *East Indies* (1727). Vol. I, p. 248.]

who took service with the E.I. Co., and quotes from Grose, *A Voyage to the East Indies*, (1772 ed.), Vol. I, p. 38.[1]]

Reitor (rector). Konk., Beng. *reytor*.

Relação (relation). Konk. *relāsáṁv*. The term is more used as the name of the 'Court of Appeal'.—Tet. *relasã*.

Religião (religion). Konk. *relijyáṁv* (l. us.); vern. terms *samurt*, *śastrasamurt*, *dharm*.—Tet., Gal. *relijiã*.

Relójio (clock, watch). Konk. *relóz*., vern. term *ghaḍyál*.—Sinh. *orlosiya*, *oralósuvā*.—*Atoralósuvā*, pocket-watch.—Tam. *orelóju*.—Malayal. *orlojjika*. –Mal. *arlóji* (Castro), *urúlis*; vern. term *jam* (from Persian).—Tet. *relóju*, *relóji*, *relósi*.—Gal. *relóji*[2].

The Portuguese dialect of Ceylon has *orlozo*.

Horlúji (Mal.), *horlóji* (Sund.), *hōrolósi* (Mac.) appear to be from the Dutch *horologie*.

Remédio (remedy). Mal. *remedio* (Haex).

Renda ('rent, hire'). Konk. *rend*. *Rendák divuṅk* or *lāvuṅk*. to let on hire or rent. *Rendák ghevuṅk* or *karuṅk*, to take on lease. *Rendāchó*, leased. *Rendkár*, the lesser, he who holds on payment of rent. *Rendêr* has lost its original meaning of 'a person who held estate on payment of rent'; it is now used to designate a sub-caste composed of the Sudras who live on the estate of another and take up, on payment of rent, coconut trees which they tap for toddy. The vernacular terms for the Portuguese *renda* are: *sāró*, *dhāró*; *ghêṇ* (us. in Kanara).—Mar. *rend*, monopoly. *Rendkari*, a monopolist. *Rendsará*, a distillery (us. in Rajapur and Savantvadi).—Guj. *rent* (perhaps from English).—Sinh. *réndaya*, hire; toll, customs. *Rēnda-karaṇavā*, to farm out the revenues of the State. *Rēndapala*, the place where the imposts are paid. *Rēndakárayā*,

1 [c. 1760.—With respect to the military, the common men are chiefly such as the Company sends out in their ships, or deserters from the several nations settled in India, Dutch, French or Portuguese, which last are commonly known by the name of **Reynols**."]

2 "Considering that the **Relogios** by which time is regulated are made in different Countries..." D. João de Castro, *Roteiro de Lisboa a Goa*, p. 183.

"The movements of the heavens which the **relogios** with difficulty show or imitate." Lucena, Bk. VII, ch. 7.

farmer of rent, tenant; farmer of toll. *Atu-rēndakárayā*, a sub-lessee, a partner in the farming of the revenue of the state.

[There are references to '**Rende Verde**' in the Surat Letters. This was evidently the name of a tax levied by the Portuguese and derived by the Company in and around Bombay. In a letter of Aungier and others, dated 7th April, 1676, it is described as follows: "The new Rent called "**Rende verde**" consists of Oyle, Opium, Bange, and Mowra. Noe person except ye farmer being permitted to retaile under a maund, it will in time wee hope prove a good addition to ye Revenue, ye Merchants and all other being well satisfyed therewith." (Forrest, *Selections* (Home Series), Vol. I, p. 92). The name shows that the tax or rent was to be levied on vegetable produce. *Verde* in Port. means 'green'.]

Renda ('lace'). Konk. *rend*; vern. terms *zāḷí*; *dál* (l. us.).—Sinh. *rénda, réndapaṭiya*.—Tam. *renda*.—Ann. *ren*.—Mal., Sund., Day., Mac., Bug. *rénda*.—Jav. *rêndô* (also 'gold or silver lace'). *Ngrendô*, to furnish with gold lace. *Rinendô*, decked with gold lace or finery.

[**Rendeiro** (in the sense of 'tax-gatherer or revenue-farmer'). Konk. *rendêr* (see above under *renda*).—Anglo-Ind. *rendero, rendere* (obs.).[1]

The primary meaning of the Port. word is 'one who holds land by paying rent, a tenant or renter'. The Anglo-Indian forms are mentioned neither in

---

[1] ["Nor durst they (the merchants of Goa) sell anything ere the police have first fixed the price. Nor durst they sell aught wholesale or retail, whether food-stuffs or other thing, that have not paid tribute to the king. So it is that with merchandise of every craft, trade or kind, however small, the power of dealing in it, making or selling it, is farmed out to the highest and last bidder. They call these farmers **Renderes**; sellers and dealers must have notes in writing from these **Renderes**." Pyrard, *Voyage*, Hak. Soc., Vol. II, p. 178.]

["The next Morning, with only sending my Servant ashore to acquaint the **Rendero**, I quitted the Pass." Fryer, *East India*, Hak. Soc., Vol. I, p. 307.]

["However this has made Volup Venny the **Rendere** of ye Customs very uneasy, finding that no vessells can pass unplundered by one sort of nation or other." Forrest, *Selections*, Home Series, Vol. I, p. 154.]

["Your Exçy &cª are noe strangers to ye **Rendeiroes** of ye last years Tobacco stand." *Idem*, p. 155.]

Hobson-Jobson nor in the *O.E.D.*].

Repique (peal, ringing of bell). Konk. *repík.* —Tet. *repíki.*

Reposta (answer). Konk. *repost*; vern. terms *uttar*, *záb*, *pratizáb.*—Tet. *reposta*; vern. term *símu.*—Gal. *resposta*; vern. term *limteha.*

Reprovar (to disapprove). Konk. *reprovár-karuṅk*, to declare that a candidate at an examination is not fit to be promoted to the higher class.—Tet. *repróva.*

Requerer (to petition). Konk. *rekerer-karuṅk.*—Mal. *requerer*, "to petition, to demand back" (Haex).

Requerimento (a petition, application). Konk. *rekriment*; vern. terms *arjí.*—Tet. *rekeriméntu.*

Resma (a ream). Konk. *rejm.*—Mar. *rejim.*—Kan. *rejmu.*

Respeito (respect). Konk. *respêt*; vern. term *mán.*—Tet. *respéitu.*

Responsável (responsible). Konk., Tet. *respoṁsável.*

Retrato (portrait). Konk. *retrát*; vern. terms *rupṇéṁ*, *rūpkár.*—Tet. *retrátu*; vern. terms *módun*, *hílas.*

Reúnião (meeting, assembly). Konk. *revunyáṁv* (l. us.); vern. terms *mêḷ*, *samáz.*—Tet. *reuniã.*

Rial, réis (a Portuguese coin equal to about 25th part of an anna, the pl. of *rial* is *réis*). Konk. *rês* (pl. *rés*).—Mar. *reṁs.* —Guj. *res.* —Sindh. *riyálu.* —Malayal. *iṛayál*, *ress.*—Tul. *reisu̥.*—Anglo-Ind. *reas*, *rees*. *res.*—Kamb. *riél*, piaster.—Siam. *rién*, piaster.[1]— | Mal, *rial* | .—Sund., Jav., Mad. *rêal.* —Ach. *ryáh.*—Mac., Bug. *réyala.*—Bal. *reyal*, *leyar.* *Pareayllan* (Jav.), a money-changer.—Pers. *riyál.*—Ar. *rial*, *riyál.*[2]

---

1 "The final *r* and *l* are both pronounced, almost universally, as *n*." Michell.

2 "For two tangas, which are two **reales**, our men used to go in a boat." Bocarro, Dec. XIII, p. 171.

["48 **Rues** (*reis*) in Rabag, is 1 *Tucca.*" Fryer, *East India*, Hak. Soc., Vol. II, p. 129.

(In Goa) "The *Vinteen*, 15 *Basrooks*.
Whereof 75 make a *Tango*
And 60 **Rees** make a *Tango.*"

(In Bombaim) "80 **Raies** 1 *Laree.*" *Idem*, pp. 130 and 131.]

["Their Accounts (Bombay) are kept by **Rayes** and *Rupees*. 1 Rupee is 400 **Rayes**...........But they (in Goa) keep their Accounts in **Rayes**." A. Hamilton, *East Indies* (1727 ed.), Vol.

[Yule says that accounts were kept at Bombay in rupees, quarters, and *reas*, down at least to November, 1834.]

? **Rinoceronte** (rhinoceros). Siam. *rĕt*. *No rĕt*, the horn of the rhinoceros.

It appears that the word is of foreign origin and that *ret* stands for (*rinoce*)-*ront*(*e*).

Ripa (the thin laths laid across the rafters of a roof to bear tiles). Mar. *ríp*.—Guj. *ríp*, *rip*.—Sinh. *ríppaya*. *Ríppataṭṭuva*, lath-work.—Kan., Tul. *rípu*.— | Anglo-Ind. *reaper* [1] | .

[Yule admits the Anglo-Indian form in *Hobson-Jobson* but is at a loss to explain its origin. He fails to trace it to Hindi but mentions that *rip* is met with in Marathi.]

Rizes (*naut.*, reef, brails). Mal. *ris* (Marre).

Roda (wheel). Konk. *ród* (especially a cart-wheel); vern. term *chák*.—L.-Hindust. *rodá*. —Sinh. *ródaya*, *róda*, *róde*; vern. terms *chakraya*, *saka*. *Jala-ródaya*, a water-wheel; vern. term *jalachakraya*. *Róda gti*, provided with a wheel. *Róda karattaya*, a wheel-cart.—Mal., Sund., Mac. *róda*. *Anak róda* (lit. 'the son of the wheel'), the spoke of a wheel.—Ach. *rúda*.—Jav., Mad. *ródô*.—Tet., Gal. *roda*.

Rôdo (corn-rake). Mal. *ródoq*.

Rolão (used in Portugal for 'brown flour', but in India for 'fine flour or semolina'). Konk. *rulámv*.—Sinh. *rulan*.—Tam. *rolam*.—Anglo-Ind. *rolong*.

Rôlo (a roll, a scroll; swell, surge). Konk. *rôl*.—L.-Hindust. *rol*.—? Tet. *lúlum*.

Ronda ('a patrol'). Konk. *rond*.—Guj. *ron*.—Beng. *rond pheran*.—Malayal. *rónda*.—Tul. *rondu*.—Mal., Sund., Mac., Bug. *ronda*.—Jav. *róndô*. *Parondan*, *prondan*, a squad of police.—Bal. *ronda*.

[Yule connects the Hindi *raund* with English (see *Hobson-Jobson*, *s.v.* round).]

Rosa (rose). Konk. *róz* (neut., the flower), *rôz* (fem., the plant).—Sinh. *rósa*, *rósamala* (lit. 'rose-flower'); vern. terms *sevvandi-mala*; *sevvandi*-

---

II, A Table of Weights, etc., pp. 6 and 7.]

[1] ["Paid the Bankshall Merchants for the house poles, country **reapers**, &c., necessary for housebuilding." In Wheeler, III, 148. See *Hobson-Jobson*, *s.v.* bankshall.]

gula ('the rose bush'). It appears to correspond to the Konk. *śivanti* (*Rosa semper florens*). *Rosa-vatura*, rose-water. *Rosa-mala samana*, rosy, roseate.—Tam. *rósa*. *Rōsā-puppóṇra*, rosy.—Mal. *rója*, ? *rôs*. Swettenham believes that *rôs* is from the English 'rose'.—? Sund. *ros*. Rigg derives it from the Dutch *roos*.—? Mac., Bug. *rósi*. Matthes connects it with *roos*.

Róz in Konkani is the 'marigold'. The rose is properly called *gulab*. *Roz de pers* stands for *rosa de Persia*, 'the rose of Persia', and *roz-ānvāló*[1] is the fruit of *Cicca disticha*.

Rosário (rosary). Konk. *ruzáy*.—Beng. *rosārí*.—Kan. *rosári*.—Tet., Gal. *rozáriu*.

Roupa (clothing). Konk. *rôp*; vern. terms *kāpḍáṁ*, *vastráṁ*; *āṅgvastráṁ*, *āṅgāvlíṁ*.—Tet. *roupa*; vern. term *náhan*.

In Konkani there is also the form *ropêr*, from *roupeiro*, 'a dealer in cloth, a mercer', in the Portuguese spoken in Goa.

Roxo (purple). Konk. *rôś*; vern. term *zāmbḷó*.—Beng. *rośú*. The term is used in connection with the purple vestments used in divine service.

Rua (street). Mal. *rúa*.

? **Rupia** (rupee). Siam. *rupia*.—Mal., Ach., Batt., Sund., Jav., Mac., Bug. *rupiya*, also 'the Dutch florin'; figuratively money in general.—Mad. *ropiya*. -Day. *rupia*, *ropia*.—Tet. *rupia*.—Malag. *rupia*.

It is an Indian word from the Sanskrit *rūpya*, 'wrought silver'. Dr. Heyligers believes that the Portuguese carried it to Insulindia. But the old Portuguese writers do not mention it, because the rupee was not then current in the south of India.[1] [The earliest reference to the 'rupee' in the *Glossario* is dated 1600.[2]]

1 According to Garcia da Orta, *rezanvoló*.

1 "The zeal must have been great, because these Religious went so far as to meet together, to give some six hundred **rupias** to Don Antonio" (in Bengal, 1682). *O Chron. de Tissuary* I, p. 317.

"The Indians have for their silver money the **Rouple.**" Tavernier, III, p. 21. [ed. O.U.P., Vol. I, p. 22].

2 [1600.—"Adding that he would collect from the Hindus 2000 **Rupias** (which are certain coins)." P. Fernão Guerreiro, *Relaçam Annual*, p. 31.]

S

Sábado (Saturday). Mal. Ach., Jav. *sábtu, sáptu.*—Sund. *sáptu.*—Mad. *sáptô.*—Day. *sábtu.*—Mac., Bug. *sáttu.*—Tet., Gal. *sábadu.*

Dr. Schuchardt and Dr. Matthes attribute to *sábtu* or *sáptu* an Arabic origin; but Dr. Heyligers is inclined to favour the Portuguese derivation of the word and supports his view by citing *mingo* from the Port. *domingo*, 'Lord's day or Sunday'.

Sabão (soap). Konk. *sābáṁv ; sābú* (m. us.).—Mar. *sábú, sābún.*—Guj. *sabu, sābú.*—Hindi, Nep. *sābún.*—Hindust. *sābún, sábun, saban.*—Or. *sábun, śābiṇí.*—Beng. *sābán. Sābānbat*, soapy.—Ass. *sában, chaban.*—Sindh. *sābuṇi.*—Punj. *sàbún, sabún. Sābūní, sabūní* (*adj.*), from soap. *Sābūní, sabūní, sābūnīá, sabūnīá*, soap-kettle, soap-boiler.—Kash. *sában, sábun.*—Sinh. *sabañ, saban.*—Tel. *sabbu.*—Malayal. *saban, sabún.*—Kan. *sabbu, sābúnu.*—Tul. *sábu, sábunu, sabúnu.*—Gar., Khas. *saban.*—Burm. *ksappyah.*—Kamb. *sabu, sabeäng.*[1] *Dŏ sabu*, to wash with soap.—Siam. *sa-bŭ, sàbŭ.*—Ann. *śabong.*—Mal. *sabon* (Haex), *sábun, sabún.*—Ach., Batt., Sund., Jav., Bal. *sábun.*—Mad., Day. *sabon.*—Mac., Bug. *sábung.*—Nic. *śaváng.*—Tet., Gal. *sabã.*—Jap. *sabon, shabon.*—Pers. *ṣābún.*—Ar. *ṣabón, ṣabún.*—| Turk. *sábun*[1] |.

Dr. Heyligers observes that the Arabs rarely make use of soap, and, on this account, it is not likely that they could have introduced the term into Malasia.[2]

[From the way the Portuguese word for soap has been introduced into almost every language or dialect of the East one might reasonably infer that soap was unknown in India before the arrival of the Portuguese; but Watt says: "The art of soap-making has been known and practised (in India)

[1] The foreign *a* is sometimes represented in Kambojan by *ea*, as for instance, *réacsa* ('to guard') from Sansk. *raksha ; roteă* ('chariot') from Sansk. *ratha.*

[1] "Saffron from Portugal, **sabão**, porcelain, and some silk cloth." Bocarro, Dec. XIII, p. 588.

[2] "The Arabic name is derived from the Latin *sapo*, which is itself derived, according to Pliny, from a Gallic word." Dr. Pierre Guiges, *Journal Asiatique*, Juillet—Août, 1905.

from a remote antiquity, the impure article produced being used by washermen and dyers" (*The Comm. Prod. of India*, 1908, p. 819). He does not give any reference in support of this statement. There is, however, plenty of evidence to show that the people used in ancient India, as they do even now, soap-nuts, the nuts of the *Sapindus trifoliatus* for washing clothes.]

Saber (to know). Pid.-Engl. *sabby, savvy* (more us.), *sha-pi* (l. us.), to know, to understand, to recognise; knowledge, science. "Used in the widest sense." Leland.

Sabre (sabre). Konk. *sábr.* —? Jap. *saberu.*

The term must have been introduced recently into Japanese from some other language. "The word is modern in Portuguese", says Gonçalves Viana, in his *Apostilas*. [In old Portuguese, instead of *sabre*, they spoke of *catana* and *espada* (*q.v.*).]

Saca-rolhas (cork-screw). Konk. *sākārôl.*—Tet., Gal. *sakarolha.*

Saco (sack). Konk. *sák*; vern. terms are *goṇ, potém̃, boksém̃.*—Sinh. *sakka-malla*; *sakuva*, pocket; vern. terms *oḍokkuva, pasumbiya.*—Tam. *sakku*; vern. term *pai.*—Malayal. *chakku* (also 'a pocket', as in corrupt Port.).—Mal. *sáku, sáko*, pocket.—Sund. *sáku.* Rigg derives it from the Dutch *zak*, purse.—? Nic. *śayo.*

In the Portuguese dialect of Ceylon *saco* is used of 'pocket, purse'.

Sacramento (sacrament). Konk. *sākrāment*; vern. term *sāoskár* (l. us.). Beng. *sākrāmentú.*—Sinh. *sakraméntuva.*—Tam., Kan., Tet., Gal. *sakraméntu.*—? Malag. *sakramenta*; perhaps from the English 'sacrament'.

Sacrário (t a b e r n a c l e). Konk. *sākrár.*—Tam. *sukkrári.* —Tet., Gal. *sakráriu.*

Sacrifício (sacrifice). Konk. *sākriphís.*—Tet., Gal. *sakrifísiu.*

Sacrilégio (sacrilege). Konk. *sākrilej.*—Tet., Gal. *sakriléjiu.*

Sacristão (sacristan). Konk. *sākristám̃v, sākistám̃v.*—Beng., Tam., Kan. *sankristán.*—Tel. *sakrístu.*—Tet., Gal. *sakristã.*

Sacristia (sacristy). Konk. *sākristí, sāṅkristí.*—Beng., Tam., Kan. *sakristí.*—Tel. *sakrístu.*—Tet. *sakristia.*

? Sagu ('farinaceous pith taken out of the stem of certain palms'). Konk. *sāgú, sâbú.*—Mar., Guj., Hindi, Hindust., Or., Beng., Punj. *sāgú.*—Sinh. * *sāgú, savgal.*—Tam. *savvu.*—Malayal. *sagu, sāgó.*—Tel. *saggu.*—Kan. *sāgo, seigo.*—Tul. *seigo* (through the influence of English).—Anglo-Ind. *sago.*—Indo-Fr. *sagou.*—Gar. *sagu.*—Khas. *sako.*—Kamb. *saku* (Kambojan has no *g*).—Siam. *sákhu.*—Mal., Batt., Sund., Jav., Mac., Bug. *ságū.*—Ach. *ságu, ságe.*—Bal. *ságu, ságo.*—Day. *sago.*—Tet., Gal. *sáku.*—| Chin. *shá-ku-mí* |.—Jap. *sagobei.*—Pers. *sābú.*[1]

Cândido de Figueiredo derives the Portuguese word from the language of New Guinea. Clough traces the Sinh. *sāgú* to Portuguese; but such a word is not met with in modern Sinhalese dictionaries. Rigg derives the Sund. *ságū* from Sinh. *saguna* (Sansk. *saguṇa*), in the sense of 'a valuable substance', but this appears to be an arbitrary derivation. According to Yule and Burnell, the original word is the Malay *ságū*; the plant is indigenous to the Indian Archipelago, and probably its original home was the region from the Moluccas to New Guinea.

It is not known for certain whether sagu was known in India before the sixteenth century; it may, therefore, be presumed that the Portuguese helped to spread the use of the word.

Saguate ('a present, an offering'). Konk. *sāguvát.*—[Anglo-Ind. *seguaty* (obs.)].—Tet. *saukáti, sauáti.*—Gal. *saguáti, sauáti.*

The word is current in the Indo-Portuguese dialects and on the eastern coast of Africa, and was much employed by old Portuguese writers. The original word is the Hindustani-Persian *saughát*, 'rarity, curiosity, present', and not the Sanskrit *svāgata*, as I at first thought it to be.[1]

---

1 "All the people of the Isles of Maluco eat a certain food which they call **Sagum**, which is the pith of a tree resembling a palm-tree." João de Barros, Dec. III, v, 5.

"There arrived a junk laden with **Çagu**, and on it he returned to the fortress." Gaspar Correia, III, p. 740.

"Five hundred bags of **Sagú**, which is a meal made from some tree and which is there eaten." Diogo do Couto, Dec. VI, ix, 12.

1 "In return for which present, the Father Provincial went to visit him

[The older and correcter form is *saugate*, now obsolete. The Anglo-Ind. 'seguaty' is neither in *Hobson-Jobson* nor in the *O.E.D.*]

Sagúeiro (*bot.*, the name applied to the Gomuti palm of the Malays or *Arenga saccharifera*, Labill., found in the Indian Archipelago). Anglo-Ind. *sagwire*.[1]

["The name is Port. *sagueira* (analogous to *palmeira*)....and no doubt is taken from *sagu*, as the tree, though not the sago-palm of commerce, affords a kind of inferior sago." Yule in *Hobson-Jobson*. He would have been correcter if he had said the Port. *sagueiro* (this is the Port. form and not *sagueira*) was built upon the analogy of *coqueiro*, coco-nut tree, from *coco*.]

Saia (petticoat, skirt). Konk. *sáy*; vern. term *ghāgró*.—Hindi, Hindust. *sāyá*.—Beng. *chhāyá*. In the sense of 'shadow' the word *chhaya* is derived from Sanskrit.—Ass. *sāyá*; vern. term *mekhlela*.—Sinh. *sáya*; vern. term *voṭiya*.—Gar. *saia*.—Ar. *ṣaya*.

Sal (salt). Nic. *śal*. With regard to the substitution of *ś* for *s*, see *sabão* and *sapato*.

It is curious that the Nicobarese should not have been acquainted with salt or not have a word for it. They have, however, the adjective *haiyé*, 'salty'. But there are other islands

with another **saguate** of a very different kind." P. Manuel Barradas, in *Hist. tragico-marit.*, II, p. 113.

"The Queen [of Onor] gave orders that they should visit the Captain-General with a big **çauguate** of many fowls, chickens, and eggs." Fernão Pinto, ch. xi.

"With their **saguates** of rice and cooked meat for the pilgrims." A. F. Cardim, *Batalhas*, etc., p. 164.

["For the obteyning the Kings ferman this Governours unckle and father in lawe, called by the name of Mammadamy, a man in great estimacion with the King, whome he would employ in this busines, and doubted not but to bring us to have trade and commerce with theis people upon good termes, if we could procure a good **seguaty** or piscash for the King." Foster, *The English Factories in India 1624–1629*, p. 255. 'Piscash' is the Pers. *pīshkash*, 'a present'.]

[1] "They could safely go in search of provisions a league from the fortress, which contained none, because the **çagueiros** had been cut down, and likewise the coco-nut trees." Castanheda, VIII, ch. 131.

"The **Çagueiro** has wood and green leaves very dark, and from this it took the name **çagu**." Gabriel Rebêlo, *Informaçao das Cousas de Maluco*, p. 169.

which have also no salt. "Pieces of the tunny fish which they dry in the sun, because in the (Maldive) Islands they have no salt." Gaspar Correia, 1, p. 341. [Pyrard says the same: "They (the fish called by the Maldivians *Cobolly masse* or 'black fish') are cooked in sea-water, and then dried in the sun upon trays, and so when dry they keep a long while..." (Hak. Soc., Vol. I, p. 191). "The fish of which I speak is cooked in sea-water and dried, for other mode of salting they have none...No salt is made at the Maldives: what they use comes from the coast of Malabar." *Idem*, p. 194.]

Sala (hall, sitting-room). Konk. *sál*; vern. term *vasró*.—? Sinh. *śala*; *sále*, *sálaya* (also 'a verandah'), *sāláva*. *Naḍu-sála*. court of justice.—Tet., Gal. *sala*.[1]

It seems that in the Sinhalese word there is the influence of, if it is not directly derived from, the Sanskrit *çālā*, to which is related the German *saal*, the sources word of the Portuguese *sala*.

Salada (salad). Konk. *sālád*; vern. term *karam* (l. us. in this sense).—Hindust. *saláta*, *salútih*, *salítih*.—Beng. *saláta*.—Sinh. *saláda* (also 'lettuce, endive').—Tam. *salládu*.—Tel. *salladam*.—Kan. *saládu*, lettuce.—Mal. *saláda*, *seláda*.—Ach. *selada*.—Sund. *saláda*. *Saláda-chai*, water-cress.—Jav. *selôdô*.—Mac., Bug., Tet., Gal. *saláda*.—Ar. *salátha*.—Turk. *salata*.

[**Salpicado** (speckled, spotted). Anglo-Ind. *salpicado*, spotted cloth.[1]

The term is neither in *Hobson Jobson* not in the *O.E.D.*]

Salva (salute, volley). Konk. *sálv*.—Tet., Gal. *salva*.

Salvação (salvation). Konk. *šalvāsáṁv*; vern. terms *mukli*, *tāraṇ*.—Tet., Gal. *salvasã*.

Samatra (sudden squalls). Anglo-Ind. *sumatra*, sudden squalls which are common in the

---

1 "And he received him in the **salla** with many honours." Gaspar Correia, IV, p. 443.

"He received him in the **sala** with great pomp." Diogo do Couto, Dec. VI, v, 4.

1 ["Wee would have you provide some **salpicadoes** flowr'd and plaine, and send us hither as soon as possible." In a Letter from Fort St. George in *Ind. Antiq.*, Vol. L, Sc. 11.]

narrow sea between the Malay Peninsula and the island of Sumatra.

The Portuguese used the term more generally of any tempest, and in this sense it is to this day employed in Goa.[1] [The *O.E.D.* omits to mention that 'Sumatra' is adopted into Anglo-Indian from Portuguese.]

Santa Maria (St. Mary). Nic. *sánta-mariá*, the name of a copper coin: half anna or quarter anna or *tanga* of the Goa currency; vern. terms *paisa* (from Hindust.), *riuid*, copper in general.

As there was no copper coin, as far as I know, called *Santa Maria*, I presume that the term denotes some place from which the Nicobarese first received the coin referred to above or one more or less like it. Perhaps it was the name of one of the islands of the Nicobar group, given by the Portuguese, which at present has ceased to exist. On the coast of Kanara, there are some small islands which go by the name of *Santa Maria*; but the name of the coin could not have originated from these.[1]

Santo (saint). Konk. *sánt*. *Sant* (*subst.*), in the sense of 'a day of obligation to rest from servile work and to hear mass', is perhaps from the Sansk. *santa* (*adj.*).—Sinh. *santuvariya* (*subst.*).—Kan. *santa* (us. among the Christians). *Santeru*.

---

1 "There was a thunder storm from the north-east which is one of the seasonal squalls which usually sweep over this island of **Çamatra.**" Fernao Pinto, ch. xxiii.

"It was not possible to avoid the loss of the galliot of Miguel de Macedo on the Ilha Grande of Malacca where he had come to anchor, when a **samatra** arose and drove the vessel on the island, reducing it to a complete wreck, though the crew and most of the cargo were saved." Bocarro, Dec., XIII, p. 626.

["Wee...had much Raine, gusts and thicke weather, which our Portugalls said is usuall in these parts att this tyme off the yeare And because such weather is incidentt to the Ile of Sumatra, thereffore such gusts, etts. are here awaies by the Portugalls Named **Sumatraes.**" Peter Mundy, *Travels*, Hak. Soc., Vol. III, pt. II, p. 320.]

["They would no doubt have succeeded in their object, had not our Lord, in His infinite mercy, in the meantime sent us a **Samatra** from the south-east, by which we distanced the Pataxes and lost sight of land." Manrique, *Travels*, Hak. Soc., Vol. II, p. 89.]

1 "The small uninhabited islands are now called **Sancta Maria**: they lie between Baçanor and Baticala." João de Barros, Dec. I, iv, 11.

saints.—Kamb. *santa* (prefixed to *Papa* ('Pope')).—Mal. *santo* ('Pope').—Tet. *sántu.*—? Jap. *seito*; this is probably from the English 'saint'.

San-Tomé (Saint Thomas, this being the name given to a coin struck in Goa). Konk. *satmém*, a gold coin with the effigy of St. Thomas. A difference is made between *navém satmém* ('new St. Thomas coins') and *parṇém satmém* ('old St. Thomas coins'). [Anglo-Ind. *St. Thomas, St. Thomae*]. [1] —Jap. *santome, santomejina*, species of striped cloth which came from San-Tomé of Mylapore near Madras. Hepburn gives as a meaning of the word the term *taffecillas*; I do not know to what language this word belongs but it occurs frequently in old writers.[1] [*Taffecilla*, or *tafe-*

1 "Gold coins which are made into **sant'-tomés** for parties who wish to have them so converted." Simão Botelho, p. 55.

"Those coins were the very *pardaos* struck like *cruzados* of the value of one thousand *réis*, having the (Portuguese) coat-of-arms on one side and on the other the figure of St. Thomas with the legend along the circumference, which read—*India tibi cessit.*" Gaspar Correia, IV, p. 434.

["Feeling the want of money in the city, the Governor commanded the issue of a gold coin of the fineness of the round pagodas which are brought from the mainland, of 43 points, equal to 20¾ carats...He directed this coin to be struck with the figure of the blessed Apostle St. Thomas, the Patron Saint of India, on one side, and the royal coat of arms of Portugal on the other.] These coins came to be called **São Thomés**, and are even now to be found in India where they are current throughout." Diogo do Couto, Dec. VI, vii, 1.

["A **St. Thomea de figura**, 16½ tangas; a **St. Thomea de Cruz**, 15 tangas." Mundy, **Travels**, Hak. Soc., Vol. III, pt. i, p. 65.]

["Their (of the people of Malabar) Coins are of Gold; a **St. Thomas** 10 *s.* a *Fanam*, 7 and ½ of which go to a *Dollar*, or *Petacha*." Fryer, *East India*, Hak Soc., Vol. I, p. 139.]

["1 Gold **St. Thomae**—5 *Xerephins.*" Hamilton, *East-Indies* (1727), Vol. II, Table of weights, etc, p 7]

1 "**Taficiras** of silk, and *beatilhas* (*q.v.*) and other sorts of cloth." Gaspar Correia, II, p. 344. "They presented one sword, and six pieces of linen, and two **taficiras.**" *Id.*, 714. "Two small bales of **tafeciras** from Cambaya and other fine cloth." *Id.*, III, 23. "Two small bales of **tafeciras** and painted cloth ('chintz') from Cambaya." *Id.*, p. 51.

"From our master and also others (from Meliapor) we learnt that at some time in the past they were all very rich because of the great gains they derived from the trade in cloth which was manufactured in that city and which was regarded as the best in the whole of the

cira, the form in which the word is more commonly met with, is the Ar. *tafṣilah*, 'woollen stuff from Mecca', and was the name given to silk or cotton fabrics, as a rule, stripped or with floral designs and much like 'chintzes'. See *Glossario, s.v. tafecira.*]

There are other Japanese words similar to the above, like *Bangarajima, Chaujima*, which indicate the place of origin (Bengal, Chaul) of the fabrics introduced into the country by the Portuguese.

[The first St. Thomas gold coins were issued in Goa by the Governor D. João de Castro; they had been struck in Portugal under the orders of King John III whose name they bore on the obverse and also the Portuguese coat of arms in the centre; on the reverse there was the figure of St. Thomas standing, letters S and T on each side of the saint, and the legend INDIA TIBI CESSIT ('India has yielded to you'). It was, however, only during the succeeding governorship, that of Garcia de Sá (1548-49), that St. Thomas gold coins were for the first time actually struck in Goa. His successor, Afonso de Noronha, struck silver St. Thomas coins; these were also known as *patacões* (see under *pataca*).]

Sapateiro (shoe-maker). Konk. *saptêr*; vern. term *chāmhár*; *mochí* (l. us.).—Sinh. *sapatéruva, sapatéṛe*; vern. term *sammariya*.—Tet. *sapatéru*.

Sapato (shoe). Konk. *sapát* (l. us.); vern. term *mocho*.—Guj. *sapát*.—Hindust. (of Bombay) *sepát*.—Sinh. *sapattu, sapattuva. Sapattu-mahanna*, shoemaker. *Slipper-sapattu*, slippers for use in the house. *Búṭ-sapattu*, boots; vern. term *us vahan* (lit. 'high sandal'). *Slipper* and *but* (= boot) are from English.—Tam. *sappattŭ*.—Tel. *sapáth*.—Mal. *sapátu. Sapátu-panjan*, boots. *Sapátu-káyu*, wooden shoes. *Buga-sapátu*, the flower of the shoe ('the Chinese rose'). *Sapátu-kuda* (lit. 'the shoe of the horse'), horse-shoe. Ach. *sepátu*.—Sund. *sapátu, sepátu. Sepátu-panjan*, boot. The term *estivel*, from the Dutch *stivel*, is also used.—Jav. *sapátu, sepátu*.—Mac., Bug. *sapátu, chapátu*.—Nic. *šapáta*.—Tet., Gal. *sapátu*.

East." João Ribeiro, *Fatalidade hist.*, III, ch. 4.

—Pers. *sabát.*—Ar. *sabbat, sebbath, sabat.*[1]

Saraça (a kind of printed cotton fabric). Konk. *sarás.*—Jap. *sarasa.*[2]

The word is of Malay origin, *sarásah.* See Gonçalves Viana, *Apostilas,* I, p. 347.

[In the *Glossario* and also in *Gonçalves Viana e a Lex. Port.,* etc., Dalgado makes the suggestion that the Malay *sarásah* may itself have come from the Sansk. *sārasa,* the zone or girdle of a woman. *Saraça* in the sense in which it is used by old Portuguese writers with reference to India or the Far East is identical with the article called in Anglo-Ind. *sarong,* in Port. *sarão,* from Malay *sárang* which is the Sansk. *sāranga,* meaning 'variegated' and also 'a garment'. See Linschoten's interesting description of 'clothes of Sarasso' (Hak. Soc., Vol. I, p. 91). Burnell's attempt to explain 'sarasso' as the Hind. *sarasā* = 'superior' is very unsatisfactory.]

Sargento (sergeant). Konk. *sārjent.*—Tet. *sarjéntu.*—Gal. *sarjéntu, saréntu.*

Sarja (serge). Konk. *sárj.*—Mal. *serja.*

The Portuguese Dictionary, *Contemporaneo,* derives *sarja* from the Latin *sericus,* and that of Cândido de Figueiredo from the Arabic *sardje.*

Satán, satanás (Satan). Konk. *satānáz.*—Sindh., Day. *setan.*—Sinh. *sátan.*—Gar. *satan.*—Gal. *satanaz.*—Jap. *satan.*

Saitán, used in some of the Indian languages, is from the

---

1 "White **çapatos,** birretas of purple silk in hand." Gasper Correia, I, p. 533.

"Sometimes patients are discharged after their recovery, but some of them for want of shirts, drawers, and **sapatos** will not go away from the hospital (1597)." *Archivo Port. Or.,* Fasc. 5th, p. 1056.

2 "With a *corja* (*q.v.*) of **çaraças,** and Malay body-cloth for his wife and daughter which is the common article of dress of that land." Fernão Pinto, ch. xxi.

"And he gave him two **sarasas,** cloth worn by women in India, which is pretty to look at." Francisco Vaz da Almada, in *Hist. tragico-marit.,* IX, p. 71.

"**Saràssas** and shirts, and all other articles of clothing they had with them, they handed over." Bocarro, Dec. XIII, p. 170.

"In the Azores Islands there is in use even to-day a woman's under-petticoat called **çaraça,** says Senhor Brito da Fonseca.... But I am inclined to think that this word **saraça** came from the East." Dr Alberto de Castro, *Flores de Coral,* p. 172.

Persian-Arabic *saiṭan*, and *satan* itself may have come directly from English. *Setan* in Dyak must be of Dutch origin, and this is the view of Hardeland.

Saúde (health). Konk. *sāvúd*, health, and also drinking to one's health. In the former meaning the vern. terms are *bhaláy*, *bhalāyki*, *ārám*, *praṇám*. *Sāvúd karuṅk*, to raise the toast, to drink to one's health.—Beng. *sāvudí*.—Sinh. *sāvódiya*, toast. —Tet., Gal. *saúdi*.

[Prof. E. M. Ezekiel, of St. Xavier's College, Bombay, informs me that it is customary in the Jewish community of Malabar at the marriage-dinner given by the bridegroom's father, for the bridegroom, before they start eating, to stand up with a glass of wine and to drink to the health of his parents in the following words: *Bāvādéum ummadeūm sāudí kebiba*. '*Sāudí kebiba*' is, I believe, the Portuguese *saude bebo* ('I drink the health'), and testifies to the extent and intensity to which the social habits of the Portuguese had influenced the life of other communities that came into contact with them.]

[**Savel** (the fish *Clupea ilisha*) Anglo-Ind. *sable-fish* (obs.).[1]

It is the same bony but savoury fish which is known in Bengal as *hilsā*, Sansk. *ilīśa*, *illiśa*, and on the Indus river as *palla*. It is said that Mahomed Toghluk, the King of Delhi (1325-1351), when on an expedition in Lower Sindh, ate this very fish to excess, which brought on fever, of which he died.]

Sé (see; the cathedral church). Konk., Tet., Gal. *sé*.

? **Secar** (to dry). Mal. *seka*.—Jav. *sékô*, *njékô* (also 'to wipe, to sweep, to brush'). *Sékat* (Mal.), *sikat* (Sund.), brush, broom.

Secretaria (secretary's office, secretariate). Konk. *sekretārí*.—Tet., Gal. *sekretariu*.

---

[1] ["A little Island, called *Apofingua* (*Ape-Fingan*)..inhabited by poor people who live by the fishing of **savels**." Fernão Pinto, ch. xviii, in *Hobson-Jobson*.]

["The fishery, we were told by these people, was of the "Hilsa" or "**Sable** Fish."......The Hilsa fish I had heard compared to a herring, but to which it bore no resemblance that I could find, either in taste or size, being at least six times as large. It is reckoned unwholesome to eat in any quantity." Heber, *Narrative of a Journey*, etc., (1828), Vol. I, pp. 126 and 127.]

Secretário (secretary). Konk. *sekretár*.—Tet., Gal. *sekretáriu*.

Sêda (silk). Konk. *séd*; vern. terms *rešim, rešim lugaṭ*. *Sedí* (*adj*.), from silk, silky.—Sinh. *séda*; vern. terms *pāṭa-redi, paṭapitiya*. *Séda paṭiya*, a silk-ribbon.— ? Mal., Sund. *sutra*. —Jav. *sutrô*.—Mad. *sotra*.—Tet., Gal. *seda*.[1]

Dr. Heyligers justifies the identity of *sutra* and *seda* by means of the change of *u* for *e* and of *t* for *d* and by the intercalation of *r*, either as the result of carelessness or for the sake of euphony. In Sanskrit, *sūtra* means 'thread'.

Seguro (safe). Konk. *sugúr*. *Sugúr-karuṅk*, to save. *Sugúr-zāvuṅk*, to be safe.—[Anglo-Ind. *seguro*, *secure* (obs.), *subst*., in the sense of 'passport, assurance' which the substantival form has in Portuguese.][2]—Mal. *seguro* (*subst*.), safety (Haex).

Sela (saddle). Konk. *sél* (more us. is *selim*); vern. terms *jīn*, *khogír*.—Mal., Tet., Gal. *séla*.—Sund. *sella*.—Jav. *sélô*.

Sêlo (revenue stamp). Konk. *sêl*.—Tet., Gal. *sêlu*.

Sem (without). Mal. *sin* (Haex).

Semana (week). Konk. *sumān*; vern. terms *sātvaḍó*, *sátoḷém*, *āṭhvaḍó*; *hāptó* (us. in Kanara). *Sumānkár*, a servant of the church who has to be on duty every alternate week; servant for the week.[1]—Sinh. *sumánaya*. *Sumána-pata*, weekly. *Sumánayak aḍangu*, weekly; vern. term *satiya*.—Mal. *semana* (Haex). Also: *sátu mingo*, lit. 'one *domingo*', i.e. Sunday; *sátu ja' mat*, lit. 'one Friday'. —Tet., Gal. *semana*.

The change of *e* into *u* in the first syllable of *sumān* is due to the *s* initial and to the *m* following. Cf. *seguro*. The form *so*-

---

[1] "Here (in China) very good **seda** is produced." Duarte Barbosa, p. 382 [ed. Dames, Vol. II, p. 214].

[2] ["I was forced to currie favor with the Jesuites to get mee a safe conduct or **seguro** from the Vice-Roy to goe for Goa, and so to Portugall, and from thence to England, thinking....that, the Vice-Roy giving his **secure** royall, there would be no danger for me." William Hawkins, in Foster, *Early Travels in India* (1921), p. 92.

[1] Derivatives of this kind are very common: Cf. *chepekár*, a man wearing a hat, from *chapeu* ('a hat'); *mortikár*, a murderer, from *morte* ('a murder'), *phontyó*, one having a seton, from *fonte* ('a seton').

mana is also to be found among the old Portuguese writers.[1]

Semana santa (Holy Week). Konk. *sumán sant.*—Tet. *semana santa.*

Seminário (seminary). Konk. *siminár*; vern. term *maṭh* (not in use among the Christians).—Tam. *seminári.*—Tet., Gal. *semináriu.*

Senhor (lord, master). Konk. *sijñór* (=*sinhor*, l. us.).—Beng. *siyor.*—Mal. *sinñor*, | *sĕnyur*, *sinyur*, | *sínyo*, *siyu* ; *sinhô* (Castro).—Sund., Mad. *sínyo.*—Jap. *sinnyoro*, master of a merchant vessel.

Bikker mentions *senyor* as meaning 'a Dutchman'; *nyung* as meaning 'a Portuguese' and *mistar* 'an Englishman'.

[It would appear from the quotation below that 'Senhor' as a form of greeting was used also of Englishmen in India in the early eighteenth century, at any rate in Bombay.][2]

Senhora (lady, madam). Konk. *sijñór* (l. us.).—Mal. *nyóra*, ? *nyonya*, *nónya*, *nóna.*—Mol. *nyora.*— ? Sund., Jav., Mad. *nyoña* (=*nionha*), *noña.*

Dr. Schuchardt is very sure that *sinyo*, *sinyor*, and *nona*, *nonya*, *nyora*, come from *senhor* and *senhora*. See *dona*.

Sentença (judicial decision). Konk. *sentems*; vern. terms *pharmaṇ*, *nivāḍó.*—Tet., Gal. *sentensa.*

Sentido (sense, meaning). Konk. *sintíd*; vern. terms *chitt*, *arth.*—Tet., Gal. *sentídu.*

Sentinela (sentinel). Konk. *sintinel*; vern. term *pahārekár* or *pahārkár.*—Tet., Gal. *sentinela.*

Sentir (to feel). Konk. *sintir-zāvuṅk*, to be sorry; vern. terms *duḥkh lāguṅk*, *vāyḷ disuṅk.*—Tet., Gal. *sínti*; vern. terms *hadômi.*

Separado (separate). Konk. *sepārád* (l. us.); vern. term *kuśin.*—Mal., Jav., Mad., Day. *separo* (*adv.*), separately, apart, by halves.—Sund. *saparo*, *paro.*—Low-Jav. *loro*, *ro* (through the intervention of *paro*, with the loss of *se*), two. *Maro*, *malih*,

[1] "To regard all the eight days of the **somana** ('week') as holidays, because of the feast." João de Barros, Dec. III, iii, 10.

[2] ["To the most Excellent, Opulent, and Renowned **Senhr** William Phipps, President and Governor General of Persia as far as Indostan, in the Port of Bombay, Conajee Angria Sarquel sends cordially Greeting." Forrest, *Selections* (Home Series), Vol. II, p. 37.]

to separate, to divide into two parts. *Paron, palikan*, in two parts, halves. See Heyligers.

? **Serão** (evening time). Mal., Sund., Low-Jav. *sore*. Properly speaking it means the part of the day from four in the afternoon to sunset.

Gonçalves Viana thinks that the resemblance of the two words is casual.

Seringa (syringe). Konk. *siring*; vern. terms *naḷ, pichkārí*.—Mal. *siring*, filtered; *Siring-an*, a filter.—Sund. *saring*.

Sério (serious, earnest). Konk. *ser*; vern. terms *bhārí, nirāḷó*.—Tet. *séri*; vern. term *matének*.—Gal. *séri*.

Sermão (sermon). Kon. *sermáṁv*.—Tet., Gal. *sermã*.

[**Serra** (an East Indian scombroid fish, *Cybium guttatum*). Anglo-Ind. *seer-, seir-fish*.[1]

Serra, in Port., means 'saw.' and the name "would appear to belong properly to the well-known saw-fish (*Pristis*)...but probably it may have been applied to the fish now in question, because of the serrated appearance of the row of finlets, behind the second dorsal and anal fins, which are characteristic of the genus". Yule in *Hobson-Jobson*. In the Bombay market it is called *Sur Mahi*.]

Serviço (service). Konk. *sirvís*; vern. terms *chākrí, sevá*. -Mal. *servício* (Haex).—Tet. *servísu*.

---

[1] ["There is a fish called **Piexe Serra**, which is cut in round peeces as we cut salmon, and salt it. It is very good, and wil indure long to carie over sea for victuals." Linschoten, *Voyage*, Hak. Soc., Vol. II, p. 11. 'Piexe' is for Port. *peixe*, 'fish'.]

["The Seas (on the 'Coast of Chormondel') produce many Sorts of excellent Fishes, and the Rivers the best Mullets ever I saw. In *November* and *December* they have great Plenty of **Seer-fish**, which is as savoury as any Salmon or Trout in *Europe*." Hamilton, *East Indies* (1827), Vol. I, p. 379.]

["Fish pickled in a preparation of tamarinds is known in Indian trade by this name (Tamarind-Fish). The species most frequently treated in this way are *Cybium guttatum*, the **seer** or **seir fish**, .. ." Watt, *The Comm. Prod of India* (1908), p. 547.]

["Of those in ordinary use (in Ceylon) for the table the finest by far is the **Seir fish**, a species of scomber, which is called *Tora-malu* by the natives" Tennent, *Ceylon*, Vol. I, p. 205.]

["*Saw Fish*.—The huge saw fish, the *Pristis antiquorum*, infests the eastern coast of the island, where it attains a length of from twelve to fifteen feet, including the powerful weapon from which its name is derived." *Id.*, p. 207. This is the fish which in Portugal is called '*serra*'.]

Servir (to serve). Konk. *sirvír-zāvuṅk*; vern. terms are *chākrí karuṅk*; *upkāruṅk*, *kamák yevuṅk*.—Mal. *servir* (Haex).—Tet., Gal. *sírvi*.

Serzideira (*naut.*, a rope or cable attached to the top-sail). Hindust. *sisidor*, *sizādor*.

Setim (satin). Konk. *setím*; vern. term *ātlá* [which is the Ar. *atlas*.]—Sinh. *sitim*; vern. term *kōseyyaya*.—Tul. *séti*.—Mal. [*sitin* (Wilkinson derives it from English)], *síten* (Swettenham traces it to Portuguese).—Jav. *kestin*.—? Mac., Bug. *sátting*; perhaps from the Dutch *satijn*.[1]

? **Sigilo** (seal). Hindust. *sijjill*.—Pers. *sijil*.—Ar. *sijjil*, decree, registry.

Perhaps imported directly from Latin or Italian.

Sinal (sign, token, earnest). Konk. *sinál* (especially in the sense of 'earnest money' after a contract).—Tet., Gal. *sinal*.

Sino (bell). Sinh. *sínuva*, *síniya*; vern. terms *ghanṭáva*, *ghanṭáraya*. *Sínuva-gahanná* (lit. 'the beater of a bell'), bell-ringer.—Mal. *siño*.—Tet., Gal. *sinu*.

Soberbo (proud). Konk. *suberb*, *suberḍó*; vern. terms *garví*, *ahankāri*.—Mal. *suberbo* (Haex).—Tet. *subérbu*.

In Teto and Galoli the form *suberba* is also used.

Sobremesa (dessert). Konk. *sobremez*; vern. term *phaḷár*.—Tet. *sobremeza*.

Sobrinha (niece). Konk. *subrính*; vern. terms *putaṇí*, *dhuvḍí*, *bāchí*.—Mal. *sobrínja* (Haex).

Sobrinho (nephew). Konk. *subrính*; vern. terms *putaṇayó*; *bhāchó*.—Mal. *subrinjo* (Haex). Tet. *subrínhu*; vern. term *manefónun*.

Sociedade (society). Konk. *sosyedád*; vern. terms *pangat*, *sangat*.—Tet. *sosiedádi*, *súsi*.—Gal. *sosiedádi*.

? **Soco** ('pedestal'). Jav. *sukh* (Heyligers).

Sofá (sofa). Konk. *suphá*.—Guj. *soppá*.—Hindust. *sufa*.—Sinh. *sōpáva*.

Sofrer (to suffer). Mal. *suffrir* (Haex).—Tet. *sofrí*; vern. term *térus*.—Gal. *sufrê*.

Solda (*bot.*, *Gallium mollugo*). Mac., Bug. *saloda*.

[1] "Very good silk is produced here (in China) from which they make great store of damask cloths in colours, **setins**, and other cloths without nap, also brocades." Duarte Barbosa, p. 382 [ed. Dames, Vol. II, p. 214].

"With a jacket of black velvet and sleeves of purple **cetym**." Gaspar Correia, *Lendas*, I, p. 533.

Soldado (soldier). Konk. *soldád*; vern. terms *šipáy, laškarí, páyk, sainik.*—Sinh. *soldáduva*; vern. terms *sévayā, hévayā.*—[Anglo-Ind. *soldado*[1] (obs.) not in *Hobson-Jobson.*]—Mal. *soldâdu, seredādu, seridādu.*—Ach. *serdádu*; *seledád*, sailor, seaman.—Sund. *soldádo, soldádu.*—Jav. *sôrôdádu.*—Mad. *sordádu.*—Bal. *suredádu, sredádu.*—Mac., Bug. *sorodádu.*—Tet. Gal. *soldádu*; vern. terms *ema fónun.*—Malag. *soridany.*

The Portuguese chroniclers spoke of the indigenous soldiers as *piães* and *lascarins.*

Sombreiro (sun-shade). Anglo-Ind. *sombrero,* [*sumbarero*], *summerhead.*—Tet. *sombréiru*; vern. term *siáti.*—Gal. *sombrélu.*

In Indo-Portuguese, *sombreiro* is used both of 'a sunshade' and 'a water-proof'.[2]

[*Sombreiro* among the Portuguese meant 'a hat' but in the

1 "This Governor used to favour **soldados** who possessed good arms." Diogo do Couto, Dec. VI, v, 3. "With a hundred **soldados** and a few *Lascaris* (*q.v.*)". *Id.*, Dec. VIII, i, 3.

["A cross-grain'd *Brachmin*, supported by an outlaw'd *Portugal*, contradicted in despight of both, seizing it by Force with Three Files of **Soldadoes.**" Fryer, *East India*, Hak. Soc., Vol. I, p. 349.]

2 "Near him (the King of Calicut) they carry a **sombreiro** ('umbrella') on a high support which keeps off the sun." Duarte Barbosa, p. 320 [ed. Dames, Vol. II, p. 26].

["As well as the page armed with a sword, ... they take also another who holds a **sombreiro** to shade them off and to keep off the rain, and of these some are made of finely worked silk with many golden tassels, and many precious stones and seed-pearls. They are so made as to open and shut, and many cost three or four hundred *cruzados.*" *Idem*, Vol. I, p. 206. The editor is of the opinion that this is the second earliest mention of umbrellas made to open and shut, the only other earlier one is that of Marignolli who died in 1355.]

"It is not permitted to any one to use torches, *andor*, **sombreiro**, without our permission or that of the Governor." *Foral* (the Revenue Settlement) of John III, in *Archivo Port. Or.*, Fasc. 5th, p. 132.

"With **sombreiros** of green and crimson satin." Fernão Pinto, ch. lxviii.

(The Archbishop of Goa) "when he goes abroad a large **sombrero** or parasol is borne over his head; and be it noted that his, and that of the viceroy and the other great lords, are very magnificent, and covered with velvet or other silk stuff, and in winter with some fine wax cloth, the stick prettily worked and painted with gold and blue". Pyrard, *Viagem*, II, p. 80 [Hak. Soc., Vol. II, p. 92].

["They (the people in Pegu) rowe too and fro, and have all their marchandizes in their boates with a great

sixteenth century it began to be used by them for 'umbrella'. Dames in Duarte Barbosa, Vol. I, p. 206, n, compares with this the use of 'bonnets' for umbrellas by John Campbell in the seventeenth century (*Travels of R. Bell and John Campbell*, ed. by Sir Richard Temple, in *The Indian Antiquary*.]

Sopa (soup, or bread soaked in broth, or wine). Konk. *sôp*.—Sinh. *sóp, sóppaya*. *Sóp-pingana*, soup plate.—? Tam. *súppu* (perhaps from the English 'soup').—Tel. *sópa*.—[Anglo-Ind. *supo* (obs.)].[1]—Mal. *sópa*.—Tet. *sôpa*.

Sūpa, in Sanskrit, is 'broth'.

Sorte ('a lottery-coupon'). Konk. *sort, soḍt*; vernacular term *chiṭṭ*.—Mar. *soḍtí*.—Guj. *sortí, surtí*.—Hindust. *shartí*.—Or. *surti*.—Beng. *surtti*.—Sinh. *sórtiya*.—Malayal., Kan., Tul. *sóḍti*.—Tet., Gal. *sóriti*, luck. *Tó-sóriti*, to enrich, to make happy.

The Portuguese *r* before *t* or *d* is easily changed in India into *ṛ* or *ḍ* cerebral. Cf. Konk. *moṛt* from Port. *morte* ('death'); Konk. *kāḍtil* from Port. *cartilha* ('booklet').

Sossegado (quiet). Konk. *susegád*; vern. terms *thanḍ*, *svasth*, *śánt*.—Tet. *susegádu*; vern. terms *hakmátek*.

Sota (queen in game of cards). Konk. *sot*.—Mac., Bug. *sóta*.

Sotaina (soutane). Tam. *sutan*.—Gal. *sotana*.

Suíssa ("a guard or corps of musketeers or riflemen founded by Afonso de Albuquerque", Cândido de Figuei-

---

sombrero or shadow over their heads to keepe the sunne from them, which is as broad as a great cart wheele made of the leaves of the coco trees and fig trees, and is very light." Ralp Fitch, in Foster, *Early Travels in India* (1921), p. 29.]

["**Sumbareros** or Catysols (see *quita-sol*) are here ('Choromandel') very Usefull and necessarie." Bowrey, *A Geo. Account*, etc., Hak. Soc., p. 85. The whole of the paragraph from which only a line is quoted above is interesting because it provides a valuable contribution to the history of the words 'roundell, sombrero, and kittysol'—all meaning umbrellas of sorts—and their uses.]

["As a protection from sun and rain, they (the people of Peroem) use, when the wind is not too high, a sort of umbrella, which the Portuguese call **sombrero**". Manrique, *Travels*, Hak. Soc., Vol. I, p. 113.]

[1] [They (the women of Goa) dress Meat exquisitely; [make] **Supoes**, Pottages, and varieties of stews." Fryer, *East India*, Hak. Soc., Vol. II, p. 28.]

redo). Konk. *suyis*. *Suyisā-chẽm kapel*, chapel of the 'Swiss guards.'—Mal. *suissa*, "a selected body of armed troops" (Haex).

In the town of Mapuca (Goa), there is a chapel dedicated to the Holy Cross which is, by the common people, spoken of as 'the chapel of the Swiss', i.e., the musketeers. On the feast day, after the church-services are over, a mock-fight is staged in a field near by between the Portuguese and the Marathas. The 'Swiss guard' was regarded as invincible.[1]

Sul (south). Konk. *súl*; vern. term *dakhiṇ*. *Sulkár*, a man from the south of Goa, i.e., an inhabitant of Kanara or of Malabar.—L.-Hindust. *sūlí*.[1]

Sumaca ('a smack, vessel with two masts'). Mal. *sumáka* (Marre).

[The *O.E.D.* says that Eng. 'sumack' is an adaptation of Port. *sumaca*. I have not come across 'sumack' in Anglo-Indian writings.]

[**Sumbaia, zumbaia** (a profound reference, a low bow). Anglo-Ind. *sumba*, *sumbra*[2]

1 "The captains of the **soyça** (Swiss) arrived at last in the ship *Conceiçam*, and with them also some men of good repute who are corporals" A. de Albuquerque, *Cartas*, I, p. 83.

"He gave orders for a register to be prepared of all the lowest class of people, with their names and the reasons which made them enlist in Portugal, and he bade them join the militia as **çoiços**. And because the **çoyça** and the militia was then something of a novelty, he had great difficulty in enlisting men, because it was considered dishonourable for a man to join the **çoyços**." Gaspar Correia, II, p. 44.

1 "The largest income which I derive from customs dues in these parts is in respect of commodities that come from China or from **Sul**." Letter from His Majesty (1591), in *Archivo Port. Or*, Fasc. 3rd, p. 312.

"And as the Island and City of Goa, the capital and metropolis of the Portuguese dominions, is situated on the same coast, it is with reference to this City and Island that we reckon the situation of all the other lands, and fortresses of the State. Those which lie towards the left, are spoken of as the **Sul**..." Fr. Luis de Sousa, *Historia de S. Domingos*, III, p. 360. [Similarly the Portuguese dominions to the north of Goa, such as Salsete, Bassein, were spoken of as '*terras do norte*' and their inhabitants as *Norteiros* ('Northeners').]

2 [1540.—"There was security for all, with liberty and freedom during the whole month of September, according to the statute of the King of Siam, for this was the month of **Çumbayas** of

(obs.); also used as a verb 'to sumbaic' (obs.).

This word is not in *Hobson-Jobson* nor in the *O.E.D.* Most Portuguese dictionaries only give the form *zumbaia*, though the older and correcter form is *sumbaia*. The *Novo Diccionário* derives it from Arabic but does not say from which Ar. word. Morais says it is an Indian word. Sir Richard Temple (Bowrey, p. 307, n.) is of the opinion that it is the Malay *sembah*, and quotes the meanings of this word from Wilkinson's Dictionary: "A salutation, a respectful address; the actual act of salutation or homage consisting in raising the hands to the face." Dalgado in his *Glossario* admits the existence of the Malay *sĕmbah* in the above meanings, but points out that Wilkinson also mentions *sĕmbahyang* in the sense of 'worship of God, prayer, ritual' (*yang*='divinity'), and is of the opinion that the source of the Portuguese word is *sĕmbahyang*. He accounts for the phonetic changes thus: Portuguese did not retain the nasal termination of the Malay word just in the same way as it did not retain *m* in the case of the Malayalam and Tamil words from which the Portuguese *jangada* (*q.v.*) is derived. The vowel of the first syllable in *sĕmbahyang* oscillates between *a* surd or *e* surd, and it

Kings." Fernão Pinto, *Peregrinação*, ch. 36, in *Glossario*.]

[1560.—"And thus they go near to the King, place their arms on the ground and make a big **çumbaya** to him with their hands joined and raised up to Heaven." Gabriel Rebêlo, *Informação de Maluco*, p 152, in *Glossario*.]

["Being aproched, we made our **sumba** or reverence to the King, and Thomas Robinson, laying the letters of Creditt which he brought upon his head, did presentlie deliver them unto him, and then both he and Peter Munday, haveing kissed his hand, were willed to sitt downe upon a large Carpott about 2 yards distant from himselfe." In Mundy, *Travels*, Hak. Soc., Vol. III, pt. i, p. 88.]

["On approaching the Puchiquē the Japanese made him profound **sumbaya** and salutations" Manrique, *Travels*, Hak. Soc., Vol. I, p. 133.]

["We read in the *Factory Records* (1642–5, 130) that Mr. Clark '**sumbaied** the Achin Queen in vain'." Editor's note to the above from Manrique.]

["He must receive them with great reverence, Standinge Up and makeinge a **Sumbra** to the Queens Windows, She all the while looketh upon us, although wee cannot See her" Bowrey, Hak. Soc., p. 307.]

is, therefore, not surprising that foreigner's should represent it by *o* surd or by *u*. The change of *s* into *z* was perhaps influenced by the Portuguese verb *zumbar* which also means 'to bow in sign of courtesy'.

With regard to the meanings of the word, Dalgado says that, though it is true, that *sĕmbahyang* signifies literally 'divine worship', it is not to be wondered at that it should also be used to denote 'reverential homage in general', in view of the fact that in Sanskrit and the Prakrits *pūjā* and *namaskār* are also used in a similar twofold meaning. Even assuming that the Malays had reserved the term *sĕmbahyang* to connote 'reverence to a divine being', it is not unnatural to expect that the Portuguese should have confounded it with *sĕmbah*, seeing that the manner in which the homage or greeting implied by the latter term was offered appeared to them little short of adoration.

Gubernatis derives *sumbaia* from the Sansk. *sandhyā*; in doing so he follows his usual bent of referring every conceivable Indian or Malay word to Sanskrit. *Sandhyā* could never become *sumbaia* or *sambaia*, but it would become *sanj* or *sanz*, and these forms are met with in some of the Prakrits.

Judging from the citations in the *Glossario*, the earliest of which goes back to 1540, it is evident the term *sumbaia* had acquired a great vogue among the Portuguese chroniclers, and there can be no doubt that such of the English writers as use the word either as substantive or verb adopted it from the Portuguese.

Sumbaia in its meaning of 'obeisance' was very similar to the Chinese *k'o-t'ou*, lit. 'knock-head', which gave 'kow-tow' to Anglo-India and English.

Sumbaia is not in *Hobson-Jobson* which, however, gives "**Somba, Sombay**, s. A present. Malay *sambah-an*". May not this Malay word be the same as *sĕmbah*, and might it not be that the 'presents' which the word implies are just those that are generally offered to a person in the East when he is treated with reverence and homage?]

Superior (superior). Konk.

superyor (l. us.); vern. terms *vartó*, *vhaḍil*.—Tet. *superior*; vern. term *bóti*.

Suspender (to suspend). Konk. *suspender karuṅk*; vern. term *maná karuṅk*.—Tet. *suspéndi*; vern. terms *tára*, *tétu*.

T

Tabaco (tobacco). Mar. *tambākhú*, *tamākhú*.—Guj. *tambáku*, *tambákuṁ*, *tamāku*.—Hindi, Hindust. *tambākú*, *tamākú*. *tamakú*. *Tambākú-vālá*, tobacconist.—Nep. *tamā-ku*.—Or. *tamákhu*. *Tamrakuḷa*, the tobacco plant.—Beng. *ta-mák*, *tāmák*, *tamáku*, *tāmakú*, *tamrakú*.—Sindh. *tamáku*. *Ta-mākí*, tobacconist.—Punj. *ta-mākú*, *tamákhú*.—Kash. *tabá-ku*, *tamók*, *tamok*.—Malayal. *tambákku*.—Kan. *tambaku*; vern. term *hoge-soppu* (lit. 'the herb of smoke'[1]).—Gar. *tama-ku*.— ? Kamb. *thuām*.— ? Ann. *thúôc*.—? Tonk. *thuōc*.—Mal. *tambáko*, *tembáko*, *tem-báku*.—Ach. *bakum*, *bakon*.—Batt. *timbako*, *bako*.—Sund. *tambako*, *bako*.—Jav. *tambako*, *embako*, *bako*.—Mad. *pôkô*.—Bal. *temako*.—Day. *tambáko*, *tamba*.—Mac., Bug. *tambáko*, —Tet., Gal. *tabáku*.—Malag. *tambáko*.—Jap. *tabako*. *Maki-tabako*, a cheerot. *Kagi tabako*, snuff.[1]—Pers. *tambākú*, *tambak*.—Ar. *tambak*[2].

The plant is an exotic and the name is Mexican, according

[1] The other Dravidian languages have different names, which are equivalent to 'leaf of smoke'.

[1] "It appears certain that we (the Portuguese) carried the plant and its uses to Japan". Wenceslau de Morais, *Day-Nippon*. Gonçalves Viana, however, attributes a Spanish origin to the Japanese *tabako* "which we certainly did not leave behind there, and which must have been introduced in much more recent times than those in which we maintained direct relations with Japan".

"In place of wine of which, as I have said, there is none, **tabaco**, which we call *herva santa*, is used; to it have been attributed throughout all the Indies so many virtues, I cannot say whether real or imaginary, and especially to the kind that grows in this Island" (of San Domingo). Gaspar Afonso (1595), in *Hist. tragico-marit.*, VI, p. 54.

[2] "The revenue from **tabaco** (in Chaul) is nine thousand seven hundred and three *patacões* (*q.v.*) per year." António Bocarro (1634), *Livro das plantas das fortalezas*, in *O Chron. de Tissuary*, IV, p, 33.

"Drinking palm-wine and using **tabaco** for smoking." João Ribeiro, *Fatalidade hist.*, Bk. I, ch. xix.

to Girolamo Benzoni (1550). The use of tobacco spread in India during the reign of the Emperor Akbar (16th-17th cent.). It was introduced into India, in all probability, by the Portuguese. But the following is taken from *Tit-Bits* of the 22nd July, 1911. "The idea that tobacco was known in Europe only after the discovery of America is erroneous. A philologist has suggested that the Greeks and the Romans used to smoke tobacco, at least in their colonies. It is said that in the Malay Archipelago the use of cheerots and cigars dates from a period before the discovery of America."[1]

It is curious that Konkani, like the Dravidian languages, has not adopted the foreign word; in this language tobacco is referred to generically as *pán*, 'leaf', or *oḍhchéṁ pán*, 'the leaf for smoking', and is thus distinguished from the betel-leaf, which is also called *pán* or, more specifically, *khāvunchéṁ pán*, 'the leaf for eating'.[1] From *pán* is derived *pānkár*, 'tobacconist'.

[There can be no doubt about the home of *Nicotiana Tabacum* being America (De Candolle, *Origine*, III). The Spaniards were the first to become acquainted with this plant when, at the close of the 5th century, they visited the Antilles, and Oviedo (*Hystoria de las Indias*, 1535) was the first to give a clear account of it. According to him *tabaco* was the name in the Carib of Hayti of the **Y** shaped tube or pipe through which the Indians inhaled the smoke. But according

---

[1] "Among them there is one which they call the smoker's weed, and which I would call '*erva sancta*' (tobacco), which they say they call (in Brazil) Betum...This plant was first brought to Portugal by Luiz de Goes." Damião de Gois, *Chron. de D. Manuel*, I, ch. 57.

[Prof. Alfred Haddon, F.R.S., in his *Head Hunters* says: "Although smoking was practised in these Islands (Papua and New Guinea) before the Whitemen came, and they grew their own tobacco, they never smoked much at a time. The native pipe is made of a piece of bamboo from about a foot to between two and three feet in length. ..They enjoy it greatly and value tobacco very highly, they usually sell almost anything they possess for the same." In *Ind. Antiq.*, Vol. XL, p. 40.]

[1] "In Arabic *cadegi indi* which means leaf of India." Garcia da Orta, Col. xxiii [ed. Markham, p. 203].

to Las Casas (*Obras* 1552), it was applied to a roll of dried leaves which was kindled at the end, and used by the Indians like a rude cigar. But Monardes, the Spanish physician, published in 1517 an account of tobacco in which he says: "This hearbe which commonly is called *Tabaco* is an Hearbe of muche antiquitie, and knowen amongest the Indians....The proper name of it amongst the Indians is *Piecielt*, for the name of *Tabaco* is geven to it of our Spaniardes, by reason of an Ilande that is named Tabaco." But the island of Tobago itself, after which the herb has been said by some to have been named, received, according to some, the name from its resemblance to an Indian pipe. Whatever, therefore, be the meaning which *tabaco* had among the Indians, the fact which remains undisputed is that the Spaniards regarded *tabaco* as the name of the herb or its leaf, and in this sense it has passed from Spanish into other European languages.

The tobacco plant was brought from America to Spain for the first time in 1558 and very soon began to be cultivated in the Iberic peninsula. In 1560 Jean Nicot, the French ambassador to Portugal, sent seeds of the plant to the Queen, Catherine de Medici. At first, great medicinal and almost miraculous properties were attributed to the plant and it was known by various names, such as, *herba panacea, herva santa.* Tobacco was first introduced into England by Thomas Harriot in 1560, and tobacco smoking became popular there thanks to Sir Francis Drake and Sir Walter Raleigh; from England the use of tobacco for smoking spread to the Continent.

It was towards the close of the 16th century that the Portuguese introduced the plant into Africa, both on the east and west coasts. The negroes took to it with the greatest readiness, and the enormous number of tiny seeds which the plant gives out facilitated its rapid propagation and dissemination in that continent. In Central Africa the names for tobacco according to Schweinfurth (*Heart of Africa*) are *ehtobboo, tab, tabba*; in Swahili *tombako;* in Ki-Galla *tambo* and in Lu-Chicongo *tabaco* and *fumu*, the last named being the Port. *fumo*, 'smoke'.

There are no references to the tobacco plant in Baber's *Memoirs* (1519–1525) nor in Garcia da Orta's *Colloquies* (1563), nor in Christoval Acosta (1578), not even in Linschoten (1589). "The first direct reference to it, in connection with India, centres around certain Portuguese missioniaries at the court of the Great Mughal. Doubtless to the Portuguese is due the credit of having conveyed both the plant and the knowledge of its properties to India and China. It is said in the *Dara-shikohi* that they had conveyed it to the Deccan as early as 1508. Asad Beg, of date 1605 (Elliot, *Hist. Ind.*, 1875, VI, 165-7), says of Bijapur that he found some tobacco and, "never having seen the like in India I brought some with me and prepared a handsome pipe of jewel work." These he presented to the Emperor Akbar, who attempted to smoke, until he was forbidden by his physician. It would thus seem to have been known in the Deccan for nearly a century before it was carried to the rest of India......By 1617 smoking had, in fact, become so general in India that the Emperor Jehangir forbade the practice, as also had Shah Abbas of Persia (Elliot, *l.c.* v., 851)." (Watt, *The Comm. Prod. of Ind.*, p. 796.)

The cultivation of the plant must have been taken up vigorously and spread with surprising rapidity, for there are references in letters and invoices received by the East India Company from its servants in the East of as early a date as 1619 to shipments of tobacco from India. These references also enable us to know the prevailing price of tobacco in India in these early years of its cultivation.[1]

---

1 ["Goods sent to the Red Sea in the *Lion*. *Mahm. Pice*
Tobacco, 155 maunds at
4 m. 18 p. .. 707 [6]
Foster, *The English Factories (1618—1621)*, p. 64.

"Tobako at rials 4 per maund of 32 sears" (in Mocha). *Op. cit.*, p. 109.

"Of the goods carried thither (Gombroon, on December 4, 1638) by the *Francis*,...the tobacco was sold for 9 lārīs per maund." *Op. cit.*, *(1637-1641)*, p. 126.

Mahmūdi, a silver coin current in

Watt very truly remarks: "As in other parts of the world, so in India, tobacco passed through a period of persecution, but its ultimate complete distribution over India is one of the numerous examples of the avidity with which advantageous new crops or new appliances have been absorbed into the agriculture and social customs and even literature of the people of India" (*op. cit.*, p. 796). On the other hand, it is but fair to mention that it has been maintained by some that the tobacco plant is indigenous to India and that tobacco was used there both for smoking and medicinal purposes centuries before the date commonly assigned for its introduction. Mr. Ganpat Ray, Librarian, Bengal National College, Calcutta, supported this view in *The Indian Antiquary* (Vols. XXV, p. 176 and XL, pp. 37–40) with many quotations: one from the poet Bāṇa to show that smoking after dinner was a common Indian habit; others from Susruta and Charaka describing the process of 'manufacturing a cigar' and also the 'efficacy of smoking'; and also one from the *Skanda-Purāṇa* (ch. 52) which is as follows:

"Smokers after death will be turned into ghosts. During the Kaliyuga, Kali himself will be incarnated as the *tambāla* leaf.

"On the advent of the Kaliyuga all the castes will be cast into hell on smoking tobacco. The worst type of men will fall victims to tobacco. Thus, losing their *dharma*, they will fall into the Mahāraurava hell..."

Mr. Ray's contention is that the Bengali term for tobacco, *tāmāku*, is a corruption of the Sanskrit word *tāmrakūṭa*—a statement which he supports by quotations from old Sanskrit works. He goes further and maintains that *tāmrakūṭa* is the same as *tamāla* of the *Skanda-Purāṇa*. But the *tamāla* plant has been identified with either *Garcinia Xanthochymus*, Hook., or *Xanthochymus Pictorius*, Roxb., or *Cinnamomum Tamala*, Nees (Watt, *Dict. Econ. Prod.*, Vol. III, p. 478).

Gujarat of the value of nearly an English shilling.

A *rial* was calculated then at about 4*s.* 6*d.* and sold for about 5 *Mamūdis*. *Lāri* was worth about an English shilling.]

It is not enough to say, as Mr. Ray does, that because *tāmrakūṭa* is mentioned along with opium, *gānjā*, and other intoxicants, it must "therefore mean 'tobacco'." Why should it not be some other narcotic like opium or *gānjā*? It requires no great philological acumen to perceive that *tabaco* could give in Bengali *tāmāku*, as it did in Marathi, in which *tamākhú* exists side by side with *tambākhū*. Moreover, botanical evidence is completely opposed to Mr. Ray's contention. (See *Ind. Antiq.*, Vols. I, p. 210 and XXXVII, p. 210.)

Taberna (tavern, pot-house). Sinh. *teberuma, teberema*; vern. terms *surāsela, surāśaláva.*

Tabernáculo (tabernacle). Konk. *tābernákl.*—Tam. *tabernákulu.*

Tacho (stew-pan). Sinh. *táchuva.*—Mal. *táchu.*—Tet., Gal. *táchu, tásu.*

Tajélo, from the Malay spoken in Amboyna, is, according to Dr. Schuchardt, composed of *tacho* and *tijela* 'bowl'.

[**Taça** (a cup). ?Anglo-Ind. *toss.*[1] 'Toss' is used by Fryer and Ovington in the sense of 'a cup', and their editors derive it from Pers. *tās*, 'a cup'. But if the Persian word was so much in use in the 17th century as to have been easily picked up by English travellers it should, without a doubt, have been adopted in colloquial Urdu or Hindi, in which, however, we do not find it. The Hindi word for 'cup', in common use, is *pyālā* or *jām*. *Taça* was used by the Portuguese for 'a cup', especially 'drinking cup', and as their *festas* accompanied by drinking had acquired a notoriety in India, it is not improbable that their name for 'cup' enjoyed considerable currency. The *O.E.D.* regards 'toss' used by Fryer as a variant or misprint for 'tass' which derived from Arabic or Persian and

[1] ["And then most of them (Persians) will freely take off their Bowls of Wine,........most of Silver, some of Gold, which we call a **Toss,** and is made like a Wooden Dish." Fryer, *East India and Persia,* Hak. Soc., Vol. III, p. 137.]

["All the Dishes and Plates brought to the Table are of pure Silver, massy and Substantial; and such are also the **Tosses** or Cups out of which we drink." Ovington, *A Voyage to Surat,* O.U.P., p. 231.]

meaning 'a cup or small goblet' has been used in English from the 14th century. But it is not only Fryer, but also Ovington who speak of 'toss'. The Portuguese *taça* has the same origin as the English 'tass'.]

Talapoi, talapõi ('a Buddhist monk'). Anglo-Ind., Indo-Fr. *talapoïn.*

The source of the word is the Pali *talapaṇṇam* (Sinh. *talapata*), a fan which the Buddhist monks carry in accordance with their liturgy.[1]

[In the supplement to the *Glossario,* Dalgado says that Señor Gabriel Ferrand has informed him that very recent investigations have disclosed the origin of this word to be the two Peguan words, *tala,* 'lord', and *pôi,* 'our', i.e., 'our lords or monsignori', a title given to Catholic prelates. This is also

---

[1] "The *Chaubainha* sent the King a letter by one of his **talapoy,** a religious who was four score years of age." Fernão Pinto, ch. cxlix [tr. Cogan, 199].

"Throughout all these kingdoms there are many religious observing different rules; some who are called in Pegu **Talapois,** and in Siam, *Biros;* and in Kamboya, *Chicús*...Their dress consists of cloaks and tunics of a dark yellow colour, a dye which they prepare from the bark of the jack-fruit tree. They carry over their heads umbrellas made of oil-paper." Diogo do Couto, Dec. V, vi, 1. "Preaching one day to the ambassadors of Bramá, and the **Talapoens** who had accompanied them, they are their Bishops, and Religious. *Id.,* Dec. VIII, 1, 12.

"He did not want for himself anything more than alms, as he was a **talapõi,** which is the same as a religious among us." António Bocarro, Dec. XIII, p. 125.

"They regard it as a sign of holiness to go about with their heads shaven and their feet unshod, and to carry in their hand a large paper-fan shaped like a buckler with which they protect their heads from the sun, and shield their looks from the gaze of the people when they pass by them." João de Barros, Dec. III, ii, 5.

["In Pegu they have many **Tallipoies** or priests, which preach against all abuses....The **Tallipoies** go very strangely apparelled, with one camboline or thinne cloth next to their body of a browne colour, another of yellow doubled many times upon their shoulder, and those two be girded to them with a broad girdle; and they have a skinne of leather hanging on a string about their necks, whereupon they sit, bare headed and bare footed, for none of them weareth shoes; with their right armes bare and a great broad sombrero or shadow in their hands to defend them in the summer from the sunne, and in the winter from the raine." (Follows a very full account of the manner of their ordination and their manner of life.) Ralph Fitch, in Foster, *Early Travels,* p. 36.]

the view of the *O.E.D.* See also *Ind. Antiq.*, Vol. XXXV, p. 267.]

Talento (high mental ability). Konk. *tālent*; vern. terms *bārkamáy*, *mardí*.—Tet. *taléntu*.

Talhamar (cut-water). L.-Hindust. *tāliyāmár*, *tāliyāvár*.

Tambaca, tambaque ('an alloy of copper and zinc prepared in Indo-China'). Konk. *tāmbak*.— | Sinh. *tambákka* | . —Tam., Malayal. *tambákku*.—Tul. *tambaku*.—Anglo-Ind. *tomback*.[1]

From the Malay *tambaga* (which is related to the Sanskrit *tamṛka*), it was introduced into India by the Portuguese.

Tambor (tambour, drum). Konk. *tambor*.—? Mar., Hindust., Punj. *tambúr*.—? Ass. *tambaru*, *tamburu*.—Sinh. *tambóruva*, *tambóreva*.—Tam., Malayal. *tambor*.—? Kan. *tambúre*.—? Mal., Sund., Jav. *tambur*.—? Ach. *támbu*.—Bug. *támboro*, *tambúru*.[1]

The source-word of *tambor* is said to be the Arabic-Persian *ṭanbúr*, which might have been directly carried to the languages in which the word ends in *úr*. | See Dozy, *s.v. atambor.* |

Tanchão (stanchion). L.-Hindust. *tenchan*.

Tangedor (player on a stringed instrument). Mal. *tanjedor*, *tanjidur*.—Jav. *tanjídur*, *panjidur*.—Bug. *tanjidóro*. A musician who plays on a European instrument.

Tanger (to play on a stringed instrument). Mal. *tanji* (*subst.*), music. *Bikin tanji*, to play music.

? **Tanque** (cistern; an artificial reservoir of water). Mar. *ṭāṅkí*, *ṭaṅkéṁ*.—Guj. *ṭāṅkí*, *ṭáṅkuṁ*.—Tul. *tánki*.—Anglo-Ind. *tank*.— | Mal. *tángki*, 'ship's tank' | .

It appears that here is an instance of a coincidence of two

---

1 ["When the King came to the First little building on the greene, hee alighted From thatt Elephant, and passing through the roome, Mounted on another thatt there stood ready For him, having the Pavillion over his head of **Tambacca**, a mixt Mettall of gold and Copper much esteemed in these parts." Mundy, *Travels*, Hak. Soc., Vol. III, pt. i, p. 125.

1 "He used to give orders to play on an **atambor** which was of such a huge size that four men could not move it." João de Barros, Dec. IV, vii, 20.

"With many bag-pipes, trumpets, kettle-drums, **tambores**, fifes." Diogo do Couto, Dec. VI, iv, 16.

terms etymologically distinct, with a meaning almost alike: the Portuguese *tanque* from the Latin *stagnum*, and the Guj. *ṭáṅkuṁ* (the etymon of the other words), which is probably from the Sanskrit *taṭāka* or *taḍāga*.

Portuguese writers speak of *tanque* when they refer to the Indian cisterns or water reservoirs, which in Konkani are called *taḷéṁ* [1].

[1] "Chaul lies over fields and cultivated lands, and contains many **tanques** of water and many groves of trees and is delightfully cool." A. de Albuquerque, *Letters*, I. p. 136.

"There was a big **tanque** four fathoms deep." *Roteiro da viagem de Vasco de Gama*, p. 95.

"Wheresoever they ('the Baneanes of Guzerate') dwell they have orchards and fruit-gardens and many water **tanques** wherein they bathe twice a day, both men and women." Duarte Barbosa, p. 268 [ed. Dames, Vol. I, p. 113].

"In order to collect the rain water, they make these **tanques** (which might be more properly called lakes) all lined with stone." João de Barros, Dec. IV, vi, 5.

["And this king ('Crisnarao of Bysnaga' (Vijayanagar) also built in his time a water **tamque**, which is situated between two high hills.....and as there was no one in his country who could construct it, he made a request to the Governor of Goa for some Portuguese masons, and the Governor sent him João de lla Ponte, a great builder of masonry work." *Chronica de Bisnaga*, ed. David Lopes, p. 55.]

Tanto (*adv.*, so much).? Mal., Mac., Bug. *tántu*, certain, determinate, steady.—Jap. *tanto* (colloquial), much, in great quantity.

Hepburn observes: "This term is derived probably from Spanish."

Tapete (carpet). Konk. *tāpêt*; vern. terms *tivāsí*, *satrangí*.—Tet. *tapêti*.

Tara (tare, abatement from the gross weight of goods). Tel. *táramu*.

Tarde (afternoon, evening). Konk. *tárd* (l. us.); vern. terms *sánz*, *uśir*.—Mal. *tarda* (Haex). —Tet., Gal. *tárdi*.

? **Tarifa** (tariff). Malayal. *taríff*.

It is possible that it may have been imported directly from Arabic or through English. [*Tarifa* is itself derived from the Ar. *ta'rif*, 'notification' ('*irf*, 'knowledge').]

Tartaruga (tortoise). Mal. *taleruga*, *tetrugo* (Haex).—Mol. *tarturugo*, turtle.

[Teca (*Tectona grandis*, Linn., and also its wood).

Anglo-Ind. *teak.*[1]—Ind.-Fr. *tek.*

The Portuguese became acquainted with this word as they did with so many others in the Malabar country: Malayal. *tekka*, Tam. *tēkku*. The Sansk. name of the tree is *sāka*, whence the Mar. and Guj. *sāg*, and the Hindust. *sāgūn* and *sāgwān*. In the 'Bombay Letters' as late as 1667 this wood is not referred to as 'teak' but as 'ye oak of India,' and Fryer is the earliest English traveller not only to refer to 'teke' but also to show first hand acquaintance with the tree as can be seen from the quotation below.]

Têmpera (used for *tempero*, "seasoning or condiments used in cooking"). Konk. *tempr*; vern. terms *sāmbhár*, *masāló*, *jiremmirém*.—Tet. *tempra*; vern. term *búdu*.—Gal. *témpera*.

In the form *tempra* or *tempr* the word is used in Indo-Portuguese dialects.

Temperado (spiced). Konk. and Tam. *temprad* (*subst.*), a vegetable stew.—Sinh. *tempráduva*, mixture. *Temprádu karaṇavā*, to season.

Tempo (time). Konk. *têmp*; vern. terms *kál*, *vêḷ*, *vagat*, *samay*.—Mal. *tempo*, duration and atmospheric condition. *Minta tempo*, to ask for time.—Jav. *tempo*. *Tempon*, period of time fixed in contracts.—Sund. *tempo*. *Rarempo*, "a modified form of *tempo* and used in the sense of:

---

1 ["The interior of Damão which is mountainous and dry and parched has many of the roughest thickets of bambus, and forests of the most plentiful and best timber that there is in the world, and that is **teca**." Diogo do Couto, Dec. VII, vi, 6.]

["Likewise all timber for shipping and houses of durance, wch wee may call ye oak of India, growes up at Cullean, Bimurly, and must necessarily passe by Tanna, where they take 33 p. cent. custome." Forrest, *Selections* (Home Series), Vol. 1, p. 120.]

["**Teke** by the *Portugueze*, *Sogwan* by the *Moors*, is the firmest Wood they have for Building, and on the account it resists Worms and Putrefaction, the best for that purpose in the World; in Height the Lofty Pine exceeds it not, nor the Sturdy Oak in Bulk and Substance; the knotty Branches which it bears aloft, send forth Green Boughs more pliant, in Form Quadrangular, fed within by a Spongy Marrow or Pith, on which at the Joints hang broad, thin, and porous Leafs, sending from the main Rib some Fibres, winding and spreading like a Fan." Fryer, *East India*, Hak. Soc., Vol. II, p. 75.]

it is all up with them; their hour has struck. It is also used of a single person, if all his little affairs have been ruined. *Gĕns rarempo jasah*, the most miserable, the most destitute." Rigg.—Day. *tempo*, limit, period.—Tet., Gal. *témpu.*

Tenaz (*subst.*, a pair of tongs or pincers). Malayal. *tanáss.*

Tenda (tent). Konk. *tend*, awning.—Sinh. *tende*, couch, bed.—Mal. *ténda*, awning.—Jav. *téndŏ*, *tíndŏ*.—Tet. *tenda.*

Tentação (temptation). Konk. *tentāsáṁv*; vern. terms *tāḷṇí*, *náḍ*, *bhúl.*—Tet. *tentasã.*

Tentar (to tempt). Konk. *tentár-karuṅk*, to tempt one to evil; to vex.—Mal. *tentar* (Haex).—Tet., Gal. *ténta.*

Têrço (a third of a rosary; a string of beads with five decades). Konk. *têrs.*—Beng. *tersú.*—Tam., Tet., Gal. *térsu.*[1]

[In Konkani the term *ters* has also come to denote the prayer with Aves and Paternosters which the string of beads was originally intended to help to count, and this is perhaps also the case in the other languages which have adopted the term.]

Terebentina (turpentine). Jap. *terementina.*— | Turk. *tèrménti* | .

Gonçalves Viana derives the Japanese *terementina* from the Spanish *trementina.* But Diogo do Couto says: '*Era semelhante á trementina*' ('It was similar to turpentine') (Dec. IV, vii, 9); and in the *Archivo Portuguese Oriental* there appears the following item (1585): "*Trementina* at 10 reis an ounce" (*Fasc.* 5, p. 1048). | Bluteau also mentions the form *trementina.* |

[**Terranquim** (a kind of small and swift bark used in the Persian Gulf and adjoining seas).

? Anglo-Ind. *trankey.*[1]

---

1 "All say the **terço** of the rozary aloud." Cardim, p. 93.

1 [" He (Noceret) fled to Komzara, and thence in a **tarranquy**, or light bark, to Lapht, a seaport in the Isle of Broct, which isle we Portuguese call commonly Queixome." Pedro Teixeira, *Travels*, Hak. Soc., p. 159.]

[" And besides these ships there were in the harbour (of Ormuz) about two hundred galleons......There were also many **terradas** (like the barques of Alcouchete) full of small guns and men wearing sword-proof dresses and armed from head to foot, most of them being archers." A. de Albuquerque,

Crooke's hypothesis that 'trankey' may be connected with the Port. *trincador* is inadmissible; it is no doubt the same word as the Port. *terranquim*. But what is the derivation of *terranquim?* Dalgado's view is that *terranquim* is either an augmentative or diminutive of *terrada* (Ar. *ṭarrād*), the name of a short boat and also of small boats for service in war used in the same parts, which is frequently referred to by Portuguese chroniclers. It is not impossible that the Portuguese spoke of the small *terrada* as *terradim*, just as they formed the diminutive *varandim* from *varanda*, and that *terradim* became subsequently transformed into *terraquim* perhaps through the influence of *terráqueo* ('terraqueous'). See *Glossario*. Both *terrada* and *terranquim* are mentioned in Vieyra's Dictionary. The derivation of 'trankey' given in the *O.E.D.* makes all the above hypotheses valueless and shows how necessary it is to seek for the explanation of a word in the language of the people by whom, and of the region where, it is used. The *O.E.D.* says 'trankey or tranky' is adopted from Pers. *trankeh*, name in Persian Gulf for a pearl diver's net, or perhaps its adjectival derivation *trānki*, applied elliptically to a pearling boat, and gives as its meaning 'a small undecked vessel, used in the pearl fishery in the Persian Gulf'.

There is no reason to suppose that 'trankey' owes anything to *terranquim* which is the Portuguese transcription of the Persian word. For the insertion of *e* after *t*, and for the nalised termination, cf. *mordexim*.]

Commentaries, Hak. Soc., Vol. I, p. 105.]

["Even the water comes (to Ormuz) from outside, from the main and from the neighbouring isles for their drinking in certain small boats which they call **teradas**, as I have said before." Duarte Barbosa, ed. Dames, Vol. I, p. 97.]

["As soon as the Contract was made, the *Arabs* went couragiously to Work, and . . . . . gave the *English* their Choice, and then got **Trankies**, (or Barks without Decks) and shipt what belonged to the *English* for *Muskat*." Hamilton, *East Indies* (1827), Vol. 1, p. 57.]

[(The King of that Province) "had provided a sufficient Number of small Vessels, called **Trankies**, for their Transports." *Idem*, p. 59.]

Terrina (tureen). Konk. *terrín.*—Tet., Gal. *terrina.*

Tesouraria (treasury). Guj. *tijorí*: also used in the sense of 'a safe'.—Malayal. *tiśóri*; perhaps from the English 'treasury.'

Tesoureiro (a treasurer). Konk. *tijrêr.*—Guj. *tijorar.*—Tam. *tijoreri.*

Testamento (will, testament). Konk. *testāment*; vern. term *maranpatr.*—Mal. *téstamen* (Castro).—Tet., Gal. *testaméntu.*

Tia (aunt). Konk. *tí, tití* (l. us.).—Beng. *tití.*—Tet. *tia.*

Tinta (ink). Konk. *tínt*; vern. terms are *śai, maśi, patrānjan.*—Sinh. *tínta* (also us. of 'colour dyes'); vern. terms *masi, deli. Tínta gánavā*, to dye, to colour. *Tínta-kuppiya, tínta-keduva*, an ink-pot.—Tam. *tintei.*—Mal., Jav. *tínta*, European ink; colour. *Mansi* is Chinese ink.—Tet., Gal. *tinta.*

[Sir Thomas Roe speaks of *Tinta Roxa* (Hak. Soc., p. 22), which Foster says is probably orchilla weed, a lichen which grows on rocks and trees near the sea-coast, and yields a purple dye. *Tinta Roxa* is Portuguese for 'purple dye', and was perhaps the then current trade name for this weed.]

Tinto (red wine). Konk. *tínt, tintāchó saró.*—Jap. *chinta.*

Tio (uncle). Konk. *tív*, the paternal uncle (us. only among the Christians); vern. term *bāpló.*—Beng. *tív* (us. among the Christians of Hashnabad, Dacca district.—Mal. *tio* (Schuchardt).—Tet. *tio.*

Tira (a strip). Konk. *tír*; vern. terms *phāḷí, chindhí, śír, paṭṭí, báṇ.*—Sinh. *tíraya, tíreva.* —Mal. *tiras*, thread, string.—Tet., Gal. *tiras*, also 'ribbon, band'. As in *apas, uvas*, in this word too, the plural form *tiras* is preferred.[1]

Tiro (a shot; range). Konk. *tir*, aim, mark; vern. terms *phár*, ('shot'); *ṭíp, mokí*, ('aim').—Sindh. *tíru*, bullet.—Tet., Gal. *tíru.*

Toalha (towel). Konk. *tuvāló*; vern. terms *hātpusṇeṁ* ('hand-towel'), *mezācheṁ chadar* ('table-towel').—Guj. *tuvál.*—Hindi, Hindust. *tauliyá* (also 'a serviette'); vern. terms *rumál, angochchá.*—Beng. *toyále.*—Sinh. *tuváya, tuvájaya,*

[1] In the sense of 'curtain', which it has in Tamil and Malayalam, *tira* is from Sanskrit.

tuváje; vern. term *pisnakaḍa.* —Tam. *tualei.*—Malayal. *tuvála.*—Tel. *tuvālā, tuvālāguṭṭa.* —Tul. *tuválu.*—Anglo-Ind. *towleea.*—Khas. *taulia.*—? Siam. *tōk.*—Mal. *tuála, tuvála.*—Tet., Gal. *tualha.*

The hiatus in *oa* was destroyed by the intercallation of *v* (=*w*), and *lh* became depalatalized, because there is no such sound in the oriental languages.

Tocha (torch). Konk. *toch.* —Tam. *tócha.*

Tomar (to take). Mal. *tóma; Tóma ánin, toma harus,* to sail near the wind, to take the current.

Tomate (tomato). Konk. *tomát*; *tamaṭ* (from the English 'tomato'); vern. term *belvāṅgeṁ.*—Tet. *tomàti*; vern. term *fái-mátak.*

Tômbo (record; archive). Sinh. *tómbuva.*

Topa (top; teetotum). Mal. *tópa*; used in a game of 'tops'.

Topaz (a dark-skinned Christian half-breed of Portuguese descent). Anglo-Ind. *topaz, topass* (obs.).—Indo-Fr. *topas.*

This term was employed in the seventeenth and eighteenth centuries as synonymous with mestizo to denote those who claimed to be Portuguese descendants, spoke Portuguese, affected the Portuguese style of dress, professed the Catholic faith and served ordinarily as soldiers in the army.

The origin of the word has been the subject of much discussion. At least three different derivations of the word, more or less plausible, are given: (1) The Turk.-Pers.-Hindust. *topchi*, 'a gunner', by profession,[1] (2) Hindust. *ṭopí* (Tam. *ṭoppi*), 'a hat' *ṭopívālá*, 'one who wears a hat'), used as a distinguishing mark, at times honour-

---

[1] "Seven hundred Portuguese, besides some **topazes** who were also musketeers." António Bocarro, Dec. XIII, p. 244.

"Gaspar Figueira was with eight companies, and in these there were two hundred and forty Portuguese, and there was one company of **topazes** in which there were thirty seven." João Ribeiro, *Fatalidade hist.*, Bk. II, ch. xx.

"In the early history of the Company these people were extensively enlisted as soldiers; [hence the term came to be applied to the Company's native soldiery generally in the Peninsula: it is now obsolete" (p. 525)]. H. H. Wilson.

able, at others opprobrious,[1] (3) Tam. *tuppási* (which is not mentioned in modern dictionaries) for *dubáshi* = Neo-Aryan *dubhāśi* or *dobāśi* = Sanskrit *dvibhāśya*, 'bilingual, interpreter'; because they spoke two languages.

In spite of Yule's censorious remark ("his usual fertility of error"), I find, as also does Dr. Schuchardt, that Fra Paolino de S. Bartolomeo had good reason in regarding *topaz* as a corruption of *dobháśya*.[2]

In the Tamil spoken by the people, *dubhāśi* or *dobāśi* ought normally to be changed into *tuppási*; because, as it possesses only soft intervocalic sounds, it changes the initial sounds of foreign words into its own respective hard ones, and very often converts the soft medials into twin hard ones, either by assimilation or by emphasis. Cf. *tāthu* = Sansk. *dhātu*, *tívu* = Sansk. *dvīpa*; *tukkam* = Sansk. *duḥkham*, *tuṭṭu* = Neo-Aryan *duḍú*. Malayalam, which passes for a dialect of Tamil, has in fact *tuppási* or *tupáyi* in the sense of 'interpreter'.[1] And Sinhalese, which occupies a place midway between the Aryan and Dravidian languages, has *tuppahiyá*, in the same sense; it is certainly a corruption (*tadbhāva*) of the Aryan *dubhāsya* or an adoption of the Dravidian *tuppási*, with *h* for the intervocalic *s*, a common phenomenon, and with the separable suffix-*yá*.

The designation of *topaz* for the 'mestizo' was more current in the south of India,[2] and it

---

1 "Metis (see *mestizo*) or **Topas**, people wearing hats are so called." A. Marre. [Wilson also thinks that this is probably the derivation of *topaz*—from Hindi *topí*, a hat.]

2 "He proposed also that it was necessary for the Church of Calicut to have a **Topaz**, or an interpreter from the Christians of the land, who should not only be competent to carry out this work but also be one to command respect, and able to carry on negotiations with the Samorim and his ministers regarding affairs of the Church and the Christians (1698)." *O Chroni. de Tissuary*, II, p. 83.

"**Tuppâsi**, that is, an interpreter, which name is also usually given to the Indian Portuguese." Ber. IV. 19 Anm. O, *apud* Schuchardt.

---

1 Gundert mentions documents of the 18th century in which *tupáyi* is employed in the sense of 'an East Indian, or half-caste'.

2 "A native Christian sprung from a Portuguese father and Indian mother

is, therefore, to be presumed that it had its origin in one of the Dravidian languages. Now, if *tuppasi* corresponds to *dubhāśi* and primarily signified an 'interpreter', it is clear that it would be applied in this acceptation to the indigenous Christians who might be acquainted with Portuguese,[1] just as well as to the descendants of the Portuguese who would speak besides Portuguese one or more of the Indian vernaculars, and as such would be frequently employed as interpreters between the Europeans and the Indians.[2] And in this sense the term is used by Portuguese and other writers. "Those who have wants manifest and set them forth very well without **topaz**, or interpreter". Lucena. "Appreciating greatly the occasion of finding himself without **topaz**". *Id.*, Bk. ii, ch. 16.

in the south of India. In the early history of the Company these people were extensively enlisted as soldiers." H. H. Wilson.

1 "There were at that time no more than five Portuguese, seven Indians, the children of Portuguese, who were born there, and six **Topazes**, by this name are called those Christians who have no Portuguese blood in them." *Conquista do Reyno de Pegu*, ch. vii.

2 "A letter patent of His Highness, dated the 25th January, 1571, in which it is ordained that the posts of *Linguas* (interpreters) be given to the new (Christian) converts." *Archivo Port. Or.*, Suppl. 2nd, p. 79.

Afterwards, when the word came to be used of one particular race, and there were interpreters from the other classes, some of the Dravidian languages, in order to avoid confusion, imported the term *dubáśi*, as *tatsama*, in order to designate an interpreter in general, as well as a factor or agent.[1] (See *Hobson-Jobson* and Schuchardt, *Beiträge*, etc.).

[With the object of settling the vexed question of the derivation of the word 'Topaz or Topass', Sir R. C. Temple collected in chronological order as many references to, and definitions of, the term as appear in *Hobson-Jobson*, the *O.E.D.*, the *Ceylon Antiquary*, and his own notes from original records and

1 In Laskari-Hindustani, 'topás' is the name of a sweeper. "It is doubtful to what language this word properly belongs. It does not mean a sweeper in Hindustani, but the Laskar 'topas' generally acts as such as his special duty in the ship." Small.

old travellers, and they are to be found in the *Ind. Antiq.*, Vol. L, pp. 106–113. I shall supplement these by a few citations from Manrique and Manucci, both of whom use the term of Indian converts to Christianity.[1]

Sir R. C. Temple's view of the derivation of the word is identically the same as Dalgado's. He says that there can be little doubt "that the word is an early Portuguese corruption, through a form *tôpâshi* in Malayalâm (the first Indian language the Portuguese learnt) of the Indian *dubhâshi* (Skt. *dvibhâshi*) one with two languages, *i.e.*, a half-breed servant of Europeans; thence a soldier, especially a gunner, and among sailors, a ship's servant, a lavatory or bathroom attendant, and incidentally, on occasion, an interpreter. In the form *topaz, topass*, the term became differentiated from *dûbhâshi* (in the mouths of Europeans, *dubash*), a superior native interpreter, and meant always a low-class half-breed. It has no relation to *tôp*, a gun, or to *tôpi*, a hat."]

Tope (the top of a mast). L.-Hindust. *tôpi*.

---

[1] "Moreover, I would be responsible also for their (Christians) maintenance and that of their wives and children for a month . . . During this period they would have sufficient time to arrange a method of livelihood, as other **topazes** do (this name of **topaz** is applied by the Portuguese of those parts to Indians and half-castes who are Christians)." Manrique, *Travels*, Hak. Soc., Vol. I, p. 279.]

["Father Fray Juan de la Cruz, a truly Apostolic man, of whom the evil spirits declared through the mouths of inspired persons, that they could not stand before him, was retreating with two Christian **Topazes.** He saw he was being pursued, ... so he told his two companions to fly, and knelt down, raising his hands to heaven. As he was in this position one of those barbarians came up to him with a large sharp sword and gave him so severe a blow on the shoulders as to cut him half through. They paid no heed to the two **Topazes** or, as they call them *Calas Franguis*, who were fleeing." *Idem*, Vol. II, p. 337.]

["For, as they call themselves Jesuits in India and Apostolic in the other place, people expect to find in them a charity which is veritably Apostolic and Christian. In this these poor men are deceived, for they are waited on in the hospital most carelessly by Canarese or **Topasses**, who frequently demand payment for even the water they require . . . . . As a relief to himself the Father Administrator entertains at this hospital a **Topass** chaplain, who looks after the patients, so they say." Manucci, ed. Irvine, Vol. III, p. 283.]

The word *topí*, *topí* or *toppi*, which is found in the Gaurian and Dravidian languages, with the meaning of 'cap or hat', is traced by some philologists to the Portuguese *tope* or *tôpo* ('the top, the uppermost end'). But the *Roteiro da Viagem de Vasco de Gama* ('*The Log Book of Vasco de Gama*') mentions *tupy* as corresponding to the Port. *barrete*, 'cap', in the list of Malabar words. Indian dictionary writers connect *topí* with *topa* or *top*, 'big hat, helmet and (in Konkani) mitre'.

[Wilson (*Glossary*, p. 525) has: "*Toppi-kuḍa*, Malayal. A hat-umbrella, a hat with a projecting brim on the crown, worn by fishermen and other castes in Malabar; the term seems to be of old, and to precede the Portuguese."]

Toranja (*Citrus decumana*, the shaddock or 'the pomelo'). Konk. *torónz* (neut., the fruit), *torônz* (fem., the plant).—Mar. *turanj*, *toranjan*.—Guj. Hindust. *turanj*.—Sindh. *turúnju*. —Tel. *turanj*, *turánju*.—| Turk. *túrunj*. |—

The plant is a native of Java, probably introduced by the Portuguese into India. The name is the Arabic *turunj*, Persian *turanj*, which appears to be the immediate source of the word in many of the languages.

[The pomelo has no Sanskrit name. It was known to the early Dutch traders as 'Pompelmoes' (=pumpkin citron), hence some of the modern names. It reached India and Ceylon in the 17th century.

The pomelo is presumed to have been introduced into India and Ceylon from Java, hence the name *batávi nebu*, and it was carried to the West Indies by a Capt. Shaddock after whom it is known there. The best quality of the pomelo is the thin-skinned Bombay variety, hence the South Indian name for it of *bombalinas*. See Watt, *The Comm. Prod. of Ind.*]

Toro ('trunk or body of a man'). Mal., Jav., *toro*, a kind of jacket. According to Dr. Heyligers it is an abbreviation of *báju-toro* (Mal.) and *rasukan-toro*.

Tôrre (tower). Konk. *tôrr*; vern. terms *gopur*, *burínz*.—Tet., Gal. *tôrri*.

Torto ('squint eyed'). Mal. *torto* (Haex).

Touca (a woman's coif). Mal. *tocca*, 'girdle' (Haex).

It appears that the meaning given by Haex is not correct because *tokka* in the Portuguese dialect of Malay signifies 'veil, mantilla, shawl'.

Traição (treason). Konk. *trãyisáṁv*; vern. term *ghát ābghát*.—Tet. *traisã*.

Traidor (traitor). Konk. *trāyidor* (l. us.); vern. terms *ghātkí, gaḷekāpó*.—Mal. *taledor*.

Tranca (bar, piece of wood to bar a door with). Sinh. *trankaya*; vern. term *agula*.

Tranqueira (palisade). Mal. *trankéyra, trankera, terankéra, telankéra*.[1]

Trapa (a trap or device to take wild beasts). L.-Hind. *trāpá*, a raft.

Traquete (the mizzen-sail). L.-Hindust. *trikat, tirkat, trinkat*.—Mal. *trinket, triaket*.[2]

Tratamento (treatment.) Konk. *trātāment*; vern. term *chāḷauṇí, keḷauṇí, upachár*.—Tet., Gal. *trataméntu*.

Tratar (to treat). Konk. *trātár-karuṅk*; vern. terms *chaḷauṅk, keḷauṅk*.—Tet., Gal. *tráta*.

Tratos ('tortures'). Mal. *tarato* (Haex), | *tarátu*. *Témpat tarátu*, 'the torture-room' |.

Trave (a beam). Tam. *trávi*.

Três (three). Malayal. *tress*, fraction of 'reis' (Gundert).

? **Tresdobrado** (threefold). Konk. *tibrád*. The term is especially used of very strong distilled liquor.—Tul. *tibralu*, liquor from the coco-nut palm thrice distilled.

I am of the opinion that *tibrád* does not come directly from the Portuguese word *tresdobrado*, but is formed on the analogy of *dobrád* (*q.v.*). As the first syllable of this word sounds like *du* which is the compositive form of *don*, 'two'

---

1 "And of these villages the principal one is Upi, which by another name is called **Tranqueira.**" Godinho de Erédia, *Declaraçam de Malacca*, fol. 5.

2 ["And as it happened that, in the act of boarding the junk, our own men were closely pressed, the Javanese wounded several of the men with arrows, and hampered the gear of the **traquete**, and the bowsprit". Afonso de Albuquerque, *Commentaries*, Hak. Soc., Vol. III, p. 63.]

["The next day we sail'd gently along, onely with the sail call'd the **Trinket.**" Della Valle, *Travels*, Hak. Soc., Vol. I, p. 143.]

(cf. *dupaṭ*, 'double', *dutonḍi*, 'double headed'), it was replaced by *ti*, from *tín*, 'three' (cf. *tipêṭ*, 'triple', *tipāyi*, 'tripod'), in order to indicate its three-fold character. Tulu must have received the word directly from Konkani, as it did so many others.

Trigo (wheat). Sinh. *tiringu*; vern. term *góduma*.—Mal. *trígu*, *terigu*; vern. term *gundum*.—Sund. *tarigo*; vern. term *gundrum*.—Jav. *trígu*.—Tet., Gal. *trígu*.

In Southern India and in Malasia no wheat is produced. The Portuguese spread the knowledge of the cereal and its use. See *pão*. *Góduma* and *gundum* are related to the Sanskrit *godhūma*.

Triste (sad). Konk. *tríst*; vern. terms *chinteśṭ*, *khantibharit*, *udás*.—Gal. *trísti*.

Trocar (to exchange). Konk. *trokár-karuṅk* (l. us.); vern. terms *badluṅk*; *vāṭāvuṅk*.—Mal., Sund., Jav. *túkar*.—Ach. *túkar*, *túka*.—Tet. *túkar*, *truka* (also us. as a subst.); vern. term *síluku*.

Trombeta (a trumpet). Konk. *turmét*; vern. terms *káḷ*, *turturí*.—Mal. | *tĕrompet* |.—Mac., Bug. *tūrumbéta*, *tūrumpéta*.—Tet. *trombeta*.[1]

Tronco ('a prison or gaol'). Mar. *turuṅg*, *turaṅg*.—Guj. *turaṅg*.—Guj. *turaṅg*. *Turaṅg adhikārí*, gaoler.—Sindh. *turungu*.—? Tam. *turukkam*, a fortress on a mountain (perhaps from the Sansk. *durgam*).—Malayal. *turungu*; vern. term *taḍavu*.—Tul. *turungu*, *torangu*, *turanga*; ver. term *bandīkhāne*.—Anglo-Ind. *trunk* (obs.).—Siam. *tárahng*.—Ann. *tú rac*.—Mal. *tronko*, *tarunku*.

"The municipal gaol, where those charged with the smaller delinquencies were locked up, was called *tronco*; the others were sent to prison. In Lisbon the *tronco* existed till the time of King Sebastian in whose reign two prisons were established." *Almanach do Occidente*, 1903.

In the East the term *tronco* was used in a generic acceptation. "The **tronco** which was the house of the chief magistrate, where the captives of Bintão were imprisoned, on account of the bribe they offer-

[1] "A great number of **trombetas**, bagpipes and kettledrums." Diogo do Couto, Dec. VII, i, 11.

ed, was kept open for them on that day." Castanheda.[1]

Tropa (troop of soldiers). Konk. *trop*. It is going out of currency; but it is preserved in such expressions as *tropāchó ghoḍo*, 'cavalry horse', to designate a person well fed and indolent.[2]—? Malayal. *truppu*, from the Engl. 'trooper', according to Gundert.—Tet., Gal. *tropa*.

[1] "As soon as we arrived at Canton, they brought us before the *porlacy* and he ordered us to be taken to certain houses used as **troncos**." Christovão Vieira, in Donald Ferguson, *Letters from Portuguese Captives in Canton*, p. 59. [*Ind. Antiq.*, Vol. XXX, p. 468, and the translation in Vol. XXXI, p. 12.]

"Simão Caeiro, and Lançarote de Seixas who were coming with him were taken to the **tronco** of Goa, and put in irons." Diogo do Couto, Dec. IV, ii. 6.

["This prison is the only one in all the town of Cochin, and is called the **Tronco**." Pyrard, *Voyage*, Hak. Soc., Vol. I, p. 429.]

["There are four general prisons at Goa, besides other private ones: the first is that of the Holy Inquisition: the second is that of the archbishop, close to his residence; the third, the **Tronquo**, at the viceroy's palace, the chief and largest of all." *Idem*, Vol. II, p. 18.]

[2] There is also a chapel in Goa which is called '*tropāchéṁ kapel* ('the chapel for the troops').

Trunfo (trump in cards). Konk. *trúmph*.—Mac. *tarúmpu*.

Tubo (tube). Konk. *túb*; vern. term *naḷí*.—? Kan. *túbu*, sluice, bore, hole.

Reeve regards the Kanarese word as a vernacular one.

? **Tudo** (all). Jav. *tutung*, having reached the end; brought to the close. *Nutung* to bring to a close, to achieve the end.—| Chin. *túd* |.

Dr. Heyligers connects *tutung* with the Portuguese *todo*, and observes that the final *g* is pronounced very faintly.

? **Tufão** (hurricane). Konk. *tuphán*, storm, tempest; ravage, damage; disturbance, disorder; rage; groundless accusation. *Tuphāní*, *tuphānkár*, one given to brawls; calumniator.—Mar. *tuphán* (has the same meanings as in Konkani). *Tuphānkhor*, calumniator.—Guj. *tophán*, tempest; tumult; wickedness. *Tophāní*, tempestuous; mischievous.—Hindust. *tūfán*, inundation; deluge; whirlwind; a disorderly person. *Tūfānī*, a boisterous, quarrelsome fellow.—L.-Hindust. *tūfán*, storm.—Or., Beng. *tuphán*, tempest; brawl. *Tuphāní*, boisterous; quarrelsome.—Sindh. *ṭuphanu*, hurricane; extravagance; calumny. *Tuphānī*, boisterous; quarrelsome; calumniator.—Punj. *tufán*, storm; strife; calumny. *Tufānī*, a disorderly fellow.—Kash. *tuphán*, tempest.—Tel. *tuphánu*.—Kan., Tul. *tuphanu*, hurricane; groundless accusation; calamity.—Anglo-Ind. *typhoon*.—Khas. *tupan*.—Mal. *ṭufán*.—Jap. *taifu*.—Pers. *ṭūfán*, *tūfán*, strong winds; inundation.—Ar. *ṭufán*, inundation; overpowering rain; cataclysm.

Portuguese dictionary-writers, with the exception of Fr. João de Sousa, point out as the original of the Portuguese word the Greek *typhōn*, which normally ought to give *typhão* or *tifão*. But was the term current in Portugal? Fernão Pinto says: "We went through such a terrible southwind which the Chinese call **tufão**". And in another place: "The storm which the Chinese called **tufão**".

The same source is indicated by Diogo do Couto,[1] and corroborated by John Barrow and Giles, who derive the word from the Chinese syllables *ta-fung*, 'great wind', and by Dr. Hirth, who derives it from the local Formosan term *t'ai* and *fung*.

Webster (*s.v.* typhoon) says that the whirlwind which raises clouds of dust was called *typhoon* "because it was regarded as the work of *Typhon* or *Typhos*, the giant who was struck with a thunderbolt by Jupiter and buried under Mount Etna". But the meaning he gives to the word is: "a violent tornado or hurricane occurring in Chinese seas".

Yule and Burnell admit that the word was first employed in the China Sea and not in the Indian Ocean, and observe that the Portuguese *tufão* distinctly

---

1 "They had very rough weather, which the inhabitants (of the port of Chincheu) call **Tufão**, which is a disturbance so great and fierce and causes so many storms and earthquakes....;" V, viii, 12. "The fly of the compass was moving as fast as do the **tufões** of China." *Id.*, VIII, i, 11.

["It was accompanied by such a furious storm of rain, with lightning and hail, that those who were familiar with these coasts declared it to be a **tufon**, a form of storm much dreaded in those parts." Manrique, *Travels*, Hak. Soc., Vol. II, p. 53.]

represents *ṭūfán* and not *tái-fung*, and presume that Vasco de Gama and his followers got the word *tufão*, as well as the word *monção* ('monsoon'), from Arab pilots.

Indian dictionary-writers regard Arabic as the source of the word. Shakespear derives *ṭūfán* from the verb *ṭūf*, 'to turn', "or, rather, from the Chaldaic or Syriac *tāfu*, from Chaldaic *taf* and *tof*, to fall, to run, to overflow"; and says it is analogous to the Greek *typhōn*. The authors of *Hobson-Jobson* identify *ṭūfán*, which occurs several times in the Koran, with *typhôn* or *typhón* and presume that it may have come to the Arabs either as the result of maritime intercourse or through the translations of Aristotle.

Robertson Smith distinguishes between two words: the one *typhôn*, 'whirlwind, water-spout', connected with *typhos*, which he says is pure Greek; and the other *ṭūfán*, 'the deluge', which he declares to be borrowed from the Aramaic. "*Tūfán*, for Noah's flood is both Jewish, Aramaic and Syriac, and this form is not borrowed from the Greek, but is derived from a true Semitic root *ṭūf*, 'to overflow'". He observes that in the sense of 'whirlwind' the word is not met with in classical Arabic, but he conjectures that this meaning was derived subsequently from the Arabic root *ṭūf*, 'to go round', or, rather, introduced from some form of *typhôn*, *typho*, or *tifone*. See *Hobson-Jobson*.

In view of this controversy, it is not certain whether the Portuguese derived the word from Arabic or from Chinese, or if they at all introduced it into India. In the Portuguese spoken in India the word *Samatra* (*q.v.*) is used, by preference, to denote 'a tempest, or storm'.

[Sir R. C. Temple appears to be inclined to accept the Ar. *tūfán*, Port. *tufão* as the original of typhoon, but he proceeds to say that "some Chinese scholars, however, ascribe a Chinese origin to the term through Cantonese *tái-fung*, a gale, *lit.*, *tái*, great, and *fung*, wind. It is possible that the form and sound 'typhoon' for *tūfān* arose out of *tái-fung*".

Mundy, *Travels*, Hak. Soc., Vol. III, pt. I, p. 164, n[1].

The *O.E.D.* distinguishes between two different Oriental words: (1) the *a* forms, like Port. *tufão*, are referred to Ar. *ṭāfa* which itself is probably an adaptation of Gk. *Typhon*, (2) *tuffoon*, *tyfoon* represent the Chinese *tai-fung*. The spelling of the second has apparently been influenced by that of the earlier known Indian word, while that now current is due to association with Typhon.

Below is a description of a storm given by Pyrard which is clearly influenced by the Greek conception of Typhon.[2]]

Tumba (a bier for the poor). Konk. *túmb.*—Beng. *tumbá.*—Tet., Gal. *túmba.*—? Jap. *fumbo*, a grave; vern. term *haka*.

The change of *t* into *f* in the Japanese word cannot be explained. Cf. *tinta, mártir*.

Tumor (bump, swelling). Konk., Mar. *ṭumbar*.

Tutanaga (a Chinese alloy of copper, zinc and nickel; also zinc). Anglo-Ind. *tootnague*. —[Indo-Fr. *toutenague*].

It appears that the immediate source of the Portuguese word is the Tam. *tuttanāgam*, 'zinc', from the Persian *tūtiā-nāk*, 'oxide of zinc'.[1]

---

1 [" Their houses (of the people of Macao) double tyled, and thatt plaistred over againe, for prevention of Hurracanes or violentt wyndes thatt happen some Yeares, called by the Chinois **Tuffaones**."

2 [" On the 24th August we passed the equinoctial line........Nothing is so inconstant as the weather, but there it is inconstancy itself; in a moment it becomes calm as by a miracle; in half an hour there is on all sides thunder and lightning, the most terrible that can be imagined: this is chiefly when the sun is near the equinox. Suddenly the calm returns, then the storm begins again, and so on. All at once the wind rises with such impetuosity that it is all you can do to lower all sail in time, and you would suppose that the masts and yards would give way and the ship be lost. Often you see coming from afar great whirlwinds, which the sailors call *dragons*; if they pass over ships they break them up and send them to the bottom. When they are seen coming the sailors take naked swords and strike them one against the other, in the form of a cross, on the bows of the ship, or in the direction where they see the storm coming, and they consider that that prevents it coming upon the ship and turns it aside." *Voyage*, Hak. Soc., Vol. I, p. 11.]

1 [" Here cometh to an end the great and wealthy Kingdom of Guzerate and Cambaya, in which are many

[Da Cunha (*Indo-Portuguese Numismatics*, *BBRAS*, Vol. XIV, p. 409) referring to 'tutenag' says: "This alloy, which has from time immemorial been used by the Chinese in the manufacture of the *gong*, is whitish in appearance, sonorous when struck, tough, strong, malleable, easily cast, hammered, and polished, and does not readily tarnish .... When analysed, it yields of copper 40·4, zinc 25·4, nickel 31·6, and iron 2·6. Its name is believed to have been given to it first by the Portuguese in India, who must have got it from the Malayalam language, in which *tuṭṭu* is the name of a tutenag coin equal to 20 cash, or ½ pice; if it is not derived from the English tutty, *tutia* in low Latin, *tuzia* in Italian, and *tuthie* in French for a sublimate of zinc or calamine collected in the furnace."]

horses......many cotton muslins.... and also other coloured cloths of divers kinds, silk muslins........gingelly oil, southernwood, spikenard, **tutenag** borax, opium." Duarte Barbosa, ed. Dames, Vol. I, p. 154.]

U

? **Umbreira** (door-sill). Konk. *umbôr*, *umbró*, *umbrí* (dim.), threshold, door-step; folding or two-leaved door; vern. term *dārvanṭó*, *devḍí*.—Mar. *umbrá*, *umrá*, *umbarṭá*, *umarṭá*. threshold, door-step; hearth, family; vern. terms *dārvaṭá*, *devḍí*, *dehalí*. *Umbarpaṭṭí*, *umbarsārá*, contribution of the house.—Guj. *umbró*, *ubharó*, threshold.

The origin of the Indian words is not known. Its meaning differs somewhat from that of the Portuguese word. The resemblance may be perhaps accidental, as in the case of *chapa*, *tunque*, *varanda*.

Uniforme (a uniform). Konk. *uniphorm*.—Tet. *unifórmi*.

Urinol (urinal). Konk. *urnôl*, *urnél*; vern. term *doṇ*.—Tet. *urinol*; vern. term *kúzi*.

V

Vacina (cow-pox: vaccination). Konk. *vāsín*.—Tet., Gal. *vasína*, also 'to vaccinate'.

? **Vagem** (pod, husk). Sinh. *bónchi*.

Valado (a mound or embankment). Anglo-Ind. *walade* (l. us.), *vellard* (used in Bombay).[1]

[Not in *O.E.D.* The term is applied to the causeways built between Bombay and the neighbouring islands, intended to exclude water and to serve as dry passages over the marshy land.

Whitworth's suggestion that the Marathi *walhâḍ*, to cross over, would supply a derivation for 'vellard or walade' would be an instance of striving after meaning, if there were such a word in Marathi. Molesworth does not mention it. *Olāndane* in Mar. is 'to cross over'.]

Valer (to be worth). Mal. *valer* (Haex).

Vapor ('a steamship'). Konk. *vāpor*; vern. term *āg-bôṭ*, lit. 'fire boat', (*bôt* is from the English 'boat').—Tet. *vapor*. —? Pers. *vāpur*.—? Ar. *vābúr*.— | Turk *vápor* | .

Belot derives *vābúr* from Italian.

Vara (a linear measure, a yard). Konk., Guj. *vár*. *Adha-vár* (Guj.), half a yard.—Malayal. *vára*.—Kan. *váru*.—Tul. *várų*, *varu*.—Mal. *vara*, a stick (Haex).[1]

The word is used in Konkani and in Tamil also in the sense of 'the pole of a canopy, and of the staff carried by the chief member of a religious sodality'.

Varanda (verandah). Konk. *varánd*, the principal part of the house which one first enters.—? Mar. *varanḍ*, *varaḍá*, *varānḍá*, *varanḍí*, parapet, a wall alongside a verandah, or a street.—Guj. *varanḍó*, gallery.—Hindi, *barāndá*, *varānḍá*, *varanḍá*, *baranḍaka*, *barāmada*. —? Hindust. *barāmada*.—Beng. *bārānḍá*.—Ass. *barandá*, a species of thatched cottage. —Sinh. *baránde*, *barándaya*, *varanḍaya*.—Tam., Malayal. *varanda*.—Kan., Tul. *varanḍa*.

1 "The Moors were also busy making a **vallado** in the river." António Bocarro, Dec. XIII, p. 81.

["The bridge over the "wide breach of land" is now called Breach Candy. It is also called "**Vellard**," a corruption of the Portuguese *Vallado*, which means a fence or hedge, properly a mud-wall with a fence of wood upon it." Da Cunha, *The Origin of Bombay*, p. 57.]

1 "All these kinds of cloths are produced in entire pieces each of which measures twenty-three or twenty-four Portuguese **varas**." Duarte Barbosa, p. 362.

—Anglo-Ind. *veranda, verandah.*[1]—Indo-Fr. *véranda vérandah.*—Gar., Khas. *baranda.*—Mal. *varánda, baránda, beránda, meranda.*—Ach. *beránda.*—Sund. *baránda.*—Tet., Gal. *varanda.*—Pers. *barāmada.*

The origin of the word *varanda* or *veranda*, 'gallery round a house or sometimes only in front', is a subject of great controversy. Three hypotheses have been put forward.

John Beames, [Whitworth,] Littré, and many others derive it from the Sansk. *varaṇḍa*, from the root *vṛ* or *var*, 'to cover, to surround, to enclose'. And this word is marked by Böhtlingk, Cappeller and Monier Williams as a pure dictionary-word, because it is not to be found in any Sanskrit books known till now; and in the dictionaries it has various meanings, such as: multitude, group, rash on the face, a pile of hay, bundle, purse, etc.

Benfey, Böhtlingk & Roth (*Dictionary of St. Petersburgh*, 1855–1875), Monier Williams (1st ed., 1874), Whitney, and Apte give it the meaning of 'verandah, gallery or portico'. And the commentator of Amarakośa (dictionary of the fifth century) quotes the authority of Hemachandra (a dictionary-maker of the twelfth century) in support of the meaning of *antaravedi* ("a veranda resting on columns", Williams) he gives to it, which in itself is also a pure dictionary term.[1]

Böhtlingk (*Sanskrit Wörterbuch in kürzerer Fassung*, 1884), Cappeller (1891), M. Williams (the edition of 1899) leave out entirely the meaning of 'gallery', as not justified.[2] And

[1] [".. Small ranges of pillars that support a pent-house or shed, forming what is called, in the Portuguese Lingua-franca **Verandas,** either round or on particular sides of the house." Grose, *A Voyage to the East Indies* (1757), p. 84.]

[1] The phrase *antarā vedirmattavāraṇayoriva*, of *Raghuvaṃśa* (XII, 93, Bombay ed.) means 'like a wall between two furious elephants'.

[2] The meaning of the compound *varandalam-buka*, which is met with in the drama *Mṛchhakaṭikā* of Kalidasa, is very obscure. Cappeller interprets it as 'fishing-line', which is also the only meaning which he gives for *varanda*, and observes that the word occurs only in the translation from the Prakrit. Monier Williams attributes to it interrogatively the same meaning. But Apte claims that it means a "projecting or overhanging wall".

Burnell observes that the meaning referred to above "does not belong to old Sanskrit, but is only to be found in works relatively modern", but does not cite any text.

Molesworth (Mar.) distinguishes between two *varandas*, one of Sanskrit origin, in the sense of 'a load of hay', and the other with the various meanings mentioned above, but does not suggest its etymology. Candy (Mar.) translates the English 'veranda' into *osrí*, *paḍví*, *paḍsál*, *paḍ-osrí*, *paḍśālā*, *paḍávi*, *oṭí*. Almost all these words, and in addition to these *osró* and *oṭó*, are current in Konkani. Gundert (Malayal.) admits the Portuguese source. Campbell (Tel.) adopts the Sanskrit derivation. Ziegler (Kan.) states that *varaṇḍu* is a foreign term but does not indicate its origin. Haex (Mal.) mentions *baranda* ('a story or balcony') as a vernacular term; but Favre attributes it to a Sanskrit and Wilkinson to a Portuguese origin. Rigg (Sund.) derives it from Portuguese.

Yule & Burnell were the first to suggest that there existed in Portuguese and Spanish the word *varanda*, independent of the Indian *varaṇḍa*. with the same or analogous meaning, because the author of the *Roteiro* (1498) employs it without explaining it,[1] and also

---

[1] "And he came to join us where we had been put in a **varanda** where there was a large candlestick made of brass that gave us light." Fernão Pinto (1540) employs the word *varanda* very often as though it was well-known: "We entered with her into another court much nobler than the first, surrounded on all sides with two kinds of **varandas**, as if it had been a cloister of monks." [Cogan renders this reference to verandas thus: "all about invironed with Galleries" (in *Hobson-Jobson*).] And Gasper Correia (1561): "The King was in a **varanda**, so that he saw everything in the order in which it happened."

[In *Chronica de Bisnaga* (1525), ed. David Lopes, both forms *varamdas* and *baramdas* are met with and nowhere is an explanation of the term offered: "The palaces of the King (of Vijayanagar) are of this kind: they have a gate leading to an open space ... and above this gate there is a pinnacle very high built like such others with their **varamḍas** ..... After going through this gate you find there is a large open space ... and you soon come to another gate very like the first ... so much so that when you have entered this you have a large open space before you, and on either side of it some low **baramdas** in which the captains and

because it occurs in *Vocabulista Arábigo* of Pedro de Alcalá (1505). And the following passage, very significant, can also be cited from João de Barros in proof thereof: "The inhabitants of Ruçotello made an open wooden gallery which in those parts serves the same purpose that *varandas* or terraces do among us." Dec. III, v, 7.

Gonçalves Viana (*Ortografia Nacional, Apostilas aos Dic. Port.*) defends this hypothesis with many arguments of great value; he connects the word with *vara* ('a rod') and *varão* ('a bar'), and concludes that "the existence of this word in India and in the Romanic languages is accidental, as the same must be the case with that of *tanque* ('tank') and of *chapa* ('mark') in Portuguese and the Indian vernaculars".

Even if the existence of *varaṇḍa* in Sanskrit and its transmission into many present day Prakrits were not open to dispute, it appears to me, for more than one reason, that the meaning of 'a gallery with columns', which is to be found in some of these languages, is not Indian, but derived from Portuguese, and has found its way into them in modern times. First, no Sanskrit or Prakrit passage with *varanda* in such a sense is found before the sixteenth century. Secondly, Konkani, Hindustani, Oriya, Sindhi, Kashmiri, to judge from the dictionaries of these languages, are not at all acquainted with the word in the form *varaṇḍa*. Thirdly, many dictionaries of the other languages do not mention it, as for instance the Gujarati Dictionary of L. Patel and N. Patel, the Sinhalese of Clough, the Punjabi of Starkey; or they derive it from another language, as the dictionary of Singh does, from the Persian *barāmada*; or they make a phonetic distinction between *barāndá* or *baránda* and *varānḍá*, as does the Hindi Dictionary of Guni Lala, the Sinhalese of Carter (*s.v.* portico). Fourthly, Marathi and Assamese do not assign to the word *varānḍá* the meaning of 'a gallery or portico'. Fifthly, in Konkani *varánd* has no

the gentry are accommodated from where to watch the festivities." p. 101.]

cerebral sounds, and is employed solely among the Christians together with other terms (*vasró*, *vasrí*) and in a meaning which is peculiar to it. Sixthly, the English form *veranda* or *verandah* betrays clearly its Portuguese, and not indigenous, origin; had it been the latter, it would have become *warand*.[1]

The third hypothesis, little probable, proposed by Webster and C. Defrémery, points out as the primary source of *varanda* the Persian *barāmada* (introduced into Hindustani), a compound of *bar* ('from above') and *āmada* ('coming'), and equivalent to 'coming forward, projecting'. Yule thinks it possible that it may be a Persian 'striving after meaning' in explanation of the foreign word which they may have borrowed.

[1] Dr. Schuchardt finds that in the Romanic languages the actual meaning of *varanda* is not brought out, because the Port. *varanda*, Sp. *baranda*, Catalan *barana* ('balustrade'), are derived from the verb '*barrar*', *Beitrage*, etc. [*Barrar* in this connection would be derived from *barra*, bar of metal or wood, and *barrar* would mean either 'to support on bars', or 'to lay bars across'.]

[The *O.E.D.* says that 'verandah' was originally introduced into English from India, where the word is found in several of the native languages as Hindi *varandā*, Beng. *bārāndā*, mod. Sansk. *baranda*, but it appears to be merely an adoption of Port. and older Sp. *varanda* (*baranda*), railing, balustrade, balcony. The Fr. *vérandа* appears to it to have been adopted from English, but to Dalgado from Indo-Fr. through Portuguese.]

[**Varela** (an idol; a Buddhist temple and monastery in Indo-China, China and in Japan). Anglo-Ind. *varella*.[1]

This word which is to be met with in the works of old Portuguese writers is believed to be the Malay *barhālā* (Jav. *brāhalā*), 'idol,' and to have

[1] [" And they consume many canes likewise in making of their **Varellaes** or idole temples, which are in great number, both great and small. They be made round like a sugar loafe; some are as high as a church, very broad beneath, some a quarter of a mile in compasse... They consume in these **Varellaes** great quantity of golde, for that they be all gilded aloft, and many of them from the top to the bottome." Ralph Fitch, in Foster, *Early Travels*. p. 35.]

been used by the Portuguese also to signify 'a temple' or 'the house of idols,' just in the same way as *pagoda* was employed by them in the sense of an 'idol' and a 'temple'. In Fernão Pinto both forms *varela* and *bralla* are met with. See *Glossario*.]

[**Várzea, vargem** or **verga** (a piece of level ground that is sowed and cultivated). Anglo-Ind. *verge* (used formerly for 'rice lands').[1] See *Hobson-Jobson*.]

Varrão (a boar-pig). Konk. *bārámv*.—Sinh. *barama*.

Vaso (vase, vessel). Konk. *váz*, flower vase.—Mal. *pásu*, *básu*.—Ach., Jav., Batav. *pásu*.—Sund., Bal., Day. *páso*.—Tet., Gal *vázu*.

Dr. Schuchardt says that *básu* proceeds probably from the Dutch *vaas* 'a vessel to put any liquor in,' notwithstanding its vowel ending. See *cámara*.

1 ["They offten dig their mimes 10 foth; and when they have a shoure of raine or two in a day, then they geet the most tinn. But when the raines are wholley seet in then they leave of their diging and goas to their **varges**" *Ind. Antiq.*, July, 1931, p. 106. It is strange that Sir R. Temple should have conjectured that 'varges' might stand for 'villages'.]

[**Vedor**, also **Veador** (an inspector, or controller). Anglo-Ind. *veador*.[1]

In the *O.E.D.* but not in *Hobson-Jobson*. This term in the English Factory records sometimes assumes interesting forms: *Veadore, Theadore*.

The *Vedor de Fazenda* was an official at Goa who had charge of all matters concerning revenue, finance, and shipping, and ranked second only to the Viceroy.]

Velho (old man). Konk. *el* (us. in a restricted sense).—Mal. *veillo*, also "an old woman" (Haex).

Veludo (velvet). Konk.

1 ["This **Viador** is overseer of all finances, and also of everything that goes on in Goa, as well affairs of war and shipping as all other affairs, he being the second personage next after the viceroy in all that pertains to the affairs of the king". Pyrard, *Voyage*, Hak. Soc., Vol. II, pt. i, p. 40.]

["He (the Viceroy of Goa) referred us unto the **Theadore** de Fazendo, from whome we received the enclosed note of his desires, both in the prices and proportion." Foster, *The English Factories, 1634–1636*, p. 99.]

["He is to proceed to Goa in the *William*; and, arriving there, to present the accompanying letters to the **Vedor**, with whom he is to treat concerning his goods". *Idem*, p. 121.]

vilúd.—Sinh. *villúdu*.—Malayal. *villúdu, velúdi*.—Mal. *veludo* (Haex), *belúdu, belúdro, beldú, beldúra*.—Ach. *belúdu*.—Batt. *bilúlu*.—Sund. *belúdru, bulúdru*.—Jav. *belúdru, bludru, belúdur*.—Mad. *blútru*.—Bal. *blúdru*.—Batav. *bilúdru*.—Mac. *bilúlu*.—Bug. *belúdu, bilúlu, valúdu, biladúra*.—Jap. *birōdo*.[1]

[Pyrard in his *Dict. of some words of the Maldive language* mentions *velouzy*, which is obviously derived from Portuguese. See Hak. Soc.'s ed. Vol. II, pt. II, p. 416.]

Belúdru in Javanese and *belústru* in Malay is also the name of a botanical plant, *Momordica charantia*. In Konkani, as also in the Portuguese of Goa, *vilud* is also the name of *Celosia cristata*.

Vendas ('sale by public auction'). Sinh. *vendésiya*. *Vendési sāláva*, the place of the auction-sale. *Vendési-karaṇavā* (lit. 'to make a sale'), *vendésiyen vikuṇanavā* (lit. 'to sell in a public auction'). *vendési damanavā* (lit. 'to place on sale'), to sell by auction. *Vendési-kárayā*, *véndu*, the seller at an auction.

[**Veneziano** (the name of an old Venetian gold coin current in India and which in the sixteenth century was worth 420 reis; afterwards the sequin). Anglo-Ind. *Venetian*.[1]

There are frequent references to this coin in the early Portuguese writers in India from as early a date as the middle of the sixteenth century.]

[**Ventosa** (cupping-glass). Anglo-Ind. *ventoso* (obs.).[2]

This form is not mentioned in the *O.E.D.*, nor is the word found in *Hobson-Jobson*.]

Verde (green). Konk. *verd*; vern. term *pāchvó*.—Beng. *berdí* (us. among the Christians).—

1 "And on the head over a coif of gold, a cap of **veludo**." João de Barros, Dec. II, x, 8.

"With jackets of black **veludo** and sleeves of purple satin." Gaspar Correia, I, p. 533.

1 ["There is another kinde of gold money (in Goa), which is called **Venetianders**: some of Venice, and some of Turkish coine, and are commonly 2. Pardawes Xeraphins." Linschoten, *Voyage*, Hak. Soc., Vol. 1, p. 243.]

["The Money which passes is a Golden **Venetian**, equivalent to our Angel." Fryer, Hak. Soc., Vol. III, p. 152.]

2 ["To Cup they use **Ventosoes**, without Scarifications." Fryer, *East India*, Hak. Soc., Vol. I, p. 286.]

Mal. *vérdi*, in *lázu-vérdi*, lapis-lazuli. [See *Rende verde.*]

Verdura ('greens'). Konk. *verdúr*; vern. terms *vārvéṁ*, *tarkāri*, *śák-bhāji*.—Anglo-Ind. *verdure* (obs.).[1]

[**Vereador** (an alderman). Anglo-Ind. *vereador*.

This term is often met with in the early settlements of disputes between the inhabitants of Bombay and the British Government.[2] Neither in the *O.E.D.* nor in *Hobson-Jobson*.

Whitworth is obviously thinking of this official when he says: "**Veador.** An appellate judge under the Portuguese Government, who heard appeals from the ouvidors; also a land factor or overseer." The way he spells the word might lead one to confound it with *vedor* (*q.v.*).]

Verniz (varnish). Konk. *verníz*; vern. term *rogaṇ*.—Tet., Gal. *verniz*.

Verónica (veronica; 'cloth with representation of Christ's face'). Konk. *verank*; vern. term *ārlúk*.—Tet., Gal. *verónika*.

Verruma (gimlet). Konk. *rum*; *barmó*, *birmó* ('auger, borer'); vern. terms *girbó*, *topaṇ*.—Hindi, Hindust. *barmá*.—Beng. *burmá*; vern. term *turpún*, *bhramar*.—Sindh. *barmá*; vern. term *sarāí*.—Punj. *varmá*, *barmá*.—Sinh. *buruma*, *burema*, *burema-katuva*; vern. term *tora-palaya*.—Malayal.

---

1 "The people were pleased with the present, and especially those ailing with the **verdura** and oranges." Gaspar Correia, I, p. 44.

2 ["**Vereador** is one who holds the staff or wand of power; is a member of Council or of the Chamber; a functionary charged with the administration of the police or the repairs of public roads; a bazaar superintendent; a magistrate or a public functionary who fires local tariffs or taxes". *Report of Cases decided in the Original Civil Jurisdiction of the High Court of Bombay*, Vol. IV, 1866-67, p. 90.

Da Cunha (*Origin of Bombay*, p. 230) makes the following comments on the above origin suggested for this word: "Now *vereador* has nothing to do with the holding of the staff or wand of power. This fanciful derivation is evidently drawn from the Portuguese word *vara*, Latin *virga*, which means a 'rod'. But *vereador* has not the remotest connection with it. *Vereador* simply corresponds to the word *procurator*, or attorney, and was in olden times equivalent to *consul* and *decurio*. He never held the staff of power in his hand, but wore a *toga* or gown, as *vereador da Camara* or member of the Municipal Corporation."]

veruma, bórmma; vern. term *turppanam, támar*.—Tel. *buruma, baramá*; vern. term *torapaḍamu*.—Tul. *burma, burmu*; vern. terms *beiraye, beiravu, beirige*.—Gar., Khas. *borma, bolma*.—Tet., Gal. *verruma*.—Pers. *barmá*.—Ar. *barrima*.

Portuguese dictionary-writers give as the certain or probable source of *verruma* the Arabic *berrima*. But Simonet says: "**Berrima.** Ar. Afr. and Or. *barríma* or *buríma*, '*borer*'; Sp. *berrima* Port. *verruma*. Ital. *verrina*. Low Lat. *verrinum* or perhaps better *verrina*: "*cum verrinis perforavit*" ('bored holes with a gimlet') Ducange, from Lat. *verruina* and this again from *veru*, from which source we have also the Low Lat. *verrubius* (*terebrus*). In consequence the Spanish word *berrima* is neither of Germanic nor Arabic origin, as some have imagined. The Arabs received it from the people of Spain as M. Dozy with much reason conjectured, and from it formed the word *berren*."

All the same, it is very probable that *barmá* or *barmó* in the Indian languages comes directly from the Persian *barmá*.[1] In Konkani *rum*, which is evidently from *verruma* (cf. *duljens*, from *indulgencia*, 'indulgence,' *pen* from *empena*, 'gable end of a house'), is distinguished from *bormó* or *birmó*.

Verso (verse). Konk. *vérs* (us. among the Christians); vern. terms *pad, charan, ślok*.—Tet., Gal. *vérsu*.

Vésperas (vespers). Konk. *vespr*.—Tam. *vesper*.—Kan. *vésperu*.—Mal. *vesporas*.—Tet., Gal. *véspera*.

Vestido (dress). Konk. *vestíd*.—Gal. *vestídu*.

Véu (veil, cover). Konk. *vev*; vern. terms *ôl, oḍhṇí*.—Beng., Tam. *vévu* (of the chalice used at mass).—Tet., Gal. *veu*.

Vidro (glass; also a tumbler). Konk. *vídr*; vern. terms *kánch* or *káz; peló, kānsó, pivanpatr, surābhánḍ* (l. us. in this sense).—Sinh. *víduruva*,

[1] "They use (in the Moluccas) only an adze, a narrow chisel, a wooden mallet, **verruma**, which is like a gouge inserted in a hollow pipe." Gabriel Rebêlo, p. 176

idureva, vídur; vern. terms *káchakaya*. *Vidurevu*, glazed. *Vídure silpiyá*, glazier.—Mal. *vídro*. Also *gilás* from the English 'glass'.—Nic. *vitore*, tumbler (cf. *libare* from *livro* ('book').—Tet., Gal. *vídru*.—Jap. *biidoro*.

In Indo-Portuguese also *vidro* means 'a tumbler'.

Vigário (vicar). Konk. *vigár*.—Tam. *vigári*.—Tet., Gal. *vigariu*.

Vinagre (vinegar). Konk. *vinágr*; vern. term *širkó*.—Sinh. *vinákiri*; vern. terms *káchi*, *kánjika*.

Vinha de alhos (the name of a species of viand). Konk. *vinjál*.—Hindust. (of the south) *bindālú*.—Tam. *vendále*.—[Anglo-Ind. *vindaloo*. Not in the *O.E.D.* nor in *Hobson-Jobson*.][1]

[In *Indian Cookery* (Bombay) there are recipes for the preparation of 'vindaloo' of various kinds.]

Vinho (wine). Konk. *vính* (l. us.); vern. term *saró* or *soró*.—Malayal. *viññu* (=*vinhu*).—Tel. *vínu*.—Nic. *víniya*, wine, liquor, brandy.

The Sinhalese *veyin* appears to be from the English '*wine*'. In the Portuguese dialect of Ceylon *vein* is 'European wine' and *vinho* 'country liquor'.

Viola (viol; guitar). Konk. *vyol*.—Sinh. *viyóle*.—Mal., Sund., Day. *biyola*, *biola*.—Ach. *biula*.—Mac., Bug. *biyóla*.—Tet., Gal. *viola*.

Virador (*naut.*, tow-line). L.-Hindust. *virādor*.

Virtude (virtue). Konk. *virtúd* (l. us.); vern. terms *guṇ*, *suguṇ*, or *seguṇ*.—Tet. *virtúde*; vern. term *díak*.

Visagra (hinge). Konk. *bizágr*.—Mar. *bijāgreṁ*, *bijogrí*.—Guj. *majāgareṁ*, *majāgaráṁ*, *misjāgaruṁ*.—Malayal. *višágari*.—Kan. *bijágri*.—Tul. *bijákri*, *bijigre*.

Visita (visit). Konk. *vizít*; vern. terms *bheṭṇí*, *bheṭ*.—Tet., Gal. *vizita*.

[**Visitador** (an official visitor; one who visits a monas-

---

1 "There is another fish (in Angola) which they call *ongulo*; it is like pork and, served in **vinha dalhos**, much resembles it" (1585), Garcia Simões, in *Jour. Geo. Soc. Lisb.*, 4th ser., p. 344.

["No water must be used in the preparation of **vindaloo**" *Indian Cookery*, by An Anglo-Indian (Bombay, 1923), p. 74.]

tery). Anglo-Ind. *visitador* (obs.).[1]

The Dutch adopted the name for one of their officials, the *Visitador General* (Foster, *Letters*, II, 165).]

Viso-rei (viceroy). Malayal. *visareyi*.—Mal. *bīsúrey*.

Viva ! (long live! hurrah!) Konk. *vivā*.; vern. terms *śabás* or *śebás*.—Tet. *viva, biba*.

Volta (turn, bend). Konk. *volt*, a band such as is worn by clergymen.—L.-Hindust. *bolta, boltá*, the twist or winding of a rope.

Voltar (to turn, in a game of cards). Konk. *voltár-karuṅk*; vern. term *partuṅk*.—Mal. *bortá*.

Voto (vow). Konk. *vot*; vern. term *āṅgvaṇ, vrat*; *vāṅgaḍ, sammati*. –Tet. *vótu*; vern. term *lia lós*.

X

[**Xerafim** (a coin formerly current in Goa and other eastern ports). Anglo-Ind. *xerafine, sherapheen, xerephin*.[2]

The original of the Portuguese word is the Ar. *ashrafī* (or *sharīfī*), 'noble', which name was originally used of the gold *dīnār* worth about 3000 reis. The Portuguese *xerafim* was originally a gold, but afterwards a silver coin; the latter was worth 5 *tangas* or 300 *reis*. The Konkani *asurpī* or *usurpī* is derived directly from *ashrafī* and not from *xerafim*.]

---

1 ["The Father **Visitador** of the *Carmelites*......persuaded the Agent to leave me at *Siras*." Fryer, *East India and Persia*, Hak. Soc., Vol. II, p. 344.]

2 ["The principall and commonest money (at Goa) is called Pardaus **Xeraphiins**. Linschoten, *Voyage*, Vol. I, p. 241.]

["Our rents were not much increased last year, though something they were our chiefe rent. The Custome is farmed for 27000 **Xs.**" Forrest, *Selections* (Home Series), Vol. I, p. 120.]

["The Vicar of Parela, Padre Antonio Barboza (a Jesuit) presented mee with the paper which is herewith sent for your perusall, by which hee endeavours to make appeare that 2000 **Sherapheens** out of the Kings rents at Maim, which comes but to 26 **Sherapheens** more per annum, were given to their Company by the King of Spaine......and confirmed unto them by the Vice Roys of India." Letter from Humfrey Cooke, in Khan, *Anglo-Portuguese Negotiations*, p. 472.]

["Their (Goa) Coin. 1 *Vintin* 15 *Budgeroocks*, 1 *Tango* 5 *Vintins*, 1 **Xerephin** or *Pardoa*, 5 *Tangos*, 1 Gold St. *Thomae*, 5 **Xerephins**." A. Hamilton, Vol. II, *Table of Weights*, p. 6.]

Z

? **Zamboa** (the Malay apple-tree, *Eugenia Malaccensis*). Jap. *zambo*, *zabon*.[1]

Gonçalves Viana is of the opinion that the word is Spanish in origin. But it is quite possible that *zambo* is related to the Sanskrit *jambū*, adopted in the Prakrits and in Malay and used to designate various trees.

[1] "In Malacca the name is **jambos** and the fruit is so called also in this country." Garcia da Orta, Col. xxviii [ed. Markham, p. 237]. "The **jambo** is the fruit of a species of *Eugenia*.... ..the *Eugenia malaccensis*." Conde de Ficalho, *Coloquios*, Vol. II, p. 27. [See *pera*.]

SUPPLEMENT[1]

Abada (rhinoceros, see p. 1). Muzaffer Shah of Gujarat included a rhinoceros among the presents he sent in 1513 to Afonso de Albuquerque—not to the King of Portugal, as is wrongly mentioned by Barbosa (see cit. p. 1). Albuquerque decided to send this strange and rare creature to King Manuel I who took a keen interest in oriental curiosities. The rhinoceros reached Lisbon safely and was kept in the royal menagerie till 1517. In that year the King was seized with the extraordinary whim to see a fight between the rhinoceros and an elephant which he also happened to own. In February of that year the two beasts were made to confront each other in a large enclosure. The rhinoceros rushed to attack the elephant, but the latter to everybody's surprise jumped over the railing of the enclosure and with loud trumpeting ran for safety to his stall, leaving the rhinoceros master of the field. Shortly afterwards the King sent the victorious beast as a present to the then Pope, Leo X. The vessel carrying the animal left Portugal in October, 1517. It put in at Marseilles and Francis I, who happened to be just then at this port, had an opportunity of seeing this strange pachyderm. When the ship continued the voyage to its destination, it was caught in a storm and sank near the coast of Italy. The rhinoceros perished but its carcass was washed up on to the shore; it was skinned and stuffed and carried to the Pope. This is the brief and tragic but remarkable history of the first and, perhaps, the only rhinoceros that found its way from Gujarat to Europe. See Correia, *Lendas*, II, 373. Damião de Góis, *Chronica*, etc., pp. 276 and 277; Ficalho, *Coloquios*, I, pp. 320 and 321.

[1] The new vocables, citations, and information set down herein came to my notice too late to be inserted in the body of the book.—Ed. and Trans.

1628–37.—"On the tops of these interlaced trees we saw large numbers of monkeys and below some **abadas** or rhinoceroses, which frequent those wilds." Manrique, *Travels*, Hak. Soc., Vol. I, p 124.

Abafado (a dish of stew, see p. 2). Anglo-Ind. *buffath.*

For recipes for preparing "Madras **Buffath**, **Buffath** of Fresh Meat, Mutton **Buffath**", see *Indian Cookery* by Anglo-Indian, pp. 75 and 76.

Achar (pickles, see p. 6). The citation below from Fryer helps to explain why Goa was noted for mango pickles.

1672–1681.—"They [the Goa women] sing, and play on the Lute, make Confections, pickle **Achars**, (the best *Mongo* **Achars** coming from them). Fryer, *East India*, Hak. Soc., Vol. II, p. 28.

1640–41.—"After numerous dishes of various kinds of flesh, both of domesticated and wild animals and birds, with stimulants of sundry **achares**, made of cucumber, radish, limes, and green chillies, soaked in strong fragrant vinegars, that served to spur the appetite." Manrique, *Travels*, Hak. Soc., Vol. II, p. 127.

Adarga (a buckler made of buffalo hide). Anglo-Ind. *adarga* (obs.). Neither in *Hobson-Jobson* nor in the *O.E.D.*

1638.—"Every Cavallero was bravely apparelled with an **adarga**, which is a great pastboard or leather buckler on his arme." Mundy, *Travels*, Vol. III. pt. i, p. 266.

Aduana (customs-house). Anglo-Ind. *aduano* (obs.). Neither in *Hobson-Jobson* nor in the *O.E.D.*

1610.—"To-morrow we purpose to send you the copy hereof by the old scrivano [*q.v.* p 149] of the **Aduano** of . . ." Danvers, *Letters*, Vol. I (1602–1613), p. 51.

Afogado (a kind of stew). Konk. *fugād*; *arros fugād*, rice boiled in broth.—Anglo-Ind. *foogath*.

"**Fooga**ths are vegetables fried with onions and the usual mussala" (condiments). *Indian Cookery*, p. 94. There are recipes for various kinds of '*foogaths*' in the book.

Águila, Áquila (aromatic wood, see p. 8).

Below is a very early Anglo-Indian form of this word which clearly discloses its connexion with the Portuguese vocable.

1619.—"As to the sale of the prize goods left at Jask, 'especially of that called by the name of **Aglia**, which we understand to bee lignum aloes, and was a fitt commodity for England." Foster, *Eng. Fact.* (*1618–1621*), p. 141.

Alcatraz (*Diomedia exulans*, L., see p. 11).

The following two quotations are not in *Hobson-Jobson*. The second is interesting because it introduces us to a new form of 'albatross' not in the *O.E.D.*

1638.—"**Allcatrazes** is againe the biggest of any Seaffowle I have yett seene, spreading Near 6 or 7 Foote with his wings, which hee seemeth not to Move att all as hee Flyeth leisurely and close to the Rymme off the water." Mundy, *Travels*, Vol. III, pt. ii, p. 360.

1690.—"The Sailers have commonly notice of this Land before they Espy it, by the Soundings which run out sixty Leagues into the Ocean, and the **Almitrosses** which is a large Sea-Fowl, and never fly very far from Land." Ovington, *Voyage to Surat*, O.U.P., p. 279.

Aldeia (a village, see p. 12).

The earliest reference for this word in the *O.E.D.* is of 1698.

1609.—See quotation under *Alfandega infra.*

1619.—"The indigo was bought 'in the **aldeas**' at 24 and 25 rupees per maund." Foster, *Eng. Fact (1618-1621)*, p. 86.

1673.—"On both sides [of the Baçein River] are placed stately **Aldeas**, and Dwellings of the *Portugal Fidalgos.*" Fryer, *East India*, Vol. I, p. 308.

Alfandega (customs-house, see p. 12).

This word which is met with frequently in the English Factory and travellers' reports assumes in Anglo-India various forms: *alfandica, alfandia, alfandira,* and *alfandiga.* It is not in the *O.E.D.*

1609.—"If you shall think it very indiscreetly done by me to trust him, I would have your Worship to take notice that . he bought of the Malabars for 30 or 40,000 pound sterling and paid all with content in a very royal manner, moreover he renting part of the **Alphandia** for 100,000 m. per year and Aldeas in the country for 110,000 m per year." Danvers, *Letters*, Vol. I, p. 25. In a postscript to the same letter (p 28) we read "Taspitas as yet holdeth both the **Alphandica** and his Aldeas".

1609.—"Neare to the castle [of Surat] is the **alphandica** where is a paire of staires for leading and unleading of goods" William Finch, in Foster, *Early Travels*, O.U.P., p. 134. On p. 128 of the same book, Finch spells the same word **Alphandira**.

1615.—"This place [the quay in Goa] is always crowded with ships and vast numbers of people. It contains a very handsome building, resembling the Place Royale at Paris in style, but not otherwise: it is called l'**Alfandequa**, and there they store and sell in gross all kinds of grain, which may not be sold or taken elsewhere. The customs dues are paid here" Pyrard, *Voyage*, Hak. Soc., Vol. II, p. 48.

"All grains, seed and other foodstuffs that come from abroad are discharged into the **Alfandeque**, and are there sold and distributed to those that want them." *Idem*, p. 177.

1615.—"For my prouisions he would see them at the **Alfandica**, and what was for the king should passe, what for other vses should paye and passe." Sir T. Roe, *Embassy*, Hak. Soc., Vol I, p. 71; see also pp. 68 and 72.

1616.—"That the goods of the English may be freely landed, and, after despatch in the **Alfandiga**..." Foster, *Letters*, Vol. IV, p. 79.

1616.—"Also a present determined to be given the Judge of the **Alfandica**, the particulars, viz.:

2 vests cloth; 1 damask piece; 2 sword-blades; 6 knives; 1 bottle strong water: 1 perspective glass; 1 dozen spectacles; 6 gorgoletts [see p. 170]; 6 wine glasses; 12 plates; 6 gilded dishes; 1 looking glass gilded." *Ibidem*, p 198.

The last citation is instructive inasmuch as it throws very interesting light on the customs-officials in India in the 17th century.

Almadia (a small boat or canoe, see p. 13). Anglo-Ind. *almadee*. The earliest instance of this word—not this form—in the *O.E.D.*, from English sources, is of 1681.

1630.—"Hari Vaisya also told them that among the Portuguese prisoners in the hands of the English is one 'of especiall noate and quallity', for whose escape a plan has been arranged with 'some Parseis or Muccadams there about Swally', the idea being to get him away (with the connivance of certain Englishmen) in one of the boats of the fleet or 'a small **almadee** of the Portingalls'." Foster, *Eng Fact. (1630–1633)*, p. 101.

Almude (a Portuguese measure for wine or oil; "twenty-six almudes make a pipe" Vieyra). Anglo-Ind. *almode*, *almoodae* (obs.). Neither in *Hobson-Jobson* nor in the *O.E.D.*

1644.—"22 **almodes** of oil." Foster, *Eng Fact. (1642–1645)*, p. 217.

1673.—"1 Barrel is six **Almoodaes.**" Fryer, *East India*, Hak. Soc., Vol. II, p. 130.

Alviçaras (a reward given for good news). Konk. *alvis*.—Anglo-Ind. *albricias* (obs.).

The word in the citation below may also be the Spanish *albricias*.

1638.—"In this 20 Daies space wee had variable News of our Merchantts att Cantan, sometymes thatt they would bee here within a Day or two, other tymes thatt itt would bee long ere they could come. Once [at Macao] the Jesuitts Man came running, calling for **Albricias** (which is a terme thatt signiffies a gratification for good newes), which was given him." Mundy, *Travels*, Vol. III, pt. I, p. 270.

Ananás (pine-apple, see p. 16).

The following quotations are of interest inasmuch as they show what value was set on this fruit in the early seventeenth century.

1615.—"Soe [the Governor of Surat] giuing me two **Pines**, with a long speech of the dayntenes, which I bade a seruante take, telling him I knew the fruict veary well, I took my leave." Sir T. Roe, *Embassy*, Hak. Soc., Vol. I, p. 66.

1·16–19.—"Their fruits are very answerable to the rest; the countrey [of the 'Great Mogol'] full of musk-melons, water-melons, pomegranats, pomecitrons, limons, oranges, dates, figs, grapes, plantans (a long round yellow fruit, in taste like to a Norwich peare), mangoes (in shape and colour like to our apricocks, but more luscious), and to conclude with the best of all, the **ananas** or pines which seemes to the taster to be a pleasing compound made of strawberries, claret-wine, rose water, and sugar, well tempered together." Edward Terry, in Foster, *Early Travels*, O.U.P., p. 297.

Apa (flat cake, see p. 22). The quotation below is of interest inasmuch as it gives the names for the different varieties of these cakes in the Punjab, and describes the way they were prepared.

1640-41.—"Bread was not lacking in these bazārs [of 'Laor'] or markets, although always made in flat cakes. It was of three different kinds with three separate names, **Apas**, *Curuchas*, and *Ragunis*. The first, which form the usual bread of the ordinary and poor people, are entirely of flour, baked on iron plates or clay dishes which are put upon live embers; it remains, thus cooked, unleavened bread: this kind of bread is generally eaten by those who travel by caravan in these parts. The second kind of bread, *Curuchas*, is a white, good bread used by the richer and more refined classes; the third the *Ragunis*, is a very fine bread, delicate in flavour and made from wheat flour and the purest *ghī*, so as to come out in thin leaves." Manrique, *Travels*, Hak. Soc., Vol. II, pp. 187 and 188.

Araca (distilled country spirit, see p. 23).

1617.—"The 5th of July the Speedwell arrived, whereof was Master John Cleare, by whom I received your kind letter with two hogshead of **rack** accordingly, for which I thank you." Foster, *Letters*, Vol VI, p. 22.

To judge from the quotations below, 'Goa arrack' in the 17th century must have been highly prized. See also quotation under *Nipa* on p. 241. It was then sent out to England, and at the present day not only is 'Goa arrack' contraband in British India, but India itself is practically inundated with foreign spirits and liquors.

1698.—"Augt. 1. Bought a half a hogshead of Goa **Arrack** to send to England to Mrs. Mounk." Entry by John Scattergood in *Ind. Antiq.*, Vol. LIX, Suppl., p. 33.

"By drawing off tody or juice, a vast quantity of arrack may be made, which in time may beat out the trade of Batavia and Goa **rack**, or at least we may share with them" *Idem*, Vol. LX, Suppl., p. 104.

Armada (a fleet of war vessels, see p. 24). Anglo-Ind. *armado* (obs.).

1642.—"Including 4,000 xerafins repaid for a similar sum advanced by Cogan at the Viceroy's request 'to the Capt. Mor of the **armado** sent to St. Tomees succour'." Foster, *Eng. Fact.* (*1642-1645*), p. 60.

1651.—See under *Terranquim* in Supplement.

1673.—"The *Portugals* striving to possess themselves of Muschat, were put to such stress, that had not their **Armado** come to their relief, they must have desisted their Enterprize." Fryer, *East India*, Vol. I, p. 193.

Arrasador (one who ruins or destroys). ? Anglo-Ind. *ransadoes* (obs.).

"The second eveninge came before our hellhound Governour, who stopeinge against all our and our frnds reasons sayd wee were **ransadoes** and one with the [Dutch?] and comanded the Cottwall to keepe us saufe till nixt, morninge." Foster, *Eng. Fact. (1622-1623)*, p. 73.

Arrendador (revenue-farmer; see also *Rendeiro*, p. 310). ? Anglo-Ind. *rendedare* (obs.).

1632.- "Our suite to this King (advised you in our last) mott with opposition by Mirza Rosvan, **rendedare** of this place, and chancellour of this kingdome." Foster, *Eng. Fact. (1630 1633)*, p 228.

Ata (custard-apple, see p. 26).

The quotation below is, according to Sir Richard Temple, the earliest notice of this fruit by European writers.

1636.—[At Goa] "A Delicate Fruit resembling a pine, butt when ripe it is offt and of an Admirable tast, called **Atae.**" Mundy, Vol. III, pt. 1, p. 58.

Atambor (a drum). Konk. *tambor*.—Malayal *tampêre* (a kind of drum).

See *Ind. Antiq.*, Vol. LVII, Nov., 1928.

Bacamarte (a blunderbuss; a gun with a bell mouth). Anglo-Ind. *boca-mortis*, *boca-mortass*, *bukmar* (obs.).

Sir Richard Temple (*Ind. Antiq.*, Vol. L, p. 227) offers an ingenious derivation of the Portuguese word, viz., Port. *boca*, 'mouth', and *mortis*, 'death', hence 'death-dealing mouth'. Death in Port. is *morte* and not *mortis*. Longworth Dames's conjecture is that the word might conceivably stand for *boca-Martis*, and thus mean 'the mouth of Mars', instead of 'the mouth of Death'. This word must not be confounded with the Port. *bracamarte* which means a broadsword or cutlass. The Portuguese dictionaries derive this latter from the French, through Low-Latin, *braquemart*, 'cutlass', but offer no derivation of *bacamarte*. The Anglo-Indian forms are neither in *Hobson-Jobson* nor in the *O.E.D.*

"They kept at a small distance firing their muskets and **bocamortasses** and flying granadoes." *Ind. Antiq.*,

Vol. XLIX, p. 10. See also *idem*, Vol. L, p. 227.

"They [the Portuguese in Goa] live with a splendid Outside, vaunting in their number of Slaves, walking under a Street of their own Umbrelloes, bareheaded, to avoid giving Distaste in not removing their Hats: They being jealous of their Honour, pardon no Affront; wherefore to ogle a Lady in a Balcony (if a Person of Quality) it is revenged with a **Bocca Mortis**, or to pass by a Fidalgo without due Reverence, is severely chastised." Fryer, *East India*, Hak. Soc., Vol. II, p. 26.

Bandel (a landing place, a harbour; also used to denote a quarter near the harbour occupied by people of one race.) ? Anglo-Ind. *bunder*, *banda* (obs.).

The Portuguese form is a corruption of the Pers. *bandar* 'port, wharf' which has been adopted by most of the Indian languages.

Bandel was used by the Portuguese as early as 1529 and it is not unlikely that the Anglo-Indian forms are indebted to Portuguese.

In the great emporiums of the East there were separate localities in which the members of the various trading communities lived, and at the head of each of these was its respective '*shabunder*,' who would correspond to the consul of the present time and with whom foreign traders and ship-masters would transact. Each of such localities was spoken of by the Portuguese as a *bandel*; thus they speak of *bandel dos guzarates*, *bandel dos quelins*, *bandel dos Portugueses*.

The term was also used of smaller ports in which there were no distinct trading communities: *bandel de Chatigão*, *bandel de Ugolim* (situated on the right bank of the Hugli). This last named place appropriated to itself the name '*Bandel*' by which it is known to this day. There was in it already in the 16th century a Portuguese factory and a large Portuguese population which built the first Catholic church in Bengal. This settlement and the Portuguese in it went through many vicissitudes but the old name of the place as also its sumptuous church edifice and the adjoining Augustinian monastery have survived them all, and the last two even yet continue to attract the reverent admiration of the people of the surrounding country. See Dalgado's *Glossário*, *s.v.*

The earliest reference for this word in the *O.E.D.* is of 1673, but the form *banda* is not mentioned.

1616.—"Besides the danger in intercepting our boats to and from the shore, etc., their firing from the **Banda**, would be with much difficulty." Foster, *Letters*, Vol. IV, p. 328.

1673.—"We fortify our Houses have **Bunders** or Docks for our vessels, to which belong Yards for Seamen, Soldiers, and Stores." Fryer, *East India*, Vol. I, p. 289.

Banean (a Gujarati trader, see p. 38).

To the compounds of this word mentioned on p. 39 two others might be added: *Banyan-day* and *Banyan-fight*. They appear to have acquired a currency as early as the seventeenth century.

The first of the following quotations is of special interest because it recalls to mind the not unsimilar efforts made by Governments and trading houses in India to combat the trade and financial depression at the present day.

The expression 'banian-fight' is not in the *O.E.D.* The earliest reference in it for 'banian-hospital' is of 1813, but though the name is not used the hospital itself is described by Fitch (*c.* 1585). See R. Fitch in Foster, *Early Travels*, pp. 14 and 25.

1634.—"As rigid economy is necessary 'in these sad deplorable tymes, whenas India affoardeth little or nothing whereon to begett a profitable trade for the Honourable Company', the commanders are charged to be as frugal as possible in regard to harbour provisions They are to deliver lists of their men and the number of their messes, 'and accordingly a computated proporcion of what they may spend in such diett for **Banyan daies** (so called) as this place affoards and the Company allowes, with promise that for the other daies care shalbe taken at Suratt that fresh meat be provided conveniently sufficient'." Foster, *Eng. Fact* (*1634–1636*), p. 38.

1690.—"Of this [Kedgeree or Kitcheree] the European Sailers feed in those parts once or twice a Week, and are forc'd at those times to a Pagan Abstinence from Flesh, which creates in them a perfect Dislike and utter Detestation to those **Bannian Days**, as they commonly call them." Ovington, *Voyage to Surat*, O.U.P., p. 183.

1666.—"The men are great clowns... they make a great noise when they have any quarrel, but what passion soever they seem to be in, and what bitter words so ever they utter, they never come to blows." Thevenot, *Travels into the Levant*, pt. III, p. 51 (Eng. tr. of 1687).

1690.—"Next to the *Moors* the *Bannians* are the most noted Inhabitants of *Suratt* who are Merchants all by Profession, and very numerous in all parts of *India*. They are most innocent and obsequious, humble and patient to a Miracle; sometimes they are heated into harsh Expressions to one another, which is seldom; and this Tongue-Tempest is term'd there a **Banian Fight**, for it never rises to Blows or Blood-shed." Ovington, O.U P., p. 163.

On p. 39, referring to *pinjrā-pole* which is the Gujarati equivalent of the Anglo-Indian 'banian-hospital,' we quoted Crooke who derived the Indian word from *pinjra*, 'a cage,' and *pola*, 'the sacred bull released in the name of Śiva.' Prof. Hodivala (*Ind. Antiq.* LVIII) has questioned this etymology and, it appears to us, rightly so. His view is that "Pole in Pinjrâpole means 'a block of houses often with a gateway', like the Poles or Pols of Ahmedabad." He says that 'Pola' the sacred bull released in the name of Śiva, can have nothing to do with the Gujarati word, as it is a Dravidian word. The 'sacred bull,' besides, is never caged. Indeed the religious merit consists in giving him his liberty.

Bangaçal (a warehouse, customs-house). Anglo-Ind. *bankshall*. Also used in the sense of 'a covered platform at the customs-house', and of 'port-dues.' These two usages are not mentioned in *Hobson-Jobson* nor in the *O E.D.*

The derivation of the word most favoured is that from the Sansk. *bhaṇḍaśāla*, Kanar. *bhaṇḍaśāle*, Malayal. *poṇḍiśāla*, 'a storehouse'. In Marathi *bhaṅgsāl* means 'a dreary big house', but Molesworth does not give its etymology. In Goa, at the present day, the use of the word is restricted to 'a timber yard', though figuratively it is also used of 'a big and badly-planned house'.

1614.—"Order was sent to prohibit us [at Musulpatam] the King's beam, and that our goods yet to land should be detained at the **Bankshall** (as they call their Custom house)." Foster, *Letters* (*1613–1615*), p. 84.

1629.—"This foresaid instrument ....was delivered to the Governour of Mesulapatam then being, and....read upon the **bancksale** and in presents of the cheefe of the Moores." Foster, *Eng. Fact.* (*1624–1629*), p. 318.

1673.—"The agreement therefore is on these terms: that any goods whatsoever or horses that are his owne ....the charges and customes, as Jaggand......**Banksoll**, and all other dues......the King does gratiously give them free." *Idem*, (*1634–1636*), p. 17.

Barrica (barrel, see p. 41). Anglo-Ind. *barrecoe*, *barreck* (obs.). The latter of these two forms is not in the *O.E.D.*

"Sends him a '**barrecoe**' of beer and desires a supply of provisions." Foster, *Eng. Fact* (*1622-1623*), p. 138.

[Safī Khān] "begs therefore a couple of '**barreckes**'." *Op. cit.*, p. 292.

Barricada (a barrier). Anglo-Ind. *barracodo* (obs.).

"The enemy's vessels were 'extraordinary great ships.... The rear-admiral was the largest of all, and had been 'built upon a carack at Cochin ...only for to make a battery and to be a **barracodo** to the rest of her fleet." *Eng. Fact.* (*1621-1629*), p 40.

Bata (subsistence allowance, see p. 41).

The citation below gives proof of a much earlier use of this word in Anglo-India than do those in *Hobson-Jobson.*

1638.—"They have received daily '**batta**' but this need not be deducted from their wages." Foster, *Eng. Fact.* (*1637-1641*), p. 51.

Batão (difference in exchange, see p. 43).

In the citations below are Anglo-Indian forms not mentioned in *Hobson-Jobson* nor in the *O.E.D.*; they are also of an earlier date than those mentioned there.

1634.—"Thus much of your silver was sould for new rupees, to be paid daily out of the mynt as it could be coyned; whereout we had hoped to have coyned some advantage, in gayneing the exchange betwixt them and mamooths here called **buttaw.**" Foster, *Eng. Fact.* (*1634-1636*), p. 68. See also Vol. of *1637-1641*, p. 100.

1651.—"When he asked Davidge he did not demand '**the vattaw** of cuzzana [khazāna=treasury] rupees due to the Company from Mr. Knipe, he with stern lookes and high words told me I was a sawcy knave to demaund of him about the Companies accompts" Foster, *Idem*, (*1651-1654*), p. 81.

The Marathi form of the Hindust. *battau* is *vāṭāv*, but it is scarcely likely that the Marathi form is used above; it appears to be a normal case of the exchange of *v* for *b* and vice versa.

Batel (a small boat, see p. 45).

With regard to this word it is useful to note what Professor Hodivalla says in *Ind. Antiq.*, Vol. LX, p. 88.

"Whatever the source of the Portuguese 'Batell', it is certain that the Bombay 'Batelo' or the Bengal 'Patello' is not directly derived from it as the form *batla* occurs in the *Târîkh-i-Fîrûzshâhî* of Baranî, which was completed in 1385 A.C. (*Bibl. Indica* Text, p. 490, l. 7)."

Portuguese dictionaries derive *batel* from the Lat. *batellum*. Dalgado does not include *batel* in his *Glossário* in which are to be found Portuguese words derived from oriental sources.

Bétele (betel, see p. 50).

The quotation below is of interest because of the form coined from *betel* to denote a carrier or box for betel-leaf, called in Hindust. *pāndān*. It is formed on the analogy of *aguadeiro* (from *agua*, water), a water jug, *aguilheiro* (from *agulha*, needle), a container for needles.

1628-37.—"Betel was then brought in, in a magnificent golden **Betelero**." Manrique, *Travels*, Vol I, p. 156.

Biombo (a moveable screen). Anglo-Ind. *beeombu*.

Did the Portuguese who had derived their word from the Japanese *byobu* or *bióbu* give it to Anglo-India or did English traders take it directly from Japanese? The form *biombo* appears to be due to the Portuguese tendency of nasalising borrowed words (cf. *palanquim*, from *pālkī*) and the Anglo-Ind. *beeombu* appears, therefore, to be indebted to Portuguese. The form *bube* in the second quotation is probably due to direct contact with Japan. Neither of the two forms are in the *O.E.D.*

1638.—"**Beeombos** are certaine skreenes of 8 or 9 Foote Deepe, made into sundry leaves which principally serve to Divide a roome or to sequester some part thereof, as allsoe for Ornament, placing them against the walles." Mundy, *Travels*, Hak. Soc., Vol. III, pt. i, p. 255.

1616.—[Here in Japan] "is also most excellent work in varnish, both chests, contors, boxes, **bubes** and other matters; but they will take up much room in shipping; it may be, more than they are worth." Foster, *Letters*, Vol. IV, p. 53.

Bispo (bishop). Malayal. *bispe*.

"It is found in old Malayalam writings of the Portuguese period, and is sometimes even now used by the Roman Catholics in Malabar." *Ind. Antiq.*, Vol. LVI, p. 85 n.

Boi (a palanquin bearer, see p. 52).

The quotation below is of interest inasmuch as it gives evidence of how efforts were made by European travellers, without knowledge of Indian tongues, to explain Indian terms by reference to European languages. Refer to derivation of 'Banyan' from Italian *bagnáre* on p. 38.

1628-37.—"These men, who bear the palanquin on their shoulders are, as it were, the bullocks (*bueyes*) for such vehicles, and not only are they so in fact but even are so in name, as they are called **bueyes** throughout India.' Manrique, *Travels*, Hak. Soc., Vol. I, p. 57.

Boi in Portuguese, *buey* in Spanish means 'a bullock'.

Bolsa (purse, bag, see p. 54). Anglo-Ind. *bulse* (obs.).

The term was used to indicate a packet of diamonds or gold dust.

1711.—"Received a **bulse**, said to be of gold, of Manuel Tavoch of Macao, merchant, sealed as above, which I promise to deliver to Mr. Frederick, the dangers of the sea excepted. J. Scattergood." *The Scattergoods and the East India Co.*, in *Ind. Antiq.*, Vol. LX, Supp. p. 77.

Botica (a shop, see p. 57).

The citation below gives evidence of earlier use of this word in Anglo-India than do those in *Hobson-Jobson*.

1668.—"Rent of the **botica**........ x 16.0.0." *Yearley Rent Rowle of Bombaim*, etc. in *Ind. Antiq.*, Vol LIV, p. 1.

Braça (a measure of extent, see p. 57). Anglo-Ind. *barsa* (obs.).

1638.—"Good drincking cuppes att 1*d*. and 1½*d*, and Fruitt Dishes att 2½*d*, each; the rest according to that rate. For a whole **barsa**, which is 2 tubbes, will cost 28 or 30 Ryall eight, and they usually contain aboutt 600 peeces little and great." Mundy, *Travels*, Hak. Soc., Vol. III, pt. i, p. 305.

'Barsa' in the passage above means a fathom, i.e., a six-foot cask. This form is not in the *O.E.D.*

Breda do mar (lit 'sea-beet', an edible seaweed). Anglo-Ind. *breda de Marr* (obs.). See *Scattergood's List of goods procurable at Malacca* in *Ind. Antiq.*, Vol. LVI, Supplement p. 76.

Brinco (curios, bric-à-brac). Anglo-Ind. *brinquo* (obs.). Not in the *O.E.D.*

"Thomas Kerridge at Surat to John Bangham at Lahore, April, 26, 1626, Sends a copy of his last, and again, urges the sale of his goods, 'least Manoell de Payva his **brinquos** cause yours to be disesteemed and this your cautious wayting produce my further prejudice'." Foster, *Eng. Fact.* (*1624-1629*), p. 130.

Búfalo (buffalo, see p. 58).

Below are some citations with Anglo-Indian forms of this word not mentioned in *Hobson-Jobson*. They help to show the tentative forms through which this word passed before the present day spelling became stabilised. One of them from Fryer contains a description of the buffalo which it would be hard to beat for accuracy.

1673.—"We passed Five Mile to the Foot of the Hill on which the City [of 'Canorein'] stands, and had passed half a Mile through a thick Wood, peopled by Apes, Tygers, wild **Buffolo's**, and Jackalls." Fryer, *East India*, Hak. Soc., Vol. I, p. 186.

1673.—"The *Moors* have it [water] brought on **Buffola's** Backs, or else on Oxen." *Ibidem*, p. 295.

"A **Buffola** is of a Dun Colour, and are all as big as their largest Oxen; they love to wallow in the Mire like an Hog; there are of them Wild, which are very Fierce and Mischievous, Trampling a Man to Death, or Moiling him to Pieces with their Foreheads; their Horns are carelessly turned with Knobs around, being usually so ordered, or rather disordered (for they retain no certain Form) that they lie too much over their Heads to do any harm with them. Their Flesh is reckon'd Hotter and Courser than Beef, which is the most common Sustinence of the *Moors*; as their Milk and boiled Butter is of the *Gentues*: for did they not boil their Butter, it would be Rank, but after it has passed the Fire, they keep it in Duppers the year round." *Ibidem*, p. 296.

1689.—"The **Buffolo** is generally larger than an Ox, but a very sowr untractable Animal, by which means he is useless to the Natives in the convenience of Riding, of Hackeries, and is generally employ'd in carrying large Bags of Fresh Water on each side, from the Tanques to the Houses." Ovington, *Voyage to Surat*, O.U.P. (1929), p. 151.

Cafre (a negro, see p. 64). Anglo-Ind. *Caffro*, *Cofferie*, *Coffer*.

The Portuguese used the term also to denote an African slave and in the citations below it will be seen how this meaning of the term was adopted in Anglo-India. The form 'caffro' is not in the *O.E.D.* wherein the earliest reference for the word in the meaning of 'slave' is of 1781.

1614.—"Signor Damian is here looking out for a **caffro** which is run from his master." Foster, *Letters*, Vol. II, p. 227.

1644.—"Send also two slaves; 'the man, being a lustie slave **coffer**'." Foster, *Eng. Fact.* (*1642–1645*), p. 81.

"East African Negroes and slaves from Madagascar, locally known as '**Cofferies**' were a well-known element of the population (of Bombay) during the early British period and continued to be imported until the middle of the nineteenth century." S. M. Edwards, *Population of the City of Bombay*, in *Ind. Antiq.*, Vol. LV, p. 215.

Cairo (fibre of the coco-nut husk, see p. 64). Anglo-Ind. *cairo* (obs.).

There is no reference from any English traveller for this form in *Hobson-Jobson*. The quotation below lends support to Yule's view that the form 'coir' appears to have been introduced in the 18th century.

1583-91.—"I went from Basora to Ormus downe the Gulfe of Persia in a certain shippe made of boordes and sowed together with **cayro**, which is threede made of the huske of cocoes, and certaine canes or strawe leaves sowed upon the seames of the bordes."

Ralph Fitch, in Foster, *Early Travels*, O.U.P., p. 11.

1644.—"She [the *Seahorse*] is then to proceed to Goa to...... buy some **cairo.**" Foster, *Eng. Fact.* (*1642–45*), p. 167.

Caju (the cashew tree and fruit, see p. 65).

The quotations below reveal some very strange forms of this word in Anglo-India. The form *cadju* though, as we have observed (p. 66), only recently noticed in India was used by Rumphius who died in 1693. The first of the following citations is of special interest because of the reference in it to Cromwell and his wife. The *O.E.D.* does not contain the forms 'cadjew' and 'cajoora', and the earliest instance it has of the word is of 1703.

1655.—"Concerning 'Generall Cromwell' he [Capt. James Martin] declared 'that before these warrs begunn hee was a pore cowardly fellow and would take a cuff on the eare from any man'; while as for Cromwell's wife, 'the stone or excrescence of a fruite called a **cadjew** would fitt her very well for a tooth'." Foster, *Eng. Fact.* (*1651–1654*), p. 123.

1638.—"**Cajooraes**: of a straunge propertye. **Cajoora** trees, whose blossome casteth a Most Fragrant smell into the ayre, the Fruit somwhatt harsh in tast and strong...." Mundy, *Travels*, Vol. III, pt. i, p. 57. There is evident confusion in Mundy's mind between *caju* and *khajūrā* or *khajūri*, the Indian name of the date-palm.

"**Cadju** is not properly speaking an Eastern fruit; but at one time it was brought there from the West Indies." Rumphius, *Herbarium Amboinense*, I, p. 177 He also mentions that in Amboyna the fruit, was called *boa franqi*, that is 'fruit from Portugal'.

Caminhar (to travel). Anglo-Ind. *caminha* (obs.).

1632.—"The Dutchman from Masulipatam arrived here on the 25th and, finding little hope of a market, hastened for 'Ninapooly and adjacent aldeas'; but being 'tardiff in **caminha**', he was overtaken by Cartwright at 'Baputly' on the 28th". Foster, *Eng. Fact.* (*1630–1633*), p. 232.

Campo (a field, see p. 72).

Here is a citation which contains an earlier instance of the use of compound in Anglo-India than those mentioned in *Hobson-Jobson* or in the *O.E.D.*

1676.—"Company's goods by reason of several thatch hovells within and round about the **compound**, which are very dangerous in respect of fire, which often happens in Dacca." Hedges, *Diary*, Hak. Soc., Vol II, p. ccxxxvi. See also instances on the same page and the next.

Canja (in the sense of 'starch used by Indian washermen, and also in that of 'rice gruel', see p. 76).

Below are instances of this word in Anglo-India older than those in *Hobson-Jobson* or in the *O.E.D.*; the last is also useful as showing how the Englishman in India. in the seventeenth century, did not disdain 'congee' as a daily beverage, and also as providing an insight into the social practices of that age.

1615.—"And finding the **Caugee** to be dangerous to delay." Foster, *Letters*, Vol. III, p. 107.

"Have been endeavouring to procure the goods required 'butt all this tyme itt hath beene soe extreame raynes thatt neather beater cann beate washer can give **cangee**, nor wee looke uppon nill." Foster, *Eng. Fact. (1622-1623)*, p. 109.

1665.—"Yet about a clock in the afternoon I went out into our Balcony, where wee commonly dine, at which time I found said Mr. Harrington looking upon a Silver hilted sword that he had newly made, and sitting down, I called to my servant for a boule of **Congee**......which to this instant is my cheifest lickuor, and seeing them merry, had a desire to participate of their mirth, and began to drink to a Portugall that was in the company, in my said liquor. Mr. Harrington, turning towards me, falsely accuses me that in those words I dishonoured him, he imagining that whereas I spake to the aforesaid Portugall, I had asked him to sell his sword, allthough all they had stood by knew and testified that there was no such word spoken; yet there was no persuading him..... To be short, he said I was what he pleased to call me, and strikes at my beare head with his naked sword I having nothing to defend myselfe but my boule of **Congee**." *A Factor's Complaint from Porakad*, in *Ind. Antiq*, Vol LI, p. 109.

Canequim (a thick cotton cloth, see p. 73). Anglo-Ind. *candykens* (obs.). Neither in *Hobson-Jobson* nor in the *O.E.D.*

1617.—"For the estate of this Achem factory, it may please you, Suratt cloth, as blue baftās.....will vent here 500 corge per year; **candykeens** of Cambaya, two thousand corge per year, yielding cento per cento profit." Foster, *Letters*, Vol. VI, p. 71.

Capado (a eunuch, see p. 77). Anglo-Ind. *capado* (obs.). Neither in *Hobson-Jobson* nor in the *O.E.D.*

1615.—"Given one of the King's **Capados** by Mr. Oxwicke: one coarse white baftā of 50 mamodes per corge, cost...." Foster, *Letters*, Vol. III, p. 97.

1615.—"The **Capado** would not deliver the said letter until the said officers were satisfied......

To the **Capado** which brought the letter....." *Ibidem*, p. 100.

Capitão mór (Captain major, see p. 78). Anglo-Ind. *Capt. mor*, *Capt. more*, (obs.).

Mór is a contraction of *maór*, the earliest form of *maior* or *major*.

1642.—"But now, say the Portugalls of St. Thoma, or rather the **Capt. More**....the peace is broke and they expect order from the Viceroy to fall on us." Foster, *Eng. Fact.* (*1642–1645*), p. 44.

See also under **Armada** in Supplement

Caro (adj. dear). Anglo-Ind. *caro* (obs.). Neither in *Hobson-Jobson* nor in the *O.E.D.*

1626.—"By reason of the Dutch's inveterate hate and malice all passages round about us are waylaid, either with a guard of Dutchmen or by the Governor, who they and Malaya together put in; which we make no doubt costs them **caro**." Foster, *Eng. Fact.* (*1624–1629*), p. 131.

Cartaz (a pass, safe-conduct). Anglo-Ind. *curtass*, *cartasse*, (obs.). See p. 82. Neither in the *O.E.D.* nor in *Hobson-Jobson.*

1618.—"If they misenforme not from Mesolapatan, there is great store of indico shipt at some ports to the sowth, all which take **curtasses** of our enemies." Foster, *Eng. Fact.* (*1618–1621*), p 3.

1618.—"Shee hath her **cartasse** without stopping at Suratt and upon conclusion sent to mee for my passe, els the merchants would not stirr." *Ibidem*, p. 4.

1621.—"The Dutch in the Red Sea gave **cartasses** or assuraunce to the juncks to pass free, and yet most treacherously, to their great infamie, made seisure of six vessels." *Ibidem*, p. 324.

Castiço (child of Portuguese parents born in India, see p. 85). Anglo-Ind. *Castilian*, *Castez.* Not in the *O.E.D.*

"Kanappa confiscated a quantity of rice, unjustly, defrauding the '**Castilian**' who brought it for sale." Foster, *Eng. Fact.* (*1651–1654*), p. 240. Foster conjectures that '**Castilian**' here is intended for *castiço* and it appears rightly so.

"Richard Trenchfield married a **Castez.**" *The Diaries of Streynsham Master* (*1675–80*), ed. Temple, Vol. II, p. 284.

Cavalaria (an establishment of horses or other animals). Anglo-Ind. *caveluriree* (obs.). Neither in *Hobson-Jobson* nor in the *O.E.D.*

1622-23.—"As for the coach, one of the oxen died and the other went lame and had to be sold; 'which is all the proceed of the **caveluriree**'." Foster, *Eng. Fact.* (*1622–1623*), p. 95 In the same volume (p 45) is also met with the form *cavyilluryoo*, in the same sense.

Cavaleiro (a horseman, a rider). Anglo-Ind. *cavallerous* (obs.).

"Had intended to keep their 'ablucks' for sale here, as ordered by the President; but their '**cavallerous**' refused to return without them." Foster, *Eng. Fact.* (*1624–1629*), p. 232. *Abluck* is Ar. *ablaq*, 'a piebald horse'. See also quotation under **Adarga** in Supplement.

Centopeia (centipede, see p. 92).

Here is an instance of the use of this word in Anglo-India.

1703.—"I shall not presume to trouble your Honours with an account of the insects of this island, only of one, it being a great curiosity, and none of us have ever seen such before; it is a small slender worme, about three inches in length much resembling a **centipee** only slenderer, and its leggs are shorter, smaller and much more numerous; wherever he creeped or moved in the night he left behind him a traine of light like a bright fire, which would also stick to his fingers and hands that but touch it." Hedges, *Diary*, Hak. Soc., Vol. II, p. cccxxxiii.

Cesta (a basket). Anglo-Ind. *cesta.* (obs.). Neither in *Hobson-Jobson* nor in the *O.E.D.*

1619.—[Sprage] "confessed there was 13 **cestas** or basketts of chenye dishes delivered Nicholas Banggam per Swaryes in Bramport, whereof two **cestas** the said Banggam caried awaye with him." Foster, *Eng. Fact.* (*1618–1621*), p. 172.

Chá (tea, see p. 93).

Below is a very early instance of the use of the form 'chawe' in Anglo-India.

1616.—"I hope you will remember me for the **chawe** I wished you to buy for me." Letter of William Eaton from Firando to Richards Wickham (at Miako), dated 22nd June, 1616, in Foster, *Letters*, Vol. IV, p. 120.

Crooke says that the earliest mention of tea in the Old Records of India is in a letter from R. Wickham, at Firando, in Japan, who writing, June 27th, 1615, to Mr. Eaton at Miaco, asks for "a pt. of the best sort of **chaw**".

After a collation of both these passages it would appear as though Miaco was then famous for its tea.

Chapa (a seal, impression).

Below are citations to show how in Anglo-India and even in Spanish this Indian term came to be used as a verb.

1618.—"That all presents being showed at the Custome house, that the officers might avoyd deceipt, being **chopped** by both parts." Sir T. Roe, *Embassy*, Hak. Soc., p. 508.

1628-37.—"The formons when prepared were read out to the King [of Arakan] who immediately had them **chapaed**, that is stamped with his Royal **chapa**, or seal as we call it, that serves as seal and signature at the same time, since no separately written signature is employed." Manrique, *Travels*, Hak. Soc., Vol I, pp. 157 and 158. The Spanish original has "*el qual los mandó luego chapar*".

1679.—"Yesterday the Mochelke (*muchalka*, bond) was **chopt** (sealed) by the Cadje." *The Diaries of Streynsham Master*, ed. Temple, Vol II, p. 276.

1698.—"*June 11th.* Diary, Wrote an answer....and order'd if such impediments continued about the Towns to get the Nishaan **chaup'd** with it for delays were dangerous." *Old Fort William in Bengal*, ed. C. R. Wilson, Vol. I, p. 37.

Here is a fairly early use of 'chop' in the sense of 'seal'.

1654.—"He also heard Winter accuse Yardley of transferring '**chopps**' from one cloth to another." Foster, *Eng. Fact.* (*1651–1654*), p. 275.

Chinche (a bug). Anglo-Ind. *chince*, *chint* (obs.).

1673.—"Swarms of Ants, *Muskeetoes*, Flies, and stinking **Chints**, *Cimices, etc.* breed and infest them: This Season we experimented; which though moderately warm, yet our Bodies broke out into small fiery Pimples.... augmented by *Muskeetoe*-Bites and **Chinces** raising Blisters on us." Fryer, *East India*, Hak. Soc., Vol. I, p. 100.

"Notwithstanding **Chints**, Fleas, and Muskeeto's torment them every Minute, [the 'Banyans'] dare not presume to scratch where it itches, lest some Relation should be untenanted its miserable abode." *Ibidem*, p. 231.

Chita (printed cotton cloth, see p. 104).

Here is an early instance of the use of this term in Anglo-India.

1690.—"In some things the Artists of *India* out-do all the Ingenuity of *Europe*, viz., in the painting of **Chites** or Callicoes." Ovington, *Voyage to Surat*, O.U.P., p. 167.

Chuname (prepared lime, see p. 105).

The following is an Anglo-Indian form of this word mentioned neither in *Hobson-Jobson* nor in the *O.E.D.*

1583–91.—"And all the time which they ('Chinians') mourne they keepe the dead in the house; the bowels being taken out and filled with **chownam** or lime, and coffined, and when the time is expired they carry them out playing and piping, and burne them." Ralph Fitch in Foster, *Early Travels*, O.U.P., p. 42.

Combalenga (a species of pumpkin). Anglo-Ind. *bolango*.

The Portuguese borrowed the word *kumbalanu*, 'a pumpkin', from one of the South Dravidian languages. The Anglo-Ind. form is not in the *O.E.D.*

1679.—"This countrey [Achin] affordeth Severall Excellent good fruites, Namely: Duryans, Mangastinos, Oranges, the best in India or South Seas, comparable with the best of China, Lemons, Limes, Ramastines [Litchis], **Bolangos**, Monsoone plums [*Zizyphus Jujuba* or *bēr*], Pumple Mooses [see under **Toranja**, p. 350], etc., and the trees beare fruite both green and ripe all the yeare alonge." Bowrey, *Countries round the Bay of Bengal*, Hak. Soc., p. 323.

Comprador (a purchaser, see p. 115).

Below is an early Anglo-Indian instance of the use of this word, earlier than any in *Hobson-Jobson* or in the *O.E.D.*

1614.—"I make John Phebe did deliver you the two fishes and letter I wrote you yesterday. He is now grown stately and will not serve in the English house for **comprador**." Foster, *Letters*, Vol. II (*1613–1615*), p. 227.

Concerto (repair). Anglo-Ind. *conserta* (obs.).

"**Consertas de Terras**" (of lands). ....xl. 19. 13. *Yearley Rent Rowle of Bombaim*, etc., in *Ind. Antiq.*, Vol. LIV, p. 1.

Covado (a cubit, see p. 126).

Below are a few other Anglo-Ind. forms of this word none of which are to be found either in *Hobson-Jobson* or in the *O.E.D.*, and they belong to an earlier date than those mentioned therein.

1615.—"The measure is called a **covett**, whereof there is two, one whereby our English cloth is only sold by, of length 35½ inches; the other, whereby all other commodity is sold by, is of length 26½ inches." Foster, *Letters*, Vol. III, p. 11.

1615.—[Carpets] "fifty-nine, to say, six long at rupies 2½ per **covedee**." *Ibidem*, p. 40.

1616.—"Good silks cost 10 rupeis their **cobda**, and mean cloth of gold 35 and 40 rupeis a **cobda**." *Idem*, Vol. IV, p. 20.

"For the crimson French 'shagge' Āsaf Khān offers fifteen rupees the **covado**, 'which is an English yard within three inches'." Foster, *Eng. Fact.* (*1618–1621*), p. 21.

"Mistake made at Surat in the length of the Patna **coved**." *Ibidem*, p. 236.

Curral (a cattle pen, see p. 130).

It would appear from an illustration in Tennent's *Ceylon* (1859), Vol. I, p. 211, that the Anglo-Indian form of this word was employed not only to denote the enclosure for capturing wild elephants but also one for catching fish.

Discalsado (barefooted). Anglo-Ind. *discalsadoe* (obs.). This form is not in the *O.E.D.* which has 'discalceate' in the same sense.

1616.—"No, he hath a **Discalsadoe** Portugall for his confessor." Sir T. Roe, *Embassy*, Hak. Soc., p. 130.

Elephanta (the name given to storms at the beginning or setting in of the Monsoon, see p. 140).

Below is a reference to the 'Elephanta' of an earlier date than the earliest mentioned in the body of this book.

1611.—"The storm of **Ofante** doth begin and endureth 2 or 3 days." Foster, *Letters*, Vol. I, p. 126.

1621.—"A crwell night of raine and thunder and of lightning .... this raine and lightning was called by the peaplle the **olliphante**, which cometh once a yeare." Foster, *Eng. Fact.* (*1618–1621*), p. 286.

It is interesting to note that, speaking of what is now called 'Elephanta Island' (see p. 142), Fryer uses the masculine form 'Elephanto' which is nearer the original '*A Ilha do Elephante*' than the present 'Elephanta', feminine in form :

1673.—"These Islands are in number seven: *Bombaim, Canorein, Trumbay,* **Elephanto,** the *Putachoes, Munchumbay,* and *Kerenjau,* with the Rock of *Henry Kenry.*" Vol. I, p. 159.

"Having in a Week's time compleated my Business, returning the same way, we steered by the *South* side of the Bay, purposely to touch at **Elephanto,** so called from a monstrous Elephant cut out of the main Rock, bearing a Young one on its Back." *Ibidem,* p. 194.

Escrito (a writing, see p. 147).

The quotation below would lead one to the view that this Portuguese word was used not only in the sense of 'a note under one's hand or attestation', but also in the sense of 'a hasty note' in which 'chit' is used to-day in India. The word in this sense is not in the *O.E.D.*

1615.—"All your letters having been liker to **screets** than letters." Foster, *Letters,* Vol. III, p. 154.

See also quotation under *Scrivão* in Supplement.

Escritorio (a writing desk, see p. 148).

The quotations below are of an early date, provide new forms of the word, some of which are not found in the *O.E.D.*, and go to show what a brisk trade there was in these desks between the Far East and India as early as the beginning of the seventeenth century.

1615-1616.—"Among other things I should mention a great number of cabinets of all patterns, in the fashion of those of Germany. This is an article the most perfect and of the finest workmanship to be seen anywhere; for they are all of choice woods, and inlaid with ivory, mother-of-pearl, and precious stones; in place of iron they are mounted with gold. The Portuguese call them **Escritorios** de la China." Pyrard, *Voyage,* Hak. Soc., Vol. II, pp. 176 and 177.

1617.—"There are two **scriptoris** which are sealed up to be delivered to you by Mr. Mothwold." Foster, *Letters,* Vol. VI, p. 27.

1617.—"I sent a gold box by Richard Kingo to buy me some **skrettores** of mackee [*maki-ye*= lacquer] work." *Ibidem,* p. 104.

1617.—"I have sent by this bearer seventeen sundry parcels of contores and **scrittores** marked with **R. W.** [Richard Wickham]. The freight of them I pray pay to the master how much it is......I have been at Meaco and talked with the makeman [maker of lacquered goods] who hath promised that in short time he will have done. He hath fifty men that worketh night and day; that, so far as I see, he doth his endeavour." *Ibidem,* p. 169.

1617.—"I give you thanks for the book of Sir Walter Rawli's which you sent me; and have no good thing to send unto you, only two small **scritoris.**" *Ibidem,* p. 266.

1690.—"It [Suratt] is renown'd for Traffick through all *Asia,* both for rich Silks......and for Agatts, Cornelians

Nigganees, Desks, **Scrutores**, and Boxes neatly polisht and embellisht, which may be purchas'd here at very reasonable Rates." Ovington, *Voyage to Surat*, O.U.P., p. 131.

"I cannot boast of the Lack upon **Scrutores** and Tables at Suratt, which is but ordinary in respect of that at Japan." *Ibidem*, p. 167.

Estanque (the shop or place where the *estanqueiro* or monopolist had licence to sell certain commodities for his own profit). Anglo-Ind. *stanck* (obs.).

1668.—"**Stanck** of tobacco imports .... x 10,225.00.00." *Yearley Rent Rowle of Bombaim*, in *Ind. Antiq.*, Vol. LIV, p. 1.

Estocada (a thrust with a rapier). Anglo-Ind. *stochado* (obs.). This form is not in the *O.E.D.*

1673.—"Tho Mass of the People [of Goa] are *Canorein*, though *Portuguezed* in Speech and Manners; paying great Observance to a White Man, whom when they meet they must give him the way with a Cringe and Civil Salute, for fear of a **Stochado**." Fryer, *East India*, Hak. Soc., Vol. II, p. 27.

Feitiço (sorcery, see p. 154). Here is an uncommon form of this word.

1690—"They (the Africans) Travel no where without their **Fateish** about them, one of which looked like the small end of a Stag's Horn, with a Bell tied to it, about the bigness of a Man's Thumb......To these **Fateishes** they ascribe their Security from Peril and Mischief." Ovington, *Voyage to Surat*, O.U.P., p. 44.

Fidalgo (one nobly descended, see p. 155). Anglo-Ind. *phydalgo, fidalgo.*

1642.—"Being truly informed which was the homicide, we. kept him and suffered the others to departe for St. Thoma; from whence wee received many letters to release him, for that he was a **phydalgo**." Foster, *Eng Fact.* (*1642–1645*), p. 43

1673.—"The **Fidalgos** have stately Dwellings, graced with covered Balconies, and large Windows two Stories high, with Panes of Oister shell, which is their usual Glazing among them in India" Fryer, *East India*, Vol. I, p. 192. See also quotations under *Aldeia* and *Bacamorte* in Supplement.

Foral (rent roll). Anglo-Ind. *forall* (obs.). Not in *O.E.D.*

1665.—"I writt about a rent that did belong to the King that might import to about 700 or 800 *li.* per annum, for the Knife that was to prune the Cocer nutt tree [known as the *Coito* tax, see *Ind. Antiq.*, LIV, p. 2], it hath proved incerte, for since by papers I find it belongs to the Owners or **Foreiros** [see below] of the ground for which they pay unto his Majesty what appeares by theyr **Foralls**, so that it proved a fals information." Khan, *Anglo-Portuguese Negotiations*, etc. O.U.P., p. 476.

Foreiro (a tenant who paid the quit rent, see p. 160).

The following quotation is illustrative not only of the early use of this term in an Anglo-Indian document but also of the hatred in which the chief 'foreiros' or revenue farmers of Portuguese days were regarded by the people of Bombay.

1664.—"Whereas this Island being formerly belonging to the Crowne of Portugall, there were in each Division thereof **Foreiros** Mayores or Cheife Farmers, men powerfule, arrogant, and Exorbitant violators, Ecclesiastiques as well as Civil; whose manner of Government was absolute, bringing the inferior sort of us so much under, and made so small accompt of them, as comparatively wee may say the Elephant doeth of the Ant......

Wherefore, we humbly beseech your Majesty for the love of God and the wounds of Jesus Christ, to take pity and compassion on us by not consenting to alienate us from your Government, and the Obedience thereof upon any Consideration or agreement whatsoever; neither to permitt any more **Foreiros** Mayores in this Island." Petition to Charles II in Khan, *Anglo-Portuguese Negotiations*, O.U.P., p. 451 *et. seq.*

Fresco (subst., a cool wind, see p. 161).

The following quotation not only illustrates the use of the above word in Anglo-India but furnishes a very vivid and interesting account of the hot season in Gujarat.

1689.—"In the Middle of *May*, before the *Southerly* Winds set in, which bring the Rains along with them, the Air at *Surat* is so very dry, that it licks up the Moisture in the Pen, before we are able to write it out; and so intensely Hot, especially about 3 in the Afternoon, that we cannot endure the standing for any long time upon the Grass, where the Sun's Beams have their full force. This causes our sprinkling the Floors of our Chambers frequently with Water, to create a kind of **Fresco** in them, during this Season, and makes us Employ our Peons in Fanning of us with Murchals made of Peacock's Feathers, four or five Foot long, in the time of our Entertainments and when we take our Repose." Ovington, *Voyage to Surat*, O.U.P., pp. 82 and 83.

Fusta (a pinnace or small ship, with sails, or oars).—Anglo-Ind. *fusto, fuste* (obs.). These forms are not in the *O.E.D.*

1614.—"The king keepeth there (Reshire) continually 100 **fustoes** and galleys with them to cut off all passengers that offer to go from Ormus to Balsora." Foster, *Letters*, Vol. II (*1613–1615*), p 146.

1615.—"It is hoped that the Osiander will be there to carry them before the **fustes** can arrive." *Ibidem*, Vol. III, p. 19.

Galeota (a small galley, see p. 164).

The following note of Foster (*Letters*, Vol. III, p 296) throws new light on the derivation of Anglo-Ind. *gallevat* which Dalgado says is derived from the

Port. *galeota*, which is also the view of the *O.E.D.*

"It has been suggested in the *Bombay Gazetteer* (Vol. XIII, p. 717) that the term *jolly-boat* is derived from galivat: the native name for large row-boats much in use on the west coast of India; and this etymology has been adopted by Sir Henry Yule (*Hobson-Jobson*) and Admiral Smyth (*Sailors' Wordbook*). But *jollyvatt* as an English word is at least as old as 1495–97 (see Oppenheim's *Naval Accounts and Inventories*, Navy Records Society, Vol. III, p. 193, etc.), and there seems to be every probability that it is simply a corruption of *galliot*, a small galley. If there be any direct relation between the English and the Indian term, it is more likely that the latter was derived from the former than the former from the latter."

Here is an Anglo-Indian form of this word not chronicled in *Hobson-Jobson* nor in the *O.E.D.*

1642.—"The Portuguese passengers were now put into their **jellowatt.**" Foster, *Eng. Fact.* (*1642–1645*), p. 240.

Gallina (a hen): Anglo-Ind. *gallina*, a name given reproachfully to the Portuguese by English sailors in the seventeenth century.

1690.—"The *Portuguese* are mightily sunk, as well in their Courage, as in their Fame and Fortune, and are found to be such contemptible Enemies, that they are seldom discours'd of but with Reproach by the name of **Gallina's**, i.e. Hen-Hearted Fellow's." Ovington, *Voyage to Surat*, O.U.P., p. 254.

Gelva, more us. **gelba** (a small vessel used in the Red Sea). Anglo-Ind. *jeloa, jellia.* Not in the *O.E.D.*

The Port. word is from the Ar. *jilba.* Did Anglo-Ind. receive the word directly from Ar. or through Portuguese? Probably from the latter, regard being had to the forms above and to the fact that Portuguese chroniclers use the word from as early as the beginning of the sixteenth century.

1634.—"And now both their and our small vessells will be more usefull than ever, for there's noe thought of trade into the Bay without them, our greater shipps ridinge so farre from the shoare, and the Kinge of Arrackans **jelliaes** or small boats of warre ever scoutinge 'twixt them and the land." Foster, *Eng. Fact.* (*1634–1636*), p. 43.

Gentio (a Hindu, see p. 167).

Here are early instances of the use of this term in Anglo-India.

1642.—"Whither Your Worshipps have imployment or no, men cannot goe naked, as the **Gentews** doe.'" Foster, *Eng. Fact.* (*1642–1645*), p. 54.

1645.—"The manning of her [the *Advice*] is a difficulty unless they take some soldiers out of the Fort and fill up with '**Jentue saylors**'." *Ibidem*, p. 282.

Below is an early instance of this term employed in the sense of the Telugu language:

1645.—"This instant wee received a letter from the King by two of our owne servants. . . The translate of that letter out of **Jentue** into English we send unto you for your perusall." Foster, *Eng. Fact.* (*1642–1645*), p. 291.

Jaca (jack-fruit, see p. 178).

The citation below is of interest, not only because it is of a fairly early date, but because it helps to show what keen observers the old travellers were, and how keenly and sympathetically they were interested in obtaining and setting down information about the fauna or flora new to them.

1637.—"The ancients called this island [Ceylon] the healthy, pleasant, fertile, flourishing and rich Taprobane. Healthy on account of its temperate climate and lovely air: fertile owing to numerous streams of excellent water...... ; pleasant owing to the fact that most of its mountains and forests are filled with aromatic cassia or cinnamon...., or else of great leafy fruit-trees like the bread-fruit which bears a sort of apple of huge size, called **Jack-fruit**. Outside they are covered with small prickles which, although sharp to the touch, do not prevent one's getting at the kernel, which is enclosed in a yellow, sweet pulp, very pleasant to the taste. From this pulp, and from the kernel many dishes are prepared which are most excellent and delicious. Mother Nature, in her foresight, perceiving that the branches would not suffice to support so great a weight, arranged for this fruit to sprout from the trunk itself, by throwing out roots or stems, which are so strong that, unless you have a knife or other sharp instrument, it is difficult to get them off." Manrique, *Travels*, Hak. Soc., Vol. I, pp. 448 and 449.

Jagra (coarse sugar, see p. 179).

The quotations from Fitch and Terry (p. 179) show how by *jagra* they meant the 'coco-nut or the coco-nut tree'. The latter of the two citations below will show how *jaggery* was a term applied to spirit obtained from palm-sugar, and the former how the form *jagra* in its correct meaning of 'palm sugar', was in vogue earlier than *jaggery*.

1630.—"April 18. Took some coconuts and '**Jagra**' from a Malabar junk." Foster, *Eng. Fact.* (*1630–1633*), p 133.

1631.—Wedell......brought a hog's head of **Jaggery** for his owne drinking at sea." *Court Minutes* for May 20, 1631.

Jangada (a raft formed by two boats lashed together with boards across them, see p. 181).

The quotations below are of interest because they contain

a new form of this word, not mentioned in *Hobson-Jobson* nor found in the *O.E.D.*

1632.—"They have got all the **sangrees** of this side Bapatly and of all the rivers unto the iland among them, and all the towne boats are to goe to them this day." Foster, *Eng. Fact.* (*1630–1633*), p. 233.

1678.—"In the morning we went downe to the River about 2 miles from Collepellee [Kallepalli] where was two great Metchlepatam Boates, and two **Sangarees** or Gun boates." *The Diaries of Streynsham Master* (*1675–80*), ed. Temple, Vol. II, p. 139.

Manga (mango).

The quotations below go to show the various forms that were current in Anglo-India before the present form became stabilised.

1615.—"Two jars of **manges** at rupees 4½." Foster, *Letters*, Vol. III (1615), p. 41.

"Two jars of **mangas**." *Ibidem*, p. 83.

"I had in her some few cloves, the rest of her cargazon being jars of pickled nutmegs and **mangoes**." *Ibidem*, p. 286.

For the form "mongoes" see quotation from Fryer under 'Achar,' in Supplement.

1608–1611.—"On the further side [near 'Nonsary Gate' in Surat] are divers faire tombes, with a goodly paved court pleasant to behold, behind which groweth a small grove of **manga** tree whither the citizens goe forth to banquet." William Finch, in Foster, *Early Travels*, O.U.P., p. 134.

Manilha (bracelet, see p. 216).

"They [the women of Goa] wear also bracelets, called **Manile** from the hand up to the elbow." Manrique, *Travels*, Hak. Soc.

"**Manila**, or wrist jewel." Hamilton, *New Account*, Vol. I, p. 303.

Marinha (a salt pan). Anglo-Ind. *marinho* (obs.).

"Pomela. A *marinho* of salt x 21.01. 35." *Yearley Rent Rowle of Bombaim*, in *Ind. Antiq.*, Vol LIV, p. 2.

Mesquita (a mosque, see p. 225).

Below is a quotation from an Anglo-Indian writer which contains a form of *masjid* neither mentioned in *Hobson-Jobson* nor in the *O.E.D.*

1664.—"A fresh recrute of men coming of about 20 more, wee than began to consider what houses neere us might be most prejuditiall, and on one side wee tooke possession of [a] pagod or Banian idol temple, which was just under our house......, on the other a Moorish **Mescete** where severall peoplo were harboured." *The Rev. John L. Escaliot's Account of Sivaji's Raid upon Surat* in *Ind. Antiq.*, Vol. L, p. 317.

Mestiço (a half-breed, see p. 226).

The following contains a very strange Anglo-Indian form of the word not mentioned in *Hobson-Jobson* but in the *O.E.D.*, as 'mostesa'.

1652.—"Friar Ephraim who was pastor or curate unto the **Mostezaes** of Madraspatam." Foster, *Eng. Fact.* (*1651–1654*), p. 92.

Monção (monsoon, see p. 229).

Below is a very strange Anglo-Indian form which, if Yule's conjecture that the Anglo-Indian *monsoon* proceeds directly from the Dutch *monssoyn* or *monssoen* is correct, perhaps marks a transition stage between the present Anglo-Indian word and the Dutch term. It is not found in the *O.E.D.*

1642.—"Wee have in this our 15 or 16 monthes residence throughly experienced the trade of this place, and doe finde that the first markets at the begining of the **monzoane** is most proffitablest.... Besids the country people, having then fully supplyed themselves, retorns not till the next **moonzoane** to replenish their wants" Foster. *Eng. Fact.* (*1642–1645*), pp. 57 and 58.

Morador (an inhabitant). Konk. *morãdor*.—Anglo-Ind. *moredor* (obs.).

In the Konkani of Goa the word is used in the specific sense of an inhabitant of a village of which he is not a member or a '*componente*'.

1632.—"Whereon one Grua Redie [Guruva Reddi], a **moredor** of Mondrero,... gathered head, to the number of three or four hundred in armes." Foster, *Eng. Fact.* (*1630–1633*), p. 233.

Morim (a thin white cloth for shirting). Anglo-Ind. *mooree, morye, moory* (obs.).

The *O.E.D.* derives the Anglo-Ind. word from Portuguese, but Sir Richard Temple (*Ind. Antiq.*, Vol. L, Supp. p. 9) is of the view that the Port. *morim* is more likely a corruption of *mûrî* than that *mûrî* is a corruption of *morim*, as it was a common custom of the Portuguese in adopting Oriental names ending in *i* to add a final *m* or *n*. *Morim* means 'Moor cloth', i.e. cloths intended primarily for Mohammedan wear. It was cotton cloth manufactured principally in the Nellore district of Madras for sale to the Mohammedans of the Malay peninsula. It is identical with *Salampore.* The earliest instance of the use of this word in the *O.E.D.* is of 1696.

1618.—"Such severall sorts of goods as Bantam requires, viz. white **moryes**, white percallaes, white salamporyes, white and redde beteles, dragons malaia, dragons salala, fine gobare serasses, fine tappy serasses, fine and course Japon tappes, tape chindees, tape anacke, caine goulons, and such like." Foster, *Eng. Fact.* (*1618–1621*), pp. 42 and 43.

1644.—"Goods most propper for this place are all sorts of Mesulapatam or Coast clothing, as long cloth, **morees** sallampores, homoomies, salooes, serasses, etc." Foster, *Eng. Fact.* (*1642–45*), p. 223.

The above citations contain some very uncommon names of textiles.

Ouvidor (a magistrate, see p. 245).

Here is an early instance of the use of this term in Anglo-India. The word is not in the *O.E.D.*

1644.—"Did their best to 'corrupt both the Kings Fitscall and **Ovedores**' with offers of money to procure leave to sell their goods this year and depart" Foster, *Eng. Fact.* (*1642–1645*), p. 224.

Padre (priest, see p. 245). Nicob. *pater.*

"In the seventeenth century at least, and probably much earlier Haensel speaks of *pater*=sorcerer, and Pere Barbe of *deos* and *reos*=God, as survivals of Portuguese missionaries." *Ind. Antiq.*, Vol. LX (Feb.), p. 38.

Pão (in the sense of 'loaf or boat shaped ingot of gold', see pp. 265 and 266). Anglo-Ind. *pam.*

1615.—"It is impossible to tell all the great riches and all the rare and beautiful things which these ships [trading between Japan and Goa] bring back; among others they bring much gold in ingots, which the Portuguese call **pandoro** (=*pão de ouro*). Pyrard, *Voyage*, Hak. Soc., Vol. II, p. 176.

1634.—"The galliots from that country brought rich cargoes, insomuch that two thousand **Loaves of gold** were registered in the royal customshouse [at Goa], to say nothing of the gold and merchandise that escape registration." Foster, *Eng. Fact.*, *1634–36*, p. 33.

1676.—"Taking all chances, he offered the piece to Marin for two **pains** of Chinese gold, and the golden **pain** is equal to 600 livres of our money." Tavernier, *Travels in India*, ed. Ball, O.U.P., Vol. II, pp. 110 and 111.

1676.—"They were instructed to present to the General of Batavia 200 **loaves** (*pains*) of gold to redeem the royal fortress." *Ibidem*, p. 238.

"We, Edward Jones and John Scattergood......confess to have received from the hands of Manuel Tavacho, resident of the city of Macao, one parcel wrapped in white cloth with fine red wax seals......in which it is said are contained fifteen **pams**, one bar and three pieces of good gold......" *The Scattergoods and the East India Co.*, in *Ind. Antiq.*, Vol. LX, Suppl. p. 77.

The term '*pão de ouro*' (and inversely *ouro de pão*, to denote a superior quality of the metal) was used by Portuguese chroniclers from as early as 1545. See Dalgado, *Glossário Lus. As.*, Vol. II, p. 165. The expression '*pão*' was also used of silver, whence the phrase '*pão de prata*' (silver ingot). In the East India Co.'s records these ingots whether of gold or silver were usually called 'shoes'. See *Hobson-Jobson*, *s.v.* Shoe of Gold.

Parau (a small vessel used in war or trade, see p. 269).

Here is an earlier instance of the use of this term in Anglo-India than any mentioned in *Hobson-Jobson.*

1653.—"Another **prau** sent to find the *Dove*... Have just heard that the Dove has been taken. She might have been saved had there been enough Englishmen here to man the **prau** instead of natives." Foster, *Eng. Fact.* (*1651–1654*), p. 190.

Fryer uses the very unusual form 'provoes'.

1673.—"They are owners of several small **Provoes,** of the same make, and Canooses, cut out of one intire piece of Wood." Fryer, *East India*, Vol. 1, p. 65.

Partido (a consignment). Anglo-Ind. *partido, partitho* (obs.). Not in *O.E.D.*

1617.—"Some good quantities we procured.... and to enlarge our investments the more, we bought also some **partidoes** on credit to pay at two and three months' time." Foster, *Letters*, Vol. VI, p. 236.

"After the **partitho** of silk he took was made up and fit to be embarked it lay there three weeks and above before he durst ship it." *Ibidem,* p. 139.

Patacho (a pinnace). Anglo-Ind. *patash* (obs.) This form is not met with in the *O.E.D.*

1630.—"Do not believe the information regarding the number of frigates and '**patashes**', for Hari Vaisya's brother writes from Damān that the force there consists only of the fourteen frigates.... and eight 'fustoes' belonging to Ruy Freire" Foster, *Eng. Fact.* (*1630–1633*), p. 98.

Pateca (water-melon, see p. 275). Anglo-Ind. *pateca, putacho* (obs.).

1673.—"From hence [Elephanta] we sailed to the **Putachoes,** a Garden of Melons (**Putacho** being a melon)....." Fryer, *East India*, Hak. Soc., Vol. I, p. 195. See also under *Elephanta.*

Fryer's *Putachoes* was called in Portuguese *Ilha de Patecas* and in Anglo-India *Island* of *Pattecas*, see *Ind. Antiq.*, Vol. LIV, p. 3. By 1724 the 'Island of Patecas or Patachoes' came to be corrupted into 'Butcher's Island', the name by which this island near Bombay is still known to this day.

Paulista (a Jesuit, see p. 277). Malayal. *Paulistákkâr.*

Sampâluppâtirimâr (San Paolo Padres) and *Yêsuvittanmár* (Jesuits). See *Ind. Antiq.*, Vol. LVI, p. 85 n.—Anglo-Ind. *Paulistine.*

1673.—" Near our Landing-place [at Bandra] stood a College, not inferior to the Building, nor much unlike those of our Universities, belonging to the Jesuits here, more commonly called **Paulistines**....who live here very sumptuously, the greatest part of the Island being theirs." Fryer, *East India*, Hak. Soc., Vol. I, p. 183.

"The **Paulistines** enjoy the biggest of all the Monasteries at St. *Roch*; in it is a Library, an Hospital, and an Apothecary's Shop well furnished with Medicines." Fryer, *East India*, Vol. II, p. 11.

Peru (turkey, see p. 283).

We have said that the turkey was introduced into India by the Portuguese (p. 284). The quotations below are links in the story of its dissemination throughout the East and go to show how by the end of the 17th century it had become a fairly common bird in India.

1615.—William Edwards from Adgmeare [Ajmere] writes to the East India Co.: "Three or four turkeycocks and hens would do well for the Mogul; he hath two cocks but no hens, and would esteem much of their brood". Foster, *Letters*, Vol. III, p. 19.

1617.—Edward Connok in Persia writes to the East India Co.: "I had almost forgotten to adjoin these other toys by this king required: ....Turkey cocks and hens, as many as you please to send. He hath caused me write for peacocks into India, where are plenty. Neither them nor turkeys he never saw; this country affordeth none." Foster, *Letters*, Vol. VI, p. 44.

1678-9.—"The Havaldar [of 'Armagon'] brought us two sheep, a goate, a Hogg, 2 Turkeys, 10 hens, a great deal of rice, butter, spice, Toddy, Corne and grass for our horses, and gave all the Peons rice." *The Diaries of Streynsham Master*, ed. Temple, Vol. II, p. 131.

Procurador (attorney, see p. 301).

Here is an early instance of the use of this word in Anglo-India. Not mentioned in the *O.E.D.*

1615.—"His name is Usseph Chann, who desired me he might present me to the king and be my **Procuradore**." Foster, *Letters*, Vol. III, p. 14.

Risco (risk). Anglo-Ind. *risgoe* (obs.).

1676.—"This Deponent answered Mr. Hall, the Company had already run the **Risgoe** thus farr and might now run it soe much further, and Reape the profitt of it themselves." *The Diaries of Streynsham Master*, ed. Temple, Vol. I, p. 485.

Scrivão (clerk or writer, see p. 149).

1615.—"To the **scrivano** of the Custom House" Foster, *Letters*, Vol. III, p. 100.

Below is an unusual form not found in *Hobson-Jobson*.

1623.—"The reason why the bakers, etc., have not come down in the behaviour of the '**screivas**', etc., in custom house, who will not give them a chittee without som feeling [feeing ?]: but on his threatening to go again to the Governor the desired 'screete' was granted." See under *Escrito*, p. 390. Foster, *Eng. Fact.* (*1622-1623*), p. 265.

Senhor (lord, see p. 325).

From the quotation below it would appear that, just as Indians used to give this title 'Senhor' to Englishmen, the latter used it of the chief foreign officials in India, not necessarily Portuguese—in the passage in question they are all Dutch.

1676.—"Concerning the affairs of the Dutch Company in this place [Metchlepatam] I understand that **Senr.** Coler....is by orders lately come from Batavia to be Governor of Pullicat... **Senr.** Peter Smith...is to be Cheife at Metchlepatam, and **Senr.** Hartsing, the Cheife at Golcondah." *The Diaries of Streynsham Master*, ed. Temple, Vol. I, p. 297. This is an earlier instance of the use of this word than the one in the *O.E.D.* which is of 1795.

Sombra (lit. shadow; also favour, protection). Anglo-Ind. *sombre* (obs.). Not found in this sense in the *O.E.D.*

"If no sales be effected, the goods should be taken on to Ahmadābād, 'under the cover of your **sombre**' and delivered to Clement." Foster, *Eng. Fact.* (*1624-1629*), p. 79.

Sumbaia (a profound reverence, see pp. 330 and 332).

1614.—"We delivered his Majesty's letter, obtaining what we required, only confined to such orders and customs (though bad) as the Dutch before us had brought in as of **Sombay** or presents, customs, rents." Foster, *Letters*, Vol. II (*1613-1615*), p. 112.

Taça (a cup, see p. 338).

In supporting the view that the Anglo-Ind. *toss* was derived from Portuguese and not from Persian, we remarked that the Persian *tās* 'a cup' had not acquired currency in Hindi or Urdu and that the word for 'cup' in the former was *pyālā*. The following quotation appears to bear out our statement.

1608-11.—"At the end are drawne many portraitures of the King [of Delhi] in state sitting amongst his women, one holding a flask of wine, another a napkin, a third presenting the **peally** [small cup]; behind, one punkawing [fanning], another holding his sword." William Finch, in Foster, *Early Travels*, O.U.P., p. 164.

Terranquim (a small swift bark, see p. 343).

We have pointed out that this Portuguese form is not the original of the Anglo-Ind. *trankey* which comes from the Pers. *trankeh*. Here are a couple of passages in which

Anglo-Indian forms of the word, different from those mentioned before, are to be found and they are of a date earlier than those in *Hobson-Jobson*.

1645.—"Their goods were transferred to a 'greate **tranka**'." Foster, *Eng. Fact.* (*1642-1645*), p. 273.

1651.—"The Arrabs of Muskatt soe much awe them [the Portuguese] with vessells which they have taken from them, and their own **tranckett**s, that they dare not at this tyme pass in the Gulph, though they are (as they tearme themselves) an Armadoe (besides theise merchantmen) of six garrobs" [see *Garopo*, p. 166]. Foster, *Eng. Fact.* (*1651-1654*), p. 64.

Topaz (a Portuguese half breed, see p. 346).

There are a number of instances of this word, used by the Jesuits in the 16th and early 17th centuries in the sense of 'interpreter', given in the *Ind. Antiq.*, Vol. LII, p. 263.

Tornado (violent storm). *Anglo-Ind. turnado, turnathe, tronado* (obs.). The last two forms are not in the *O.E.D.*

1617.—"And being in the latitude of the Cape we steered away S.S.E. with a meridian compass till we came into 0° 24′ of N. latitude, where we met the **turnath**[es?] and lay becalmed and troubled with the variable winds twenty-one days." Foster, *Letters*, Vol. VI, p. 290.

1617.—"But to proceed: you may please to know that the last of April we passed the **turnathes**." *Ibidem*, p. 291.

1690.—"Here likewise we were affrighted with a **Turnado** which, without Care and speedy handing of our Sails, might have endanger'd our Ship." Ovington, *Voyage to Surat*, O.U.P., p. 27.

1630.—"From the 10th May unto the 6th currant, we accompted ourselves to bee in the **Tronados**, it being extraordinary variable weather, as Calmes, sodaine and violent gusts, the wind on all points of the compasse in 24 howeres." Mundy, *Travels*, Vol. III, pt. I, p. 30.

Toronja ('the pomelo', see p. 350).

In connection with this fruit and the question about its introduction into India, it is useful to quote Prof. S. H. Hodivala (*Ind. Antiq.*, LXI, p. 32) who says that the *Citrus decumana* is mentioned in the *Bâburnâma*, if Erskine's and Mr. Beveridge's interpretation of the emperor's description of the *Sadâphal* is to be relied on. "The *Sadâphal*," he writes, "is another orange-like fruit. This is pear-shaped, colours like the quince, ripens sweet, but not to the sickly-sweetness of the orange" (*naranj*). Tran. A. S. Beveridge, p. 512. If the *Sadâphal* of Bâbur was the *Citrus decumana*, the fruit must have been known in India long before the XVII century".

Tromba (a species of reed met with near the Cape of Good Hope).—Anglo-Ind. *strumblowes*. Not in the *O.E.D.*

1615.—"Fifty or sixty leagues out are seen floating in vast numbers the stalks of reeds, with about nine or ten reeds (more or less) attached to each stalk, these are called *trombas*." Pyrard. *Voyage*, Hak. Soc., Vol. I, p 20.

"These *trombas* are a kind of great canes, about the bignesse of a man's arm, and three or four foot long, which flote upon the water with their roots." Mandelslo, *Travels*, cit. by Gray in note to passage above.

1624.—"*March* 27. Sailed from the Downs. *July* 13. 'Mett with weeds called **strumblowes**, a good sine of neerness' to land." Foster, *Eng. Fact.* (*1624–1629*), p. 23.

Tufão (hurricane, see p. 353).

Below is an early Anglo-Indian reference:

1617.—"Two of these Dutch ships were full laden with silk and stuffs which they had taken from the Chinas, as also two junks with the like; but by means of a storm or **tuffon** the two Holland ships and one junk were driven ashore." Foster, *Letters*, Vol. VI, p. 260.

Tutanaga (an alloy, see p. 356).

The following quotation contains an Anglo-Indian form of this word unrecorded in *Hobson-Jobson* or in the *O.E.D.*

"Their **tutinggle** they [the Dutch] bring from Tiwan" [Taiwan, i.e., Formosa]. *Eng. Fact.* (*1642-1643*), p 36.

Varanda (verandah, see p. 358).

The citations below give evidence of earlier use of this term in Anglo-India than do those in *Hobson-Jobson.*

1718.—"But if the making of such a Compound and **Virandas** for depositing and securing the Merchants Goods will be so great a convenience....we permit you to make it" *Old Fort William in Bengal*, ed. Wilson, Vol. I, p. 37.

1755.—"Ordered Mr. Bartholomew Plaisted to survey the **Verandah.**" *Ibidem*, p. 34.

1756.—"They [the Nabob's troops] had infinitely the advantage over us in this attack as they could fire upon our men from the tops, windows and **verandas** of houses which stood close to and overlooked our lines and batteries." *Ibidem*, Vol. III, p. 295.

Visitador (official visitor), see pp. 367 and 368.

The quotation below bears out the statement made before (p. 368) that the Dutch adopted this Portuguese word for one of their officials.

1614.—"The first of this month arrived here a Dutch ship coming in three months from Bantam, and in her there comes the **Visitador** General for the Dutch to visit these coasts." Foster, *Letters*, Vol. II (1613–1615), p. 165.

ALPHABETICAL LISTS OF WORDS IN ASIATIC LANGUAGES DERIVED FROM OR INFLUENCED BY PORTUGUESE

Attention to the following points will facilitate reference: Against every Asiatic vocable is set the Portuguese word from which it derives. Vocables printed in italics are not listed herein for reasons mentioned in the Introduction and in all such cases the English equivalent of the Portuguese word is given after it within brackets. The vernacular idiom is sometimes mentioned after the Asiatic word derived from Portuguese in which case it is invariably enclosed within brackets, thus: *Negosiānt* (*yepāri*) Negociante (merchant). The peculiar sense which a word has acquired is set in quotation marks and brackets. The following additional abbreviations occur: S=Supplement; (S) denotes that the word to which it is annexed must be looked for in the Supplement, and (C) that the word is current only among Christians; eccles=ecclesiastical term; mus=musical term; leg=legal term; med=medical term; arch=archaic; us. fig.=used figuratively.

1. Achinese

Achinese		*Portuguese*	*Achinese*		*Portuguese*
Ambar	..	Ambar	? Masigit, mesígit, misígit		Mesquita
? Amin	..	Amen	Meja súrat	..	Mesa
Ánas, anus	..	Ananás	Menátu	..	Mainato
? Apam	..	Apa	Menisan, melisan		Munição
Bakum, bakon		Tabaco	Mentiga	..	Manteiga
Bandála	..	Bandola	Mestol	..	Pistola
Banké	..	Banco	Miskina	..	Mister
Bási, besoi	..	Bacia	Nona, ñoña	..	Dona
Boludo	..	Veludo	Pásu	..	Vaso
Beranda	..	Varanda	Pilor	..	Pelouro
Biula	..	Viola	Pingan	..	Palangana
? Bói	..	Bolo	Pípa	..	Pipa
? Chap	..	Chapa	? Piring	..	Pires
Dádu	..	Dado	Rúda	..	Roda
Fítah, pita	..	Fita	? Rupiya	..	Rupia
Gagab	..	Gago	Ryah	..	Rial
Gáji	..	Gago	Sábtu, sáptu	..	Sabado
Júdi	..	Jogar	Sábun	..	Sabão
Kafíri	..	Cafre	? Ságu, ságe	..	Sagu
Kamija, kaméja		Camisa	Selada	..	Salada
*Kápal	..	Cavalo	Seladád, serdádu		Soldado
Kapitan	..	Capitão	Sepatu	..	Sapato
Kásut	..	Calçado	Sita	..	Citar
Kerábu	..	Cravo	? Támbu	..	Tambor
? Kértas	..	Carta or Cartaz	Túkar, túka	..	Trocar
? Khandél	..	Candil			
Lamári	..	Armário			
Lélang	..	Leilão			

2. Anglo-Indian

Anglo-Indian		*Portuguese*	*Anglo-Indian*		*Portuguese*
Abada	..	Abada	Adarga	..	Adarga (S)
Achar	..	Achar, also in S	Aduano	..	Aduana (S)

Anglo-Indian	*Portuguese*
Albacore ..	Albacora
Albatross ..	Alcatras, also in S
Albricias ..	Alviçaras (S)
Aldea ..	Aldeia, also in S
Alfandica, alfandia, alfandira, alfandiga	Alfândega, also in S
Aljofar ..	Aljôfar
Alligator ..	Lagarto
Almadee ..	Almadia (S)
Almirah, almyra	Armário
Almode, almoodæ	Almude (S)
Amah ..	Ama
Ananas ..	Ananás
Anile, neel ..	Anil
Ap, hopper ..	Apa
Areca ..	Areca
Armado ..	Armada (S)
Arrack, rack ..	Araca
Assegay ..	Azagaia
Atæ ..	Ata (S)
Ayah ..	Aia
Balachong, blachong	Balchão
Balty ..	Balde
Bamboo ..	Bambu
Banana ..	Banana
? Banda ..	Bandel (S)
Bandejah ..	Bandeja
Bangue ..	Bangue
Bankshall ..	Bangaçal (S)
Banyan, Banyan-day, Banyan fight, Banyan hospital	Banean, also in S
Barracodo ..	Barricada (S)
Barreck, barrecoe	Barrica (S)
Barsa ..	Braça (S)
Batel, batelo, botella, botilla	Batel, also in S
Batta ..	Bata, also in S
Batta ..	Batão, also in S
Batte, batty ..	Bate
Bayadère ..	Bailadeira
Beatello, betteela	Beatilha
Beech-de-mer	Bicho do mar
Becombu, bube	Biombo (S)
Benzoin, benjamin	Beijoim, benjoim
Betel ..	Bétele, bétel betle, bétere, betre
Bilimbi, blimbee	Bilimbim
Boca-mortis, bocamortass, bukmar	Bacamarte (S)
Bolango ..	Combalenga (S)
Bonito ..	Bonito
Bonze ..	Bonzo
Botickeer ..	Botiqueiro
Botica ..	Boutique, also in S
Boy ..	Bói, also in S

Anglo-Indian	*Portuguese*
Brab ..	Brava
Breda do Marr	Breda do Mar (S)
Brinjaul ..	Beringela
Brinquo ..	Brinco (S)
Budgrook ..	Bazaruco
Buffalo, buffola, buffolo	Búfalo, also in S
Buffath ..	Abafado (S)
?Buggalow, budgerow	Bairel
Bulse ..	Bolsa (S)
Bumba ..	Bomba
? Bus ..	Basta
Cabook ..	Cabouco
Caffer, caffre, caffro, coffer, cofferie	Cafre, also in S
Calabash ..	Calabaça
Calputtee ..	Calafate
Calumba, Colombo root	Calumba
Cameeze ..	Camisa
Caminha ..	Caminhar (S)
Campoo ..	Campo, also in S
? Compound	Campo
Canada (us. in Ceylon)	*Canada* (a liquid measure)
Candykens ..	Canequim (S)
Cangue ..	Canga
Capado ..	Capado (S)
Captain mor ..	Capitão mór (S)
Carambola ..	Carambola
Caravel, Carvel	Caravela
Caro ..	Caro (S)
Cash ..	Caixa
Cashew, cadju, cadjew	Caju, also in S
Caste ..	Casta
Castees ..	Castiço, also in S
Catechu, cutch caut	Cate, cato, cáchu
Cattanar, cassanar	Catãnar, caçanar
Cavallerous ..	Cavaleiro (S)
Cavally ..	Cavala
Cavelurire ..	Cavalaria (S)
Centipede centipse	Centopeia, also in S
Cesta ..	Cesta (S)
Chabee ..	Chave
Chaw, chawe ..	Chá, also in S
Chince, chint ..	Chincho (S)
Chite ..	Chita (S)
? Chop, chapa chapaed, chopt, chaup'd	Chapa, also in S
Chunam, chinam, chownam	Chuname, also in S
Cobra ..	Cobra
Cobra de capello, cobra capella	Cobra de capelo
Cobra manilla, minelle	Cobra manila
Cocoa, cocoanut	Côco

Anglo-Indian	Portuguese	Anglo-Indian	Portuguese
Coco de mer ..	Côco do mar	? Factory ..	Feitoria
Coir ..	Cairo	? Falaun ..	Fulano
Comprador, compradore	Comprador, also in S	Fazendar, fazendari	Fazendeiro
Conjee, cangee, caugee	Canja, also in S	Fetish, fateish	Feitiço, also in S
Conserta ..	Concerto (S)	Fidalgo, phydalgo	Fidalgo (S)
Coprah ..	Copra	Flamingo ..	Flamengo, flamenco
Corge, coorge	Corja	Foogath ..	Afogado (S)
Cornac ..	Cornaca	Fogass ..	Fogaça
Corral ..	Curral, also in S	Forall ..	Foral (S)
Covid, covedee, cobda	Côvado, also in S	Foras, forasdárs	Fôro
Cranny ..	Carrane	Foreiro ..	Foreiro (S)
Cumra ..	Câmara	Freguezia ..	Freguesia
Curry ..	Caril	Fresco ..	Fresco (S)
Curtass, cartasse	Cartaz (S)	Fusto, fuste ..	Fusta (S)
Cuspadore ..	Cuspidor	Gallevat ..	Galeota, also in S
Cuttanee ..	Cotonia	Gallina ..	Gallinha (S)
Cutter ..	Catur	Gentoo, gentue, gentew, jentue	Gentio, also in S
Discalsadoe ..	Discalsado	Ghamella ..	Gamela
Dispense [1] ..	Despensa (S)	Girga ..	Igreja.
Dorado ..	Dourado	Godown ..	Gudão
Eagle-wood ..	Águil, áquila, also in S	Goglet ..	Gorgoleta
Elephanta, ofante, olliphante	Elephanta, also in S	Grab ..	Garopo
? Factor ..	Feitor	Gram ..	Grão
		Guava ..	Goiaba
		? Hackery ..	Carreta
		Hollander ..	Holandês (Dutchman)
		Imprest (us. in Ceylon)	Emprestimo (a loan)

[1] ["Pucka built Bungalow ... the accommodations comprise a sitting room with open veranda on three sides, ... **Dispense,** cook room, etc., ..." *The Bombay Courier,* 2nd May, 1835.]

Anglo-Indian	*Portuguese*
Jack	Jaca
Jaggery, jagri, jagra	Jagra, also in S
Jangar, sangree, sangaree	Jangada
Jeloa, jellia	Gelva (S)
? Jillmill	Janela
Joy	Joia
Kalay	Calaim
Keby	Quebe
Kittysol, kitsol	Quita-sol
Lacre, lacquer, lacker	Lacre
Ladúru (us. in Ceylon)	Lázaro
Lanchara	Lanchara
Lanho, lagne, lanha	Lanha
Lascar, lascarin, lascoreen	Lascarim
Lawad	Louvado
Leelam, neelam	Leilão
Lime	Lima
Linguist	Lingua
? Lorcha	Lorcha
? Macareo	Macaréu
Maioral (us. in Ceylon of the head of the irrigation staff)	*Maioral* (superior)
Maistry, mistry, mistery	Mestre
Maladoo, manadoo	Malhado or Molhado
Manchua	Manchua
Mandadore	Mandador
Mandarin	Mandarim
Manga Voluchoes	Mangas de veludo
Mangelin	Mangelim
Mango	Manga, also in S
Mangosteen	Mangostão
Manilla	Manilha, also in S
Margosa	Amargosa
Marinho	Marinha (S)
Martil, martol	Martelo
Maune, maund	Mão
Medeeda	Medida
Moley	Môlho
Monsoon	Monção, also in S
Moorah	Mura
Mooree, morye	Morim (S)
Moor, moorman	Mouro
Morador	Morador (S)
Mort-de-chien	Mordexim
? Mosque, muskeet, mescete	Mesquita, also in S
Mosquito	Mosquito
Muncheel, manjeel	Machila
Mungoose	Manguço, mangusto
Mustees, mestiz, mustechees, mostesa, mistaradoes	Mestiço, also in S
Muster	Mostra
Mustira	? Mosteiro

Anglo-Indian	*Portuguese*
Nabob	Nababo
Naik, naique	Naique
Nair	Naire
Neep, nipa	Nipa
Nigger	Negro
Oart	Horta
Ollah	Ola
Ortolan	Hortulana
Ovidore	Ouvidor, also in S
Padre, padri	Padre
Padroadist	Padroadista
Padroado	Padroado
Pagar	Pagar
Pagoda	Pagode
Palanquin, palankeen	Palanquim
Palmyra	Palmeira
Pam	Pão (S)
Pamplee, pamplet, paumphlet, pomfret	Pâmpano
Payapa, papaw	Papaia
Pardao, pardaw perdao	Pardáo
Parao, praw, prow	Parau, paró, also in S
Partido, partitho	Partido (S)
Pataca	Pataca
Patacoon	Patacão
Patash	Patacho (S)
Pattamar, patimar	Patamar

Anglo-Indian	*Portuguese*
Pattarero, pateraro petarero, paterero	Pedeiro, pederero
Paulist, Paulistine	Paulista, also in S
Pedareea, pedaeria	Pedraria
Peirie	Peres
Peon	Peão
? Penguin	Pingue
Pial	Poial
Pertenças	Pertenças
Picotta, picottah	Picota
Pindar	Pinda
Pintado	Pintado
? Poonac	Pinaca
? Porgo, pork, purgo	Piroga
Povo	Povo
Procurador, procuradore	Procurador, also in S
Propagandist	Propagandista
Puckery	Púcaro
Putacho	Pateca (S)
Raia	Raia
? Ransadoes	Arrasador (S)
Raseed	Receibo
Reaper	Ripa
Reas, rees, res, rayes, rues	Rial, réis
Rolong	Rolão
Recado, recarder	Recado
Reinol, reynol reynold	Reinol

Anglo-Indian	*Portuguese*
Rende ..	Renda
Rendedare ..	Arrendador (S)
Rendero, rendere	Rendeiro
Risgoe ..	Risco (S)
Sable-fish ..	Savel
? Sago ..	Sagu
Sagwire ..	Sagúeiro
Salpicado ..	Salpicado
Screetore, screwtore, scriptor, scritoire	Escritório, also in S
Scrito, screet	Escrito, also in S
Scrivan, scrivano	Escrivão, also in S
Seer,—seir fish	Serra
Seguaty ..	Saguate
Senhor ..	Senhor (S)
Soldadoe ..	Soldado
Sombre ..	Sombra (S)
Sombrero, sumbarero, summerhead	Sombreiro
Stanck ..	Estanque (S)
Stevedore ..	Estivador
Stochado ..	Estocada (S)
Strumblowes	Tromba (S)
St. Thomas, St. Thomae	San-Tomé
Sumack ..	Sumaca
Sumatra ..	Samatra
Sumba, sumbaia, sumbra, sombay	Sumbaia, zumbaia, also in S
Supo ..	Sopa
Talapoin ..	Talapoi
Tank ..	Tanque
Teak ..	Teca
Tomback ..	Tambaca
Tootnague, tutinggle	Tutanaga, also in S
Topass, topaz	Topaz, also in S
? Toss ..	Taça
? Trankey ..	Terranquim
Trunk ..	Tronco
Turnado, turnathe, tronado	Tornado (S)
? Typhoon ..	Tufão, also in S
Varella ..	Varela
Veadore, Theadore	Vedor, Veador
Vellard, walade	Valado
Venetian ..	Veneziano
Ventoso ..	Ventosa
Veranda, verandah	Varanda
Verdure ..	Verdura
Vereador, veador	Vereador
Verge ..	Varzea, vargem, verga
Vindaloo ..	Vinha de alhos
Visitador ..	Visitador, also in S
Xerafine, sherapheen, xerephin	Xerafim
Yam ..	Inhame

3. Annamite

Annamite	*Portuguese*	*Annamite*	*Portuguese*
Át ven tô ..	Advento (Advent)	Lê missa ..	Missa
Bánh, bánh mì	Pão	Sábong ..	Sabão
? Calicê ..	Cális	*Thánh Ju de* ..	São José (St. Joseph)
? Cà-phe ..	Café		
? Chè ..	Chá	*Than Lô-ren-sô*	São Lourenço (St. Lawrence)
Cõc ..	Copo		
Gisang Baotishita	S. João Baptista (St. John Baptist)	? Thúôc ..	Tabaco
		Tú rac ..	Tronco

4. Arabic

Arabic	*Portuguese*	*Arabic*	*Portuguese*
Aainunnās ..	Ananás	? Dāyá ..	Aia
Anjar, anjara	Anchora	Espinkh, esfinkh, isfonkh, isfánkh, safankh, sifahk, sufank	Esponja
Arganún, argan, organ, orgon	Órgão		
Arshidiak ..	Arcediago		
Bābā, bābāvi..	Papa		
Bálsam balsám, bolasán, bolsán	Bâlsamo	Falaskiya, balaskiya	Frasco (us. in Egypt)
Bandeira, bandera, bandira, bandaira	Bandeira	Forn, furn ..	Fôrno
		Gabia ..	Gávea
		Galion ..	Galeão
? Baqalá ..	Baixel	Galitha ..	Galeota
Barkús ..	Barcaça	Kabút, kabábit	Capote
Barmíl, bermil, birmil, beramil, varil	Barril	Kalsat ..	Calçado
		Kastána, kastánia	Castanha
Barrima ..	Verruma	* Kirub ..	Querubim
Bāsāburth ..	Passaporte	Koba ..	Copo
Bobra, bubra	Abóbora	? Marmar, marmer	Marmore
Buqál ..	Bocal		
Chess, chiss ..	Gesso	Mez ..	Mesa

Arabic	Portuguese	Arabic	Portuguese
Musika, muzika, musikay, musiki, musikari	Música	Sabbat, sebath, sabat	Sapato
		Ṣabón, ṣabun	Sabão
? Naulun ..	Naulo	Salátha ..	Salada
? Qabá ..	Capa	Ṣaya ..	Saia
Qālāfat, qalfat, qāllaf	Calafate	Shāí ..	Cha
		Spáda ..	Espada
? Qamis ..	Camisa	Tambak ..	Tabaco
Qitár ..	Guitarra	Usthúra ..	História
Qumandán ..	Comandante	Vābúr ..	Vapor
Rial, riyál ..	Rial	Vérdiyán ..	Guarda

5. Assamese

Assamese	Portuguese	Assamese	Portuguese
Āchár ..	Achar	Istrí ..	Estirar
Āiyá ..	Aia	Jalangani ..	Janela
Álmārí ..	Armário	Juá, jūá khelá	Jogar
Álpin ..	Alfinete	? Kampás ..	Compasso
Ātlas ..	Ata	? Káphi ..	Café
? Básan ..	Bacia or bacio	Káphri ..	Cafre
? Báp ..	Bafo	Lilám ..	Leilão
Barandá ..	Varanda	Mastúl ..	Mastro
Bhoyám ..	Boião	Mej ..	Mesa
Boma-gola ..	Bomba	Mistrí ..	Mestre
Chábi, sábi ..	Chave	Nemú ..	Limão
Cháh, chái ..	Chá.	Pāti-hámh ..	Pato
? Cháp, chápa, chapi, chāpái, chapá, chapalá, chapkhāná, chap, or chabmar	Chapa	Perú ..	Peru
		? Phaṭaká ..	Foguete
		Phitá ..	Fita
		Piris ..	Pires
		Rachita ..	Recibo
		Sában, chaban	Sabão
Girja, girjaghar	Igreja	Sāyá ..	Saia
Gūdám ..	Gudão	Tambaru, tamburu	Ṭambor
Ingráji ..	Inglês		

6. Balinese

Balinese	*Portuguese*	*Balinese*	*Portuguese*
Bandéra	Bandeira	Palúngan, pingan	Palangana
Blúdru	Veluda	Páso	Vaso
? Bedil	Fuzil	Piring	Pires
Botol	Botelha	Prada (gilding, gold-foil)	Prata
? Hechap, chap-chap	Chapa	Reyal, leyar	Rial
Jendila, gendéla	Janela	Ronda	Ronda
* Kápal	Cavalo	Sábun	Sabão
Kaput	Capote	*Sagu, sago	Sagu
Katela	Castela	Suredadu, sredádu	Soldado
Manas	Ananás	Temako	Tabaco
Miskin	Mesquinho		

7. Batavian

Batavian	*Portuguese*	*Batavian*	*Portuguese*
Bilúdru	Veludo	Noña or nyónya	Dona
Gágu	Gago	Pásu	Vaso
Honas	Ananas	Pingan	Palangana
Karĕpus	Carapuça	Sidádi	Cidade
Kintal	Quintal		

8. Batta

Batta	*Portuguese*	*Batta*	*Portuguese*
Bandéra	Bandeira	Kámar	Camara
? Bedil	Fuzil	? Kansa	Ganso
Bilúlu	Veludo	*Kapal (a large ship)	Cavalo
? Botol	Botelha	Kareta, kreta	Carrêta
? Chap	Chapa	Kasut	Calçado
Dadu	Dado	? Lampu	Lampada
Honas	Ananás	Lélang	Leilão
Júdi, erjúdi, njudiken, perjudin	Jogar	Mandur	Mandador
		Máte	Matar

Batta	*Portuguese*
Méja ..	Mesa
Pasar ..	Passear
? Pataroli ..	Patrulha
Péchu ..	Fecho
Pijer ..	Fechar
Pelur, pinúru..	Pelouro
Pestúl ..	Pistola
Pingan ..	Palangana
? Rupiya ..	Rupia
Sábun ..	Sabão
Ságu ..	Sagu
Timbako, bako	Tabaco

9. Bengali

Bengali	*Portuguese*
Ābdú (C) ..	Hábito
Ag-bent ..	Água benta
Aiyá ..	Aia
Ālamp (C) ..	Alâmpada
Ālkatrá ..	Alcatrão
Ālmāri, almārí	Armário
Almús ..	Almôço (breakfast)
Alpinêt, ālpín	Alfinete
Altár ..	Altar
Ȧlva ..	Alva
Ambar ..	Ambar
Amen ..	Amen
Amit (C) ..	Amito
Anārasí ..	Ananás
Anjeūl (C) ..	Em joelhos (on knees)
Āpostôl ..	Apostolo
Ātá ..	Ata
Ave Māri ..	Ave Maria
Āvò (C) ..	Avó
? Bajrá ..	Bairel
Balcham ..	Balchão
Baldí, baltí ..	Balde
Bánk ..	Banco
Bāphādú ..	Abafado
Baranda ..	Varanda
Básan ..	Bacia
Bavtijma ..	Baptismo
Bayá ..	Boia
Berdí (C) ..	Verde
Bhoyám ..	Boião
Biskuṭ ..	Biscoito
Bispa ..	Bispo
Biyala ..	Viola (guitar)
Bolinos (C) ..	Bolinho
Bomá ..	Bomba
Boroga ..	Verga (rafter)
? Botal, botol	Botelha
Botam ..	Botão
Bovas noiti (C)	Boas noites (good night)
Bovás tardiyá (C)	Boas tardes (good evening)
Burmá ..	Verruma
Chá ..	Chá
Chābi, sābi ..	Chave
? Cháp, chhāp	Chapa
Chhāyá ..	Saia
Dalmatic (C) ..	Dalmatica
Damás ..	Damasco

Bengali	*Portuguese*
Deus boms diyá (C) (God good day)	Bom dia
Deus boms nouti (C. God good night)	Bom noite
Devus (C) ..	Deus
Ejmolá (C) ..	Esmola
Entrudú (C) ..	Entrudo
Estol (C) ..	Estola
Garādiyá ..	Grade
Girgá, girjjá ..	Igreja
Gudam ..	Gudão
Ingláj ..	Inglês
Insensú (C) ..	Incenso
Irmáñ (C) ..	Irmão
Isopa (C) ..	Hissope
Ispát ..	Espada
Istrí ..	Estirar
Jānālá, janālá	Janela
Kābár ..	Acabar
Kaderá, kadārá	Cadeira
Káj ..	Casa
Kājú ..	Caju
Kālāpāti ..	Calafate
Kāldó ..	Caldo
Kális ..	Cális
? Kāmán ..	Canhão
Kamíj ..	Camisa
? Kampás ..	Compasso
Kāppa (C) ..	Capa
Karābu ..	Cravo
Karṇel ..	Coronel
Kárūbim ..	Querubim
Kasūl (C) ..	Casula (chasuble)
Kātekísma (C)	Catechismo
Katholika ..	Católico
Kintal ..	Quintal
Kobi, kobi śák	Couve
? Kôch ..	Coche
Koindú ..	Cunhado
Komādri ..	Comadre
Komedori (C)	Comedoria
Kompādri ..	Compadre
Komphisáñ ..	Confissão
Komuniyāñ ..	Comunhão
Konsuvādá ..	Consoada
Korjmu ..	Quaresma
Krisma ..	Crisma
Kristāñ ..	Cristão
Kruś, kruśa-kriti	Cruz
Lantará ..	Lanterna
? Lebu ..	Limão
Lona ..	Anona
Madi ..	Madrinha
Māldisán ..	Maldicão
Maná (C) ..	Mana
Maná (C) ..	Maná
Mānú (C) ..	Mano
Mārtel ..	Martelo
Māstul ..	Mastro
Mej ..	Mesa
Misán ..	Missão
Misiyonár ..	Missionário
Minta mercê (C)	Minta mercê
Nātál ..	Natal
Nilám, nilām, nilāmá	Leilão

Bengali	*Portuguese*
Novená	Novena
Ol	Óleo
Opá	Opa
Orgán	Órgão
Osti	Hóstia
Pādrí	Padre
Pādrovādú	Padroado
Pādú	Padrinho
Pāpá (C)	Papá
Papayá	Papaia
Paṛtikul (C)	Particula (sacred wafer)
Pāskuvá	Páscoa
Páti-hams	Pato
Paum	Pão (bread)
Pená	Pena
Perek	Prego
Perú, piyará	Pera
Perú	Peru
? Pilurí	Pelouro
Pipá, pipe, pimpa	Pipa
Pirij	Pires
Pistol	Pistola
Piyá	Pia
Pobrí (C)	Pobre
Provijor (C)	Provisor
Purgātori (C)	Purgatório
Rêndá	Renda (lace)

Bengali	*Portuguese*
Resto (C)	Resto (remains)
Rituál (C)	Ritual (ritual)
Reytor	Reitor
Rond pheran	Ronda
Sābán, sābānbat	Sabão
Sākrāmentú	Sacramento
Sakrúr (C)	Sacrário (tabernacle)
Salálā	Salada
Sankristán	Sacristão
Sāvudí	Saude
Siyor	Senhor
Sobrepeliz (C)	Sobrepeliz (surplice)
Spanj	Esponja
Spiritú Sāntú	Espírito Santo
Stānti	Estante
Surtti	Sorte
Tamák, tamáku etc.	Tobaco
Tersú	Terço
Tiv (C)	Tio
Titi (C)	Tia
Toyále	Toalha
Tumbá	Tumba
? Tuphán	Tufão
Turibúl	Turibulo
Vévu (C)	Véu

10. Bugui

Bugui	*Portuguese*
Aláhoya	Algoz
Ambarā	Ambar
? Amin	Amen
Angarisi	Inglês

Bugui	*Portuguese*
? Anīsí (áda, ádassa)	Anis
? Ápang	Apa
Arapa	Harpa

Bugui	*Portuguese*
Arúda	Arruda
Ássā	Az
Balasáng	Bálsamo
Bandéra	Bandeira
Bandóla	Bandola
Baraló	Bordo
Basáttu	Basto
? Batará	Batel
? Bátili	Bátega
Bisatirida	Bastarda
Bisésetu	Bissexto
Biyóla	Viola
? Chá	Chapa
? Chalana	Pantalona
Chapiyo	Chapéu
Chamalóti	Chamalote
Charaméle	Charamela
Chí	Chita
Dádu	Dado
Dílu	Codilho
Dóbalō	Dôbro
? Dórtorō	Doutor
Gága	Gago
Gáji	Gage
Gále	Galé
Gánho	Ganho
Garéja	Igreja
Garidmong	Cardamomo
Isitāraluga	Astrólogo
Jandéla	Janela
Jinerála	General
Jugarā	Jogar
? Júmba	Jibão
Kamáli	Câmera
Kamándarē	Comendador
Kanhão (gun)	Canhão
Kápa	Capa
Kapitan-moro	Capitão mor
? Káppala	Cavalo
Karubiyúna	Querabim
Korabu	Cravo
? Karátassa	Cartaz
Karatúsa	Cartucho
Karéta	Carreta
*Kasatúri	Castor
Kaválu	Cavalo
Kéju	Queijo
Kóndi	Conde
Kópasa	Copas
? Kopi	Café
Kóntara	Contrato
? Kútang	Cotão
Lagarisi	Algarismo
Lamári	Armário
Lapéresè	Alferes
Lelang	Leilão
? Lémo	Limão
Lóji	Loja
Manila	Manille
Mantéga	Manteiga
Marinio	Meirinho
Matadóro	Matador
Máte	Matar
Méjan	Mesa
? Nómoro	Numero
Nona, nhonha	Dona
Palakko	Falcão
Panniti	Alfinete
Paráda	Prata
Paráguta	Fragata
Paraséro	Parceiro
? Pasa	Bazar

Bugui		Portuguese	Bugui		Portuguese
Pasikála	..	Fiscal	Saláda	..	Salada
Peseta	..	Festa	Saloda	..	Solda
Píja	..	Fechar	Sapadila	..	Espadilha
Piluru	..	Pelouro	Sapátu	..	Sapato
Pináchu	..	Penacho	Sáttu	..	Sábado
? Pinjan	..	Palangana	? Satting	..	Setim
? Piring	..	Pires	Sorodádu	..	Soldado
Píta	..	Fita	Sóta	..	Sota
Póntu	..	Ponto	Tambáko	..	Tabaco
Réi	..	Rei	Támboro, tamboru	..	Tambor
Rénda	..	Renda	Tanjidóro	..	Tanjedor
Réyala	..	Rial	? Tantu	..	Tanto
Ronda	..	Ronda	Tūrumbéta	..	Trombeta
Rósi	..	Rosa	Valudu, beludu, bilulu		Veludo
? Rupiya	..	Rupia			
Sábung	..	Sabão			
*Ságu	..	Sagu			

11. Burmese

Burmese		Portuguese	Burmese		Portuguese
? Bú-zo	..	Bucha	Nan-na-si	..	Ananás
Kap-pa-li	..	Cafre	Ngan	..	Ganso
? Kap-phe	..	Café	Lay-lan	..	Leilão
? Kyane	..	Cana da Índia	Ksap-pyah	..	Sabão

12. Chinese

Chinese		Portuguese	Chinese		Portuguese
Akee	..	Aqui	Pa-ti-li, pa-té-le		Padre
Fáh-lán-jin	..	Flanela	Pí-pá-tung	..	Pipa
? Kiá-fe	..	Café	Sabby, savy, sha-pi		Saber
Kiá-tsú	..	Caju	? Shá-ku-mí	..	Sagu
Máng-koo	..	Manga	? Túd	..	Tudo
? Mien-páu	..	Pão	Yélong, lélang, loylang		Leilão
Misáh	..	Missa			
Pá-pá	..	Papá			

13. Dayak

Dayak	Portuguese	Dayak	Portuguese
? Apam, abam	Apa	Lelang ..	Leilão
Badil ..	Fuzil	Liman ..	Limão
Bandéra ..	Bandeira	Mandúr ..	Mandador
Banko ..	Banco	? Matei ..	Matar
Bijola, viola ..	Viola	Meja ..	Mesa
? Búyong ..	Boião	Mingo, mengo	Domingo
? Chap ..	Chapa	Ñoña ..	Dona
Chita, sita ..	Chita	Páso ..	Vaso
Gása ..	Ganso	Pingan ..	Palangana
Gudang ..	Gudão	? Piring ..	Pires
Judo ('luck, destiny')	Jogar	Práda, paráda	Prata
Kamandan ..	Comandante	Rénda ..	Renda
Kaméja ..	Camisa	? Rupia, ropia	Rupia
Kanas ..	Ananás	Sabon ..	Sabão
*Kápal ..	Cavalo	Sábtu ..	Sábado
Kápir ..	Cafre	*Sago ..	Sagu
Kapítan ..	Capitão	Separo (adv.) ..	Separado
? Karatas ..	Carta or cartaz	Setan ..	Satan
Karéta ..	Carrêta	Tambáko ..	Tabaco
? Kúpi ..	Café	Tempo ..	Tempo

14. Galoli

Galoli	Portuguese	Galoli	Portuguese
Abril ..	Abril	Aidúda ..	Ajudar
Achar ..	Achár, asár	*Alegra* ..	Alegrar (to gladden)
Adeus ..	Adeus	Alerta ..	Alerta
Admira ..	Admirar (to admire)	Alfándega ..	Alfândega
Adorasã ..	Adoração (Adoration)	Alféris ..	Alferes
Advogádu ..	Advogado	Alfinêti ..	Alfinete
Agôstu ..	Agôsto	*Alforg* ..	Alforge (portmanteau)
Agradéci ..	Agradecer		

Galoli		*Portuguese*
Algem	..	Algemas (manacles)
Algiber	..	Algibeira (pocket)
Alinháv	..	Alinhavo (basting)
Alkatifa	..	Alcatifa
Almonik	..	Almôndega
Almúsa	..	Almôço
Altar	..	Altar
Álva	..	Alva
Amen	..	Amen
Amostra	..	Amostra
Amu Deus	..	Deus
Ananaz	..	Ananás
Animar	..	Animal
Ánju	..	Anjo
Ánu	..	Ano
Antig	..	Antigo (old)
Apa, apas	..	Apa
Argola	..	Argola
Argolinha	..	Argolinha
Assísti	..	Assistir
Avestruz	..	Avestruz (ostrich)
Avizu	..	Aviso
Baban baú	..	Baú
Baionêta	..	Baioneta
Báldi	..	Balde
Bandeira	..	Bandeira
Bandeja	..	Bandeja
Bándu	..	Bando
Bánha	..	Bainhar
Bánku	..	Banco
Barreti	..	Barrete
Barril	..	Barril
Básár	..	Bazar
Basia	..	Bacia
Batalhã, batayã		Batalhão
Bensã	..	Bençâo
Beringela	..	Beringela
Bíphi	..	Bife
Biskóitu	..	Biscoito (biscuit)
Bíspu	..	Bispo
Bôba	..	Bouba
Bôbu	..	Bobo
Bolacha	..	Bolacha (biscuit)
Bolsa	..	Bôlsa
Bôlu	..	Bôlo
Bomba	..	Bomba
Boné	..	Boné
Bonéka	..	Boneca
? Bótir	..	Botelha
Búli	..	Bule (tea-pot)
Cabo ('corporal')		Cabo
Chá	..	Chá
Chávi	..	Chave
Chikara	..	Chícara
Chokaláti	..	Chocolate
Consêlu	..	Conselho
Daia	..	Daia (Ind.-Port. 'midwife')
Dedál	..	Dedal
Despáchu	..	Despacho
Despénsa	..	Despensa
Devosã	..	Devoção
Diamánte	..	Diamante
Diné	..	Dinheiro

Galoli		Portuguese
Dispensa	..	Dispensa (dispensation)
Distérra	..	Desterrar
Divinha	..	Adivinhar (to foretell)
Dom	..	Dom
Dona	..	Dona
Dótor	..	Doutor
Dotrina	..	Doutrina
Dúra	..	Durar
Dúzi, dúsi	..	Dúzia
Ermida	..	Ermida
Esa	..	Essa
Escola	..	Escola
Eskolta	..	Escolta
Eskomunhã	..	Excomunhão
Eskôva	..	Escova
Eskriván	..	Escrivão
Esmola	..	Esmola
Espoleta	..	Espoleta
Estribu	..	Estribo
Estrika	..	Esticar
Evanjélhu	..	Evangelho
Ezámi	..	Exame
Ezémplu	..	Exemplo
Fáma	..	Fama
Farda	..	Farda (uniform)
Farol	..	Farol
Favor	..	Favor
Fé	..	Fé
Feira	..	Feira
Ferias	..	Férias (holidays)
Festa	..	Festa
Figura	..	Figura
Filtru	..	Filtro (filter)
Finta	..	Finta

Galoli		Portuguese
Fita	..	Fita
Flanela	..	Flanela
Forsa	..	Força
Fôrnu	..	Fôrno
Fórti	..	Forte
Fráku	..	Fraco
Fragata	..	Fragata
Fraskeira	..	Frasqueira
Freguezia	..	Freguesia
Friu	..	Frio (cold)
Fuma	..	Fumar (to smoke)
Funil	..	Funil
Furtuna	..	Fortuna
Galã	..	Galão
Gavèta	..	Gaveta
Gloria	..	Glória (glory)
Gorgoleta	..	Gorgoleta
Gôstu	..	Gôsto
Govêrnu	..	Govêrno
Grasa	..	Graça
Guarda	..	Guarda
Inférnu	..	Inferno
Insénsu	..	Incenso
Intensã	..	Intencão
Ispirítu	..	Espírito
Ispirítu Santu		Espírito Santo (Holy Ghost)
Ispital	..	Hospital
Istôri	..	História
Janela	..	Janela
Jara	..	Jarra
Jardim	..	Jardim (a garden)
Jaro	..	Jarro (pitcher)
Jenebra	..	Genebra

Galoli	*Portuguese*
Jentiu, sentiu	Gentio
Jerasã ..	Geração
Jinjum, jijum	Jejum
Jugador ..	Jogador (gambler)
Júga ..	Jogar
Juiz, juis, duis	Juiz
Julho ..	Julho
Junho ..	Junho
Juraméntu, duraméntu	Juramento
Júra ..	Jurar
Júru ..	Juro
Justisa ..	Justiça
Kabáya ..	Cabaia
Kabídi ..	Cabide
Kadeira ..	Cadeira
? Kafé ..	Café
Kafri ..	Cafre
Kajús, kaidú	Caju
Kakau ..	Cacau
Kális ..	Cális
Kalsa ..	Calcas
Kama ..	Cama
Kámara ..	Câmara
Kamclu ..	Camelo (camel)
Kamiza ..	Camisa
Kamizola ..	Camisola (chemise)
Kampainha ..	Campainha
Kámpu ..	Campo
Kanapé ..	Canapé
Kanfora ..	Canfora
Kanivéte ..	Canivete
Kánu ..	Cano
Kápa ..	Capa, capar

Galoli	*Portuguese*
Kápadu ..	Capado
Kapás ..	Capaz
Kapéla ..	Capela
Kapítan ..	Capitão
Karíl ..	Caril
Karreta ..	Carrêta
Kartús ..	Cartucho
Kasímbu ..	Cachimbo (tobacco pipe)
Kastígu ..	Castigo
Kásu ..	Caso (case)
Katána ..	Catana
Katáru ..	Catarro
Keiju ..	Queijo
Kestã ..	Questão
Kóbi ..	Couve
Koêlho ..	Coelho
Kófri ..	Cofre
Konfésa ..	Confessar
Kónsul ..	Consul
Konta ..	Conta
Konténti (adj.)	Contente (content)
Kontrátu ..	Contrato
Kópi ..	Cópia
Kópu, kóbu ..	Copo
Koresma ..	Quaresma
Korneta ..	Corneta
Korôa ..	Coroa
Koronel ..	Coronel
Kortina ..	Cortina
Kostumu ..	Costume (custom)
Kostumadu ..	Costumado (accustomed)

Galoli	Portuguese
Kovadu	Covado
Koyabas	Goiaba
Kréda	Igreja
Kriadu	Criado
Kriar	Criar
Krisma	Crisma
Kruz	Cruz
Kudir	Acudir
Kunha	Cunha
Ladainha	Ladainha
Lámpa	Lâmpada
Lampiã	Lampião
Lansa	Lança
Lápis	Lápis
Lata	Lata
Lavanka	Alavanca
Lei	Lei
Leilã, lelã	Leilão
Lénsu	Lenço
Letra	Letra
Linhu	Linho (linen)
Lisã	Lição
Lisensa	Licença
Lista	Lista
Lívru	Livro
Loisa	Loiça
Lumінári	Luminárias
Lúva	Luva
Maldisã, malisã	Maldição
Malkriádu	Malcriado
Mantéga	Manteiga
Marcha	Marchar
Marfim	Marfim
Marrafa	Marrafa
Marsu	Março
Martelú	Martelo
Mãrtir	Mártir
Mas	Mas
Meia	Meia, meias
Méstri	Mestre
Meza	Mesa
Milágri	Milagre
Mimútu	Minuto
Mirínhu	Meirinho
Misa	Missa
Misã	Missão
Misál	Missal
Multa	Multa
Mundu (*rea*)	Mundo (world)
Munisã	Munição
Músika	Música
Mustarda	Mostarda
Nasã	Nação (nation)
Natál	Natal
Néga	Negar
Noda	Nódoa (stain)
Nota	Nota
Notísi	Notícia
Númeru	Número
Ofísiu	Ofício
Oku	Oco
Okulu	Óculos (spectacles)
Onra	Honra
Ópa	Opa
Ophisyál	Oficial
Ora	Hora
Orasã	Oração
Oragu	Orago (patron saint of a church)
Órgão	Órgão

Galoli	*Portuguese*
Ostia	Hóstia
Pã	Pão
Pádri	Padre
Páliu	Pálio
Palmatória	Palmatória
Pápa	Papa
Parabem	Parabêm
Pássi	Passe
Pataka	Pataca
Pateka	Pateca
Patrónu	Patrono
Pátu	Pato
Péna	Pena
Penhor	Penhor (pawn)
Perdã	Perdão (pardon)
Pestí	Peste
Pia	Pia
Piã	Pião (a top)
Pintar	Pintar
Píris	Pires (saucer)
Pistola	Pistola
Pomba	Pomba
Póntu	Ponto
Posta	Posta
Pregos	Prego
Prêsu	Preço
Prima	Prima
Prokurãdor	Procurador
Prokurasã	Procuração
Proséssu	Processo
Prosisã	Procissão
Pulga	Pulga (flea)
Púkaru	Púcaro
Púlpitu	Púlpito
Purga	Purga
Purgatóri	Purgatório

Galoli	*Portuguese*
Rabeca	Rabeca
Repuga	Refogar (dressed meat)
Regedor	Regedor
Regra	Regra
Rekádu	Recado
Religiã	Religião
Relóji	Relojio
Renda	Renda (rent)
Reposta	Reposta
Résã	Raçao
Resíbu	Recibo
Rezã	Razão
Riku	Rico (rich man)
Roda	Roda
Romã	Romã (pomegranate)
Rosa	Rosa (a rose)
Rozáriu	Rosário
Sabã	Sabão
Sábadu	Sábado
Sagúati, sauáti	Saguate
Sakraméntu	Sacramento
Sakráriu	Sacrário
Sakrifísiu	Sacrifício
Sakriléjiu	Sacrilégio
Sakristã	Sacristão
? Sáku	Sagu
Sala	Sala
Saláda	Salada
Salva	Salva
Salvasã	Salvação
Sangra	Sangrar (to let blood)
? Sapa	Chapa
Sapátu	Sapato

Galoli		*Portuguese*
Sarjentu, saréntu		Sargento
Sarúto	..	Charuto
Satanaz	..	Satan, satanas
Sauda	..	Saudar (to drink to one's health)
Saúdi	..	Saúde
Sé	..	Sé
Seda	..	Sêda
Sekretariu	..	Secretaria
Sekretáriu	..	Secretário
Séla	..	Sela
Sêlu	..	Sêlo
Semana	..	Semana
Semináriu	..	Seminário
Semitéri	..	Cemitério
Sentensa	..	Sentença
Sentídu	..	Sentido
Sentinela	..	Sentinela
Séri	..	Sério
Sermã	..	Sermão
Sifra	..	Cifra
Sikóuro	..	Socorro (aid)
Silensiu	..	Silencio (silence)
Sinal	..	Sinal
Sinela	..	Chinela
Sínti	..	Sentir
Sínu	..	Sino
Sírvi	..	Servir
Sita	..	Chita
Soberba	..	Soberba (pride)
Soldádu	..	Soldado
Sombrélu	..	Sombreiro
Sóriti	..	Sorte
Sosiedádi	..	Sociedade

Galoli		*Portuguese*
Sotana	..	Sotaina
Splíka	..	Explicar
Sufrí	..	Sófrer
Tobáku	..	Tabaco
Táchu, tásu	..	Tacho
Tárdi	..	Tarde
Témpera	..	Têmpera
Témpu	..	Tempo
Tenda	..	Tenda (tent, booth)
Tenente	..	Tenente (lieutenant)
Ténta	..	Tentar
Terrina	..	Terrina
Térsu	..	Têrço
Testaméntu	..	Testamento
Tinta	..	Tinta
Tiras	..	Tira
Tíru	..	Tiro
Tôrri	..	Torre
Tráta	..	Tratar
Trataméntu	..	Tratamento
Trígu	..	Trigo
Triśti	..	Triste
Tropa	..	Tropa
Tualha	..	Toalha
Túmba	..	Tumba
Usu	..	Uso (use)
Uvas	..	Uvas (grapes)
Vasina	..	Vacina
Varanda	..	Varanda
Vázu	..	Vaso
Verniz	..	Verniz
Verónika	..	Verónica
Verruma	..	Verruma

Galoli	*Portuguese*	*Galoli*	*Portuguese*
Vérsu ..	Verso	Vídru ..	Vidro
Véspera ..	Vésperas	Vigariu ..	Vigário
Vestídu ..	Vestido	Viola ..	Viola
Veu ..	Véu	Vizita ..	Visita

15. Garo

Garo	*Portuguese*	*Garo*	*Portuguese*
Alkatra ..	Alcatrão	Joa ('game')	Jogo
Almari ..	Armário	Joa kala ..	Jogar
Balti, baltin ..	Balde	Kamij ..	Camisa
Baranda ..	Varanda	Kapi ..	Café
Borma, bolma	Verruma	Kartus ..	Catucho
? Botal ..	Botelha	Kóbi ..	Couve
Burus ..	Bruça	Mistri ..	Mestre
Butam ..	Botão	Pipa ..	Pipa
Cha ..	Chá	Pistol ..	Pistola
Chabi ..	Chave	Saban ..	Sabão
? Chapa ..	Chapa	? Sagu ..	Sagu
? Diabol ..	Diabo	Saia ..	Saia
Gilja ..	Igreja	? Satan ..	Satan
Ilam ..	Leilão	Tamaku ..	Tabaco

16. Gujarati

Gujarati	*Portuguese*	*Gujarati*	*Portuguese*
Āmā ..	Ama	? Báph ..	Bafo
Anenás, annas	Ananás	? Baptijhma	Baptismo
Angrêj angrejí	Inglês	? Barát ..	Baralho
Āphús ..	Afonsa	Bārkas ..	Barcaça
Armár, ārmá	Armada	Bārotium ..	Barrote
Armārí ..	Armário	Basí ..	Bacia
Āyá ..	Aia	Batātā ..	Batata
? Baglo ..	Baixel	Bateló ..	Batel
Bāldí ..	Balde	Bāú, bávuṁ ..	Baú
Bamb, bambô	Bomba	? Borás ..	Bórax
Bánk ..	Banco	Bôyu, bôyuṁ	Boia

Gujarati	Portuguese
Búch	Bucha
Buddu	Bordo
Burákh	Buraco
Chá, cháha, cháhe	Chá
? Chháp, chhāp-khánum, etc.	Chapa
Dhumás, dumás	Damasco
Gája	Casa
Garád	Grade
Gárdí, gaḍdi	Guarda
Iscotri, iscutri, iskotarô	Escritório
Istrí, astrí, astarí	Estirar
Jāphran	Açafrão
Jugár, jugáru, juô, juveṁ, etc.	Jogar
Káju	Caju
Kampás	Compasso
? Kandil	Candil
? Kaphí	Café
Kaphlád	Acafelar
Kaptán, kapat-tán	Capitão
Karnel	Coronel
Kārtús	Cartucho
Katholik	Católico
Kobi, kobij	Couve
Kôch	Coche
Kolerô	Cólera
Krus, krús	Cruz
Kurtaní	Cortina
Lavád	Louvado
Lilám, nilám	Leilão
? Limbu, límbu	Limão
Majagarem, ma-jagaram, mis-jagarúm	Visagra
Marmar	Mármore
Mej	Mesa
Mīstri, mistarí	Mestre
Nātál	Natal
Pader (*khanuṁ*)	Padeiro
Pādrí	Padre
Pagár	Paga
Páj	Passo
Palmantrí	Palmatória
Paránch	Prancha
Parej	Preso
Pásum	Página
Páum, páṁu	Pão
Pāyri	Peres
Pegám	Pregão
Pên	Pena
Per, perum	Perar
? Phalánum	Fulano
Pháltu	Falto
Phám	Fama
Phárm, pharmô	Forma
Phit, phint	Fita
Píp	Pipa
Pistol	Pistola
Polís	Polícia
Purāvó, purvāri	Prova
Purvár karvuṁ	Provar
Rasíd	Recibo
Ratal	Arrátel
? Rent	Renda
Res	Rial, pl. réis
Ríp, rip	Ripa

Gujarati	*Portuguese*
Ron	Ronda
Sabu, sābú	Sabão
? Sāgú	Sagu
Sapát	Sapato
Sindor (us. in Damaun)	Senhor (Master)
Soppá	Sofá
Sortí, surtí	Sorte
Survál, suravála	Ceroilas
Tambáku, tambákum	Tabaco
? Tāṅkí, tāṅkuṁ	Tanque
Tijori	Tesouraria
? Tikam	Picão
? Tophán	Tufão
Turang	Tronco
Turanj	Toranja
Tuval	Toalha
? Ubharó, umbró	Umbreira
Vár	Vara
Varandó	Varanda

17. Hindi

Hindi	*Portuguese*
Achár	Achar
Ālmārí, almārí	Armário
Ambar	Ambar
? Amin	Amen
Anannás	Ananás
Angrezí	Inglês
Át, ātá	Ata
? Baptismá	Baptismo
Barāndá, barandaka, barāmada	Varanda
Barmá	Verruma
Basan	Bacia
? Bháph	Bafo
? Botal	Botelha
Chá, cháh, cháy, chaé	Chá
Chábí	Chave
? Chhāpá, chapna, etc.	Chapa
Girjá	Igreja
Ispát (also aspát)	Espada
Juá, juá khelna, juạ̄ri, juvāri, juanḍi	Jogar
Kālapatti	Calafate
Kamrá	Câmara
Kaptán	Capitão
Karnel	Coronel
Katholika	Católico
Kobí, gobí, gobhí	Couve
? Kôch	Coche
Krús, krussa, etc.	Cruz
? Marmar	Mármore
Martaul	Martelo
Mez, menz, mench	Mesa

Hindi	Portuguese	Hindi	Portuguese
Nilám, nīlám ..	Leilão	Rasíd ..	Recibo
Pādri ..	Padre	Sābún ..	Sabão
Parát, parāti	Prato	? Sāgú ..	Sagu
Papayá ..	Papaia	Sāyá ..	Saia
Pav-roṭí ..	Pão	Tambākú, ta-mākú, etc.	Tabaco
Phāltu ..	Falto		
Phitá ..	Fita	Tauliyá ..	Toalha
Pīpá ..	Pipa	Varāndá, va-randá	Varanda
Qamiz ..	Camisa		
? Qandil ..	Candil	Viskut ..	Biscoito

18. Hindustani

Hindustani	Portuguese	Hindustani	Portuguese
Achár ..	Achar	Berinjal ..	Beringela
Almāri ..	Armário	Bilambú ..	Bilimbim
Ālpín, alpín, alpin	Alfinete	Bindālú ..	Vinha de alhos
		Biskut ..	Biscoito
Āmá ..	Ama	? Botal, bottal	Botelha
Ambar ..	Âmbar	Bótám ..	Botão
? Āmin ..	Amen	Boyam ..	Boião
Ananás ..	Ananás	Bumbá, bamba	Bomba
Angrejí ..	Inglês	Chá, cháh, cháy, cháe	Chá
? Anīsún ..	Anis		
Argan, argha-núm	Órgão	? Chháp, chhā-pa, chhāp-khana, etc.	Chapa
Át, ātá ..	Ata		
Āyá ..	Aia	Chāvi, chābí, chābhí	Chave
Bāldí, bāltí ..	Balde		
Balsán ..	Bálsamo	Farmá ..	Forma
Bāolá ..	Baú	Fitá, fīta, phitá	Fita
? Báph ..	Bafo		
? Baptismá ..	Baptismo	? Fulan, fulaná	Fulano
Barmá ..	Verruma	Gārad ..	Guarda
? Bas ..	Basta	Garādiyá ..	Grade
Basan ..	Bacia	? Garandíl ..	Granadeiro

Hindustani	*Portuguese*
Garnál ..	Granada
Girjá ..	Igreja
Godám ..	Gudão
Ispát ..	Espada
Istrí ..	Estirar
Juá, juá khelná, juā khāna; juāri, juābáj	Jogar
Jinjalí ..	Gergelim
Jhilmil ..	Janela
Juláb, jullab ..	Jalapa
Káj ..	Casa
Kalpatti, kalāpatiyá	Calafate
Kāmará, kamará, kámra	Câmara
Kāmpas ..	Compasso
Kampú ..	Campo
Kaptán ..	Capitão
? Karabín ..	Carabina
Kārtús ..	Cartucho
Kardhani ..	Cordão
Kārūbín ..	Querubim
Kobí ..	Couve
? Kochbán ..	Cocheiro
Kuñya, kuñiyañ, koniyá	Cunha
? Lamp ..	Lâmpada
Langūchá ..	Lingùiça
? Līmú, lemú, nimbú	Limão
Man ..	Maná
Mājkabár ..	Mês
? Marmar ..	Marmore

Hindustani	*Portuguese*
Mārtil, martaul, mārtol, martol	Martelo
Mastisa ..	Mestiço
Mastúl ..	Mastro
Mej, mez ..	Mesa
Mistrí ..	Mestre
Mūsiki, mūsigí	Música
? Naul, nuval	Naulo
Nīlám ..	Leilão
Pādrí ..	Padre
Pagár ..	Paga
Pámvroṭí, paoroṭi	Pão
Papayá ..	Papaia
Parát, parátí	Prato
Perú ..	Peru
Pháltu ..	Falto
? Phatakhá ..	Foguete
Pīpá ..	Pipa
Pirich ..	Pires
Pistaul, pistol	Pistola
? Polís ..	Policia
Preg, pareg ..	Prego
Qamij, qamis	Camisa
? Qandil ..	Candil
Rasíd ..	Recibo
Ratal ..	Arrátel
Sābún, sábun, saban	Sabão
? Sāgū ..	Sagu
Sangtara ..	Cintra
Salátā, salútih, salitih	Salada
Sāyá ..	Saia
Sharti ..	Sorte

Hindustani	*Portuguese*
Sufa	Sofá
Tambākú, tāmākú, tamakú	Tabaco
Tambúr	Tambor
Tauliyá	Toalha
? Tūfán	Tufão
Tūranj	Toranja

19. Indo-French

Indo-French	*Portuguese*
Abada	Abada
Achar, achars	Achar
Albatros	Alcatraz
Aldée	Aldeia
Alfandeque	Alfândega
Ananas	Ananás
Anil, anir	Anil
Anone	Anona
Arack, rack	Araca
Arec, areque, arequier	Areca
Argamasse	Argamassa
Arratel	Arrátel
Arroyo	Arroio
Baladine, bayadère	Bailadeira
Bambou	Bambu
Banane, bananier	Banana
Bangue	Bangue
Benjoin	Beijoim, benjoim
Bétel	Bétele
Biche-de-mer	Bicho do mar
Bonite	Bonito
Bonze	Bonzo
Caire	Cairo
Cange	Canja
Caoutchouk	Cate, cato, cáchu
Carambole, carambolier	Carambola
Carry	Caril
Caste	Casta
Cipaye	Cipai
Cobra-de-capello, cobra-capello	Cobra, cobra-de-capelo
Coco, cocotier	Côco
Coco-de-mer	Côco do mar
Comprador	Comprador
Copre	Copra
Corge, courge	Corja
Cornac	Cornaca
Dorade	Dourado
Goyave, goyavier, gouave	Goiaba
Igname	Inhame
Jagra, jagara, jagre	Jagra
Jaque, jaquier	Jaca
Loje	Loja
Mainate	Mainato
Mandarin	Mandarim
Mangelin	Mangelim

Indo-French	Portuguese
Mangostan, mangonstan	Mangostão
Mangouste ..	Manguço, mangusto
Mangue, manguier	Manga
Margosier ..	Amargosa
Mousson ..	Monção
Merigne ..	Meirinho
Métis ..	Mestiço
Mort-de-chien	Mordexim
Nabab ..	Nababo
Naïque ..	Naique
Naïre ..	Naire
Ortolan ..	Hortulana
Pagode, pagodin	Pagode
Paillote ..	Palhota
Palanquin ..	Palanquim
Pample ..	Pâmpano
Papaye ..	Papaia
Pastèque ..	Pateca
Patemar, patmar	Patamar
Pintade ..	Pintada
Poyal ..	Poial
Sagou ..	Sagu
Topas ..	Topaz
Toutenaque ..	Tutanaga
Véranda, vérandah	Varanda

20. Japanese

Japanese	Portuguese
Abito ..	Hábito
Ama-gappa ..	Capa
Amen ..	Amen
? Améndō, ammento	Amêndoa
Anjo ..	Anjo
Azna ..	Asna
Bánku ..	Banco
Baputesuma ..	Baptismo
Bársan, bārusamo	Bálsamo
Basara ..	Bezoar
Báteren ..	Padre
Biidoro ..	Vidro
Bírōdo ..	Veludo
Bisukóto, bisuko	Biscoito
Bóbura ..	Abóbora
Bóru ..	Bôlo
Bútan, bótan	Botão
Charumera, charumeru	Charamela
Chinta ..	Tinto
Conféto, kompeito, kómpéto	Confeito
Ekirinjiya, ekirinji	Igreja
? Fumbo ..	Tumba
? Furasuko ..	Frasco
? Gacho, gan..	Ganso
Garasa ..	Graça
Gomu ..	Goma
Hiryúzu ..	Filhó

Japanese	*Portuguese*
Inferno, imberno	Inferno
Iruman ..	Irmão
Ishikiriban ..	Escrivão
Jaketsu ..	Jaqueta
Jejun ..	Jejum
Jiban, juban ..	Jibão
Kanekim ..	Canequim
? Kantera ..	Candil
? Kapaibe ..	Copaíba
Kapitan ..	Capitão
Kappa ..	Capa
? Karameiru, karumera, karumeira	Caramelo
Karisu ..	Cális
Karusan ..	Calção
Karuta ..	Carta
Kasováru, kasvaruchō	Casoar
Kareuta [1] ..	Galeota
Kastéra, kasutera	Castela
Katáru ..	Catarro
Katoríkku ..	Católico
Kerubin, kerubu	Querubim

[1] ['Galliot, which in its Portuguese form of *galeota* became naturalised as a Japanese word **Kareuta** in Kyūshū' C. R. Boxer, *Portuguese Commercial Voyages to Japan*, etc., *Trans. Japan Soc. of London*, Vol. xxxi, p. 30. The existence of this word and of *Kunishimento* (infra) in Japanese was brought to my notice by Mr. Boxer. Ed. and Tr.]

Japanese	*Portuguese*
Kirishtan, kirishitan	Cristão
Kirismo ..	Crisma
Kohisan ..	Confissão
? Kompasu ..	Compasso
Kompra ..	Compra
Kompradoru ..	Comprador
Kontasu ..	Contas
Kóppu ..	Copo
Koreijo ..	Colégio
*Korera ..	Cólera
Kunishimento [1]	Conhecimento (bond or receipt)
Kurusu, kurosu	Cruz
Maki-tábako ..	Tabaco
Mana ..	Maná
Manteka ..	Manteiga
Manto ..	Manto
Maruchiriyo ..	Martirio
Maruchiru ..	Mártir
Maruméru ..	Marmelo
? Onsu ..	Onça
Orashyo ..	Oração
? Orogan ..	Órgão
Óstiya ..	Hóstia
Pan, paung, pan-ya	Pão
Pappu ..	Papa
Paraizo ..	Paraíso

[1] ['*Chōginsu shijū Kwamme no* **Kunishimento** *Kwanci jūgonen Kugwatsu minichi.*' C. R. Boxer, Portuguese Commercial Voyages to Japan, etc. *Trans. Japan. Soc. of London*, Vol. xxi, p. 73.]

Japanese	Portuguese
Pistoru, pisutoru	Pistola
? Rampu ..	Lâmpada
Ranseta ..	Lanceta
Rasha ..	Raxa
? Saberu ..	Sabre
Sabon, shabon	Sabão
Safuran ..	Açafrao
? Sagobei ..	Sagu
Santome, santomejiná	San-Tomé
Sarasa ..	Saraça
? Seito ..	Santo
Sinnyoro ..	Senhor
Superansa ..	Esperança
Tabako ..	Tabaco
? Taifu ..	Tufão
Tanto ..	Tanto
Teromentina ..	Terebintina
? Yarapa ..	Jalapa

21. Javanese

Javanese	Portuguese
Alpérès ..	Alferes
Ambar ..	Ambar
Amin ..	Amen
Antéro ..	Inteiro
? Arum, rum ..	Aroma
Baluvárti, balovárti, balurti	Baluarte
Bandérô, gandérô	Bandeira
Bánku ..	Banco
Bási, bési ..	Bacia
? Bedil ..	Fuzil
Belúdru, bludrú, beládur	Veludo
Bersérô, besérô	Parceiro
Bóla ..	Bola
Bonékô ..	Boneca
Chinélô, chanélô	Chinela
Chitó ..	Chita
? Echap ..	Chapa
Gaji ..	Gage
Galadri, gladri	Galeria
Gárdu, gerdu, gredu	Guarda
Gréjô, grijô, garinjô	Igreja
Kabáya ..	Cabaia
Káldu, káldo ..	Caldo
Kámar ..	Câmara
Kaméjô ..	Camisa
? Kampong, kampung	Campo
? Kang ..	Canga
*Kápal ..	Cavalo
Kapitan ..	Capitão
Kardamon ..	Cardamomo
Karéta, karéto, kréta	Carrêta
Kárpus, krapus	Carapuça
Kártu ..	Carta
Kásut ..	Calçado
Katelo ..	Castela

Javanese	*Portuguese*
Kéju ..	Queijo
Kestin ..	Setim
Komendadór, komendúr	Comendador
Korsãn ..	Coração
? Kotang ..	Cotão
Koubis, kúbis	Couve
Kras, keras ..	Crasso
Lamári, lemári	Armário
Lantérô ..	Lanterna
Legójo ..	Algoz
Lélang ..	Leilão
Loji ..	Loja
Manátu, nenatu	Mainato
Mandôr, mandúr	Mandador
Mantégô ..	Manteiga
Máski, méski..	Mas que
? Máti ..	Matar
Méjô ..	Mesa
Míngu ..	Domingo
? Misigit, mesigit, masigit	Mesquita
Nanas ..	Ananás
Panjer ..	Penhor
Pásu ..	Vaso
? Patrol ..	Patrulha
? Pegen ..	Pegar
Pelánki, plánki	Palanquim
Pesiyar, besiyar	Passear
Pĕsti, pasti ..	Mister
Péstô, pistô ..	Festa
Pétor ..	Feitor
Pilar ..	Pilar
Pingan ..	Palangana
? Piring ..	Pires

Javanese	*Portuguese*
Pitô ..	Fita
? Pómpô ..	Pompa
Rasan, ransan	Raçaô
Rêndô ..	Renda
Rial ..	Rial, réis
Ródô ..	Roda
Róndô ..	Ronda
? Rôtô ..	Raso
? Rupiya ..	Rupia
Sábtu, sáptu ..	Sábado
Sábun ..	Sabão
* Ságũ ..	Sagu
Sapátu, sepátu	Sapato
? Sékô, nyékô	Secar
Sélô ..	Sela
Selôdô ..	Salada
Separo (adj.) ..	Separado
Seruval ..	Ceroilas
Setóri ..	História
Skólah ..	Escola
? Sore ..	Serão
Sôrôdádu ..	Soldado
? Suku ..	Soco
Sutrô ..	Sêda
Tambako, embako, bako	Tabaco
Tambur ..	Tambor
Tanjidur, panjidur	Tanjedor
Tarvéla, trevela	Coelho
Tempo ..	Tempo
Téndô, tendô..	Tenda
? Tjelônô ..	Pantalona
Toro ..	Toro
Tukar ..	Trocar
? Tutung ..	Tudo
Urdi ..	Ordem

22. Kambojan

Kambojan	Portuguese	Kambojan	Portuguese
Áncgris ..	Inglês	Manŏs ..	Ananás
Bôn natal ..	Natal	Mārtir ..	Mártir
Bŏn Păs ..	Páscoa	Metis ..	Pimentos
? Cafê ..	Café	Minŭt ..	Minuto
*Capăl, capal chŏmbăng, capăl phlúng, capăl kdong	Cavalo	Missa ..	Missa
Cărsa, crâsa ..	Garça	Nŏm păng ..	Pão
*Congsul ..	Consul	(Santa) pap (see under Santo)	Papa
? Credas ..	Carta	Pay (pope) (C)	Pai
Crus, chhúcrus	Cruz	Riél (piaster)..	Rial
? Crol ..	Curral	Sabu, sabeăng	Sabão
Kristăng ..	Cristão	? Saku ..	Sagu
		? Thuăm ..	Tabaco

23. Kanarese

Kanarese	Portuguese	Kanarese	Portuguese
Āmá ..	Ama	Chávi ..	Chave
Almāri, almáru	Armário	Damásu ..	Damasco
Ámen ..	Amen	Dôse ..	Doce
Ananásu ..	Ananás	*Estolu* (C) ..	Estola
Apōstalánu ..	Apóstolo	Evanjélu ..	Evangelho
Apōstalara ..	Apostolico	Gadangu ..	Gudão
Āspatri ..	Hospital	Insénsu (C) ..	Incenso
Bámbu ..	Bomba	Istri ..	Estirar
Bási ..	Bacia, bacio	Julábu ..	Jalapa
Baṭāṭé ..	Batata	Jugáru, jugu, jūgugára, jūjáḍuvava, jūjuna paḍe, jūjuna kôli	Jogar
Bátu ..	Pato	Kamísu ..	Camisa
Bijágri ..	Visagra	? Kandíla ..	Candil
Biráku, biríku, birúku	Buraco		
Bispu ..	Bispo		
Chá ..	Cha		

Kanarese	*Portuguese*
? Káphi ..	Café
Káphri ..	Cafre
Kathólika ..	Católico
Kiristánu ..	Cristão
Kōbisu ..	Couve
Komphisáñ ..	Confissão
Komuniyāñ ..	Comunhão
Krúji ..	Cruz
Kuśini ..	Cozinha
Lántaru ..	Lanterna
Leylam, lilámu, yálam, yélamu	Leilão
? Limbe, nimbe	Limão
? Manu ..	Maná
Mējódu ..	Meia
Meju ..	Mesa
Mestre ..	Mestre
Mīsayagavu ..	Missa
Misiyonár ..	Missionário
Natalu ..	Natal
Novenú ..	Novena
Óstu ..	Hóstia
Pádri, pádari ..	Padre
? Pagadi ..	Paga, pagar
Phaláni ..	Fulano
Pangayu ..	Pangaio
Pappáya (v.t. parangi-haṇṇu)	Papaia
Papósu ..	Papuses
Pápu (pope) ..	Papa
Parata ..	Prato
Páska ..	Páscoa
Pénu (sisa-pénu, pencil)	Pena
Pérla-mara, pérla-haṇṇu	Pera
Phannále ..	Funil
? Phaṭóki ..	Foguete
Pingáni ..	Palangana
Pipe, pipái, pīpáyi	Pipa
Pistúlu ..	Pistola
? Polis ..	Policia
Pulpitu ..	Púlpito
Rabaku ..	Rabeca
Rasídi, raśidi, raśidu	Recibo
Rátalu ..	Arrátel
Rejmu ..	Resma
Ripu ..	Ripa
Sābbu, sābúnu	Sabão
? Sāgo, seigo ..	Sagu
Sakraméntu ..	Sacramento
Sakristi ..	Sacristia
Saládu ..	Salada
Sankristán ..	Sacristão
Semitéri ..	Cemitério
Sóḍti ..	Sorte
Spanju ..	Esponja
Spiritu Sántu (C)	Espírito Santo
Tambaku ..	Tabaco
? Tambure ..	Tambor
? Tubu ..	Tubo
? Tuphanu ..	Tufão
Turibulu (C) ..	Turíbulo
Váru ..	Vara
Varanḍa ..	Varanda
Vésperu ..	Vésperas

24. Kashmiri

Kashmiri		*Portuguese*	*Kashmiri*		*Portuguese*
Chai	..	Chá	Tabáku, tamók, tamok		Tabaco
Mez	..	Mesa	? Tuphán	..	Tufão
Sában, sábun	..	Sabão			

25. Khassi

Khassi		*Portuguese*	*Khassi*		*Portuguese*
? Aiah	..	Aia	Lilam	..	Leilão
Almari	..	Armário	? Linten	..	Lanterna
Baranda	..	Varanda	Mastul	..	Mastro
Borma	..	Veruma	Mez	..	Mesa
Budam	..	Botão	Pādri	..	Padre
Buiam	..	Boião	Peru, pirú	..	Peru
? Butol	..	Botelha	Phiris	..	Pires
Garod, karod	..	Guarda	Phita, fita	..	Fita
Istri	..	Estirar	Pipa	..	Pipa
Juvari	..	Jogar	Prek	..	Prego
Kamra	..	Câmara	Raj-misteri	..	Mestre
Kaphi	..	Café	Saban	..	Sabão
? Kaptan, koptan		Capitão	? Saku	..	Sagu
			Sha	..	Chá
Kartus	..	Cartucho	Shabi	..	Chave
Kirja	..	Igreja	? Shap	..	Chapa
Kubi	..	Couve	Taulia	..	Toalha
Kudam	..	Gudão	? Tupan	..	Tufão

26. Konkani

Konkani		*Portuguese*	*Konkani*		*Portuguese*
Ab ('*pākhoṭó*')		Aba (a skirt of a garment)	*Ābilydād* (*sakti*)		Habilidade (ability)
Ābāl ('*dāuṁdalṇi*')		Abalo (uneasiness)	*Ābrās* ('*veṅg*')		Abraço (embrace)
Ābesí	..	ABC	Ābríl	..	Abril

Konkani	Portuguese	Konkani	Portuguese
Ābsolusāṁv ..	Absolviçao (absolution)	*Ākānh* (*bhīḍ*)	Acanho (bashfulness)
Ābusār-karuṅk (*māthyār basuṅk*)	Abusar (to abuse)	*Akānhād* (*bhidest*)	Acanhado (bashful)
		Ākolt (eccles.)	Acólito (acolyte)
Ādes ..	Adeus	*Ākoṁpāmhāment* (*pāvṇi*)	Acompanhamento (bridal party)
Ādministrador	Administrador		
Ādministrāsāṁv (*chalauṇi*)	Administração (administration)	*Ākoṁpānhaṅt* (*pavṇó*)	Acompanhante (member of a bridal party)
Ādr ..	Adro		
Ādūph ..	Adufa	*Ākt* ..	Acta (record)
Ādveṅt (eccls.)	Advento (advent)	*Ākt* ..	Acto (religious function)
Ādvogād ..	Advogado	*Ākuzār-karuṅk* (*parivâduṁk*)	Acusar (to accuse)
Advogār-karuṅk (*vakili-karunk*)	Advogar (to plead)	*Ākuzāsāṁv* (*phiryād*)	(Açusacão (accusation)
Ag-bént, ālmét, almént	Água-benta	*Āldrāv* (*khil*) ..	Aldrava (door-latch)
Āgeṁt (' *kārbhāri* ')	Agente (agent)	*Ālegāsāṁv* (*dakhauṇ*)	Alegação (allegation)
Āgôst ..	Agôsto	*Ālegar* (*samtośi*)	Alegre (cheerful)
Āgphurtād ..	Aguas-furtadas (garrets)	*Ālegrêt* (*kuṁḍi*)	Alegrete (flower-pot)
Āgsál ..	Agua e sal (kind of curry)	*Ālekri* ..	Alecrim (rosemary)
Āgvādôr ..	Aguador (watering-can)	*Āleluī* ..	Aleluia (alleluia)
Ājud (*pichkāri*)	Ajuda (enema)		
Ājudāṅt ..	Ajudante	Āletô ..	Alerta
Ājudār-karuṅk	Ajudar	Ālgārijm ..	Algarismo
Ājust (*khand*)	Ajuste (contract)	Ālgôj ..	Algoz
		Āliment (*ann*)	Alimento (sustenance)
Ājustar-karuṅk (*khaṁduṅk*)	Ajustar (to contract)		
		Ālkātíph ..	Alcatifa

Konkani	*Portuguese*
Ālkātrāṁv ..	Alcatrão
Ālkúṅh ..	Alcunha
Ālm, pl. *ālmāṁ* (souls in purgatory)	Alma (soul)
Ālmānāk (*paṁcháṅg*)	Almanaque (almanac)
Ālmār ..	Armário
Ālmirānt ..	Almirante (admiral)
Ālmir ..	Almeirão (wild endive)
Ālmopharij (*vān*)	Almofariz (mortar)
Ālmoreṁ ..	Almorreimas (hemorroids)
Ālmús ..	Almôço
Ālpāk ..	Alpaca (alpaca)
Ālphājem ..	Alfazema (lavender)
Ālphānd ..	Alfândega
Alphāz ..	Alface (lettuce)
Ālphér ..	Alferes
Ālphinêt ..	Alfinete
Ālphyād (*darji*)	Alfaiate (tailor)
Āls (*dasturi*) ..	Alça (perquisite)
Ālsāpāṁv (*chordār*) ..	Alçapão (trapdoor)
Ālt (*uṅch*) ..	Alto (tall)
Āltār ..	Altar
Ālthe ..	Alteia (hollyhock)
Ālv ..	Alva
Ālvís ..	Alviçaras (S)
Ālvorād ..	Alvorada
Āmā ..	Ama

Konkani	*Portuguese*
Āmbar ..	Âmbar
Āmen ..	Amen
Āmend, āmén	Amêndoa
Amig (*iśt*) ..	Amigo (friend)
Āmijād (*iśtigat*)	Amizade (friendship)
Āmikt (eccles.)	Amito (amice)
Āmór (*tut*) ..	Amora (mulberry)
Āmostr ..	Amostra
Ānanês ..	Ananás
? Andôr, andôl	Andor
Ānijet (*sepāṁcho soro*)	Anisete (aniseed liqueur)
Ānimál ..	Animal
Āniversār ..	Aniversário
Āṅj ..	Anjo
Ānón ..	Anona
Āntikrist ..	Anticristo (Anti Christ)
Ānuṁs (*kabar, praghat*)	Anúncio (announcement)
Ānzli (*gari*) ..	Anzolo (fishing-hook)
Āpār ..	Aparo (nib)
Āpelāsāṁv ..	Apelação (appeal)
Āpelāsāṁv karuṅk (*ilaj māguṅk*)	Apelar (to appeal)
Āpharāmeṅt ..	Aforamento (leasehold estate)
Āphekt (*moypas*)	Afecto (affection)

Konkani	Portuguese
Āphektuoz (mogal)	Afectuoso (affectionate)
Āphinār-karuṅk (svar meḷauṅk)	Afinar (to tune)
Āphliksāṁv (duḥkh)	Aflição (affliction)
Āphlit (duhkvaṁt)	Aflicto (grieved)
Āphons, āphonsāchó āmbó	Afonsa
Āpontār karuṅk	Apontar
Apost (vaḍhā)	Aposta (a wager)
Āpóstl ..	Apóstolo
Āppopleśi (ragat chaduṁk)	Apoplexia (apoplexy)
Āpprovād zāvuṅk	Aprovado (to be approved)
Āprovār karuṅk	Aprovar (to approve)
Āprovāsāṁv ..	Aprovação (approval)
Ār ..	Ar (palsy)
Ārām ..	Arame
Ārārūt ..	Araruta (arrowroot)
Ārgāmās ..	Argamassa
Ārgól ..	Argola
Ārgolinh ..	Argolinha
Árk ..	Arco
Ārk ..	Arca (ark)
Ārkānj ..	Arcanjo (archangel)
Ārm (banduk)	Arma (gun)
Ārmād ..	Armada

Konkani	Portuguese
Ārmād ..	Armado (armed)
Ārmādor ..	Armador (a decorator)
Ārmār karuṅk (*neṭauṅk*)	Armar (to decorate)
Ārmāsāmv ..	Armação (decoration)
Ārmónyu ..	Harmónio
Āros fugād ..	Arroz refugado (a kind of pilau)
Ārp ..	Harpa
Ārremātādor (pavnekar)	Arrematador (auctioneer)
Arremātār karuṅk (pāvuṅk)	Arrematar (to put up for auction)
Arremātāsāṁv	Arrematação (auction)
Ārsebisp ..	Arcebispo (archbishop)
Ārsebispād ..	Arcebispado (archbishopric)
Arsedyāg ..	Arcediago (archdeacon)
Ārsenāl ..	Arsenal
Ārt ..	Arte
Artig (paik) ..	Artigo (article of faith)
Artig (leg.) ..	Artigo (article)
Ārtilheri (tophkhano)	Artilharia (artillery)
Āsād ..	Assado
Āsistir-zāvuṅk	Assistir

Konkani	Portuguese
Āspirānt ..	Aspirante (a subaltern)
Āt, āṅt ..	Ata
Ātak ..	Ataque (attack)
Atākar karunk (*āmgār yevuṅk*)	Atacar (to attack)
Atemsāṁv ..	Atenção
Ātrevid ..	Atrevido
Āut (*vyavahār*)	Auto (complaint)
Autor (*pushtakkār*)	Autor (author)
Āvaliadôr (*ajmāsi, motāytolô*)	Avaliador (appraiser)
Āvaliār karuṅk (*molāvuṅk*)	Avaliar (to appraise)
Āvāliāsāṁv ..	Avaliação (valuation)
Āvdyeṁs (*aykaṇi*)	Audiência (audience)
Āvémari, aimori	Ave Maria
Āveṁs (‘*ghodepāval*’)	Avença (bot. maiden-hair)
Āviz ..	Aviso
Āvizār-karuṅk	Avisar
Āyá ..	Aia
Āz ..	Az
Āzeton ..	Azeitona
Āzúl ..	Azul
Āzil (*āśram*) ..	Asilo (asylum)
? Baglo ..	Baixel
Bāil (*nāch*) ..	Baile (dance)
Bājū ..	Baju (woman's blouse)
Bākālhāṁv ..	Bacalhau
Bākulh (*koṁkeṁ*)	Báculo (pastoral staff)
Bālāṁv ..	Balão (balloon)
Balchāṁv ..	Balchão
Bāldi ..	Balde
Balkāṁv ..	Balcão (balcony)
Bālsm ..	Bálsamo
Bālsamār karuṅk (*maḍyāṁt parmal bharuṁk*)	Embalsamar (to embalm)
Bāṁkāl ..	Bancal (carpet)
Bāṁket (*bhojan, jevan*)	Banquete (banquet)
Bāṁket (eccles.)	Banqueta
Bānd ..	Banda
Bānd ..	Bando
Bāndêj ..	Bandeja
Bander ..	Bandeira
Banh (*nahāṇ*)	Banho (bath)
Bāṅhar karuṅk	Bainhar
Bāṅk ..	Banco
Bānkiṇ ..	Banquinho (a small wooden seat)
Bāph ..	Bafo
Bāphād ..	Abafado
Bārálh ..	Baralho
Bārālhār karuṅk	Baralhar
Bārāṁv (*desāy*)	Barão (baron)
Bārbêr (*nhāvi*)	Barbeiro (barber)
Bārkas ..	Barcaça

Konkani	Portuguese
Barl	Barril
Barmo, birmo	Verruma
Barrāṁv	Varrão
Barrêt	Barrete
Barsál	Braçal
Barsalat (*kām-kaṇ*)	Bracelete (bracelet)
Bās ('*jarḍi*')	Baço (spleen)
Bāś (*mus.*) (*nichasavan*)	Baixo (bass)
Baśão	Baixão (bassoon)
Basí, baśí	Bacia or Bacio
Bást	Basta
Bastāṁv	Bastão
Bātālhāṁv	Batalhão
Batatim (*kaṇgi*)	Batatinha (medicinal tuber)
Batató	Batata
Bātedor (*peṭṇeṁ*)	Batedor (a rammer)
Bateló	Batel
Bāteri	Bateria
Bātk	Bátega
Bāú	Baú
Bāvtíjṁ	Baptismo
Bāynêt	Baioneta
Báyś (uṇav)	Baixa
Beāt	Beata (a religious woman who does not live in a community but by herself)
Bebdó	Bêbado
Bej (*umāṁv*)	Beijo (kiss)
Beṁjimeṅt	Benzimento (blessing)
Beṁs	Bens (property)
Bemsáṁv	Bênção
Benhār karuṅk	Benzer
Bentín	Bentinho
Bêr	Beira (brink, eaves)
Bhobḷó (also bobr)	Abóbora
Bibliotek (*pustaksāḷ*)	Biblioteca (library)
Bík (*naḷ, naḷī*)	Bica (spout)
Bilambí, bimblí, bilambeṁ, bimbleṁ	Bilimbim
Bilhêt (*chit*)	Bilhete (card)
Binokl	Binóculo
Bíph	Bife
Bisêst	Bissexto
Biskút	Biscoito
Bísp	Bispo
Bispād	Bispado (bishopric)
Bizágr	Visagra
Bob	Bobo
Bobd (*ghumaṭ, bhuṁyār*)	Abóbada (vault)
Bôb decamᵉd	Bobo de comedia (buffoon)
Boḍad	Bordo
Bokād ('*ghāms, kuṭko*')	Bocado (morsel, small piece)
Ból	Bola

Konkani	Portuguese
Boletiṁ (*varta-mānpatr*)	Boletim (official periodical)
Bolính ..	Bolinho
Bôl ..	Bôlo
Bóls ..	Bôlsa
Bômb ..	Bomba
Boṁ dí ..	Bom dia
Bonéṁ ..	Boné
Boniphrāt (*sutribāhuli*)	Bonifrate (puppet-show)
Bord (deg; kinaró)	Borda (border, selvedge)
Bordāṁv (mus. *gor*)	Bordão (base string)
Bordār karuṅk	Bordar (to embroider)
Bórl ..	Borla
Bôrr ..	Bôrra
Bót ..	Bota
? Bôt ..	Bote
? Botl ..	Botelha
Brāṁk ..	Branco (white wine)
Brāṁdāṁv .	Brandão (large wax candle)
Brév ..	Breve (Pope's letter)
Brevyār ..	Breviário (Breviary)
Bríṁ ..	Brim (strong linen fabric)
Bruś (*ghāḍin*)	Bruxa (a hag; witch)
Brut (*monjāt, mūrkh*)	Bruto (brute)
Búch ..	Bucho (tripe)
Bujī ..	Bugia (small candle)
Bukál ..	Bocal
Búl ..	Bula
Búl ..	Bule
Bulach ..	Bolacha
Burāk ..	Buraco
Burāp ..	Borrado (blotted out)
Búrr ..	Burro
Burrāṁv ..	Borrão (first draft of a writing)
Burrāruṅk (*śai ghāluṅk*)	Borrar (to blur)
? Burús ..	Bruça
Busét ..	Boceta
Butámv ..	Botão
Butidor (*khamchṇār*)	Embutidor (inlayer)
Chá, cháv ..	Chá
Chāg (*ghāy*) ..	Chaga (wound)
Chāl, śāl (*āḍvol*)	Chale(shawl)
Chālās (khesṭāy)	Chalaca (joke)
Chamādôr ..	Chamador
Chāṁtr ..	Chantre (chanter)
Chāprús (*kachar*)	Chapuz (wedge)
Charôl (*āṁdal*)	Charola (a litter for carrying images of saints; see andór)
Chaurīs ..	Chouriço

Konkani	*Portuguese*
Chāvêr ('a bunch of keys'), chāví	Chave
Chepéṁ ..	Chapéu
Chermel ..	Charumela
? Chhāp, śáp; chhāpunk; chhāpṇí; chhāpkár; chhāpí; chhāpó; chhāpekár	Chapa
Chikān (*taṭ-ḍoṁg*)	Chicana (chicanery)
Chikanêr (*taṭ-ḍhoṁgi*)	Chicaneiro (one up to chicanery)
Chíkr ..	Chícara
Chinel, chinel-kārṇ	Chinela
Chirpāṁ ..	Chiripos
Chit ..	Chita
Chokolāt ..	Chocalate
Dād ..	Dado
Dālmātik (ec-cles.)	Dalmatica (dalmatic)
Dām ..	Dama
Dāṁs ..	Dança
Damāsk ..	Damasco
Dāt (*tārikh*) ..	Data (date)
Defêyt (*aguṇ; khoḍ*)	Defeito (defect)
Degrāv ..	Degrau
Degred (*kālyā pāṇyāk dhād-ṇeṁ*)	Degredo (exile)

Konkani	*Portuguese*
Degredād (*kālyā pāṇyāk dhāḍ-lalo*)	Degredado (exiled)
Dejembr ..	Dezembro (December)
Dejm ..	Décima (tithe)
Dekór (*toṅḍpaṭh*)	De cor (by heart)
Dekrét ..	Decreto
Delegād ..	Delegado (deputy)
Demānd (*myāy*)	Demanda (lawsuit)
Demāndist, *demāndkār* (*nyāyi*)	Demandista (litigious person)
Demón (us. fig.)	Demónio (devil)
Depôr karuṅk (*gvāhiki divuṁk*)	Depor (to testify to)
Depóst (*thev-ṇeṁ*)	Depósito (deposit)
Deputād(*vakil*)	Deputado (deputy)
Deseṁh (*nakśó*, *chitr*)	Desenho (design, drawing)
Despāch ..	Despacho
Despêz ..	Despesa
Desprezār karuṅk	Desprezar
Devosāṁv, Devót ('religious serenade')	Devoção
Devôt (*bhakti-vaṁt*)	Devoto (a devout man)

Konkani	Portuguese
Didāl ..	Dedal
Dilikad (*nājūk*)	Delicado (delicate)
Diplóm (sanad)	Diploma (diploma)
Direktôr (*nāyak*)	Director (director)
Dirêt (*adhikār*)	Direito (right)
Desidir karuṅk (*nichāv karunk*)	Decidir (to decide)
Disijāṁv nivāḍó)	Decisão (decision)
Diskomphyād (*dubhāvi*)	Desconfiado (diffident)
Diskoṁphyār-zāvuṅk	Desconfiar
Diskónt (*sôḍ, súṭ*)	Desconto (discount)
Diskontár-karuṅk	Descontar
Diskulph (*bogsaṇéṁ*)	Desculpa (forgiveness)
Diskūrs (*sabhāvād*)	Discurso (speech)
Dispedid (*rajā*)	Despedida (farewell)
Dispeṁs ..	Despensa
Dispeṁs (*māphī*)	Dispensa (dispensation)
Dispemsêr ..	Despenseiro (pantry-man)
Dispūt (*jhagḍeṁ*)	Disputa (dispute)
Ditād (*opār*) ..	Ditado (maxim)
Ditār karuṅk (*sāṁguṁk*)	Ditar (to dictate)

Konkani	Portuguese
Disyonār ..	Dicionário
Disypl (*śis, siknār*)	Discipulo (disciple)
Dizgôst (*khaṅt*)	Desgôsto (sorrow)
Dizord (*gaḍbaḍ*)	Desordem (disorder)
Dizôrdêr (*tuphāni*)	Desordeiro (disorderly fellow)
Dizgrās ..	Desgraça
Dó (*kāḷeṁ*) ..	Dó (mourning)
Dôbr ..	Dobro
Dobrād ..	Dobrado
Dobraṁv ..	Dobrão
Doṁ ..	Dom
Dôs ..	Doce
Dosél ..	Dossel
Dôt (*kanyādhār*)	Dote (dowry)
Dotôn, dotín	Doutrina
Dotôr ..	Doutor
Drāgon ..	Dragona (epaulet)
Dúk ..	Duque (two points in cards)
Dulgeṁs ..	Indulgencia
Durāk ..	Duraque
Duveṁs (*piḍā*)	Doença (illness)
Duveṅt (*piḍevant*)	Doente (a patient)
Dūz ..	Duzia
Dyāb ..	Diabo
Dyākn ..	Diácono (deacon)

Konkani	Portuguese
Dyāmāṅt ..	Diamante
Dyāṁv ..	Deão (dean)
Editāl (*dākhló*)	Edital (proclamation)
Efêt (*guṇ*) ..	Efeito (effect)
El ..	Velho
Elephāṅt ..	Elefante
Elesāṁv (*viṁchap*)	Eleição (election)
Empātār karuṅk (*bād karuṅk*)	Empatar (to make equal)
Emprêg ..	Emprêgo
Empregād ..	Empregado (person employed)
Emprestār-karuṅk	Emprestar
Eṅsāy (*parikśā*)	Ensaio (rehearsal)
Entrād ..	Entrada (hall)
Entrād (*svāri*)	Entrada (entry)
Entrār zavuṅk (*bhitar saruṅk*)	Entrar (to enter)
Entreg (*deṇéṁ*)	Entrega (delivery)
Entregār karuṅk	Entregar (to deliver)
Epākt ..	Epacta (epact)
Epistl (eccles.)	Epistola (epistle)
Érāṁs (*dāyz*) ..	Herança (inheritance)
Erdār-karunk	Herdar
Érdêr (*dāyji*) ..	Herdeiro (heir)
Eréj ..	Herege (heretic)
Ereji ..	Heresia (heresy)
Ervādôs ..	Erva doce (dill herb)
Erveläd (*jhāḍ-palacho voiz*)	Ervenário (herbalist)
Es ..	Essa
Eskānd ..	Escândalo
Eskolt ..	Escolta
Eskomumgād (*sirāp paḍlalo*)	Excomungado (excommunicated)
Eskomumgār karuṅk	Excomungar (to excommunicate)
Eskomunhāṁv	Excomunhão
Eskôv ..	Escôva
Eskūs (*nīb*) ..	Excusa (excuse)
Esmālt ..	Esmalte (enamel)
Espādílh ..	Espadilha
Espārtilh ..	Espartilho (corset)
Espérāṁs ..	Esperança
Eśpért ..	Esperto
Espertêz (*huśarki*)	Esperteza (smartness)
Esplikār-karuṅk	Explicar
Esplikāsāṁv (*vivaraṇ*)	Explicação (explanation)
Esponj ..	Esponja
Espozisāṁv (eccles.)	Exposição (exposition of the Blessed Sacrament)
Estād (*bhês*) ..	Estado
Estānt ..	Estante
Estāsāṁv ..	Estação (catheeism)
Estāsāṁv ..	Estação (station)

Konkani	*Portuguese*
Estimār-karuṅk	Estimar (to esteem)
Estimasāṁv (*āpurbāy*)	Estimação (esteem)
Estríb ..	Estribo
Estudar, istud karuṅk	Estudar
Ezám ..	Exame
Ezaminadôr (*parikśa ghetalo*)	Examinador (examiner)
Ezekutor (leg.)	Executor (executor)
Ezeṁpl ..	Exemplo
? Gāg ..	Gago
Gal (*dabājo*) ..	Gala (gala)
Gālāṁv ..	Galão
Gāleri ..	Galeria
Galhêt (*śimsli*)	Galheta (cruet)
Gāṁāṁv ..	Gamão (backgammon)
Gamél ..	Gamela
Gāṁg, kāṁg ..	Ganga (kind of khaki cloth)
Gāṁgren ..	Gangrena (gangrene)
Ganch ..	Gancho
Gānh (*joḍ*) ..	Ganho
Gānhār karuṅk (*zoḍuṅk*)	Ganhar (to earn)
Garād ..	Grade
Garnāl ..	Granada
Gārph ..	Garfo
Gārsó, garsuló (*niḷo, niḷsār*)	Garço (blue-eyed)
Garvāt ..	Gravata (necktie)

Konkani	*Portuguese*
Gāst ..	Gasto
Gāstār karuṅk (*kharchuṅk*)	Gastar (to spend)
Gavét ..	Gaveta
Gāzet (*vartta-mānpattr*)	Gazeta (gazette)
Gitār ..	Guitarra
Giyāṁv ..	Guião (religious banner)
Gizād ..	Guisado
Gizāmeṅt ..	Guisamento (wine, candles, for mass)
Glôb ..	Globo
Gól ..	Gola
Gomār karuṅk (*pej ghāluṁk*)	Engomar (to starch)
Góm ..	Goma
Gôst ..	Gosto
Govêrn ..	Govêrno
Governādor ..	Governador
Gracioz (*keśṭā-yaṁcho*)	Gracioso (humorous)
Grādārī ..	Gradaria (railing)
Gráṁv ..	Grão
Grás ..	Graça
Grāś ..	Graxa
Grāv (*pāunḍo*)	Grau (step, rung)
Grilyāṁv (*sori*)	Grilhão (chain)
Guer (*zūz*) ..	Guerra (war)
Gurūd lāvuṁk (*chikṭāvuṁk*)	Grudar (to glue)
Gudāṁv ..	Gudão
Gurud ..	Grude

Konkani	Portuguese
Gurgulét ..	Gorgoleta
Guvārd ..	Guarda
Guvārdanáp ..	Guardanapo
Guvārnisāṁv	Guarnição (trimming of a garment)
Igraz, igarz ..	Igreja
Iló (*ḍoḷo*) ..	Ilhó (eyelet)
Imāz ..	Imagem
Imgrāt (*anupkāri*)	Ingrato (ungrateful)
Iṁphern ..	Inferno
Imphormāsāṁv (*dād*)	Informação (information)
Imyn (*sadgit*)..	Hino (hymn)
Inglêz, ingrêz	Inglês
Inimig (*duśmān*)	Inimigo (enemy)
Inimizād (*duśmāṅkāy*)	Inimizade (enmity)
Injustis ..	Injustiça
Inoseṁs ..	Inôcencia
Inoseṅt (*gunyaṁv nāslalo*)	Inocente (innocent)
Iṁspektôr (*adhikārī*)	Inspector (inspector)
Iṁstāṁs (leg.)	Instância (legal tribunal)
Iṁstrument ..	Instrumento
Iṁsultār karuṅk (*mān kāduṁk*)	Insultar (to insult)
Iṁsult (*akmān*)	Insulto (insult)
Inteṁsāṁv ..	Intenção
Iṁtentār karuṅk (leg.; *nitin ghāluṅk*)	Intentar (to commence legal action)
Iṅteresād (*bhāgidār*)	Interessado (shareholder)
Intêr (*puruṁk, mātiyek lavuṁk*)	Enterrar (to bury)
Interés (*ādāv*)	Interêsse (interest)
Iṅtimāsāṁv (*kaḷauṅi*)	Intimação (intimation)
Iṅtimār-karuṅk (*kaḷauṇk*)	Intimar (to cite)
Intuvār karuṅk (*svaruṁk*)	Entoar (to hum)
Intuvāsāṁv (*svarṅi*)	Entoaçao (air, tune)
Intrūd ..	Entrudo
Iṅvéj (*nichkuchār, nirduḥkh*)	Inveja (jealousy)
Iṅvejoz (*nichkuchāri*)	Invejoso (jealous)
Iṅveṁtār (*zhaḍti*)	Inventario (inventory)
Ipokrésy (*dhoṁg*)	Hipocrisia (hypocrisy)
Irmāṁv ..	Irmão
Irmit ..	Ermida
Isād, iśad ..	Enxêrto
Iskād ..	Escada
Iskādor ..	Esquadro
Iskalér ..	Escaler
Iskól ..	Escola
Iskrivāṅki (*śeṇaypaṅ*)	Escrivania (clerkship)
Iskrivaṁv ..	Escrivão
Isóp ..	Hissope

Konkani	*Portuguese*
Ispād ..	Espada
Ispīlêt ..	Espoleta
Istór ..	História
Istud ..	Estudo
Istudāṅt (*śikpi*)	Estudante (student)
Izmól ..	Esmola
Jākêt ..	Jaqueta
Jāner (*pauśmag*)	Janiero
Janot (*kāsphīs*)	Janota (dandy)
Jār ..	Jarra
Jārd ..	Jarda (a yard measure)
Jel (*baraph*) ..	Gêlo (ice)
Jelek ..	Jaleco (a doublet)
Jen (*guṇ, svabhāv*)	Génio (disposition)
Jenebr ..	Genebra
Jeneral ..	General
Jervasāṁv ..	Geraçao
Jes (*khêḍ*) ..	Gêsso (chalk)
Jest (*môḍ*) ..	Gesto (gesture)
Jet (*kuvet*) ..	Geito (knack)
Jintu ..	Gentio
Jinvar (subet), jinvār dharuṅk	Jejuar (to fast)
Jiresaḷ (*suryākamal*)	Gira-sol (sunflower)
Jôgādor, jogo	Jogar
Jornal ..	Jornal
Jubilev ..	Jubileu (jubilee)
Jūdi ('*short coat*')	Judia (a long coat formerly worn by Jews)
Jugār, jugār kheḷ, jugár kheluṅk, jugārí	Jogar
Julgāmeṅt (*nivāḍó*)	Julgamento (trial)
Jūlh (*Sravaṇ*)	Julho
Jūnh (*Aśaḍh*)	Junho
Jūṅt (*jamo, meḷ*)	Junta (council)
Jūr ..	Juro
Jurāment ..	Juramento
Jurār-zāvuṅk	Jurar
Júst ..	Justo
Justiphikāsāṁv (*rujvāt*)	Justificação (legal proof)
Justis ..	Justiça
Juyiz ..	Juiz
Kabaler (*purn*) ..	Cabeleira (false hair)
Kabār karuṅk (*sampauṅk*)	Acabar
Kabay ..	Cabaia
Kābid ..	Cabide
Kabo ..	Cabo (a corporal)
Kāchor (us. as interjection)	Cachorro (a puppy)
Kader, kadel	Cadeira
Kāderinh ..	Cadeirinha (a stool)
Kādern ..	Caderno (copy book)
Kādey (*baṁdkaṇ*)	Cadeia (gaol)
Kāḍṭil (*paṭṭi, pothi*)	Cartilha (booklet)

Konkani	Portuguese
Kājáṁv ..	Ocasião
Kākāv ..	Cacau
Kāld ..	Caldo
Kālderijn ..	Calderinha (kettle)
Kāldin ..	Caldinha (a kind of curry)
Kālkul (gaṇam)	Cálculo (reckoning)
Kālor (garmi, ubáḷ)	Calor (heat)
Kālot (phaṣauṇeṁ)	Calote (swindling)
Kāls ..	Cális
Kālsād ..	Calçado ..
Kālsādor ..	Calçador (shoehorn)
Kālsāmv ..	Calção
Kām ..	Cama
Kāmād (gānthaṅ)	Cambata (string of fish)
Kāmbrād ..	Camarada
Kāmbrist ..	Camarista (Municipal Counsellor)
Kāmizol ..	Camisola
Kāmp ..	Campo
Kāṁphr ..	Cânfora
Kāmpín ..	Campainha
Kāmr, kambr	Câmara
Kānitor (gāṇār)	Cantor (singer)
Kāṁv (ghoḍo)	Cão (trigger)
Kān ..	Cano
Kānāl ..	Canal
Kānāpó ..	Canapé
Kānār ..	Canário

Konkani	Portuguese
Kānel ..	Canela
Kānhāṁv ..	Canhão
Kāṅkr (chāḷaṃpuli)	Cancro (cancer)
Kānokl ..	Canóculo (perspective glass)
Kānt (gāyan)	Canto (singing)
Kāntār, kāntār-karuṅk *(gāvuṁk)* ..	Cantar
Kantrel ..	Cantareira (niche to keep bottles, etc.)
Kānvêt ..	Canivete
Kāp ..	Capa
Kapāṁv ..	Capão
Kapāṁv-karuṅk (āṁḍ khāḍuṁk)	Capar (to castrate)
Kapāz ..	Capaz
Kapél ..	Capela
Kapelāṁv ..	Capelão (chaplain)
Kāphi, kāphó	Café
Kāphlār karuṅk	Acafelar
Kāpitaṁv ..	Capitão
Kāpitl (āṁk) ..	Capitulo (chapter)
Kāpôt ..	Capote
Kapsél (māthem)	Capitel (capital of a column)
Kaphlād ..	Capelada (uppers of a shoe)
Karāb ..	Cravo

Konkani	Portuguese
Kārdyāl ..	Cardeal (cardinal)
Karél (a species of mango)	Carreira
Karét ..	Carreta
Kārg (*jāgó, adhikār*)	Cargo (office)
Karga (*oghem̐*)	Carga (load)
Kāridād ..	Caridade
Kārṭ, kāṭ (*chauto*)	Quarta (fourth part)
Kārt ..	Carta
Kartel ..	Quartel
Karto (*pustak*)	Cartapácio (note-book)
Kārtor ..	Cartório (notary's office)
Kārtuś ..	Cartucho
Kās (*śikār*) ..	Caça (chase, hunting)
Kāsādor (*śikāri*)	Caçador (hunter)
Kasāg (*ḍaglo*)	Casaca (a coat)
Kāsk (*lāschem̐ okhat*)	Cáustico (caustic)
Kāst ..	Casta
Kāstig (*khāst*)	Castigo (punishment)
Kāstijm ..	Castismo (caste mindedness)
Kāstisāl ..	Castiçal
Kāstist ..	Castista (one keen on caste distinctions)
Kāstôr ..	Castor
Kāsuvād (*khebād*)	Caçoada (teasing)
Kāsuvār kāruṅk (*kem̐ḍum̐k*)	Caçoar (to tease)
Kātesijm ..	Catechismo
Kātolik ..	Católico
Kātr (*pālki*) ..	Catre (a small bedstead)
Kauz (*kārān*)	Causa (cause)
Kāyād ..	Caiado (white-washed)
Kāyādor ..	Caiador (one who gives white colour wash)
Kayār-karuṅk (*chuno kāduṃk*)	Caiar (to white-wash)
Kāyś (*peṭ*) ..	Caixa (a box)
Kāyśām̐v ('a coffin')	Caixão (big chest, coffin)
Kāz ..	Caso
Kāz ..	Casa
Kāzār; kāzār-karuṅk; kāzār zāvuṅk	Casar
Kāzro; kāzāri; kāzārāchó; kāzu; kāz; kajel, kāzū-goḷá	Caju
Kāzul ..	Casula (chasuble)
Kerubim ..	Querubim
Keś (*gārāṇem̐*)	Queixa (complaint)

Konkani	*Portuguese*
Khāpri ..	Cafre
Khuris ; khuris kāḍuṅk ; khursār kāḍuṅk ; khursār zaḍuṅk ; khursar māruṅk ; khuris karuṅk	Cruz
Kirit (*khoḍi kaḍneṁ*)	Critica
Kirit māruṅk (*khoḍi karuṅk*)	Criticar
Kistel ('reproof')	Clister (enema)
Klāret ..	Clarete (claret)
Klārinet ..	Clarinete (clarinet)
Klās (*varg*) ..	Classe (class)
Klaustr (*maṭh*)	Claustro (cloister)
Kleriji ..	Clerezia (clergy)
Kobrador (*patkār*)	Cobrador (bill collector)
Kobrāṁs (*pat*)	Cobrança (bill collection)
Kobrār karuṅk (*path geuṁk*)	Cobrar (to collect bills)
Koch ..	Coche
Kochêr ..	Cocheiro
Kodjudôr ..	Coadjutor (coadjutor)
Kokād ..	Cocada (cocoanut sweet in Indo-Port.)
Kolār (*galebaṁd*)	Colar (neck band)
Kolārinh ..	Colarinho (men's collar)
Kolun ..	Coluna
Kophr ..	Cofre
Koym ('cattle pound')	Coima (a fine)
Kob ..	Couve
Kobd ..	Côvado
Koléj ..	Colégio
Komāndānt ..	Comandante
Komd ..	Cómoda (chest of drawers)
Komed (*nāṭikā*)	Comedia (comedy)
Komend ..	Comenda
Komendador	Comendador
Komesār karuṅk (*āḍāvuṁk, ārāṁbhuṁk*)	Começar (to begin)
Komgṙ ..	Congrua (allowance to a priest)
Kompanher (*sāngāti*)	Companheiro (companion)
Komphet ..	Confeito
Komphôrt (*kuśalpaṇ*)	Confôrto (comfort)
Komphrāri, komphr	Confraria
Komphujāṁv (*goṁdhaḷ*)	Confusão (confusion)
Komphuz (*ghābro*)	Confuso (confused)

Konkani	Portuguese
Komphyāṁs ..	Confiança
Kompositor (ghadnār)	Compositor (composer)
Komsāgrār karuṅk (saṁskaruṅk)	Consagrar (to consecrate)
Komsalāsāṁv (santôś)	Consolação (consolation)
Konselh ..	Conselho
Konserv (murambo)	Conserva (a preserve)
Konservador ..	Conservador (recorder)
Konservator ..	Conservatória (record office)
Komsyems (amtaskharn)	Consciência (conscience)
Koṁsyeṁsos (baryā aṁtashkarṇācho chaltalo)	Consciencioso (conscientious)
Komungār ..	Comungar
Komunhāmv	Comunhão
Koṁveṅt (maṭh, aśram)	Convento (convent)
Koṁversāṁv (dharmbhed)	Conversão (conversion)
Koṁvit ..	Convite
Kond ..	Conde (knave in cards)
Kond ..	Conde (a count)
Kondenād *(sikśecheṁ pharman dilalo)*	Condenado (one convicted)
Kondisāṁv (daśa)	Condição (condition)

Konkani	Portuguese
Konezi ..	Conezia (canonry)
Kong (eccl. t.)	Conégo (a canon)
Konkêr (phātor mārnār)	Cabouqueiro (quarryman)
Konsêlh (prānt)	Concelho (district)
Konsêrt *(saṁgit)*	Concêrto
Konsertār-karunk (sudhāruṁk)	Concertar (to repair)
Konsertin ..	Concertina (concertina)
Konstipāsāṁv (bārkhaṇ)	Constipação (cold, chill)
Koṅsul ..	Consul
Koṅsult (buddh māgṅeṁ)	Consulta (consultation)
Konsumir (lāsuṁk)	Consumir (to be consumed)
Kont ..	Conta
Kont ..	Contas
Kontādôr (mejtalo)	Contador (accountant)
Kontādori (hiśabāchem ghar)	Contadoria (accountant's office)
Kontr (partó) ..	Contrário (contrary)
Kontr ..	Contra
Kontraband (jakātchori)	Contrabando (contraband)
Kontrādāṁs ..	Contradança (quadrille)

Konkani	*Portuguese*	*Konkani*	*Portuguese*
Konträfort (*dhiró*).	Contraforte (a buttress)	*Krizm divuṅk*	Crismar (to give confirmation)
Konträord (*uḷaṭ hukum*)	Contra-ordem (counter-order)	*Kryäd* ..	Criada (servant girl)
Konträpez .. (*sambhär*)	Contrapeso (counter-poise)	*Kryäd* ..	Criado (man servant)
Konträt ..	Contrato	*Kubert* (*olcheṁ*)	Coberta (bed sheet)
Konträvontäd (*khuśibhäyr*)	Contra vontade (unwillingly)	Kuidäd (*phikir*)	Cuidado
Kóp ..	Copo	Kuitäd ..	Coitado
Kóp ..	Cópia	*Kujner* (*raṁdhpi*)	Cozinheiro (cook)
Kopäṃ ..	Copas	*Kujumeṅt* (*kaḍo*)	Cozimento (infusion)
Kopist (*sarekär*)	Copista (drunkard)	Kuläs ..	Colaça
Kôr ..	Côr	Kulchäṁv .. (*däpḍi*)	Colchão
Kôr ..	Côro	Kulchêt ..	Colchete
Kórd ..	Corda	Kulér (*doy*, (*davli*)	Colher
Kordäṃv(' gold chain ')	Cordão	Kulêt ..	Colete
Korejm ..	Quaresma	*Kulp* (*chûk*) ..	Culpa (fault)
Kórj ..	Corja	*Kumäṁv* (*käkūs*)	Comua (latrine)
Kornél ..	Coronel	Kumär, kumärki	Comadre
Kornêt ..	Corneta	Kumpär, kumpärki	Compadre
Korporäl (eccles.)	Corporal (corporal)	Kumpäs ..	Compasso
Korrimäṁv (*kaṭhḍo*)	Corrimão (bannister)	*Kumsädôr* ..	Confessadouro (confessional)
Kortesi (*mansugi*)	Cortesia	Kumsär-karuṅk (kumsar-zävuṅk)	Confessar
Kota ..	Cota (a lawyer's gown)	Kuṁsvär ..	Consoada
Kota (eccles.)	Cota (surplice)	Kunh, kunj ..	Cunha
Kristäṁv ..	Cristão		
Krizm ..	Crisma		

Konkani	*Portuguese*
Kunhād (*mehuṇo, der, naṇḍayo*)	Cunhado
Kūr ..	Cura (curate)
Kurār karuṅk (*baro karuṅk*)	Curar
Kurāsāmv ..	Coração
Kurātiv ..	Curativo (medical treatment)
Kurov ..	Coroa
Kurredôr ..	Corredor
Kurrênt ..	Corrente
Kurrey (*tapāl*), *kurrey kar* ('postman')	Correio (post-office)
Kurtid (*kutlalo*)	Cortido (versed in)
Kurtín ..	Cortina
Kurtir (*rāṁpauṅk*)	Cortir (to cure leather)
Kurvār-karunk (*mukuṭ ghaluṅk*)	Coroar (to crown)
Kurvêt ..	Corveta
Kuryoj (*tajvitecho*)	Curioso (eager to learn)
Kuskurāṁv (*kūt*)	Coscorão (a rap on the head with knuckles)
Kuspidôr ..	Cuspidor
Kust (*kharch*)	Custa (cost)
Kustár-zavuṅk	Custar
Kustod (eccles.)	Custodia (monstrance)
Kustum ..	Costume

Konkani	*Portuguese*
Kutāmv ..	Cotão
Kutní ..	Cotonia
Kuzid ..	Cózido (subst. soup meat)
Kuzidād (*bārkāy, tajvit*)	Curiosidade (intellectual keenness)
Kvādrād (*chaukoṇo*)	Quadrado (square)
Kvādril ..	Quadrilha (dance)
Kvárt ..	Quarto
Ladín ..	Ladainha
Lāmn ..	Lâmina
Lāmpt ..	Lâmpada
Laṁpyāṁv ..	Lampião
Lāṁs (*zāmvó*)	Lanço (bid at auction)
Lāṁs gāluṅk	Lançar em leilão (to bid at auction)
Lāmsét ..	Lanceta
Laṁv (*kheṁs*) ..	Lã (wool)
Lāṅch ..	Lancha
Lāṅtern (*phāṇas*)	Lanterna
Lāps ..	Lápis
Lārāṁj (*nāriṁg*)	Laranja (orange)
Lās ..	Laço
Laśkari ..	Lascarim
Lāt ..	Lata
Leṁs ..	Lenço
Létr ..	Letra
Letrad (see Advogado)	Letrado(lawyer)

Konkani	*Portuguese*
Ley ..	Lei
Leylāṁv ..	Leilão
Leytaṁv (*dhukurlo*)	Leitão (sucking pig)
Libr ..	Libra (pound sterling)
Liberdād (*sattyā*)	Liberdade (liberty)
Lig (*bhāmdhap*)	Liga (garter)
Likor ..	Licor (liqueur)
Limb ..	Limbo (limb)
? Limbó, nimbó, nimbu	Limão
Limonād ..	Limonada (lemonade)
Lingís ..	Linguiça
Linhār karuṅk (*dāgo baruṅk*)	Alinhavar (to baste, to tack)
Liseṁs ..	Licença
Lisāṁv ..	Lição
Lisev ..	Liceu (Lyceum)
List ..	Lista
Lívr ..	Livre
Lívr ..	Livro
Livrār karuṅk	Livrar
Livrārí (*pustakaśālā*)	Livraria (library)
Lôb ..	Loba
Loj ..	Loja
Lôjêr, lôjkār paśārkār)	Lojeiro (shopkeeper)
Lôt (*vāṁto*) ..	Lote (share)
Loterí ..	Lotaria
Lovād ..	Louvado
Lôys ..	Loiça
Luí (' influence of moon on lunatics ')	Lua (moon)
Luminād ..	Luminária
Lunêt ..	Luneta (eyeglass)
Lut ..	Luto
Lúv (' phases of the moon ')	Lua (moon)
Lúv ..	Luva
Māchíl, mānchíl	Machila
Māchpheṁ (*kaḷāsi*)	Macha-fêmea (tongue and groove)
Madan, madín	Madrinha
Madér ..	Madeira
Mādr ..	Madre
Madrupēl (*motyāchi śiṁpi*)	Madrepérola
Magnes (med.)	Magnesia (magnesia)
Mājor, mānjor	Major
Māk (*dol*) ..	Maca (stretcher)
Mākinet ..	Maquineta
Mākn ..	Máquina
Mākinist (*yaṁtraṁ chalaitolo*)	Maquinista (machinist)
Māl ..	Mala
Mālāssād ..	Mal-assado (half-boiled egg)
Māldisāṁv ..	Maldição

Konkani	*Portuguese*
Mālis ..	Malícia
Mālisyoz (*kusḍo*)	Malicioso (malicious)
Mālkyryād ..	Malcriado
Malto, malti, mālteló (' bowl ')	Matula (arch. urinal)
Mām ..	Mama
Māmāṁ ..	Mamã
Maṁtimeṅt .. (*varav*)	Mantimento (victuals)
Mān ..	Mano
Māṇā ..	Mana
Mānā ..	Maná
Māṅdād (*hukuṁ*)	Mandado (writ)
Māndār-karuṅk (*hukūm divuṅk*)	Mandar
Maṅg (*hāt*) ..	Manga (sleeve)
Māngāsāṁv ..	Mangação
Maṅgil (*peṭneṁ*)	Mangual
Maṅgustaṁv	Mangostão
Māngād ..	Mangada (mango cheese)
Māníl ..	Manilha (manille)
Māníp l (eccles.)	Manipulo (maniple)
Maṁter (*barpāchí vahí; reṁd*)	Materia (copyplate; pus)
Māṅt (*ol*) ..	Manto
Mānuāl ..	Manual (prayer-book)
Mānz ..	Manha

Konkani	*Portuguese*
Māp (*nakśo*) ..	Mapa (map)
Mārchār-zāvuṅk (*pāṁ ulām uḍauṁk*)	Marchar
Māre (*pānī*) ..	Maré (tide)
Mariāsāṁv (' astuteness, tact ')	Mareação (seamanship)
Mārinher (*tārvaṭi*)	Marinheiro
Mārk ..	Marca
Mārphiṃ ..	Marfim
Mārmelād ..	Marmelada (marmalade)
? Mārmar ..	Mármore
Mārráph ..	Marrafa
Mārs (*phālguna chaitr*)	Março
Mārsiner (*sāṁdpí*)	Marceneiro (joiner)
Martél ..	Martelo
Mārtír ..	Mártir
Mās (*puḍó*) ..	Maço (packet)
Mas (*lugḍó*) ..	Massa (dough)
Mātāburrāṁv (*tipāvuṁchem kāgad*)	Mataborrão (blotting paper)
Mātin (eccles.)	Matinas (matins)
Mātrāk ..	Matraca
Mātrikl (*nāvaṁchi śivdi*)	Matricula (register)
Matrikulāchi ezam	Exame de Matricula (us. in Goa. Matriculation examination)

Konkani	*Portuguese*	*Konkani*	*Portuguese*
Māy, māvśimāy, māy-tí, Vhaḍlí-māy, dhākṭi-māy)	Mãe	*Meter, menter-zāvuṅk (ghusauṁk)*	Meter-se (to intermeddle)
Māy (vaiśākh jyeshṭh)	Maio (month of May)	Mey ..	Meia
Māynel (*kaṭhḍo*)	Mainel	*Mey (mājvelo)*	Meio (middle)
Meāṁv (mus.)	Meão (string)	Méz ..	Mesa
Mech (gaṁd-khādi, vāt)	Mecha (suppository; tent for a wound)	*Mijer (daḷdir)*	Miséria (wretchedness)
Medālh	Medalha	*Mijerikord* ..	Casa de Misericordia (a charitable institution in Goa)
Medisin (vaijipaṇ)	Medicina (Medicine)	*Mijerāvel (dalḍiró)*	Miseravel (wretched)
Mel (moṁh) ..	Mel (honey)	Milāgr ..	Milagre
Metar-karuṅk (mhoṁvavuṁk)	Melar (to coat with sugar)	Militār ..	Militar
Melās (kākai)	Melaço (treacle)	Ministr ..	Ministro
Membr (sāṁdho)	Membro (limb)	*Minut (khardo)*	Minuta (draft of a writing)
Meṅdāṁv ..	Mandioca (manioc)	*Minut karuṅk (khardo karuṅk)*	Minutar (to make a draft)
Menorist (eccles.)	Menorista (one with the four minor orders)	*Minut* ..	Minuto (a minute)
Mereṅd ('sweets for afternoon-tea')	Merenda (afternoon-tea)	*Minuyet* ..	Minuete (minuet)
Miran, mirní ..	Meirinho	Mis, misācho pādri	Missa
Mest, mestir, mestirn, mestírpan	Mestre	Misāl ..	Missal
		Misāṁv ..	Missão
		Misiyonār ..	Missionário
		Mistér ..	Mistério
		Mistis, mistis bonchurdi	Mestiço
		Mitr (bispāchó tōp)	Mitra (mitre)

Konkani	Portuguese
Mistur (*misaḷ*)	Mistura (mixture)
Mistur karuṅk (*melauṅk*)	Misturar (to mix)
Mizrikāṁv ..	Mangerição (sweet basil)
Mód ..	Moda
Modél ..	Modêlo
Modijñ (*pad*)	Modinha (popular song)
Moir ..	Mouro
Mol ..	Môlho
Monsāmv ..	Monção
Monument (*yādgiri*)	Monumento (monument)
Mordom (*kārbhāri*)	Mordomo (steward of estate)
Morālist (*nitiśāstri*)	Moralista (moralist)
Morgād ('first born')	Morgado (heir through primogeniture)
Mort ('violent death')	Morte (death)
Mortālh ('cigarette paper')	Mortalha (winding sheet)
Motet (mus.)	Motete (motet)
Mud ('suit of clothes')	Muda (moulting of birds)
Mudāṁs (*badli*)	Mudança (change)
Mudār karuṅk (*badluṅk*)	Mudar (to change)
Mulāt ..	Mulato
Múlt ..	Multa
Multar-karuṅk (*daṁd ghāluṅk*)	Multar (to fine)
Munisāṁv ..	Munição
Muram ..	Morrão
Murmurāsāṁv (*chāḍi*)	Murmuração (back biting)
Mūrs ..	Murça (pallium, a garment without sleeves)
Mustārd (*saṁ-* (*sāṁsūṁ*)	Mostarda (mustard)
Muzeu (*ajāpācheṁ ghar*)	Museu (museum)
Múzg ..	Música
Múzg (*vājpi*, *vajaṁtri*)	Músico (musician)
Natal ..	Natal
? Naul ..	Naulo
Negār zāvuṃk, negār vachuṃk	Negar
Negos (yepār)	Negócio (business)
Negosiānt (yepāri)	Negociante (merchant)
Nerv (*taṁtu*) ..	Nervo (nerve)
Nāvet (*dhuṁpāl*)	Naveta (incense-pan)
Nomeār-karuṅk (*nimyaruṅk*)	Nomear (to nominate)
Nomeāsāṁv (*nimyārni*)	Nomeação (nomination)
Nortêr ..	Norteiro (a Northener, see pp. 299 and 330)

Konkani	*Portuguese*
Nót ..	Nota
Notar-karuṅk (*khún karuṅk*)	Notar (to mark)
Notís ..	Notícia
Novembr (*kār-ttik mārgaśirsh*)	Novembro (November)
Novén ..	Novena
Numr ..	Número
Objeksāṁv (*āḍ*)	Objecção (objection)
Oboy ..	Obóe (hautboy)
Obr (*kam*) ..	Obra (work)
Obrey ..	Obreia (wafer)
Obrigād ..	Obrigado
Obrigar-karuṅk	Obrigar
Obrigāsāṁv ..	Obrigação
Oitád ..	Oitava (a drachm)
Okl ..	Óculos
Okupād (*kāmi*)	Ocupado (busy)
Okupāsāṁv ..	Ocupação
Ól ..	Óleo
Oṁs ..	Onça
Onr, mān ..	Honra
Op ..	Opa
Ophendêr karuṅk	Ofender
Opheresêr-karuṅk	Oferecar
Ophart (*deṇeṁ*)	Oferta (gift)
Ophis ..	Ofício
Ophisyāl ..	Oficial
Ór (*ghaḍi*) ..	Hora
Orag ..	Orago (patron Saint)

Konkani	*Portuguese*
Orāsāṁv ..	Oração
Oratôr ..	Oratório (place for private worship)
Ord ..	Ordem
Ordenāsāṁv ..	Ordenação (ordination)
Org, orgāṁ ..	Órgão
Orgānist ..	Organista
Órt ..	Horta
Orteláṁv (*pudinā*)	Hortelã (peppermint)
Ôspīs ..	Hospicio (hospice)
Ospitāl, ispaṭal	Hospital
Ôst ..	Hóstia
Ôṭél ..	Hotel (hotel)
Otūbr (*āśvina-karthik*)	Outubro (October)
Padan, padin ..	Padrinho
Padêr ..	Padeiro
Padrí, pādri-pan, pādri-lok	Padre
Padrovād ..	Padroado
Pādtiv ..	Padre tio (reverend uncle)
Pág ..	Paga
Pākāu ..	Pacau (a kind of card game)
Pāl ..	Pala (the uppers of a shoe)
Pál ..	Pális
Palās (*manidr*)	Palácio (palace)
Palgaṇ ..	Palangana
Pālmātór ..	Palmatória

Konkani	Portuguese	Konkani	Portuguese
Pālmi	Palmilha (sole of a stocking)	*Pārtil* (*dāybhāg*)	Partilha (partition)
Pámpl	Pâmpano	*Pās*	Passa (raisin)
Pāṁv	Pão	Pás	Passe
Pān (*lugat*)	Pano (cloth)	Pás	Passo
Pangáy	Pangaio	*Pāsādis*	Pasadiço (passage)
Panniṅh	Panninho (thin cloth)	Pāsāport	Passaporte
Pānorām	Panorama (panorama)	Pāsār-zavuṅk	Passar
Páp	Papa (poultice)	*Pāsey* (*phirṇeṁ*)	Passeio (a walk)
Páp (sāheb)	Papa (pope)	Pásk	Páscoa
Pāpá	Papá (daddy)	*Pāssāj* (*tar*)	Passagem (ferry)
Papáy	Papaia	*Pāst*	Pasta (portfolio)
Papelāṁv	Papelão (cardboard)	Pastel	Pastel
Pār	Par	*Pastoral* (eccles.)	Pastoral (pastoral)
Paránch	Prancha	Pasyeṁs	Paciência
Pārāpêt (*pāḷ*)	Parapeito (rampart)	Pātāk	Pataca
Pārār-karuṅk (*thāmbuṅk*)	Parar (to stop)	*Pāten* (eccles.)	Patena (paten)
Parāt	Prato	Pātrāt	Patarata
Parbém	Parabêm	*Pātrātêr* (*baḍāykhor*)	Patarateiro (braggart)
Pārent	Parente	*Pātrimon*	Património (patrimony)
Pārl (*gajāl*)	Parla (talk)	*Pātrīs*	Patricio (one born in the same country)
Pārlāment	Parlamento (parliament)	Pātron	Patrono
Parsêr	Parceiro	*Pātryārk*	Patriarca
Párt	Parte	*Pau*	Paus (clubs in cards)
Pārtid (*pako, mat*)	Partido (party)	Pāvlist	Paulista
Pārtidār (*pāthlāvkār*)	Partidario (partizan)	*Paut* (*paṭṭi*)	Pauta (schedule of customs' duty)
Pārtikl (eccles.)	Particula (sacred wafer)		

Konkani	Portuguese
Páy, páy-tiv, vhadlo páy, dhākto páy	Pai
Pāy ..	Paio (a thick sausage)
Pāyri ..	Peres
Pāyśāṁv (*ras, rag*) ..	Paixão (passion)
Páz ..	Passo
Pázu, paséṁ ..	Página
Pél (*chenḍú*) ..	Péla (ball)
Pén ..	Pena
Pen ..	Empena (the gable end)
Penāṁv ..	Penão (pennon)
Penêd ..	Pendente (pendant)
Peniteṁs, pinteṁs	Penitência
Pemsāṁv (*baiṭhāpagār*)	Pensão (pension)
Pér, perad ..	Pera
Perdāṁv ..	Perdão
Perdid ..	Perdido
Pergāṁv ..	Pregão
Perīg (*kaḷ*) ..	Perigo (danger)
Perjuṅt ..	Presunto (ham)
Pern ('pāy, jaṁghli')	Perna (leg)
Perturbad (*uchaṁbaḷ*)	Perturbado (perturbed)
Perturbār-karuṅk (*uchaṁbaḷavuṅk*)	Perturbar (to annoy)
Perúṁ ..	Peru
Pés ..	Peça
Pesārmār ('to worry')	Peça, (cannon) and Armar (to arm)
Pest ..	Peste
Pestān ..	Pestana (edging on a garment)
Pêt ..	Peito
Petrol ..	Petróleo (petroleum)
Phābrik (eccles.)	Fábrica (parish committee)
Phābrikêr ..	Fabriqueiro (warden of a church)
Phāgot ..	Fagote (bassoon)
Phajeṅd ..	Fazenda (revenue department)
Phajendār ..	Fazendeiro
Phākâr ..	Faqueiro (one skilled in carving) us. restrict.
Phāl ..	Fala (Speech)
? Phalāṇo ..	Fulano
Phālhār-zāvuṅk	Falhar (to fall short of)
Phāls ..	Falso
Phālt ..	Falta
Phált ..	Falto
Phāltār-zāvuṅk	Faltar
Phām ..	Fama
Phāmil (*kuṭāmb*)	Familia (family)

Konkani	Portuguese
Phārd ..	Farda (uniform, livery)
Phārdāmeṅt	Fardamento (uniform)
Phargát ..	Fragata
Pharm ..	Forma
Pharn, kharn	Fôrno
Phaski (*kāṁb*)	Fasquia (frame)
Phāt (*gharsāmaṇ*)	Fato (furniture)
Phāti ..	Fatia
Phāvôr ..	Favor
Phāvt (*pirluk*)	Flauta (flute)
Phé-bāvārth	Fé
Phebrêr ..	Fevereiro (February)
Pher (*peṁth*)	Feira (a fair)
Phér (see under Estirar)	Ferro (smoothing iron)
Pherrêr (lohar)	Ferreiro
Pheryād ..	Feriado
Phest ..	Festa
Pheti (*kriti*, *ghaḍnī*)	Feitio (making)
Pheygá (us. as interj.)	Pega (get hold of)
Pheytôr ..	Feitor
Pheytorí ..	Feitoria
Phidālg ..	Fidalgo
Phigād ..	Figada (banana cheese)
Phig de hórt ..	Figo de horta (a species of banana)
Phigúr ..	Figura
Philhós ..	Filhó

Konkani	Portuguese
Philjophy ..	Filosofia (philosophy)
Philjophér ..	Filósofo (philosopher)
Phint (*daṁd*)	Finta (tax)
Philó ..	Filó (net)
Phirgaz ..	Freguesia
Phirgej (*gihrāyk*)	Freguês (customer)
Phiskāl ..	Fiscal
Phit, phint ..	Fita
Phitís (*kamvṭāl*)	Feitiço
Phitśel ..	Frechal (piece of wood into which the feet of the principal rafters are fixed)
Phitsér (*ghāḍi*)	Feiticeiro (a sorcerer)
Phivel ..	Fivel (shoe-buckle)
Phlānel ..	Flanela (flannel)
Phlāt (*vāy*) ..	Flato (wind)
Phôg ..	Fogo (fireworks)
Phôl ..	Fôlha
Pholér ..	Farol
Pholg (*dil*) ..	Folgado (loose)
Pholgé (pl.) ..	Folga (frolic)
Pholiṅh ..	Folinha (tin can)
Pholiyiṅh ..	Folhinha (almanac)

Konkani		Portuguese
Phônt	..	Fonte
Phôr	..	Fôro
Phorkajay (*as-aktāy*)		Fraqueza (weakness)
Phorr	..	Fôrro
Phorrār karuṅk		Forrar
Phôrs	..	Fôrça
Phórt	..	Forte
Phosphor	..	Fósforo (safety match)
Phót	..	Fota (fine cloth)
Phrád, pharád		Frade
Phrāk, pharāk		Fraco
Phrāsk	..	Frasco
Phrāskêr	..	Frasqueira
Phre	..	Frei (friar)
Phresk	..	Fresco
Phrey	..	Freio
Phri (*thaṇd*)	..	Frio (cold)
Phrontal (eccles.)		Frontal (altarpiece)
Phrut (*phaḷ*)	..	Fruta (fruit)
Phugāṁv ('chicken pox')		Fogagem (pimples)
Phujāṁv	..	Fugião (a coward)
? Phugaṭi	..	Foguete
Phuṁch	..	Funcho (fennel)
Phuṁksāṁv (*chalauṇi*)		Função (function)
Phuṅd (*pôt*)	..	Fundo (fund)
Phunel	..	Funil
Phuri, *khurī* (*kaḍkaḍo*)		Fúria (fury)
Phurtún	..	Fortuna
Phuslán	..	Porcelana
Phustāṁv	..	Fustão (fustian)
Phyād (*udhar*)		Fiado (on credit)
Phyādor (*jamin*)		Fiador
Phyāṁs (*jaminki*)		Fiança (surety)
Phyrm (*thir*, *ghaṭṭ*)		Firme (firm)
Pi	..	Pia
Pidrêr	..	Pedreiro
Pikāṁv	..	Picão
Pikándar	..	Picadeira
Pilôt	..	Piloto
Pimsel ('kalam')		Pincel (painter's brush)
Ping	..	Pingo (grain of gold)
Pính	..	Pinho
Pinhor	..	Penhor
Pintālgeṁ	..	Pintada
Pintar-karuṅk		Pintar
Pintor (*chitāri*)		Pintor (painter)
Pintúr	..	Pintura
Pip	..	Pipa
Piphn (*pirluk*)		Pifano (fife)
Pir	..	Pires
Pirder-zavuṅk (*sāṁduṅk*)		Perder (to lose)
Pirdisāṁv	..	Perdição
Pirzent	..	Presidente
Pirzep	..	Presepe (stable, crib)
Pismat	..	Posponto (running stitch)

Konkani	*Portuguese*
Pistol ..	Pistola
Pluvial (eccles.)	Pluvial (pluvial)
Pobr ..	Pobre
Polegād (*ākanḍó*)	Polegado (inch)
? Polis ..	Policia
Politik (*rājniticho*)	Politico (politic)
Politika (*rajrit*)	Politica (politics)
Polk ..	Polka (polka)
Polkist ('a dandy')	Polkista (a polka dancer)
Polvorinh ..	Polvorinho
Pont ..	Ponta
Pónt ..	Ponto
Poṁtāri (*mokni*)	Pontaria
Port (*baṁdir*) ..	Pôrto (harbour)
Port ..	Vinho de Porto (Port wine)
Portādor (*vharṇār*)	Portador (bearer of letter, etc.)
Portādór ..	Portādora (woman bearer)
Portāri (*hukum nāmā*)	Portaria (order, decree)
Portêr ..	Porteiro (doorkeeper)
Portést ..	Protesto
Portuguêz ..	Português
Pos (*bhogni*) ..	Posse (possession)
Póst ..	Posta
Pôst ..	Pôsto
Postur ..	Postura (municipal law)
Pot ('*kaḷso*')	Pote (earthen pot)
Pratik (*rahāṭ*)	Practica (practice)
Prāy (*véḷ*) ..	Praia (shore)
Preg (*dodi*) ..	Prega (plait)
Preg ..	Prego
Pregādôr ..	Pregador (preacher)
Pregar-karuṅk (*sāṁguṅk*)	Prègar (to preach)
Prejuiz (*nuskān*)	Prejuizo (loss)
Prem (*inám*) ..	Premio (reward)
Prepār (*tayāri*)	Preparo (preparation)
Prepārār-karuṅk	Preparar
Prijāṁv (*bandkhaṇ*)	Prisão (prison)
Prim ..	Prima
Prim ..	Primo
Prim (*mus.*) ..	Prima (E string)
Primāj ..	Primaz (primate)
Pres ('*magṇeṁ*')	Prece (prayer)
Prês ..	Preço
Prêz ..	Preso
Prezent ..	Presente
Prokurādor ..	Procurador
Prokurāsāṁv ..	Procuração
Promés ..	Promessa
Prometer-karuṅk (*uttar-divuṅk*)	Prometer (to promise)
Promt ..	Pronto
Prophesi ..	Profecia (prophecy)

Konkani		*Portuguese*
Prophesor (*śe-nay, guru*)		Professor (teacher)
Prophet	..	Profeta
Propr	..	Próprio
Prosés	..	Processo
Protestāṅt	..	Protestante (Protestant)
Prov	..	Prova
Provār-karuṅk		Provar
Provisor	..	Provisor
Provizaṁv (*pu-rav*)		Provisão (provision)
Provizāṁv	..	Provisão (bestowal of a church living)
Puyal	..	Poial
Pujñ	..	Punho (sleeve)
Púkr	..	Púcaro
Pulpút	..	Púlpito
Pultran	..	Poltrona
Púrg	..	Purga
Purgator	..	Purgatório
Purím	..	Prumo
Pursāṁv	..	Procissão
Puzád	..	Poisada (inn)
Pyāṁv	..	Peão
Pyān	..	Piano (piano)
Rābān (*ḍum-ḍumeṁ*)		Rabana (kettle-drum)
Rabar (*sāṇ*)	..	Rebôlo (a grind stone)
Rajār (*prārthan*)		Reza (prayer)
Rajār-karuṅk (prāthan karuṅk)		Rezar (to pray)
Rām	..	Ramo

Konkani		*Portuguese*
Rāmālyet (*bu-chko*)		Ramalhete (nosegay)
Ráṅch	..	Rancho
Rāsāṁv	..	Ração
Rātér	..	Ratoeira (rat-trap)
Razāṁv	..	Razão
Rebek	..	Rabeca
Rebekaṁv	..	Rabecão (double bass)
Rebekist	..	Rabequista (violinist)
Rebeṁ	..	Rebem (bull's pizzle)
Rechêr-karuṅk (*baruṅk*)		Rechear (to stuff)
Rechey	..	Recheio
Rêd	..	Rêde
Regr	..	Regra
Regrāṁv	..	Regrão (a lined sheet of paper in Indo-Port.)
Regulameṅt (*vyavasthā*)		Regulamento (regulation)
Reinol	..	Reinol
Rejedor (patel)		Regedor (a village official)
Rejedory	..	Regedoria (the office of the 'regedor')
Rejimeṅt (*pal-tan*)		Regimento (regiment)
Rejin (*râḷ*)	..	Resina (resin)
Rejist	..	Registo
Rejistār karuṅk		Registar (to register)

Konkani	Portuguese
Rejm	Resma
Rekãd	Recado
Rekerer karuṅk	Requerer
Rekolimeṅt	Recolhimento (retreat for religious exercises)
Rekriment	Requiremento
Rekūrs (leg.)	Recurso (appeal)
Rekyāṁv	Réquiem (requiem)
Relāsāṁv	Relação
Relijyāṁv	Religião
Relijyoz (*dharmachari*)	Religioso (a religious)
Relik	Relíquia (relic)
Relojer	Relogoeiro (watchmaker)
Relóz	Relójio
Remātijm (*vāt*)	Reumatismo (rheumatism)
Reṁdimeṅt (*ādāv, yeṇeṁ*)	Rendimento (income)
Rend, rendāchó, rendkar	Renda (rent)
Rend	Renda (lace)
Rendêr	Rendeiro
Repartisāṁv (*kacheri*)	Repartição (department)
Repheg (*peṭi*)	Refêgo (tuck)
Rephetor (*jevuṁchi kūd*)	Refeitório (dining room)
Rephorm (*baiṭhāpagār*)	Reforma (pension)
Rephormād	Reformado
Repik (*ghant oḍhṇeṁ*)	Repique
Repost	Reposta
Reposter (*paḍdo*)	Reposteiro (curtain)
Reprejemtasāṁv (*arji*)	Representação (representation)
Reprovād	Reprovado (unsuccessful in examination)
Reprovār karuṅk	Reprovar
Reprovāsāṁv	Reprovação (reprobation)
Republik	República (republic)
Rês	Rial
Resét	Receita (prescription)
Resib	Recibo
Resignasaṁv (*jāgo-soḍṇeṁ*)	Resignação (resignation)
Respér (*lagn*)	Recebimento (nuptials)
Respêt	Respeito
Respoṁs (eccles.)	Responso (response)
Respoṁsāvel	Responsável
Responder karuṅk (*parteṁ samguṅk*)	Responder (to reply)
Restrusaṁv	Restituição (restitution)
Retābl	Retábulo (picture)

Konkani	Portuguese
Retorn (*vāṭāv*)	Retôrno (exchange)
Retrāt ..	Retrato
Rev (*prativādi*)	Réu (accused person)
Revolt (*baṁḍ*)..	Revolta (revolt)
Revunyáṁv ..	Reúnião
Rey ..	Rei
Reytor ..	Reitor
Risk (*regh*) ..	Risca (line)
Risk (*kāḷ, zokh*)	Risco (risk)
Riskad (*reghāṁcho*)	Riscado (ruled)
Ritvāl ..	Ritual (ritual)
Rod ..	Roda
Rojêt, rojvêt ('star-shaped ornament')	Roseta (the rowel of a spur)
Roklo ..	Rocló (cloak with sleeves)
Rôl ..	Rôlo
Romāṅs (*kadambāri*)	Romance (romance)
Rond ..	Ronda
Rôp ..	Roupa
Ropêr ..	Roupeiro (a dealer in cloth)
Rôst ..	Rosto (the Holy Winding Sheet)
Rot (*vet*) ..	Rota (walking stick)
Rotêr ..	Roteiro (one who bottoms chairs, in Indo-Port.)
Róz ..	Rosa
Roz de pers ..	Rosa de Persia
Rubim (*mānik*)	Rubi (ruby)
Ruṁ ..	Verruma
Rutāṁv ..	Rolão
Ruzáy ..	Rosário
Sabāṁv, sābú	Sabão
Sābr ..	Sabre
Śādrej (*chaturang*)	Xadrez (chess)
Sāgrād (*pavitr*)	Sagrado (sacred)
Sagrāsāṁv (*saṁskār*)	Consagração (consecration)
? Sāgú, sābú	Sagu
Sāguvāt ..	Saguate
Sāk ..	Saco
Sākād ..	Sacada (balcony)
Sākādor ('patkar')	Sacador (collector of dues)
Sākādôry ..	Sacadoria (the office of the '*sacador*')
Sākarôl ..	Saca-rôlhas
Sākr ..	Sacra (each of the three tablets on the altar)
Sākrāmeṅt ..	Sacramento
Sākrār ..	Sacrário
Sākrilej ..	Sacrilégio
Sākriphis ..	Sacrificio
Sākristāmv ..	Sacristão
Sākristi, sāṅkristi	Sacristia
Sál ..	Sala
Sālād ..	Salada

Konkani	Portuguese
Salêr (*mithā-cheṁ āydan*)	Saleiro (salt-cellar)
Sālitri (*sor-miṭh*)	Salitre (salt-petre)
Sālm (*gīt*) ..	Salmo (psalm)
Sālsāpāril (*ka-vaḷ kāṁṭi*)	Salsaparrilha (salsaparilla)
Sālv ..	Salva
Sālv (*namaskār*)	Salve (Hail !)
Sālvār-karuṅk (*vātāvuṁk*)	Salvar (to save)
Sālvāsaṁv ..	Salvação
Sāṁgijñ (eccles.)	Sanguinho (cloth used to wipe chalice after receiving blessed Sacrament)
Saṁgri (*ud-kācho māg*)	Sangria (water dram)
Sāṁṭism ..	Santissimo (Most Holy)
Sāṁṭism Sākrā-ment	Santíssimo Sacrament (Most Holy Sacrament)
Saṁt Krus ..	Santa Cruz (Holy Cross)
Sanphon ..	Sanfona (hurdy-gurdy)
Sānt ..	Santo (saint)
Sāntesāṁv ..	Santa Unção (Extreme Unction)
Sāpāl (*khajan*)	Sapal (marshy land)

Konkani	Portuguese
Sapāt . ..	Sapata (plinth)
Sāpāt ..	Sapato
Saptêr ..	Sapateiro
Sarás ..	Saraça
Sārj ..	Sarja
Sārjent ..	Sargento
Śārop (*śar-but*)	Xarope (syrup)
Sarpatel ..	Sarapatel (a viand prepared from the blood of the pig)
Satanáz ..	Satanás
Sātisfāsāṁv (kuśāli)	Satisfação (satisfaction)
Satméṁ ..	San-Tomé
Sāvūd ..	Saúde
Sāy ..	Saia
Sé ..	Sé
Séd ..	Sêda
Segred (*gūḍh*) ..	Segredo (secret)
Seguṁd ..	Segunda (A string)
Seguṁd ..	Segundo (second performer)
Sekestr (*japti*)	Sequestro (sequestration)
Sekretār ..	Secretário
Sekretāri ..	Secretaria
Sekulār (*saṁ-sāri*)	Secular (secular)
Sél ..	Sela
Sêl ..	Sêlo
Selād ..	Selado (stamped)

Konkani	Portuguese
Seliṁ	Selim (English saddle)
Sempr (*sadām*)	Sempre (always)
Sentimeṅt	Sentimento (grief)
Séṁsur (*jhaḍṇi*)	Censura (censure)
Seṁsurār karuṅk (*jhāduṁk*)	Censurar (to censure)
Senteṁs	Sentença
Sepārād	Separado
Sepūlkr ('Holy Sepulchre')	Sepulchro (sepulchre)
Ser	Sério
Seraphim (*mogācho bhaḍvo*)	Serafim (seraphim)
Serezámv (*naka jālaleṁ*)	Sem-razão (unreasonably)
Sermāṁv	Sermão
Sermón	Cerimónia
Serpênt (*sarrap*)	Serpente (snake)
Sert (*kharo*)	Certo (certain)
Sertez (*kharepan*)	Certeza (certainty)
Serúl	Ceroilas
Servej	Cerveja
Sesm	Sesma (sixth part)
Seteṁbr	Setembro (September)
Setím	Setim
Sidād	Cidade
Sigār	Cigarro
Sij	Cisa (cess)
Sijñôr	Senhor
Sijñór	Senhora
Sīlb (*akśar*)	Silaba
Siminár	Seminário
Simitér	Cemitério
Simphoni (*saṁgit*)	Sinfonia (symphony)
Siṁser ('*bhoḷó*')	Sincero
Sinál	Sinal
Sinapijm	Sinapismo (mustard plaster)
Sintid	Sentido
Sinturāṁv	Cinturão
Sintinel	Sentinela
Siṅz (eccles.)	Cinza (ash)
Siphr	Cifra
Siphlin	Disciplina (mortification by penance)
Sīr (*vhaḍli vāt*)	Cirio (large candle)
Sirdāmv (*chiṭṭ*)	Certidão (certificate)
Sirgīr	Sirgueiro (silk-throwster)
Siring	Seringa
Sirkulār (*subst. prasiddhpatr*)	Circular (a circular)
Sitār karuṅk (*satten āpauṁk*)	Citar
Sitsāṁv (*serkāri āpauneṁ*)	Citação
Sirventi	Serventia (passage)

Konkani	*Portuguese*
Sirvir-zāvuṅk	Servir
Sirvís ..	Serviço
Sobrad (*māḷoy*)	Sobrad (upper floor)
Sobregol ..	Sobregola (cape of a garment)
Sobrekājāk ..	Sobrecasaca (frock coat)
Sobremez ..	Sobremesa
Sobrepilij ..	Sobrepeliz (surplice)
Sobresev ..	Sobrecéu (tester of a bed)
Sod ..	Soda (soda)
Sol ..	Sola (sole of shoe)
Soldád ..	Soldado
Solidev ..	Solidéu (calotte)
Solph (*svar*, *sūr*)	Solfa (a musical note)
Soltêr (*ānkuvār*)	Solteiro (bachelor)
Soltér ('a hoyden')	Solteira (spinster)
Soṁ (*nād*, *āvóz*)	Som (sound)
Sôp ..	Sopa
Sopêr ..	Sopeira (soup-plate in Indo-Port.)
Sort, soḍt ..	Sorte
Sós (*bhageli*) ..	Sócio (partner)
Sosyedád ..	Sociedade
Sot ..	Sota
Subdiākn ..	Subdiácono (subdeacon)
Suberb, suberdo	Soberbo

Konkani	*Portuguese*
Subrính ..	Sobrinha
Subrính ..	Sobrinho
Sugúr ..	Seguro
Sugur-karuṅk (*ghaṭṭ karuṅk*)	Segurar
Sūj (*meḷó*) ..	Sujo (dirty)
Sujār-karuṅk (*meḷaunk*)	Sujar (to soil)
Sujidād (*mel*)..	Sujidade (dirt)
Súl (*dakhín*), sulkar	Sul
Sumān ..	Semana
Suman Sant ..	Semana Santa
Superyor ..	Superior
Suphá ..	Sofá
Surjāṁv (*śastra-vaid*)	Cirurgião (surgeon)
Suseg (*svasthi*)	Sossêgo (calmness)
Susegād (*thaṁd*, *svasth*)	Sossegado (quiet)
Suskrever-karuṅk (*kabûl-karuṅk*)	Subscrever (to subscribe)
Suskrisāṁv (*sāi*)	Subscrição (subscription)
Suskritor (*sai kartalo*)	Subscritor (subscriber)
Suspeṁs (*baṁd jâlalo*)	Suspenso (suspended)
Suspender-karuṅk	Suspender
Suspeṁsāṁv (*amânatpan*)	Suspensão (suspension)
Suspeṁsor ..	Suspensório (braces)

Konkani	Portuguese	Konkani	Portuguese
Suspet (*dhubav*)	Suspeita (suspicion)	*Tarbáz* (*kaśṭ*)	Trabalho (labour)
Sustemt (*anpāṇi*)	Sustento (sustenance)	Tārd ..	Tarde
Sustentār-karuṅk (*posuṅk*)	Sustenter (to maintain)	*Tarimb* (*sipāyāchem khāṭlem*)	Tarimba (bed for soldiers)
Sustitut (*badlecho*)	Substituto (substitute)	*Tarpāsêr* (*labōd*)	Trapaceiro (a cheat)
Suyis ..	Suíssa (Swiss)	*Tarsād* (*tarvār*)	Terçado (a sabre)
Tabád (*ankzáḷ*)	Tabuada		
Tābel (*paṭṭi*) ..	Tabela (tariff)	*Taś* (*dhāraṇ, paṭṭi*)	Taxa (rate, tax)
Tabelyāmv ..	Tabelião (notary)	*Tekl* ..	Tecla (organ-key)
Tabernākl ..	Tabernáculo		
Tābl ..	Tabula (a piece in draught)	Telegram (*tár*)	Telegrama (telegram)
Tābler (*chaupat*)	Tabuleiro (draught-board)	*Tem* (*māñj*) ..	Teima (obstinacy)
		Temdilyāmv ..	Tendilhão (a small tent)
Tadalsānt ..	Todos os Santos (All Saints day)	*Templ* (*dev-mandir*)	Templo (temple)
Tālemṭ ..	Talento	*Tempr* (eccles.)	Têmporas (temple)
Tālhār-karuṅk (*kātruṅk*)'	Talhar (to cut clothes)	Tempr ..	Têmpera
Tālher ..	Talher (set of knife, fork and spoon at table)	Temprād ..	Temperado
		Temsāmv (*man*)	Tenção (intention)
		Tend (*tambū*) ..	Tenda
Tāmbak ..	Tambaca	*Tenent* (*nāyb*)	Tenente (lieutenant)
Tambor ..	Tambor		
Tambret (*chauki*)	Tamboreti	*Tenor* (*madhyasavan*)	Tenor (tenor)
Tāpêt ..	Tapete		
Tāphetā, tāphtā	Tafetá (taffeta)	Tentār-karuṅk (*nādumk*)	Tentar
Tāpyok ..	Tapioca (tapioca)	Tentāsāṃv ..	Tentação

Konkani	*Portuguese*
Term (*vaydo*)..	Termo (limit)
Tern ..	Terno (three points in cards)
Terrin ..	Terrina
Ters (*tisro vāṁto*)	Têrça (a third of an inheritance)
Têrs ..	Têrço
Testāment ..	Testamento
Testimujñ (*gvāhi*)	Testemunha (witness)
Ti (*ākay, māvśi*)	Tia
Tibrād ..	Tresdobrado
Tijrêr ..	Tesoureiro
Tiṇ ..	Tina (tub)
Tingir karuṅk (*rangauṅk*)	Tingir (to dye)
Tint ..	Tinta
Tintācho saro	Tinto (red wine)
Tinter (*daut*)	Tinteiro (ink-pot)
Tipl ..	Tiple (treble in music)
Tír ..	Tira
Tir ..	Tiro
Tirāṁt ..	Tirante (trace or strap to draw a vehicle)
Tirép ..	Trevo (trefoil)
Titl (*śironām, barad*)	Titulo (title)
Tív ..	Tio
Tizāl ('a big earthen cooking pot')	Tigela (a porringer)

Konkani	*Portuguese*
Tizān ('*pej*')..	Tisana (ptisan)
Tizuló (*iṭ*) ..	Tijolo (tile)
Toch (*ujvādi*)..	Tocha
Tocher ..	Tocheiro (a stand for a torch)
Toga (*chogo*) ..	Toga (toga)
Told (*sezó*) ..	Tolda (fore part of the deck)
Told (*ḍero*) ..	Tôldo (awning)
Toṁ (*svar, sūr*)	Tom (tone)
Tomāt	Tomate
Toṅt (*sairbair*)	Tonto (silly)
Torónz ..	Toranja
Tôrr ..	Tôrre
Tort (*kajloḷi*) ..	Torta (tart)
Tôrt (*vānkḍo*)..	Torto (crooked)
Trāduzir karuṅk (*utruṅk*)	Traduzir (to translate)
Trāt (*salgi*) ..	Trato (dealing with)
Trātament ..	Tratamento
Trātár-karuṅk	Tratar
Trayidor ..	Traidor
Trāyir-karuṅk (*vikuṅk*)	Trair (to betray)
Trāyisāṁv ..	Traição
Tremo ..	Tremó (a large looking-glass)
Tribūn ..	Tribuna (rostrum)
Tribunal (*nyāyāsan*)	Tribunal (tribunal)
Trinidād ..	Trinidade (Trinity)
Trist ..	Triste

Konkani	*Portuguese*
Trokār-karuṅk	Trocar
Troṁbon ..	Trombone (trombone)
Trop ..	Tropa
Trúmph ..	Trunfo
Túb ..	Tubo
Túmb ..	Tumba
Tumbar ..	Tumor
Tūnk (*āṁglem̐*)	Túnica (tunic)
? Tuphān ..	Tufão
Tūrm (*penḍém̐*)	Turma (a company)
Turmét ..	Trombeta
Tusin (*dhukrachi charab*)	Toucinho (fat in pork)
Tután (*meṁdu*)	Tutano (marrow)
Tutor (*rakhnār*)	Tutor (guardian)
Tuvāló ..	Toalha
Tyātr (*nāṭakśāl*)	Teatro (theatre)
Tyolg ..	Teólogo (a student of theology)
Tyology (*dev-jñañ*)	Teologia (theology)
Typ (*chhāp*)	Tipo (type)
Typogrāphy (*chhapkhāno*)	Tipografia (printing press)
? Umbôr ..	Umbreira
Uniphorm ..	Uniforme
Urnôl, urnel ..	Urinol
Urre (*intej.*) ..	Hurrah (hurray)
Usād (*parṇo*) ..	Usado (used)
Uz (*saṁvay*) ..	Uso (habit)

Konkani	*Portuguese*
Vāj ..	Vasa (a trick in cards)
Vāl ('*ṭappālachi huṅdi*')	Vale (postal money order)
Valāmt ..	Volante (gauze)
Vāls ..	Valsa
Vanjel ..	Evangelho
Vanjelist ..	Evangelhista (evangelist)
Vāpor ..	Vapor
Vār ..	Vara
Varánd ..	Varanda
Vāret (*gaj*) ..	Vareta (ramrod)
Vāsimbór ..	Va-se-embora (get out !)
Vāsín ..	Vacina
Vāskiṇ (*ghāgró*)	Vasquinha (skirt)
Vāz ..	Vaso
Veṁtoz ..	Ventosa (cupping-glass)
Verank ..	Verónica
Verd ..	Verde
Verdúr ..	Verdura
Verniz ..	Verniz
Vérs ..	Verso
Vespr ..	Vésperas
Vestid ..	Vestido
Vestiment ..	Vestimenta (vestment)
Vev ..	Véu
Vid (*jivit*) ..	Vida (life)
Vídr ..	Vidro
Vigār ..	Vigário
Vigi (*terluk*) ..	Vigia (night-watch)

Konkani	*Portuguese*
Vijnêr (*yamtrakār*)	Engenheiro (engineer)
Vilúd	Veludo
Vinagr	Vinagre
Vính	Vinho
Viṅjāl	Vinha de alhos
Virgul, vīrgl	Virgula (comma)
Virtud	Virtude
Virvil	Ervilha
Viryādor (*vasaunar*)	Vereador (alderman)
Viryāsāṁv (*vasauni*)	Vereação (meeting of aldermen)
Vís (*aguṇ*)	Vício (vice)
Visioz (*aguṇi*)	Vicioso
Viskoṅd	Visconde (viscount)
Vist (*diśt*)	Vista (sight)
Vívā !	Viva !
Vizit	Visita
Vizitār-karuṅk (*bhetuṅk*)	Visitar (to call on)
Volt	Volta
Voltār-karuṅk	Voltar
Vot	Voto
Vyāz	Viagem (voyage)
Vyol	Viola
Zanél	Janela
Zāphi (*bhāśabhāś*)	Desafio (a wager)
Zelādor (eccles.)	Zelador
Zubāṁv	Jibão
Zuksāṁv (leg.)	Execução (execution of a decree)
Zulāb	Jalapa

27. Laskari-Hindustani

Laskari-Hindustani	*Portuguese*
Ābês	Avêsso
Ábít, habít	Abita
Ālá	Alar
Ānila	Anel
Ariyá	Arrear
Bāldi, bālti	Balde
Bambá, bumbá	Bomba
Bánk	Banco
Bolta, boltá	Volta
Boyá	Bóia
Brándal, brāndál, barándal, baranda	Brandal
Brás, barás	Braça
Búch	Bucha
Bulín	Bolina
Būrdú	Bordo
? Chápas	Chapa
Chāvi, chābi	Chave
Dubrál	Dobrado
Fālká	Falca
Fūndál, pūndāl	Fundal
Gāvi	Gávea
Ghaset, ghaseth, ghanset, ghansit	Gaxeta

Laskari-Hindustani	*Portuguese*
Hamár, már ..	Amarra
Iskát ..	Escada
Istap, istúb ..	Estopa
Istingí ..	Estingue
Jāket ..	Jaqueta
Kalmariyá ..	Calmaria
Kalpatti, kalāpatiyá	Calafate
Kamra ..	Câmera
Karva ..	Curva
Kasturá ..	Costura
Katarnál ..	Cadernal
? Kátvāi ..	Catavento
Kavila, kabíla	Cavilha
Kuñiyáñ ..	Colchão
Kuñya, kuñiyañ, koniyá	Cunha
Kurdam ..	Cordão
Kurdami ..	Cordame
Kustád ..	Costado
Largá ..	Largo
Lás ..	Lais
Madár ..	Mandar
Mantēlá, mantelá, mantel, matelá	Amantilho
Mārká ..	Marca
Martil, martol, martaul	Martelo
Mej ..	Mesa
Mistri ..	Mestre
Mutám, motám matám	Moutão
? Naul, nuval	Naulo
Páo ..	Poa
Parānchá ..	Prancha
Pāsādor ..	Passador
Perchá ..	Percha
Phāltú, faltú ..	Falto
Phanel, fannel	Funil
Pharal (karná)	Forrar
Pont, ponta, puntá	Ponta
Prum ..	Prumo
Prek ..	Prego
Resan ..	Ração
Rikáda ..	Arraigada
Rodá ..	Roda
Rol ..	Rôlo
Sabdorá, subdhará	Cevadeira
? Salúp ..	Chalupa
Sinta, sit ..	Cinta
Sisidor, sizādor	Serzideira
Sūlí ..	Sul
Taliyāmár, taliyavár	Talhamar
Tenchan ..	Tanchão
Tôpi ..	Tope
Trāpá ..	Trapa
Trikat, tirkat, trinkat	Traquete
? Tufán ..	Tufão
Virādor ..	Virador

28. Macassar

Macassar	*Portuguese*
Alahója	Algoz
? Ámbarā	Âmbar
? Amin	Amen
Angarisi	Inglês
? Ánisi	Anis
? Ápang	Apa
Ássā	Az
? Bádili	Fuzil
Balasáng	Bálsamo
Bandeja	Bandeja
Bandéra	Bandeira
Bandóla, bandala	Bandola
Basáttu	Basto
? Batará	Batel
Bátili	Bátega
Biyóla	Viola
Bôlu	Bôlo
Bong	Bomba
Boroló, baraló	Bordo
? Bótelo	Botelha
? Chá	Chapa
Chamalóti	Chamalote
Chapíyo	Chapéu
Charaméle	Cháramela
Dádu	Dado
Dilu	Codilho
Dóbalō	Dôbro
? Gaga	Gago
Gáji	Gage
Gánhu	Ganho
Garéja	Igreja
Garididong	Cardamomo
Héra	Era
Isitāraluga	Astrólogo
Jandéla	Janela
Júgarā	Jogar
Kadéra	Cadeira
? Kampong, kampung	Campo
Kápa	Capa
Káppalā	Cavalo
Karábu	Cravo
Karatúsa	Cartucho
Karéta	Carrêta
Kasatéla	Castela
Kásu	Calçado
Kéju	Queijo
Kobáyā	Cabaia
Kóndi	Conde
? Kópi	Cafe
Kora	Cora
Kútang	Cotão
Lagarísi	Algarismo
Lakari, alkári	Lacre
Lamári	Armário
Lantéra	Lanterna
Lélang	Leilão
Lémo	Limão
Lóji	Loja
Manila	Manilha
Mantéga	Manteiga
Marínio	Meirinho
? Masígi	Mesquita
? Máte	Matar
Méjan	Mesa
? Misĕkin	Mesquinho
Nóna, nhónha	Dona
Paniti	Alfinete
Paráda	Prata

Macassar		*Portuguese*	*Macassar*		*Portuguese*
Paraséro	..	Parceiro	Sábung	..	Sabão
? Pásarã	..	Bazar	? Ságu	..	Sagu
Pásu	..	Passar	Saláda	..	Salada
Pétorõ	..	Feitor	Saloda	..	Solda
Pijarã, pijã	..	Fechar	Saluvára	..	Ceroilas
Pilúru	..	Pelouro	Sapada	..	Espada
? Pinjen	..	Palangana	Sapadila	..	Espadilha
Pípa	..	Pipa	Sapátu, chapátu		Sapato
? Piring	..	Pires	Sáttu	..	Sábado
Réi	..	Rei	Sorodádu	..	Soldado
Rénda	..	Renda	Sóta	..	Sota
Réyala	..	Rial	Tambáko	..	Tabaco
Róda	..	Roda	? Tantu	..	Tanto
Ronda	..	Ronda	Tarúmpu	..	Trunfo
Rósi	..	Rosa	Turumbéta, turumpéta		Trombeta
Rupiya	..	Rupia			

29. Madurese

Madurese		*Portuguese*	*Madurese*		*Portuguese*
? Arom	..	Aroma	Kéju	..	Queijo
Banko	..	Banco	Kértô	..	Carta
? Bedil	..	Fuzil	Kóbis	..	Couve
Blútru	..	Veludo	Lamári, lemári		Armário
Bóla	..	Bola	Lanas	..	Ananás
Chinélô	..	Chinela	Lantérô	..	Lanterna
Chita	..	Chita	Mandôr	..	Mandador
? Galdri	..	Galeria	Mejô	..	Mesa
Gréjô, grijô	..	Igreja	Mentégô	..	Manteiga
Káldu, káldo	..	Caldo	Nyoña, noña		Senhora
Kámar	..	Câmara	Pálsô	..	Falso
Kaméjô	..	Camisa	? Patrol	..	Patrulha
? Kampong, kampung		Campo	Pélar	..	Pilar
			Pélor	..	Pelouro
Kápal	..	Cavalo	Péta	..	Fita
Karétô	..	Carrêta	Pôkô	..	Tabaco

Madurese	*Portuguese*	*Madurese*	*Portuguese*
? Pómpô ..	Pompa	Separo (adj.) ..	Separado
Rêal ..	Rial, réis	Setóri ..	História
Ródô ..	Roda	Sinyo ..	Senhor
? Ropiya ..	Rupia	Sordádu ..	Soldado
Sabon ..	Sabão	Sotra ..	Sêda
Sáptô ..	Sábado	? Tjelônô ..	Pantalona

30. Malagasy

Malagasy	*Portuguese*	*Malagasy*	*Portuguese*
? Apostoly ..	Apóstolo	Kozina ..	Cozinha
? Barika ..	Barrica	Laraka ..	Araca
Basi ..	Bacia	? Mana ..	Maná
Batata ..	Batata	Mananasy ..	Ananás
Batisa ..	Baptismo	Manga ..	Manga
Bolina ..	Bola	? Marika ..	Marca
? Bomba, bumba	Bomba	? Mati ..	Matar
? Burusi ..	Bruça	Mozika ..	Música
? Elifanta ..	Elefante	Ora ..	Hora
Empelastra ..	Emplastro	Palankina ..	Palanquim
? Gamela ..	Gamela	? Papa ..	Papá
? Gisa ..	Ganso	Papai ..	Papaia
Guavy ..	Goiaba	Pipa ..	Pipa
? Hisitoria ..	História	? Rupia ..	Rupia
? Indiana ..	Indiano	? Sakramenta	Sacramento
? Kafé ..	Café	Soridany ..	Soldado
? Kapoti ..	Capote	Tambáko ..	Tabaco

31. Malay

Malay	*Portuguese*	*Malay*	*Portuguese*
Abit ..	Ábita	Agradecer ..	Agradecer
Acerca ..	Acêrca	Aguabenta ..	Água benta
Áchar ..	Achar	Ajudán ..	Adjudante
Açotar ..	Açoitar	Alabanka, albanka	Alavanca
Agôstu, agústu	Agôsto		

Malay		Portuguese	Malay		Portuguese
Alcatifa	..	Alcatifa	? Báluq	..	Falua
Alcobitera	..	Alcoviteira	Baluvárdi	..	Baluarte
Alcunia	..	Alcunha	Bandeja, bandeya		Bandeja
Alfiate	..	Alfaiate	Bandéra	..	Bandeira
Algójo, algója, algújo, algúju		Algoz	Bandóla, bandála		Bandola
Almaria, almári, lamári, lemári		Armário	Bánku	..	Banco
Almursar	..	Almoçar	? Bartion	..	Bastião
Alpéres	..	Alferes	Bási	..	Bacia
Alpineto	..	Alfinete	Basta	..	Basta
Amah	..	Ama	Batattas	..	Batata
Ambar, amber		Ambar	Bateria, teria	..	Bateria
? Amin	..	Amen	? Bátil	..	Bátega
Ananas, anas, nãnas, ninas		Ananás	? Bedil	..	Fuzil
? Apam	..	Apa	Bem-ensinado		Bem-ensinado
? April	..	Abril	Ben pode	..	Bem pode
Aría	..	Arrear	Berinjal	..	Beringela
Árku	..	Arco	Ber-júdi	..	Jogar
Arlóji	..	Relójio	Bīsúrey	..	Viso-rei
Armada	..	Armada	Bitíla	..	Beatilha
Arroyo	..	Arroio	Boba	..	Bouba
Arrúda, arúda		Arruda	Boetta, bosséta		Boçeta
Arúm	..	Aroma	? Bókar	..	Bocal
A saber	..	A saber	Bóla	..	Bola
Asegay	..	Azagaia	Bolsa	..	Bôlsa
Assar	..	Assar	Bomba	..	Bomba
Avés	..	Avêsso	Bembardero	..	Bombardeiro
Áya	..	Aia	Bonéka, bonika		Boneca
? Bahatra	..	Batil	Bórdo, bórdu		Bordo
Bála	..	Bailar	Bortá	..	Voltar
? Balasan	..	Bálsamo	? Bot	..	Bote
Báldi	..	Balde	Botafóra, botapóra, batapóra		Bota-fora
Báloq	..	Balão	? Bótol, bótul		Botelha

Malay	*Portuguese*
Bóya	Bóia
Brús, berus	Bruça
Bulin	Bolina
Bótam, bútan	Botão
Búyong	Boião
? Ca	Cá
Camma	Cama
Capa	Capa
Castigar	Castigar
Cear	Cear
Cerco	Cêrco
? Chap	Chapa
Chapéu, chapíyu	Chapéu
Chaping	Chapinha
? Cherpu	Chiripos
Chinela	Chinela
Chita	Chita
? Coa, kua	Coa
Coitado	Coitado
Concierto	Concêrto
Conseillo	Conselho
Consentir	Consentir
Contento	Contente
Costume	Costume
Crear	Criar
Crescer	Crescer
Cudir	Acudir
Cudir	Cuidar
Cuidado, cudado	Cuidado
Cuniada	Cunhada
Cuniado	Cunhado
Curar	Curar
Dádu, dadu	Dado
Dam	Dama
Dánsa, dánsu	Dança
Deos	Deus
Desmorecer	Desmorecer
Dídal, bídal, deidál, lídal	Dedal
Diné	Dinheiro
Dispén, spens, spen, sepén	Despensa
Distérra	Desterrar
? Dogtor	Doutor
Domingo, dumingo, míngo, mingu	Domingo
Durar	Durar
Enganar	Enganar
Entaon	Então
Entendimento	Entendimento
Entregar	Entregar
Espingarda, istingarda	Espingarda
Fadiga	Fadiga
Falka	Falca
Fáltu	Falto
Fantasma, pantasma	Fantasma
Fastio	Fastio
Feitór, fetór, pētór	Feitor
Ferrero	Ferreiro
Festa, pesta, péstu	Festa
Fidalgo, hidalgo	Fidalgo
Figura	Figura
Fita, pita	Fita
Forsa, parúsa	Fôrça
Franga	Franga

Malay	*Portuguese*
? Fulán, púlan	Fulano
Fusta ..	Fusta
Gade, gáji, gádei, gádeikan	Gage
? Gágap ..	Gago
Gaganet ..	Baioneta
Galari, galri ..	Galeria
Gallo ..	Galo
Galôjo ..	Guloso
Galyúm ..	Galeão
Gánchu ..	Gancho
? Gánsa, gása	Ganso
Gárdu, gărdu	Guarda
Gárfu, gárpu	Garfo
Gargalét, bargalét	Gorgoleta
Gávei ..	Gávea
Getéra ..	Guitarra
Grado, gerádi	Grade
Grosso ..	Grosso
Gubernadúr, gubernúr, gurnadúr gurundúr	Governador
Hora ..	Hora
Igresia, gréja, gríja	Igreja
Imagem ..	Imagem
Incenso ..	Incenso
Ingeolar ..	Ajoelhar
Inginio ..	Engenho
Ingris ..	Inglês
Ismola ..	Esmola
Istrika ..	Esticar
Intero, intéru, enteiro, entéro, antéro	Inteiro
Janéla, janalá, jinelá, jandéla, jendéla, jindéla	Janela
Jangkar, dyankar	Âncora
Jaspe, jasbe ..	Jaspe
Jendral ..	General
Julu ..	Julho
? Jun ..	Junho
Kabáya ..	Cabaia
Kabos ..	Caboz
Kadéra ..	Cadeira
Kajar ..	Caçar
Káju, gajus ..	Caju
Káldo, káldu ..	Caldo
Kalépet, kalpát	Calafate
Kámar ..	Câmara
Kamija, kaméja	Camisa
? Kampong, kampung	Campo
? Kandíl ..	Candil
? Kang ..	Canga
Kantar ..	Cantar
Kántu ..	Canto
Kapitán, kapítan	Capitão
Kápor (subst.)	Acafelar
Kápri, káfris	Cafre
Kardamon ..	Cardamomo
Karéta, keréta, kréta, krita	Carrêta

Malay	*Portuguese*	*Malay*	*Portuguese*
Karnel ..	Coronel	Lanchong, lanchang	Lanchão
Karpús, karpúz	Carapuça	Lantérna, lantéra	Lanterna
Karta, kártu ..	Carta	Lélan, lélon, lélong	Leilão
? Kártas, kertas	Carta or cartaz	Levantar ..	Levantar
Kasrol ..	Caçarola	Liao ..	Lião
Kásta ..	Casta	Libro ..	Livro
Kastúri, kastóri	Castor	Licensa ..	Licença
Kásut ..	Calçado	Limon, liman, limán, limun	Limão
Katólika ..	Católico	Lis ..	Lista
Keju, kíju ..	Queijo	Listro ..	Lesto
Kembesa ..	Cabeça	Lóji ..	Loja
Kestén ..	Castanha	Lústo ..	Justo
Koba ..	Cova	Mai ..	Mãe
Kóbis, kúbis ..	Couve	Maldiçaon ..	Maldição
Kobra ..	Cobra	Mal ensinado ..	Mal-ensinado
Koménda ..	Comenda	? Mandil ..	Mandil
Komendadór	Comendador	Mandôr, mandúr	Mandador
Kofíah, kópiah, kúpia	Coifa	Manisan ..	Munição
? Kópi ..	Cafe	Mantéga ..	Manteiga
? Koridor ..	Corredor	Márka ..	Marca
Korsang, krusang, krunsang	Coraçao	Marcadjota ..	Marquesota
? Kosnil ..	Cochonilha	Marsu ..	Março
Kósta ..	Costa	Martello ..	Martelo
Kovélu, tarvélu	Coelho	Maskára ..	Máscara
Kras, keras ..	Crasso	Máski, miski ..	Mas que
Kunta ..	Conta	Matelote ..	Matalote
Kurpinyu ..	Corpinho	? Máti ..	Matar
Lagárti ..	Lagarto	Meja, méza, mésa	Mesa
Lamina ..	Lâmina	Merecer ..	Merecer
Lámpu, lámpo	Lâmpada	Meriniyu ..	Meirinho
Láncha ..	Lancha		

Malay	*Portuguese*
? Meskin, miskin	Mesquinho
Mester, místi	Mister
Mĕstĕri, mester	Mestre
Milagro ..	Milagre
Mísa ..	Missa
? Misigit, mesígit, masigit	Mesquita
Moler ..	Mulher
Mostárdi, mustárdi	Mostarda
Muran ..	Morrão
Músik ..	Música
Natal ..	Natal
Negociar ..	Negociar
Nen ..	Nem
Nyóra, ? nyonya nónyá, nóna	Senhora
Obrigacion ..	Obrigação
Ordi, úrdi, rúdi, rodi	Ordem
Organ, orgam, organon	Órgão
Orivis ..	Ourives
Pádri ..	Padre
Pálsu ..	Falso
Panjar ..	Penhor
Paon ..	Pão
Papa ..	Papá
Papáya, peppáya, pápua	Papaia
Para ..	Para
Parecha ..	Frecha
Parente ..	Parente
Parésku ..	Fresco
Paresser ..	Prazer

Malay	*Portuguese*
Par forsa, per forsa	Por força
Paris ..	Par
Parséru, parséro	Parceiro
Paskil, paskvil	Pasquim
Pasiyar ..	Passear
Pastel, pastil	Pastel
Pasu, básu ..	Vaso
Pātarána ..	Poltrona
Patrás, patráz	Patarata
? Patrol ..	Patrulha
? Patuley ..	Patuleia
Páu ..	Pau
Pavam ..	Pavão
Pay ..	Pai
? Pĕgan ..	Pegar
Peito ..	Peito
Pelánki, planki	Palanquim
Pelúru, pélor, pilóru, pilor	Pelouro
Pena ..	Pena
Péna ..	Pena
Pepinio ..	Pepino
Permísi ..	Permissão
Persén ..	Presente
? Pétas, petásan	Petardo
Píchu ..	Fecho
Píjar ..	Fechar
Pingan, ping-gan	Palangana
Pípa ..	Pipa
? Piring ..	Pires
Piskal ..	Fiscal
Pistol ..	Pistola
Pitár ..	Fitar

Malay	*Portuguese*
Pomba, pombaq, pamba, pambaq	Pomba
? Pompa ..	Pompa
Por ..	Por
Portero ..	Porteiro
Práda, paráda	Prata
Prego ..	Prego
Pregoaçaon ..	Pregoação
Pregoar ..	Pregoar
Prima ..	Prima
Primo ..	Primo
Proveito ..	Proveito
Prum, parum	Prumo
Pulpito ..	Púlpito
Quanto ..	Quanto
Quanto mas ..	Quanto mais
Ramo ..	Ramo
Ranson ..	Ração
? Rata ..	Raso
Recado ..	Recado
Rede ..	Rêde
Regalas ..	Regalo
Remedio ..	Remédio
Rénda ..	Renda
Requerer ..	Requerer
Resít ..	Recibo
Rial ..	Rial
Róda ..	Roda
Ródoq ..	Rôdo
Rója, ? rôs ..	Rosa
Ronda ..	Ronda
Rúa ..	Rua
? Rupiya ..	Rupia
Sabon, sábun, sabún	Sabão
Sábtu, sáptu ..	Sábado
? Ságū ..	Sagu
Sáku, sáko ..	Saco
Saláda, seláda	Salada
Santo ..	Santo
Sánto pápa ..	Papa
Sapátu ..	Sapato
Seguro ..	Seguro
? Seka ..	Secar
Séla ..	Sela
Semana ..	Semana
Sentar ..	Jantar
Sin ..	Sem
Sinñor, sinyo, siyu, sínhô	Senhor
Siño ..	Sino
Siríng ..	Seringa
Sita ..	Citação
Sita ..	Citar
Sitin, síten ..	Setim
Skola, sakola, sekola	Escola
Sobrinja ..	Sobrinha
Sobrinjo ..	Sobrinho
Soldādu, seredādu seridādu	Soldado
Sópa ..	Sopa
? Sore ..	Serão
Spada ..	Espada
Spera ..	Espera
Suberbo ..	Soberbo
Suissa ..	Suíssa
Sumáka ..	Sumaca
? Sutra ..	Sêda
Táchu ..	Tacho

Malay	Portuguese	Malay	Portuguese
Taledor ..	Traidor	Tocca ..	Touca
Tambáko, tembáko, tembáku	Tabaco	Tóma ..	Tomar
		Tópa ..	Tofa
		Toro ..	Toro
? Tambur ..	Tambor	Torto ..	Torto
? Tángki ..	Tanque	Trígu, terigu	Trigo
Tanjedor, tanjidur	Tangedor	Tronko, tarunku	Tronco
Tanji ..	Tanger	Tuála, tuvála	Toalha
Tántu ..	Tanto	? Tufán ..	Tufão
Tarda ..	Tarde	Túkar ..	Trocar
Tateruga, tetrugo	Tartaruga	Valer ..	Valer
		Varánda, baránda, beránda, meranda	Varanda
? Telana, tjalana, tjilona	Pantalona		
Tempo ..	Tempo		
Ténda ..	Tenda	Veillo ..	Velho
Tentar ..	Tentar	Veludo, belúdu, belúdro, beldú, beldúva	Veludo
Tĕrompet ..	Trombeta		
Téstamen ..	Testamento		
Tínta ..	Tinta	Vérdi ..	Verde
Tio ..	Tio	Vesporas ..	Vésperas
Tiras ..	Tira	Vidro ..	Vidro

32. Malayalam

Malayalam	Portuguese	Malayalam	Portuguese
Ádi ..	Ádem	Aruda ..	Arruda
Ālnāri ..	Armãrio	Āspatri ..	Hospital
Amár ..	Amora	Ātta ..	Ata
Ambar, amber	Ambar	Balam ..	Balão
Ananás ..	Ananás	Batatas ..	Batata
Andólam ..	Andor	Bispe ..	Bispo (S)
Ánju ..	Anjo	Bôrmona ..	Fôrno
Anona ..	Anona	Burchcha ..	Bucha
Apostalañ ..	Apóstolo	? Buruss ..	Bruça

Malayalam	*Portuguese*
Chá, cháya ..	Chá
Chakku ..	Saco
Chappiñña ..	Chapinha
? Cherippu ..	Chiripos
? Chháppa ..	Chapa
Chiññer ..	Cinzel
Chippuli ..	Cepilho
Diyáb ..	Diabo
Dôś ..	Doce
Girádi, grádi, grási	Grade
Governṇador..	Governador
Góvi, goviṇṇu	Couve
Guḍḍam ..	Gudão
Ingirisu ..	Inglês
Iṛayál, ress ..	Rial, réis
Istrí ..	Estirar
Janarál ..	General
Janel, chenel, chenárel, janavātil	Janela
Kabalarikka ..	Acafelar
Kábu ..	Cabo
Kāl-chchaṭṭa..	Calção
Kamis, khamis	Camisa
Kāppa ..	Capa
Kapparikka ..	Capar
? Kāppi, káppikhuru	Cafe
Káppiri ..	Cafre
Kappitán ..	Capitão
Karal ..	Cairel
Karámbu, karayabu	Cravo
Karpu ..	Garfo
? Karuvaḍu ..	Cravado

Malayalam	*Portuguese*
Kasêla ..	Cadeira
Katólika ..	Católico
Kasú, kasúmáru	Caju
Kheruba ..	Querubim
Kiristanmár ..	Cristão
Koḍudam ..	Cordão
Kompasárikka	Confessar
Konta ..	Contas
Kóppa ..	Copo
Kórja, kórchchu	Corja
Krittikka ..	Critica
Krúśu, kurisá	Cruz
Kulér ..	Colher
Kura ..	Curar
Lanchi, lenji ..	Lenço
Lántar ..	Lanterna
Lelam, élam ..	Leilão
Léyam ..	Lião
List ..	Lista
Meśa, més ..	Mesa
Mestarí ..	Mestre
? Miskín, maskin	Mesquinho
Nāváli ..	Navalha
Oḍam ..	Horta
Olamári, ōlamári	Almadia
Orlojjika ..	Relógio
Pádiri, padriyár	Padre
Pangáyar ..	Pangaio
Páppà ..	Papa
Pappáyam ..	Papaia
Pattáchu ..	Patacho
Pattāká ..	Pataca

Malayalam	Portuguese
? Paṭṭaka	Foguete
Páttu	Pato
Péna	Pena
Pērá	Pera
Peridéri	Pedreiro
Phiṭṭa, phiṭṭu	Fita
Pikkam	Picão
Piññа	Pinho
Pintárani	Pintura
Pintārikā	Pintar
Píppa	Pipa
Pirzent	Presidente
Pórkku	Porco
Prakuka, pirākuka	Praga
Rabekka	Rabeca
Raśidu, rasdi	Recibo
Rattal	Arrátel
Rónda	Ronda
Saban, sabún	Sabão
? Sagu, sāgó	Sagu
Sódti	Sorte
Spoñu	Esponja
Tambákku	Tabaco
Tambákku	Tambaca
Tambor	Tambor
Tanáss	Tenaz
? Tariff	Tarifa
Tishóri	Tesouraria
Tital̤	Dedal
Tress	Três
Truppu	Tropa
Turungu	Tronco
Tuvála	Toalha
Vára	Vara
Varanda	Varanda
Varkkas	Baracaça
Vássi	Bacia
Vattakka	Pateca
Vattéri	Bateria
Veruma, bórmma	Verruma
Vilimbi, velumba	Bilimbim
Villúdu, vellúdi	Veludo
Viññu	Vinho
Visareyi	Viso-rei
Viśagari	Visagra

33. Marathi

Marathi	Portuguese
Āchár	Achar
Āmá	Ama
Ambar	Ambar
Ananás ananas	Ananás
Aphôs	Afonso
Ark	Arco
Ārmár, armár, ārmar, aṛmar	Armada
Armāri	Armāri
Ayá	Aia
? Baglá, bagalá	Baixel
Bāldí	Balde
Bamb	Bomba
Bánk	Banco
Baptismá	Baptismo
Barát	Baralho

Marathi	*Portuguese*
Barkatá	Barqueta
Barkín	Barquinha
Basi, bāsí, bāśi	Bacia
Batelá	Batel
Bhoplá, bhomplá	Abóbora
Bijāgrem bijogrí	Visagra
Bilambi, bimbla	Bilimbim
Boḍad	Bordo
? Bôt	Bote
Burákh	Buraco
Butāvém	Botão
Búz	Bucha
Chahá	Chá
Chepém	Chapéu
? Chháp	Chapa
Dhumas	Damasco
Ekpharmá	Forma
Gamel	Gamela
Garád, garág, garadá	Grade
Gārdí, gāḍdi	Guarda
Garnál	Granada
Gudámv	Gudão
Inglejí	Inglês
? Isáḍ, isāḍá	Enxêrto
Istád	Estado
Istrí (karṇem)	Estirar
Jingalí	Gergelim
Jugár, juvá, juvebāji, júvá kheḷṇem	Jogar
Kabáy, kabāi	Cabaia
Káj	Casa
Kamíg, khamis	Camisa
Kampú	Campo
? Kāphí	Café
Karneḷ	Coronel
Katholik	Católico
Kāzú	Caju
Kôb, kobí, koí	Couve
Kontrát	Contrato
Krús	Cruz
Kulás	Colaça
Kurêl	Carreira
Kust hoṇeṁ	Custar
Kutní	Cotonia
Lavád	Louvado
Lilámv, lilám	Leilão
Máma	Mama
Mej	Mesa
Mestarí, mest	Mestre
Milāgri	Milagre
? Miskín, miskíl	Mesquinho
Nātal, natāḷéṁ	Natal
Org, ork	Órgão
Pādrí	Padre
Pág, pagár	Paga
Páp	Papa
Pāpá	Papá
? Pāpliśt	Pampano
Parānchí	Prancha
Parát	Prato
Pasár	Passar
Pasár	Passear
Pāyri	Phres
Páz	Passo
Pên	Pena
Peru	Pera
Phajindár	Fazendeiro
? Phalaṇá	Fulano

Marathi		*Portuguese*	*Marathi*		*Portuguese*
Pháls	..	Falso	Rend	..	Renda
Phāltu	..	Falto	Ríp	..	Ripa
Phargád	..	Fragata	Sábú, sábún	..	Sabão
? Phatkaḍi	..	Foguete	? Sāgú	..	Sagu
Phidālkhôr	..	Fidalgo	Soḍtí	..	Sorte
Phít, phínt	..	Fita	Tambākhu, tamākhú		Tabaco
Phôl	..	Folha	? Tankí, tankém		Tanque
Pidrêl	..	Pedreiro	Tumbar	..	Tumor
Pikándar	..	Picadeira	? Tuphán	..	Tufão
Pikáṁv, ? pikás		Picão	Turanj, toranjan		Toranja
Píp, pimp	..	Pipa	Turung, turang		Tronco
Pistol, pistúl	..	Pistola	? Umbrá, umra, umbartá, umartá		Umbreira
Popáy, popayá, phopai		Papaia	? Váph	..	Bafo
? Pot	..	Ponta	Varanḍ, varaḍá, varānḍá, varanḍí		Varanda
? Pot, pont, ponth		Fonte			
Ratal	..	Arrátel			
Rejim	..	Resma			
Rems	..	Rial, réis			

34. Molucan

Molucan		*Portuguese*	*Molucan*		*Portuguese*
Bariga	..	Barriga	Lés	..	Ler
Cabessa	..	Cabeça	Mainato	..	Mainato
Cheyro	..	Cheiro	Maman	..	Mamã
Espera	..	Espera	Martélo, martelu		Martelo
Graia	..	Gralha	Milo, mīlu	..	Milho
Ingeniyo	..	Engenho	Papá	..	Papá
Kertu, kérto	..	Carta	Pees	..	Pés
Lénsu	..	Lenço			

35. Nepali

Nepali		*Portuguese*	*Nepali*		*Portuguese*
? Báf	..	Bafo	? Chháp	..	Chapa
Chābí	..	Chave	Chiyá	..	Chá

Nepali		Portuguese	Nepali		Portuguese
Fālto	..	Falto	Mej	..	Mesa
Godám	..	Gudão	Pīpá	..	Pipa
Juvá	..	Jogar	Sābún	..	Sabão
Līlám	..	Leilão	Tamākú	..	Tabaco
Mārtāul	..	Martelo			

36. Nicobarese

Nicobarese		*Portuguese*	*Nicobarese*		*Portuguese*
Biskut	..	Biscoito	Paráta	..	Prata
Chá	..	Chá	Patáta	..	Batata
Chumbo	..	Chumbo	Pípa	..	Pipa
Deṁ	..	Rei	Pistola	..	Pistola
Deuse	..	Deus	Popai	..	Papaia
Kápre	..	Cabra	Sál	..	Sal
Katére	..	Cadeira	Sánta-mariá	..	Santa Maria
Koyabas	..	Goiaba	Sápáta	..	Sapato
Lébare	..	Livro	Sapéo	..	Chapéu
Lenśe	..	Lenço	Śaváng	..	Sabão
Lévere	..	Lebre	Sayo	..	Saco
? Lifanta	..	Elefante	Víniya	..	Vinho
Menśa	..	Mesa	Vitore	..	Vidro

37. Oriya

Oriya		*Portuguese*	*Oriya*		*Portuguese*
Āchár	..	Achar	Istrí	..	Estirar
Āiyá	..	Aia	Jua	..	Jogar
Anáras	..	Ananás	Kalāpāti	..	Calafate
Át	..	Ata	Kamrā	..	Câmara
? Bájan	..	Bacia	? Kāphi	..	Café
? Bháp	..	Bafo	Kobi	..	Couve
Chá	..	Chá	? Lemu, nemu, nimu		Limão
Chābí	..	Chave			
? Chháp	..	Chapa	Mástul	..	Mastro
Girjá	..	Igreja	Mej	..	Mesa
Gudáma	..	Gudão	Nilám	..	Leilão

Oriya		*Portuguese*	*Oriya*		*Portuguese*
Pati-hams	..	Pato	Sábun, śābiṇí		Sabão
Perú	..	Peru	? Sāgú	..	Sagu
Phitá	..	Fita	Tamákhu	..	Tabaco
Rasid	..	Recibo	? Tuphán	..	Tufão

38. Punjabi

Punjabi		*Portuguese*	*Punjabi*		*Portuguese*
Āchár	..	Achar	Lalám, nilám		Leilão
Almāri	..	Armário	? Marmar	..	Mármore
? Bájan	..	Bacia	? Maskin	..	Mesquinho
? Bháph	..	Bafo	Mastari	..	Mestre
? Bodal	..	Botelha	Mastul	..	Mastro
Bujá, bujja, bujji		Bucha	Perú	..	Peru
Chāha	..	Chá	? Phalāná, phalāni, phalāuná		Fulano
Farmá	..	Forma	Pīpá	..	Pipa
Fītá	..	Fita	Pistaul	..	Pistola
Girjá	..	Igreja	Rasíd	..	Recibo
Ispát	..	Espada	Sābún, sabún		Sabão
Istrí	..	Estirar	? Sāgú	..	Sagu
Jūá, khelna, jūá mārná		Jogar	Tamākú, tamákhú		Tabaco
Karābiní	..	Carabina	? Tambúr	..	Tambor
Kārtús	..	Cartucho	? Tufán	..	Tufão
Kumedan	..	Comandante	Varmá, barmá		Verruma

39. Persian

Persian		*Portuguese*	*Persian*		*Portuguese*
Anjar, anjara		Ancora	? Marmar	..	Mármore
Barmá	..	Verruma	Mez, miz	..	Mesa
? Bas	..	Basta	Mūsīgí	..	Música
Chāí	..	Chá	Póta, móta	..	Ponta
Chit	..	Chita	Purtughál	..	Portugal
? Dāya	..	Aia	Rasíd	..	Recibo
? Foran	..	Fôrno	Riyál	..	Rial

Persian		Portuguese	Persian		Portuguese
Sabát	..	Sapato	? Sijil	..	Sigilo
? Sābú	..	Sagu	Tambākú, tambak		Tabaco
Sābún	..	Sabão	? Vāpúr	..	Vapor
? Saiṭan	..	Satán			
Sangtara	..	Cintra			

40. Pidgin-English

Pidgin-English		Portuguese	Pidgin-English		Portuguese
Amah	..	Ama	Joss, Josh	..	Deus
Bangee	..	Bangue	Maskee, mashkee, ma-sze-ki		Mas que
Cab-tun	..	Capitão	Molo-man	..	Mouro
? Cango	..	Canga	Na	..	Não
? Chop	..	Chapa	Pa-ti-li, pa-tele		Padre
Compradore, compladore, kam-pat-to		Comprador	? Pidgin	..	Ocupação
? Consu	..	Consul	Sabby, savvy, shapi		Saber
Galanti, ka-lanti		Grande			

41. Rabbinical

Rabbinical		Portuguese
Kamaron	..	Câmara
Espáthe	..	Espada
Forni ..	..	Fôrno

42. Siamese

Siamese		Portuguese	Siamese		Portuguese
? Ahbam	..	Apa	? Cháping, tápping		Chapinha
? Áni	..	Anis	Cŏngsul	..	Consul
Bāt	..	Padre	Fárān̄	..	Açafrão
? Bote	..	Bote	Kāb	..	Capa
? Chabap	..	Chapa			

Siamese		Portuguese	Siamese		Portuguese
? Kafē, khǎofe		Café	Pet	..	Pato
Kāmpān	..	Cavalo	Pib	..	Pipa
Khrĭstǎng	..	Cristão	? Pliuěk	..	Pelouro
? Kra-dart	..	Carta or cartaz	? Rēt	..	Rinoceronte
? Kra-sá, ka-sá		Garça	Rién	..	Rial
Kra-tā	..	Carrêta	? Rupia	..	Rupia
Kratu	..	Grade	Sá	..	Chá
Kravhn	..	Cravo	Sa-bŭ, sǎbŭ	..	Sabão
Lelǎng	..	Leilão	? Sákhu	..	Sagu
? Mǎnao	..	Limão	Tárahng	..	Tronco
Miśa	..	Missa	? Tau	..	Dado
Monsúm	..	Monção	? Tēng	..	Pateca
? Pa-thǎt	..	Petardo	? Tōk	..	Toalha

43. Sindhi

Sindhi		Portuguese	Sindhi		Portuguese
Ācháru	..	Achar	? Līmò	..	Limão
Ambāru	..	Ambar	Meza, mesu	..	Mesa
Anānásu	..	Ananás	Nilámu, nilámu		Leilão
? Bápha	..	Bafo	Pagháru	..	Pagar
Barmá	..	Verruma	? Pāsô	..	Página
? Bas	..	Basta	? Phalānô	..	Fulano
Bateló	..	Batel	Phaliṭu	..	Falto
Bunji	..	Bucha	? Phatakô	..	Foguete
? Buti	..	Botelha	Phíta	..	Fita
Chá, cháhi	..	Chá	Pípa	..	Pipa
? Chhápa, chhā-pô		Chapa	Pistola	..	Pistola
			Rasíd	..	Recibo
Istirí	..	Estirar	Riyálu	..	Rial
Jhirmíri	..	Janela	Sābuni	..	Sabão
Juá khelṇu	..	Jogar	Tamáku	..	Tabaco
Kadela, gadela		Cadeira	? Tíru	..	Tiro
? Karabinu	..	Carabina	? Tuphanu	..	Tufão
Kháju, kházo		Caju	Turungu	..	Tronco

44. Sinhalese

Sinhalese	*Portuguese*
Adŭ́ppuva, adíppuva	Adufa
Agôstu ..	Agôsto
Alavắnguva ..	Alavanca
Almāriya ..	Armário
Almúsu, almúsuva	Almôço
Alpenêtiya, alpêntiya	Alfinete
Āmá ..	Ama
Amen ..	Amen
Annási, anahsí annắsiya	Ananás
Anōná ..	Anona
Attá ..	Ata
Aṭṭalaya ..	Atalaia
Avánaya, avánē, aváne	Abano
Āyá ..	Aia
Bájan ..	Bacia
Baḷama ..	Balão
Báldiya, báliya	Balde
Bandêsiya ..	Bandeja
Bănkuva ..	Banco
Barama ..	Varrão
Barándе, barándaya, varanḍaya	Varanda
Baraseḷ ..	Braçal
Batála ..	Batata
Bastắmu ..	Bastão
Bavtísmaya ..	Baptismo
Bayinettiya, bayinêttuva	Baioneta
Bêbaduva, bêbaduvu, bêbadda, bêbayiyā	Bêbado
Biskóttu, viskóttu, viskottuva	Biscoito
Boku ..	Oco
Bólaya ..	Bola
Bômbaya ..	Bomba
? Bónchi ..	Vagem
Bônikka ..	Boneca
Bora ..	Bôrra
? Bótale, bótalaya	Botelha
Bottama ..	Botão
Bujắma ..	Boião
Búliya ..	Bule
Buruma, buṛema, buṛema-kaṭuva	Verruma
Búruva búṛeva	Burro
Chinélaya ..	Chinelas
Chitta ..	Chita
Dáduva ..	Dado
Didálaya, didále	Dedal
Diyamántiya ..	Diamante
Don ..	Dom
Dôsi ..	Doce
Garádiya ..	Grade
Gástuva ..	Gasto
Golôva ..	Globo

Sinhalese	*Portuguese*
Gudama	Gudão
Guruléttuva	Gorgoleta
? Hisop	Hissope
? Hôrā, hôrāva	Hora
Indiyánu	Indiano
Ingrisi	Inglês
Ispiritále	Hospital
Jalúsi	Gelosia
Janélaya, janele	Janela
Kabáya	Cabaia
Kabuka	Cabouco
Kaju, kajju	Caju
Kaldérama, kaldarama	Caldeirão
Kálduva	Caldo
Kalisama, kalasama	Calção
Kámaraya, kámarê	Câmara
Kamise, kamisaya, kamiseya	Camisa
Kanáde	Canada
Kanåppuva	Canapé
? Kandalåruva	Candelabro
Kánuva	Cano
Kappádu, kappádukala	Capado
Kappaláruvā	Acafelar
Kappita, kappeta	Capitão
Kardamúnga	Cardamomo
Karette, karettiya, karåttiya, karéttuva	Carrêta
Kasádaya, kasáda bẹndima	Casado
Katekísmaya	Catecismo
Katólika	Católico
Kéju	Queijo
Kittárama	Guitarra
Kôntaya, kontêya	Contas
? Kópi	Café
Kóppaya, kóppe	Copo
Kórnel	Coronel
Kôssiya	Coche
Kottama	Cotão
Kóvi	Couve
Krábu, karábu	Cravo
Kulachchama	Colchão
Kuluna, kulunna	Coluna
Kúññaya, kúññeya	Cunha
Kurůsiya, kurẹsiya.	Cruz
Kůssiya	Cozinha
? Lámpuva	Lâmpada
Lånsaya, lanse	Lança
Lantẹruma, lantẹrẹma	Lanterna
Lásuru	Lázaro
Lémsuva	Lenço
Lésti, lestiya	Lestes
Linguyis, lingus	Linguiça
Lottarẹya, lotaruyiya	Lotaria
? Malla	Mala
? Mariyá	Marear

Sinhalese	Portuguese
Masan ..	Maçã
Mês ..	Meia, meias
Midulu ..	Medula
Móstraya, móstaraya, mostra, mostare	Mostra
Mūnissama ..	Munição
Nattal ..	Natal
Nómare, nommaraya	Número
Nónā ..	Dona
Orgalaya, orgale	Órgão
Orlosiya, oralósuvā	Relójio
Pádiri, pádeli	Padre
Palanchiya ..	Prancha
Palangana, palangánama	Palangana
Páṅ, pán, páṅgediya	Pão
Páppa ..	Papa
Pápus ..	Papuses
Páskuva ..	Páscoa
? Paspórtuva	Passaporte
Patágaya, pattakka gediya	Pateca
Pāttayá, pātti (fem.)	Pato
Pedaréruvā, pedarérẹva	Pedreiro
Pẹna, pẹne, tatupẹna	Pena
Penéraya, penēréya	Peneira
Peragama ..	Pregão
? Petta ..	Fatia
Pikama, pikásiya	Picão
Pintáruva, pintárẹma, pintüraya	Pintura
Pipiññа ..	Pepino
Píppaya, píppe, pippa-vaḍuvá	Pipa
Pirissya ..	Pires
Pistólaya, pistóle	Pistola
Pítta-pataya, pítta-paṭiya	Fita
Piyon ..	Peão
Pôrṇuva, poraṇuva	Fôrno
Pôrke ..	Forca
Prophétaya ..	Profeta
Púkuruva, púkiraya	Púcaro
Punílaya ..	Funil
Purgatóriya ..	Purgatório
Pusalana, kuslána	Porcelana
Rábu ..	Rabão
Ránchuva ..	Rancho
Ráttala ..	Arrátel
Rénda, réndapaṭiya	Renda
Réndaya ..	Renda
Ródaya, róda, róde	Roda
Rósa, rósamala	Rosa
Rulan ..	Rolão
Sabañ, saban..	Sabão

Sinhalese	*Portuguese*	*Sinhalese*	*Portuguese*
? Sāgú, savgal	Sagu	Sóp, sóppaya..	Sopa
Sakkamalla ..	Saco	Sōpáva ..	Sofá
Sála, sále, sálaya	Sala	Sórtiya ..	Sorte
Saláda ..	Salada	Sprítuva ..	Espírito
Santuvariya ..	Santo	? Stalaya, istálaya, istále	Estala
Sapatéruva, sapatére	Sapateiro	Sumánaya ..	Semana
Sapattu, sapattuva	Sapato	Táchuva ..	Tacho
Satán, satanás	Sátan	Tambóruva, tambóreva	Tambor
Sāvódiya ..	Saude	Tebẹruma, tẹberẹma	Taberna
Séda ..	Sêda	Tempráduva	Temperado
Sideran, sidaran	Cidrão	Tínta ..	Tinta
Sínuva, siniya	Sino	Tíraya, tirẹva	Tira
Sitásiya, sitāsikeríma	Citação	Tiringu ..	Trigo
Sitim ..	Setim	Tómbuva ..	Tômbo
Skólaya, iskóle, skólayê sahakáriya	Escola	Trankaya ..	Tranca
? Sokalat ..	Chocolate	Tuváya, tuvájaya, tuváje	Toalha
Soldáduva ..	Soldado	Vendésiya ..	Vendas
		Vẹyin ..	Vinho
		Víduruva, vidurẹva, vidur	Vidro
		Vinákiri ..	Vinagre

45. Sundanese

Sundanese	*Portuguese*	*Sundanese*	*Portuguese*
Almári ..	Armário	Bási ..	Bacia
Âmbar ..	Ambar	? Bedil ..	Fuzil
Amin ..	Amen	Belúdru, bulúdru	Veludo
Bálla ..	Bailar	Bídal ..	Dedal
Bandéra ..	Bandeira	Biyola, biola	Viola
Bánku ..	Banco	Bóla ..	Bola
Baránda ..	Varanda		

Sundanese	*Portuguese*
Bonéka ..	Boneca
? Chapa, echap	Chapa
Chapeó ..	Chapéu
Chinela ..	Chinela
Chita, sita ..	Chita
Dádu ..	Dado
Danas, ganas ..	Ananás
? Gágu ..	Gago
Gáji ..	Gage
Gánsa ..	Ganso
Gárpu ..	Garfo
Gréja, gríja ..	Igreja
Ingris ..	Inglês
Kabáya ..	Cabaia
Káju ..	Caju
Káldu, káldo	Caldo
Kámar ..	Câmara
Kaméja ..	Camisa
? Kápal ..	Cavalo
Kapitan ..	Capitão
Kampong, kampung	Campo
Karābu, kurābu	Cravo
Karéta, kréta	Carrêta
Kártas, kértas	Carta or Cartaz
Kártu ..	Carta
Kásut ..	Calçado
Kerĕpus ..	Carapuça
Kiju ..	Queijo
? Kópi ..	Café
Kósta ..	Costa
? Kutang, kutung	Cotão
Lámpu, lampo	Lampada
Lantéra ..	Lanterna

Sundanese	*Portuguese*
Lélang ..	Leilão
Limó ..	Limão
Mandôr ..	Mandador
Mantéga ..	Manteiga
Marínio ..	Meirinho
Mása ..	Mas
Méja ..	Mesa
Minátu ..	Mainato
Místi ..	Mister
Móri ..	Mouro
Nóna ..	Anona
Nóna, nunya	Dona
Nyoña ..	Senhora
Pádri ..	Padre
Palsu ..	Falso
? Panel ..	Mainel
Paníti ..	Alfinete
Panjer ..	Penhor
? Pas ..	Passe
Páso ..	Vaso
Pastel ..	Pastel
Pélor ..	Pelouro
Pésta ..	Festa
Péstol ..	Pistola
Pétor ..	Feitor
Pingan ..	Palangana
Piring ..	Pires
Pita ..	Fita
Práda, parāda	Prata
Rêal ..	Rial
Rénda ..	Renda
Róda ..	Roda
Ronda ..	Ronda
? Rupiya ..	Rupia
Sabun ..	Sabão
? Ságū ..	Sagu

Sundanese	*Portuguese*
Sáku	Saco
Saláda	Salada
Saparo, paro	Separado
Sapátu, sepátu	Sapato
Sáptu	Sábado
Sella	Sela
Serável	Ceroilas
? Sikat	Secar
Sínyo	Senhor
? Sore	Serão
Stóri	História
Sutra	Sêda
Tambako, bako	Tabaco
Tambur	Tambor
Tarigo	Trigo
? Telana, tjalana, tjilona	Pantalona
Tempo	Tempo
Túkar	Trocar

46. Tamil

Tamil	*Portuguese*
Ádru	Adro
Alavángu	Alavanca
Almond	Almôndega
Alpinêti	Alfinete
Altár	Altar
Alumári	Armário
Alvei	Alva
Amár	Amarra
Ambar	Ambar
Annási	Ananás
Appostolamam	Apóstolo
Aráttal	Arratel
Asádu	Assado
Attá	Ata
Balcham	Balchão
Báldi	Balde
Bánku	Banco
Bási	Bacia
Bíphi	Bife
Bispu	Bispo
Bôlu	Bôlo
Bótan	Botão
Bulei	Bule
Canhão	Canhão
Chá	Chá
Chāmādôr	Chamador
? Cherippu	Chiripos
Chinelei	Chinela
Damásu	Damasco
Dósei	Doce
Élam	Leilão
Galobei	Globo
Gánchu	Gancho
Gavêti	Gaveta
Garáde, girádi	Grade
Golla	Gola
Goyá palam	Goiaba
Ilansi	Lenço
Iskiriván	Escrivão
Iskolei	Escola
Isopei	Hissope
Jānalá, jannal	Janela
Jūdádu, jūávilaiyádu	Jogar

Tamil	*Portuguese*	*Tamil*	*Portuguese*
Kabáy ..	Cabaia	Miriñ ..	Meirinho
Kadêra ..	Cadeira	Misál ..	Missal
Káju-p a l a m, kaju-maram	Caju	Misán ..	Missão
		Misiyonár ..	Missionário
Kalapparradip-pal	Calafate	? Molei ..	Môlho
		Nattal ..	Natal
Kal-chattei ..	Calção	Novenei ..	Novena
Kamisei ..	Camisa	Ópa ..	Opa
Kăppa ..	Capa	Orelóju ..	Relójio
? Káppi, kóppi	Café	Orgán ..	Órgão
Kapelei ..	Capela	Óstu ..	Hóstia
Karámbu, ki-rámbu	Cravo	Pádiri, padriyár	Padre
		Padrovádu ..	Padroado
Karesmai ..	Quaresma	Pálli ..	Pálio
? Karuvádu ..	Cravado	Páppa, páppu, páppanavan	Papa
Kastisál, kas-trisál	Castiçal	Pappai ..	Papaia
Katólik ..	Católico	Paská ..	Páscoa
Kiristavan ..	Cristão	Pattaká, vatta-kei	Pateca
Kompádri ..	Compadre		
Komphisáñ ..	Confissão	? Paṭṭake ..	Foguete
Komuniyāñ ..	Comunhão	Péna, pennei	Pena
Kordan ..	Cordão	Pērá ..	Pera
Kóvi ..	Couve	Peśkār ..	Fiscal
Krismei ..	Crisma	Pingān ..	Palangana
Kujíd ..	Cozido	Píppā ..	Pípa
Kumádri ..	Comadre	Píris ..	Pires
Kurus ..	Cruz	Pirzent ..	Presidente
Kusini ..	Cozinha	Piyá ..	Pia
Kuttán ..	Cotão	Pulpitu ..	Púlpito
Lántar ..	Lanterna	Ramade ..	Remada
Lobei ..	Loba	Renda ..	Renda
Masuvádu ..	Amancebado	Rolam ..	Rolão
Mesei ..	Mesa	Rósa ..	Rosa
Mey-jódu, kal-mês, kai-mês	Meia	Sakkrári ..	Sacrário
		Sakraméntu ..	Sacramento

Tamil		Portuguese	Tamil		Portuguese
Sakristí	..	Sacristia	Temprád	..	Temperado
Sallâdu	..	Salada	Térsu	..	Têrço
Sankristán	..	Sacristão	Tijoreri	..	Tesoureiro
Sappattu	..	Sapato	Tintei	..	Tinta
Sávi	..	Chave	Tócha	..	Tocha
? Savvu	..	Sagu	Trávi	..	Trave
Seminári	..	Seminário	Tualei	..	Toalha
Semitére	..	Cemitério	? Turukkam	..	Tronco
Sīdári	..	Cidade	Varanda	..	Varanda
Spíritu Sántu		Espírito Santo	Vattu	..	Pato
Stantei	..	Estante	Vendále	..	Vinha de alhos
? Súppu	..	Sopa	Venjan-pradu		Benzer
Sutun	..	Sotaina	Vesper	..	Vésperas
Tabernákulu		Tabernáculo	Vévu	..	Véu
Tambákku	..	Tambaca	Vigári	..	Vigário
Tambor	..	Tambor	Viskan	..	Biscoito

47. Telugu

Telugu		Portuguese	Telugu		Portuguese
Almár	..	Armário	Battéri, phattéri		Bateria
Amáru, amáru-tádu		Amarra	Bátu	..	Pato
Anānásu, anásu, anás-paṇṭu, anās-ávanasa-paṇṭu		Ananás	Biskotthu	..	Biscoito
Áno	..	Ano	Boda	..	Bordo
Āspatri	..	Hospital	Buruma, barama		Verruma
Ayá	..	Aia	Butaum, bottam		Botão
Bāldi, bādlí	..	Balde	? Gadangu, gidding		Gudão
Bankatí	..	Banco	Galan	..	Galão
? Baptismam		Baptismo	? Garandilu	..	Granadeiro
? Baredo	..	Baralho	Istiri	..	Estirar
? Barusu	..	Bruça	? Istuva, istuva		Estado
Bási	..	Bacia	Janalu	..	Janela
			Kalapati	..	Calafate

Telugu	*Portuguese*	*Telugu*	*Portuguese*
Kāmará, kamera, kamra, kamiri	Câmera	Pádiri ..	Padre
		Pápa ..	Papa
		Pāpásum ..	Papuses
Kamisu, kamsu	Camisa	Paranja, paranju	Prancha
Kanáli ..	Canal		
? Kápi ..	Café	Páska ..	Páscoa
Káppiri ..	Cafre	Payal, payálu	Poial
Kappu ..	Capa	Pēná ..	Pena
Kātarusu, kātanusu, ? kakitamu	Cartucho	? Phatóki ..	Foguete
		Phita, píta ..	Fita
		? Phulána, phaláni	Fulano
Kathóliku ..	Católico		
Kómánu ..	Comando	Pingáni, pīngáni	Palangana
Kōpá ..	Copo	Pípaya ..	Pipa
Krismu ..	Crisma	Polísu ..	Policia
Kumbadri ..	Compadre	Puroya ..	Prova
Kumandán ..	Comandante	Raśidu ..	Recibo
Kusinikára, kusini-vádu	Cozinha	Sabbu ..	Sabão
		? Saggu ..	Sagu
Lélām, yálam, yalam, yélamu	Leilão	Sakrístu ..	Sacristão
		Sakrístu ..	Sacrístia
		Sapáth ..	Sapato
Mádiri ..	Madeira	Sávi, chevi ..	Chave
Manna ..	Maná	Spanji ..	Esponja
Mariyansu-át ..	Maria	Spíritu Sántu ..	Espírito Santo
Mayóru ..	Major	Táramu ..	Tara
Meláma ..	Melão	? Tuphánu ..	Tufão
Méja ..	Mesa	Turanj, turánju	Toranja
Mējódu, mejóllu	Meia	Tuvālā, tuvālāgutta	Toalha
Nimma ..	Limão		
Novéna ..	Novena	Vínu ..	Vinho

48. Teto

Teto	*Portuguese*	*Teto*	*Portuguese*
Abril ..	Abril	Achár, asár ..	Achar
Abuzar (*bôsok*)	Abusar (to abuse)	Adeus ..	Adeus

Teto	*Portuguese*
Admirar (*sarebak*)	Admirar (to admire)
Adorar	Adorar (to worship)
Adorāsāṁv (*akruúku*)	Adoração (adoration)
Adulteriu (*séluku*)	Adultério (adultery)
Advogádu	Advogado
Afrikan (*malai meta*)	Africano (African)
Agora (*orasnéi*)	Agora (now)
Agôstu	Agosto
Agradar (*akonôku*)	Agradar (to please)
Agradéci	Agradecer
Aidúda	Ajudar
Ajul	Azul
Alfándega	Alfândega
Alfayáti	Alfaite
Alféris	Alferes
Alfinêti	Alfinete
Algema (*uenlima*)	Algema (fetters)
Alkatifa	Alcatifa
Almónik	Almôndega
Almúsa, almósa	Almoçar
Altar	Altar
Alva	Alva
Alvorada	Alvorada
Amar (*adomi, dóben*)	Amar (to love)
Ambisāṁv (*karak*)	Ambição
Ámen	Amen
Amora	Amora
Amostra	Amostra
Ananaz, nánas	Ananás
Andor	Andor
Animal	Animal
Ánju	Anjo
Aniversáryu	Aniversário
Antigu (*kleur*)	Antigo (ancient)
Apa, apas	Apa
Apitu (*fúi*)	Apito (whistle)
Aprender (*aténi*)	Aprender (to seize)
Apresentar (*hatúdu*)	Apresentar (to present)
Aradu	Arado (a plough)
Arámi	Arame
Argola	Argola
Argolinha	Argolinha
Arkabuz (*kiláti boti*)	Arcabuz (harquebus)
Armada	Armada
Ārsenál	Arsenal
Árti	Arte
Assísti	Assistir
Asu ('nib of a pen')	Aço (steel)
Atensã	Atenção
Auxiliar (*túlun*)	Auxiliar (to help)
Avestruz	Avestruz (ostrich)
Avízar	Avisar
Avízu	Aviso
Azeitona	Azeitona
Bakalhau	Bacalhau
Banda	Banda

Teto	*Portuguese*
Bandeira	Bandeira
Bandeja	Bandeja
Bándu	Bando
Bánku	Banco
Barálha	Baralhar
Barreti	Barrete
Barril	Barril
? Básar	Bazar
Basía	Bacia
Batalhã, batayã	Batalhão
Bátik	Bátiga
Batina	Batina (cassock)
Baviu	Pavio (wick)
Bemditu (*kmanek*)	Bemdito (well spoken)
Bénsa	Bênção
Bentinh	Bentinho
Beringela	Beringela
Bilhet (*súratikik*)	Bilhete (ticket)
Binokulu	Binóculo
Bíphi	Bife
Biskóitu	Biscoito
Bispadu	Bispado (bishopric)
Bíspu	Bispo
Boa noite	Boa noite (good night)
Boa tárde	Boa tarde
Bôba	Bouba
Bôbu	Bobo
Bolacha	Bolacha
Bolsa	Bôlsa
Bôlsu	Bôlso (pocket)
Bôlu	Bôlo
Bomba	Bomba
Bom dia	Bom dia
Bonéka	Boneca
Borla	Borla
Borrão	Borrão (blot)
Bota	Bota
? Botel	Botelha
Breve	Breve (a brief)
Bula	Bula
Búli	Bule
Butã	Botão
Cabo	Cabo
Chá	Chá
Chavena	Chávena (a cup)
Chávi	Chave
Chíkara	Chicara
Chokoláti	Chocolate
Consêlu	Conselho
Daia	Daia (midwife)
Dedál	Dedal
Degrau	Degrau
Dekretu	Decreto
Deseju (*hakárak*)	Desejo (a wish)
Desgosta	Desgostar (not to like)
Deskobrir (*loke*)	Descobrir (to discover)
Deskonfiá	Desconfiar
Deskónta	Descontar
Deskulpa (*haróhan*)	Desculpa (excuse)
Despáchu	Despacho
Despénsa	Despensa
Despeza	Despesa
Despréza	Desprezar
Desprézu (*tos*)	Desprézo (contempt)

Teto	*Portuguese*	*Teto*	*Portuguese*
Desterradu ..	Desterrado (exiled)	*Enśofre* ..	Enxôfre (sulphur)
Destêrru ..	Destêrro (banishment)	Enśu ..	Enxó (adze)
		Entã ..	Então (then)
Determina (*haménu, haruka*)	Determinar (to fix)	*Entender* (*haténi*)	Entender (to understand)
Dever (*hatúsan*)	Dever (to owe)	Entendimentu	Entendimento
Devosã ..	Devoção	Entréga ..	Entregar
Diábu ..	Diabo	Entrúdu ..	Entrudo
Diamánti ..	Diamante	*Epistola* (*surati*)	Epístola
Disionári ..	Dicionário	Érda ..	Herdar
Dispensa ..	Dispensa	Ermida ..	Ermida
Distérra (*phó lákon*)	Desterrar	Ervilha ..	Ervilha
		Esa ..	Essa
Divisa ..	Divisa (emblem)	Escola ..	Escola
Dom ..	Dom	Eskolta ..	Escolta
Domingu ..	Domingo	Eskomunhã ..	Excomunhão
Dona ..	Dona	Eskôva ..	Escôva
Dormitóriu ..	Dormitório (dormitory)	Eskriván ..	Escrivão
		Esmola ..	Esmola
Dosel ..	Dossel	Espértu ..	Esperto
Dótôr ..	Doutor	Esplíka ..	Explicar
Dotrina ..	Doutrina	Espoleta ..	Espoleta
Dôsi ..	Doce	Estádu ..	Estado
Dragã ..	Dragão (dragon)	Estribu ..	Estribo
Dúra ..	Durar	Estríka ..	Esticar
Dúzi, dúsi ..	Duzia	*Estrondu* (*baláun*)	Estrondo (loud noise)
Edisã ..	Edição (edition)		
Edukasã ..	Educação (education)	Estuda ..	Estudar
		Estúdu ..	Estudo
Embarasa (*hakahik, hatáu*)	Embaraçar (to embarrass)	*Eternidād* ..	Eternidade (eternity)
Empáta ..	Empatar	*Eukaristia* ..	Eucaristia (eucharist)
Emprêgu ..	Emprêgo		
Empréata ..	Emprestar	Evanjélhu ..	Evangelho
Enśada ..	Enxada (axe)	Ezámi ..	Exame

Teto		Portuguese
Ezémplu	..	Exemplo
Fálsu	..	Falso
Fálta	..	Faltar
Fáman	..	Fama
Farol	..	Farol
Favor	..	Favor
Fé	..	Fé
Fechadura	..	Fechadura (lock)
Feira	..	Feira
Feriádu	..	Feriado
Festa	..	Festa
Figura	..	Figura
Finta	..	Finta
Fita	..	Fita
Fivela, fiela	..	Fivela
Flanela	..	Flanela
Fogádu	..	Refogado (rice or meat basted in butter, onion, etc.)
Fóra	..	Forrar
Fórma	..	Forma
Fôrnu	..	Fôrno
Forsa	..	Fôrça
Fórti	..	Forte
Frádi	..	Frade
Fragata	..	Fragata
Fráku	..	Fraco
Fraskeira	..	Frasqueira
Frásku	..	Frasco
Freguezia	..	Freguesia
Fréyu	..	Freio
Frontal	..	Frontal

Teto		Portuguese
Fukar (*réko, rego*)		Refogar (altar piece) (see 'Refogado' *supra*)
Funil	..	Funil
Furtuna	..	Fortuna
Gaiola	..	Gaiola (cage)
Gala	..	Gala (feasting)
Gala	..	Galão
Galheta	..	Galheta (cruet)
Gavêta	..	Gaveta
Gizádu	..	Guisado
Glória	..	Glória
Golilha	..	Golilha (iron collar)
Goma	..	Goma
Gorgoleta	..	Gorgoleta
Govêrno	..	Governo
Gracha	..	Graxa
Grasa	..	Graça
Grúdi	..	Grude
Guarda	..	Guarda
Guarnecer (*hudiak*)		Guarnecer
Guia	..	Guia (permit)
Importa (*klétak*)		Importar-se (to come to)
Indistã (*tuan móras*)		Indigestão
Indignu	..	Indigno (unworthy)
Indulgénsia	..	Indulgência
Inférnu	..	Inferno
Injustisa	..	Injustiça
Inosénsi	..	Inocência
Insénsu	..	Incênso

Teto	Portuguese
Inspirasã ..	Inspiraçâo
Instanti (*láis ôan*)	Instante (instant)
Instruméntu ..	Instrumento
Intenta (*hakárak*)	Intentar (to commence)
Intrépiti (*duru bása*)	Intérprete
Inveja ..	Inveja (envy)
Iskalér ..	Escaler
Iskandalu ..	Escândalo
Iskapulariu ..	Escapulário (Scapulary)
Ispirítu ..	Espírito
Ispirítu Santu	Espírito Santo
Ispital ..	Hospital
Istilu ..	Estilo
Istóri ..	História
Janeiru ..	Janeiro (January)
Janela, jinela ..	Janela
Jantar ..	Jantar
Jara ..	Jarra
Jardim ..	Jardim (garden)
Jarru ..	Jarro (pitcher)
Jejum ..	Jejum
Jenebra ..	Genebra
Jeneral ..	General
Jentiu ..	Gentio
Jerasã ..	Geração
Jogador ..	Jogador (gamester)
Jornál ..	Jornal
Júga, dúka, dôka, yóka	Jogar
Juiz, duiz ..	Juiz
Juizu (*néon*) ..	Juizo (reason)
Júlga, *dúlga*, *dúlka*	Julgar (to judge)
Julho ..	Julho
Junho ..	Junho
Júra ..	Jura
Juraméntu, duraméntu	Juramento
Júru ..	Juro
Justisa ..	Justiça
Kabàya ..	Cabaia
Kabārési ..	Cabresto (halter for cattle)
Kabídi ..	Cabide
Kada ..	Cada (each)
Kakau ..	Cacau
Kadeadu (*hénu*)	Cadeado (padlock)
Kadeia ..	Cadeia (chain)
Kadeira ..	Cadeira
Kafé ..	Café
Kajus, kaidu	Caju
Kális ..	Cális
Kamelu ..	Camelo (camel)
Kamiza ..	Camisa
Kamizola ..	Camisola
Kampainha ..	Campainha
Kámpu ..	Campo
Kanapé ..	Canapé
Kandeiru ..	Candieiro (lamp)
Kandu ..	Quando (when)
Kanela ..	Canela
Kaneta ..	Caneta (a pen)
Kánfora ..	Cânofora
Kanivéti ..	Canivete
Kanudu ..	Canudo (a cigar)

Teto	*Portuguese*
Kápa	Capa
Kápa	Capar
Kapadu	Capado (castrated)
Kapás	Capaz
Kapéla	Capela
Kapitan	Capitão
Kapóti	Capote
Kaprichu (*dekur*)	Capricho (caprice)
Karábu	Cravo
Karíl	Caril
Karreta	Carrêta
Kartel	Quartel
Kartús	Cartucho
Karu (*dóben*)	Caro (dear)
Kastelu	Castelo (a castle)
Kastisál	Castiçal
Kastidad	Castidade (chastity)
Kastígu	Castigo
Kásu	Caso
Katána	Catana
Katáru	Catarro
Keiju	Queijo
Kestã	Questão (question)
Kintal	Quintal
Klima	Clima (climate)
Kóbi	Couve
Kochéiru	Cocheiro
Koêlhu	Coelho
Kófri	Cofre
Koléju	Colégio
Komandánti	Comandante
Kominhu	Cominho (cummin seed)
Komparasã	Comparação (comparison)
Komparar (*bádan*)	Comparar (to compare)
Kompásu	Compasso
Komúnga	Comungar
Konderádu	Conderado
Kónegu	Cónego
Konfeitu	Confeito
Konfésa	Confessar
Konfiansa	Confiança
Konforme (*simú*)	Conforme (accordingly)
Konsagrar (*sarani*)	Consagrar (to consecrate)
Konsagrasã	Consagração (consecration)
Konselhu	Concelho (Council)
Konsénti	Consentir
Konsolar (*hakśolak*)	Konsolar (to console)
Kónsul	Cônsul
Konta	Conta
Kontas	Contas
Konténti	Contente
Kontra	Contra
Kontrátu	Contrato
Kontrã vontádi	Contra vontade
Konvíti	Convite
Kopa	Copa (cup)
Kópi	Cópia
Kópu, kóbu	Copo
Kôr	Côr

Teto	*Portuguese*	*Teto*	*Portuguese*
Kôr ..	Côro	*Lakre* ..	Lacre
Koral (*morten*)	Coral (coral)	Lámpa ..	Lâmpada
Koresma ..	Quaresma	Lampiã ..	Lampião
Korneta ..	Corneta	*Lancha* (*róoan*)	Lancha
Korôa ..	Coroa	Lápis ..	Lápis
Koronel ..	Coronel	Lásu ..	Laço
Korrénti ..	Corrente	*Lata* ..	Lata (tin-box)
Kortezia ..	Cortesia	Lei ..	Lei
Kortina ..	Cortina	Leilã, lelã ..	Leilão
Kostúmi ..	Costume	Lénsu ..	Lenço
Kóvadu ..	Côvado	*Lensol* ..	Lençol (bed-sheet)
Kreda ..	Igreja		
Kreditu ..	Credito (credit)	Letra ..	Letra
Kriádu ..	Criado	Lião ..	Lião
Kriatura (*hakálak*)	Criatura (creature)	*Lima* ..	Limar (to file)
		Linho (*fúka*) ..	Linho (flax)
Krisma ..	Crisma	*Liriu* ..	Lirio (lily)
Kruz ..	Cruz	Lisã ..	Lição
Kudir ..	Acudir	Lisensa ..	Licença
Kúida ..	Cuidar	Lista ..	Lista
Kuidádu ..	Cuidado	Lívra ..	Livrar
Kulchã ..	Colchão	Lívre ..	Livre
Kulchête ..	Colchete	Lívru ..	Livro
Kulpa (*sala*) ..	Culpa (fault)	*Lobu* ..	Lobo (wolf)
Kumadre ..	Comadre	Logu (*ôri-lái*)	Logo (soon)
Kumprir (*hálu*)	Cumprir (to fulfil)	Lona ..	Lona (canvas)
		Luminári ..	Luminárias
Kura (*báli*) ..	Cura (cure)	Lútu ..	Luto
Kurveta ..	Corveta	Lúva ..	Luva
Kústa ..	Custar	*Machadu* (*balium*)	Machado (hatchet)
Kustódia ..	Custodia (monstrance)		
		Machila ..	Machila
Kustumadu ..	Costumado (customary)	*Major* ..	Major
Ladainha ..	Ladainha	*Mal* (*aáti*) ..	Mal (evil)
Lagosta (*knáse*)	Lagosta (lobster)	Mala ..	Mala
		Maldisã, malisã	Maldição

Teto	*Portuguese*
Malísi	Malicia
Mangasã	Mangação
Malkriádu	Melcriado
Manha	Manha
Mantéga	Manteiga
Márcha	Marchar
Marka	Marca
Marfim	Marfim
Mársu	Março
Martélu	Martelo
Mãrtir	Mártir
Mas	Mas
Maskê	Mas que
Matraka	Matraca
Meda (*boú*)	Meda (hay rick)
Medalha	Medalha
Mèdiku	Médico
Meias	Meias
Meiu (*naknótak*)	Meio (adj., half)
Meiu dia	Meio dia (mid-day)
Meréci	Merecer
Mersê	Mercê
Méstri	Mestre
Meza	Mesa
Milagru	Milagre
Militar	Militar
Minístru	Ministro
Minútu	Minuto
Mirínhu	Meirinho
Misa	Missa
Misã	Missão
Misál	Missal
Mitra	Mitra (mitre)
Moleiru	Moleiro (miller)

Teto	*Portuguese*
Momentu (*láis ôan*)	Momento (moment)
Multa	Multa
Mundu	Mundo (world)
Munisã	Munição
Músika	Música
Mustarda	Mostarda
Nabu	Nabo (turnip)
Nasã	Nação (nation)
Natál	Natal
Nora	Nora (daughter-in-law)
Nossa Senhora	Nossa Senhora (Our Lady)
Nota	Nota
Notísi	Notícia
Novembru	Novembro (November)
Númeru	Número
Obedeser (*halu-ktúir*)	Obedecer (to obey)
Obediensia	Obediência (obedience)
Obrigasã	Obrigação
Obríga	Obrigar
Obrigádu	Obrigado
Ofender	Ofender
Ofereser	Oferecer
Okaziã	Ocasião
Ókulu, óku	Óculos
Onra	Honra
Ópa	Opa
Ophisyál	Oficial
Ophisyu	Ofício
Ora	Hora
Orasã	Oração

Teto	Portuguese
Órdi	Ordem
Órgão	Órgão
Óstia	Hóstia
Ostra	Ostra (oyster)
Pã	Pão
Pádri	Padre
Pádri Nossu	Padre Nosso (Our Father)
Pagódi	Pagode
Paiol	Paiol (store room)
Palmatória	Palamatória
Pápa	Papa
Papu (*kakalúku*)	Papo (bird's mow)
Para	Para
Parabêm	Parabêm
Parénti	Parente
Párti	Parte
Pasiar	Passear
Pasiénsi	Paciência
Páskua	Páscoa
Pássi	Passe
Pastu	Pasto (pasture)
Pataka	Pataca
Pateka	Pateca
Patarata	Patarata
Patena	Patena (paten)
Patria	Patria (native country)
Patriarka	Patriarca (Patriarch)
Patrónu	Patrono
Pátu	Pato
Paz (*dámi*)	Paz (peace)
Pekadu	Pecado (sin)
Pelu sinal	Pelo sinal (by the sign)
Péna	Pena
Peniténsi	Penitência
Perdã	Perdão
Perdidu	Perdido
Perdisã	Perdição
Perdoar	Perdoar (to pardon)
Pesa	Peça
Pésti	Peste
Phyādór	Fiador
Phyadu	Fiado (retail)
Phyltru	Filtro (filter)
Pia	Pai
Piã (*lúru*)	Pião
Piku	Pico (summit)
Polôtu	Piloto
Pimenta (*ai manas*)	Pimenta (pepper)
Pinta (*tádan*)	Pinta (spot)
Píris	Pires
Pistola	Pistola
Plantasã (*ai kúda*)	Plantação (plantation)
Polisia	Polícia
Polvorinhu	Polvorinho
Pomba	Pomba
Ponte (*iambáta*)	Ponte (bridge)
Póntu	Ponto
Portuguêz	Português
Pôstu	Pôsto
Pôvos (*éma, dátu*)	Povo
Praga	Praga

Teto	Portuguese
Prasa	Praça (market square)
Prátika	Prática (practice)
Pregar (*hédi*)	Pregar (to nail)
Prègar	Prègar (to preach)
Prègasã	Prègação (sermon)
Pregos	Prego
Prémiu	Premio (reward)
Prender	Prender (to seize)
Prepára	Preparar
Presizar	Precisar (to need)
Presizo	Preciso (adj., needed)
Présu	Preço
Prezénti	Presente
Prezidénti	Presidente
Prokurasã	Procuração
Prokurãdor	Procurador
Promesa	Promessa
Próntu	Pronto
Própi	Próprio
Proposta	Proposta
Proséssu	Processo
Prosisã	Procissão
Protestant	Protestante (Protestant)
Prostestu	Protesto
Provincia	Provincia (province)
Pudim	Pudim (pudding)

Teto	Portuguese
Púlpitu	Púlpito
Purga	Purga
Purgatório	Purgatório
Púrsu('*courage*')	Pulso (pulse)
Rabeka	Rabeca
Rádè	Ádem (a duck)
Rédi	Rêde
Reformádu	Reformado
Regent (*nai úlun*)	Regente (regent)
Regra	Regra
Regua	Régua (carpenter's rule)
Reinu	Reino (kingdom)
Rejístu	Registo
Rekádu	Recado
Rekeriméntu	Requerimento
Relasã	Relação
Religíã	Religião
Relóju, relóji, relósi	Relójio
Remata	Rematar (to finish)
Rénda	Renda (lace)
Renova	Renovar (to renew)
Repíki	Repique
Reposta	Reposta
Repróva	Reprovar
Resã	Ração
Resibu	Recibo
Resina	Resina (resin)
Respéitu	Respeito
Respomsável	Responsável
Retiru	Retiro (retreat)

Teto	Portuguese
Retrátu	Retrato
Reuniã	Reúnião
Reza	Reza (prayer)
Rezã	Razão
Riku	Rico (rich)
Riska	Risca (a dash with a pen)
Romã	Romã (pomegranate)
Ronda	Ronda
Roska	Rosca (twisted loaf)
Roupa	Roupa
Roza	Rosa
Rozáriu	Rosário
Rude (*aáti*)	Rude (rude)
Rufu	Rufo (red-haired)
? Rupia	Rupia
Sabã	Sabão
Sábadu	Sábado
Sakarolha	Saca-rolhas
Sakraméntu	Sacramento
Sakráriu	Sacrário
Sakrifísiu	Sacrificio
Sakriléjiu	Sacrilégio
Sakristã	Sacristão
Sakristia	Sacristia
? Saku	Sagu
Sala	Sala
Saláda	Salada
Salsa	Salsa (garden parsley)
Salva	Salva
Salvasã	Salvação
Sangra	Sangrar (to let blood)
Santa Kruz	Santa Cruz (Holy Cross)
Santisimu	Santissimo (Most Holy)
Santisimu Sakramentu	Santissimo Sacramento (most Holy Sacrament)
Sántu	Santo
? Sapa	Chapa
Sapatéru	Sapateiro
Sapátu	Sapato
Sardinha ('ikan')	Sardinha (a pilchard)
Sarjéntu	Sargento
Sarútu	Charuto
Sáuda	Saudar (to greet)
Saúdi	Saúde
Saukáti, sanáti	Saguate
Sé	Sé
Seda	Sêda
Sedu	Cedo (early)
Segundu	Segundo (second)
Sekreta (*laklo*)	Secreta (a privy)
Sekretaria	Secretaria
Sekretáriu	Secretário
Séla	Sela
Sêlu	Sêlo
Semana	Semana
Semana Santa	Semana Santa
Semináriu	Seminário
Semitéri	Cemitério
Senteiu	Centeio (rye)

Teto	*Portuguese*	*Teto*	*Portuguese*
Sentensa ..	Sentença	Soldádu ..	Soldado
Sentídu ..	Sentido	Sombréiru ..	Sombreiro
Sentinela ..	Sentinela	Sôpa ..	Sopa
Sentopê (*lalyan*)	Centopeia	Sóriti ..	Sorte
		Sosiedádi ..	Sociedade
Sepilho, sebilo	Cepilho	Subérbu ..	Soberbo
Séri ..	Serio	Subrinhu ..	Sobrinho
Serimóni ..	Cerimónia	*Sumu Pontifice*	Sumo Pontifice (the Pontifex)
Sermã ..	Sermão		
Serveja ..	Cerveja	Superior ..	Superior
Servent (*ata*)	Servente (servant)	Surisa ..	Chouriço
		Suseder ..	Suceder (to happen)
Servísu ..	Serviço		
Sidadã ..	Cidadão	Susegádu ..	Sosegado
Sidádi ..	Cidade	Suspéndi ..	Suspender
Sifra ..	Cifra	Tabáku ..	Tabaco
Sigára ..	Cigarro	Táchu, tásu ..	Tacho
Signifikar ..	Significar (to signify)	Taléntu ..	Talento
		Talher ..	Talher (a set of knife, fork and spoon)
Sikóuro (*túlun*)	Socorro (help)		
Silênsiu ..	Silêncio		
Silha ..	Cilha (saddle-girth)	Tapêti ..	Tapete
		Tárdi ..	Tarde
Sinal ..	Sinal	Tasu ..	Taco (wad of a gun)
Sinela ..	Chinela		
Sínti ..	Sentir	Tempra ..	Tempêra
Sinturã ..	Cinturão	Témpu ..	Tempo
Sínu ..	Sino	Tenda ..	Tenda
Sita ..	Chita	*Tenent* ..	Tenente (lieutenant)
Sirvi ..	Servir		
Sobremeza ..	Sobremesa	Ténta ..	Tentar
Sobreskritu ..	Sobrescrito (superscription)	Tentasã ..	Tentação
		Terrina ..	Terrina
Sofrí ..	Sofrer	Térsu ..	Têrço
Soldada (*sê-lu-kóli*)	Soldada (wages)	Testaméntu ..	Testamento
		Tia ..	Tia

Teto	Portuguese	Teto	Portuguese
Tigr ..	Tigre (tiger)	*Venera* ..	Venera (scallop shell)
Tinta ..	Tinta		
Tio ..	Tio	Verniz ..	Verniz
Tira ..	Tiro	Verónika ..	Verónica
Tiras ..	Tira	Verruma ..	Verruma
Tomáti ..	Tomate	Vérsu ..	Verso
Tôrri ..	Tôrre	Véspera ..	Vésperas
Torsida ..	Torcida (a wick)	Veu ..	Véu
Traisã ..	Traição	Vídru ..	Vidro
Trataméntu ..	Tratamento	Vigáriu (*nai-lúlik*)	Vigário
Trátar ..	Tratar		
Tribunal ..	Tribunal (tribunal)	*Vila* ..	Vila (a small town)
Trígu ..	Trigo		
Trombeta ..	Trombeta	*Vintem* ..	Vintem (a penny)
Tronko	Tronco		
Tropa ..	Tropa	Viola ..	Viola
Tualha ..	Toalha	Virtude ..	Virtude
Túkar ..	Trocar	*Vitória* (*mánan*)	Vitória
Túmba ..	Tumba	Viva, biba ..	Viva
Unifórmi ..	Uniforme	*Vizinhu* (*máluku, bésik*)	Vizinho
Urinol ..	Urinol		
Usu ..	Uso (use)	Vizita ..	Visita
Uvas ..	*Uvas* (grapes)	*Vontad* (*hakárak*)	Vontade (will)
Vapor (*ró áhi*)	Vapor		
Varanda ..	Varanda	Vótu ..	Voto
Vasalu ..	Vassalo (vassal)	*Zelador* ..	Zelador (overseer)
Vasina ..	Vacina		
Vázu ..	Vaso (vase)	*Zinku* (*kálen*)	Zinco (zinc)

49. Tibetan

Tibetan	Portuguese
? Ch'a, sö-ch'a ..	Chá
Ko-pi	Couve
? Pá-le, sh'e-pa ..	Pão

50. Tonkinese

Tonkinese	*Portuguese*
? Bat ..	Batéga
Banh ..	Pão
? Cà-phe ..	Café
? Chè ..	Chá
Côc ..	Copo
Cù-lac ..	Chocolate
? Thúõc ..	Tabaco

51. Tulu

Tulu	*Portuguese*
Almārí, almêru	Armário
Āmá ..	Ama
Apóstale ..	Apóstolo
Áriya ..	Arrear
Árka árkhu̥ ..	Arco
Aspatri ..	Hospital
Áya ..	Aia
Báldi ..	Balde
Bási ..	Bacia
Baṭaṭé, paṭaṭé	Batata
Battu ..	Pato
Bijákri, bijigre	Visagra
Bilimbi, bimbali, bimbili, bimbule	Bilimbim
Bórdu ..	Bordo
Burma, burmu	Verruma
Chá ..	Chá
Chávi ..	Chave
Damása ..	Damasco
Dôse ..	Doce
Dubrálu, dibrálu	Dobrado
Gadangu ..	Gudão
Garnalu ..	Granada
Góbi ..	Couve
Igreje ..	Igreja
Istri ..	Estirar
Jangálu, jangalu, jangaru	Jangada
Jugārigobbuni	Jogar
Julábu ..	Jalapa
Kamísu ..	Camisa
? Káphi ..	Café
Kápri, kapiri ..	Cafre
Karnélu ..	Coronel
Kathólika ..	Católico
Kerubi ..	Querubim
Kópu ..	Copo
Kórji ..	Corja
Krussu, kursu, krúji	Cruz
Kulér ..	Colher
Kumpádri, kombári	Compadre
Kumusáku ..	Confessar
Kusinu, kusini, kusni	Cozinha
Lándaru ..	Lanterna
Leilámu, yelamu, yélamu	Leilão
Listu, liśṭu ..	Lista
Manchilu ..	Machila
Manna ..	Maná
Mátri ..	Madre
Mestre ..	Mestre

Tulu	Portuguese
Mírne	Meirinho
Mulatta	Mulato
Mungárụ, mungarụ	Mangual
Pádri, pádre	Padre
Pangayu	Pangaio
Pápasu, pāpásu	Papuses
Paráta	Prato
Parenji, pareji	Prancha
Penụ, pénụ	Pena
Péranggáyi	Pera
? Phaláne	Fulano
? Phatóki	Foguete
? Pikkasu, pikkásu	Picão
Pingana, pingani, pingáni	Palangana
Pistulu	Pistola
Pulli	Fôlha
Rasídi	Recibo
Rátalu, rátelu	Arrátel
Reisu	Rial, réis
Rípu	Ripa
Rondu	Rámda
Sábu, sábunu,	Sabão
Sábu, sáburu, sabúnu	Sabão
? Seigo	Sagu
Séti	Setim
Sódti	Soıte
Tambaku	Tambaca
? Tánki	Tanque
? Tibralu	Tresdobrado
? Tuphanu	Tufão
Turungu, torangu, turanga	Tronco
Tuválu	Toalha
Varanda	Varanda
Váru, varu	Vara

52. Turkish

Turkish	Portuguese
Bándara	Bandeira
Bánqa	Banco
Cancha	Gancho
Cháy	Chá
Firgatéyn	Fragata
Gordéla	Cordão
Kestáne	Castanha
Līmón	Limão
Mákina	Máquina
Massa	Mesa
Móda	Moda
Mòdèl	Modêlo
Pàssàpòrta	Passaporte
Pishtow	Pistola
Pòrtugál	Portugal
Pósta	Posta
Qàmara	Câmara
Qànapé	Canapé
Qáptan	Capitão
Qáput	Capote
Qàrabína	Carabina
Qordéla	Cordão
Sábun	Sabão
Salata	Salada
Tèrménti	Terebintina
Túrunj	Toranja
Vápor	Vapor
Váril	Barril

Gaekwad's Oriental Series

CATALOGUE OF BOOKS

1936

ORIENTAL INSTITUTE, BARODA

SELECT OPINIONS

Sylvain Levi: The Gaekwad's Series is standing at the head of the many collections now published in India.

Asiatic Review, London: It is one of the best series issued in the East as regards the get up of the individual volumes as well as the able editorship of the series and separate works.

Presidential Address, Patna Session of the Oriental Conference: Work of the same class is being done in Mysore, Travancore, Kashmir, Benares, and elsewhere, but the organisation at Baroda appears to lead.

Indian Art and Letters, London: The scientific publications known as the "Oriental Series" of the Maharaja Gaekwar are known to and highly valued by scholars in all parts of the world.

Journal of the Royal Asiatic Society, London: Thanks to enlightened patronage and vigorous management the "Gaekwad's Oriental Series" is going from strength to strength.

Sir Jadunath Sarkar, Kt.: The valuable Indian histories included in the "Gaekwad's Oriental Series" will stand as an enduring monument to the enlightened liberality of the Ruler of Baroda and the wisdom of his advisers.

The Times Literary Supplement, London: These studies are a valuable addition to Western learning and reflect great credit on the editor and His Highness.

GAEKWAD'S ORIENTAL SERIES

Critical editions of unprinted and original works of Oriental Literature, edited by competent scholars, and published at the Oriental Institute, Baroda

I. BOOKS PUBLISHED.

Rs. A.

1. **Kāvyamīmāṁsā:** a work on poetics, by Rājaśekhara (880–920 A.D.): edited by C. D. Dalal and R. Anantakrishna Sastry, 1916. Reissued, 1924. Third edition revised and enlarged by Pandit K. S. Ramaswami Shastri of the Oriental Institute, Baroda, 1934 .. 2–0

This book has been set as a text-book by several Universities including Benares, Bombay, and Patna.

2. **Naranārāyaṇānanda:** a poem on the Paurāṇic story of Arjuna and Kṛṣṇa's rambles on Mount Girnar, by Vastupāla, Minister of King Vīradhavala of Dholka, composed between Samvat 1277 and 1287, *i.e.*, A.D. 1221 and 1231: edited by C. D. Dalal and R. Anantakrishna Sastry, 1916 .. .. .. *Out of print.*

3. **Tarkasaṅgraha:** a work on Philosophy (refutation of Vaiśeṣika theory of atomic creation) by Ānandajñāna or Ānandagiri, the famous commentators on Śaṅkarācārya's Bhāṣyas, who flourished in the latter half of the 13th century: edited by T. M. Tripathi, 1917. *Out of print.*

4. **Pārthaparākrama:** a drama describing Arjuna's recovery of the cows of King Virāṭa, by Prahlādanadeva, the founder of Pālanpur and the younger brother of the Paramāra king of Chandrāvatī (a state in Mārwār), and a feudatory of the kings of Guzerat, who was a Yuvarāja in Samvat 1220 or A.D. 1164: edited by C. D. Dalal, 1917 .. .. .. *Out of print.*

5. **Rāṣṭrauḍhavaṁśa:** an historical poem (Mahākāvya) describing the history of the Bāgulas of Mayūragiri, from Rāṣṭrauḍha, king of Kanauj and the originator of the dynasty, to Nārāyana Shāh of Mayūragiri, by Rudra Kavi, composed in Śaka 1518 or A.D. 1596: edited by Pandit Embar Krishnamacharya with Introduction by C. D. Dalal, 1917 .. .. *Out of print.*

6. **Liṅgānuśāsana:** on Grammar, by Vāmana, who lived between the last quarter of the 8th century and the first quarter of the 9th century: edited by C. D. Dalal, 1918 0–8

7. **Vasantavilāsa:** an historical poem (Mahākāvya) describing the life of Vastupāla and the history of

Rs. A.

Guzerat, by Bālachandrasūri (from Moḍheraka or Moḍhera in Kaḍi Prant, Baroda State), contemporary of Vastupāla, composed after his death for his son in Samvat 1296 (A.D. 1240): edited by C. D. Dalal, 1917 1–8

8. **Rūpakaṣaṭkam** : six dramas by Vatsarāja, minister of Paramardideva of Kalinjara, who lived between the 2nd half of the 12th and the 1st quarter of 13th century: edited by C. D. Dalal, 1918 .. *Out of print.*

9. **Mohaparājaya** : an allegorical drama describing the overcoming of King Moha (Temptation), or the conversion of Kumārapāla, the Chalukya King of Guzerat, to Jainism, by Yaśaḥpāla, an officer of King Ajayadeva, son of Kumārapāla, who reigned from A.D. 1229 to 1232: edited by Muni Chaturvijayaji with Introduction and Appendices by C. D. Dalal, 1918 .. 2–0

10. **Hammīramadamardana** : a drama glorifying the two brothers, Vastupāla and Tejaḥpāla, and their King Vīradhavala of Dholka, by Jayasiṁhasūri, pupil of Vīrasūri, and an Ācārya of the temple of Munisuvrata at Broach, composed between Samvat 1276 and 1286 or A.D. 1220 and 1239: edited by C. D. Dalal, 1920 .. 2–0

11. **Udayasundarīkathā** : a romance (Campū, in prose and poetry) by Soḍḍhala, a contemporary of and patronised by the three brothers, Chchittarāja, Nāgārjuna, and Mummuṇirāja, successive rulers of Konkan, composed between A.D. 1026 and 1050: edited by C. D. Dalal and Pandit Embar Krishnamacharya, 1920 .. 2–4

12. **Mahāvidyāviḍambana** : a work on Nyāya Philosophy, by Bhaṭṭa Vādīndra who lived about A.D. 1210 to 1274: edited by M. R. Telang, 1920 2–8

13. **Prācīnagurjarakāvysaṅgraha** : a collection of old Guzerati poems dating from 12th to 15th centuries A.D.: edited by C. D. Dalal, 1920 2–4

14. **Kumārapālapratibodha** : a biographical work in Prākṛta, by Somaprabhāchārya, composed in Samvat 1241 or A.D. 1195: edited by Muni Jinavijayaji, 1920 7–8

15. **Gaṇakārikā** : a work on Philosophy (Pāśupata School), by Bhāsarvajña who lived in the 2nd half of the 10th century: edited by C. D. Dalal, 1921 1–4

16. **Saṅgītamakaranda** : a work on Music, by Nārada: edited by M. R. Telang, 1920 2–0

17. **Kavīndrācārya List** : list of Sanskrit works in the collection of Kavīndrācārya, a Benares Pandit (1656 A.D.): edited by R. Anantakrishna Shastry, with a foreword by Dr. Ganganatha Jha, 1921 0–12

18. **Vārāhagṛhyasūtra** : Vedic ritual (domestic) of the Yajurveda: edited by Dr. R. Shamasastry, 1920 .. 0–10

19. **Lekhapaddhati** : a collection of models of state and private documents, dating from 8th to 15th centuries A.D.:

Rs. A.

edited by C. D. Dalal and G. K. Shrigondekar, 1925 2–0

20. **Bhavişayattakahā or Pañcamīkahā**: a romance in Apabhraṁśa language, by Dhanapāla (*circa* 12th century): edited by C. D. Dalal and Dr. P. D. Gune, 1923 6–0

21. **A Descriptive Catalogue of the Palm-leaf and Important Paper MSS. in the Bhandars at Jessalmere**, compiled by C. D. Dalal and edited by Pandit L. B. Gandhi, 1923 3–4

22. **Paraśurāmakalpasūtra**: a work on Tantra, with commentary by Rāmeśvara: edited by A. Mahadeva Sastry, B.A., 1923 .. .. *Out of print.*

23. **Nityotsava**: a supplement to the Paraśurāmakalpasūtra by Umānandanātha: edited by A. Mahadeva Sastry, B.A., 1923. Second revised edition by Swami Tirvikrama Tirtha, 1930 5–0

24. **Tantrarahasya**: a work on the Prābhākara School of Pūrvamīmāṁsā, by Rāmānujācārya: edited by Dr. R. Shamasastry, 1923 .. .. *Out of print.*

25, 32. **Samarāṅgaṇa**: a work on architecture, town-planning, and engineering, by king Bhoja of Dhara (11th century): edited by Mahamahopadhyaya T. Gaṇapati Shastri, Ph.D. Illustrated. 2 vols., 1924-1925 10–0

26, 41. **Sādhanamālā**: a Buddhist Tāntric text of rituals, dated 1165 A.D., consisting of 312 small works, composed by distinguished writers: edited by Benoytosh Bhattacharyya, M.A., Ph.D. Illustrated. 2 vols., 1925–1928 14–0

27. **A Descriptive Catalogue of MSS. in the Central Library, Baroda**: compiled by G. K. Shrigondekar, M.A., and K. S. Ramaswāmi Shastri, with a Preface by B. Bhattacharyya, Ph.D., in 12 vols., vol. I (Veda, Vedalakṣaṇa, and Upaniṣads), 1925 6–0

28. **Mānasollāsa or Abhilaṣitārthacintāmaṇi**: an encyclopædic work treating of one hundred different topics connected with the Royal household and the Royal court, by Someśvaradeva, a Chalukya king of the 12th century: edited by G. K. Shrigondekar, M.A., 3 vols., vol. I, 1925 2–12

29. **Nalavilāsa**: a drama by Rāmachandrasūri, pupil of Hemachandrasūri, describing the Paurāṇika story of Nala and Damayantī: edited by G. K. Shrigondekar, M.A., and L. B. Gandhi, 1926 2–4

30, 31. **Tattvasaṅgraha**: a Buddhist philosophical work of the 8th century, by Śāntarakṣita, a Professor at Nālandā with Pañjikā (commentary) by his disciple Kamalaśīla, also a Professor at Nālandā: edited by Pandit Embar Krishnamāchārya with a Foreword by B. Bhattacharyya, M.A., Ph.D., 2 vols., 1926 .. 24–0

	Rs. A.
33, 34. **Mirat-i-Ahmadi**: by Ali Mahammad Khan, the last Moghul Dewan of Gujarat: edited in the original Persian by Syed Nawab Ali, M.A., Professor of Persian, Baroda College, 2 vols., illustrated, 1926–1928 ..	19–8
35. **Mānavagṛhyasūtra**: a work on Vedic ritual (domestic) of the Yajurveda with the Bhāṣya of Aṣṭāvakra: edited with an introduction in Sanskrit by Pandit Rāmakrishna Harshaji Śāstri, with a Preface by Prof. B. C. Lele, 1926	5–0
36, 68. **Nāṭyaśāstra**: of Bharata with the commentary of Abhinavagupta of Kashmir: edited by M. Ramakrishna Kavi, M.A., 4 vols., vol. I, illustrated, 1926, vol. II, 1934 Vol. I (*out of print*).	11–0
37. **Apabhraṁśakāvyatrayī**: consisting of three works, the Carcarī, Upadeśarasāyana, and Kālasvarūpakulaka, by Jinadatta Sūri (12th century) with commentaries: edited with an elaborate introduction in Sanskrit by L. B. Gandhi, 1927	4–0
38. **Nyāyapraveśa**, Part I (Sanskrit Text): on Buddhist Logic of Diṅnāga, with commentaries of Haribhadra Sūri and Pārśvadeva: edited by Principal A. B. Dhruva, M.A., LL.B., Pro-Vice-Chancellor, Hindu University, Benares, 1930	4–0
39. **Nyāyapraveśa**, Part II (Tibetan Text): edited with introduction, notes, appendices, etc., by Pandit Vidhusekhara Bhattacharyya, Principal, Vidyabhavana, Visvabharati, 1927	1–8
40. **Advayavajrasaṅgraha**: consisting of twenty short works on Buddhist philosophy by Advayavajra, a Buddhist savant belonging to the 11th century A.D., edited by Mahāmahopādhyāya Dr. Haraprasad Sastri, M.A., C.I.E., Hon. D.Litt., 1927	2–0
42, 60. **Kalpadrukośa**: standard work on Sanskrit Lexicography, by Keśava: edited with an elaborate introduction by the late Pandit Ramavatara Sharma, Sahityacharya, M.A., of Patna and index by Pandit Shrikant Sharma, 2 vols., vol. I (text), vol. II (index), 1928–1932	14–0
43. **Mirat-i-Ahmadi Supplement**: by Ali Muhammad Khan. Translated into English from the original Persian by Mr. C. N. Seddon, I.C.S. (*retired*), and Prof. Syed Nawab Ali, M.A. Illustrated. Corrected reissue, 1928	6–8
44. **Two Vajrayāna Works**: comprising Prajñopāyaviniścayasiddhi of Anaṅgavajra and Jñānasiddhi of Indrabhūti—two important works belonging to the little known Tantra school of Buddhism (8th century A.D.): edited by B. Bhattacharyya, Ph.D., 1929 ..	3–0
45. **Bhāvaprakāśana**: of Śāradātanaya, a comprehensive work on Dramaturgy and Rasa, belonging to A.D. 1175–1250; edited by His Holiness Yadugiri Yatiraja Swami, Melkot, and K. S. Ramaswami Sastri, Oriental Institute, Baroda, 1929	7–0

Rs. A.

46. **Rāmacarita**: of Abhinanda, Court poet of Hāravarsa probably the same as Devapāla of the Pāla Dynasty of Bengal (cir. 9th century A.D.): edited by K. S. Ramaswami Sastri, 1929 7–8

47. **Nañjarājayaśobhūṣaṇa**; by Nṛsiṁhakavi *alias* Abhinava Kalidāsa, a work on Sanskrit Poetics and relates to the glorification of Nañjarāja, son of Vīrabhūpa of Mysore: edited by Pandit E. Krishnamacharya, 1930 5–0

48. **Nāṭyadarpaṇa**: on dramaturgy, by Rāmacandra Sūri with his own commentary: edited by Pandit L. B. Gandhi and G. K. Shrigondekar, M.A. 2 vols., vol. I, 1929 4–8

49. **Pre-Diṅnāga Buddhist Texts on Logic from Chinese Sources**: containing the English translation of *Śataśāstra* of Āryadeva, Tibetan text and English translation of *Vigraha-vyāvartanī* of Nāgārjuna and the re-translation into Sanskrit from Chinese of *Upāyahṛdaya* and *Tarkaśāstra*: edited by Prof. Giuseppe Tucci, 1930 9–0

50. **Mirat-i-Ahmadi Supplement**: Persian text giving an account of Guzerat, by Ali Muhammad Khan: edited by Syed Nawab Ali, M.A., Principal, Bahauddin College, Junagadh, 1930 6–0

51. **Triṣaṣṭiśalākāpuruṣacaritra**: of Hemacandra, translated into English with copious notes by Dr. Helen M. Johnson of Osceola, Missouri, U.S.A. 4 vols., vol. I (Ādīśvaracaritra), illustrated, 1931 15–0

52. **Daṇḍaviveka**: a comprehensive Penal Code of the ancient Hindus by Vardhamāna of the 15th century A.D.: edited by Mahamahopadhyaya Kamala Kṛṣṇa Smṛtitīrtha, 1931 8–8

53. **Tathāgataguhyaka or Guhyasamāja**: the earliest and the most authoritative work of the Tantra School of the Buddhists (3rd century A.D.): edited by B. Bhattacharyya, Ph.D., 1931 4–4

54. **Jayākhyasaṁhitā**: an authoritative Pāñcarātra work of the 5th century A.D., highly respected by the South Indian Vaiṣṇavas: edited by Pandit E. Krishnamacharyya of Vadtal, with one illustration in nine colours and a Foreword by B. Bhattacharyya, Ph.D., 1931 .. 12–0

55. **Kāvyālaṅkārasārasaṁgraha**: of Udbhaṭa with the commentary, probably the same as Udbhaṭaviveka of Rājānaka Tilaka (11th century A.D.): edited by K. S. Ramaswami Sastri, 1931 2–0

56. **Pārānanda Sūtra**: an ancient Tāntric work of the Hindus in Sūtra form giving details of many practices and rites of a new School of Tantra: edited by Swami Trivikrama Tirtha with a Foreword by B. Bhattacharyya, Ph.D., 1931 3–0

Rs. A.

57, 69. **Ahsan-ut-Tawarikh:** history of the Safawi Period of Persian History, 15th and 16th centuries, by Hasan-i-Rumlu: edited by C. N. Seddon, I.C.S. (*retired*), Reader in Persian and Marathi, University of Oxford. 2 vols. (Persian text and translation in English), 1932–34 19–8

58. **Padmānanda Mahākāvya:** giving the life history of Ṛsabhadeva, the first Tīrthaṅkara of the Jainas, by Amarachandra Kavi of the 13th century: edited by H. R. Kapadia, M.A., 1932 14–0

59. **Śabdaratnasamanvaya:** an interesting lexicon of the Nānārtha class in Sanskrit compiled by the Maratha King Sahaji of Tanjore: edited by Pandit Viṭṭhala Śāstrī, Sanskrit Paṭhaśāla, Baroda, with a Foreword by B. Bhattacharyya, Ph.D., 1932 11–0

61. **Śaktisaṅgama Tantra:** a voluminous compendium of the Hindu Tantra comprising four books on Kālī, Tārā, Sundarī and Chhinnamastā: edited by B. Bhattacharyya, M.A., Ph.D., 4 vols., vol. I, Kālīkhaṇḍa, 1932 2–8

62. **Prajñāpāramitās:** commentaries on the Prajñāpāramitā, a Buddhist philosophical work: edited by Giuseppe Tucci, Member, Italian Academy, 2 vols., vol. I, 1932 12–0

63. **Tarikh-i-Mubarakhshahi:** an authentic and contemporary account of the kings of the Saiyyid Dynasty of Delhi: translated into English from original Persian by Kamal Krishna Basu, M.A., Professor, T.N.J. College, Bhagalpur, with a Foreword by Sir Jadunath Sarkar, Kt., 1932 7–8

64. **Siddhāntabindu:** on Vedānta philosophy, by Madhusūdana Sarasvatī with commentary of Puruṣottama: edited by P. C. Divanji, M.A., LL.M., 1933 .. 11–0

65. **Iṣṭasiddhi:** on Vedānta philosophy, by Vimuktātmā, disciple of Avyayātmā, with the author's own commentary: edited by M. Hiriyanna, M.A., Retired Professor of Sanskrit, Maharaja's College, Mysore, 1933 .. 14–0

66, 70, 73. **Shabara-Bhāṣya:** on the Mīmāṁsā Sūtras of Jaimini: Translated into English by Mahāmahopādhyāya Dr. Ganganath Jha, M.A., D.Litt., etc., Vice-Chancellor, University of Allahabad, in 3 vols., 1933–1936 48–0

67. **Sanskrit Texts from Bali:** comprising a large number of Hindu and Buddhist ritualistic, religious and other texts recovered from the islands of Java and Bali with comparisons: edited by Professor Sylvain Levi, 1933 3–8

71. **Nārāyaṇa Śataka:** a devotional poem of high literary merit by Vidyākara with the commentary of Pītāmbara: edited by Pandit Shrikant Sharma, 1935 2–0

Rs. A.

72. **Rājadharma-Kaustubha**: an elaborate Smṛti work on Rājadharma, Rājanīti and the requirements of kings, by Anantadeva: edited by the late Mahamahopadhyaya Kamala Krishna Smṛtitirtha, 1935 10–0

74. **Portuguese Vocables in Asiatic Languages**: translated into English from Portuguese by Prof. A. X. Soares, M.A., LL.B., Baroda College, Baroda, 1936 .. 12–0

II. BOOKS IN THE PRESS.

1. **Nāṭyaśāstra**: edited by M. Ramakrishna Kavi, 4 vols., vol. III.
2. **Mānasollāsa** or Abhilaṣitārthacintāmaṇi, edited by G. K. Shrigondekar, M.A., 3 vols., vol. II.
3. **A Descriptive Catalogue of MSS. in the Jain Bhandars at Pattan**: edited from the notes of the late Mr. C. D. Dalal, M.A., by L. B. Gandhi, 2 vols.
4. **Alaṁkāramahodadhi**: a famous work on Sanskrit Poetics composed by Narendraprabha Sūri at the request of Minister Vastupāla in 1226 A.D.: edited by Lalchandra B. Gandhi of the Oriental Institute, Baroda.
5. **Sūktimuktāvalī**: a well-known Sanskrit work on Anthology, of Jalhaṇa, a contemporary of King Kṛṣṇa of the Northern Yādava Dynasty (A.D. 1247): edited by Pandit E. Krishnamacharya, Sanskrit Pāṭhaśālā, Vadtal.
6. **Triṣaṣṭiśalākāpuruṣacaritra**: of Hemacandra: translated into English by Dr. Helen M. Johnson, 4 vols., vol. II.
7. **Gaṇitatilaka**: of Śrīpati with the commentary of Simhatilaka, a non-Jain work on Arithmetic with a Jain commentary: edited by H. R. Kapadia, M.A.
8. **Dvādaśāranayacakra**: an ancient polemical treatise giving a résumé of the different philosophical systems with a refutation of the same from the Jain standpoint by Mallavādi Suri with a commentary by Simhasuri Gani: edited by Muni Caturvijayaji.
9. **Nāyakaratna**: a commentary on the Nyāyaratnamālā of Pārthasārathi Miśra by Rāmānuja of the Prābhākara School: edited by K. S. Ramaswami Sastri of the Oriental Institute, Baroda.
10. **Haṁsa-vilāsa**: of Haṁsa Bhikṣu: forms an elaborate defence of the various mystic practices and worship: edited by Swami Trivikrama Tirtha.
11. **Tattvasaṅgraha**: of Śāntarakṣita with the commentary of Kamalaśīla: translated into English by Mahamahopadhyaya Dr. Ganganath Jha.

III. BOOKS UNDER PREPARATION.

Rs. A.

1. **A Descriptive Catalogue of MSS. in the Oriental Institute, Baroda**: compiled by the Library staff, 12 vols., vol. II (Śrauta, Dharma, and Gṛhya Sūtras).

2. **Prajñāpāramitās**: commentaries on the Prajñāpāramitā, a Buddhist philosophical work: edited by Prof. Giuseppe Tucci, 2 vols., vol. II.

3. **Śaktisaṅgama Tantra**: comprising four books on Kāli, Tārā, Sundarī, and Chhinnamastā: edited by B. Bhattacharyya, Ph.D., 4 vols., vols. II–IV.

4. **Nāṭyadarpaṇa**: introduction in Sanskrit giving an account of the antiquity and usefulness of the Indian drama, the different theories on Rasa, and an examination of the problems raised by the text, by L. B. Gandhi, 2 vols., vol. II.

5. **Gurjararāsāvalī**: a collection of several old Gujarati Rāsas: edited by Messrs. B. K. Thakore, M. D. Desai, and M. C. Modi.

6. **Paraśurāma-Kalpasūtra**: an important work on Tantra with the commentary of Rāmesvara: second revised edition by Swami Trivikrama Tirtha.

7. **Tarkabhāṣā**: a work on Buddhist Logic, by Mokṣākara Gupta of the Jagaddala monastery: edited with a Sanskrit commentary by Pandit Embar Krishnamacharya of Vadtal.

8. **Mādhavānala-Kāmakandalā**: a romance in old Western Rajasthani by Gaṇapati, a Kāyastha from Amod: edited by M. R. Majumdar, M.A., LL.B.

9. **A Descriptive Catalogue of MSS. in the Oriental Institute, Baroda**: compiled by the Library staff, 12 vols., vol. III (Smṛti MSS.).

10. **An Alphabetical List of MSS. in the Oriental Institute, Baroda**: compiled from the existing card catalogue by the Superintendent, Printed Section.

11. **Nītikalpataru**: the famous Nīti work of Kṣemendra: edited by Sardar K. M. Panikkar, M.A., of Patiala.

12. **Chhakkammuvaeso**: an Apabhramsa work of the Jains containing didactic religious teachings: edited by L. B. Gandhi, Jain Pandit.

13. **Saṁrāṭ Siddhānta**: the well-known work on Astronomy of Jagannatha Pandit: critically edited with numerous diagrams by Pandit Kedar Nath, Rajjyotisi, Jaipur.

14. **Vimalaprabhā**: the famous commentary on the Kālacakra Tantra and the most important work of the Kālacakra School of the Buddhists: edited with comparisons of the Tibetan and Chinese versions by Giuseppe Tucci of the Italian Academy.

Rs. A.

15. **Niṣpannayogāmbara Tantra**: describing a large number of maṇḍalas or magic circles and numerous deities: edited by B. Bhattacharyya.

16. **Basatin-i-Salatin**: a contemporary account of the Sultans of Bijapur: translated into English by M. A. Kazi of the Baroda College and B. Bhattacharyya.

17. **Madana Mahārṇava**: a Smṛti work principally dealing with the doctrine of Karmavipāka composed during the reign of Māndhātā son of Madanapāla: edited by Embar Krishnamacharya.

18. **Triṣaṣṭiśalākāpuruṣacaritra**: of Hemacandra: translated into English by Dr. Helen Johnson, 4 vols., vols. III-IV.

19. **Kṛtyakalpataru**: of Laksmidhara, minister of King Govindachandra of Kanauj: edited by Principal K. V. Rangaswami Aiyangar, Hindu University, Benares.

20. **Bṛhaspati Smṛti**, being a reconstructed text of the now lost work of Bṛhaspati: edited by Principal K. V. Rangaswami Aiyangar, Hindu University, Benares.

For further particulars please communicate with—

The Director,
Oriental Institute, Baroda.

THE GAEKWAD'S STUDIES IN RELIGION AND PHILOSOPHY.

Rs. A.

1. **The Comparative Study of Religions**: [Contents: I, the sources and nature of religious truth. II, supernatural beings, good and bad. III, the soul, its nature, origin, and destiny. IV, sin and suffering, salvation and redemption. V, religious practices. VI, the emotional attitude and religious ideals]: by Alban A. Widgery, M.A., 1922 15–0
2. **Goods and Bads**: being the substance of a series of talks and discussions with H.H. the Maharaja Gaekwad of Baroda. [Contents: introduction. I, physical values. II, intellectual values. III, æsthetic values. IV, moral value. V, religious value. VI, the good life, its unity and attainment]: by Alban G. Widgery, M.A., 1920. (Library edition Rs. 5) 3–0
3. **Immortality and other Essays**: [Contents: I, philosophy and life. II, immortality. III, morality and religion. IV, Jesus and modern culture. V, the psychology of Christian motive. VI, free Catholicism and non-Christian Religions. VII, Nietzsche and Tolstoi on Morality and Religion. VIII, Sir Oliver Lodge on science and religion. IX, the value of confessions of faith. X, the idea of resurrection. XI, religion and beauty. XII, religion and history. XIII, principles of reform in religion]: by Alban G. Widgery, M.A., 1919. (Cloth Rs. 3) 2–0
4. **Confutation of Atheism**: a translation of the *Hadis-i-Halila* or the tradition of the Myrobalan Fruit: translated by Vali Mohammad Chhanganbhai Momin, 1918 .. 0–14

Conduct of Royal Servants: being a collection of verses from the Viramitrodaya with their translations in English, Gujarati, and Marathi: by B. Bhattacharyya, M.A., Ph.D. 0–6